Time Out

Boston

timeout.com/boston

Penguin Books

PENGUIN BOOKS

Published by the Penguin Group
Penguin Books Ltd, 27 Wrights Lane, London W8 5TZ, England
Penguin Books USA Inc, 375 Hudson Street, New York, New York 10014, USA
Penguin Books Australia Ltd, Ringwood, Victoria, Australia
Penguin Books Canada Ltd, 10 Alcorn Avenue, Toronto, Ontario, Canada M4V 3B2
Penguin Books (NZ) Ltd, 182-190 Wairau Road, Auckland 10, New Zealand

Penguin Books Ltd, Registered Offices: Harmondsworth, Middlesex, England

First published 1999
Second edition 2001
10 9 8 7 6 5 4 3 2 1

Colour reprographics by Icon, Crown House, 56-58 Southwark Street, London SE1
and Precise Litho, 34-35 Great Sutton Street, London EC1.
Printed and bound by Cayfosa-Quebecor, Ctra. de Caldes, Km 3 08 130 Sta, Perpètua de Mogoda, Barcelona, Spain.

Edited and designed by
Time Out Guides Limited
Universal House
251 Tottenham Court Road
London W1P 0AB
Tel + 44 (0) 20 7813 3000
Fax + 44 (0) 20 7813 6001
Email guides@timeout.com
www.timeout.com

Editorial
Editor Christi Daugherty
Consultant Editor Chris Wright
Deputy Editor Kevin Ebbutt, Richard Lines, Lesley McCave
Listings Researchers Michael Endelman, Heather Kissell, Megan Morley
Proofreader Marion Moisy
Indexer Alison Bravington

Editorial Director Peter Fiennes
Series Editor Ruth Jarvis
Deputy Series Editor Jonathan Cox
Editorial Assistant Jenny Noden

Design
Art Director John Oakey
Art Editor Mandy Martin
Senior Designer Scott Moore
Designers Benjamin de Lotz, Lucy Grant, Kate Vincent-Smith
Picture Editor Kerri Miles
Deputy Picture Editor Olivia Duncan-Jones
Scanning & Imaging Dan Conway
Ad make-up Glen Impey

Advertising
Group Commercial Director Lesley Gill
Sales Director Mark Phillips
International Sales Co-ordinator Ross Canadé
Advertising Assistant Catherine Shepherd

Administration
Publisher Tony Elliott
Managing Director Mike Hardwick
Financial Director Kevin Ellis
Marketing Director Christine Cort
Marketing Manager Mandy Martinez
Group General Manager Nichola Coulthard
Production Manager Mark Lamond
Production Controller Samantha Furniss
Accountant Sarah Bostock

Features in this guide were written and researched by:
Introduction Chris Wright. **History** Camille Dodero, Tim Rowbottom, Christi Daugherty, Art Corriveau. **Boston Today** Camille Dodero. **Architecture** Camille Dodero, Art Corriveau. **Literary Boston** Camille Dodero, Art Corriveau. **College Town** Michael Endelman. **Accommodation** Alex Shapiro. **Sightseeing: Boston Common & Downtown, Beacon Hill & West End** Camille Dodero; **Introduction, Back Bay & South End, The North End, South & The Waterfront, Guided Tours** Alex Shapiro; **Cambridge & Somerville** Michael Endelman; **Further Afield** Holly Monacelli; **Museums** Randi Hopkins. **Restaurants & Cafés** Alex Shapiro. **Pubs & Bars** Mike Millard, Chris Wright, Michael Endelman. **Shops & Services** Robin Vaughan, Michael Endelman. **By Season** Camille Dodero. **Children** Holly Monacelli. **Dance Clubs** Robin Vaughan. **Film** Rosie McCobb. **Galleries** Randi Hopkins. **Gay & Lesbian** Robert David Sullivan. **Music: Rock & Roots** Robin Vaughan. **Performing Arts** Sean Richardson. **Sport & Fitness** Alex Shapiro. **Trips Out of Town: Introduction** Christi Daugherty; **Colonial New England, Mass Beaches & Ocean** Alex Shapiro. **Western Mass** Michael Endelman, Steve Ellman. **Heading South, Heading North** Steve Ellman. **Directory** Michael Endelman.

The editor would like to thank the following: Aimee O'Brien at the Greater Boston Convention & Visitors Bureau, Ken Lanclos, Martha Daugherty, Eileen Lee at the Boston Park Plaza, Ferne Mintz at the Bed & Breakfast Agency of Boston, Myra Burson, Tim Rowbottom, Gerald Sibon, Lesley McCave, Richard Lines, Will Fulford-Jones, Cath Phillips, Nicholas Royle, Sally Davies, Jonathan Cox, Chris Stringer, Chris Moore, Matt Ashare, Sean Metagh and Alan Quinn.

Maps by JS Graphics, 17 Beadles Lane, Old Oxted, Surrey RH8 9JG.
Map on page 316 reproduced with the kind permission of the MBTA.

Photography by Adam Eastland except: page 6 Mary Evans Picture Library; pages 10, 11, 33 AKG; page 17 Allsport; pages 15, 23, 35, 193 Associated Press; pages 31, 245 Corbis; page 213 Marco Breuer; pages 235, 236 and 242 Popperfoto; page 244 Mystic Seaport; page 248 Robert Deschene/Salem Chamber of Commerce; page 251 Jim McEkholm/Marblehead Chamber of Commerce; page 253 Cape Cod Chamber of Commerce; page 257 Jim McElholm/Martha's Vineyard Chamber of Commerce; page 258 K Clineff/Provincetown Chamber of Commerce.

The following photographs were supplied by featured establishments: pages 45, 49, 56, 57, 58, 59, 89, 113, 114, 115, 116, 117, 119, 209, 212, 229, 243, 255, 270-276, 261, 263, 265-269.

Contents

Introduction 2

In Context

History 6
Boston Today 17
Architecture 24
Literary Boston 31
College Town 37

Accommodation

Accommodation 44

Sightseeing

Introduction 62
Boston Common & Downtown 63
Beacon Hill & West End 71
Back Bay & South End 78
The North End 89
South & The Waterfront 95
Cambridge & Somerville 103
Further Afield 109
Guided Tours 111
Museums 113

Eat, Drink, Shop

Restaurants & Cafés 122
Pubs & Bars 156
Shops & Services 171

Arts & Entertainment

By Season 192
Children 198
Dance Clubs 203
Film 206
Galleries 210
Gay & Lesbian 214
Music: Rock & Roots 221
Performing Arts 227
Sport & Fitness 234

Trips Out of Town

Getting Started 244
Colonial New England 245
Mass Beaches and Ocean 252
Picturesque Western Mass 260
Heading South 265
Heading North 270

Directory

Getting Around 278
Resources A-Z 281
Further Reference 292
Index 294
Advertisers' Index 300

Maps

Trips Out of Town 303
Greater Boston 304
Downtown Boston 306
Central Boston 308
Back Bay 309
Beacon Hill 310
Cambridge 311
Coastal Boston 312
Street Index 313
MBTA Subway Map 316

Introduction

Pick up most Boston guidebooks, and you'll be bombarded with Pilgrims and Patriots. You'll get Bunker Hill and Paul Revere and the Shot Heard Around the World. Pretty soon, you'll have visions of Redcoats dancing in your head and the Declaration of Independence ringing in your ears. The Revolution is, after all, Boston's defining moment. The city sits on a historical fault line, the fissure which marks the breakaway point of the Old World and the New. And yet this fact barely begins to scratch the surface of what makes today's Boston such an interesting place to visit and to live. Boston is the Cradle of Democracy and the birthplace of the Internet. It is in equal parts the land of Henry David Thoreau and John F Kennedy, and of Ben Affleck and Matt Damon.

Actually, the really interesting thing about this city is that almost anything you say about it demands an immediate 'and yet'. Boston is the town which first spurned European influence, and yet today it is known as the most European of American cities. It is the site of America's oldest subway system and some of its worse traffic, and yet it remains a walkable city. It is as vibrant and diverse as any city in the US, and yet it retains that small-town feel. It is the premier college town in the country, with a massive transient population, and yet it is divided into deeply entrenched neighbourhoods, each of which clings steadfastly to its identity.

Indeed, even Boston's 'most European' status is fraught with kaleidoscopic contingency. Are we talking the Italian Europe of the North End or the English Europe of Beacon Hill? The Irish Europe of South Boston or the Prada-wearing, cell phone-toting Europe of the city's seething nightclubs? And where does Chinatown fit into all this? Or Roxbury, with its large African American population? Or Allston, with its Vietnamese and Brazilian immigrants? The fact is, Boston's Pilgrims never stopped arriving. In this sense, it is the most American of American cities.

Make your way to the Cambridge side of the Charles River, a hundred yards east of the Longfellow Bridge, and you'll not only be treated to one of the most exquisite views imaginable, you'll also get insight into Boston's dynamism and complexity. First, there's the river itself, the resource that attracted settlers here in the first place. Then, beyond the river – the blue water and the green trees and the lily-white sails – a snarl of traffic lurches along Storrow Drive. Beyond this is the scribble of Boston's skyline: the redbrick clutter of Beacon Hill, the gleaming towers of the Financial District. Standing here, it's as if you were looking at a cross-section of a palimpsest, the story of Boston unfolding before you in a series of ascending layers. Meanwhile, at your back you have the future: the labs of MIT, humming with the business of technological invention.

And so Boston, this bastion of Yankee decorum and conservatism, is actually anything but. Or it is, but it is much more besides. It is cosmopolitan and parochial, progressive and Puritanical, obsessed with preservation and desperate to forge ahead. It is a mixture of the earthy and the ethereal, of transcendence and common sense. That's the thing about this city, the thing that this guidebook has tried to capture: there is always an 'and yet'. Boston is full of surprises, and that's why we love it here, why some of us, visitors ourselves, never left.

ABOUT THE TIME OUT CITY GUIDES

The *Time Out Boston Guide* is one of an expanding series of *Time Out* City Guides, now numbering over 30, produced by the people behind London and New York's successful listings magazines. Our guides are all written and updated by resident experts who have striven to provide you with all the most up-to-date information you'll need to explore the city, listen to its music, meet its residents, enjoy its history and architecture or read up on its background, whether you're a local or a first-time visitor.

THE LOWDOWN ON THE LISTINGS

Above all, we've tried to make this book as useful as possible. Addresses, telephone numbers, websites, transport information, opening times, admission prices and credit card details are all included in our listings, which were all checked and correct as we went to press. However things change rapidly,

There is an online version of this guide, as well as weekly events listings for over 30 international cities, at www.timeout.com.

so before you go out of your way, we'd advise you to phone ahead and check opening times and other details. While every effort has been made to ensure the accuracy of the information in this guide, the publishers cannot accept responsibility for any errors it may contain.

PRICES AND PAYMENT

We have noted where venues such as shops, hotels and restaurants accept the following credit cards: American Express (**AmEx**), Diners Club (**DC**), MasterCard (**MC**) and Visa (**V**). Many businesses also accept other cards, including Switch, Delta and JCB. In addition, some shops, restaurants and attractions take travellers' cheques issued by major financial institutions.

THE LIE OF THE LAND AND MAPS

We have divided the city into its best-known sections. To make your task easier, our listings include the address, plus the area of town in which each hotel, restaurant or bar is located. There's also a map reference, indicating the page and square on which an address will be found on our maps at the back of the book.

TELEPHONE NUMBERS

The area code for metropolitan Boston (including Cambridge, Somerville, and Brookline) is 617. The first ring of suburbs is in the 781 area code and is considered a local call from metropolitan Boston. The northern suburbs and north coast are served by 978; the western and southern suburbs (including Cape Cod and the islands) are served by 508. These are both long distance calls from metropolitan Boston. As of April 2001, a new area code 857 (known as an 'overlay' code) is being added to the region. This won't change any of numbers listed in this guide (only new customers will be assigned the 857 code), but it will alter the way that calls are made. All calls made within Eastern Massachusetts (617, 781, 508, 978 and 857) should be dialled using all 10 digits – area code + plus seven-digit phone number. So, when calling from one side of Boston to the other, it is necessary to include 617 before the bulk of the number. The listings in this guide do not include the 617 area code, but you will quickly become used to dialling 617 before the seven-digit numbers listed. All other area codes are included in the listings, where appropriate.

ESSENTIAL INFORMATION

For all the practical information you might need for visiting the city, including emergency phone numbers and details of local transport, turn to the **Directory** chapter at the back of the guide. It starts on page 278.

LET US KNOW WHAT YOU THINK

We hope you enjoy the *Time Out Boston Guide*, and we'd like to know what you think of it. We welcome tips for any places that you feel we should include in future editions and take note of your criticism of our choices. There's a reader's reply card at the back of this book, or email us on bostonguide@timeout.com.

Advertisers

We would like to stress that no establishment has been included in this guide because it has advertised in any of our publications and no payment of any kind has influenced any review. The opinions given in this book are those of *Time Out* writers and editors and are entirely independent.

In Context

History 6
Boston Today 17
Architecture 24
Literary Boston 31
College Town 37

Feature boxes

Listen my children 8
Seven Boston firsts 12
The Great Molasses Massacre 13
The devil made them do it 14
Key events 16
Tattoo you 19
From Beantown to Athens 22
Just make mine red brick, thanks 30
Where the wordsmiths are 36
Best quads 38
Coolest college hangouts 42

History

You say you want a revolution; well, you know, someone had to change the world.

Boston has always been a city of extremes. Its nicknames tell the tale of its past reputation – the Cradle of Liberty, the Centre of Abolition, the Athens of America. The 19th-century US author and essayist Ralph Waldo Emerson once wrote of this city: 'I do not speak with any fondness but the language of coolest history when I say that Boston commands attention as the town which was appointed in the destiny of nations to lead the civilization of North America.'

Yet, while Boston, in many ways, has lived up to those names, it also has a much less glorious side. It's worth noting, for instance, that Boston's route to being the cradle of liberty began with citizens who made their fortunes in the slave trade. A century later, however, Boston became one of the first cities in the nation to abolish slavery, something it did 30 years before the US Civil War began. Yet, 100 years after that, this same city made a name for itself as a centre of intolerance after it burst into an angry firestorm of racism over school integration.

Boston has always been a fascinating hybrid of puritan intolerance and rampant liberalism. Thus, while Massachusetts is heralded as a centre of intellectual prowess and liberalism, it is also notorious for landmark death sentences such as the Salem Witch Trials and the infamous Sacco and Vanzetti Case in the 1920s. Is Boston intellectual or emotional? Progressive or reactionary? Puritanical or liberal? The answer to all those questions seems to be an infuriating, 'yes'. In that ambivalence, though, lies the city's attraction, and, in many ways, the impressive strengths and devastating weaknesses of this entire nation.

THE BIRTH OF BOSTON

Strictly speaking, Boston was not truly 'settled' until the arrival of the Puritans in 1620. Of course, that's the Anglocentric way of looking at it. In fact, the area had human occupants as far back as 7500 BC. The area was heavily populated with Native Americans by 1497, when John Cabot's explorations in search of the North-west Passage to the Orient led him to claim Massachusetts for King Henry VII of England. Just over a quarter of a century later, in 1524, Giovanni Verrazano claimed the same land for Francis I of France, thus setting up more than 200 years of squabbling over what had become known as the New World.

Word of this 'paradise' reached John Brewster, leader of a strict religious sect known as the Puritans. Facing persecution in England, he began an effort to establish a Puritan colony in America. And so it was that the *Mayflower*, filled with 102 passengers, set sail in September 1620 bound for 'some place about the Hudson River'. It landed nowhere near the Hudson, actually, anchoring instead, after 65 days at sea, at the tip of Cape Cod, near what is now Provincetown. Finding the area too wild for their new town, the Puritans soon moved on, crossing the bay and ultimately establishing their colony on a protected stretch of sandy beach close to several cornfields maintained by local tribes. They called it Plymouth.

'Nearly half of the Pilgrims died of pneumonia and smallpox that first winter.'

Utopia it surely wasn't. Winters are brutal here, and the Pilgrims had little understanding of the land, the kinds of crops that would grow there and the edible native vegetation. They also brought diseases with them that wrought devastation on their population and on the Native American tribes. Nearly half of the Pilgrims died of pneumonia and smallpox that first winter. But in the spring, local tribes taught them how to plant corn, dig clams and fish for cod. By harvest time, the settlers were enough established to host a three-day feast – celebrated today as Thanksgiving.

Once things were running more smoothly on the new shores, word spread back to England about the Puritan's settlement. By 1630, 1,000 more settlers had arrived. They established Salem, on the north shore of Massachusetts Bay. These new settlers would ultimately form the foundation for what is now Boston. Choosing as their leader John Winthrop, many of them migrated south from Salem to the area now known as Charlestown. This didn't last, however, as the lack of fresh water forced them to relocate to a neighbouring peninsula, known to the natives as Shawmut. Winthrop's settlers bought the narrow 440-acre (177-hectare) peninsula from a hermit bachelor and renamed it Tremontaine after its three surrounding hills. In short order, though, they changed their minds and renamed it again. This time they called it Boston, after the Lincolnshire village from which many of them had come. It quickly became the centre of activity for the colony.

PURITY IS STRENGTH

By 1636, there were some 12,000 colonists, primarily Puritans, spread between the townships of Plymouth, Salem and Boston, with new settlements springing up almost monthly. In fact, the lack of qualified ministers to keep up with the growing population led Puritan elders to establish America's first training college, which they later named after a young minister, John Harvard, who died and left the college his library. Early colonists found Massachusetts curiously easy to settle and rather empty of the anticipated hostile Indians. The fact was, epidemics of smallpox, pneumonia and influenza brought over by early explorers and settlers had decimated the once robust native population.

Relations with the remaining tribes rapidly deteriorated. The fundamental Puritan notion of a righteous life leading to the accumulation of wealth clashed with native beliefs that it was impossible to own the land. Unlike the French to the north, who converted native populations to Catholicism, the Puritans took a more aggressive tack. They attempted to rid Christianity of the heathen devil by burning out the Indian's settlements and appropriating their land. The Algonquin nation, under the leadership of Chief Metacomet (known to colonists as King Philip), retaliated in 1675 by raiding several outlying English settlements. But it was all in vain. Metacomet was betrayed by one of his own warriors the following year and gruesomely executed.

The Indians were not the sole targets of Puritan intolerance. Quakers and Baptists arriving in the colonies were sometimes prevented from leaving their ships; those who practised their faith publicly were hanged for heresy. Such religious paranoia ultimately led to the witch trials of Charleston (1648), Boston (1665) and – most infamously – Salem (1692), where 100 colonists were imprisoned and 19 were hanged in a mass hysteria that became known as the Salem Witch Trials (*see p14*).

IN COD WE TRUST

By 1700, Boston had grown into the third largest port of the burgeoning British Empire. Some of the Puritans grew wealthy, thanks primarily to the export of dried cod to the Caribbean and Mediterranean. (To this day, a carved pine cod – known as 'the Sacred Cod' – hangs above the entrance to the House

Listen my children

Of all America's founding fathers, only George Washington is more famous among US schoolchildren than Paul Revere. Part of the reason for his popularity is the incredibly catchy poem written in 1863 by another Bostonian, Henry Wadsworth Longfellow. 'Paul Revere's Ride' is one of the first poems many kids learn, for the simple reason that it is both historical and, well, kind of fun:

Listen my children, and you shall hear
Of the midnight ride of Paul Revere,
On the eighteenth of April, in Seventy-five;
Hardly a man is now alive
Who remembers that famous day and year...

Let's start at the beginning. Revere was a silversmith in Boston at the time of the Revolution. He was also one of the key rebels in the city, heavily involved in overthrowing the British government in the colonies. An artist, Revere's drawings of the Boston Massacre were widely published throughout the colonies, and helped to inflame the anger against the British.

Despite his artistic efforts, in large part, Revere's primary role was as a messenger. He frequently travelled between Boston and Philadelphia – where the Continental Congress was meeting to form the country's early government – carrying messages from Boston's rebels to the leaders.

By 1775, the Boston colonists had created an extensive underground network to monitor the British troops occupying the area, and to alert the rebel leaders of any activity by the Redcoats. In particular, the well-positioned Old North Church at the top of a hill was a prime location for spying. The sexton, Robert Newman, had offered to signal by placing lanterns in the church's steeple – one lantern meant the troops were moving on the ground; two would mean they were coming in from the ocean. 'One if by land, two if by sea.'

On 18 April 1775, the British troops began marching toward Lexington, where the rebels had stockpiled munitions. Newman placed one lantern in the steeple. Revere and two other horsemen (William Dawes and Samuel Prescott) hit the road. Their mission was to beat the British to Lexington and then to Concord (where rebels were assembling), to warn the militia, giving them enough time to mount a defence.

The three succeeded in arriving in Lexington in time to gather the Minutemen and to rouse Patriot leaders John Hancock and Samuel Adams, both of whom were spending the night at a Lexington inn. Hancock and Adams escaped safely, but as the three rebels headed for Concord they encountered a British patrol. The two other riders escaped and rode on, though only Prescott ultimately reached Concord. Interestingly, Revere, who was well-known to the British for his work with the rebels, was held for several hours and then deprived of his horse. He finally walked into Concord. Now, there's something nobody ever tells US schoolkids.

of Representatives in the State House, pointing to the party in power.)

Some got very rich in a notorious triangular shipping trade where sugar cane was harvested by slaves in the West Indies and shipped to Boston to be distilled into rum. The Puritans shipped most of the rum to West Africa to be traded for more slaves who were, in turn, delivered to the Caribbean sugar plantations.

One of the by-products of the city's rum production was molasses (Boston was the largest American producer of the stuff until the early 20th century). Another was the introduction of slavery to American soil. By 1705, there were more than 400 black slaves – and a small number of free blacks – living in Boston.

At about the same time, England was mired in a serious financial crisis. The crown had incurred enormous expenses during its lengthy (and inconclusive) wars with France. As some of the battles were fought in New England, and as the colonists were virtually voiceless in Parliament, it established the Revenue Act of 1764, which placed heavy duties on silk, sugar and wine from the West Indies. The colonists were irate and began the first of a series of boycotts of the imports involved.

BREAKING THE TIES THAT BIND

Ignoring their protest, Parliament enacted another set of taxes a year later. The Stamp Act required a heavy duty to be paid on all commercial and legal documents printed in the colonies, including newspapers. This was viewed by the colonists as an attempt to remove what little voice they had through the freedom of the press. Again they fumed. Again they felt no sympathy from England Again they boycotted, but this time, with more force. They branded their now more organised protest with the

The **Boston Massacre** took place in front of the Old State House.

tagline, 'No taxation without representation', on the grounds that they had no voice in government in England. They were heard, and the Stamp Act was hastily repealed a year later, but the British still attempted to keep their rebellious cousins in line. They next imposed the Townshend Acts of 1767 – a litany of levies on imported lead, glass, paint, paper and tea.

Britain's attempts to pull political rank enraged the colonists, especially those in Boston. Governmental meeting houses such as Faneuil Hall, the Old South Meeting House and the Old State House became hotbeds for revolutionary plotting. Rebels like Samuel Adams, Daniel Webster, Paul Revere and James Otis gathered secretly to discuss the benefits of splintering off from the British Empire. Prodded by growing public outcry, civil unrest grew so clamourous it carried across the Atlantic and back to the monarch. To quiet the rumblings, George III reluctantly sent troops overseas in 1768, but military occupation in the colonies created more problems than it solved.

Lt Gen Thomas Gage, commander-in-chief of British forces in the colonies, was faced with a near impossible situation. Perhaps understandably, he hated Boston and disliked the Bostonians virtually to a man. 'I wish this cursed place was burned,' he wrote of Boston in 1770. 'America is a mere bully, from one end to the other, and the Bostonians by far the greatest bullies.'

But it was the British who looked like bullies when, on 5 March 1770, a group of unarmed anti-royalists sparred with English soldiers in front of the Old State House. During the fray, the British troops opened fire. Five colonists were fatally shot. The colonists were outraged over the attack, and dubbed the incident the 'Boston Massacre'. The shooting became a rallying cry for those who supported plans for a revolution

FIGHT THE POWER

Word of the incident quickly spread throughout the colonies, causing King George III to fear (and rightly so) that this bloodshed might be the match that would light the powder keg. To avert such an outcome, the king quickly abolished the Townshend Acts – all except for the provisions on tea, a little jab from the king to his subjects as George III knew that colonists loved their tea (it was the most popular beverage in America). Instead of easing the mood of revolt, the move added fuel to the flames and the colonists continued to plot and to boycott.

With the situation growing heated – and with the East India Company (Britain's chief exporter of tea) teetering on the brink of bankruptcy – in 1773, Parliament attempted rescue by exempting that company's tea from taxation, hoping to flood the colonial markets with the product. No such luck: every American port slammed shut to English tea ships – except Boston. The state's British governor, Thomas Hutchinson, stuck to the party line, ignoring the incensed citizens, and insisting that all ships could dock in Boston Harbor until the other ports accepted the tea.

The rebels hit back. On the night of 16 December 1773, a group of 60 men, calling themselves the 'Sons of Liberty', disguised themselves as Mohawk Indians (then seen as a symbol of freedom in the new world), stormed the blockaded ships in the harbour and dumped 342 chests of tea into the harbour. This defiant act, known as the Boston Tea Party, electrified

Colonists make world's biggest cup of tea.

the colonies and seemed to fan the flames of rebellion among its residents.

The following September, the first Continental Congress for Independence convened in Philadelphia. Massachusetts sent prominent delegates such as John Adams and John Hancock to represent it and to help in the writing of the country's manifestos. At the same time, throughout the colonies, local militia began training for a fight.

'BLOWS WILL DECIDE IT'

The first shots of the revolution were fired in Boston on 19 April 1775. British garrisons lodged in the area heard about an arms store located in the nearby township of Concord. When the Redcoats left Boston to seize the Concord stockpiles, rebels Paul Revere, William Dawes and Samuel Prescott set out on horseback to warn the local militia that the British troops were on their way (*see p8*). That wild and brave ride by horseback became one of the most famous acts of the War of Independence. The message was sent, the British marched forth and early the next morning the world's David and Goliath came to blows.

The first shot of the battle, called by the rebels the 'shot heard round the world', rang out on Lexington Green where 77 Minutemen – an elite force of local militia members – crouched waiting to ambush the Redcoats. The king's men quickly smothered the skirmish, killing eight rebels, and the war was underway. By then, King George was no longer reluctant about going to war. He is said to have told his counsellors: 'I am glad that blows will decide it.'

It was to be a lengthy, bitter fight, marked by heroism on the part of the out-gunned, out-manned rebels, and rugged determination on the part of the British. The Americans were led by military leaders who knew only too well that their troops were fighting more with heart than skill. They certainly wouldn't win because they outgunned the British. The colonists were plagued by a shortage of ammunition and weaponry. In the first full-scale battle of the revolution, two months after the shots at Lexington, General Israel Putnam is said to have ordered his American troops 'Don't one of you fire until you see the white of their eyes.' Part of the reason Putnam gave the order was to prevent the troops from wasting scarce ammunition.

That famous command came during the gory battle of Charlestown, which started on 17 June 1775, when the British attacked a group of colonists who had fortified themselves at the top of Breed's Hill. (This battle was later mistakenly identified as the battle of Bunker Hill, which was, in fact, the next mound over.) Having learned from their mistakes earlier in the war, the unflinching colonists waged a tactically masterful fight: British casualties were double that of the Minutemen – more than 1,000 Redcoats were killed to 440 rebels. Unfortunately for the Americans, the fight was so heated that they ultimately exhausted their ammunition supplies. The Redcoats won that battle, but reports of the bravery of the American troops helped to inspire the spirit of insurrection throughout the colonies.

THE UNITED COLONIES

Meanwhile, in Philadelphia the Second Continental Congress was establishing a new government. Using as an excuse the fact that King George III had not replied to a petition for redress of grievances sent by the First Continental Congress, the second Congress gradually took on the responsibilities of a national government. In June 1775 the group established the Continental Army as well as a continental currency. By the end of July of that year, it had also created a post office for the 'United Colonies.'

In August 1775 England issued another proclamation, this one declaring (a bit belatedly) that the colonies were 'engaged in open and avowed rebellion.' Later that year, Parliament passed the American Prohibitory Act, which declared that all American vessels and cargoes were the property of the Crown.

It all reached a crescendo in Philadelphia on 7 June 1776. On that date the Congress heard Richard Henry Lee of Virginia read a resolution which began: 'Resolved: That these United Colonies are, and of right ought to be, free and independent states, that they are absolved from all allegiance to the British Crown, and that all political connection between them and the state of Great Britain is, and ought to be, totally dissolved.'

SOME TRUTHS ARE SELF-EVIDENT

The valour (or traitorousness, depending on your perspective) of the rebels in Boston ultimately resulted in the penning of the

The bloody **Battle of Bunker Hill** convinced the colonists that they could win the war.

Declaration of Independence. The document, still considered one of the world's great governmental manifestos, has been taught in political science classes ever since. Its introductory paragraph is blunt and unapologetic and tells the story of how America viewed its strength in comparison to England's: 'When in the course of human events, it becomes necessary for one people to dissolve the political bands which have connected them with another ... a decent respect to the opinions of mankind requires that they should declare the causes which impel them to the separation. We hold these Truths to be self-evident, that all men are created equal; that they are endowed by their Creator with certain unalienable rights, that among these are Life, Liberty and the pursuit of Happiness.'

On 4 July 1776 in Philadelphia, John Hancock of Boston signed his name to the document with a flourish. His is the largest signature by far – he is said to have written large enough that George III could read it without spectacles. Even today in America a 'John Hancock' is a euphemism for one's signature.

STARTING OVER

At that point, of course, the war was far from over. The fight would last for another five years, but while much of it was fought in New England, there were no more battles in Boston. When America finally did achieve its independence in 1781, Massachusetts was one of the original 13 states in the fledgling United States of America.

As might be expected, when it was all over, the war relegated the US to England's doghouse and trade was cut off. The loss of the English market caused Boston's status as a major port to suffer. The US economy continued to sputter until Boston embraced whaling and Far East trade; eventually when the demand for fishing clippers grew, Boston's shipyards – especially Nantucket, New Bedford and Salem – grew into some of the largest in the world. Other Boston inventions that helped the economy were Eli Whitney's cotton gin, Charles Goodyear's vulcanised rubber, Elias Howe's sewing machine and Alexander Graham Bell's telephone.

As the city's wealth and power grew, so did its immigrant population. By 1822, fleets of immigrants turned up in droves on its shores looking for a better life. Later they arrived in a flood. The Irish arrived in 1845, escaping the potato famine; they were followed by tens of thousands of European immigrants seeking financial opportunity and religious freedom. By 1860, it was estimated that more than 60 per cent of Boston's population had been born elsewhere in the world.

Boston's skinny peninsula could hardly accommodate such an enormous influx of new citizens, so resourceful denizens looked to the fetid swamps of Back Bay for real estate. To

Seven Boston firsts

First African-American author
Phillis Wheatley, the slave of a Boston merchant, started writing at the age of 13. Her first book, *Poems on Various Subjects,* was published in 1773 in London.

First American sighting of a house rat
Occurred in Boston in 1775. A dubious distinction at best. Not indigenous to the US, the rodents came by ship. As you'll notice if you look around Boston, they stayed.

First painless surgery with a general anaesthetic
In 1846, a dentist named William Morton demonstrated the first surgical use of ether at Massachusetts General Hospital. Dental work is such fun now, thanks to him.

First telephone
On 10 March 1876 Alexander Graham Bell made the very first phone call in history to his assistant, Dr Watson.

First North American subway system
Trains started rolling out of Park Street Station on 1 September 1897.

First computer
Developed at MIT in 1897, the world's first computer was called a 'differential analyser'.

First successful kidney transplant
Surgeon Joseph E. Murray stitched up the first successful kidney swap at Peter Bent Brigham Hospital in 1952.

make the bogs liveable, two of Boston's three hills were levelled and several feet were shaved off the top of Beacon Hill. But the real work of filling in the marshy Back Bay didn't begin until 1858, when 3,500 loads of gravel a day were railed in and dumped into the muck. It took more than 30 years to complete the project – the largest engineering feat of its day. The result was 450 more acres (181 hectares) of land, which doubled the city's size.

Unfortunately, the new neighbourhoods encouraged ethnic ghettoisation. As waves of immigrants poured into the North End and slowly crept up the 'wrong' side of Beacon Hill, it alarmed the lily-white 'Brahmins' (as those who lived on the hill were called). These were the self-proclaimed First Families of Boston – or FFB, as the Cabots, Lodges, Codmans and Lowells referred to themselves – and they promptly abandoned the 'right' side of the Hill and began building mansions in Back Bay as quickly as acres were added. Always the least desirable neighbourhood, the North End was to change population several times during the 19th century, from black to Irish to Jewish to Portuguese. Only in the past 60 years has the North End become the lively Italian quarter of the present day.

THE ATHENS OF AMERICA
'Their hotels are bad. Their pumpkin pies are delicious. Their poetry is not so good,' Edgar Allan Poe once wrote about Bostonians. And Poe was right. For a while, Boston's poetry wasn't so good. But it wasn't just the city's stanzas that lacked finesse; it was the entire notion of crafted aesthetics that escaped the community's inhabitants. Why had the arts been so neglected? In essence, Massachusetts housed many Puritans and Puritans were, well, Puritans. They didn't consider the arts a godly practice. As for the other early colonists, many were preoccupied with gaining independence. ('I must study politics and war so that my sons may have liberty to study mathematics and philosophy in order to give their children a right to study painting, poetry, music, architecture,' wrote patriot and future US President John Adams to his wife Abigail in 1780.)

Luckily, economic prosperity in the 19th century was to beget a cultural awakening. When the Cabots and Lowells began to travel abroad, they realised just how unenlightened their city was – and it didn't take them long to rectify the situation. In the short span between the 1840s and 1880s, Boston gleaned a music hall, a magnificent public library, a museum of natural history, a museum of fine arts and a symphony orchestra. These new arts showcases, coupled with the talent they attracted, earned the city the sobriquet 'the Athens of America'.

THE CENTRE OF ABOLITION
In 1800, Boston was home to the oldest and largest population of free black people in America (a full 5 per cent of its then total population of 25,000) and the black community already had its heroes: Crispus Atticus was a martyr of the Boston Massacre, Peter Salem a hero of Bunker Hill. Although the black population hadn't yet been granted suffrage, they were allowed to earn wages as servants,

street cleaners, shipbuilders, blacksmiths and barbers. They could also meet freely, worship as they pleased and educate themselves. The first African Meeting House in America was built on Beacon Hill in 1806, as was the first school, Abiel Smith, in 1835. And taught to young Boston children were the ABCs of Abolition:

A is an abolitionist
A man who wants to free
The wretched slave
And give to all
An equal liberty
B is a Brother with a skin
Of somewhat darker hue,
But in our Heavenly Father's sight
He is as dear as you

Hence, it wasn't surprising that, as tensions over slavery mounted between the north and south, Boston became the centre of the abolition movement. The New England Anti-Slavery Society was founded in 1832, and prominent blacks such as Frederick Douglass, William Nell and Maria Miller Stuart began condemning slavery publicly with the support of wealthy white people. Lewis and Harriet Hayden's house at 66 Phillips Street became a station on the Underground Railroad (a network of abolitionists whose members smuggled slaves from the south to freedom in the north).

When the Civil War broke out, the first free black regiment of the Union Army – the 54th Regiment of Massachusetts – was organised on Beacon Hill, trained in Jamaica Plain and sent to battle in the Carolinas. All of those soldiers died in war. Their story was largely forgotten for the better part of a century. It gained attention only in recent years, and is commemorated by a sculpture in the Public Garden, and was explored in the 1989 film *Glory*.

IRELAND WEST

It might be hard to believe in these days of pubs shipped over brick by brick from Dublin, but Boston didn't always ooze unconditional love for the Irish. When the potato famine of the mid-19th century first sent over a 100,000 people from Ireland to Boston, the reported life expectancy of an Irish immigrant living in Boston was 14 years. In this traditionally Brahmin city, blatant discrimination was common. Job postings often bore the clause 'No Irish Need Apply'.

After generations of political struggle, though, prejudices began to subside as the city's Irish political machine fought its way into power. The election of the first Irish-Catholic mayor of Boston, Hugh O'Brien, started to chip away at racial biases – so much so, that eventually Irish leaders couldn't lose a race.

'Boss' James Michael Curley was perhaps the finest example of this relative invincibility. Curley was nicknamed The Purple Shamrock – and as the moniker suggests, he was a colourful character. Curley served as congressman, governor and mayor, and over a checkered 40-year career, he bought votes, got re-elected to the position of alderman while in the clink and allegedly acquired the mayoral office after threatening to expose the incumbent, (John F Kennedy's maternal grandfather) John 'Honey Fitz' Fitzgerald, for having a mistress. And

The great molasses massacre

As catastrophes go, this was a fairly novel one. At midday on 15 January 1919, a huge iron tank of molasses (a thick, dark syrup) spontaneously ruptured, launching a sweet tsunami on the unsuspecting residents of Boston's North End. Two million gallons of the stuff washed in an enormous sugary wave over the neighbourhood.

The *New York Times* reported: 'A dull, muffled roar gave but an instant's warning before the top of the tank was blown into the air.' The sticky mass crushed buildings and consumed anyone unlucky enough to be within the harbourside neighbourhoods of Commercial Street and Copps Hill. The wave overtook a group of city workers lunching in a nearby building. It demolished a local fire station. It hit with such force that it cracked a train trestle suspended high above the wharf.

The next day, the *Boston Post* described its fatal impact this way: 'Once it smeared a head – human or animal – there was no coughing off the sticky mess. To attempt to wipe it with hands was to make it worse. Most of those who died, died of suffocation.' Those who survived had to have their clothes cut off, as the glue-like substance simply would not let go.

The glutinous flood killed 21 people and injured more than 50. In the weeks following the catastrophe, wild speculation as to the cause of the explosion absorbed the town. In the end, the Purity Distillery Company was found responsible for storing the molasses in a shoddily engineered container.

To this day, local lore maintains that on very hot days in the North End you can still smell the sickly sweet scent of molasses.

holding true to his crooked ways, Curley spent much of his fourth and last term as mayor in a federal penitentiary, serving his sentence for his conviction on charges of mail fraud.

PROBLEMATIC PROGRESS

By the late 1940s, Boston had lost its major port status to the West Coast and its manufacturing to the south. What's more, Boston became the only major US city in the post-World War II baby boom to see a decline in population (plummeting from 800,000 to 560,000). Both its middle and upper classes migrated to the suburbs, and its infrastructure went along. With downtown crime on the rise and student demonstrations blocking the streets, tourism began to suffer, and the city entered an economic crisis. By the mid 1960s, Boston had officially become one of the worst places to live in America.

Panicked by Boston's decline, city officials attempted to hit the brakes. Under Mayor John Hynes and the newly established Boston Redevelopment Authority (BRA), officials began a 'clean up' of the city's problem areas. The 1960s saw the completion of three massive urban renewal projects with controversial results. The Prudential Tower rose out of Back Bay's abandoned Boston & Maine railyards. The West End, Boston's only ethnically mixed neighbourhood, was razed to make way for a modern apartment complex called Charles River Park. Seedy Scollay Square, home to Boston's then few gay bars and jazz joints, was levelled to make way for the squeaky-clean pavement of a new Government Centre. Basically, in the name of progress, the city's character and eclecticism were systematically erased. They called it urban renewal. To this day, the name remains a cruel joke.

However inept, though, these first efforts at re-urbanisation had their positive side. Organisations like the Beacon Hill Historical

The devil made them do it

'An Army of Devils is horribly broke in upon the place which is our centre.' So wrote the Puritan preacher Cotton Mather in July 1692 as the madness that became known as the Salem Witch Trials swept through the small village just north of Boston.

The legacy of the shocking proceedings in Salem Village between February and September of 1692 has proved a lengthy one which has remained a point of fascination in American folklore. By the time the witch hunt ended, 19 convicted witches were executed, at least four accused witches had died in prison, and one man had been pressed to death. Over 100 others were arrested and imprisoned on witchcraft charges. Even animals were not immune to the mass hysteria – two dogs were executed as suspected accomplices.

It all started with the peculiar symptoms of Betty Parris, the six-year-old daughter of Village minister Samuel Parris. With little provocation, she dashed about, dove under furniture, contorted in pain and complained of fever. When three of Betty's playmates developed similar symptoms, Tituba, the Parris' slave, attempted a remedy; a 'witch cake' composed of rye and the urine of an afflicted victim. Unfortunately for Tituba, her technique and her knowledge of voodoo placed her under immediate suspicion of witchcraft. Under tremendous pressure, Tituba confessed to consorting with the devil.

The 'victims', now numbering seven, were encouraged by their new-found power, and their accusations flowed. The paranoia and fear spread, and suddenly it seemed nobody was immune from allegations of witchcraft.

Even as they went about the business of killing their neighbours, the townspeople were stunned by the devil's intrusion into their quiet community. 'It cannot be imagined that in a place of so much knowledge, so many in so small a compass of land should abominably leap into the Devil's lap all at once,' wrote the Reverend John Hale in September 1692.

Over time, though, as accusations fell upon even those with the purest of characters, the villagers began to have doubts. By the fall of 1692, even the zealous father-and-son preaching team of Cotton and Increase Mather began to question the validity of the proceedings, and the sorry mess was brought to an end.

Throughout the centuries since, memories of the event refuse to die. Countless books have been written about it. In the 1950s, the playwright Arthur Miller wrote *The Crucible* to highlight the similarities he saw between activities in Salem in 1692 and the anti-Communist 'witch hunts' of his time. In the end, it seems the fascination in Salem lies not only in the mysticism of it all, but in the speed with which this brave new world of freedom and democracy turned on itself.

Integration of Boston's public schools in the 1970s led to months of ugly riots.

Society were established to protect other neighbourhoods from suffering the fate of the West End. Public outcry caused subsequent developers to be attentive to architectural and historical significance. Today the city maintains many of its most important historical buildings despite the ravages of the 1960s and 1970s.

FIGHT THE POWER, REDUX

In the midst of financial chaos, Boston then entered an emotional and moral morass. The city's 1970s race riots are notorious to this day. Possibly the most striking image from those days was shot on City Hall Plaza, when a white student tried to spear a black passer-by with a flagpole bearing an American flag. Presages of such bigotry began in 1974, when federal Judge Arthur Garrity Jr ordered the city to desegregate its public school system. Before the ruling, proximity had dictated school assignment, leaving poor children (often racial minorities) going to school only with other poor children and receiving a poor education. The court saw this as a violation of civil rights and forced an end to the practice. It ordered a racial integration policy designed to give each school a ratio of black to white children that reflected Boston's overall population. That September, under heavy police security, the Board of Education began busing white students into black neighbourhoods and black students into white neighbourhoods.

It was ugly. Enormous riots developed. Crowds of angry white parents and children filled the streets. Rocks were thrown at the black students. Blood was spilled, bedlam ensued – most particularly in Irish South Boston and the largely black section of town known as Roxbury.

While the violence exposed Boston's ugly underbelly to the nation, critics of busing – future Mayor of Boston Ray Flynn, President Gerald Ford, state politician William Bulger – argued fervently that this fight concerned more than just pure racism. Many believed that Boston's ethnic ghettos had evolved into closely-knit neighbourhoods – both blacks and whites feared losing their hard-earned sense of community. The court disagreed, and busing remained for many years.

Finally, in 1999, precisely 25 years after the racial integration programme began, the Boston School Committee voted to stop using racial quotas for school placement, saying it would never achieve its goal making the schools truly equal. The ending was anti-climactic, nobody emerged a winner. And in the eyes of many – fairly or not – Boston will always be associated with those scenes of racial intolerance and hatred.

THE MASSACHUSETTS MIRACLE

In the 1970s, City officials courted the emerging hi-tech industry aggressively and, by the mid-1980s, Boston had reinvented itself once again. 'The Massachusetts Miracle' – as the media touted Boston's resuscitated economy – was due largely to the leadership of mayors such as Kevin White and Raymond Flynn.

Within the last 15 or 20 years, Boston has become a popular location for the headquarters of national corporations and the chosen home for thousands of urban professionals. The flip side to this urban renaissance is not so nice, though. The days of cheap living in Boston are long gone. And while much of Boston's historical past has been preserved much of the city's colourful social character has been homogenised, as local independent businesses have been elbowed out by larger chains.

Once again, it seems, Boston has found a way to reinvent itself.

Key events

1497-1524 Explorations of Massachusetts Bay by John Cabot, Miguel Corte Real and Giovanni Verrazano – among others.
1614 Captain John Smith explores and maps the Massachusetts Bay area, calling it a 'Paradise' in his memoirs.
1620 Puritans set sail aboard the *Mayflower* to establish the first colony in New England. They land on 9 November on Cape Cod. They found Plymouth on 10 December.
1630 John Winthrop and his Puritans establish Boston on the Shawmut peninsula.
1636 The first college in the New World is established; it's given the name Harvard College in 1638.
1665 Boston witch trials.
1675 Chief Metacomet (King Philip) raids several Massachusetts Bay Colony settlements. A year later he is captured, drawn and quartered and then beheaded.
1692 Salem witch trials.
1765 Parliament imposes the Stamp Act on all commercial and legal documents, including newspapers. It's repealed one year later.
1767 The Townshend Acts are passed by Parliament, placing duties on any glass, lead, paint, paper and tea imported to the colonies.
1768 Troops are dispatched to Boston by George III to quiet civil unrest.
1770 George III repeals all duties levied in the Townshend Act except those on tea. Clash on 5 March between Bostonians and English soldiers results in the 'Boston Massacre'.
1773 Sons of Liberty host the 'Boston Tea Party' on 16 December by dumping 342 chests of East India tea into the harbour.
1774 Boston port is closed and colonists prohibited from meeting publicly. Delegates from Massachusetts are sent to the First Continental Congress in Philadelphia, convened on 5 September.
1775 Battles of Lexington and Concord take place on 19 April, when British march to Concord to take an arms store. Battle of Bunker Hill takes place on 17 June.
1776 British troops evacuate Boston in March. Declaration of Independence signed in Philadelphia on 4 July.
1783 Slavery is abolished in the state of Massachusetts.
1793 Eli Whitney introduces his cotton gin in Boston.
1835 Abiel Smith School is opened, the first black schoolhouse in the USA.
1839 Charles Goodyear invents vulcanised rubber.
1854 Boston Public Library opens, the first free public library in the USA.
1862 54th Massachusetts, the first black regiment of the Union Army, is commissioned, trained and sent to battle in the Civil War.
1872 The Great Fire of Boston destroys most of what is now downtown Boston.
1876 Alexander Graham Bell introduces the telephone. The Museum of Fine Arts is opened.
1887 Park Street and Boylston Street stations open, part of the first subway in the USA.
1897 First Boston Marathon is run.
1912 Fenway Park opens. The Red Sox win the World Series for the first and only time.
1905 James Curley begins political career as alderman, campaigning from jail.
1928 World's first computer is developed at MIT.
1946 John F Kennedy is elected congressman.
1947 Curley serves final term as mayor from a federal penitentiary.
1960 John F Kennedy becomes 35th president of the USA.
1963 John F Kennedy is assassinated.
1974 Federal district court orders the desegregation of Boston schools. Cross-town busing begins.
1980 City celebrates its 350th anniversary.
1988 Governor Mike Dukakis runs unsuccessfully as Democratic candidate for president.
1990 Boston's population increases in the census for the first time in four decades.
1993 Thomas Menino is elected mayor, the first non Irishman to hold the post in 63 years.
1998 200th birthday of *USS Constitution* ('Old Ironsides'), commemorated by its first sail in over a century.
1999 Race-based admissions end in Boston public schools.
2000 A few days after Christmas, technical support worker Michael McDermott shoots seven of his co-workers dead at a suburban Boston computer technology firm.

Boston Today

Suffering from status envy, the Athens of America longs to be world class.

In 1993, when Massachusetts state Representative James T Brett lost the Boston mayoral race to District Councillor Thomas M Menino, the conceding candidate offered these words: 'I pledge to stand shoulder-to-shoulder with you in an effort to make Boston the world-class city we know it can be.' Brett's speech recognised the one thing that eats away at this town's ego. Even in its boom days, Boston isn't yet respected as world class. This town has a serious case of status-envy.

With its brawny business sector, esteemed universities and rich local history, Boston feels itself positioned within striking distance of international repute, but even so, at both the international and the national level, the Hub is a stepping stone rather than the higher ground

Sox it to 'em: Babe Ruth is long gone, but Bostonians are still big on baseball.

itself; an agent rather than a celebrity; a catalyst rather than the explosion. Though it is the founding city of the most powerful nation on Earth, and the chosen home of some of the world's greatest minds, Boston wants more. So, like a candidate scrambling for votes, it is doing everything within its power to win over the world.

RED SOX AND GREENBACKS

It shouldn't matter, but it does. Boston's baseball team, the Red Sox, haven't won the World Series since 1918, and that's a major source of insecurity for this baseball-mad city. To proud Massholes (an, er, polite term of affection Massachusetts natives bestow upon one another), Red Sox insults are as personal as mother jokes; even non-baseball fans are sensitive about their town's ill-fated team.

While baseball doesn't define an entire community, it does hint at one of Boston's dirtiest secrets: a quiet but robust jealousy of New York. The two cities are so geographically close to one another (three hours away by train), that it's like a weird case of metropolitan sibling rivalry. As with all domestic disputes, there's a history here. And as with many things in Boston, it all comes down to baseball. The covetousness began early in the 20th century, when the Boston Red Sox had on their roster one of the greatest players of all time, Babe Ruth. The story of what happened to The Babe is now American baseball lore. You see, the Sox traded him to the Yankees because the Boston team's owner, Harry Frazee, was a fan of musicals, and he needed funds to put on a production of 'No No Nanette'. With the auctioning off of Babe Ruth, Frazee got $100,000, and put on his show. The Sox never won another pennant. And the city never got over it.

Boston's sense of inadequacy hasn't subsided since – and in most ways, it's become even more palpable. In 2000, for instance, the US sports magazine *Sports Illustrated* predicted the Boston Red Sox would win the World Series. In a scenario more horrible than Sox fans could have imagined, they lost in the playoffs to their arch-enemies, the New York Yankees.

Even outside the realm of sports, Boston feels the power of New York constantly. The New York Times Company owns the city's well-respected daily newspaper, the *Boston Globe*; Macy's, the archetypal New York department store, has replaced Boston's longtime stalwart Jordan Marsh. In the late 1990s, in a particularly ignoble event, former Massachusetts Governor William Weld publicly jettisoned Beantown for the Big Apple.

In the same way big brothers know their younger siblings simultaneously revere and despise them, New Yorkers love to jab Bostonians. One easy target is the city's New England conservatism – especially aspects like the city's 2am pub closing time (New Yorkers call their home 'the city that never sleeps') and Massachusetts' Blue Laws. Some say the colourful term for the rules that enforce the state's morality comes from the blue paper on which the legislation was first written; others suggest the name was derived from the colour skin takes on after someone has been beaten for disobeying them. Either way – paper dye or skin contusion – the intention behind the Blue Laws is to preserve the sanctity of the Christian sabbath. To this day antiquated legislation still on the state's books proscribes the retail sale of alcohol on Sundays, along with full-day open hours for businesses and shops. In theory, such prim provisions seem like an homage to the state's forebears, but in practice, the laws are a priggish annoyance to virtually everybody.

Even with such rules, and such bad luck at baseball, the city genuinely has little reason to feel insecure. Certainly, local business doesn't seem to be bothered. The top US business magazine *Fortune* recently heralded Boston as one of the 'top ten places to do business in America.' In 1998, Boston was ranked as the world's third largest city for money management, behind New York (naturally) and London. Widely viewed as the king of the mutual fund, Boston houses the headquarters of world class financial companies like Fidelity, Putnam and John Hancock Investments. The boom and bust high-tech sector continues to be one of the city's biggest growth industries, and Boston is home to 3,000 software and Internet companies.

GENTRIFICATION AND DISCONTENT

With the Boston business scene dazzling the North-east with so much dizzying cash, the real estate market suddenly became extremely competitive in the late 1990s. By 2000, Boston's vacancy rate hovered at a chillingly low 1 per cent. There simply isn't anything to buy, even if you could afford it in the first place, which you probably couldn't because prices went through the roof. A modest one-bedroom

Tattoo you

It is the eternal dichotomy of Boston – on one hand, the city likes to portray itself as a liberal, intellectual, international city with the kind of status and amenities one finds in New York or Paris, albeit on a smaller scale. On the other hand, it can't quite shake its reputation as an uptight, puritanical town with restrictive laws dating back beyond the days of Prohibition. Liquor stores are required to close on Sundays, for example, while all bars must close at 2am. And, until 2001, if the impulse struck you to adorn any part of your body with a tattoo, you were out of luck, for until then tattooing was illegal throughout the state.

Massachusetts was one of only three states in the US (South Carolina and Oklahoma were the other two) to outlaw the practice of ink-art. The Mass state law read, in part: 'Tattooing the body of a person by other than a qualified physician ... shall be punished by a fine of not more than $300, or by imprisonment for not more than one year, or both.' Now, trying to find a doctor willing to tattoo a rose on your arse was not an easy task, so, for all intents and purposes, tattooing was completely outlawed.

This all started in 1962, when a hepatitis outbreak in New York heightened fears that practices like tattooing could transmit infectious diseases, and the Massachusetts Legislature decided to ban the practice in the interest of public health.

Of course, the law never stopped anybody from adorning their bodies with intricate artwork. Within an hour's drive, Rhode Island and New Hampshire both boast a healthy number of tattoo parlours eager for the out-of-state traffic. At the same time, as always seems to happen when something is banned, an intricate underground network sprang up. Those in search of a good tattoo found their artists the same way people have always found drug dealers – those with tattoos made referrals to their artist, cash was exchanged under a table and the deal was struck. Anybody with an especially good tattoo could expect to be asked where they had it done, and entrepreneurial tattoo artists made surreptitious house calls. Tattoo parties, in which a group would gather at a friend's home for a drink and some ink, became as common in the 1990s as speakeasies were in the 1920s.

It's all ending now though. With improved sterilisation standards, and no indication that tattoos are spreading disease elsewhere, the state Legislature reversed the anti-tattoo law at the end of 2000. By mid-2001, Boston-area tattoo artists were lining up to apply for a permit from their local governmental agencies to open shops. The great tattoo ban was over.

apartment in Back Bay now rents for around $2,000 a month and sells for around $300,000. Between the years 1999 and 2000 the median monthly rent for the entire city, including its least attractive areas, increased from about $1,350 to more than $1,450.

While the city is doing well economically, clearly not everyone in Boston can afford such steep prices. In the past, anyone who wasn't lugging home a huge pile of financial bacon – students, lower-wage workers and struggling families in particular – looked to nearby burgs like Allston, Cambridge or Somerville for cheap rent. But once the economy boomed and rent control ended, the moneyed classes started pouring into the city and fringe neighbourhoods became younger and wealthier. Today, high rents are pushing working-class families and the elderly even further away from the centre of city life.

'Booming development had the side-effect of killing off much of Boston's underground party scene.'

In the worse cases, of course, exorbitant rents have kicked people to the curbside. From 1989 to 1999, city streets saw a 52 per cent increase in the number of homeless. Walking around downtown Boston today, you will see them everywhere. Estimates, which some social agencies feel are hugely conservative, place the total homeless population at about 5,000 – a little under one per cent of the city's total population. Slapped with these statistics, in November 2000 Mayor Menino unveiled a five year plan of attack, a plan which includes increasing funds for job training, adding beds to shelters and devoting a percentage of new city-approved renovations to house the homeless.

Gentrification has also changed long-standing ethnic neighbourhoods. Although there are still ethnic strongholds such as South Boston, Dorchester, Roxbury and Mattapan, Boston's neighbourhoods have begun to mix. Today, the South End and Jamaica Plain are two of the most multicultural. Just over half of Boston's residents are white, nearly a quarter are black, 10 per cent are Hispanic and 10 per cent are of Asian descent. These days even the North End – long the city's centre of Italian culture – feels a little less Italian, while the South End is less black and Chinatown is less Chinese.

PORTRAIT OF AN ARTIST AS A TENANT

City development and a bustling economy have had the side-effect of killing much of Boston's infamous underground party scene – the all-night raves, the ticket-only loft parties and the mad warehouse bashes that hallmarked the city during the late 1980s and early '90s. That was an era of cheap living, and hundreds of local artists creatively searched for affordable housing and studio space, often by squatting in hollowed-out buildings, dusty warehouses and abandoned lofts along the edge of downtown and waterfront. Landlords often agreed to let the squatters stay, as long as no one complained.

These makeshift homes afforded the new residents with a neighbourless venue for raves, art galleries and alternative theatres. Gradually the artists' efforts to make their new environs safe and comfortable proved successful – so successful in fact, that it caught the attention of those with much deeper pockets (namely rich corporations). For their trouble, the artists received thank-you notes in the form of eviction notices. Since the tenants' upheaval, marathon underground parties aren't completely extinct in the area, but they tend to take place outside the city limits, in low-profile towns like Chelsea, Dorchester and Roxbury.

BOSTON'S BIG DIG

A year or so ago, while trying to gain favour with Beantown's college crowd, the Coors Brewing Company toyed around with the idea of printing up promotional T-shirts that used the tagline 'Boston, you've got a Big Dig' alongside a phallic image of a crane. *Double entendres* aside, the much discussed Big Dig – the city's attempt to drive its central traffic artery underground while keeping the elevated expressway open to traffic – is, well, huge. Begun in 1991, the Dig's original estimated cost was $2.6 billion. Over time, that figure skyrocketed to $11 billion, and then to a whopping $14 billion. The ballooning expenses have caused quite a hubbub in the Hub, with the press and other local officials haranguing the Dig's project manager and the governor for alleged mismanagement and ineptitude.

Official estimates have the project finished in 2004 – believe it when you see it. In the meantime, Bostonians and visitors to the city are routinely confronted by inconveniences: constant pounding and crashing, huge mountains of sand and gravel, unpleasant and nervous displaced water rats and inexplicable traffic jams at all hours of the day and night. Locals have grown

The problems: bumper to bumper traffic and damaging pollution.

The solution: the $14 billion Big Dig aims to move the freeway underground by 2004.

accustomed to the labyrinth of scaffolding, road signs and hard hats in the northern end of the city, expecting exit ramps that open and close without warning, one-way street systems that shift daily, ruined suspensions on their cars, flat tyres and the need to weave in and out of stark cement towers and underneath ominous steel girders that seem to lead to nowhere. Stay for long, and you'll get used to it too.

When completed, however, the system will be the most advanced in the nation. Moving traffic underground will not only make the town look better – its extensive interstate system hides some of the nicest property in the city – it will also reduce carbon monoxide levels in car-loving Boston by 12 per cent. Neighbourhoods long isolated by the central freeway system – the North End and Charlestown in particular – will again be connected to downtown. And once the elevated freeway system is torn down, about 30 acres (12 hectares) of land in the very heart of Boston will once again open up. Most of that land is to be set aside for park land.

And so Boston endures its position as the biggest construction site in the world by promising itself that the future will be much greener, once the last shovelful of earth is nestled into place.

THE NAKED TRUTH

The problems began with bare breasts. In the summer of 1999, stunt double Gidget Churchill impulsively flashed a photographer during a raucous harbour 'booze cruise'. Little did she know, the snapping shutterbug worked for the *Boston Herald* newspaper – a detail that probably would not have reverberated to the Massachusetts State House if the cruise hadn't been organised by a high-ranking state official and paid for with taxpayers' money. Word of the incident got out, the state official was dismissed and Gidget's naked flesh signaled the first of a series of scandals for Massachusetts Governor Paul Cellucci's administration.

Other highly publicised State House debacles in recent years: the aforementioned swelling of the Big Dig's price tag; the lieutenant governor roping State House staff into helping her move, having her aides babysit her daughter and arranging for a police helicopter to whisk her home for Thanksgiving; allegations that the governor appointed a leader of the Teamsters (an enormous, controversial and powerful union of lorry drivers) to the Massachusetts Port Authority, despite concerns that the appointee had been accused of extortion. Needless to say, Cellucci's popularity plummeted.

From Beantown to Athens

There is just something about Boston that brings out the creativity in everybody. Or, at any rate, it seems everyone wants to call the city something besides Boston. The Native Americans called it **Shawmut**, or 'unclaimed land'. When John Winthrop and his fellow Puritans defied the Indians by claiming it after all, they promptly renamed it **Tremontaine** ('three mountains') after the three local hills that dominated the place. In no time flat, though, the homesick settlers had re-dubbed their village **Boston** (a corruption of 'St Botolph's Town') after the Lincolnshire village from which most of them had come. A torrent of other names followed, all of which have stuck around for centuries.

Take, for instance, **Beantown**. In the 18th century Boston was fairly awash with molasses, a by-product of rum production. Because of its cheap cost and plenitude, the syrup was frequently used by colonial housewives to sweeten ordinary foods. A favourite food of the day was beans that had been stewed in the sugary stuff for hours. Travellers dubbed the town Beantown, for this ubiquitous dish.

In the early 1800s, Boston became America's undisputed capital of culture. It's little wonder, then, that the city became known as the **Athens of America**.

Later in the 19th century, the writer Oliver Wendell Holmes gave the city the name that Bostonians love the most. Holmes so admired the city's artistic and civic achievements that he described Boston as the 'hub of the Solar System' in his popular 1858 essay 'The Autocrat of the Breakfast Table'. It took Bostonians no time to embrace that concept, and, ever since, the nickname you're most likely to hear Bostonians call their city is the **Hub**.

On the other hand, Boston Mayor Tom Menino remained very popular. Since his 1994 inauguration, Menino – nicknamed 'Mumbles' because his speaking style sounds as if he is talking through a mouthful of mashed potatoes – has successfully fought large-scale problems like crime, education and unemployment. Menino won voters' favour during the 1993 mayoral race against representative Brett with his frank, get-tough attitude and won by a landslide, carrying 18 of the city's 22 ward districts. He became the first non-Irish man to hold the position in 63 years. And even Menino's most strident critics have to admit that it was action that got him re-elected in 1997. During his first term, the unemployment rate dropped to almost zero, crime plummeted to its lowest levels in 30 years and school exam scores finally began to climb. Menino seemed to be everywhere: cutting ribbons at new homes for the elderly, marching in the Gay Pride parade, meeting with other mayors in Washington and speaking to the city's youth at graduation ceremonies.

Still, all has not been sunshine for the mayor. Menino has been criticised for borrowing the ideas of others and passing them off as his own. He's also had to apologise for favouring South Boston over other city districts – most expressly in a deal that would have sucked millions out of the city's general budget and over to South Boston's waterfront development. But in the past, Bostonians haven't seemed to care where the idea comes from or who he favours, as long as it all works. The next mayoral race will be in late 2001. Will Menino keep mumbling? You tell us.

CRIME STORIES

When city officials decided to make Boston a leading tourist destination, they knew their first job was to make the streets safer for visitors. Crime prevention has been a major priority ever since. In the past decade or so, the Boston Police Department has put more police officers on the street, neighbourhoods all over the city have organised crime watches and schools have instituted anti-gang programmes. State legislators, who have provided Massachusetts with the toughest gun control laws in the country, have also taken up the crime hue-and-cry. The results have been pretty spectacular: both violent crime and crimes against property are at their lowest levels in 30 years. Homicide is at its lowest level in 40 years, with a stunning 75 per cent reduction in homicides involving a firearm. Before leaving office, former President Clinton described Boston as a nationwide model in crime prevention.

SECOND-TIER CITY

With college students who seem to treat the city like bivouac, pedestrians who jaywalk like suicidal goats in Third World countries and bicycles that are little more than target practice for car drivers – it's not hard to see why locals become disenchanted after spending many years in Boston. Although repeated public opinion polls have shown that the city is now viewed by those who live elsewhere as one of the nation's most attractive places in which to live, the fact is, Boston is really third base on the baseball diamond of American life.

Still smiling: Boston grad Hillary Clinton.

THE MEANS TO AN END

Many powerful figures have lodged in Boston on the way up: Hillary Rodham Clinton graduated from Wellesley College, Bill Gates dropped out of Harvard, astronaut Edwin 'Buzz' Aldrin walked through the halls at MIT before he ever stepped foot on the moon. Hell, even US nemesis Ho Chi Minh worked as a dishwasher at the old Parker House Hotel. Hundreds of other famous folks have done time here, including former US Vice President (and almost-US President) Al Gore, his mortal enemy Ralph Nader, late-night comedy hosts Conan O'Brien and Jay Leno and talk-show host Rosie O'Donnell.

Still, Boston is tired of losing talent after it trains it – it wants to be the end rather than the means. Will the City on a Hill ever be on top of the world? Will the Athens of America live up to its oldest nickname?

Like we said. You tell us.

Architecture

Sculpted by fire and war, modern Boston's architecture mixes and mingles its eras.

Although fires have plagued Boston since its settlement – the city suffered devastating blazes with numbing regularity in 1653, 1676, 1679, 1711 and 1761 – the Great Fire of November 1872 was the most catastrophic. It started in a hoop skirt warehouse on the corner of Kingston and Summer Streets and swept on to destroy most of Boston's early cityscape. Thus, very little architecture exists that was built before that year, and virtually all of the city is made of brick – which was the city's answer to the flames.

In fact, the only 17th-century wooden construction that remains within Boston's city limits is the **Paul Revere House** (19 North Square). Built in 1680 for merchant Robert Howard, the Paul Revere House lodged its eponymous inhabitant for 30 years from 1770 to 1800. After periods as a flop-house, souvenir shop, cigar factory and grocery store it was saved from the wrecking ball in 1902 by one of Revere's descendants and restored to its original two-storey frame; everything but one door of the interior is now reproduction. Today the house is a National Historic Landmark and museum furnished with period antiques and displays of Revere's remarkable silverwork.

Next to Revere's house is **Pierce/Hichborn House** (29 North Square), a three-storey brick structure built in 1711 for glazier Moses Pierce and later owned by Revere's cousin, shipbuilder Nathaniel Hichborn. Although the

Pierce/Hichborn House was constructed only 30 years after its neighbour, there is a stark contrast between the two. Organic Tudor gives way to orderly English Renaissance; clapboard to brick; diamond to gridded panes; a cramped winding staircase to one that is extravagantly straight. The Pierce/Hichborn House was restored in the 1950s and four of its rooms are open to the public.

The **Old State House** (206 Washington Street, at State Street, *see also p68*) is another remnant of Boston's Georgian past. Designed and constructed in 1713, this small building served as the colonial governor's offices – hence the lion and unicorn ornamentation. It was then used as a public meeting place until the Revolution when it became the headquarters of the British Army. Topped with a richly ornamented steeple, the three-storey brick building is now the Bostonian Society's museum and the State Street T station.

A LOAD OF BULFINCH

Charles Bulfinch (1763-1844) was America's first notable – though never formally trained – architect. Born in Boston to great wealth, Bulfinch travelled extensively in England and Europe and developed an affinity for the fashionable Greek Revival style of architecture he saw. He returned to America and began designing his friends' houses for free. This led to public commissions such as designing the **State House** (Beacon & Park Streets; *see also p72*) and the remodelling of **Faneuil Hall** (*see also p65*).

Bulfinch is best known for the development of the Federal style – an Americanisation of Georgian Greek Revival and his crowning glory outside of Massachusetts was the US Capitol building in Washington, DC. Typical of this genre is the austere, three-storey brick **Harrison Gray Otis House** (141 Cambridge Street), one of the three houses Bulfinch designed for his close friend Otis. Completed in 1796, the flat-faced estate is a masterpiece of symmetry and proportion. Rooms contain false doors, intricately carved fireplaces and shockingly garish colour schemes – all typical of the period. Though the brick building nearly crumbled in the early 1900s, it was rescued in 1916 by the Society for the Preservation of New England Antiquities and painstakingly restored to its original state. Most of the rooms are now open to the public.

The State House, Boston's gold crown, is also a Bulfinch creation. In 1795, when Boston decided it needed a proper state house, the city chose Beacon Hill as its setting and commissioned Bulfinch to orchestrate its appearance. Considered one of his best works, the State House sits atop the hill, and its gleaming gold dome can be seen for miles. Bulfinch's building has a red-brick façade, supported by white Corinthian pillars and flanked by Palladian windows. Bulfinch's dome – his signatory flourish – originally bore a layer of white wood shingles. In 1802, Paul Revere covered the curvature with copper sheeting and painted it grey. Then, as the nation's wealth grew, a coating of 23-carat gold leaf was applied in 1872. That elegant finishing touch has been maintained to this day.

'The Victorian era was as frilly as a doily and as intricate as a wedding dress.'

Bulfinch's architectural impact extended beyond buildings he designed himself. His influence can be spotted around town in green wooden doors topped with fanlights, wrought-iron grillwork and bay windows – a Boston invention. The preponderance of black shutters you see today are a Victorian afterthought.

One of the few Beacon Hill houses you can get inside is the **Charles Nichols House Museum** (55 Mount Vernon Street; *see also p72*).

VICTORIAN VERTICALITY

Frilly as a doily and as intricate as a wedding dress, the Victorian architectural era is manifested nicely in two of Boston's neighbourhoods – the South End and the Back Bay. Until 1858 neither neighbourhood existed. The first of the two to spring up was the South End. Stacked with red brick and bay windows, the South End's architecture tends to reflect Beacon Hill's Federal tradition; many of the side streets emulate Bulfinch's beloved English square design. Two wonderfully preserved examples of this can be seen at Union and Rutland squares. Yet, the South End stands apart from Beacon Hill in several notable ways. The scale of its townhouses is noticeably larger than those on Beacon Hill – apparently because 19th-century folk were taller than their 18th-century counterparts. High ceilings, soaring windows and mansard roofs also speak of a Victorian preoccupation with slenderness and verticality. Ground floors don't really exist in this upwardly mobile, middle-class neighbourhood. Parlour level is now a half-storey above the street while the kitchen and servants' quarters are a half-floor below, at garden level.

Back Bay, on the other hand, takes most of its cues from France's Second Empire. This is where Boston's upper class moved when

Boston Public Library – Charles McKim's creation has Italian and French influences.

Beacon Hill became crowded with immigrant families. The area favours Parisian avenues over English squares and the house façades tend towards marble and sandstone rather than red brick. Small public alleys were added between streets.

In essence, Victorian Boston's private and public architecture has all the unnecessary glamour of a diamond-studded tiara. The **Ames-Webster House** (306 Dartmouth Street), for example, sports an elaborate *porte cochère* that kept the ladies dry as they descended from their carriages. The **Burrage Mansion** (314 Commonwealth Avenue) is a grotesque neo-Gothic confection modelled on the Vanderbilt mansion in Newport, which was modelled on Chateau Chenonçeau in the Loire.

Throughout the Victorian era, the city embraced such ostentation. The favoured styles of the time were Italian Renaissance, neo-Gothic and neo-Romanesque. An area then known as Art Square was one of the first parcels of land set aside in Back Bay purely to showcase the city's fledgling cultural institutions. Later renamed **Copley Square** (*see also p79*), it housed great examples of institutional architecture, such as the Museum of Fine Arts (later torn down to make way for the **Fairmont Copley Plaza**), the Museum of Natural History (now the **Louis** department store) and the magnificent Boston Public Library.

Charles McKim's (1847-1909) original wing of the **Boston Public Library** (*see also p79*) is usually attributed to the Italian Renaissance style, though he claimed its ornate stone façade was equally inspired by a library in Paris, a temple in Rimini and the Marshall Fields department store in Chicago. The library was not an easy project. It was finally completed after a 10-year construction period in 1895. The lobby doors were designed by Daniel Chester French (the artist who also created the Abraham Lincoln statue in the Washington, DC memorial, and the statue of John Harvard in Cambridge). McKim didn't spare any expense when it came to the library's interior, commissioning murals by John Singer Sargent and Pierre Puvis de Chavannes and sculptures by Saint-Gaudens.

While the modern wing of the museum (built in 1972 by Philip Johnson adjacent to the historic wing on Boyleston Street) is seen by many as a blight on McKim's work, the historic portion of the structure is worth a visit. Its grand staircase, vaulted reading room and enchanting cloistered garden have all been meticulously restored and lovingly maintained. McKim would be proud.

RICHARDSON'S BACK BAY

Henry Hobson Richardson (1838-86) is considered one of the greatest American architects. And he was to Victorian Boston what Charles Bulfinch was to Colonial Boston. Although he lived in New York, New Orleans and Paris before moving to Boston – and constructed only two major buildings in the city – Richardson is inextricably linked to

Moving on up: the 1980s economic boom brought skyscrapers to the city's skyline.

the Bay State because of the designs of his masterpiece, the **Trinity Church** (236 Clarendon Street, Copley Square; *see also p79*) and the lovely **First Baptist Church** (110 Commonwealth Avenue; *see also p81*). A student of the Ecole des Beaux Arts in Paris, Richardson was influenced by the heavy lines and solid arcs of medieval French architecture, which he masterfully tempered with delicate Byzantine detailing. Richardson introduced himself to Boston by designing the First Baptist Church. Completed in 1871, it offers a mix of stone and wood surfaces set against a belltower bas-relief from Frederic Auguste Bartholdi – sculptor of the Statue of Liberty. His finest work, the Trinity Church, though commissioned in 1872, didn't open until 1877, at a cost of almost four times the original budget – few question the added expense today as it is often cited as one of the most successful pieces of architecture in America.

As is characteristic of most of his works, Richardson crafted Trinity with the stone walls and solid arcs prevalent in medieval French architecture and decorated them with delicate Byzantine etching. Richardson modelled the central tower after one in Salamanca, though it had to be built considerably shorter than the original or its weight would have sunk the structure into the marshy Back Bay. The church rests on 4,502 pilings driven into the mud.

Richardson's Romanesque style is evident in a number of flagrant imitations around town, including buildings such as the **New Old South Church** (645 Boylston Street) and the **Flour & Grain Exchange Building** which is located right off Quincy Market.

GOING GREEN

A bleak irony shrouds the epilogue to Frederick Law Olmsted's prolific land sculpting career. Nationally renowned for shaping such urban greenery as New York's Central Park and Boston's 'Emerald Necklace', Olmsted (1822-1903) also refurbished the grounds of McLean Hospital in Massachusetts – a sanatorium where, sadly, he later spent his final days.

Yet long before Olmsted was born, Boston tried to temper the lifelessness of its paved streets with the vibrancy of grassy plots. **Boston Common** (*see also p63*) is the oldest public park in America – colonists used it to graze their sheep, train their militia and hang their heretics. The country's oldest botanical gardens are the **Public Garden** (*see also p63*), built on reclaimed land in 1837. When city officials considered selling the Public Garden to developers in 1857, such an uproar broke out that they opted, instead, to add more green space to the burgeoning Back Bay area.

By the time the Back Bay was fully developed, the Metropolitan Parks Commission (now the Metropolitan District Commission, or MDC) had been established and they hired Olmsted to create an 'Emerald Necklace' – a string of lush green plots stretching from Boston Common to Jamaica Plain. Olmstead, known as the father of landscape architecture in America, added

The **John Hancock Tower** and other modern monsters dwarf the likes of **Trinity Church**.

jewels to the Common, the Gardens and Commonwealth Avenue, including the **Back Bay Fens**, **Olmsted Park**, **Jamaica Pond**, **Franklin Park** and the **Arnold Arboretum**. The **Charles River Esplanade**, although conceived by Olmsted, wasn't developed until after his death in the 1930s. And after the MBTA extended the Orange Line to the South End, the **Southwest Corridor Park** joined the 'Emerald Necklace' in the 1980s.

UGLY URBAN RENEWAL

Boston's first attempt to scrape the sky came in 1915, when a 30-storey, neo-Gothic tower was inexplicably added to the **Customs House**. Shortly thereafter, though, the city slumped into a recession. Virtually no important buildings were constructed until the 1960s. Then began a brutal and controversial effort at urban renewal. Swathes of buildings in the inner-city were torn down and replaced with ugly modern architectural behemoths. The city wiped away several culturally and historically rich communities as the concept of 'progress' eclipsed aesthetics throughout the 1960s and early 1970s.

'The Prudential Center is a cheese grater-like tower that's consistently voted Boston's ugliest structure.'

Most of the **West End** was razed to make way for **Charles River Park**, a bland slab of high-rise apartment buildings. One of the first architectural monstrosities was the **Prudential Center** (*see also p80*), a cheese grater-like tower that's consistently voted Boston's ugliest structure. Rising up out of the historical Boston & Albany railyards, the surface of the 52-storey torso resembles a metallic nail file. At its base stands a 27-acre (11-hectare) shopping complex, one so outdated by the early 1990s that most Bostonians forgot there were even stores there. (A few years back, the complex was gutted, and primly renamed the Shops at the Prudential.)

Not long after the West End fell prey to anxious metropolitan surgeons, sordid Scollay Square – in its less-sketchy days, it was where Alexander Graham Bell invented the telephone, but in the 20th century it ended up a hotbed of gin joints and brothels – went under the city's knife, clearing out space for **Government Center** and **City Hall Plaza**.

The respected architect IM Pei designed the master plan for Government Center, which paved red brick over 56 acres (23 hectares) and reduced 22 city streets to six. Architects Kallman, McKinnel and Knowles designed City Hall itself, and Architects Collaborative (Walter Gropius' firm) created the **JFK Buildings**. Despite the pedigree of the people behind the project, the results are flat and uninviting. Plonked in the middle of the seemingly barren Government Center is the awkward City Hall, a checkerboard on stilts.

REACHING FOR THE SKY

Today, most of the city's skyscrapers are downtown – the area annihilated by the Great Fire of 1872 – and only a handful of historically interesting buildings remain. **The Batterymarch** (60 Batterymarch Street) is a decent example of art deco and the **Winthrop** (276 Washington Street) was Boston's first building to make use of a steel frame.

With the 1980s economic boom came a forest of new skyscrapers, many of which were designed by America's most prominent architects. Three firms in particular have been responsible for shaping modern Boston's appearance: IM Pei Associates, Graham Gund Associates and Philip Johnson.

Besides the stolid fortress of the Government Center complex, IM Pei is also responsible for the new wing of the **Museum of Fine Arts**, **Harbor Towers** on the waterfront (off Atlantic Avenue), the gleaming layout of the **Christian Science Center** (175 Huntington Avenue; *see also p83*), the **John F Kennedy Library** (Columbia Point, Dorchester) and **MIT's Media Lab** (on the MIT campus, Massachusetts Avenue, Cambridge). But Pei's most spectacular – and controversial – contribution is the **John Hancock Tower** (*see also p79*).

According to Pei, the concept behind the severe rhomboid shape was to not overwhelm Copley Square's older buildings – the tower is 62 storeys tall, but only a sliver of it shows from the square. It's made more pleasing to look at by the images of Back Bay and the sky reflected in its glass sides. Though instantly more popular than 'The Pru' with most Bostonians, the Hancock did not escape controversy. While it was still under construction in 1973, a structural flaw caused the windows to pop out and crash down into the street below. Every one of its 10,344 panes had to be replaced – at a cost of $8 million. In addition, the historic Trinity Church was slightly damaged in the process.

Philip Johnson's most important – and hugely controversial – contribution to Boston architecture is the stark 1972 addition to the **Boston Public Library**. A guru of postmodernism, Johnson also masterminded **500 Boylston Street** and **International Place** (on Atlantic Avenue), which is said to contain more Palladian windows than does the whole nation of Italy.

Just make mine red brick, thanks

Like the three little pigs, early Bostonians experimented with hay and wood until a Big Bad Wolf came along in the form of ravenous fire and destroyed all the homes made of wood and straw. Bostonians scrambled for refuge, turning to clay blocks for reliable shelter and thus eventually making itself into a city of bricks.

You have to go back centuries to find a time when central Boston was not built nearly entirely of monochromatic red brick buildings. The original township located at the tip of the Shawmut Peninsula (today's North End) in the early 1600s was a maze of two- and three-storey clapboard wooden houses called saltboxes. After a couple of harrowing near misses, in 1631 the city's first ever ordinance designed for fire prevention banned thatched roofs and chimneys made of wood. Unfortunately, that didn't do the trick and it was followed by the catastrophic fire of 1676, in which virtually the entire city burned to the ground. After that, the city went further with building restrictions, mandating that builders use slate for roofs and red brick for walls. Some attention was paid to this 17th-century regulation, but for the most part it wasn't enforced. Much of what you see now when walking through the streets of Boston came into existence after the North End fire, although two more devastating blazes tore through the region before the 20th century. Because of these trials by fire, and the city's subsequent fear of flames, today the streets of Boston are lined end-to-end with row houses in rosy red brick.

No one seems to be precisely sure what percentage of the city is bricked in – one local historical society estimates 75 per cent of the landscape is hued red, while urban developers report a little more than half – but every eyeful of Boston includes at least one stack of rust-coloured blocks. From the Old North Church to MIT dorms to hole-in-the-wall Irish pubs, the city is a bastion of bricks. And no matter how hard you huff and puff, that's hard to blow (or burn) down.

Sylvia Plath was just as miserable in Boston as she was everywhere else.

Literary Boston

Like Memphis draws musicians, and Las Vegas gamblers, Boston sings a siren's song to writers.

Henry David Thoreau axed pine, squatted in a cabin for two years and composed *Walden* in a forest about 45 minutes north of Boston. Black Power crusader Malcolm X tarried in Roxbury, maintained a burglary operation out of his Harvard Square apartment, and converted to Islam in a Charlestown prison. And 20th-century novelist Edwin O'Connor dawdled in South Boston pubs, gathered slurred anecdotes from the barflies, and strung them together for his fictional portrait of former Boston Mayor James Michael Curley, *The Last Hurrah*.

Yes, Boston's literary lore is rich with odd characters, seminal works and quirky anecdotes. With its Brahmin caste, Athens sobriquet and academic prestige, Boston's lettered reputation has much merit, but little permanence. While many have written here, few have stayed for long. Rather than a glorious literary home, Boston is more like a damp, drafty bus station for scribes – sometimes the writers are coming, sometimes they're going, and often they're just thumbing through the *New Yorker* until their ride shows.

THE PURITAN POETS

Since the only acceptable muse for Puritans was God, everything written down had to have a purpose, so prose took the form of journal entries, sermons and historical records. Respectable examples of all three do exist. Just like every waiter in New York is really an actor, it seems everybody who settled in Massachusetts was a writer at heart. William Bradford (1590-1657), Mayflower Puritan and second governor of Massachusetts, kept a detailed account of those first harsh years, which was eventually published in 1856 as *Of Plymouth Plantation 1620-1647*. The first governor, John Winthrop (1588-1649), also recorded his impressions in *The History of New England*, which was also published posthumously in 1790.

The most successful author of his day was Cotton Mather (1663-1728). Respected for *Magnalia Christi Americana* (1702), his chronicle of the American Protestant movement, Mather is most remembered for fanning the flames of the Salem witchcraft hysteria.

'The fight for national independence consumed most Bostonians until late in the 18th century.'

There were a few other early Puritans who, in complete secrecy, did scribble verse. Anne Bradstreet's (1612-72) poems fell into the hands of a cousin and he published them without her knowledge as *The Tenth Muse Lately Sprung up in America* (1650) and an authorised volume with her corrections, *Poems* (1678), was published after her death. The Rev. Edward Taylor (c1642-1729) was not known as a poet in his lifetime, although he did publish a few elegies while he ministered to his congregation, but the majority of his more domestic and spiritual musings were not published until 1937. The only poet, in fact, whose work was published while he was alive, was Michael Wigglesworth (1631-1705), whose treatise on Calvinistic theory, *Day of Doom* (1662), was a sort of *Paradise Lost* of the New World.

THE NEW ENGLAND RENAISSANCE

The fight for national independence consumed most Bostonians until late in the 18th century, preventing much in the way of literary art. It was only after the war that locals were able to focus on the arts. In 1807, a group of wealthy Beacon Hill Brahmins established 'a reading room, a library, a museum and a laboratory'. Called the Athenaeum after a temple devoted to the goddess Athena, it served as a model for Boston Public Library, which was the first in the country when it opened. By 1811, the Athenaeum was already publishing the influential *North American Review*. And, over the course of the century, it claimed Daniel Webster, Ralph Waldo Emerson, Henry Wadsworth Longfellow and Amy Lowell as members.

In 1829, Timothy Harrington Carter opened the Old Corner Bookstore at the corner of Washington Street and School Street downtown. It quickly became another locus for Boston's fledgling literary scene – especially between 1845 and 1865, when William Tichnor and Jamie Fields owned it. The latter focused on printing and encouraging local talent like Emerson, Longfellow, Oliver Wendell Holmes and James Russell Lowell. They were also the first to bring European authors such as Charles Dickens to America, the first to publish literary magazines such as the *Atlantic Monthly* and the first to pay their authors royalties on sales rather than a flat fee.

HAWTHORNE, MELVILLE AND DICKINSON

One of the first great authors to come out of the New England Renaissance was Nathaniel Hawthorne (1804-64). A native of Salem, Hawthorne is believed to have altered the spelling of his last name to distance himself from his infamous ancestors, William Hathorne (who harassed Quakers) and Judge John Hathorne (who presided over the 1692 Salem witch trials). A scion of religious persecutors and an alumni of Maine's Bowdoin College, Hawthorne seemed haunted by the sins of his judgmental ancestors – so much so that his most revered work, *The Scarlet Letter*, examines the oft-ignored point of view of a condemned victim in early America.

Living as a recluse in early adulthood, Hawthorne absorbed local legends, some of which resulted in his first literary success, *Twice Told Tales* (1837). In his own day, however, Hawthorne was hard-pressed to support his family. Financial need drove him to manoeuvre himself into a political appointment at the Salem Customs House, though – as it turned out – he didn't prove particularly well suited to government work. His drafting of *The Scarlet Letter* was nearly jeopardised by a politically motivated dismissal from his post for alleged malfeasance.

To escape the Customs House controversy, Hawthorne fled with his family to the village of Lenox in western Massachusetts, where he wrote *The House of the Seven Gables* and crossed paths with Herman Melville (1819-91), a denizen of the nearby township of Pittsfield. Melville had already achieved moderate literary success in New York with his first two novels of the sea, *Typee* (1846) and *Omoo* (1847). His close friendship with Hawthorne so inspired him to finish *Moby Dick* (1851) that he dedicated the novel to him. Unfortunately, *Moby Dick* wasn't recognised as the quintessential American novel until the 1920s – well after the deaths of Melville and Hawthorne.

Also writing in western Massachusetts at the time was Emily Dickinson (1830-86), acknowledged today as the greatest American poet of the 19th century. Cloistering herself in nearby Amherst, Dickinson had a bitter distaste for the city of Boston, scoffing at its pomp and circumstance even though she barely ever visited the place. Only seven of her poems made print in her lifetime, yet she wrote more than 1,800 – only 24 of them with titles. Drawn to the rhythm of Protestant hymns and Transcendentalism, Dickinson used verse to feel around her heart and soul – only occasionally, in love poems no less, did she redirect her gaze outside of herself.

Nathaniel Hawthorne, author of *The Scarlet Letter.*

THE TRANSCENDENTALISTS

According to the New England Transcendentalists, spirituality was as essential to the human body as food, intuition was more important than intellectual knowledge and the purest ideas came from reason and not sensual discovery. Transcendentalism's chief prophet was Ralph Waldo Emerson (1807-82), a Harvard alumni and Boston native born to a long line of Unitarian ministers. Although Emerson deftly weaved nature's nuances into a metaphor for the human mind in his first work, *Nature* (1836), he is most noted for his collections of essays (1841, 1844) on 'Self-Reliance', 'Compensation' and the 'Oversoul'.

It took 12 years to sell the initial 500 copies of *Nature*, yet the book resonated immediately with a diverse group of writers called the Transcendentalist Club. The club regularly communed at Emerson's house and produced *Dial* (1840-42), a quarterly of poetry and essays dedicated to 'literature, philosophy, and religion'. Among *Dial*'s most noted contributors were Margaret Fuller (journalist, critic and feminist), Amos Bronson Alcott (founder of Boston's controversial Temple School, founder of the short-lived Utopian community Fruitlands and father of author Louisa May Alcott), George Ripley (founder of the Utopian artist's community Brook Farm), Emerson and Henry David Thoreau (1817-62).

Probably the most poignant and talented writer of the group was Thoreau, the curious fellow who penned *Walden* (1854) during the two years, two months and two days he spent in isolation in a cabin near Walden Pond. Thoreau's other crucial work, *Civil Disobedience* (1849), sprung from another form of self-imposed isolation – a brief jail sentence for refusing to pay his taxes as part of an abolitionist protest against the expansion of slavery into western territories.

Tutored at home by both Emerson and Thoreau, Louisa May Alcott (1832-88) achieved worldwide fame for her novel *Little Women* (1868) and its sequel *Little Men* (1871). Lack of formal education didn't impair her from making a career of novel writing – or creating characters that Hollywood would still be embracing more than a century later.

THE CAMBRIDGE POETS

The Transcendentalists were not nearly as popular in their day, however, as a group of writers that became known as the Cambridge Poets. Primarily well-heeled academics, the Cambridge Poets were associated with Harvard and influenced by the work of English Romantic poets such as Wordsworth and Coleridge. Chief among them was Henry Wadsworth Longfellow (1807-82). Though Longfellow's singsong verse has fallen out of fashion, he was the first literary artist in America to support himself completely by his own pen (and the first to earn a place in Poet's Corner in Westminster Abbey). He swept Paul Revere out of historical obscurity when he canonised the courier in 'Paul Revere's Ride'. He consecrated the love affair between Priscilla and John Alden in 'The Courtship of Miles Standish' (1858) and created a myth around the Native American Hiawatha in 'The Song of Hiawatha' (1855), a poem, incidentally, which was not based on American Indian lore but on the Finnish epic *Kalevala*.

Often loitering around Longfellow's magnificent Craige House at 105 Brattle Street were his Cambridge cronies Oliver Wendell

Holmes and James Russell Lowell. Holmes (1809-94) was a master of light verse. His 'Breakfast Table' pieces for the *Atlantic Monthly* (1858) combined fictional settings, characters and dialogue with poems and essays. (It was Holmes, in fact, who suggested the name for the magazine.) And although James Russell Lowell (1819-91) was actually suspended from Harvard in his senior year (he spent the time with Emerson and Thoreau in Concord), he ultimately returned there to take Longfellow's professorship when the poet retired to write full-time. In the intervening years, he wrote for the *National Anti-Slavery Standard* in Philadelphia, became the first editor of the *Atlantic Monthly* and co-edited the *North American Review* with Charles Eliot Norton.

Also influenced by the English Romantics (but not considered nearly as urbane as the Cambridge Poets) were John Greenleaf Whittier (1807-92) and William Cullen Bryant (1794-1878). Whittier's somewhat sentimental and homespun poems became the texts for several hymns. Bryant was regarded as the leading American poet of the 1830s, though his best-known poem, 'Thanatopsis' (1815), is one of his first. Bryant's popularity eventually garnered him the position of the *New York Evening Post*'s most influential editor.

BANNED IN BOSTON

In the midst of a morality phase just after the turn of the century, in 1904 Boston transformed itself from an incubator of classic literature into a closet of condemned works. That was the year in which the city appointed a city censor – one who forbade the publication of morally corrupt literature and limited local creativity to state-sanctioned morals. This set off a sort of literary Dark Ages that lasted for an astonishing 40 years and prohibited works by Ernest Hemingway, Sinclair Lewis and Eugene O'Neill. Even Lillian Hellman's award-winning play, *The Children's Hour* (1935), wasn't allowed to open in Boston because it contained lesbian undertones.

It's no surprise, then, that the centre of America's writing and publishing focus shifted to New York. Or that native Bostonian Henry James moved to England, obtained citizenship from Britain and sifted through his lasting impressions of Boston from abroad; or that TS Eliot, who found his voice at Harvard, became a British citizen in 1927, despite preserving many New England emotions and values in his lifetime work. Writers did still sojourn around Boston – usually drawn to the area's stellar universities – but more and more budding scribes collected their educational spoils here and then promptly relocated.

TWENTIETH CENTURY

Still, despite stifling free speech early on, Boston managed to nurture talented authors, poets and journalists during the 20th century. Living in the small Massachusetts town of Lenox, Edith Wharton (1862-1937), Pulitzer Prize winner for *The Age of Innocence* (1920), derived influence from Hawthorne's bleak portrait of New England for two of her works – *Ethan Frome* (1911) and *Summer* (1917). Future Pulitzer winner Edwin O'Connor (1918-1968) bolted from his Rhode Island birthplace to Boston, finding both a job at the *Boston Herald* and fodder for his first novel, *The Last Hurrah*, a thinly veiled story about former Beantown Mayor James Michael Curley.

'As Plath wrestled with her emotional demons, Kerouac fought his own intellectual war on the streets, in the bars and on freight trains.'

Another Pulitzer winner who sauntered around Boston in the 1950s was poet Robert Lowell (1917-77). Praised for his emotionally rich verse and stark confessional poetry, Lowell taught at both Boston University and Harvard. Known for his chronic drinking, three marriages and time at Belmont's McLean Hospital, Lowell had a messy personal life – a commonality he shared with his BU grad students Sylvia Plath and Anne Sexton. Lowell was respected for holding open office hours to aspiring poets during his Harvard time, and revered as a source of inspiration for budding young talent. At around the same time as Lowell's reign as Boston's poet *non pareil*, the equally talented Elizabeth Bishop taught at Harvard. Suddenly, Boston was again the hub of literary America.

Meanwhile, at the other end of the literary spectrum was Lowell native Jack Kerouac. His masterful novel, *On The Road,* was stunning the country with its jazz-influenced writing style and utter lack of literary pretension. As Plath was wrestling with her emotional demons in intellectual fashion, and describing that battle in *Ariel* and *The Bell Jar*, Kerouac fought his own intellectual war on the streets, in the bars and on freight trains. In their own way, each was changing the way people read. Kerouac from his position at the centre of the Beat movement heralded the age of hippies, rock 'n' roll, and experimental literature. He became, and remains, a poet laureate for teenagers. Plath, who made her name writing about being misunderstood, even abused, by

Jack Kerouac's love of beat poetry was probably not honed while he lived in these parts.

the men in her life, became a poet laureate for women. Both, it's worth noting, moved away from Massachusetts.

AN EMBARRASSMENT OF RICHES

Boston today is a hive of notable thinkers, poets and journalists. Famous writers are always stopping by, some to teach, some to learn and others to gain experience before trying to conquer the world.

Boston University boasts among its faculty Saul Bellow, Derek Walcott, Elie Wiesel and Robert Pinsky, former Poet Laureate of the United States. Other literary greats live within a stone's throw: John Updike in Beverly, Norman Mailer in Provincetown. Novelist James Carroll kicks around Boston. *Orchid Thief* author, and heiress to Joan Didion's throne, Susan Orlean, resided here. And chapters of Elizabeth Wurtzel's *Prozac Nation* recall her depressive debacles while at Harvard.

And the list goes on. Novelists Margot Livesey (*The Missing World*) lives here, as does up-and-comer Tom Perrotta (*Election*), and best-seller Arthur Golden (*Memoirs of a Geisha*). Literary critics Sven Birkerts, Helen Vendler and Christopher Ricks have homes, and teaching positions, in the area. Boston's crop of world-renowned poets includes Frank Bidart, Louise Glück and Seamus Heaney. Playwright extraordinaire David Mamet has a home in suburban Boston. And with each year's crop of literary awards, Boston ties abound: young Pulitzer Prize-winning fiction writer Jhumpa Lahiri interned at *Boston Magazine* and attended Boston University.

Boston may not have a literary 'movement' as such any more, but the list of writers who live and work here puts the city somewhere near the centre of American letters. Sometimes writers are coming, sometimes they're going, sometimes they're just waiting for a ride. But they're here.

Where the wordsmiths are

Fenway Park is the last place you'd expect to find a world-class author. Hell, it's hard enough getting a world-class baseball player to go there. Yet horror writer **Stephen King** is a regular at Red Sox home games. Legend has it that watching the Sox inspired King to write his book *Misery*.

But the ball park isn't the only place to find writers in Boston. In a town this literary, exchanging author sightings is a vaguely entertaining bar pasttime, much like celebrity sightings in Los Angeles, only infinitely more intellectual, of course. Here are a few other places you can hang out if you want to get an author's autograph.

If you're lucky, your post-game trip through nearby Kenmore Square might lead to a chance encounter with one of Boston University's stellar creative writing staff (maybe even the elusive **Saul Bellow**). But these guys are probably too smart to subject themselves to the thrum of Kenmore. Visiting writers at the Barnes & Noble bookstore on Kenmore Square, however, don't know any better. **Martin Amis** once hung out long enough to play pool at the nearby Boston Billiards (126 Brookline Avenue). **Irvine Welsh** was spotted making minced meat of a jerked turkey sandwich at the Audubon Circle (*see p160*).

Harvard Square, of course, is a wonderful place for literati-spotting. Try the Grolier Poetry Book Shop (*see p174*), which has long attracted famous versifiers. **Allen Ginsberg** and **Jack Kerouac** used to be regulars here. These days you might catch a glimpse of former Poet Laureate **Robert Pinsky**, or maybe Harvard's heavy-hitting critic **Helen Vendler**. She'll be the one looking down her nose at the books.

Harvard Square's bars often provide boozy respite for writers taking part in the university's reading series. If the authors aren't instantly recognisable, their jittery, blathering PR people will be. The Casablanca is a popular spot, as is the Harvest (the author **Christopher Hitchens** was once witnessed scarfing a plateful of oysters here – not a pretty sight). **Seamus Heaney** has been known to venture out of Harvard to enjoy a nice pint of Guinness at the Plough & Stars (*see p169*).

Even further afield, in Somerville, the Thirsty Scholar (*see p170*) is the official meeting place for the professional writers' group PEN/New England. Somerville is fast becoming known for its artists and writers, many of whom have been priced out of Cambridge and Boston. Expect no Pulitzer winners or Poet Laureates here. This is home to countercultural types like **Pagan Kennedy**, or up-and-comers like **Elizabeth McCracken**.

If you're having trouble distinguishing the literati from the merely literary, try yelling 'Movie rights!' The writers are the ones who start drooling.

College Town

Welcome to Boston, the biggest college town on earth.

When you're walking down a Boston street, look around you. One out of every two people you pass is likely to be a college student. Of the city's 550,000 residents, an estimated 250,000 are students. The area is home to more than 60 colleges and universities. In other words, famous though Athens, Georgia, and Oxford, England, might be, there is no bigger college town than Beantown. Several US presidents, including John F Kennedy, sought their educations in Boston. Future kings, presidents and world leaders undoubtedly still roam the city's campuses, which abound with Nobel laureates, writers, researchers and former heads of state.

Funnily enough, all of this happened by accident. Boston's centrality in education is the result of a convergence of factors which occurred over hundreds of years. Starting with Harvard, of course. Harvard is the oldest college in the country, founded before America was a nation in 1636. It was developed by the Puritans who, as the Massachusetts population grew, needed a local source for educated preachers. Over the centuries, the school developed a reputation as one of the world's best universities. Its presence meant that both Cambridge and Boston became known as places of learning. Because many students didn't move out of the city once they graduated, over the years Boston became the country's intellectual centre. By the 19th century, the city was, as it is today, home to many of the country's most esteemed writers, poets and scientists. Because of the wealth of knowledge just hanging about in the area, over time many small liberal arts schools sprang up nearby. That, in turn, brought in still more talent. It is a trend that has continued to this day.

This massive student enrolment has an indelible effect on the city, influencing everything from the traffic to the book stores to the club scene. Several sections of the city are little more than student ghettos filled with cheap Chinese take-out joints, low-budget pizzerias and supermarket-sized liquor stores. With their ratty buildings and couches on front porches, these littered student 'hoods stand in sharp contrast to the rest of central Boston's crisply mowed lawns, neatly painted rowhouses and sharp New England attention to detail. The clutter and clatter of college life is largely forgiven by the rest of the city, though, for a variety of reasons. Starting, for example, with the city's much-vaunted cultural scene.

It is thanks in part to the presence of so many colleges that Boston is known for its abundance of high-quality musical performances, film screenings, lectures and museum exhibits, as many are tied in some way to the local colleges. The art museums at Harvard rank among the best university collections in the world. At the same time, the large population of young adults attracts rock bands like big red flowers attract bees. So a steady stream of national touring acts pass through the area.

Talent doesn't need to be bused in from outside, though, because Boston abounds with arts colleges and music schools, each of which produces musicians and artists of its own while also bringing in artistically talented faculty. Boston's music scene is immeasurably improved, for example, by the presence of the Berklee School of Music and the New England Conservatory, two of the country's most respected musical training grounds, which turn out virtuosic classical, jazz and rock musicians year after year.

Similarly, the literary circuit is boosted by the presence of high-profile residents like Nobel Prize-winner Eli Wiesel, poet Robert Pinsky and author Saul Bellow, all of whom lecture at local universities and occasionally speak in open lectures that can be attended by non-students.

While that might be reason enough to forgive the beer cans and occasional bouts of highly literate graffiti, the city also has plenty of financial encouragement to be accepting of such youthful peccadilloes. Academic institutions in the city generate an estimated 125,000 jobs and $10 billion in income each year. Graduates from the Massachusetts Institute of Technology have contributed heavily to the growth of Boston's high-tech sector, helping to make the city one of the centres of America's e-commerce boom.

Still, there is no question that the presence of the colleges represents a double-edged sword of sorts. Together with spending and brain power come reckless partying and crowds of sometimes arrogant youngsters. Then there's the issue of high rents, which can be worsened by an influx of students willing to cram 10 friends into a flat to make it affordable, which causes the landlord to raise the rent further, which means families and couples are often priced out of the market.

Amid housing and parking shortages, late-night noise, festering trash and heavy traffic, sometimes the city's patience shows signs of wear and tear. In the student-heavy Allston-Brighton area, for example, permanent residents have tried to get rid of student party houses by demanding higher levels of on-campus student housing. The schools have tried to appease their neighbours – both Boston University and Northeastern University are in the process of building massive skyscraper dorms, although

Best quads

The teaching might take place inside the lecture halls, but anybody who has ever gone to college in the US knows that the real action goes on outside on the grassy geometrically shaped parks that form the central meeting place and pick-up joint for virtually any college anywhere. Boston has more than its share of quads. Here's what you can expect if you're off to meet the co-ed of your dreams, or if you're just dying for a wicked game of frisbee.

Harvard Yard, Harvard University

More tourists than actual Harvard students. Thus, a bit disappointing. Red brick and ivy, both present and accounted for.

Killian Court, MIT

Immortalised in the film *Good Will Hunting*. Lots of shirtless guys wandering about pretending they've got clothes on.

Harvard University

The Quad, Tufts University

Atop a hill, this one has the best view. You can see all the suburbs from here.

The Beach, Boston University

This sad, short strip of grass behind the student centre on Comm Ave is so named because the hum of nearby traffic approximates the sound of waves lapping against the shore.

The statue of John Harvard looks out over his namesake university.

this is more in response to housing shortages than neighbourhood complaints – but the problem remains unresolved.

The students, meanwhile, are perceived by residents as comfortably oblivious to their impact on the city, fretting more about their party schedule and mid-term exams than the state of their temporary homes. While this is surely a stereotype, it is clear that this issue continues to bedevil the city, and thus the love-hate relationship between Boston's grown-up residents and its youngsters is a perennial point of discussion.

There is less concern, interestingly, over the fact that the universities exert extraordinary control over the rhythm of life in Boston. The city has simply become used to the fact that, instead of following the typical January to December calendar, Boston follows the cycles of the academic year. Few would deny the city is at its most vibrant from September to May, when school is in session. During the university recesses – Christmas holiday for example, and throughout the entire summer – a noticeable hush settles over the city. Then, when the fall semester begins, the roads bottleneck with overloaded station wagons and out-of-state rental vans and weepy parents bidding their children goodbye. June is similarly harried; students rushing off for the summer litter the sidewalks with all types of detritus – used futons, soiled couches and scattered textbooks abound. This time of year is also graduation season, and thus the month of May, like September, brings on another deluge of tearful relatives. Universities deck out their campuses to create an impression of tuition money well spent, hotel rates soar and restaurant reservations are hard to come by. Then, suddenly, the city settles in for a quiet summer vacation. But even as it does, Boston's ever-changing, temporary population is already beginning to rejuvenate itself. The respite is only temporary.

HARVARD UNIVERSITY

Founded in 1636, Harvard University is the most prestigious institution of higher learning in America, and one of the best-known colleges in the world. Thousands of tourists come strolling through Harvard Yard every year just to soak up the atmosphere of heady intellectualism, historical importance and, let's face it, family money.

Harvard's high standing attracts tens of thousands of hopeful applicants each year, ignoring the limitations of its extremely inclusive admission policy – only 11 per cent of applicants were accepted into the entering class of 1999. They're also paying little mind to the fact that a Harvard education doesn't come cheap – tuition, room, board and fees for a year here costs $34,350. Though the student body is far more diverse, both ethnically and economically, than it was 20 years ago, the standing stereotype about Harvard undergrads remains that they are arrogant, rich and better bred than they are raised. It's hard to say if this viewpoint is based more on jealousy than fact, but there's one generality that appears to be applicable: Harvard students take their work, and themselves, very seriously. Considering the stature of the university, that could be seen as quite understandable.

Along with top students, Harvard attracts world-renowned faculty as well. Trial lawyer and best-selling author Alan Dershowitz – who has represented boxer Mike Tyson, OJ Simpson, Claus von Bulow, Mia Farrow and many other celebrities – teaches here, as does evolutionary biologist Edward O Wilson and Nobel Prize-winning poet Seamus Heaney. The undergraduate programme is accordingly rigorous and many students enter the school well on their way to fast-track careers in politics, business and public service. Or just to fame. Recent alumni include jazz saxophonist Joshua Redman, talk-show host Conan O'Brien and actress Natalie Portman. Even Harvard's most famous drop-out, Bill Gates, has done pretty well for himself.

▶ For addresses and phone numbers of Boston area colleges see Chapter **Directory**

The studious and career-driven atmosphere doesn't make Harvard much of a party school, but students manage to blow off steam in their own inimitable way. Forbidden by long-standing tradition to have the kinds of fraternities and sororities that most US colleges rely on to create a (usually drunken) centre for university social life, some students turn to the 'Final Clubs' – exclusive, upper-crust student organisations that offer membership by invitation only. Still, those who are not invited needn't weep into their double mocha cappuccinos. With a virtually endless number of campus-sponsored dances, concerts and social events, it's not unusual to see packs of undergraduates in formal wear strolling through Harvard Yard on the weekends.

'Harvard's endowment hovers around $11 billion. Oh my, so much to spend, and what to spend it on?'

Harvard is also one of the largest land-owners in the Boston area. In addition to the central undergraduate campus, the Divinity School and the Law School stretch further north along Mass Ave; the Harvard School of Business lies directly across the Charles River from Harvard Square and the university's entire real estate holdings include over 360 acres (146 hectares) in Boston and Cambridge. Not surprisingly, these assets contribute to Harvard's massive endowment, which hovers around $11 billion. Oh my, so much to spend, and what to spend it on? Never fear, the school has found plenty of ways to blow its dough, including buildings by Walter Gropius and Le Corbusier; then there's the Widener Library which holds over 13.4 million volumes. In addition, many of Harvard's residence houses feature stately fireplaces, antique furniture and indoor squash courts. It's a tough life.

MIT

Just a few miles – and one T stop – down Mass Ave from Harvard is the Massachusetts Institute of Technology. Known throughout the country as MIT, this is one of the finest science and technology universities in the world. Research at MIT's cutting-edge labs has led to many technological innovations – including radar, high-speed photography and magnetic core memory (which led to the development of digital computers).

Nearly 70 per cent of the research at MIT is supported by funding from the US government – particularly federal agencies like the Department of Defence, the Department of Energy and NASA. If we told you what they were doing in there, we'd have to kill you. According to a recent MIT study, its inventions add $20 billion and 150,000 jobs to the American economy every year. As US universities go, MIT is a fairly serious and career-oriented school, with students making headlines for spinning off their undergrad research into Internet start-ups or selling their services to high-tech industry giants like Microsoft.

Stretching along the Charles River in East Cambridge, much of the architecture of the school is mostly modern and unattractive, though several outstanding buildings designed by IM Pei (an MIT alumnus) and Eero Saarinen stand out among the gray concrete structures. Walking through the campus can be quite a dehumanising experience, as the imposing scale of the landscape makes one feel like a cog in a machine (or more appropriately, like a microchip inside a mainframe). One architectural oddity worth viewing is the 'infinite corridor.' Running through the neo-classical main administration building called Killian Court, this seemingly endless walkway connects the main campus with Mass Ave. At 940 feet (287 metres) long, it's not infinite, but it is impressive.

It is interesting to note that the student population at MIT does not attempt to defy stereotypes. It is around 60 per cent male, and generally proud of its 'geekness,' but that's still a generalisation. Pocket protectors are as rare as cheerleaders on this campus. This is a new generation of geeks. These guys stand to make millions. Or billions. Still, the social scene is somewhat hampered by the overwhelming workload, though fraternities are quite active on campus. This is partly due to an on-campus housing shortage; it seems plenty of students would rather live in a plush frat house than a crowded, aesthetically underwhelming dorm. The 1997 death of an underage MIT fraternity brother from alcohol poisoning set the university in a negative light, but much of the bad publicity was unfounded; MIT is far from a beer-swilling party school. Most students here would rather die than risk spilling a Michelob on their keyboard.

BOSTON UNIVERSITY (BU)

With a location adjacent to the nexus of Boston's nightlife – Lansdowne Street – Boston University's student population is somewhat more lighthearted and frivolous than their Cambridge counterparts. BU's acceptance policy is also more lenient, though, being a private institution, the tuition is just as astronomical, exceeding $100,000 for four years. But the quality of education is very high, with particularly strong programmes in journalism, communications and drama.

The **MIT** campus.

Famous faculty and alumni abound at BU, and current professors include Nobel-prize winner Elie Wiesel and author Saul Bellow, while Dr Martin Luther King Jr, actress Geena Davis and National Public Radio broadcaster Nina Totenberg are all graduates.

With an undergraduate enrolment of around 16,000, it's hard to classify BU students as anything in particular. Every facet of US youth culture – jocks, nerds, frat boys, hippies, ravers, b-boys – is on display here. As at most Boston schools, there is also a significant contingent of heavily accented, cell-phone waving and Prada-wearing international students.

Despite its large size, BU doesn't have much of a physical or architectural presence. Stretching east along Commonwealth Avenue from the bustle of Kenmore Square out towards Allston-Brighton, the university blends blandly into the urban landscape. The actual social and cultural centre of the university lies in the Allston-Brighton neighbourhood, a centre of all things cheap and collegiate.

BOSTON COLLEGE (BC)

Further east in the exclusive Chestnut Hill neighbourhood lies Boston College, a private Jesuit institution founded in 1863. The picturesque and leafy campus stretches over 115 acres (47 hectares) and seems far removed from the urban buzz of BU – though it's only a short T-ride away. With excellent sports teams, strong school spirit and a study-hard-party-hard reputation, BC's image is that of a traditional Animal House-style university. To a large extent, this is a traditional sort of college where students still dress nicely for class, study hard all week, head en masse to football games on the weekends, and then stop off at Mass on Sundays.

The Jesuit tradition contributes to academic life as well. The school's departments of theology and philosophy are well regarded, and volunteerism is quite popular among BC undergrads. Two of the biggest social events on the calendar include the yearly hockey game against cross-town rival BU, and the football game against the fellow Jesuits at Notre Dame University.

EMERSON COLLEGE

Slightly closer to the centre of town than BC, Emerson College is the nation's only four-year college devoted to the study of communication and the performing arts. Emerson's campus is barely distinguishable from its very urban surroundings – located, as it is, between Boston Common and the Theatre District. In fact, most Bostonians only know of Emerson from its excellent radio station, 88.9 FM WERS, which is distinguished by its eclectic play list (blocks of folk, jazz, world music, reggae and hip hop daily) and exclusive on-air performances.

NORTHEASTERN UNIVERSITY

Like Emerson, Northeastern University emphasises hands-on experience and pre-professional training. The second largest

Coolest college hangouts

The Crimson Grille
59 JFK Street, at Harvard Square, Cambridge, (868 5900). Harvard Square T. **Open** noon-1am Mon-Wed, Sun; noon-2am Thur-Sat. **Credit** AmEx, DC, MC, V.
This unassuming sports bar attracts a lively crew of Harvard jocks and preppies, along with female students bused in from Wellesley and Simmons, making it a buzzing pick-up scene for khaki-wearing undergrads.

Our House
1277 Commonwealth Avenue, at Spofford Street, Allston (782 3228). Harvard Avenue T. **Open** 4pm-2am daily. **Credit** MC, V.
With weathered couches, plentiful TVs and retro board games, this BU-BC stalwart cultivates an atmosphere similar to a grubby student apartment, without the pesky neighbours.

Wally's Cafe
427 Massachusetts Avenue, at Columbus Avenue (424 1408). Mass Ave T. **Open** 9am-2am Mon-Sat; noon-2am Sun. **No credit cards.**
Not a college hangout in the traditional sense, this minuscule nightclub on the Roxbury-South End border attracts young jazz virtuosos from the New England Conservatory and Berklee, who come for the smouldering sessions.

Algiers Coffee House
40 Brattle Street, at Harvard Square, Cambridge (492 1557). Harvard Square T. **Open** 8am-midnight daily. **Credit** MC, V.
Harvard students convene here after taking in an art film at the Brattle Theatre downstairs, while Harvard professors discuss Middle Eastern politics over the strong Turkish coffee.

Panini
406 Washington Street, at Beacon Street, Somerville (666 2770). Harvard Square T. **Open** 7am-7pm Mon-Fri; 8am-5pm Sat-Sun. **No credit cards.**
Nine-to-fivers blaze through this cosy coffeeshop on their way to the T in the mornings. Harvard students take over for the rest of the day, nibbling on home-made scones; research papers in tow.

Toscanini's
899 Main Street, at Massachusetts Avenue, Cambridge (491 5877). Central Square T. **Open** 7am-11pm Mon-Fri; 7am-midnight Sat-Sun. **No credit cards.**
When life in the lab gets too stressful, MIT students flock towards this ice-cream store and café that features oddball flavours like Guinness and burnt caramel.

university in Boston, Northeastern boasts a 'co-operative' education programme where students spend a quarter of their school year interning and working in their field of study. The campus is unremarkable, fitting neatly into Back Bay between Symphony Hall and the Museum of Fine Arts.

NEW ENGLAND CONSERVATORY
Just across the street from Northeastern is the New England Conservatory – the oldest independent school of music in America. It's worth seeking out a concert at NEC's Jordan Hall, a beautiful performance space that, some say, has far better acoustics than Boston's revered Symphony Hall.

BERKLEE COLLEGE OF MUSIC
The Berklee College of Music is beautifully placed at the very edge of Back Bay. Less than 50 years old, Berklee is far from a traditional music conservatory. Jazz, rock, film scoring, music engineering and production are Berklee's strongest programmes. The school is largely populated by male, guitar-toting, rock-star hopefuls. They have good reason to hope, as the popular music world is dotted with Berklee graduates. Among their ranks are producer/arranger Quincy Jones, Steely Dan's Donald Fagen and singer and songwriter Melissa Etheridge.

A FEW OF THE REST
More colleges – some of them nationally renowned – are located just outside the city of Boston. **Tufts University**, which straddles the Medford-Somerville border, is a small liberal arts college that regularly ranks in the top 25 in the country.

Located a short distance outside Boston, **Wellesley College** is an all women's school located in the manicured and exclusive town of Wellesley. Former first lady and New York Senator Hillary Rodham Clinton is an alumnus.

The quiet town of Waltham is home to **Brandeis University**, which is named after the esteemed former Supreme Court judge Louis Brandeis (a former Boston resident and Harvard professor). The school is notable for the fact that a large percentage (more than half) of its students are Jewish.

Accommodation

Accommodation 44

Feature boxes

The best hotels 48
Chain gang 55
Their house is your house 57
Think boutique 58

Accommodation

The combination of too many visitors and not enough hotels in Boston means one thing – get your wallet out.

Blink in this town and you'll miss a hotel going up. Boston is in the midst of a massive hotel construction boom. They're throwing them together like it's going out of style, and still there are not enough rooms to meet the demand. The city fell behind in hotel construction years ago, and even though it is now hurrying to catch up, it's still got a long way to go. What that means for visitors is predictable but depressing – skyrocketing prices and a complete lack of bargaining power. When it comes to getting a room in these parts, you take what you can get. That's the bad news. The good news is, change is on the horizon. Between 1999 and 2000, 3,059 more hotel rooms were added. By mid-2003, another 4,350 more rooms will be completed.

The new hotels in Boston are coming in all shapes and sizes. Between 1999 and 2003, a total of 32 hotels were scheduled for completion. Among these new facilities are the upscale, business-class 362-room Boston Wyndham, which opened in the Financial District in 1999, the 62-room boutique hotel, XV Beacon, completed in 2000, and the massive 1,120-room Starwood Hotels Sheraton, due to open in 2003.

With all this new blood, even the city's regal traditional hotels – the Ritz-Carlton, the Regal Bostonian, the Park Plaza – have been spurred to action. The Regal Bostonian and the Park Plaza have both undergone major renovations, while the Ritz-Carlton is building a sister hotel on Boston Common.

So, when all the rooms are open and the renovations complete, prices are going to drop to reasonable levels, right? Not likely. Based on the high occupancy rates of recent years, projections indicate that even after the new hotels are completed this city will fill up fast. During the busy autumn season, as it has for years, the entire town will still 'sell out'.

In addition to the bustling autumn, it's worth noting that rooms are also nearly impossible to find during May and June, when 64 college graduation ceremonies take place over the course of a month. Then there are the hundreds of conventions and expositions that snatch up thousands of hotel rooms each year. Think it's easy to get a room when 20,000 dentists come to town to talk teeth? No. Book ahead.

WHAT YOU'LL PAY

When it comes to cost, the average room rate in Greater Boston in 2000 was around $200 per night and rising. Even in the off-season, prices here can be outrageous. That's not to say there aren't some budget options in town, but they are very limited. There are also agencies (*see p57*) that will help you to book rooms in B&Bs or unhosted apartments, which can save you a few bucks. But, in general, when you're staying in Boston get ready to pay.

WHERE TO STAY

Of course, where you stay depends largely on why you've come here. Just about everybody wants to stay in Back Bay. With its astonishing array of restaurants, bars and shops, that is certainly understandable, and it is Boston's most popular hotel area. But it's worth noting that there are other exceptional areas of town in which to set up camp. Beacon Hill, with its leafy streets and easy access to Boston Common, makes a peaceful and romantic getaway. The section of downtown around Kenmore Square is lined with cheap restaurants and funky shops, and can be a raucous place to let your hair down. Those in town on business, on the other hand, could find the Financial District or the Waterfront more convenient options for making it to meetings on time. Meanwhile, the funky South End, with its miles of brick rowhouses and cobblestone streets, is rapidly emerging as a popular offbeat choice for regular visitors. Most hotels in this neighbourhood are of the small and intimate variety.

AND BEAR IN MIND

Many hotels have now adopted a no-smoking policy in all rooms. Smokers are advised to call ahead so they don't end up having to trudge outside every time they want a quick puff.

Even guesthouses and B&Bs now charge for phone use, including local calls. Some hotels charge as much $2.50 for each local call. A few now charge for 'free' 1-800 calls. If you have to make a lot of calls while in town, check the hotel's phone policy.

In terms of tipping: give bellhops $1 per bag; room service waiters 10-15 per cent of the total bill (this is often included in the check, be sure to read it before you tip); and staff members a token amount for any special favours.

Accommodation

Get a panoramic view of Boston from the windows of the **Regal Bostonian**. *See p54.*

ABOUT THE LISTINGS
Prices may change according to season. Prices do not include the 12.75 per cent sales tax. Note that, unless otherwise stated, breakfast is included in the following rates.

Back Bay & Downtown

Deluxe

Four Seasons

200 Boylston Street, Boston, MA 02116, at the Public Garden (338 4400/1-800 332 3442/fax 351 2051/www.fourseasons.com). Arlington T. **Rates** (breakfast not included) $495-$745 single; $535-$785 double; $1,450-$3,900 suite. **Credit** AmEx, DC, Disc, MC, V. **Map** p308 F5; p309.

Not exactly architecture's gift to Boston, the Four Seasons makes up in assiduous, professional service and luxurious amenities what it lacks in (exterior) charm. Built on the site of the Playboy Club, in the middle of what was once known as the Combat Zone, the hotel overlooks the beautiful Public Gardens. Guests can stop for a drink at the quietly elegant Bristol Lounge. The tony 24-hour room service here even extends to a pet menu. The rooftop pool, though on the small side, boasts good views of the city. The hotel offers several (relatively) bargain-priced deals tied in with local events which are well worth asking about.

Hotel services *Air-conditioning. Bar. Business services. Concierge. Disabled: adapted rooms. Gym. Laundry. Limousine service. No-smoking rooms. Parking ($30 per night). Restaurants (2). Swimming pool (indoor).* **Room services** *Dataport. Mini-bar. Room service (24hr). Turndown. TV: cable/pay movies/satellite.*

Ritz-Carlton

15 Arlington Street, Boston, MA 02117, at Newbury Street (536 5700/1-800 241 3333/fax 536 1335). Arlington T. **Rates** $335-$585 single/double; $410-$3,000 suite. **Credit** AmEx, DC, Disc, MC, V. **Map** p308 F5; p309.

Truly the Grande Dame of Boston hotels, the Ritz opened in 1927 with the intention of catering to a very select clientele – the Duke and Duchess of Windsor, Winston Churchill and Charles Lindbergh among them – and the hotel has never deviated appreciably from this policy, although it has long-since stopped screening bookings with the Social Register (a formal listing of old money families in the US). If you prefer old-world charm and extremely elegant service, this is your place. There are said to be two employees for every guest here. Great care is taken to make sure the Ritz feels familiar to loyal customers (though the hotel's 278 French Provincial rooms have been completely overhauled in the past three years). For Beacon Hill Brahmins, tea at the Ritz is an institution, its ballroom the site of legendary soirées. It is still the epitome of elegance. The hotel is in the process of building a sister institution across Boston Common. The Ritz-Carlton Boston Common (2 Avery Street, Boston, MA 02111; 556 8222) is scheduled to open by August 2001.

Hotel services *Air-conditioning. Bar. Beauty salon. Business services. Concierge. Disabled: adapted rooms. Gym. Laundry. No-smoking rooms. Parking ($31 per night). Restaurant.* **Room services** *Dataport (High-speed). Iron. Mini-bar. Room service (24hr). Turndown. TV: cable/pay movies.*

High End

Boston Park Plaza

64 Arlington Street, Boston, MA 02116, at Boston Common (426 2000/1-800 225 2008/fax 423 1708 www.bostonparkplaza.com). Arlington T. **Rates** (breakfast not incl) $129-$299 single/double; $309-$349 suite. **Credit** AmEx, DC, Disc, MC, V. **Map** p308 F5; p309.

Among the oldest of Boston's hotels, the Park Plaza has finally thrown down the cash – $60 million, in fact – for a major revamp. The vast, chandeliered lobby will always scream 'fancy old hotel,' but the rooms have taken on a much more modern feel with the addition of new, streamlined and upscale furniture, silky, natural-fibre fabrics piled on the enormous beds, and chic new touches like post-modern-looking exercise bicycles tucked away in the corner. The upgrade used enough new (subtle beige) carpeting for 250 two-bedroom homes (or so we're told). Just be sure to ask for a renovated room – not all have been upgraded, and those that are not are more than a little worn around the edges. Other new additions at the Plaza include its very trendy bar, Whiskey Park (*see p159*) and a branch of the pricey seafood restaurant chain McCormick and Schmick's (*see p131*).

Hotel services *Air conditioning. Bar. Beauty salon. Business services. Concierge. Disabled: adapted rooms. Gym. Laundry. No-smoking rooms. Parking ($27 per night). Restaurant.* **Room services** *Dataport. Iron. Room service (6.30am-midnight). TV: cable/pay movies.*

Colonnade

120 Huntington Avenue, Boston, MA 02116, at the Prudential Center (424 7000/1-800 962 3030/fax 424 1717). Prudential T. **Rates** (breakfast not incl) $250-$495 single/double; $750-$1,000 suite. **Credit** AmEx, DC, Disc, MC, V. **Map** p306 E5; p309.

The best feature of the Colonnade's somewhat sterile 1970s architecture is its rooftop swimming pool – nothing beats it on a sticky summer afternoon. The hotel's 285 rooms are generous in size if somewhat anonymous in decor (though there's always the complimentary rubber ducky for the tub). But what the hotel lacks in charm it makes up for in its location, right next to Symphony Hall and the Prudential Center shopping mall.

Hotel services *Air-conditioning. Bar. Business services. Concierge. Disabled: adapted rooms. Gym. Laundry. Limousine service. No-smoking rooms.*

Parking ($24 per night). Restaurant. Swimming pool (outdoor). **Room services** *Dataport. Iron. Mini-bar. TV: cable/pay movies/VCR (on request).*

Eliot

370 Commonwealth Avenue, Boston, MA 02215, at Massachusetts Avenue (267 1607/1-800 443 5468/fax 536 9114). Hynes/ICA T. **Rates** (breakfast not incl) $215-$335 single; $255-$335 double; $295-$415 suite. **Credit** AmEx, DC, MC, V. **Map** p306 E5; p309.

Built in 1925, the Eliot was looking a little tattered until a few years ago when it renovated its 95 rooms and suites, without losing its original atmosphere. The main lobby is cosy and relatively small-scale. On the ground floor is Clio, one of Boston's hottest upmarket restaurant/bars (*see p122*), which also provides room service for the hotel guests. Most of the Eliot's accommodation consists of suites – bedrooms and sitting rooms equipped with small kitchenettes and fold-out sofas. Perfect for families, or those who just like a little extra space.

Hotel services *Air-conditioning. Bar. Business services. Disabled: adapted rooms. Gym. Laundry. No-smoking rooms. Parking (valet). Restaurant.* **Room services** *Dataport. Fax. High-speed Internet. Iron. Kitchenette. Mini-bar. Room service (24hr). Turndown. TV: cable/pay movies/VCR (on request).*

Fairmont Copley Plaza

138 St James Avenue, Boston, MA 02116, at Copley Square (1-800 441 1414/fax 375 9648/ www.fairmont.com). Copley or Back Bay T. **Rates** (breakfast not incl) $199-$389 single; $229-$469 double; $479-$669 suite. **Credit** AmEx, DC, Disc, MC, V. **Map** p306 F5; p309.

Overlooking Copley Square, this hotel was originally built in 1912 as the sister establishment to New York's Plaza. Over the years, it has lost none of its style or elegance. The mirrored and gilded lobby is nothing short of spectacular. In contrast to the almost over-the-top lobby, the hotel's 379 rooms combine discreet opulence with every modern amenity. The rooms are large and exquisitely outfitted. Those with views of the square are particularly coveted. Most have helpful touches like quick Internet access and fax machines with direct numbers. Every US president since Taft has stayed here (except Clinton). Service is the best in town – bar none. The concierges here know what you're thinking before you do. The Fairmont's restaurant, the Oak Room (*see p127*), is a perennial contender for best steak house in Boston.

Hotel services *Air-conditioning. Bar. Beauty salon. Business services. Concierge. Disabled: adapted rooms. Gym. No-smoking rooms. Parking ($29 per night). Restaurant.* **Room services** *Dataport. Iron. Mini-bar. Room service (24hr). TV: cable/pay movies.*

Lenox

710 Boylston Street, Boston, MA 02116, at Copley Square (536 5300/1-800 225 7676/fax 266 7905/ www.lenoxhotel.com). Copley T. **Rates** (breakfast not incl) $308-$348 single/double; $428-$508 suite. **Credit** AmEx, DC, Disc, MC, V. **Map** p306 F5; p309.

The Lenox, which first opened in 1900, boasts a prime location next to the spectacular architecture of the Boston Public Library. The hotel's old-style gold and blue decor has earned it design awards for years. Several of the Lenox's 212 beautifully appointed rooms boast working fireplaces, as does the charmingly restored lobby.

Hotel services *Bar. Business services. Concierge. Disabled: adapted rooms. Gym. Laundry. No-smoking rooms. Parking (valet). Restaurants.* **Room services** *Dataport. Room service (6.30am-midnight). TV: cable/pay movies/web TV.*

Mid-range

Buckminster

645 Beacon Street, Boston, MA 02215, at Kenmore Square (236 7050/1-800 727 2825/fax 262 0068). Kenmore T. **Rates** (breakfast not incl) $99-$129 single/double; $139-$169 suite. **Credit** AmEx, DC, Disc, MC, V. **Map** p306 D5; p309.

With its perfectly acceptable rooms and its close vicinity to Kenmore's clubs and bars – and, of course, Fenway Park – the Buckminster is one of the best bargains in Boston. None of its 96 rooms will win any design awards, but all are equipped with cheaper versions of the same amenities that the deluxe hotels offer.

Hotel services *Air-conditioning. Cooking facilities. Disabled: adapted rooms. Laundry (self-service). No smoking rooms.* **Room services** *Dataport. Iron. TV: cable.*

Copley Square

47 Huntington Avenue, Boston, MA 02116, at Exeter Street (536 9000/1-800 225 7062/fax 236 0351/www.copleysquarehotel.com). Back Bay or Copley T. **Rates** (breakfast not incl) $255-$295 single; $295 double; $405 family unit; $405 suite. **Credit** AmEx, DC, Disc, JCB, MC, V. **Map** p306 E5; p309.

Across the street from the Lenox (*see above*) is its more modest turn-of-the century sister, the Copley Square. This understated hotel has a distinctly

The best Hotels

For loud, blushing affairs
Wyndham Boston. *See p54.*

For people who hate children
Newbury Guest House. *See p49.*

For inconspicuous consumption
Charles. *See p56.*

For serious oenophiles
XV Beacon. *See p58.*

For techno-geeks
University Park Hotel @ MIT. *See p56.*

The concierges at the **Fairmont Copley Plaza** can read your mind. *See p48.*

European feel about it, from the snippets of French and German you'll hear in the comfortable lobby lounge to the traditional Hungarian food served up at Café Budapest. True, the corridors are a bit dingy and the decor in the 143 rooms is a bit spare, but it's a solid, comfortable choice.
Hotel services *Air-conditioning. Babysitting. Bar. Business services. Concierge. Disabled: adapted rooms. Laundry. No-smoking rooms. Parking. Restaurant.* **Room services** *Dataport. Iron. Room service (until 10pm). TV.*

Gryphon House

9 Bay State Road, at Beacon Street, Boston, MA 02215 (375 9003/fax 425 0716/ www.innboston.com). Kenmore T. **Rates** *Mar-Nov* $185-$245 double. *Dec-Feb* $149-$208 double. **Credit** AmEx, Disc, MC, V. **Map** p306 D5; p309.
The first things you'll notice when you walk inside Gryphon House are its walls. Papered with scenic French wallpaper, the walls here explore the flora and fauna of Africa, Asia and Europe. All of the eight colourful rooms are decorated with similarly heavy-handed hand-painted murals. Our decor vocabulary eludes us on this one. On the other hand, most rooms have cute gas fireplaces.
Hotel services *Air-conditioning. High-speed Internet. No smoking. Parking (free).* **Room services** *CD player. Dataport (DSL). Fireplace. Iron. Kitchenette. TV: cable/VCR.*

Newbury Guest House

261 Newbury Street, Boston, MA 02116, between Gloucester & Fairfield Streets (437 7666/fax 262 4243/www.hagopianhotels.com). Hynes/ICA T. **Rates** $140-$190 single/double. **Credit** AmEx, DC, Disc, MC, V. **Map** p306 E5; p309.
One of Boston's sweetest small hotels, the Newbury is actually three refurbished townhouses joined together. The 32 rooms are tastefully outfitted, with

The swanky **Newbury Guest House** offers a perfect excuse to leave the kids behind.

wooden floors, high ceilings and bay windows. Continental breakfast is served in a sunny little room that opens onto a patio terrace; the staff are relaxed and charming. About half the clientele here is gay men, but all are made to feel welcome. Except families with children. Note that no children between the ages of two and 13 are allowed. Despite that fact, this hotel can get a bit noisy – light sleepers would do well to request rooms away from the hustle and bustle of lively Newbury Street.
Hotel services *Air-conditioning. Disabled: adapted rooms. No-smoking rooms. Parking ($15 per night).* **Room services** *Dataport. Iron. TV: cable.*

Oasis Guest House

22 Edgerly Road, Boston, MA 02115 (267 2262/ fax 267 1920/www.oasisgh.com). Hynes/ICA or Symphony T. **Rates** $80 single; $90-$135 double; Winter rates 20% lower. **Credit** AmEx, MC, V. **Map** p306 E6; p309.

The name says it all. Though it's just a few blocks from Symphony Hall and the city's hottest nightclubs, the hotel's location on a leafy, quiet side street makes you forget the busy city outside. The 16 rooms are nicely decorated, and most offer private baths. Continental breakfast is served in the cosy lounge, and the two outdoor decks are great places to hang and relax. The clientele here is a mix, with about half the guests being gay men. But, again, all are made to feel welcome. As of April 2001 the Oasis will also have at its disposal a further 14 rooms in a nearby townhouse.
Hotel services *Air-conditioning. No-smoking rooms. Parking ($10 per night).* **Room services** *TV: satellite.*

Budget

Boston International American Youth Hostel

12 Hemenway Street, Boston, MA 02115, behind Symphony Hall (536 1027/1-800 909 4776 ext 07/fax 424 6558). Hynes/ICA T. **Rates** (breakfast not incl) $27-$30 dorm; $81-$87 private single/double. **No credit cards. Map** p306 E6; p309.

Before you get all excited about the price, find out what an American Youth Hostel is. This one, at the edge of Back Bay, can accommodate up to 190 people, but the rooms are dormitory style (single sex), with up to six beds each. And you have to bring your own sheets or rent them for $2 a night. The saying 'you get what you pay for' was never more apt.
Hotel services *Air-conditioning (private rooms and lounge only). Cooking facilities. Internet access. Laundry (self-service). Payphone. No-smoking. TV room.* **Room services** *No phone.*

Florence Frances Guest House

458 Park Drive, Boston, MA 02215, at Beacon Street (267 2458). Fenway or Kenmore T. **Rates** (breakfast not incl) $80 single; $90 double. **No credit cards. Map** pp306 D6.

If you want to stay in this 150-year-old townhouse you'll have to share it with Florence Frances, the proprietor, who lives here. All four rooms are done up according to a different, and slightly over-the-top, theme, such as the 'Spanish' double room with a display of fans and Spanish paintings, white fabric on the walls and black lacquered furniture. Each room has a colour TV, but no telephone

or private bath. Honeymooners can request satin sheets. There's a sports bar, a comfortable lounge, a roof terrace, laundry facilities and free parking at the back. The owner, a self-confessed collector of china figurines, is an added feature of your stay here – if you don't mind her participating a little.
Hotel services *Air-conditioning. Cooking facilities. No smoking. Parking. Public phone.* **Room services** *Iron. TV.*

YMCA

316 Huntington Avenue, Boston, MA 02115, at Northeastern University (536 7800/fax 267 4653). Northeastern T. **Rates** $45 single; $65 double. **Credit** MC, V. **Map** p306 E6; p309.

This one is men only. But the Y has a surprisingly friendly atmosphere and its private rooms certainly make it a step up from the Youth Hostel. The rooms look austere, but are comfortable enough. Bathrooms are down the hall. No phone in rooms.
Hotel services *Gym. Laundry (self-service). No-smoking rooms. Restaurant. Swimming pool. TV lounge.*

YWCA/Berkeley Residence

40 Berkeley Street, Boston, MA 02116, between Warren Avenue & Appleton Street (375 2524/fax 375 2525). Arlington or Back Bay T. **Rates** $56 single; $86 double; $99 triple. **Credit** MC, V. **Map** p309 F6; p309.

This is the YWCA, which means women only. In fact, Y-chromosome types can barely get in the door. No men are allowed beyond the public areas. This is your basic youth hostel, albeit a fairly nice one. Thus, the rooms, as might be expected, are a bit threadbare, but clean. Bathrooms are down the hall. Breakfast, included in the price, is served in the surprisingly pleasant restaurant-cum-cafeteria, where dinner is also dished up at decent prices. Weekly, monthly and permanent rates are available. No phone in rooms.
Hotel services *Laundry (self-service). Payphone. Restaurant. TV room: cable.*

Beacon Hill

High End

Beacon Hill Hotel & Bistro

25 Charles Street, Boston, MA 02114, at Chestnut Street (1-888 959 2442/www.beaconhillhotel.com). Charles/MGH or Arlington T. **Rates** $225-$285 single/double; $345 suite. **Credit** AmEx, DC, Disc, MC, V. **Map** p307 F4; p310.

This new hotel, which opened in November 2000 in a converted 1830s townhouse, is Boston's first real stab at importing the European idea of the 'independent small hotel'. Among the attractions are a French bistro – where locals actually outnumber guests – 24-hour room service, and, surprisingly, all the conveniences you'd expect from a much larger place. The size of the hotel – 12 rooms, one suite – means that owners Peter and Celia Rait shower personal attention on each and every guest (though they also know when to leave well enough alone). This hotel is elegant and easy to handle. The rates include full breakfasts in the bistro.

You can have a patriotic moment, American style, in the **YMCA** lobby.

The lovely lobby matches the friendly staff at the **John Jeffries House**.

Hotel services *Air-conditioning. Business services. Disabled: adapted rooms. Laundry. No-smoking. Restaurant.* **Room services** *Dataport. Iron. Room service (24hr). TV: satellite/pay movies.*

Mid-range

John Jeffries House

14 David G Mugar Way, Boston, MA 02114, at Charles Street (367 1866/fax 742 0313). Charles T. **Rates** $90 single; $105 double; $125-$145 suite. **Credit** AmEx, DC, Disc, MC, V. **Map** p306 F4; p310.

This 19th-century B&B is more like a small hotel. The quality of the warm and elegant decor, and amenities like 24-hour coffee and tea service, well exceed the price. The staff here is so welcoming you almost believe they're really glad to see you. A continental breakfast of fruit, muffins and scones is served each morning in the common room on the ground floor. A further bonus comes in the form of the shops and restaurants of Charles Street, which are right on the doorstep. Dollar for dollar, this is one of the best deals in town.

Hotel services *Air-conditioning. Fax. Garden. No smoking. Parking ($18 per night).* **Room services** *Dataport. Iron. Kitchenette. TV.*

Financial District & Government Centre

High End

Le Méridien

250 Franklin Street, Boston, MA 02110, near Post Office Square (451 1900/1-800 543 4300/fax 423 2844). State/Citizen's Bank T. **Rates** (breakfast not incl) $310-$450 single/double; $440-$800 suite. **Credit** AmEx, DC, Disc, MC, V. **Map** p307 G4.

Many believe Le Méridien is Boston's most elegant hotel. We wouldn't go that far, but it's certainly in the upper echelon. Its architects made marvellous use of the former Federal Reserve Bank's Renaissance revival architecture – polished bronze, ornate woodwork and coffered ceilings abound. The hotel includes two of the most popular French restaurants in town: Julien and Café Fleuri (*see p136*).

Hotel services *Air-conditioning. Bar. Business services. Concierge. Disabled: adapted rooms. Gym. Laundry. Limousine service. No-smoking rooms. Parking. Restaurants (2). Swimming pool (indoor).* **Room services** *Dataport. Iron. Mini-bar. Room service (24hr). Turndown. TV: cable/pay movies/ VCR (on request).*

Omni Parker House

60 School Street, Boston, MA 02108, at Tremont Street (227 8600/1-800 843 6664/fax 742 5729). Gov't Center or Park St T. **Rates** (breakfast not incl) $139-$235 single; $235-$315 double; $295-$395 suite. **Credit** AmEx, DC, Disc, MC, V. **Map** p307 G4.

First opened in 1855 as the Parker House, this is the oldest continuously operating hotel in America. It's also one of the largest in Boston, with 552 rooms. In the city's literary heyday, the Parker House was host to the Saturday Club, a group of distinguished authors (including Longfellow, Hawthorne and Emerson), who would meet here once a month for lunch. Though the elegance of the lobby doesn't extend to the rooms, the service is up to scratch.

Hotel services *Air-conditioning. Bars (2). Concierge. Disabled: adapted rooms. Gym. Laundry. No-smoking rooms. Parking (valet). Restaurant.* **Room services** *Dataport. Iron. Mini-bar. Room service (24hr). Turndown. TV: cable/pay movies.*

Regal Bostonian

Faneuil Hall Marketplace, Boston, MA 02109 (523 3600/1-800 222 8888/fax 523 2454/ www.millennium-hotels.com). Gov't Center or Haymarket T. **Rates** (breakfast not incl) $269-$375 single/double; $450 junior suite; $700 suite. **Credit** AmEx, DC, Disc, MC, V. **Map** p308 G4.

Housed in two adjoining converted red brick warehouses, and arranged around a central brick courtyard, the Regal is close to the madding crowds of Faneuil Hall and Quincy Market. Noise aside (ask for a room at the back), the hotel's rooms are neutrally decorated with small, covered balconies and well-equipped bathrooms (featuring vast bathtubs). A fire crackles in the lobby hearth on cold days and the sound of jazz wafts in from the piano bar. Seasons, the hotel's rooftop restaurant, has been a launching pad for some of the city's best-known chefs and is an ideal spot for a power breakfast or lunch.

Hotel services *Air-conditioning. Bar. Business services. Concierge. Disabled: adapted rooms. Gym. Laundry. Limousine service. No-smoking rooms. Parking (valet, $30 per night). Restaurant.* **Room services** *Dataport. Iron. Mini-bar. Room service (24hr). Turndown. TV: cable/pay movies.*

Tremont House

275 Tremont Street, at Stuart Street, Boston, MA 02116 (426 1400/1-800 331 9998/fax 338 7881). Boylston and New England Medical Center T. **Rates** (breakfast not incl) $149-$319 single; $169-$339 double; $225-$395 suite. **Credit** AmEx, DC, Disc, MC, V. **Map** p308 G5.

This hotel was originally built in 1925 as the national headquarters for the business organisation the Elks Club (look out for the authentic elk head doorknobs). The recent renovation of the hotel kept such touches but softened up the icy marble and patriotic murals with period-appropriate art deco furniture and fixtures. Ideal for young urban types, the hotel has two popular nightclubs on the premises and a decent restaurant and bar, and the city's hectic nightlife is only steps away.

Hotel services *Air-conditioning. Bar. Concierge. Disabled: adapted rooms. Gym. No-smoking rooms. Parking (valet). No-smoking rooms. Restaurants.* **Room services** *Dataport. Iron. Mini-bar. Room service (until 11pm). TV: cable/pay movies/satellite.*

Wyndham Boston

89 Broad Street, Boston, MA 02110, at Franklin Street (556 0066/fax 556 0053/www.wyndham.com). Aquarium T. **Rates** (breakfast not incl) $265-$375 single/double; $340-$450 suite. **Credit** AmEx, DC, Disc, MC, V. **Map** p308 H4.

Much has been made of the Wyndham's recent architectural triumph – its costly renovation of the 1928 art deco Batterymarch Building downtown. Still, though, there is an overwhelming air of newness to the hotel, only slightly balanced by the few, charming historical elements of the old building that remain. As with other Wyndhams, comfort and efficiency are the name of the game here. Amenities in the rooms include well-lit, oversized desks, funky ergonomic desk chairs, virtually soundproof walls, cordless telephones, and Net access in every room. For those who care more for aesthetics than stock prices, there are a few nice touches that help to keep it all from being completely cold and businesslike – the library downstairs, for example, with dark, oak walls and a fireplace glowing on cold days, is a spectacular place to while away a rainy afternoon. That aside, however, much of the building's spirit has been subdued by its new modern look. And that's a shame.

Hotel services *Air-conditioning. Bar. Business services. Concierge. Disabled: adapted rooms (25). Gym. Laundry. No-smoking rooms. Parking (valet). Restaurant.* **Room services** *Dataport. Iron. Mini-bar. Room service (6am-2am). TV: cable/pay movies/web TV.*

South End

Mid-range

Chandler Inn

26 Chandler Street, Boston, MA 02116, between Columbus & Warren Avenues (482 3450/1-800 842 3450/fax 542 3428/www.chandlerinn.com). Back Bay T. **Rates** *Dec-Mar* $105 single; $115 double. *Apr-Nov* $139 single; $149 double. **Credit** AmEx, MC, V. **Map** p308 F5.

Chandler Inn is what you'd call 'straight-friendly': its primary clientele is gay, but all visitors are welcome – as long as they're cool. The Chandler's location in the South End is as appealing as its price. This is a sweet, little hotel, with a truly lovely staff who go out of their way to help their guests. Still, it does have its weaknesses. This building was once a military barracks, and it shows. The 56 rooms, while clean and tasteful, are more than a little worn, and the furniture is more particle board than solid pine. Television reception can be intermittent. The bathrooms are tiny and have no impressive touches. There's no lobby to speak of, no restaurant and no lounge. Still, Fritz, the gay bar on the ground floor, (*see p215*), offers a decent brunch on the weekend, and serves free coffee and fresh, warm muffins to guests in the morning. Nonetheless, unless you're there to party, it's a good idea to ask for a room above the third floor – Fritz is also outrageously loud, and even heavy sleepers may be kept up by its raucous late-night party atmosphere.

Hotel services *Air-conditioning. Bar. No-smoking rooms.* **Room services** *Dataport. Iron. TV: satellite.*

Clarendon Square Inn

198 West Brookline Street, between Tremont Street & Warren Avenue, Boston, MA 02118 (536 2229/ www.clarendonsquare.com). Back Bay T. **Rates** $129-$259 double. **Credit** AmEx, MC, V. **Map** p308 F6.

The centrepiece of this newly converted 1860s townhouse is an original Victorian parlour with soaring ceilings, period detail and a grand piano. Rooms are stylish in a 19th-century kind of way, and also well appointed, with all the modern amenities you wouldn't usually expect of a place with so much old-world charm. The focus here is definitely on romance – straight or gay; if you're squeamish about sharing the rooftop hot tub with a couple of another sexual orientation, you might be better off hanging out, so to speak, in your room's own two-person shower.

Hotel services *Air-conditioning. Business services. No smoking. Parking ($15 per night).* **Room services** *CD player. Dataport. Iron. TV: cable/VCR.*

Waterfront & Seaport

High End

Boston Harbor

70 Rowes Wharf, Boston, MA 02110 (439 7000/ 1-800 752 7077/fax 345 6799). South Station T. **Rates** (breakfast not incl) $365-$535 single/double; $400-$800 suite. **Credit** AmEx, DC, Disc, MC, V. **Map** p308 H4.

Just outside this waterfront hotel, the clangour of Big Dig construction rattles the nerves and batters the eardrums seemingly without end. Inside the hotel, however, it's another story. The elegant lobby looks out peacefully over the sparkling harbour. Aside from its gorgeous views, what makes this such a spectacular hotel is its attention to detail. The restaurant's china is by Tiffany. More than half of the hotel's 230 rooms boast harbour views; some have private balconies and all of them feature sound-proof glass and separate seating areas, as well as other little niceties – fresh flowers in the bathroom, two pairs of slippers by the bed, bottled water – that make all the difference. You'd hardly know you were smack dab in the middle of the biggest construction project in US history.

Hotel services *Air-conditioning. Babysitting. Bar. Business services. Concierge. Disabled: adapted rooms. Gym. Laundry. Limousine service.*

Chain gang

There are a number of chain hotels, mostly business class, in central Boston. Listed below are their locations and toll-free central reservation numbers.

First class

Hilton *(1-800 445 8667)*
Back Bay (Hynes Convention Center) and Dedham.

Hyatt *(1-800 233 1234)*
Cambridge Regency and Harborside Logan Airport.

Westin *(1-800 228 3000)*
Copley Place and Waltham.

Mid-range

Holiday Inn *(1-800 465 4329)*
Cambridge Street (Government Center), Beacon Street (Brookline) and Somerville.

Marriott *(1-800 228 9290)*
Copley Place, Long Wharf, Cambridge, Newton and Burlington.

Radisson *(1-800 333 3333)*
Radisson 57 (Theatre District) and Chelmsford, Marlboro and Milford.

Sheraton *(1-800 325 3535)*
Prudential (Hynes Convention Center), Cambridge, Newton and Braintree.

Budget

Howard Johnsons *(1-800 654 2000)*
Kenmore Square and Fenway Park.

Motels

Most of the economy hotel and motel chains offer several places to stay in suburban Boston. Here's a list of the most common with their toll-free central reservation numbers.

Best Western (1-800 528 1234)
Comfort Inns (1-800 228 5150)
Days Inn (1-800 222 3297)
Motel 6 (1-800 466 8356)
Ramada Inn (1-800 272 6232)
Suisse Chalet (1-800 524 2538)
Travelodge (1-800 255 3050)

Business amenities with an ocean view are the speciality at **Seaport**.

No-smoking rooms. Parking. Restaurants (2). Swimming pool (indoor). **Room services** *Dataport. Iron. Mini-bar. Room service (24hr). Turndown. TV: cable/pay movies/VCR (on request).*

Seaport

One Seaport Lane, Boston, MA 02210, at the World Trade Center (385 4000/385 4001/1-877-SEAPORT/fax 385 4001/www.seaporthotel.com). South Station T. **Rates** (breakfast not incl) $139-$399 single/double; $450-$1,700 suite. **Credit** AmEx, DC, Disc, MC, V. **Map** p307 J5.

If you're coming to Boston on business, the Seaport is the place for you. Situated directly across the street from the Boston World Trade Center, very close to the Financial District and a few minutes from the airport by cab, this hotel has every modern convenience imaginable. It is the kind of place where not a moment is spared. Even the elevators have screens that constantly flash stock prices. For the CEOs among us, there's a private yacht available upon request. To cap it all, the Seaport boasts what is arguably the best hotel health club in town. Aura, the hotel restaurant (*see p144*) may look like a sectioned-off part of the lobby, but the excellent continental food and service are a secret not even the locals have caught on to yet. The hotel also has a 'service-inclusive' policy, so you can save your cash for other things.

Hotel services *Air-conditioning. Babysitting. Bar. Business services. Concierge. Disabled: adapted rooms. Gym. Laundry. No-smoking rooms. Parking. Restaurant. Swimming pool (indoor).* **Room services** *Dataport. Iron. Mini-bar. Room service. Turndown. TV: cable/VCR.*

Cambridge

High End

Charles

1 Bennett Street, Cambridge, MA 02138, off Harvard Square (864 1200/1-800 882 1818/ fax 864 5715). Harvard T. **Rates** (breakfast not incl) $250-$500 single/double; $550-$3,000 suite. **Credit** AmEx, DC, MC, V. **Map** p311 B2.

The Charles Hotel bills itself as 'simply elegant', and it is. The 296 rooms epitomise New England decorative restraint: all are done in blond woods, with muted carpets and calm fabrics. Most have stereos and feather duvets. Don't miss the hotel's exceptional restaurant, Henrietta's Table (*see p149*), and the Regatta Bar (*see p225*), which hosts excellent jazz ensembles.

Hotel services *Air-conditioning. Babysitting. Bar. Beauty Salon. Business services. Concierge. Disabled: adapted rooms. Gym. Laundry. Limousine service. No-smoking rooms. Parking ($25 per night). Restaurants (2). Swimming pool (indoor).* **Room services** *Dataport. Iron. Room service (24hr). TV: cable/pay movies.*

University Park Hotel @ MIT

20 Sidney Street, Cambridge, MA 02139 (577 0200/fax 494 8366/www.hotel@mit.com). Central Square T. **Rates** (breakfast not incl) $99-$379 single/double; $329-$550 suite. **Credit** AmEx, DC, Disc, MC, V. **Map** p306 D4.

The Hotel @ MIT is just that. Not only is it affiliated with the Massachusetts Institute of Technology (MIT), it's located on MIT property. But this is no

Their house is your house

If you find it hard to get familiar with a city and its people from the 33rd floor of a hotel, you're not alone. More and more visitors to Boston are using bed-and-breakfasts as a more intimate alternative. Whether you opt to stay in an elegant brownstone, a quaint colonial house or a rustic seaside cottage, B&Bs offer a more 'authentic' experience of the area.

At the low end of the price scale, you can score a clean bed and a shared bathroom for around $100. For closer to $150, the room should come with a private bath. As you approach $200 (which is about as expensive as these rooms get), you will often find a bigger bed, more upscale amenities, a nice view and a fireplace.

Bed & Breakfast Agency of Boston

A new B&B spin-off that has appeared in the past few years are 'unhosted apartments'. Staying at these places – which range between $135 to $200 per night – is like having your own little pied-à-terre. Many can sleep up to four people.

These agencies promise to hook you up with just the right B&B for you:

Bed & Breakfast Agency of Boston

47 Commercial Wharf, Boston, MA 02110 (720 3540/1-800 248 9262/UK freephone 0800 89 5128/fax 523 5761/ www.boston-bnagency.com).

This agency offers some of the highest-quality accommodation in central Boston. There are more than 150 possibilities, from waterfront lofts to rooms in historic Victorian Back Bay homes. It is especially good at finding short-term studios and apartments.

Bed & Breakfast Associates Bay Colony

PO Box 57166, Babson Park Branch, Boston, MA 02157 (781 449 5302/1-800 347 5088/fax 449 5958/www.bnbboston.com).

This agency lists accommodation in some 150 B&Bs, inns, suites and furnished apartments with waterfront, Back Bay, Beacon Hill or South End locations. The agency also has places to stay throughout eastern Massachusetts and Cape Cod, as well as the islands.

Bed & Breakfast Reservations

11A Beach Road, Gloucester, MA 01930 (964 1606/1-800 832 2632/ www.bbreserve.com).

Susan and Shirl, operators of B&B Reservations, offer a personal touch. Their forté is matching clients with rooms that fit their needs – both in downtown Boston or out along Cape Cod. They offer a wide variety of facilities from small inns to suites to beach houses, with a similarly wide range of prices.

New England Bed & Breakfast

PO Box 9100, Suite 176, Newton Center, MA 02159 (244 2112).

A one-man operation offering home stays in suburban Boston – most within a short walk of public transportation. Catering for special needs (no smoking, pets, allergies) is a speciality.

Think boutique

The lobby of the **XV Beacon** is all but designed to death.

Relatively new on the US hotel scene, the genre of luxurious independents known as 'boutique hotels' is just beginning to set down roots in Boston. There is only one authentic boutique in Beantown at the moment, the recently opened **XV Beacon**. Located, as the name implies, on swanky Beacon Street, XV has quickly made a name for itself with its extraordinary look and astonishing level of service. It joins the ranks of these largely new, trendy hotels catering to those who are weary of the enormous skyscraper hotels, but not ready for the intrusive intimacy, and unpredictable quality, of a B&B. Boutiques tend to have fewer than 150 rooms, and to shower their guests with attention. In addition, of course, there are other benefits: large bottles of Kiehl's products in the bath, pure cotton and linen sheets on the thick mattresses, brushed copper bathroom sinks and showers so big you need a map to find your way out. Plus boutique hotel restaurants tend to defy – nay, laugh in the face of – the humdrum eateries found in many ubiquitous hotel chains. Their restaurants are a gourmet's dream. So, if you feel like splashing out on somewhere individualistic and luxurious, think boutique.

XV Beacon

15 Beacon Street, Boston, MA 02108, at Park Street (670 1500/fax 670 2525/ www.xvbeacon.com). Park Street T. **Rates** $395-$550 single/double; $1,200 suite; $3,500 private floor. **Credit** AmEx, DC, Disc, MC, V. **Map** p308 G4.

This place has every extra touch you can imagine. Its lobby is designed within an inch of its life. It has interesting 1920s-style lifts with sliding metal grills and glass doors. The rooms feature an equally manic attention to detail. The fireplaces are controlled through a switch on the wall by your pillow, as are the stereo and television. Small cable televisions are built into the bathroom walls. Exotic orchids rest languorously on shelves. In essence, XV is modern luxury personified.

Who is that behind the chandelier?

After dinner downstairs at the Federalist, one of the finest restaurants in Boston (which features a 21,000-bottle wine cellar holding $2 million worth of wine; *see also p141*), you can retire to your room and relax on the queen-size canopy bed with crisp Italian linens. In the morning, don the complimentary thick, soft bathrobe, brush your teeth in the deep, free-standing bowl and dry your hands on a towel freshly toasted on the warmer. Thus refreshed, proceed with the important business of the day with a pocketful of the hotel's complimentary, personalised business cards. Isn't life beautiful?
Hotel services *Air-conditioning. Bar. Business services. Concierge. Disabled: adapted rooms. Gym. Laundry. Limousine service. No-smoking rooms. Parking. Restaurant.* **Room services** *CD player. Dataport. Fax. Iron. Mini-bar. Room service (24hr). Turndown. TV: cable/ pay movies/VCR.*

glorified dorm. No less an authority than the popular, upscale US food and decor magazine, *Bon Appétit*, has lauded it and its funky American-style restaurant, Sydney's Grille. Decorated like a chic high school science fair, the hotel verges on elegant surrealism. There are robotic sculptures in the lobby, atomic energy signs stitched into the elevator carpet and circuit boards in all the most unexpected places, including engraved into the frosted glass of the light fixtures in the hallways. The rooms are sleek, well appointed and decorated with exactly the kind of witty techie cartoons and photos you would expect from MIT. Truly unique.
Hotel services *Air-conditioning. Bar. Business services. Concierge. Disabled: adapted rooms. Gym. Garden. No-smoking rooms. Parking ($15 per night). Restaurant.* ***Room services*** *Dataport. Iron. Room service (24hr). TV: cable/pay movies/satellite.*

Mid-range

Cambridge House Bed & Breakfast

2218 Massachusetts Avenue, at Rindge Avenue, Cambridge, MA 02138, north of Harvard Square (491 6300/1-800 232 9989/fax 868 2848/ www.acambridgehouse.com). Davis or Porter T.
Rates $129-$239 single; $149-$289 double. **Credit** AmEx, DC, Disc, MC, V. **Map** p311 B2.
A lovely little Greek Revival house built in 1892, the Cambridge House Bed & Breakfast has 16 rooms furnished with period antiques; two of the rooms also have working fireplaces. A full hot breakfast is included in the room price, along with a hot and cold buffet in the early evening. There's free off-street parking – a godsend in the Hobbesian world of Metro Boston traffic.
Hotel services *Air-conditioning. No-smoking rooms. Parking (free).* **Room services** *Dataport. Iron. TV: cable.*

Inn at Harvard

1201 Massachusetts Avenue, Cambridge, MA 02138, off Harvard Square (1-800 458 5886/fax 491 6520/www.theinnatharvard.com). Harvard T.
Rates (breakfast not incl) $189-$349 single/double. **Credit** AmEx, DC, Disc, MC, V. **Map** p311 B2.
This little gem of a place is a stone's throw from Harvard Yard, and it shows. Designed by Harvard alumnus Graham Gund in 1992, the red brick structure is intended to mimic the architectural style of America's most prestigious university. Inside it's much nicer than a college dormitory, thankfully. All 113 rooms are arranged over four floors around a skylit central courtyard reminiscent of an Italian villa. The atrium is the ideal place for morning coffee, afternoon tea or a quiet dinner. The rooms themselves are somewhat predictable, but are comfortable enough, with all the usual amenities.
Hotel services Air conditioning. Business services. Concierge. Disabled: adapted rooms. No-smoking rooms. Parking ($30 per night). Restaurant. Room services Dataport. Iron. Room service (7am-10pm). TV: cable/pay movies/VCR (on request).

Sightseeing

Introduction	**62**
Boston Common & Downtown	**63**
Beacon Hill & West End	**71**
Back Bay & South End	**78**
The North End	**89**
South & The Waterfront	**95**
Cambridge & Somerville	**103**
Further Afield	**109**
Guided Tours	**111**
Museums	**113**

Feature boxes

Top five cemeteries	67
Freedom's just another word	68
Nobody knows your name	75
Speaking only to God	76
Malcolm X in Roxbury	86
The best parks	91
The best churches	93
Good will changing	97
Hangin' in Central Square	107
Top five museums	117
Going public	119
Stealing beauty	120

Introduction

Wander in the footsteps of George Washington and JFK.

Boston is so rich with history it can all be pleasurably dizzying. Trip in the North End and you'll skin your knee on the same cobblestones upon which Paul Revere rode his horse to warn the residents that the British were coming. Try picking up some babe in a Charlestown bar and chances are George Washington, or at least a Kennedy, once stood right where you are and tried to do the same.

Of course, tourism is one of the city's largest industries, and most of the obvious stuff (Old North Church, the Benjamin Franklin Statue) is pretty easy to find – just follow the well-marked Freedom Trail. But not everything is what it seems. The Cheers Bar, for example, is not Cheers. It's the Bull & Finch Pub, and the only thing it shares in common with the television show is its stairwell. What's most amazing about the sights in Boston is the way the city works in and around them. Boston's best details are not found behind glass in a stuffy museum; they're on a corner by an old lady selling lemonade. So, buy yourself a sugary glass, and get going.

ORIENTATION

Newcomers to Boston face several challenges. Meeting these challenges will give you licence to wander this town with impunity. To fall short will mean you have to dust yourself off and try again. The first thing you will notice while moving around is a lack in many Bostonians of anything resembling patience. Your waiter or waitress will be quite put out if made to wait for you to decide between the chicken and the pork. Cars will honk if you are slow in crossing the road. This impatience is a rude affliction, a learned behaviour, but one they can do nothing about. It is best avoided by learning to think a few steps ahead and to make quicker decisions. Or by ignoring them, as they so often ignore one another.

Then there is the famous language barrier. It's only sort of true. The vast majority of people living in Boston speak perfectly intelligible English. Still, some do violate grammar rules by dropping their Rs after As, and reattaching them after words that end with an 'uh' sound. It's even more complicated than that, and this is especially important to be aware of on public transportation, as conductors and drivers tend to be loud and proud of their 'Boston' pronunciation. Just keep your eye on the map, ask questions when necessary and don't be surprised if people snap at you. Their bark is worse than their bite. However, as with the British and the royal family, don't bring up the Kennedys unless you have something nice to say. Actually, the same goes for Boston sports teams as well.

Finally, a few words on finding your way around town: despite its relatively diminutive size, Boston happens to be a very easy town in which to get lost. If this happens, take a deep breath, relax and realise that it takes years to figure out these cursed cow paths now glorified with names like 'street'. Here's a simple trick: look for the biggest building or highest steeple and walk towards it. Suddenly you'll know just where you are. Never fails. Well, almost never.

► For more on **getting around Boston**, see page 278, and for **guided tours**, see page 111. To learn more about the notorious **Boston accent**, see chapter **Directory**.

Boston Common & Downtown

Red brick and green parks make this a most unusual downtown.

The city's history is represented in sculptures throughout **Boston Common**.

Second only to Back Bay, the area stretching from Boston Common to Government Center is the main attraction for most visitors to Beantown. The bucolic, historic greenery that is the Common – celebrated for centuries in artworks commemorating its unique tranquillity – forms Boston's answer to Central Park. Not far away stand the buildings in which this nation's government was forged. In many ways, this area is truly the heart of Boston.

Boston Common & The Public Garden

As surprising as it may seem, given the lush greenery that is its signature, the 48-acre (19-hectare) **Boston Common** – America's oldest public park, established in 1634 – originally had no trees at all, save one giant specimen that served as a central meeting place for the Puritans who settled here. The 'Great Elm', as it was called, was also handy for hangings, but the park was originally a grazing pasture for cattle, and later became a military training ground. The tree eventually fell victim to a series of ferocious storms that blew through the area in the late 1860s or early 1870s, but by then the Common's use as a rallying point was already a permanent tradition – tree or no tree.

Today, the Common is an arena for public rallies, protests and pick-up sports (impromptu games of frisbee, basketball and the like). Despite their urban moorings, the Common's grassy hillocks, intersecting byways, various statues, playground and its ever-popular **Frog Pond** (city dwellers totter in circles around it during the winter skating months) comprise a relatively calm knoll; a soothing oasis for office workers and downtown denizens seeking a respite from the daily grind.

The 25-acre (10-hectare) **Public Garden** sits shoulder-to-shoulder with Boston Common. Dating from 1837, the Garden is much younger than the Common. It acts as the end-point for the grand expanse of Commonwealth Avenue. It was America's first public botanical garden, a showcase for the then burgeoning greenhouse technology. The dazzling display of flower power continues today, albeit with a few newer attractions. One of them, a statue tribute to Boston writer Robert McCloskey's story *Make Way For Ducklings*, features eight of his characters following their quacking mother.

A more sombre monument of a good Samaritan holding an individual under the influence of ether commemorates the 'discovery that the inhaling of ether causes insensibility to pain'. This landmark in medicine – first demonstrated at Boston's Massachusetts General Hospital – was apparently the source of a skirmish between two individuals who each claimed credit for the discovery. So the decision was made to offer a tribute to neither individual, but, rather, to ether itself.

A third attraction that stands centre stage in the Garden, surrounded (in season) by a brilliant yellow bed of dandelions, is a regal-looking bronze statue of General George Washington sitting astride his horse. It has been said that the statue features one of the most detailed, true-to-life examples of a horse (the only part of the animal missing is its tongue). Unfortunately, late-night pranksters regularly remove the good general's sword as a souvenir, keeping statue sword-makers in steady business.

Benjamin Franklin must have learned a lot in his school days.

In winter, if the Frog Pond in the Common is too crowded you can skate on the **Pond** in the Garden, and in summer, if you're looking for a true tourist experience, take out one of the famous **Swan Boats** out onto its waters. Just don't pet the (real) swans or drink the water – a few years ago there was an outbreak of what the locals called 'mad swan disease.'

Beyond the Common

On the north-east corner of the Common, up Tremont Street from the entrance to the Park Street T, is the tall and gloomy **Park Street Church** (*see p65*). Its primary claim to fame, aside from its adjacent burial ground, is the fact that this is the place where abolitionist William Lloyd Garrison gave his first anti-slavery address in 1829. Beside the church is the **Granary Burying Ground** (*see p65*), a historic cemetery that houses the bones of the famous American patriots Paul Revere and John Hancock. Stepping into this cemetery is like taking a walk in America's past. The gravestones lean toward one another over the hilly ground, and the light is dimmed by the surrounding buildings and a scattering of trees. Sometimes a hazy fog blows across the graveyard, making it as spooky as a setting for a Nathaniel Hawthorne story.

Across the street and tucked into a wide alley is the **Orpheum Theatre** (1 Hamilton Place), a refurbished music hall with a rickety balcony and proscenium seating. Hundreds of multi-platinum acts have climbed onto the Orpheum's stage and Tchaikovsky's First Piano Concerto had its world première here in 1875.

Further north, heading towards Government Center, is the **King's Chapel & Burying Ground** (*see p65*). Originally the first Anglican church in Boston, the chapel is perched on the corner of Tremont and School Streets. Nearby on School Street, in front of the site of Boston's **first public school** (hence the street name), stands a statue of the Man Who Flew a Kite in a Thunderstorm and Lived To Tell About It – **Benjamin Franklin**. Author, inventor, scientist, patriot and scholar, this long-haired pioneer attended the school, which was built in 1635, along with fellow patriots and writers Sam Adams, Cotton Mather and John Hancock. (The schoolmasters must've instilled some serious leadership qualities.) Later, it became the Boston Latin School.

Old South Meeting House – inside and out.

Also on School Street, at Washington Street, is the site of what was once the **Old Corner Bookstore**. Emerson, Dickinson, Hawthorne, Longfellow, Harriet Beecher Stowe and Thackeray all thumbed through tomes in this scholarly nook at one point or another when it was a bookshop. *Walden, The Scarlet Letter* and *The Song of Hiawatha* were all published in the building. Across the street is the **Old South Meeting House** (*see below*) – the largest building in colonial Boston and a sparring ground for anti-British debate before the Revolution.

Granary Burying Ground

at Tremont & Bromfield Streets (635 4505). Park St T. **Open** dawn-dusk daily. **Admission** free. **Map** p308 G4.

Despite being boxed into downtown Boston, the Granary Burying Ground's crooked gravestones look like they could be the backdrop of a classic horror film. Established in 1660, the weathered cemetery lays adjacent to Boston's first granary (hence the name). In addition to Paul Revere and John Hancock, famous figures buried here are Samuel Adams, Peter Faneuil, Ben Franklin's parents, the victims of the Boston Massacre and Samuel Sewall (famous because he was the only Salem Witch Trial magistrate to admit later that he was wrong). Note that there are two tombstones for Revere – the obvious one is a more recent and elaborate pillar. But beside it is a tiny ancient headstone that says only 'Revere.' No headstone rubbing allowed.

King's Chapel & Burying Ground

58 Tremont Street, at School Street (227 2155). Gov't Center T. **Open** *15 Apr-15 June* 9am-4pm Mon, Fri, Sat; *16 June-Labor Day* 1-3pm Sun; *Labor Day-15 Oct* 9am-4pm Mon, Thur-Sat; *16 Oct-14 Apr* 10am-2pm Sat; also by appointment. **Admission** free. **Map** p308 G4.

Never having had enough money to build a steeple, King's Chapel became the First Unitarian church after the Revolution. The adjoining burial ground is Boston's oldest. Laid to rest here – among other notable Bostonians – is Elizabeth Pain (supposedly the model for Hester Prynne in Nathaniel Hawthorne's *The Scarlet Letter*).

Park Street Church

1 Park Street, at Tremont Street (523 3383). Park St T. **Open** *July, Aug* 9am-3pm daily. **Map** 308 G4.

This was known as 'Brimstone Corner' during the War of 1812, as the Park Street Church stored gunpowder in a crypt in the basement, and thus the smell of sulphur was constant, and sometimes overwhelming. Sunday services are still held here.

Old South Meeting House

310 Washington Street, between Milk & Water Streets (482 6439). Downtown Crossing or State/Citizen's Bank T. **Open** 9.30am-5pm daily. **Admission** $1-$3. **Credit** MC, V. **Map** p308 G4.

With its handsome white interior and pew-style seating, this meetinghouse was second only to Faneuil Hall in vocalising Boston's dissonance during Revolutionary times. The building was also a departure point for the enraged 'Mohawk Indians' who chucked 342 crates of tea into Boston Harbor on the night of 16 December 1773.

Faneuil Hall & The Cradle of Liberty

Following either Washington Street or Tremont Street further along will bring you to Government Center, which is dominated by **City Hall Plaza** (Congress Street, at Court Street. Gov't Center T). The result of the same 1960s urban renewal scheme that levelled other historic parts of the city, City Hall Plaza used to be the site of Scollay Square, a raucous, seedy milieu of burlesque shows, jazz joints and gay bars. City planners chose to banish that red-light district and, in its place, built this vast, brick expanse for public performances, special events

and festivals. The open brick plaza is anchored by the hulking City Hall, the daytime home of the mayor and many city officials. Bordering the area is **Haymarket** (by the Central Artery), a small open-air fruit, veg and fish market that operates on Fridays and Saturdays.

The main attractions of the area for most tourists, however, are the historic colonial structures that make up **Faneuil Hall** (*see p69*) and **Quincy Market** (*see p69*). Once the seat of the American Revolution – the very Halls of Liberty – today these two buildings are little more than glorified shopping malls. How the mighty have fallen. What would Paul Revere say if he saw these historic structures today? Maybe he wouldn't mind. Or maybe he'd think that a Crate & Barrel (trendy US homewares chain store) was a poor use for such illustrious property. Maybe he'd think that the ugly outdoor bars that surround the two buildings, and fill them with blustering drunks late on weekend afternoons, was an unfortunate development. At any rate, that is what you will find here. But you must go there anyway. The history of the place renders its current condition secondary. (Interestingly, the conversion of the buildings into shopping centres is considered a huge success, and representatives from other cities frequently study them for tips on how best to convert their own historic buildings into tourist traps.)

Faneuil Hall (pronounced alternately *fan-nail* and *fan-yell*) is the companion piece to Quincy Market, which stands adjacent. Locals refer to the two interchangeably, and the current uses of the two buildings are so similar that this is understandable. In the earliest days of the American struggle for independence, the patriots frequently met – in tense, secret gatherings under pain of execution for sedition – at Faneuil Hall. It was here that they first fomented their plans for revolution. Because of the role it played in their schemes, the building itself became known as the Cradle of Liberty. As the war began, Faneuil Hall was the heated centre of the struggle for the minds and hearts of the people of the colonies. It is where the rebels who dumped the English tea into the sea during the so-called Boston Tea Party met and organised their rebellious feat. It is where the firebrand Samuel Adams rallied the citizens of Boston to fight for freedom. It was in Faneuil

Sightseeing

Top five Cemeteries

As is often the case with historic cities, Boston is rich with buried history. Here is a quick guide to its most interesting cemeteries.

Granary Burying Ground
Samuel Adams is buried here. So is Paul Revere and Crispus Attuck, the first black man shot in the Revolutionary War. *See p64.*

Mt Auburn Cemetery
Such Boston luminaries as Oliver Wendell Holmes, Charles Bulfinch and Henry Wadsworth Longfellow rest here. *See p107.*

Copp's Hill Burial Grounds
Thousands of 17th-century graves; and a beautiful view from the top of a hill. *See p91.*

King's Chapel & Burying Ground
Elizabeth Pain (supposedly the model for Hester Prynne in Nathaniel Hawthorne's *The Scarlet Letter*) lies here. *See p64.*

Bunker Hill Monument
Not technically speaking a cemetery but still, this is where hundreds of men died in the Battle of Bunker Hill. It is a very profound resting place. *See p98.*

Stunningly peaceful **Granary Burying Ground**.

Ah, romance. Even the cold can't kill it in the **Public Garden**'s bucolic setting. *See p63.*

Hall that George Washington toasted the giddy new nation on its first birthday. Through the years, the walls at Faneuil Hall have heard the nation's most impassioned speakers, from the writer Oliver Wendell Holmes and early US feminist Susan B Anthony, to Bill Clinton and US Senator Ted Kennedy.

Directly across very busy Congress Street from the marketplace is the site where the Boston Massacre took place. One of the most significant historical sites in the area, it was under the balcony of the colonial-style **Old State House** (*see p69*) that British troops fired on protesting rebels, providing critical fire to fuel the flames of American rebellion. Today, it is one of the very few buildings connected to the Revolutionary War that is properly used – it serves as a museum to the war and those who fought it. It is one of the most affecting and important historical sites in the city. Included in its collection is a drawing by Paul Revere of Redcoats firing on rebels, with the Old State House in the background. In typical Boston fashion, however, even this building is not deified as it might be. Almost unthinkably, its basement also serves as an entrance to the T.

Freedom's just another word

The red brick line of the Freedom Trail covers the best-known historical sites in Boston. A relatively good starting point for viewing the city, the 2.5-mile (4-kilometre) trail links some 16 different sites starting in downtown Boston and ending in Charlestown.

The Freedom Trail begins on Boston Common at the Visitor Information Center (147 Tremont Street; 426 3115; open Mon-Fri), where you can pick up maps of the trail. The sites on it are as follows (and in this order):

The **State House** (*see p68*); **Boston Common** (*see p63*); the **Park Street Church** (*see p64*); the **Granary Burying Ground** (*see p64*); the **King's Chapel & Burying Ground** (*see p64*); the **First Public School/Benjamin Franklin Statue** (*see p64*); the site of the **Old Corner Bookstore** (*see p65*); the **Old South Meeting House** (*see p65*); the **Old State House** (*see p68*); the **Boston Massacre Site** (*see p68*); **Faneuil Hall** (*see p67*); the **Paul Revere House** (*see p89*); **Old North Church** (*see p91*); **Copp's Hill Burying Ground** (*see p91*); the **Bunker Hill Monument** (*see p98*); **USS Constitution** (*see p98*).

From the marketplace, walk north up Congress Street and you come to **Blackstone Block** (the block of streets off Blackstone Street, between Hanover Street and North Street). Cosy pubs, and one of the city's most famous restaurants, the **Union Oyster House** (*see p137*), line this cobblestoned area, making it an agreeable place to recover with a pint of Guinness after a long afternoon's touring. As an antidote to all that history, one of the city's newest landmarks, the **New England Holocaust Memorial**, is directly across the street in **Carmen Park** (at Congress and Union Streets). Six glass towers covered with six million etched numbers stand as a memorial to those who died in the Holocaust. At night, steam rises out of the transparent towers and the dancing vapours make the monument particularly haunting.

Faneuil Hall

15 State Street, at Congress Street (242 5642). Gov't Center or State/Citizen's Bank T. **Open** 9am-5pm daily. **Admission** free. **Credit** *shop* AmEx, MC, V. **Map** p307 G4.

Built for the city by the wealthy merchant Peter Faneuil in 1742, the hall was later remodelled by that ubiquitous architect Charles Bulfinch. During Revolutionary times it was known as the 'Cradle of Liberty' – colonial heroes like Samuel Adams regularly roused the Boston populace against the British here. These days, as a nod to its history Faneuil Hall hosts the occasional political debate and symposium, but the rest of the time it serves as a mishmash marketplace, with a comedy club lodged on the second-level, and the ground floor market hall is full of tacky souvenir shops.

Old State House

206 Washington Street, at State Street (720 3290). State/Citizen's Bank T. **Open** 9am-5pm daily. **Admission** $1-$3. **Credit** AmEx, DC, MC, V. **Map** p308 G4.

Elegantly set in the midst of modern skyscrapers and congested traffic, like a reminder of things past, the former legislative house is the oldest surviving public building in Boston. It was built in 1713 for the Massachusetts Bay Colony governmental offices. Proclamations, including the Declaration of Independence, were read in this building, often from the balcony on the east side. The area below the balcony was the scene of the Boston Massacre on 5 March 1770 (commemorated by a ring of cobblestones), when British soldiers fired on an unruly crowd, killing five men. After the Revolution, the State House continued as the seat of Massachusetts government until Bulfinch finished his new legislative building on Beacon Hill.

Quincy Market

Chatham & Quincy Streets (338 2323). Gov't Center or State/Citizen's Bank T. **Open** food hall 10am-9pm Mon-Sat; noon-6pm Sun. **Map** p307 G4.

The innermost hall of the central building is lined with fast food stands, where tourists and local office workers grab platefuls of dim sum, hotdogs, clam chowder or burritos and eat them in the indoor courtyard or on benches outside. On either side of the central hall (which gives its name to the whole complex), rows of carts loaded with souvenirs and crafts lure tourists to part with still more dollars, as do the street performers who flock to the place, some of whom are quite good. Flanking Quincy Market on either side are the North and South Markets, which are likewise filled with shops ranging from Gap and Disney to local oddities such as Kites of Boston.

Long Wharf & the Aquarium

Almost directly behind the Faneuil Hall area (under an overpass and through a brief, but unattractive area) lies Long Wharf. It was known as Boston Pier in 1710, when a group of merchants first built brick warehouses here. The shoreline has changed since then: when the **Customs House**, Boston's first skyscraper, was built (in 1847 in the style of an Italian Renaissance campanile), it stood on the edge of the water. The landmark now lies on State and India Streets, several streets inland. The scenic space at the border of Long Wharf is **Christopher Columbus Park**. A huge wooden arbour, with vine-covered trellises and

Old State House, dwarfed by the new kids on the block.

Sightseeing

benches from which to admire the waterfront views, gives the spot an unexpectedly romantic air; it forms the border with the nearby Italian neighbourhood, the North End. Long Wharf is the place to go to find tickets for whale-watching cruises or tours of the harbour islands (*see p111*). A courtyard at the very edge of the wharf offers great waterfront views of barges, sailing boats and planes flying in and out of Logan airport, and the ubiquitous swooping sea gulls, of course. The striking glass **New England Aquarium** (*see below*) sits on neighbouring Central Wharf; while every city seems to have one of these things these days, this is one of the country's best and it's worth a trip even if you don't like fish.

New England Aquarium

Central Wharf, at Atlantic Avenue & Milk Street (973 5200). Aquarium T. **Open** *1 July-Labor Day* 9am-6pm Mon, Tue, Fri; 9am-8pm Wed, Thur; 9am-7pm Sat, Sun. *Day after Labor Day-30 June* 9am-5pm Mon-Fri; 9am-6pm Sat, Sun. **Admission** $5.50-$12.50. **Credit** AmEx, DC, MC, V. **Map** p307 H4.

There's a seal tank outside, a huge indoor penguin exhibit (constructed so that almost all of the balconies overlook it) and a colossal 187,000-gallon salt-water replica of a Caribbean coral reef. Forty feet in diameter and three storeys tall, this cylindrical tank is alive with moray eels, stingrays, huge sea turtles and sharks. There's also a display where you can stick your hands into the cold water of a tidal basin and get up close and personal with starfish, sea urchins and hermit crabs.

The Financial District

If there is one section of Beantown that feels ever-so-slightly like its dreaded competitor, New York, it's the Financial District. Down here, in an area bordered roughly by Congress, Purchase and State Streets, is a concrete labyrinth of one-way streets. You'll find only a handful of attractions down here, although it's interesting enough with its tucked-away galleries and lofts (though both are getting sparse), and a handful of eclectic bars buried among the skyscrapers. It's impersonal, a little claustrophobic, and it's the essence of a big city. This 'hood is a maze of quirky, often picturesque streets. Don't bother to bring a car to explore: those numbered streets in downtown New York have got nothing on the zig-zag of baffling intersections here.

During the day, Boston's business types fill the byways of this money-making district, the heart of America's trust fund industry. Shiny, square, featureless buildings sprinkle the area around **Post Office Square Park** (between Pearl and Congress Streets), where you can find suits nibbling their sandwiches and grabbing a breath of fresh air during their lunch breaks, or talking busily on their mobile phones. At 185 Franklin Street is the giant edifice of the **New England Telephone Building** (it now belongs to NYNEX), which is where the world's first telephone exchange was developed.

Tourists mill through the streets during the day on their way to Faneuil Hall or to catch a glimpse of the waterfront, and, though the Financial District used to empty pretty quickly after hours, hip restaurants and bars like **Vertigo** (126 State Street; 723 7277) and **The Exchange** (148 State Street; 726 7600) have begun popping up recently, giving outsiders an incentive to enter the area after nightfall.

Chinatown & The Theatre District

Originally known as South Cove, Chinatown is a small neighbourhood lined with Asian bakeries, tailors, antique shops and, of course, restaurants. Towards the end of the 19th century, Chinese immigrants began arriving in the city to work on the railroads and as cheap labour in factories. By the early 20th century there were over a 1,000 mostly Asian residents in Chinatown, and the number expanded hugely after World War II. Today the area is contained within a few blocks next door to the Theatre District, and roughly based around Kneeland, Essex, Beach and Tyler Streets.

It's still the best place in the city to see roasted ducks hanging in storefront windows, to gawk at market aisles lined with whole plucked chickens (feet included) or to get a taste of authentic Asian cuisine. Because of its proximity to the Theatre District, restaurants are often packed with theatre-goers before and after shows, and many stay open late into the night to catch the after-hours trade. Remnants of the **Combat Zone** (the once notorious red-light district that was located around Washington Street between Essex and Kneeland Streets) linger in the form of a handful of X-rated video stores, a couple of peepshows and the only strip joint left within city limits. Whether the Combat Zone disgusts or arouses you, be alert if you're there after dark, because, perhaps unsurprisingly, you can find some shady characters in the area.

Next door to Chinatown, on Tremont Street, is what's known as the **Theatre District**. You can find almost any sort of entertainment within this block, be it comedy, dance, musicals, cabaret or drama. The almost stadium-like **Wang Center** is where the big shows play, but there are several more intimate and elegant theatres situated close by as well.

Beacon Hill & West End

Hang around like you own the place in Boston's swankiest neighbourhood.

Life is always beautiful on **Beacon Hill**.

If you had to pick one word to describe Beacon Street, that word would have to be 'long'. The street extends from the heart of downtown Boston through Brookline to the suburbs of Cleveland Circle – over four miles (six kilometres) away. Another word you might use is 'lovely'. Beacon Street is a classic Back Bay grand avenue, with Victorian mansions on either side, often encased in ivy. It is, in essence, exactly what it seems to be on the surface – Boston's wealthiest street, and one of the nation's richest stretches of pavement. It was here in the 1800s that the powerful Boston Brahmins joined together to shape their city and, ultimately, their country. Their descendants still live there today.

Beacon Hill

A neighbourhood that fashioned itself as a breeding ground of refinement, Beacon Hill's most sordid aspect is probably the statue of **Major General 'Fighting Joe' Hooker**, which stands beside the State House. A native of Hadley, Massachusetts, Fighting Joe didn't only distinguish himself as a Civil War general, he also became notorious for his bodily appetites. An accomplished boozer, Major Hooker would allow loose women to prowl his troops' tents at night. These nocturnal guests became known as 'Hooker's Ladies', and, later, as 'hookers'. Get it?

There's little else that openly references anything even remotely subversive in Boston's most prestigious neighbourhood. Originally a messy tangle of cow paths and downtrodden footways, this nest of wealth and power has been home, at one point or another, to famous folk like the patriot John Hancock, authors Louisa May Alcott and Nathaniel Hawthorne and the architect Charles Bulfinch. Bulfinch, who designed the State House, part of the Massachusetts General Hospital, and enhanced the original Faneuil Hall, left indelible imprints on the city's architecture Even today, his style continues to be imitated by architects throughout the country.

These days, the city's elite still occupy the Hill. Musician Carly Simon bought a house here, while writers Robin Cook and Robert Frost have also been Hill residents. Further evidence of high-brow society is to be found in the area's super-abundance of Saabs, BMWs and pearl-necked, loafer-shod residents, who will try assiduously not to notice you, without ever being overtly rude. That's class, that.

In fact, class is what it's all about. While Beacon Hill is tremendously rich, its overflowing flower boxes and gas lamps still manage to be more quaint than outwardly opulent. This has been the case ever since the Beacon Hill Historic District came into existence in 1955, and began enforcing architectural restraints that required the neighbourhood to keep its colonial, rustic charm. This old-fashioned beauty is especially prevalent in the byways of the hill, beyond the brick townhouses of places like **Acorn Street** (between Mount Vernon and Chestnut Streets), probably one of the tiniest and quaintest lanes in town, still bearing some

Acorn Street's cobblestones.

of its original cobblestones. The most central and the largest of three inclines on a larger hill once known as Tremontaine, Beacon Hill earned its name during colonial times. A lookout would be posted at the top of the hill and would light a beacon if enemy ships were sighted out at sea. Before the American Revolution even concluded, Bulfinch had begun designing a seat for the Massachusetts legislature here, to replace the old building at the corner of Washington and State Streets. When word spread that the site of the new **State House** (*see p73*) was to be on the southern slope of Beacon Hill (where John Hancock's livestock once grazed), everyone who was anyone began to relocate in that direction. Other historical and architectural points of interest on Beacon Hill include the **Harrison Gray Otis House** (*see p73*), built by the omnipresent Bulfinch, and the **Charles Nichols House Museum** (um, Bulfinch again. Did that guy ever sleep?), as well as the **Boston Athenaeum** (10 Beacon Street; 227 0270; *see also p117*).

Also in the area, the local branch of the **German Goethe Institute** (170 Beacon Street; 262 6050) is between Clarendon and Berkeley Streets, and offers lectures, films, exhibitions and events, focusing on all aspects of German culture and society. At 150 Beacon Street is the mansion where **Isabella Stewart Gardner** lived in the late 1800s until her move to a palazzo in the Fenway in 1902 (*see p114*). When she lived on Beacon, her home was number 152, but when Gardner moved she ordered that the number never be used again – and apparently she was obeyed. The building is now a college.

If you want to know what these mansions look like inside, **Gibson House** (*see p73*), will give you a taste. The six-story brownstone has been turned into a 'Victorian House Museum'. Nearby, opposite the Public Garden on Beacon Street is one of the city's most popular tourist attractions, the **Bull and Finch Pub**, better known as the inspiration for the long-running television show *Cheers* (*see p75*).

At the foot of the hill lies the area's main thoroughfare, Charles Street. Lined with antique shops and fancy restaurants, the street contributes considerably to the village-like charm of the neighbourhood and is the ideal end point of any exploration. If you can swing it, splash out on dinner at one of the local restaurants: perhaps the **Federalist** (*see p141*), located in the neighbourhood's poshest new resident, the **XV Beacon** hotel (*see p68*). Or you could pinch your pennies and drop in for a cup of coffee at **Panificio** (144 Charles Street; 227 4340).

Scale the heights of **Beacon Hill**.

Charles Nichols House Museum

55 Mount Vernon Street, at Joy Street (227 6993). Park St T. **Open** *May-Oct* 12.15-4.15pm Tue-Sat. *Nov, Dec, Feb-Apr* 12.15-4.15pm Thur-Sat. **Admission** $5. **No credit cards. Map** p308 G4; p310.

The Charles Nichols House Museum, also a Bulfinch design, was the home of the slightly wacky spinster Rose Standish Nichols who lived a Beacon Hill life of leisure and wealth. One of the few Beacon Hill homes left open to the public, you can wander her halls and learn how the other half lived.

Gibson House

137 Beacon Street, between Arlington & Berkeley Streets (267 6338). Arlington T. **Open** *May-Oct* 1pm, 2pm, 3pm Wed-Sun. *Nov-Apr* 1pm, 2pm, 3pm Sat, Sun. **Admission** $5. **No credit cards. Map** p308 F4; p310.

Though the 1859 façade of Gibson House is unspectacular, the interior offers a rare glimpse at how wealthy Bostonians lived 100 years ago. Its six floors of pure Victoriana are original to the house (a member of the Gibson family lived here until the 1950s) and are open to the public. For an upstairs/downstairs perspective, take a look at the kitchen and servants' quarters as well.

Harrison Gray Otis House

141 Cambridge Street, at Staniford Street (227 3956). Gov't Center T. **Open** tours only 11am-5pm Wed-Sun. **Admission** $4; $2-$3.50 concessions. **Credit** MC, V. **Map** p308 G4; p310.

A Harvard graduate who was known as 'the irrepressible social lion', Otis had his house built by Bulfinch in 1796. Both mayor of Boston and representative in the US Congress, Otis was fortunate enough to inhabit what was at the time one of the finest homes in Boston. Today it is an interesting look back at homes of his time.

State House

Beacon & Park Streets, Beacon Hill (727 3676). Park St T. **Open** 9am-5pm Mon-Fri; 10am-4pm Sat. **Admission** free. **Map** p308 G4; p310.

The architectural goose commissioned to lay this structure's huge golden egg was Charles Bulfinch. Covered in 23-carat gold, to this day, that bright bulb is one of Boston's best-known landmarks. The building is the seat of government for the state. It is today, as it has been for hundreds of years, the stomping ground of the Senate and House of Representatives of the Massachusetts State Legislature, with the House holding its political ceremonies under the Sacred Cod, a wood carving symbolizing the state's reliance on the fish industry (*see p25*).

Downtown Crossing

Across Tremont Street from Beacon Hill stands this gritty monument to modern consumerism. Real Bostonians don't go shopping in Quincy Marketplace or Faneuil Hall. Instead, they spend their money here, in the far less touristy, and much more urban environs of Downtown Crossing. This shopping and business strip is tucked away among enormous concrete buildings between Beacon Hill, the Theatre District and the Financial District. Locals

Where nobody knows your name

It never fails. You near the top of the hill on Beacon Street at the edge of Boston Common and there they are. The queue of hopeful, eager, vaguely confused *Cheers* fans, all lined up in front of the place where it all started. The Bull and Finch Pub (84 Beacon Street, at Arlington Street), known to all who loved it on the small screen as the *Cheers* Bar. Or is it?

From the outside, the pub looks quite satisfyingly like the opening shot of the series. Which it should, as the shot was filmed right here. It's got the stairs leading down into the basement, the flags blowing in the breeze, the maroon awning crisp overhead. But that's it. The rest of the place looks nothing like the set of the television show. It's not even a bar, really. It's mostly a restaurant. It's tiny and crowded, and smells perpetually of ketchup. The workers look more like college kids than Sam, Coach and the gang. They're busy and a bit short-tempered, and all wearing matching baseball hats, and they certainly don't have time to get to know you.

Nobody comes here often enough for anybody to shout their name when they walk in the door, unless you count putting your name on a waiting list and getting a cheap thrill when called for your table. And don't count that because it just isn't the same and you know it.

search here for basics like CDs, clothes and electrical goods. Just follow the sweet smell of roasted peanuts to the street vendors who line the walkways throughout this unattractive but useful district. Walk down Washington Street, where Winter Street becomes Summer Street (so cute, that). The area is closed off to cars during the day, making it somewhat like a industrial postmodern open market. This place is like Covent Garden-meets-*Bladerunner*.

Pushcart vendors peddle cheap jewellery and T-shirts in front of the huge department stores like Macy's, Filene's and the famous discount house, **Filene's Basement** (*see p171*). Weirdly, the T at Downtown Crossing shares its entrance with Filene's Basement, so you push past commuters to get inside. It's all very congested and harried, but if you love expensive clothes sold cheap – or just expensive clothes – it's worth it all.

Sightseeing

Speaking only to God

When MTV's *Real World* foisted itself on Boston in 1999, the setting of the 'real-life' drama was a renovated Beacon Hill firehouse on the corner of Mount Vernon and River Streets. (Interestingly, that same location had previously served as a backdrop for the 1980s television series *Spenser For Hire.*) If that doesn't say something about the neighbourhood – namely that Hollywood regards Beacon Hill as cosmopolitan and trendy enough for the airwaves – then maybe telling you that it's also the fictional home of *Ally McBeal*, America's archetypal neurotic single woman, will.

Beacon Hill's aristocratic reign began in the 19th century, when Boston's upper crust became flustered by the droves of immigrants settling into the North End. These well-heeled families, most of them members of the First Families of Boston – or the FFBs, as the Cabots, Lodges, Codmans and Lowells called themselves – moved up to the heights of the then freshly developed Beacon Hill.

The FFBs were so repugnantly exclusive that in 1910 local wit JC Bossidy delivered a half-mocking toast about them that remains famous here to this day:

This is good old Boston
The home of the beans and cod
Where the Lowells speak only to Cabots
And the Cabots speak only to God

The early 20th-century author Oliver Wendell Holmes further ridiculed their exclusivity and self-righteousness by labelling the FFBs as 'Boston Brahmins' in his very popular column in the high-profile literary magazine *Atlantic Monthly.* The name was a stinging reference to the caste system in India. The sobriquet stuck, later evolving into a synonym for old Yankee riches.

The West End

On the other side of Beacon Hill from Downtown Crossing, this neighbourhood was once a large residential area that formed a sort of bridge between the North End and Beacon Hill. For many years the West End housed a considerable low-income population who inhabited its winding streets and cramped tenements. Despite the problems that such neighbourhoods tend to endure – overcrowding and a run-down infrastructure being the most basic – the West End was a gritty but solid niche for minority families, many of whom dearly loved their neighbouhood. In the 1960s, though, urban planners decided to give the area a bit of renewal by way of architectural cosmetic surgery. Amputation is a more appropriate term, actually, as they essentially levelled the neighbourhood in favour of luxury high-rises and the expanding Massachusetts General Hospital.

This so-called 'urban renewal' displaced thousands of residents – many of them African-American and Hispanic families. The memory of the destruction sticks sharply in Boston's collective memory – so much so that former West End denizens preserve the spirit of their crushed homes with a quarterly publication called *The West Ender*, as well as a local access TV show in Somerville.

This is not exactly a tourist hotspot, but a few of the original neighbourhood buildings are worth seeing if you're in the area. Looking like dwarfs beside the tacky high-rises are the **West End Public Library** (151 Cambridge Street; 523 3957) and the synagogue, **Vilna Shul** (14 Phillips Street). Bordering what remains of the West End is the **FleetCenter** (*see p235*), a characterless stadium that was plopped on the former site of the late, lamented Boston Garden sports arena. Though the Garden was mildewed, rickety and weathered, it was the place where the Boston Celtics won numerous NBA Championships in the 1980s, and where Boston Bruins legend Bobby Orr regularly sprayed ice with his skates. Lacking the legacy, personality and obstructed views (as well as the chipped yellow seats) of the Garden, the relatively new FleetCenter is a waxed, antiseptic fortress of corporate branding, high-priced concession stands and a pixelated JumboTron video screen. Yet it's the only arena in town where major sporting events unfurl, pro wrestling matches explode, and platinum selling recording artists like Britney Spears and Mariah Carey wail.

So, bypass the FleetCenter unless you're seeing the Rolling Stones there, and head instead across the highway to the banks of the West End side of the Charles River, where you will find the complex that houses the **Museum of Science & Hayden Planetarium** (*see p118*). This is where you can see the Gemini space capsule which orbited the Earth more than 200 times in 1965, before splashing down safely on national television, and you can watch the stars projected on a giant screen above you.

Don't be fooled; the sun never really sets on beautiful **Beacon Hill**.

Back Bay & South End

Where the hoi meet the polloi; where the watched go to be seen.

Far-reaching view over Boston from the **John Hancock Tower**. *See p79.*

Boston's Back Bay and South End stand today as friends and neighbours, happily united in their joint rule over Boston's most beautiful beings; holders of much of its cosmopolitan flare and affluent sophistication. Their residents are the city's party pages personified; their buildings adored by architectural digests; their dramas ready-made for television.

But this wasn't always the case. Though both neighbourhoods were erected on adjoining marshland landfill sites in the 1850s – and both share a rich social and architectural heritage – by the early 1900s, the South End was very much the Back Bay's poor relation, suffering a long-standing reputation as, well, a bit of a dump. Meanwhile, its neighbour to the north had established itself as a haven for the great and the good of Boston.

In time, Back Bay's Newbury Street became to Beantown the equivalent of London's King's Road, a destination for the fashionable and the wealthy, and for those who want to ogle them. Grand hotels seemed to spring up everywhere. Blue bloods, dignitaries, and super-rich merchants settled into the Back Bay's elegant red-brick townhouses. Exotic lap dogs availed themselves of the area's ornate street lamps. Streets with English-sounding names were created – Marlborough, Beacon, Newbury – that even today remain the most coveted addresses in town.

By the mid 1970s, however – despite boasting some pretty nifty red brick architecture of its own – the South End was largely run-down and economically depressed. Many original buildings had been demolished, and what was left was neglected. Some buildings were unoccupied. Others fell victim to arson. The area became known as a hotbed for drugs, crime and urban decay. The neighbourhood was scorned to the extent that imposingly large buildings were built all along Huntington Avenue to keep the South End out of sight.

But you'd never know that now. The South End – with all of its glorious Victorian swell-front architecture – has effectively licked itself clean. As the city's affluence grew, and it looked for new places to expand, in the late 1980s and early 1990s it looked to the South End, and a period of renewal began. Today, in addition to being home to scores of popular restaurants, the South End has become a centre for the arts. Audiences at the Boston Center for the Arts here swelled from 8,000 in 1990 to 40,000-plus in 2000.

Renewed and restored, the Back Bay and South End combined contain enough bars, boutiques, cafés, restaurants and salons to satisfy even the most ambitious drinker, consumer, diner or people-watcher. And there are, of course, dozens of culturally significant landmarks to check out.

Roughly defined, the Back Bay's centre is the area stretching from Copley Square up to Newbury Street. It's the obvious starting point for exploring both the Back Bay and the South End. If you are coming by T, take the Green Line and exit at Copley.

Copley Square

Copley Square is one of Boston's most attractive spots, with the stunning **Trinity Church** (*see below*) on one side and the vast and impressive **Boston Public Library** (*see below*) on the other. Music festivals often take place in the square on spring and summer weekends, and it's also the finishing point for the annual Boston Marathon.

No guidebook on Boston would be complete without a shot of the neo-Romanesque Trinity Church, completed in 1877. The church, with exquisite Moorish details, took five years to build. Today, the steps of the church make for a perfect place to sit and enjoy lunch on a sunny day. Directly opposite the church, kids skateboard down the entrance ramps of the Boston Public Library – a neo-classical masterpiece. The historic part of the library was recently restored, with great attention to detail. However, critics still turn their noses up over the modern wing of the building, which stands in stark contrast to the main structure.

Just across St James Avenue from Copley Square, but light years away in terms of architectural styles, is the 62-storey **John Hancock Tower** (*see below*). Best known to Boston visitors for the observatory deck at the top, it offers spectacular views and, at night, the colour of the lights on the tower forecasts the next day's weather.

Boston Public Library

666 Boylston Street, at Copley Square (536 5400/ www.bpl.org). Copley T. **Open** 9am-9pm Mon-Thur; 9am-5pm Fri, Sat; 1-5pm Sun. **Admission** free. **Map** p306 F5; p309.

Founded in 1848, designed by Charles McKim and built between 1887 and 1895, this is the oldest public library in the country. The ornate exterior is usually described as Italian Renaissance style, although McKim claimed it was equally inspired by a library in Paris, a temple in Rimini and the Marshall Fields department store in Chicago. Go inside to explore its courtyard gardens and imposing reading rooms. On the way up the stairs are murals by Puvis de Chavannes, and there are others elsewhere in the building by John Singer Sargent. The star attraction is the Bates Hall, which features a majestic barrel-arched ceiling enclosed by half domes at each end. Adjacent to the old public library is its newer wing, a bland, featureless edifice built by Philip Johnson in the early 1970s. Known as a leader of the postmodern movement, Johnson built a wing as smooth and lacking in detail as McKim's is filled with flourishes. The library holds more than seven million books, including over one million rare manuscripts covering many key moments in US history.

John Hancock Tower

200 Clarendon Street, at Copley Square (247 1977/ www.hancock.com). Copley T. **Open** *Apr-Oct* 9am-11pm daily. *Nov-Mar* 9am-11pm Mon-Sat; 9am-5pm Sun. **Admission** $6; $4 concessions. **Credit** AmEx, MC, V. **Map** p306 F5; p309.

According to architect IM Pei, the idea behind the severe rhomboid shape of the tower (built in 1973) is to not overwhelm Copley Square's older buildings. Only a sliver of it shows when viewed from the historic square. Alternatively, from the observatory deck, on a good day, you can see landmarks more than 100 miles (160 km) away. The construction of the skyscraper had its share of controversy. While it was still being built, its windows began popping out and crashing into the street below. Caused by a structural flaw, the problem was nearly catastrophic. Every single one of the building's 10,344 panes had to be replaced, at an additional cost of $8 million. In addition, Trinity Church was damaged during the tower's construction. The top floor has an audio-visual presentation charting the development of Boston. Interspersed with flowery accounts of the 1773 Boston Tea Party and the Revolution that followed, it shows how Boston gradually reclaimed land from the River Charles and the ocean.

Trinity Church

236 Clarendon Street, Copley Square (536 0944). Copley or Back Bay T. **Open** 7am-6pm daily. **Admission** $3. **Map** p306 F5; p309.

The different faces of **Copley Square**.

Sightseeing

Trinity Church, dominating one side of Copley Square. *See p79.*

Before it was a tourist landmark, back in the 19th century, Trinity was the place of worship for the city's elite. Yet it's surprising in some ways that the staid Boston Brahmins approved of the church's architectural flamboyance. It is highlighted by windows and frescos by John LaFarge and sculptures by Saint-Gaudens. Its architect, Henry Hobson Richardson, modelled the central tower after one in Salamanca, though it had to be built considerably shorter than the original or its weight would have sunk the structure into Back Bay.

Boylston Street

To reach Newbury Street from Copley Square, you must first cross Boylston Street. Until recently, Boylston Street was a rather run-down stretch of road, but thanks to a major clean-up initiative by the city, and the opening of a few trendy bars and several moderately priced restaurants, the street has grown popular enough to challenge even mighty Newbury for sheer number and variety of eating and drinking establishments.

Architecturally, Boylston Street is a bit of a mishmash: traditional Back Bay style meets brutal Modernism. This is particularly true at its south-western end, around the **Prudential Center** (*see below*). This undercover shopping mall and apartment complex is centred on the huge tower universally known as 'The Pru.' It is a largely unspectacular modern building, with rather pricey mainstream shops inside. It is the starting point for the boisterous **Boston Duck Tours** (*see p202*).

Also at this end of Boylston Street is the **Boylston Fire Station** (955 Boylston, at Massachusetts Avenue). Dating from 1887 and built in the same Romanesque style as Trinity Church, it is still operational today, and houses two fire engines. Part of the building was once a police station, but in 1976 that section became the **Institute of Contemporary Art** (*see p114*), which exhibits lesser-known as well as big-name modern artists.

If you like your buildings chintzy, take a look at **The Berkeley**. On the southern side of Boylston, on the corner of Berkeley Street, this 20th-century edifice looks like a giant wedding cake, with gleaming white spires and fussy adornments. Somewhat less tacky, at the other end of Boylston and abutting the **Public Garden** (*see p63*), is the **Arlington Street Church** (351 Boylston Street, at Arlington Street). One of Back Bay's earliest buildings, the church was built in the 1800s by Arthur Gilman, and boasts 16 Tiffany stained-glass windows. Boylston actually carries on towards the downtown area, but beyond the Public Garden there is little to interest the historically minded.

Prudential Center & Tower

800 Boylston Street, between Dalton & Exeter Streets (1-800 746 7778). Prudential T. **Open** *Skywalk* 10am-10pm daily. *Stores* 10am-8pm

Mon-Sat; 11am-6pm Sun. *Food court* 7am-9pm Mon-Sat; 9am-7pm Sun. **Admission** Skywalk $6; $4 concessions. **No credit cards**. **Map** p306 E5; p309.
This is a fairly typical example of the American phenomenon of shopping-mall-based-office-skyscrapers. There's no telling why US cities feel they must have downtown combinations of this sort, but they clearly do think it's a good idea. This is an unspectacular 27-acre (11-hectare) shopping complex which forms a base for the 52-storey tower above. It was so unsuccessful with locals that in the early 1990s the whole thing was gutted and completely redesigned. The building is so unimpressive that locals have come to love it. The 'Skywalk' viewing platform in the Prudential Tower is more rewarding than the one in the Hancock building, if only because you get to view the impressive, looking-glass architecture of the Hancock and not the oversized Lego Land structure that is the Pru.

Newbury Street

The city's hype merchants like to call Newbury Street Boston's Rodeo Drive, after the exclusive shopping street in Beverly Hills. There's no doubt that Newbury is the priciest shopping avenue in Boston, and it's the place to find most of the international fashion outlets in the city – including names such as Armani and DKNY. But it's more than that. Commercial art galleries have also made Newbury their home, as have dozens of hairdressing salons, cafés, restaurants, bars and bistros all of which line the length of the street – many are known as much for their intimidatingly stylish hostesses as for their food and drink.

At the Arlington Street end, towards the downtown area, Newbury Street has a reserved atmosphere, with more conservative fashion outlets, high-end jewellers and the occasional furrier. As you go south-west along the street towards Massachusetts Avenue, the shops – and the prices – become less exclusive while the number of pierced eyebrows increases. So does the traffic, especially in summer, when convertibles and SUVs (sports utility vehicles) crawl along the street, rollerbladers and skateboarders zipping between them.

One of the ultimate Newbury shopping experiences is a visit to **Louis Boston** (*see p179*), a grand clothes shop based in a four-storey mansion. The building stands alone, between Boylston and Newbury Streets, with mannequins in glass cabinets outside. Not far from here is the **Armani** (*see p128*) store and café, home of break-the-bank suit jackets and second-mortgage cappuccinos.

The far end of Newbury Street, near Massachusetts Avenue, is as hip as it gets in Boston, thanks to an interesting mix of cafés and shops. **Trident Booksellers and Café** (338 Newbury Street) specialises in 'alternative' books on anything from medicine to lifestyles to modern primitives. Directly opposite this is the second-hand **Avenue Victor Hugo Book Shop** (*see p175*), which, as its name suggests, stocks a wide range of foreign-language titles.

Newbury Street – as pricey as Boston gets.

Commonwealth Avenue

Running parallel with Newbury is Commonwealth Avenue, the grand boulevard of Back Bay and easily the most imposing street in Boston. A wide, tree-lined mall, it is hallmarked by the lovely gardens that run along its centre. Statues and memorials are dotted along the length of the mall, beginning near Massachusetts Avenue and ending at Arlington Street. It's a popular stroll for locals, who try not to get too close to the many homeless who also enjoy the mall in the warmer months. It's also a popular spot for dogwalkers, so beware of 'droppings'.

Classic Victorian mansions run the length of the avenue on both sides, although not all are as exclusive as they look – some serve as student dorms. One house, at 72 Commonwealth, is the **Boston Center of the International Society for Krishna Consciousness**. Not far away, on the corner with Clarendon Street, is another Back Bay landmark – the striking tower of Henry Richardson's 1871 **First Baptist Church**. Like much of Richardson's other work, it was also designed in the

Taking a stroll through the Public Garden, bordered by Arlington Street.

Romanesque style, and some joke that it was Richardson's warm-up to creating the more lavish Trinity Church in Copley Square.

Stroll along the Comm Ave mall and you'll encounter the granite likeness of Alexander Hamilton, the first secretary of the Treasury, an aide to George Washington, and the face on the US $10 bill. Hamilton, who was responsible for financing the Revolutionary War, met his end the old-fashioned way: he was killed in a duel with vice-president Aaron Burr after Hamilton offended him.

Criss-crossing Comm Ave are a series of roads that run in alphabetical order (Arlington Street, Berkeley, Clarendon, Dartmouth, and so on). Cut down one of these streets, going north towards the river, and you'll come to Marlborough Street. Because of traffic restrictions, Marlborough is the quietest of the Back Bay's grand streets. It's also one of the prettiest, and well worth a stroll, just for the meditative aspects.

First Baptist Church

110 Commonwealth Avenue, at Clarendon Street (267 3148). Copley T. **Open** 11am-2pm Tue-Fri. **Admission** free. **Map** p306 F5; p309.

Completed in 1871, a year before Richardson began work on Copley Square's Trinity Church, this building is a similar mix of stone and wood surfaces. Richardson commissioned the bas-relief encircling the top of the belltower from Frédéric Auguste Bartholdi, the sculptor of the Statue of Liberty.

Imposing **First Baptist Church**. *See p81.*

Massachusetts Avenue

From Beacon Street as far as Boylston Street, the section of Massachusetts Avenue that forms the western boundary of Back Bay is a motley mixture of shops, bars, restaurants and colleges. Just after Boylston (going south), at 136 Massachusetts Avenue is the **Berklee Performance Center**, linked with the adjacent **Berklee College** (*see p42*), one of the country's top music schools. The performance centre puts on shows by both students and big-name acts.

Further down, the triangle of space formed by Mass Ave and Huntington Ave is dominated by the world headquarters of the L Ron Hubbard's Christian Scientists (175 Huntington Avenue). It is known by all here as the **Mother Church**. It's an eye-catching, weird as hell collection of buildings designed by IM Pei. You'll see a concrete tower on one side and an ornate pastiche concrete basilica on the other. Along the middle is a very American concrete piazza centred on a delightful pool. At one end is a fountain which, in the summer, is filled with frolicking children.

Behind the church, next to Mass Ave (no one in Boston says Massachusetts Avenue), is the Christian Science Publishing Society building, which contains one of the more unusual attractions in Boston – the **Mapparium**. This is a 30-foot (nine-metre) globe made up of more than 600 stained-glass panels, which allows you to get 'inside' the earth by means of a glass bridge through the middle. National boundaries are drawn to scale. The Mapparium has been closed for renovations and repairs since 1999, and it is not scheduled to reopen until 2002.

Almost directly across Mass Ave is **Symphony Hall**, headquarters of the **Boston Symphony Orchestra** (*see p231*), which was completed in 1900.

Landmark District

A five-minute stroll south of Copley Square casts you into the Landmark District near the junction of Clarendon and Tremont Streets. This is the South End's core. Here, a cluster of trendy cafés and fancy stores create a hip urban-village identity. Many of the businesses are either gay-owned or gay-aimed and rainbow flags are everywhere. Here you will also find the largest collection of Victorian cast iron and rowhouse property in the country. When you're done gawking at that, it is also here that you will find many of Boston's most outrageous sex-toy shops, creative chef-owned restaurants and kitschy trinket boutiques.

The great architect Charles Bulfinch (*see p25*) laid out the original street plan here in 1801. While some of his work has been lost, what remains has risen from the ashes of the South End's bad old days as a beautifully designed neighbourhood with a thriving arts scene. There are many galleries open to the public. The Jorge Hernandez Cultural Center, a performance space in the **Villa Victoria Church** (85 West Newton Street; 739 4567), is known to host biweekly salsa, flamenco and Afro-Caribbean bashes, plus the occasional well-known Latin rhythm and song performer; The baroque **Church of the Immaculate Conception** (775 Harrison Avenue; 536 8440) is appreciated by even the most irreligious for the way its organ cranks out amazing gospel music; and the **Ebenezer Baptist Church** (157 West Springfield Street; 262 7739), started by former slaves, always has some kind of classical or gospel concerts going on.

Another South End site of cultural significance is the recently erected statue honouring **Harriet Tubman**, a runaway slave and key organiser of the Civil War-era 'Underground Railroad', an escape route to the north for southern slaves seeking freedom. Tubman ended up living in the South End and her house still stands today (566 Columbus Avenue; 536 8610).

The landmark around these parts is the **Boston Center for the Arts**. The BCA has three theatres and a large, airy gallery that displays a wide range of contemporary and experimental art. The BCA's centrepiece is the **Cyclorama**: a circular, domed structure built in 1884 to exhibit the huge painting by Dominique Philoppoteaux of the Civil War battle of Gettysburg. The painting went on tour five years later, but never returned – it's now on display in Gettysburg. The Cyclorama itself has served as a rollerskating arena, flower market and factory – one Albert Champion invented the spark plug here in 1907. Today, it's an exhibition space and venue for flea markets and fetish paraphernalia fairs.

Just behind the BCA and a short walk up Clarendon Street is the cheap and deservedly popular local watering hole called the **Delux Café** (*see p157*).

From Clarendon Street take a walk up **Appleton** or **Chandler** Streets, two of the most desirable in the neighbourhood. The Victorian architecture manages to look good in any season. The South End is a great neighbourhood in which to simply wander, stumbling across tiny little parks or the occasional public garden sandwiched in-between buildings.

When you reach Columbus Avenue, it's hard to believe that this drab main road was once touted as the finest residential avenue in the city. But that was 1869, and times have changed. Still, there are several great restaurants in the section between Dartmouth Street and Concord Square. If you are in the neighbourhood anywhere close to lunchtime, **Charlie's Sandwich Shoppe** (429 Columbus Avenue; 536 7669) is worth a visit. The classic diner decor and menu have barely changed since the 1930s. Charlie's turkey hash is a divine way of clogging your arteries.

The Fens

It's impossible to talk about, or traverse, this area of Boston without mentioning a name that is all but inseparable from the Boston park system: **Frederick Law Olmsted** (1822-1903). Generally acknowledged to be the father of landscape architecture, Olmsted is perhaps best known as the designer (along with Calvert Vaux) of New York's Central Park. After he moved his offices from New York to the Boston suburb of Brookline in 1883, Olmsted undertook one of his greatest endeavours, designing the Boston park system – a continuous string of nine parks that stretch through, and offer a respite from, some of the city's busiest districts. It is known collectively as the **Emerald Necklace**. It is feasible to walk the Necklace from end-to-end (it's about a seven-mile/11-kilometre trek from Boston Common to Franklin Park), although sensible walking shoes and a motivated frame of mind are advisable at the outset of such a journey. The Boston Park Rangers (*see p112*) offer a walking and biking tour of the Necklace every season that is both spirited and informative.

Walking through the rose-vined archways of the **James P Kelleher Rose Garden** – established in 1930 – can be a sumptuous experience, especially in late April or May, when the flowers blush in crimson and pink.

The **Museum of Fine Arts** (*see p114*) has work by Degas, Renoir, Rembrandt, Sargent and Picasso, as well as art ranging from African sculpture to 16th-century Chinese furniture and Egyptian artefacts.

The palatial **Isabella Stewart Gardner Museum** nearby (*see p114*) is an equally impressive showcase, with three floors of galleries that house an array of antique furnishings and masterpieces by Rembrandt, Botticelli and Whistler, among others.

Continuing along the Riverway portion of the Emerald Necklace is the Olmsted-designed, man-made **Muddy River** (it isn't actually that muddy), which leads towards **Olmsted Park** (between Jamaica Way and Riverdale Parkway). With its strategically steep banks designed to

The Fens, Boston's glorious showpiece of park design. *See p84.*

block out what were once carriageways (and are now roadways) and its inviting paths, the 28-acre (11-hectare) Muddy River remains one of the purest examples of Olmsted's vision of rural sanctuary in an urban setting. Olmsted Park, once known as Leverett Park after the man-made Leverett Pond, features a well-travelled path for cyclists and pedestrians and its 180 acres (73 hectares) provide ample space in which to pedal or walk.

Roxbury

This area of the city, located next door to the South End, once served as a port of entry to Boston (first for Irish immigrants, then Jewish immigrants and then African-Americans). Today, Roxbury is populated mostly by long-settled African-American families and has a small immigrant population.

In its heyday, Roxbury was a bustling hub of activity, but in the 1970s and 1980s it fell into poverty, the victim of 'white flight' to the suburbs, poor investment in the public schools, and institutional neglect. Today, there is a growing middle class, but residents still face higher rates of unemployment than in other areas of the city, as well as a higher crime rate. Still, for the adventurous, a slice of life can be seen in Roxbury that simply doesn't exist elsewhere in Boston, and the area provides an interesting view of what the city must have looked like 100 years ago.

One of the sights worth visiting is the beautiful **First Church of Roxbury** (10 Putnam Street, at Dudley Street; 445 8393; Roxbury Crossing T), the oldest wooden church in Boston. This is about eight blocks from the Prudential Center in downtown Boston and sits on a slight hill overlooking John Eliot Square; the patriot and silversmith Paul Revere cast the bell in its tower.

The **Shirley-Eustis House** (*see p86*) is another of the city's hidden gems. Largely unknown to all but a small group of preservationists and historians, it was built in 1747. In 1867 it was moved 60 feet (18 metres) to make way for a new street, and was also divided into small apartments. Now a museum, it is currently undergoing restoration.

In 1900 there were no fewer than 30 active breweries in full operation in Boston. In fact, the city had more breweries per capita than any other US city. Today, there are just two (the Samuel Adams Brew House in Jamaica Plain and Tremont Ale in Charlestown). But the ornate brick buildings that once housed the breweries (owned and operated mostly by Irish and German immigrants) are still standing. Many of them were located along the banks of Stony Brook in Roxbury. Of particular interest is the **American Brewing Company** building (235 Heath Street), an ornate, 107-year-old brick building that still retains its original granite sign. The structure is topped with a pointed tower,

Malcolm X in Roxbury

His street name was Red, and his Muslim name was El-Hajj Malik El-Shabazz, but when the infamous man best known as Malcolm X first moved to Boston in 1941, he was just 16-year-old Malcolm Little. Malcolm made the transition from naïve, country bumpkin to street-savvy, small-time hustler after meeting his half-sister Ella for the first time in 1940. In his autobiography, Malcolm stated: 'She was the first really proud black woman I had ever seen in my life.' It was Ella who invited the young Malcolm to come and live with her in Roxbury.

X marks the spot where Malcolm was.

The house Ella owned with her husband Frank was on Waumbeck Street in an exclusive neighbourhood, Sugar Hill. The Hill encompasses a section of upper Roxbury bordered by Humboldt, Blue Hill and Walnut avenues, branching up towards Franklin Park.

Though Malcolm lived on the Hill, he spent most of his time hanging out in bars, clubs and pool halls in what is today referred to as Lower Roxbury. This section of the neighbourhood flanks Tremont and Columbus Avenues and is intersected by the short block of Massachusetts Avenue. Here Malcolm was introduced to petty crime, the bursting jazz scene and young, zoot suit-wearing hipsters when he worked as a shoe shine boy in the men's room of the Roseland Ballroom on the corner of Huntington and Mass Avenues. Today, the Roseland has been replaced by an unspectacular hotel called the **Midtown Hotel**, but the spirit of the jazz scene is still very much alive up the street at **Wally's** on Mass Ave (*see p226*). One of the most popular jazz clubs in the 1940s and 1950s, Wally's has stood the test of time and today still sponsors cookin' jam sessions. Around the corner from Wally's on the corner of Northampton Street and Columbus Avenue is another Malcolm favourite, **Bob the Chef's Café** (*see p132*). This soul food joint has gotten a serious make-over in the past couple of years, and now looks more upscale bistro than down home hangout, but it still serves quality soul food at reasonable prices, and features regular sets by popular jazz trios.

Sadly, with Boston's skyrocketing real estate prices and the expansion of Northeastern University, most of Malcolm's former stomping grounds have been bulldozed and turned into municipal car parks and student dormitories.To get a glance of what Roxbury was like during Malcolm's days, visit **Dudley Square**, near the corner of Washington and Dudley Streets. Most of the original architecture is intact, and both **Ferdinand's Furniture** building and **Dudley Station** are impressive examples of what Roxbury looked like in Malcolm's day.

and has two false clocks built into its façade: one is set at seven o'clock and the other at five o'clock – brewers' hours.

Just down the street is the former home of the **Alley Brewing Company** (123 Heath Street). It's a massive brick structure, though it lacks the interesting architectural details of the American Brewing Company.

Other streets in the area worth exploring include Alleghany, Calumet and Iroquois Streets, and Parker Hill Avenue. These reveal a mix of once grand houses, some painstakingly restored, but others suffering the rude fate of a century of neglect – or worse, vinyl siding. The impression is one of a neighbourhood struggling to regain its lost glory.

Shirley-Eustis House

33 Shirley Street, at Massachusetts Avenue (442 2275). JFK/UMass T. **Open** *June-Sept* noon-4pm Thur-Sun. *Oct-May* by appointment only. **Admission** $5; $3 concessions. **No credit cards.**

Over the years this noble house has housed two Massachusetts governors (William Shirley, who served as the royal governor of the Massachusetts Bay Colony, and Dr William Eustis, who served as governor from 1823 to 1825). It has received visits

Sightseeing

L Ron Hubbard's eclectic Christian Scientists' HQ, aka the **Mother Church**. *See p83.*

from George Washington, Benjamin Franklin and Daniel Webster. During the Revolutionary War, it served as a barracks and hospital for the British. In 1970, work began on restoring the house to what it looked like in the Federal era. Open as a museum today, it is America's last remaining country house built by a British Royal Colonial Governor.

Jamaica Plain

Ask the people who reside in the area to describe Jamaica Plain and they'll usually say it's like living in the country within the city. That's an apt description of a place once known as the Eden of America because of the wealth of green space that all but surrounds it. Several tales, some of them quite tall, surround the naming of the village that was originally a part of the neighbouring community of Roxbury. One of the stories claims Jamaica Plain earned its moniker because residents in the northern part of Roxbury happened to enjoy Jamaican rum and what's more, they liked it plain. The Jamaica Plain Historical Society, however, puts the name down to a Native American woman called Jamaica who once lived on the shores of Jamaica Pond.

The area, settled in 1639, blossomed into a farming community during the 18th century and was eventually annexed by the city of Boston in 1874. During the 19th century, JP, as it's known today, became increasingly industrialised, as tanneries, shoe factories and breweries were built following waves of German and Irish immigration. Jamaica Plain was also the area where many of Boston's most wealthy and powerful movers-and-shakers chose to build idyllic getaways from city life. Walk along Jamaica Pond and you'll be able to see the imposing Victorian mansions that once dominated the landscape. James Michael Curley, Boston's flamboyant four-term mayor, two-term congressman and one-term governor, built a majestic Georgian Revival mansion at 350 Jamaicaway, which had shamrock shutters to identify its owner as being of Irish descent.

Other notable sites include the granite monument in **Eliot Square**, which pays tribute to the 23 residents of West Roxbury who died in the service of the Union during the Civil War. Eliot Square is considered the heart of JP. It is bordered by Centre and South Streets. Nearby is the **Loring-Greenough House** (*see p88*), where British loyalist Joshua Loring once lived. A host of progressive-minded notables have lived in JP, including Judith Windsor Smith, an Abolitionist and suffragist who voted for the first time at the age of 99 when women were finally granted that right in 1919.

Jamaica Plain's tradition of liberal politics continues today. The area has a reputation for being a bastion of racial, ethnic, sexual and class diversity – although it has become increasingly gentrified as city dwellers seek to escape congestion and concrete, a fact that has inevitably driven real estate prices through the roof and forced some longstanding residents out. In recent years, a bevy of boutiques, cafés, healthfood shops and upmarket restaurants catering to a younger, more affluent clientele have moved in alongside the older bars and five-and-dime shops that were once staples of Centre Street, JP's main thoroughfare.

Two of the most celebrated sites of the Jamaica Plain neighbourhood are the 265-acre (107-hectare) **Arnold Arboretum** (*see below*) and the 120-acre (49-hectare) stretch of **Jamaica Pond** (Jamaicaway, at Pond Street; 635 7383), and for good reason. Jamaica Pond, a kettlehole caused by an ancient glacier, is the largest body of water in Boston, and much celebrated by a steady stream of joggers, walkers and picnickers who populate its paths and sit on the grassy slopes leading to the water's edge. Although most people prefer to fish in it rather than drink it, one could down a glass of the stuff: Jamaica Pond's water is so clean that Boston has designated it as its back-up city reservoir.

In the early 19th century, the blue waters of the pond lured Boston's wealthiest residents to build lavish summer homes facing it. Olmsted convinced the city to buy out and demolish many of these properties when he began his plans to develop the Emerald Necklace of parks around Boston's centre. Today only one of those spacious homes remains standing, albeit in dilapidated condition. Sadly holding out against the elements on the northern side of the pond, the **Pinebank Estate** is a three-storey brick affair built in 1870 by James Newton Perkins. It exists in limbo, awaiting a consensus between the city and local preservation groups. Its restoration is expected to cost somewhere between $3 million and $4 million. Other far more pleasant sights along the edges of the pond include a boathouse (where canoes and rowing boats can be hired) and an outdoor bandstand, which regularly hosts live jazz bands and small-piece orchestras.

Not far away are the 13,000 trees, shrubs and vines of the Arnold Arboretum. Its gently rolling hills and lush expanses of lawn and marshland are a magnificent study in science, courtesy of scientist Charles Sprague Sargent, who collected and catalogued the plant specimens, and of design (Olmsted who else?).

The sprawling 527-acre (213-hectare) **Franklin Park** (*see below*) was rightfully considered by Olmsted to be his Boston masterwork – a scenic country park intended, first and foremost, to be used for recreation and enjoyment by city dwellers seeking escape from the pressures of workday life. The park, which features a woodland preserve, 18-hole golf course (the nation's first public one) and zoo (a baby gorilla was born there in 1999), took several years to build and the effort shows: inside the park, medieval-looking stone steps lead to picture-perfect vistas of colour and detail; splashes of yellow and orange dominate the treescapes in autumn. Seemingly endless lawns roll out into other distant wonders and there's not one car to be seen for what, quite literally, is miles of unbroken country.

Arnold Arboretum

125 Arborway, at Routes 203 & 1, (524 1718). Forest Hills T. **Open** *Grounds* dawn-dusk daily. *Visitors' centre* May-Oct 9am-4pm Mon-Fri; Nov-Apr 10am-2pm Sat, Sun. **Admission** free. Free public tours one Sat each month.

The Arboretum is named after James Arnold, who financed its development and left his fortune (including the Arboretum) to Harvard University, which subsequently sold it to the city. The city in turn leased it back to the university for one dollar a year for 1,000 years. Today, the place looks like a spectacular, three-dimensional painting of peaceful water lily decorated ponds, exotic bonsai trees and intoxicating lavender-coloured lilac trees, among other numerous seasonal delights. The Arboretum is more than just a showplace, however. Its living, breathing tree museum is a bountiful resource for botanists and other scholars, students and teachers.

Franklin Park & Zoo

Franklin Park Road (park 635 7383/zoo 541 5466). Forest Hills T, then 16 bus. **Open** *Park* dawn-dusk daily. *Zoo* Oct-Mar 10am-4pm daily; Apr-Sept 10am-5pm Mon-Fri; 10am-6pm Sat, Sun. **Admission** *Park* free. *Zoo* $7; $4 concessions. **Credit** AmEx, MC, V.

The Tropical Forest, complete with gorillas, leopards, pygmy hippos and tropical birds, is the main draw here. There is also the Kalahari Kingdom's lions, and wallabies and emus on the Outback Trail. And little ones can meet llamas, goats and chickens out in the Contact Corral.

Loring-Greenough House

12 South Street, at Centre Street (524-3158). Forest Hills T, then 39 bus or Green St T. **Open** by appointment; tours in summer noon-3pm Sat. **Admission** $3. **No credit cards.**

This house was used as a hospital for General George Washington's troops. The home was purchased in 1924 by the Jamaica Plain Tuesday Club, an organisation formed in 1868 to 'improve female minds' in the neighbourhood.

The North End

When the moon hits your eye like a big pizza pie, you're in Little Italy.

As long as you don't park your car in one of those spaces marked with a 'You take-a my space; I break-a your face' sign, it's all about love in the North End, an area locals have begun to call their own 'Little Italy'. It's the type of neighbourhood where a lively beat owns the streets, everyone seems to know the butcher and the little old ladies sell home-made lemonade when it's nice out. And it doesn't matter if you're British, Polish or straight off the boat from Finland; anyone who can order an espresso can be Italian in the North End.

The area brims with history that extends back to pre-Revolutionary days, from its settlement shortly after the Puritans landed on Plymouth Rock to the famous ride of its early resident Paul Revere to the birth of the Kennedy clan. The North End was a locus of great wealth before the Revolution, but as the wealthy moved out to the swankier environs of Beacon Hill, waves of immigrants moved in. For decades the area has been mostly Italian.

The North End's architecture has been affected by the number of fires it has, only barely, survived. It also was the site of the great molasses flood of 1919 (*see p13*). In that memorable incident, an enormous tank of molasses that was being stored for the purpose of rum-making, exploded and sent 2.5 million gallons of the stuff cascading through the streets. The 12-foot wave sank a boat, and dragged 23 people (and 12 horses) to a sugary grave. Some claim that on a hot day you can still smell molasses on Commercial Street.

Sightseeing

The house where the US patriot **Paul Revere** raised his 16 children. *See p90.*

The North End is best navigated by foot. One of the best ways to experience the neighbourhood vibe is to check out one of the summer street fairs called 'feasts'. Every weekend during the warmer months, residents hold religious-inspired parades, set up food carts and sell locally made crafts, each household trying to outdo the next in good-natured competition.

North Square

Three of the Freedom Trail's sites (*see p68*) are in the North End. The best known of these is the house of the area's biggest star, Paul Revere. Every year, 200,000 people visit the **Paul Revere House** (*see below*). He owned the house for 30 years and was residing here the night he set off on his famous midnight ride to Lexington and Concord. Revere worked as a silversmith in a workshop on nearby Clark's Wharf and some of his handiwork can be seen in the house today. What has not lasted is the third storey he added to accommodate his many children (he had 16 of them). Thirty years separated the oldest and youngest and no more than eight lived under his roof at any one time. While the house is interesting, representing as it does a rare example of wooden 17th-century colonial architecture, in the end it is Revere's own history that makes it worth a visit.

More impressive architecturally is the three-storey brick mansion next door, the **Pierce/ Hichborn House**. It was built in 1810, and Revere's cousin Nathaniel Hichborn bought it to be closer to his relative. The contrast between the two houses is fascinating – Revere's being far more primitive than Hichborn's, showing how the nation's wealth had advanced over the course of a century (*see below*).

Walt Whitman's old house of worship, the **Sacred Heart Church** (*see below*), is across the cobblestoned North Square plaza from the Pierce/Hichborn House. It's also worth taking a glance at the **Mariners' House** (11 North Square, between Moon and Prince Streets). This was a hotel that rented rooms to sailors for $3.75 a night from the 1870s up until 1997.

While Revere is the most widely visited figure in the area, it's only fair to point out that the North End boasts other famous sons and daughters. Congressman and former Boston mayor John 'Honey Fitz' Fitzgerald was born on Ferry Street and later lived at **4 Garden Court**, where he reared a daughter named Rose who later married a fellow named Kennedy. Her sons included President John F Kennedy, Attorney General Robert F Kennedy and Senator Ted Kennedy, who still serves in the US Congress. Despite many personal ups and downs, especially among the family's younger generations, the liberal Kennedy clan remains undefeated in Massachusetts elections.

Paul Revere House & Pierce/Hichborn House

19 & 29 North Square, between Richmond & Prince Streets (523 2338/www.paulreverehouse.org). Haymarket T. **Open** *Apr-Oct* 9.30am-5.15pm daily; *Nov-Mar* 9.30am-4.15pm daily. **Admission** $2.50; $2 concessions; combined ticket $1.50-$4. **Credit** *shop only* AmEx, MC, V. **Map** p308 H3.

Built in 1680, the Paul Revere House was originally designed for a local merchant named Robert Howard. The two-storey clapboard building seems modest by Boston standards, but its leaded diamond panes and extravagant Elizabethan overhang indicate it was home to families of means. Revere lived here from the late 1700s through the early 1800s. The third storey was removed in the 19th century, when the house fell into disrepair (during that time it was briefly a flop-house and then a souvenir shop). It was saved from the wrecking ball in 1902 by one of Revere's descendants, and restored. However, nothing you'll see here, aside from one interior door, is original to the house. The Pierce/Hichborn House was built in 1810 for local resident Moses Pierce, and later purchased by Revere's cousin, a shipbuilder named Nathaniel Hichborn.

Sacred Heart Church

12 North Square, at Prince Street (523 5638). Haymarket T. **Open** 7am-8pm daily. **Map** p308 H3.

Founded in 1833, this was originally known as Seamen's Bethel, and was devoted solely to the needs of the sailors who lived and worked in the area. It adapted to the ethnic mix of the neighbourhood over the years, and today one mass every Sunday is delivered in Italian.

Hanover & Salem Streets

No visit to the North End would be complete without a good Italian meal, and chances are that exploring Hanover and Salem Streets will reveal one or two … hundred. Food rules here, and everyone has some kind of sign in their window laying claim to being the best something in Boston. There are dozens of bustling little coffee and pastry shops lining the streets, particularly Hanover Street. And it's not all hype, either. The food here is some of the best Italian cooking in the country, so it's hard to go wrong. (*See chapter* **Restaurants & Cafés**.)

If you can put down your fork for a minute, waddle on down to one of the more notorious sites in the area – the **Langone Funeral Home** (383 Hanover Street). This is where Nicola Sacco and Bartolomeo Vanzetti were executed in 1927, following a controversial robbery and murder trial that preyed on the xenophobia of the era. Many believed the two

The best Parks in Boston

Boston Common is one of the city's best parks.

As great as urban life can be, there's something positively exquisite about trading the concrete jungle for fields of soft fluffy grass. Boston's parks are great places to relax, throw a Frisbee and meet people who enjoy doing the same. As with any other open urban spaces, however, it's wise to avoid them after dark.

Arnold Arboretum

When it's time to see (not pick) the flowers, head to this gigantic arboretum. Each season brings with it a host of special flora and fauna for your sight and smell pleasure. *See p88.*

Boston Commons & Public Garden

The city's most popular escape by far. Swans, swan boat rides, floral arrangements and, commonly, lots of young people making out on benches, punctuate this green expanse. *See p63.*

Castle Island

Not only does this 22-acre park have historical value, it's also perfect for running, swimming, fishing, picnicking or swinging from the jungle gym. *See p96.*

Charles River Esplanade

For lovers of athletics, this park along the Charles River offers biking, jogging, Frisbee, boating and all sorts of other sweat-building activities. For the rest of us, however, there's plenty of soft grass to lounge around on while grooving to music from the Hatch Shell. *See p102.*

Boston Harbor Islands National Park

Actually a string of many natural parks located in Boston Harbor and accessed by ferry, they are the perfect setting on which to act out your own homespun version of *Survivor*. *See p100.*

Sightseeing

were innocent, and were railroaded through the court system to appease the angry, anti-immigrant zeitgeist. The story of their fate remains a *cause célèbre* among anti-death penalty groups worldwide. On the other hand, a nicer memory lies at 168 Hanover Street, where in 1851 Eben Jordan started a store that evolved into the Jordan Marsh empire. A few years later, Rowland H Macy began his own store nearby, called Macy's. All went well for both for more than a century until Macy's absorbed Jordan Marsh in 1996 – effectively killing Jordan's dream as part of a massive consolidation trend among US stores and chains nationwide. Well, maybe this isn't such a nice story after all.

Nearby on Prince Street is **St Leonard's Church** (at Hanover Street, 523 2110), the first Italian Catholic church in New England. It houses a beautiful flower garden and still functions as a place of worship. Not far from St Leonard's is **St Stephen's Church** (*see below*), the only remaining church in Boston designed by Charles Bulfinch. The church also has a part in the history of the Kennedys – Rose was baptised and had her funeral here.

St Stephen's Church

24 Clark Street, at Hanover Street (523 1230). Haymarket T. **Open** 7am-dusk daily. **Map** p308 H3.

Bulfinch didn't build this church from scratch. Instead, he remodelled an existing structure in 1804. Shortly thereafter, the church's congregation purchased a set of bells cast by Paul Revere's foundry for $800. Those who are most familiar with elaborate cathedral architecture will find this church's colonial plainness unusual. The building was renovated in 1965, at which point it was painstakingly returned to its original appearance. Which is very, very simple, as historic churches go.

The Prado

In 1933 the North End's favourite son got his own memorial. The **Paul Revere Mall**, located in the quaint, brick-paved park known as the Prado, features as its centrepiece a statue of Revere first designed by Cyrus E Dallin in 1865 but only cast in 1940. The mall (between Hanover and Unity Streets) serves as a social epicentre of the North End, with neighbourhood folks doing neighbourhood things – playing cards, gossiping and arguing over sport scores

Cops Hill Burying Ground. *See p94.*

The best Churches

Boston was founded by Puritans and populated by Irish Catholics, so its feet have always been in the baptistery and its head near the pulpit. There are many variations on the theme, but when those bells ring on any given Sunday, baby, there's one thing for sure: people come running like supper's ready. And it's not even necessarily about God. It's about church. Hell, even atheists go to church in Boston.

Old North Church

Where the lantern was placed to signal Paul Revere to hit the road and start a revolution. *See p94.*

First Baptist Church

The bas-relief encircling the top of the belltower was sculpted by Frédéric Auguste Bartholdi, the sculptor of the Statue of Liberty. *See p83.*

Trinity Church

Top five churches in Boston? Please. The American Institute of Architects ranks the Trinity among the ten greatest public buildings in the country. *See p79.*

First Church of Christ, Scientist

Aka the 'Mother Church'. A granite-and-concrete behemoth that looks like a space alien's interpretation of Renaissance architecture. It's fun to roll up your trousers and walk through the long pool on a hot summer day. *See p83.*

Arlington Street Church

This church has 16 Tiffany stained glass windows, but more than that, it is a Unitarian-Universalist church with the most diverse congregation in town – Buddhist, pagan, atheist, 'recovering Catholic', you name it. Its leader, the Rev Kim Crawford Harvie, is the first openly lesbian minister to lead a church in Boston. *See p80.*

One if by land at the **Old North Church**.

(yes, the Red Sox still suck). In the square, engraved tablets on the walls list famous residents and places in the North End. Another social spot further towards the waterfront and on the very edge of the North End is Christopher Columbus Park, and, no, he did not live in the North End.

One of the most important Freedom Trail landmarks in the North End is the **Old North Church** (*see below*). It was originally called Christ Church in Boston, but local custom dictated that the oldest church in the area be known as Old North.

The last Freedom Trail stop in the North End is **Copp's Hill Burying Ground** (*see below*) on Charter Street, the final resting place of roughly 10,000 early Bostonians. It's the highest point in the North End, and an especially good spot for taking pictures of the USS *Constitution* across the harbour in Charlestown. Puritan preachers Cotton Mather and his father Increase are buried on Copp's Hill. The Mathers were arch-conservative theologians. Cotton Mather was famed for his literary prolificacy. He is believed to have written more than 400 books and pamphlets. Both Cotton and Increase fell out of favour in subsequent years over their handling of the Salem Witch Trials. Both were influential enough to have halted the Salem inquisition, but neither condemned the mass hysteria that occurred among the religious residents of Salem until far too late.

Also buried on Copp's Hill is the slave and soldier Prince Hall, an early African-American leader in Boston. Hall lived in the free black community that originally settled the hill, and earned fame for his bravery in the Battle of Bunker Hill.

Nearby is a symbol of the sometimes eccentric rudeness of some Bostonians. You'll note that 44 Hull Street barely looks like a house. After all, it's the narrowest in Boston – only ten feet (three metres) wide. According to local lore, the sole purpose its original owners had in building it was to block their neighbours' view. Welcome to Boston, pal.

Copp's Hill Burying Ground

Charter Street, at Snowhill Street. North Station T. **Open** dawn-dusk daily. **Admission** free. **Map** p308 G3.

Developed on the most northern hill of the Shawmut Peninsula, this cemetery was founded in 1659. Once the site of the community's mill, it was originally called Windmill Hill. The British used the site's geographical advantage to launch cannon balls at the rebel army during the Battle of Bunker Hill; it is said that they warmed up by using some of the cemetery's gravestones for target practice.

Old North Church

193 Salem Street, at Hull Street (523 6676). Haymarket T. **Open** *Nov-May* 9am-5pm daily. *June-Oct* 9am-6pm daily. **Admission** $2. **Map** p308 H3.

This is believed to be the oldest church in Boston. Built in 1723 in the style of Christopher Wren, the church played a critical role in the earliest days of the American Revolution. It houses the famous steeple from which lanterns were hung to warn the Minutemen of the movements of British troops. One lantern was to be placed in the steeple if the troops were seen moving by land, two if they were coming in by sea. They came by sea, and two it was. It was the signal from the lanterns in that steeple that spurred Paul Revere to take his midnight ride. The steeple wasn't part of the original church, and was only added in 1740. Replacement steeples were built in 1806 and 1954 after a pair of hurricanes knocked the previous versions down. In the original window where the two lanterns were hung sits a third lantern, lit by President Ford on 18 April 1975, symbolising hope for the nation's next century of freedom. More trivia about the church: its 175-ft (53 m) spire has been used as a reference point by sailors for hundreds of years. It still appears on modern nautical maps. Famous visitors to the church have included US presidents James Monroe and Theodore and Franklin Roosevelt. And, finally, the bust of George Washington inside the church is said to have been the first memorial ever dedicated to the country's founding father.

South & The Waterfront

Yo. Wear your hat backward when you're hangin' in Southie.

Gorgeous water views are luring the upper classes to tough **South Boston**.

It's been more than 200 years since South Boston (universally known here as 'Southie') was a meadow. Then, or so it is said, a wooden gate was extended across the path at the present junction of Dorchester Avenue and Dorchester Street to contain the livestock. Even now, in the court of public perception, Southie remains something of a gated community. Of all Boston's neighbourhoods, this one has carried on with the smallest amount of change to its ethnic, social and religious make-up: for more than a century Southie has been working-class, blue-collar, conservative-Democrat and Irish-Catholic. As a result of fighting to keep it so – violently opposing school desegregation and forced busing in the 1970s, for example – Southie has also earned a reputation as one of the toughest and most controversial of Boston's neighbourhoods.

In its earliest days, circa 1630, South Boston was known as 'Mattapanock' by the Neponset tribe of Massachusetts Indians and as 'Great Neck' by the Puritans who settled in nearby Dorchester. The 560-acre (227 hectares) peninsula afforded perfect pasturage for the Puritans' cattle, and remained roughly undeveloped until the first decade of the 19th century. Dorchester Street, leading to Broadway, corresponds to the old cow path.

When it was thought in 1804 that Boston could not physically handle many more inhabitants (read: immigrants), the city scratched its collective snobby head and decided to annex the cow pasture. The dozen families living in the area were paid off, and two surveyors from Dorchester – Mather Washington and Stephen Badlam – came up with a grid plan for the new neighbourhood. From A Street at Broadway Station to P Street at City Point; cross streets going from First upwards, it is all as they designed it. The first real bridge across the Fort Point Channel into Southie was built in 1805 and horse-drawn streetcars were soon operating along Dorchester Avenue to and from Boston.

The community grew rapidly. Shipbuilding, glassworks, iron foundries, distilleries and breweries began to flourish in the area and many of the workers took up residency in South Boston for the proximity to these mills and factories. Back in those days, the Irish were considered undesirables and dealt with heavy prejudice – help wanted signs in Boston famously read, 'Irish need not apply'. Faced with intractable bigotry, the Irish immigrants banded together and made this undesirable plot of land their own.

The 20th century was, in general, good to Southie. Industry prospered. The waterfront was beautified. On the other hand, crime-wise, over time fists gave way to guns as dispute solvers and a tough group of organised criminals cornered the market on murder and shakedowns. Still, locals recall the 1940s as the area's heyday, when to be from Southie was to have 'Southie Pride'.

There is still some of that pride today, but things have changed. None of the following attractions are widely advertised; there are no organised tours in Southie. But it represents the last vestige of true 20th-century Boston.

Southie

The main drag in South Boston is West Broadway, and as you walk down it you will pass one of Southie's sweet little touches. The **West Broadway Clock** (346 West Broadway) was created as part of one of those weird little acts of civic duty or pride that cities are sometimes inspired to do. Nobody quite remembers why, but in the 1870s, a street clock was installed for the people. The historic timepiece has lovely carved wood details and is believed by many to be the last working gas-illuminated clock in the country.

One of the first things you'll notice when you arrive at the Broadway Station T is a bar across the street with the name **Triple O's Lounge** (28 West Broadway Street). Now, before you rush in for a cold one, there are a few things you should know. According to a book written by *Boston Globe* reporters Dick Lehr and Gerard O'Neill, *Black Mass: The Irish Mob, The FBI and A Devil's Deal*, this bar earned the nickname 'Bucket of Blood' for a pretty straightforward reason – and it has nothing to do with rare steaks. The book alleges that members of the so-called Winter Hill Gang committed some pretty heinous crimes here, and that their then leader, James 'Whitey' Bulger – who has been on the FBI's 'Top Ten Most Wanted' list since 1999 – kept his offices upstairs at Triple O's at some point. Caution: Triple O's is not exactly 'tourist friendly' and is probably more safely viewed from the outside, but it has become a local landmark nonetheless.

On the other side of fame is **Woody's L Street Tavern** (195 L Street). For decades, this tavern was just a random place to knock 'em back, but then Matt Damon and Ben Affleck put it up on the silver screen in the Oscar-winning film *Good Will Hunting*. Now there's a big sign on the wall outside reminding passersby of its connection to the popular flick. Things just haven't been the same since. But it's still a great place to have a drink with the locals, and bitch about the Red Sox.

Not far from Broadway, on Dorchester Heights, is one of the best places to take a picture in South Boston (locals seem to think it's one of the best places to have a smoke, actually). The **Dorchester Heights Monument** surely wasn't intended to encourage the act of smoking. The spot marks the site of a former military encampment used by the troops of General George Washington when he was pushing the British out of Boston. It is said that when Washington brought his forces up to Dorchester Heights on 17 March 1776, he was culturally prescient enough to order the troops to use the password 'Saint Patrick'. This explains why St Patrick's Day here is also called Evacuation Day. The Boston architectural firm of Peabody and Stearns designed the white marble monument. It has recently undergone a massive restoration and now its weather vane can be seen for miles.

Just down Dorchester from the monument to a war victory stands a monument to Catholicism in Boston. It wasn't easy being a Roman Catholic in the predominantly Protestant Boston of the early 1800s. Before the massive Irish immigration began, a small community led by Bishop John-Louis Lefevre de Cheveurs tired of burying their dead in Protestant burial grounds. When Father François Antoine Matignon, a colleague of Bishop Cheveurs, passed away in 1818, Cheveurs built the **St Augustine Chapel** (on Dorchester Street between Tudor and West 6th Streets) as a funeral chapel and burial site. The small church was enlarged and dedicated as a parish church in 1831, and though it is no longer used for services, the red brick Gothic Revival-style structure is the oldest surviving Catholic church in Massachusetts – with the oldest Roman Catholic cemetery in New England.

Castle Island

As forts go, **Fort Independence**, on Castle Island at the very tip of South Boston, is right up there among the best. It's seen its share of action and of celebrities (the writer Edgar Allen Poe was stationed there as a young soldier). It offers a sweet view of the ocean, plenty of pretty green lawn to roll around on, a nice jungle gym for the kiddies and a great little shack that sells ice-cream, hot dogs and grilled

Good will changing

In the movie *Good Will Hunting*, Matt Damon played a troubled young maths genius living in Southie. His version of Southie is a rough-and-tumble, hard drinking blue-collar area ruled by primal city law. And so it was in South Boston for the past 50 years. Recently, though there has been a change. Real estate is up; revival and renovation are in, yuppies are everywhere. And though it is still largely a working class district, it seems it won't be long before Southie becomes another neighbourhood filled with middle class professionals. Clusters of affluent young workers are scrambling for living space and discovering Southie for its wide streets, beautiful water accessibility and convenience to downtown. As the population becomes increasingly cosmopolitan, the local shops and restaurants are evolving. The Newbury Street-style Larry Barron Salon and Spa (*pictured right;* 699 East Broadway; 269 7699) has appeared. And a rowdy Irish pub called Molly Darcy's has been overhauled by one of Boston's most acclaimed restaurant designers to make way for the Playwright Café (658 East Broadway; 269 2537).

A ripple effect has set in. Not only are luxury condominiums popping up left and right, but a three bedroom family apartment that sold for $200,000 just two years ago now sells for at least double that amount.

Of course, this growth does not come without cost to the locals, whose families have been renting in South Boston for generations and who can't all afford to spend the kind of loot that the new economy demands. 'Growing up, Ma never told us we were poor,' jokes Dan 'Farnue' McCole, an artist and local pundit.

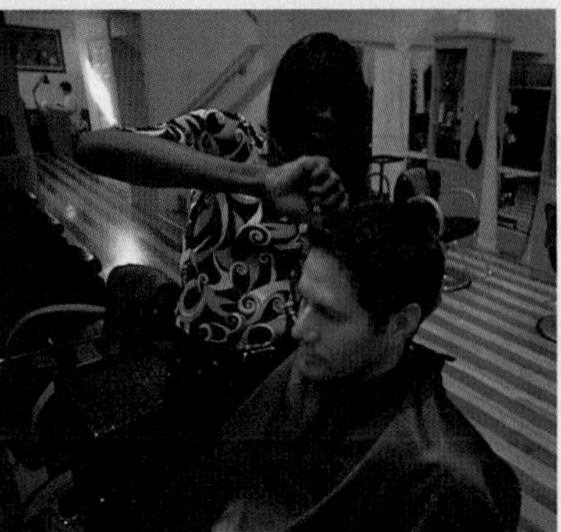

McCole created a series of paintings he called *South Boston: Lost but Not Forgotten*. Among the things McCole points to as lost are the old Strand Theater, the City Point Head House, the City Point Aquarium, and, er, his house. When his mother passed away recently, he found himself effectively priced out of Southie.

Despite all the changes, of course, the neighbourhood is still about as far away as you can get from being a shopping mall. And for every Carhartt-clad money-manager sipping a gin and tonic at the Playwright on a Friday night, there are ten guys with hard-hats at their feet pounding back Guinness down the street at Shenanigan's (332 West Broadway; 269 9509). The question that bothers many locals is: will Southie continue to take care of itself and retain its flavour? 'Any neighbourhood that doesn't fight for its own survival,' quotes McCole from something he says he remembers having read, 'is not a neighbourhood'.

cheese sandwiches wrapped in wax paper. Still, unless you really know what you're looking at – tours are infrequent and placards only go so far – it might be hard to get a charge out of the experience. So, as they say in Southie, listen up.

It was while serving as a 16-year-old soldier on Castle Island that Poe received the inspiration for the tale of the unfortunate Fortunato in his short story *Cask of Amontillado*. That inspiration came in the form of a duel that occurred between two soldiers named Massie and Drane on Christmas Day 1817, in which the more popular of the two was killed. It is said that spectators to the event revenged the death by entombing the less popular man alive.

Castle Island Park and Fort Independence

East end of William J Day Boulevard (268 5744). Broadway T, then 9 or 11 bus. **Open** 6am-11pm daily. **Admission** free.

First fortified by the British as Castle William (hence Castle Island) in 1634, Fort Independence has been restored four times for the purpose of fulfilling its role in harbour defence, which it did from the Revolutionary War through World War II. Today the pentagonal, five-bastioned, granite fort is the centre of an urban park and is just as peaceful as can be – though we wouldn't suggest you hang out there after dark or that you should pick a fight with anyone more popular than yourself.

Charlestown

This tough old shipbuilding neighbourhood has quite a reputation in this city. There used to be an ironic saying around Boston that, despite its rough, working class streets, Charlestown was one of the safest areas to live in town; this was ostensibly because the Mob was so powerful in the area that it kept the petty criminals in line. Nowadays this is more legend than truth and, even as the economic boom seems to be entering its waning days, the well heeled are still snapping up its real estate like crazy.

A trip to Charlestown wouldn't be complete without a visit to the **Charlestown Navy Yard** (*see below*) which first opened in 1800. By the beginning of World War II, the Navy Yard employed 47,000 workers, almost as many as lived in the the Charlestown area at that time. President Richard Nixon closed it down in 1974 (shortly before his resignation in the Watergate scandal), supposedly as a final act of revenge against the liberal state of Massachusetts which never supported him in anything he ever did (it's also the birthplace of his nemesis, John F Kennedy). The closure devastated Charlestown, where, even then, most of the residents still worked at the shipyard. The area was never the same again. Today the navy yard serves as a museum of American naval history.

The most famous ship at the yard (if not in the country) is the **USS *Constitution***, 'Old Ironsides'. The ship earned her nickname during the war of 1812, when shots fired by the British supposedly bounced off her hull. A sailor on another ship in the battle, the USS *Gerriere*, is said to have shouted 'Her sides are made of iron!' Sadly, it's unlikely that sailor lived to tell the tale as his own ship sank just a few minutes later. Old Ironsides has largely remained in dry dock since the late 19th century, although she did set sail for the first time in 116 years in 1997 – the year of her bicentennial – and she is towed out into the harbour and turned once a year, to ensure that her hull weathers evenly. The **USS Constitution Museum** (*see below*) adjacent to the ship includes an interactive gallery in which visitors can load and fire a cannon or simulate steering a square-rigger at sea. Nearby is the **Charlestown Visitor's Center** which is also located in the navy yard adjacent to the USS Constitution Museum. Here a re-enactment of the Battle of Bunker Hill is shown on video every 30 minutes.

From the yard, you can see the obelisk of the **Bunker Hill Monument** (*see p100*) shining in the near distance. It commemorates one of the earliest, goriest battles of the Revolutionary War. Started on 17 June 1775, the fight began when the British attacked a group of rebellious colonists who had fortified themselves at the top of Breed's Hill. This battle was later, and for all time, mistakenly identified as the Battle of Bunker Hill, which was actually the next hill over. The clash was critical to the war effort, in that the rebels came very close to winning it, though they ultimately lost. More than 1,500 men lost their lives in that battle – of those more than 1,000 were British. The rebels' near-success emboldened the fledgling nation to rally to the cause. To find out more it's worth visiting the informative **Bunker Hill Pavilion** (*see p100*) nearby, which offers an educational multi-media presentation on the bloody battle.

Not far from Bunker Hill, at 10 City Square near Main Street, you'll find **Olives** restaurant (*see p143*). This is one of Boston's favourite upmarket eateries, and has been for several years. Chef Todd English has influenced Boston cooking like nobody else. But he doesn't accept reservations, so if you feel like lunching here, leave your name at the door, and wander off for a while. You could do worse than passing some time over a drink at the **Warren Tavern** (2 Pleasant Street, at Main Street; 241 8142). Named after Joseph Warren, a revolutionary who died in the Battle of Bunker Hill, the tavern was built just after most of the Charlestown neighbourhood was burnt in the late 1700s, which makes it one of the oldest structures in Charlestown. Paul Revere presided over Masonic meetings as a grand master here, and George Washington visited after he became president. The tavern was closed for a while in the 1960s, then re-opened as a bar and restaurant in 1972 and it has thrived ever since.

Charlestown Navy Yard

Outside Gate 1 of the Charlestown Navy Yard, Constitution Road, Charlestown (241 7575). North Station T/92, 93 bus. **Open** *summer* 9am-6pm daily; *winter* 9am-5pm daily. **Admission** free. **Map** p308 G3.

Built on the spot where the Mystic and Charles rivers converge, the first hammer was slammed onto a piece of wood in the shipyard as the 18th century turned into the 19th. It was, for many years, the nation's premier navy yard. As you enter it through the main gate, there is a helpful visitor information centre to your right, which provides free leaflets with maps and information about the site. In the yard are both the USS *Constitution* (free tours are given of the ship and its 44 guns daily), and the USS *Cassin Young*, a destroyer which saw action in the Pacific during World War II.

USS Constitution Museum

Charlestown Navy Yard, Charlestown (242 5671). Community College T. **Open** 9.30am-3.50pm (last tour 3.30pm) daily. **Admission** free. **Map** p308 G3.

Sightseeing

The **USS *Constitution***. Sailors once swore her sides were made of iron.

The Southie waterfront is lined with parks.

Located inside the Charlestown Navy Yard, this museum is worth a detour as it offers exhibits related to the ship itself and to naval history in general. The interactive portion includes computer games that allow players to devise an escape from an enemy ship, and to see an attack through the eyes of various crew members. Costumed staff demonstrate ship-related skills such as knot tying.

Bunker Hill Monument

Monument Square, Breed's Hill, Charlestown (242 5641). Community College T. **Open** 9am-5pm daily. **Admission** free. **Map** p308 G3.

The memorial consists largely of a towering obelisk in Monument Square. To reach the top you climb 294 steps (it takes about 15 minutes). The cornerstone of the monument was laid in 1825 by the Marquis de Lafayette, the French officer who was viewed by the American revolutionaries as the only foreign leader brave enough to offer his help in their fight. It was dedicated in 1842 by Daniel Webster. The monument is part of the Boston National Historical Park and park rangers give free informative talks hourly (call ahead in winter months to check the frequency of their presentations).

Bunker Hill Pavilion

55 Constitution Road, near Charlestown Navy Yard, Charlestown (241 7575). Haymarket T. **Open** *June-Nov* 9.30am-5pm daily. *Sept-Nov* 9.30am-4pm daily. **Admission** free. **Map** p308 G3.

A multi-media presentation explores and explains the Battle of Bunker Hill, using a variety of screens and modern technology to simulate battle sounds. The story is skillfully narrated by actors.

On the waterfront

What's most stunning about Boston's 43 miles (69 kilometres) of coastline – beyond its natural beauty and utility – is that, until recently, a good deal of it was barren wasteland more commonly used for dumping bodies than strolling hand-in-hand with a loved one, or, for that matter, hosting an international meeting on the human genome project. With the new **Seaport District** fast taking shape and the Big Dig (*see p20*) putting the city's highways underground, however, a good deal of waterfront property is opening up for redevelopment, and private and public interests are battling furiously over almost every inch.

It's about time. This is, in many ways, an essential part of Boston's past. Until the late 1860s, the city of Boston survived on maritime activities. The city was centred on shipbuilding, water commerce and fishing. Although today the economics of the area have less to do with the sea than ever before, it is still a powerful part of the city's economic base. The Port of Boston remains extremely active. Boston's **Fishing Pier** (Pier 6), constructed in 1914, is the oldest working fishing pier in the country. Boston Harbour welcomed almost 200,000 cruise ship passengers in 2000, and handled container ships carrying more than $8 billion worth of goods. For tourists, it offers a variety of water-related sights, and a gorgeous day out on the ocean blue.

Boston Harbour Islands

One of the finest introductions to the waterfront is a visit to the **Boston Harbour Islands** – 30 small islands left by a retreating glacier about 12,000 years ago. Seventeen of them were designated the **Boston Harbour Islands National Park** by former president Bill Clinton; of these, six are open to the general public. Today, wildlife is thriving in the water and on the islands. Rare and endangered species of birds such as the plover and osprey have been spotted here. Grey and harp seals also live in the harbour. The islands don't seem to have been discovered by most of the general public yet, which means they can still be enjoyed in relative comfort, even on a sunny summer day.

Short of bringing your own boat, taking a ferry cruise from **Long Wharf** to the islands with **Boston Harbor Cruises** (*see p101*) is the best way to see it all. The 28-acre (11-hectare) **Georges Island** is where you'll land first. The front part of the island is dominated by **Fort Warren**, a massive structure used during the Civil War as a Union training base and a prison for captured Confederate soldiers (including, most famously, the vice-president of the Confederacy, Alexander Hamilton Stephens). You can either take a guided tour or explore it on your own. A free shuttle service takes you to other islands in the park. **Bumpkin Island**, covering about 35 acres (14 hectares), is tucked away in Hingham Bay and doesn't see much traffic. From the early part of the 20th century to the 1940s, it was used to quarantine children with polio. Today it's one of four harbour islands where camping is permitted. Peddocks, Grape and Lovells

Lovely in the winter, South Boston's **waterfront** is more fun in the summer.

islands also allow camping. In all cases, reservations must be made in advance with park officials (223 8666/www.nps.gov/boha/). Also note that, inexplicably – chalk it up to prim New England culture – alcohol is not permitted on the islands.

Gallops Island, at just 16 acres (six hectares), is the smallest of the harbour islands open to the public. During the Civil War, it was put to use by Union soldiers; in the 19th century it served as a popular summer resort. Today it offers hiking trails, picnicking spots and some of the best views of Boston's skyline.

Grape Island has never been developed; the remains of a 19th-century farmhouse are the only clue that the 50-acre (20-hectare) island was once inhabited. The island has pristine shell and gravel beaches, camp-sites and berries to pick.

Lovells Island covers 62 acres (25 hectares) and has a public swimming beach, hiking trails, wooded hills and dunes. **Peddocks Island**, at 188 acres (76 hectares), is the largest of the harbour islands. During the 1960s, a 4,100-year-old skeleton was excavated on its shores. It's the only island with residents all year round; when the harbour islands were first turned into a state park, the state granted these residents, almost all of them fishermen, life-long leases; upon their death the land reverts back to state ownership. Peddocks also allows camping, picnicking and hiking. With its salt marshes, wildlife sanctuary and heavily wooded inlands, the island is a mini paradise.

Boston Harbor Cruises

1 Long Wharf, next to New England Aquarium, Downtown (227 4321). Aquarium T.
Rates sightseeing & whale-watching $8-$28.
Credit AmEx, MC, V. **Map** p308 H4.
Specialising in historic sightseeing tours, inner harbour cruises, whale watch safaris, George's Island ferry, sunset cruises, commuter services, private functions and special events, they're the first folks to call when you've got water in mind.

Fort Point Channel

Fort Point, 16 December 1773: a group of 60 colonists disguised as Mohawk Indians dumps 342 chests of tea into Boston Harbour in protest at the tea tax imposed by King George. Good luck trying to visit the spot where this occurred. A landfill now obscures the site – on Pearl Street across Route 93 by what is now **Carl's Deli** (147 Pearl Street; 542 1965) – and the actual ships involved are, of course, long gone. What remains is the interesting to look at, but generally disappointing **Boston Tea Party Ship and Museum** (*see p102*), which is best viewed from the outside. When you've had enough of the American Revolution, stop by the **Milk Bottle** (312 Congress Street). As the name implies (well, sort of), it's a restaurant shaped like a giant milk bottle. It has been serving fast food since 1934.

The area on the eastern side of Fort Point Channel, between Northern Avenue and Summer

Some of the best views in the city can be found along the **Charles River**.

Street, is sometimes called the Museum Wharf because of a handful of museums and galleries located along the harbour front. In particular, the **Children's Museum** (*see p201*) is located here. It focuses on early childhood education and teaching resources, and has hands-on displays to entertain children of all ages.

Continuing along Northern Avenue, you come to **Boston's Fishing Pier** (Pier 6). This is the place to discover the city's traditional harbourside fishing shacks, including **Jimmy's Harborside** (242 Northern Avenue; 451 3663) and **Anthony's Pier 4** (140 Northern Avenue; 423 6363), where baked cod, finnian haddie and salty oyster crackers can be eaten while you sit among the driftwood and fishing nets.

Boston Tea Party Ship and Museum

Congress Street Bridge (338 1773/ www.bostonteapartyship.com). South Station T. **Open** *spring & autumn* 9am-5pm daily. *Summer* 9am-6pm daily. **Admission** $8; $4 concessions. **No credit cards. Map** p308 H5.

The Beaver II is a full-size working replica of the original tea-carrying ship. In general, this is more theatrical show than actual museum. Costumed guides do a feeble re-enactment of the Tea Party, and visitors have little choice but to join in, as the museum itself is a disappointment. Let's face it, there's just not much to put in a museum of this sort. Nothing remains of the actual tea party – not the tea, not the ship, not the crate the tea was in; so there's nothing to look at here but words on paper in glass cases describing the historical event and, on a recent visit, the history of tea. It's all mostly aimed at kids who don't mind wearing green (why green?) feathers in their hair and chanting 'Dump the tea into the sea!' However, some parents look truly miserable as they take part in this interactive exhibit and learn very little from it except perhaps to be very careful what they pay for in the future. The gift shop here is shockingly expensive, but worth a visit if only for the tiny models of the USS *Constitution* in a bottle, for sale for $14, each of which bears a stamp on the bottom reading, 'Made in China'. Lovely.

The Charles River Basin

The Boston Harbour is hard to beat, but it's not the only waterfront space the city has to offer. The Charles River Basin runs from the river's end at the **Museum of Science** *(see p118)* to the Boston University Bridge.

The **Charles River Esplanade** is located on the Boston side of the basin just after the Harvard Bridge as you head toward Boston. It's a grassy field criss-crossed by numerous walking paths and anchored by the **Hatch Memorial Shell** (Charles River Esplanade, between Longfellow & Harvard Bridges; 266 1492), a pavilion best known for the annual Fourth of July concert by the **Boston Pops**, an extravaganza which attracts hundreds of thousands of concert-goers each year (*see p230*). Bicycle paths and grassy banks hug both sides of the river. On summer days, sun-worshippers lie on towels, impeding the frolicking of frisbee players, dog walkers, cyclists and rollerbladers. On sunny weekends it can get quite crowded here. One of the best views of the city skyline is from the Cambridge side of the basin along Memorial Drive between the Boston University and Longfellow Bridges.

Farther up the path behind the Hatch Shell is **Charlesbank Park**. This is a sweet space with room to roam alongside tennis courts, playgrounds for children, and the useful **Community Boating Center** where sailing boats can be hired during the summer.

Cambridge & Somerville

See how smart you look among the ivy-covered walls and dazzling bookshops around Harvard.

Harvard Square is for people-watching, but not when the snow is falling. *See p104.*

Boston is famous for being a college town, but Cambridge is the real academic centre, boasting two of the world's best universities – Harvard and MIT – just a few miles apart. Though it's just across the river from Boston, Cambridge is a very different place from its neighbour. Nicknamed by locals 'the People's Republic of Cambridge', the city boasts a diverse and decidedly liberal population of academics, artists, immigrants and students. Rising housing costs, triggered by the end of rent-control and an influx of dotcom rich kids, has threatened the leafy community's bohemian atmosphere, but Cambridge is still the type of place where cab drivers have PhDs, school teachers play in rock bands and multiculturalism is a mantra.

Cambridge was only briefly anything other than a college town. It was founded in 1630 by one of the first waves of Puritans who came from England to settle in Massachusetts. Originally called Newtowne, it was a farming community for exactly six years before the city elders established the country's first college there in 1636. A short time later the college was renamed after the clergyman John Harvard who, upon his death in 1638, left the school half his estate and all the books from his personal library. Newtowne was then renamed after that other famous university town in England, where many of the settlers had received their education.

Harvard University

Harvard has more than 400 buildings scattered around 360 acres (146 hectares) in Boston and Cambridge, but its nerve centre is **Harvard Yard** (tours available by calling 495 1573), a grassy, tree-lined quadrangle surrounded by colonial red-brick buildings that date back to 1720. First-year students still live in dormitories in the Yard, and you'll find them studying and reading (or flirting or sleeping) on the grassy sections of the quad.

As you enter the Yard (opposite Harvard T stop) by the gate on Massachusetts Avenue opposite Dunster Street, the first thing you'll see is **Massachusetts Hall** diagonally opposite. Built between 1718 and 1720, during the Revolutionary War the Hall sheltered the soldiers of the fledgling Continental Army.

Today the president of the university, vice presidents and other university officials live on the lower floors, while the upper floors are used as living space by first-year students. The hall just edges out the **Wadsworth House** (built in 1726) as the oldest building in the yard, though the latter, yellow clapboard structure, is the more picturesque. This building served as temporary headquarters for George Washington when he was leading the nation's army in 1775.

University Hall, designed by Charles Bulfinch in 1813, sits directly in front of what is probably the biggest tourist magnet in Harvard: the statue of **John Harvard**. Cast in 1884 by Daniel Chester French (who also sculpted the Lincoln Memorial in Washington, DC), the statue is known as the 'statue of three lies'. Its inscription reads 'John Harvard, Founder, 1638', three times untrue since John Harvard was a donor, not a founder; the college was set up in 1636; and nobody knows what he really looked like – French used a Harvard student as a model. Touching John Harvard's shoe is rumoured to bring good luck, so students (and tourists) line up accordingly.

Though most visitors to the campus don't venture beyond the main quad, it's worth exploring further in order to see the neo-Gothic **Sanders Theater** and the **Carpenter Centre of the Arts** (designed in 1963 by the respected French architect Le Corbusier). Other notable Harvard buildings include the **Science Centre** – which is one of several on campus designed by Josep Lluis Sert; the others are the **Peabody Terrace** (built in 1964), **Holyoke Centre** (built in 1967), and the **Centre for the Study of World Religions** (built in 1959).

On the quiet quad directly behind University Hall, you'll find the imposing, classically styled **Widener Library**, the oldest university library in the country and the largest academic library in the world. It holds more than 13 million volumes. Getting through the doors of the library without a student ID is almost as difficult as getting into the college itself, but even anyone can appreciate the Titanic tie-in of the place. Harry Elkins Widener, after whom the library is named, graduated from Harvard in 1907, then went down with the famous ship when he failed to swim 50 yards to reach a lifeboat. The following year, his mother donated $2 million to Harvard for this library. Legend has it that she stipulated all undergraduates must pass a 50-yard swimming test.

Outside Harvard Yard

The extraordinary collections on display in the **Harvard Art Museums** (*see p115*), which lie behind Harvard Yard on Quincy Street, are definitely worth a visit. Among the collection of museums here are the **Museum of Natural History** (26 Oxford Street), the **Peabody Museum of Archaeology and Ethnology** (11 Divinity Avenue), and the **Semitic Museum** (6 Divinity Avenue) – all located a couple blocks north of the Yard.

Lying between Harvard Yard and Memorial Drive is the **Harvard Lampoon Castle** (44 Bow Street), a haven for writers and editors of the satirical publication the *Harvard Lampoon*, which has spawned countless writers and comedians, including Conan O'Brien and John Updike. Not open to the public, the Castle is worth seeing from the outside. It is wedged onto a tiny sliver of land between Mt Auburn and Bow Street, but architects Wheelwright & Haven have made the most of the awkward site, creating a cartoonish, miniaturised castle that reflects its mischievous inhabitants.

Harvard Square

Cambridge and Somerville are all about squares. The two towns are divided into small neighbourhoods, themselves divided into a matrix of squares – though many are little more than glorified intersections. The most well-known, and certainly one of the most popular of these, is **Harvard Square**.

Harvard Square is not just for readers, however, it is also a people-watcher's paradise, as the bustle of aristocratic Harvard students, mohawked punks, camera-toting tourists, homeless panhandlers and harried, suit-wearing businesspeople creates a diverse and colourful street scene.

Coming out of the Harvard Square T station, the biggest local landmark is right in front of you – **Out of Town News**, which stocks a wide selection of periodicals from all over the world, is the area's popular meeting place. Right next to it is a pedestrianised space known as 'the Pit' – not much to look at when nobody's around, but it has been a haven for street kids since punk-rock broke in the 1970s.

Similar to the area around Government Center in central Boston, there are usually plenty of street performers on every corner of the square when the weather is fine, but the area is much less touristy than Faneuil Hall, and more musically focused. Another favourite spot for street musicians is outside the local branch of **Au Bon Pain** (Massachusetts Avenue, at Harvard Square; 354 4144), which makes an ideal spot for relaxing outdoors and observing the local street life. An added bonus is the numerous chess experts who set up at the outdoor tables; for a buck or two they'll let you challenge them, or for a few more, you can get a one-on-one lesson.

Central Square is a popular local hangout, filled with clubs and restaurants. *See p106.*

The winding streets surrounding the square are best navigated on foot – lanes suddenly merge or disappear without warning and free parking is only for those with Zen-like patience and eagle eyes. To best experience Harvard Square, exit from the main subway entrance, and just start walking. No matter which way you head – left, right or straight ahead – you'll find something of interest.

The streets of Harvard Square are lined with restaurants, street performers, cafés and shops, though the influx of mega-chains like the Gap, Tower Records and Starbuck's over the past 15 years has diminished the neighbourhood feel of the area a great deal. The recent demise of the Tasty, a tiny greasy spoon diner once frequented by JFK and featured in the film *Good Will Hunting*, is yet another indication of the widespread gentrification of the area.

Though it may not be the bohemian enclave it once was, Harvard Square has a lot to offer, including the independent cinema, **Brattle Theatre** (*see p206*). The other top-line arts venue in the area is the legendary **Club Passim** (*see p222*), a folk club which helped to launch the careers of Joan Baez and Suzanne Vega, among others. Other highlights in the area are **Cardullo's** (6 Brattle Street; 491 8888), a wonderful gourmet food shop and deli counter; and **Leavitt & Peirce** (1316 Massachusetts Avenue; 547 0576), an old-fashioned tobacconists that's been in the same location for over 100 years.

Bibliophiles will be in heaven in Cambridge, which is said to have the most booksellers per square mile of any city in America. Among the best-loved are **Grolier Poetry Book Shop** (6 Plympton Street; 547 4648); and the **Harvard Book Store** (1256 Massachusetts Avenue; 661 1515), a scholarly shop where you can get happily lost for hours among the shelves.

From Harvard Square, it's a short stroll to the **Charles River**. Just walk down John F Kennedy Street and you'll soon run directly into the river embankment. There are walking paths in both directions. It's especially pleasant on summer Sundays when Memorial Drive is closed to automobiles, and scores of runners, rollerbladers and bikers take over the street.

In the opposite direction, at Garden Street and Massachusetts Avenue, is **Cambridge Common**, a lovely 16-acre (six hectare) stretch of grass by day and a bad place to be found at night. William Dawes rode across it before the battles of Lexington and Concord; it's also where George Washington took control of the Continental Army in 1775 and a plaque marks the elm tree under which the troops were mustered. Established in 1631, the common is the only surviving part of colonial Cambridge. Nearby, **Christ Church** (*see p106*) is the site where George and Martha Washington once worshipped. Right next to the church is the **Old Burying Ground**, also known as 'God's Acre'. It first began life as a cemetery in 1635, and thus contains the remains of early settlers.

Brattle Street was once called Tory Row, and several of the mansions of its former wealthy merchant residents remain. The further you venture from Harvard Square on Brattle, the older and grander the houses become. The **Longfellow National Historic Site** (*see p33*), is a 28-room mansion where the poet lived from 1837 until his death in 1882. It is also one of the many spots in Cambridge where George Washington spent time during the Revolutionary War. Appropriately enough, a few doors down is the headquarters of the Cambridge Historical Society, who have set up shop in the oldest house in Cambridge, the 1688 **Hooper-Lee-Nichols House** (159 Brattle Street; 547 4252).

Another pleasant walk, with a more modern slant, is along Massachusetts Avenue north from Harvard Square to **Porter Square**. Starting at the Cambridge Common, the broad avenue passes **Harvard Law School** and an array of small independent restaurants and shops – including clothing boutiques, antique stores, health food shops and record stores – before running into Porter Square. This is a fairly affluent part of Cambridge, though the mood is more ageing hippie than ostentatious yuppie. From Porter Square, it's a short subway or bus ride back to Harvard Square.

Christ Church

Zero Garden Street, at Massachusetts Avenue, Cambridge (876 0200). Harvard T. **Open** 7.30am-6pm Mon-Fri, Sun; 7.30am-3pm Sat. **Map** p311 B2.

Designed in 1761 by the country's first trained architect, Peter Harrison, Christ Church was a hotbed of rebel activity during the Revolutionary War. The walls are still peppered with bullet-holes. While much here is original to the building, the organ's pipes are not. They were melted down to make bullets in the war.

Old Burying Ground

Massachusetts Avenue, at Garden Street, Cambridge (Cambridge Historical Commission 349 4683). Harvard T. **Open** dawn to dusk daily. **Map** p311 B2.

This was one of the country's first cemeteries. It contains the remains of several early Puritan settlers as well as Revolutionary War victims and veterans.

Kendall & Central Squares

Harvard notwithstanding, some very bright folks attend that other school in Cambridge, the **Massachusetts Institute of Technology** in Kendall Square. MIT was founded in 1861 and rose to prominence during World War II when radar was invented in its labs. The architecture of its various buildings is wildly diverse, ranging from the neo-classical walls of **Building 10**, the main administration building, to the modern **Wiesner Building**, on which IM Pei collaborated. MIT also boasts its fair share of impressive museums, from **Doc Edgerton's Strobe Alley** to the multimedia **MIT Museum** (*for both, see p116*). One of the most amusing of the exhibits on the campus is the 'MIT Hall of Hacks' installation at the MIT Museum, a permanent exhibition that chronicles the various pranks pulled by MIT students over the years.

MIT doesn't have the same symbiotic relationship with Kendall Square that Harvard has with its square, so Kendall doesn't really have its own identity. It isn't visually exciting, consisting mostly of imposing industrial architecture and large office complexes. Recently, many of these buildings have been occupied by biotechnology companies and Internet start-ups – most staffed with fresh-faced MIT grads. Kendall does have some good restaurants, however, and a popular art house cinema (the **Kendall Square Cinema**; *see p207*). It also has a few shops worth checking out, including vintage and second-hand clothing emporiums. But the area doesn't lend itself to wandering or sightseeing.

Central Square is the polar opposite of Kendall. Central is animated by a never ending hustle and bustle, from early morning rush hour to late-night club crawls. It's a lower-income section of Cambridge, and has attracted a younger population alongside a large African-American and immigrant community. Over the past few years, though, it's become a desirable neighbourhood for recent college grads and young professionals. Upmarket bistros, high-rise condos and the Gap have followed. Still, Central Square maintains a strong ethnic and counter-culture vibe, and it's hard to imagine that vanishing anytime soon.

Most Bostonians head to Central Square at night, to eat at one of the area's various inexpensive ethnic restaurants or visit one of the many nightclubs and bars in the area (*see p107*). During the day, an assortment of Indian markets, record shops, cheap clothing stores, cafés, and one sexual fetish shop, make it an interesting browse for the left-of-centre shopper.

A short drive from Central is **Inman Square**, an area distinguished primarily by a high concentration of restaurants. Unfortunately, it's not accessible by subway, so it takes a dedicated foodie to make the trip.

A short drive to the edge of Cambridge brings you to **Fresh Pond**, at the end of Fresh Pond Parkway (take the 72 bus from Harvard T). The Pond was used in the 1800s as an ice source and today is a peaceful reservoir with a two mile (4-kilometre) perimeter and constantly changing scenery. To its south lies **Mount**

Hangin' in Central Square

In a clear case of becoming too popular for its own good, the encroaching commercialisation and corporatisation of Harvard Square has turned that historic area into less a destination for locals than an attraction for tourists and day-tripping suburbanites. When young Cantabridgians want to eat, drink and socialise they are more likely to head to Central Square, one T stop south of Harvard on the Red Line. Once viewed askance as a run-down and seedy area, Central Square is now being gentrified too, but it's far from losing its distinctive flavour. It's the kind of neighbourhood where ragged punks, dreadlocked Rastafarians, and business moguls regularly bump elbows at the bus stop.

Central Square originally became a night-time destination thanks to the **Middle East** (*see p225*) and **TT the Bear's Place** (*see p225*), two long-standing rock clubs on the same block. Other venues have followed: the **Green Street Grill** (280 Green Street) has a cosy back room offering experimental jazz, indie-rock and world music; the **Good Life** (720 Massachusetts Avenue) is a swanky, retro Martini bar with surprisingly good live jazz; the **Cantab Lounge** (*see p223*) is a working-class dive with righteous blues and R&B courtesy of local soul legend Little Joe Cook; while the **Phoenix Landing** (*see p205*), an Irish pub, has become the unlikely midweek home for Boston's rave community – excellent local and international DJs spin techno, house and jungle Tuesday through Thursday nights here. Close by, the **Western Front** (343 Western Avenue) and **Rhythm & Spice** (315 Mass Ave) cater to the local neighbourhood's large population of West Indian immigrants, booking reggae and soca bands on the weekends. Everything's in such close proximity that you can club-hop on foot, checking out punk, jazz and calypso over the course of one evening. Which, of course, is exactly what the locals do, making it a good place to get off the tourist track.

Auburn Cemetery, the country's first garden cemetery (*see below*). This is a lovely and peaceful place, where many of the city's most famed residents, including Charles Bulfinch, are buried.

Mount Auburn Cemetery

580 Mount Auburn Street, Cambridge (547 7105). Harvard T, then 71 or 73 bus. **Open** *Cemetery* 8am-5pm daily. *Greenhouse* 8am-3.30pm Mon-Fri; 9am-1pm Sat. **Admission** free. **Map** p311 A3.

This is the final resting place for Oliver Wendell Holmes, Winslow Homer, Charles Bulfinch, Henry Wadsworth Longfellow and some 86,000 others. In fact, the cemetery is now so full that locals who want to spend eternity at Mount Auburn have to settle for cremation. But there's plenty of life here too. There are 4,000 kinds of trees and 130 species of shrub alone on its 174 acres (70 hectares), and excellent free guided tours to help you distinguish them.

Somerville

Rising rents in Cambridge have led many students, artists and young professionals to move into Somerville, a densely populated neighbourhood just to the north. So similar are the two towns where they interesect that you can wander from Cambridge into Somerville without ever noticing you've done so. In fact, they were once both one town. There's not much to see here, in traditional sightseeing terms. It's mostly known for cheap shopping and eating options, a handful of lively bars and its feeling of relaxed college life.

Tufts University (*see p41*), ranked as one of the nation's top 25 schools, rises on a hill just to the north. Straddling the Somerville-Medford border, Tufts boasts a glorious panoramic view of the Boston skyline from the centre of its campus.Though Somerville stretches far east towards Charlestown, the hub of its bohemian renaissance is in the west, where **Davis Square** – a tightly knit cluster of shops, bars, cafés and restaurants – attracts hip urbanites and college students. Within this small area you'll find one of Boston's best second-hand CD stores, **Disc Diggers** (*see p184*); a scholarly used bookshop, **McIntyre and Moore** (255 Elm Street) and the world-class roots-rock nightclub **Johnny D's** (*see p222*). Nearby, the barbecue joint **Redbones** (*see p154*) and **The Burren**, a raucous Irish pub (*see p169*), both attract large local crowds in the evenings.

Finally, there's one last historic site to see. A ten-minute walk down College Avenue will bring you to **Powder House Park** (at College Avenue and Broadway). This is the site of the first hostile act of the Revolutionary War. In 1774, a British battalion successfully raided the West Somerville Powder House in search of the 250 barrels of gunpowder stored there. A small castle built in 1903 now marks the site.

Further Afield

Head to the suburbs; it's Kennedy country.

The birthplace of John, Bobby and Ted Kennedy is a landmark in **Brookline**.

Brookline

Dotted with unique shops, blessed with hilly scenery and crowded with beautiful homes, Brookline is one of Boston's sweeter suburbs. Located four miles (six kilometres) west of downtown, the young families, upper crust retirees and struggling singles living here make for a multicultural mix. Brookline High School boasts students from more than 50 countries.

This area is only vaguely interesting to most tourists, but there are two sights that make the trip worthwhile. One is for garden lovers – the **Frederick Law Olmsted National Historic Site** (99 Warren Street, at Dudley Street; 566 1689). This is the former home of the creator of the Emerald Necklace (*see p84*). It features attractive gardens and an interesting exhibition about his life. The other is for baby boomers and political types – **83 Beals Street**, just off Beacon, is the birthplace and boyhood home of former President John F Kennedy. It has been lovingly restored and is maintained by the US Parks Service and a team of volunteers (*see p110*).

Beyond those two places, though, Brookline isn't much of a draw. It does seem as if Beacon Street, its central avenue, has a restaurant for every nationality. The beautifully decorated **Golden Temple** (1651 Beacon Street; 277 9722) can supply a fix of Chinese food. The critically acclaimed **Elephant Walk** (900 Beacon Street; 247 1500) offers an unusual split menu of French and Cambodian cuisine.

Nearby, an eclectic mix of shops can be found in the **Coolidge Corner** area (at the corner of Beacon and Harvard Streets). **Fire Opal** (320 Harvard Street; 739 9066) sells art and jewellery and offers soap-making and herbal healing classes. The **Perrin Gallery** features up-and-coming artists in the space it shares with framing experts the **Picture Place** (320A Harvard Street; 277 4357). The area is also the home of the **Coolidge Corner Theater** (*see p206*), in its restored art deco digs. It's best known for showing quirky independent films.

Avid golfers might feel drawn to the **Country Club** (191 Clyde Street; 566 0240), an 18-hole golf course which hosted the 1999 Ryder Cup. Incidentally, this course was the site of the controversial scene in which an upstart and overly rambunctious US team celebrated their victory on the green (prematurely, as it turned out) and upset just about everybody.

John F Kennedy Birthplace

83 Beals Street, at Harvard Avenue (566 7937). Coolidge Corner T. **Open** *Apr-Nov* 10am-4.30pm Wed-Sun. **Tours** every half hour from 10am-4pm. **Admission** $2; free under 17.

The former home of the country's 35th president has been restored to the way it looked in 1917. It is designed to offer an insider's view to the Kennedy family through the past century. The site is part of the US National Park Service, and is shown only as part of a tour guided by a park ranger at regular intervals throughout the day. Call ahead for times.

Sightseeing

Kenmore Square

Just minutes from central Brookline, **Kenmore Square** is a bustling traffic triangle between Commonwealth, Brookline and Massachusetts Avenues and the **Boston University** (*see p39*) campus. Fraternities, dorms and classroom buildings are scattered among coffee shops, fast food joints and the Ho Jo (the simultaneously revered and despised Howard Johnson's hotel). The HoJo's top floor is home to one of the city's best dance clubs, **Lava** (*see p205*), which offers spectacular views of the city. The area teems with college kids during the school year, and most businesses cater primarily to them. You'll have no problem trading used CDs, buying vintage clothing or grabbing a beer in this area.

The square can be easily identified by the giant Citgo sign above the **Barnes and Noble** book store (660 Beacon Street; 267 8484). This particular branch of the enormous book chain carries any college paraphernalia you could ever want – and a lot you don't. Bit of trivia: The Citgo sign has been a fixture in Kenmore for 33 years. When the company announced plans to take it down in 1983, thousands of outraged residents petitioned. Like a giant, neon star, its bright light continues to help club-goers stumble home.

Those aforementioned clubbers have probably been to nearby **Landsdowne Street**. When the sun goes down, young scholars (and their older counterparts) come out in knee-high boots and mini skirts. Oh, and leather trousers, hair gel and heavy eyeliner. Landsdowne offers everything from enormous dance clubs, such as **Axis** and **Avalon** (*see p204*) to the intimate yet funky **Bill's Bar** (*see p160*). If none of those appeal, wander down to the **Modern** (36 Landsdowne Street; 536 2100), a sleek dance club that is almost as good-looking as its patrons. Not up for a trendy scene? Shoot pool or play games in **Jillian's** (145 Ipswich Street; 437 0300, *see p160*) or sing along with the duelling pianos at **Jake Ivory**'s (1 Landsdowne Street; 247 1222). Or, sit quietly and bemoan the fate of the now defunct Mama Kin, the former club hangout of Aerosmith.

Just steps from Landsdowne sits historic **Fenway Park**, home of the Boston Red Sox (*see p234*). The baseball stadium opened on 20 April 1912 – the same day the *Titanic* sank. It may have been an omen, as the Sox haven't won a World Series since 1918. Nonetheless some of the best played here, including Babe Ruth, Cy Young and Roger Clemens. The most famous part of the stadium is its 37-foot-high (11 metres) left-field wall, affectionately known as the Green Monster. See it while you can, as plans are afoot to knock it all down.

Chestnut Hill

Located some six miles (ten kilometres) north-west of the city, the actual boundaries of the affluent suburb of Chestnut Hill are blurry. Most agree that it is squeezed in between Newton, Brookline and Brighton. Its primary claim to fame is that it is the home of **Boston College** (*see p40*). Its students are quick to point out that BC is utterly misnamed as it is neither a college (it's a university) nor in Boston. It lies between Commonwealth Avenue and Beacon Street and its 10,000 students live in a quaint campus setting among 115 acres (44 hectares) of rolling lawns and shady trees.

On the edge of BC's campus is an area known as the **Reservoir** – a pleasant spot to walk or jog. However, a better area for outdoor activities can be found at the nearby **Hammond Pond Reservation** (Hammond Pond Parkway; 698 1802), where those with no fear of heights can indulge in rock climbing and hiking, while the rest of us sit around lazily waiting for them to fall.

For those whose interests are more in consuming than in the countryside, Chestnut Hill is a shopping paradise. The **Atrium Mall** (300 Boylston Street; 527 1400) is packed with shops, while on the opposite side of Boylston Street is **Chestnut Hill Mall** (199 Boylston Street; 965 3037), which has the distinction of being the site of the only Bloomingdale's in New England.

Just as its malls reflect Chestnut Hill's somewhat upmarket residents, so do its restaurants. Locals crowd into their branch of respected chef Todd English's **Figs** chain of upmarket pizzerias (1208 Boylston; 738 9992), and pack into the pricey, faux-Parisian bistro, **Aquitaine** (1 Boylston Street; 734 8400), which first made a name for itself in Boston's South End.

Guided Tours

Sometimes it's nice to have your hand held.

Whether it's a bus that floats on water or fake trolley cars that ride without rails, Boston offers dozens of variations on the tour theme. Whatever form they take, most of these trample the same trail, so in the end it comes down to which one has the vehicle that strikes your fancy, or what approach they take to the city's architecture and history.

Amphibious

Boston Duck Tours

Prudential Center Court, 800 Boylston Street, at Fairfield Street (723 3825/ www.bostonducktours.com. Hynes/ICA or Prudential T. **Open** *Apr-Nov* 9am-sunset. **Tickets** $22; $12-$19 concessions. **Credit** Disc, MC, V. **Map** p306 E5.

The most unusual ride in the city is this strange part-aquatic tour. The vehicles owned by this company are impossible to miss on the streets of Boston, and they have an interesting historical genesis as World War II amphibious landing craft. Today, they travel through historic sites in the Back Bay, Beacon Hill, downtown and the North End, restored, painted in bright colours and renamed as Duck Tours. The duck theme is endless – they are manned by so-called conDUCKtors. Despite this silliness, the tours are surprisingly good, but they are geared at kids, and group participation is encouraged in the form of shouting 'quack-quack' all the time.

Bicycle tours

Bike Boston Urban Bike Tours

Meets on the Commonwealth Mall between Gloucester and Hereford Streets, Back Bay (695 2153). **Open** *Apr-Sept* hours vary. **Rates** vary; phone for details. **Map** p306 E5.

While this tour does not ignore history, it specialises in showing you the Boston of today, pointing out hot restaurants and art galleries along with architecture. Of course, the best part is when the guides forget about the transmitters they're using to narrate the tour and start muttering swear words at car drivers. Bring your own bike or rent one through Back Bay Bicycles (336 Newbury Street; 247 2336).

Boston Bike Tours

Meets at the beginning of the Freedom Trail on Boston Common, Back Bay (308 5902/ www.bostonbiketours.com) Park Street T. **Open** 1-4pm Mon-Sat; 12.30pm Sun. **Rates** (include bike rental) $18 daily tours; $25 on Sun. **Map** p307 G4.

This company offers daily two-hour bike tours through many of the city's historic neighbourhoods and parks. It has the added benefit of providing bicycles for those who don't have one of their own. The guides are interesting and helpful.

Boat tours

Bay State Cruise Lines

164 New Northern Avenue, at World Trade Center, Downtown (748 1428/ www.baystatecruisecompany.com). South Station T, then 7 bus. **Open** entertainment cruises *June-Sept* 8.30pm Fri, Sat. Ferries *May-Sept* 8am, 9am, 4pm, 5pm daily. **Rates** entertainment cruises $15-$25; ferry $18-$49; $14-$39 concessions. **Credit** AmEx, MC, V. **Map** p307 J5.

Cruises with this company are music based, and feature local talent playing jazz, blues and rock. The company also offers ferry services to points along Cape Cod and around the Boston coastline.

Boston Harbor Cruises

1 Long Wharf, next to the New England Aquarium, Downtown (227 4321/ www.bostonharborcruises.com). State/Aquarium T. **Open** *Apr-Oct* noon-7pm daily. **Rates** $10-$29; $8-$23 concessions. **Credit** AmEx, MC, V. **Map** p307 H4.

One of the biggest cruise companies in town, BHC provides ferry services to the islands throughout the harbour, as well as cruises up to and around old Ironsides, the USS *Constitution*.

Charles River Boat Company

Cambridgeside Galleria Mall, 100 Cambridgeside Place, at Charles Street, Cambridge (621 3001/ www.charlesriverboat.com). Lechmere T. **Open** *Apr, May, Oct* 10.30am-5pm Sat, Sun; *June-Sept* 10.30am-5pm daily. **Rates** $8-$10; $6-$7 concessions. **Credit** MC, V. **Map** p306 F3.

This company specialises in cruises of the Cambridge side of the river, touring the Charles River basin and the area beyond.

Massachusetts Bay Lines

60 Rowes Wharf, at Boston Harbor Hotel, Downtown (542 8000/www.massbaylines.com). State/Aquarium or South Station T. **Open** *May-Oct* 11am-8.45pm daily. **Rates** $10-$29; $7-$22 concessions. **Credit** AmEx, Disc, MC, V. **Map** p308 H4.

This company offers a huge array of cruises, with one for everybody who is not afraid of the water. They feature everything from watching the sunset to watching whales gambol in the waves.

Trolly tours are omnipresent in Back Bay.

Odyssey Cruises

Rowes Wharf, at Boston Harbor Hotel, Downtown (654 9700/1-888 741 0282/ www.odysseycruises.com/odyssey/boston). State House or Aquarium T. **Open** 11am-6pm daily; midnight Fri, Sat. **Rates** $28-$85. **Credit** AmEx, DC, Disc, MC, V. **Map** p308 H4.

Take your brunch, lunch or dinner on the water, as this company offers meal cruises with musical entertainment. The summertime midnight cruises are a big hit with locals and tourists.

Specialty tours

Fenway Park Tour

Fenway Park, Gate D, Yawkey Way and Van Ness Street, Fenway (236 6666/www.redsox.com) Fenway or Kenmore T. **Open** *May-Sept* 10am-4pm daily. **Rates** $5; $3-$4 concessions. **Credit** MC, V. **Map** p306 D5.

Check out the press box, the dugout, the Red Sox' private suite, the '600' club, and behind the scoreboard; then walk around the field. The players probably don't know as much about the park as you will by the end of this tour. This one is great for kids. The way things are going, these sights may soon be confined to the history books as Fenway may be replaced. see it while you can (*see p240*).

Harvard University

Harvard Events & Information Office, Holyoke Centre, 1350 Massachusetts Avenue, Cambridge (495 1573/www.harvard.edu). Harvard T. **Open** tours *Sept-May* 10am, 2pm Mon-Fri; 2pm Sat. *June-Aug* 10am, 11.15am, 2pm, 3.15pm Mon-Sat; 3pm Sun. **Rates** free. **Map** p311 B2.

Just hanging out with these student tour guides and looking at the old buildings like the Science Centre and Memorial Hall is enough to make you feel just that much smarter. Plus, a picture taken by the John Harvard statue can be used as proof you actually attended Harvard. Sure you did.

Michele Topor, L'Arte di Cucinare

6 Charter Street, at Hanover Street, North End (523 6032/www.cucinare.com). Haymarket T. **Open** *tours* 10am, 2pm Wed, Sat; 3pm Fri. **Rates** $38. **Credit** MC, V. **Map** 308 H3.

Topor's market tour of the North End is excellent – albeit a wee bit long at three hours – and legendary among locals, all of whom she seems to know and many of whom you'll catch listening as she leads you off the beaten path to see, smell and taste the very best of the North End. Go with comfortable footwear and bring a notebook.

Trolley tours

Boston Old Town Trolley Tours

Old Atlantic Avenue, at New England Aquarium, Downtown (269 7150/www.trolleytours.com). Aquarium T. **Open** *Mar-Oct* 9am-4pm Mon-Fri; 9am-5pm Sat, Sun. *Nov-Feb* 9am-3pm Mon-Fri; 9am-4pm Sat, Sun. **Rates** $23; $10-$21 concessions. Specialised tours up to $50. **Credit** MC, V. **Map** p308 H4.

These faux trolley cars (they ride on wheels instead of rails) are omnipresent in Boston. One always seems to be passing you no matter where you are. This company offers a host of seasonal specialised tours – from a decadent chocolate tour to the life of John F Kennedy. If you approach sightseeing more like bird watching – leisurely and with binoculars – a trolley tour is for you. Hop aboard and get ready for an hour's worth of bad puns and old Boston history and architecture. It helpfully offers customers the right to leave and rejoin the tour as they wish, so they can get a better look at their favourite buildings or neighbourhoods.

Walking tours

Boston Adventures

These tours leave from a variety of locations. Call for information (430 1900/331 1729/ www.bostonscavengerhunts.com). **Open** tours 10am, noon, 2pm, 5pm daily. **Rates** $20; $10-$15 concessions. **No credit cards**.

From the tame Freedom Trail to the morose Boston Strangler Tour to drunken 3-hour pub-crawls, this group tries to cover it all. It can also arrange for limousines and scavenger hunts.

Boston by Foot

These tours leave from a variety of locations. Call for information (367 2345/367 3766/ www.bostonbyfoot.com). **Open** *May-Oct* hours vary. **Rates** $8; $6 concessions. **No credit cards**.

By Foot offers an impressive selection of walking tours through the city's historic neighbourhoods. Tours vary thematically from women's history to art deco art in Boston. Included are Back Bay, North End, the Big Dig and the waterfront.

Boston Park Rangers

145 Tremont Street, at West Street, Back Bay (635 7383). Park St T. **Open** 9am-5pm Mon-Fri. **Rates** free. **Map** p308 G4.

For those interested in exploring the scenery of the ring of parks known as the Emerald Necklace, the Boston Park Rangers offer a free tour.

Museums

Art lovers wake up smiling when they dream about Boston.

The Fraser Garden Court and Terrace at the **Museum of Fine Arts**. *See p114.*

Things have changed in Boston. It's not just about Paul Revere's Midnight Ride here any more. The visual arts are moving and shaking, with expansions in the works at major art institutions such as the **Museum of Fine Arts** and the **Institute of Contemporary Art**. New spaces for art are planned at some of the area's colleges and universities, many of which house significant collections and mount some of the best exhibitions in town. World-class shows at the MFA and at Harvard's **Fogg Museum** have put Boston on the map as a cultural destination. And although the Impressionists remain popular – the MFA loves to put on shows with Monet in the title – new curators and directors at many institutions are bringing in fresh energy and important shows.

The 21st century finds new enthusiasm – and new venues – for art in and around Boston. Go the extra mile to seek out fine exhibitions in art museums, libraries, universities, art colleges and galleries located in all corners of the city.

Visual arts museums

Though Boston's museum scene does not rival New York's in terms of exhibiting ground-breaking contemporary art, it runs a strong second. At the same time, changes in recent years have brought growth and increasing variety. It all heralds much promise for the city's art future.

For the **Children's Museum**, *see p201.*

Addison Gallery of American Art

Phillips Academy, Main Street, Andover (1-978 749 4027/www.andover.edu/addison). **Open** 10am-5pm Tue-Sat; 1-5pm Sun. **Admission** free.

This place in suburban Andover can be worth the drive if you can get your hands on a car. It is home to a fine permanent collection that includes major works by Winslow Homer, Thomas Eakins and Maurice Prendergast, and a basement-full of scale models of American ships. It also hosts contemporary art exhibitions from the likes of Sol LeWitt and Alice Neel.

Boston Center for the Arts

Mills Gallery and Cyclorama, 539 Tremont Street, at Clarendon Street, Back Bay (426 8835/ www.bcaonline.org). Back Bay or Copley T. **Open** for exhibitions only 7-10pm Thur-Sat, 1-4pm Sun. **Admission** free. **Map** p308 F6.

Expect the unexpected at the Mills Gallery, which focuses on presenting new works by artists with ties to Boston and New England, and which has been the site of memorable exhibitions including artist Sheila Pepe's transformation of the space with miles of crocheted yarn. Large, experimental installation works feature in the remarkable Cyclorama next door:

a huge brick rotunda of a building constructed in the latter part of the 19th century in which large-scale Civil War re-enactments were staged.

DeCordova Museum & Sculpture Park

51 Sandy Pond Road, off Route 2 or 128, Lincoln (1-781 259 8355/www.decordova.org). **Open** 11am-5pm Tue-Sun. **Admission** $6; $4 concessions; free under-12s. **Credit** MC, V.

West of Boston on a sprawling site, DeCordova showcases the work of New England artists in its recently expanded, castle-like museum. Recent noteworthy exhibitions included an in-depth survey of photography in Boston and an annual exhibition of emerging talent. The grounds are studded with large sculptures next to which visitors can picnic or listen to concerts – do bring mosquito repellent in the summer.

Institute of Contemporary Art

955 Boylston Street, at Massachusetts Avenue, Back Bay (266 5152/www.icaboston.org). Hynes/ICA T. **Open** noon-5pm Wed, Fri; noon-9pm Thur; 11am-5pm Sat, Sun. **Admission** $6; $4 concessions; free under-12s. Free to all 5-9pm Thur. **Credit** AmEx, MC, V. **Map** p306 E5.

Currently in a converted 19th-century fire station just off Newbury Street, the ICA plans to construct a grand new building in Boston's waterfront area in the next few years. Meanwhile, it continues its ambitious programme of presenting solo exhibitions of renowned contemporary artists, including Olafur Eliasson and Cornelia Parker, as well as imaginative group shows such as 'Gothic' and 'Customized: Art Inspired by Hot Rods, Low Riders and American Car Culture'. The ICA is one of the few institutions in this smart city that takes big intellectual and political risks with the content of its shows. The results don't please all the people all the time, but the ICA always aims high.

The **DeCordova Museum & Sculpture Park**.

Isabella Stewart Gardner Museum

280 The Fenway, at Palace Road, Fenway (566 1401/www.boston.com/gardner). Museum of Fine Arts T. **Open** 11am-5pm Tue-Sun. **Admission** $11; $5-$7 concessions; free under-18s. **Credit** AmEx, Disc, MC, V. **Map** p306 D6.

This lavish Venetian-style palace, where socialite Isabella Stewart Gardner lived and entertained early in the 20th century, houses her idiosyncratic collection of art and objects, displayed entirely according to her personal instructions. The museum boasts work by Rembrandt, Botticelli, Raphael and Titian, and offers a variety of unexpected delights, from its breathtaking interior courtyard to the famous portrait of Gardner herself by John Singer Sargent. What's more, since 1992, the Gardner has hosted an artist-in-residence programme, allowing it to mount important solo shows by current artists.

Museum of Fine Arts

465 Huntington Avenue, at Museum Street, Fenway (267 9300/www.mfa.org). Museum of Fine Arts T. **Open** 10am-4.45pm Mon, Tue; 10am-9.45pm Wed-Fri (only West Wing Galleries open after 4.45pm Thur, Fri); 10am-5.45pm Sat, Sun. **Admission** $12; $5-$10 concessions; free under-17s on weekends and school holidays; free under-6s at all times. Free to all 4.45-9.45pm Wed. **Credit** AmEx, Disc, MC, V. **Map** p306 D6.

The largest, oldest and most expansive of Boston's mainstream institutions – and it plans to expand even further. The museum has recently selected British architect Norman Foster to renovate its historic building, making way for more art in its already impressive galleries. With extensive holdings in areas ranging from the art of Asia to American Colonial and Federal portraits, and with smaller collections studded by gems (European Impressionists and ancient Egyptian artefacts significant among them), the MFA earns a place on most itineraries. Seek out John Singer Sargent's famed ceiling murals – recently restored to their original colourful condition. And check out the MFA's film programme, which hosts some of this city's favourite film festivals (*see p208*). While the MFA has been criticised in the past for its blockbuster shows, recent endeavours, including the scholarly crowd-pleaser 'The Art of the Guitar' and the smaller but hugely moving 'Charlotte Salomon: Life? Or Theater?', highlight what a big museum can do best, and show that the increasingly commercial activity here still hasn't taken all the spirit out of it.

Museum of the National Center of Afro-American Artists

300 Walnut Avenue, at Crawford Street, Roxbury (442 8614/www.afamnet.com/ncaaamuseum). Ruggles T, then 42 bus. **Open** 1-5pm Tue-Sun. **Admission** $4; $3 concessions. **No credit cards.**
The Museum of the NCAAA has been affiliated with the Museum of Fine Arts since the late 1960s, and is the only museum in New England committed exclusively to African, Caribbean and Afro-American fine arts. In a neo-Gothic Victorian mansion in Roxbury, exhibitions include selections from the permanent collection, and changing exhibitions like 'Aspelta: a Nubian King's Burial Chamber'.

Worcester Art Museum

55 Salisbury Street, Worcester (1-508 799 4406/ www.worcesterart.org). **Open** 11am-5pm Wed-Fri, Sun; 10am-5pm Sat. **Admission** $8; $6 concessions; free under-17s. Free to all 10am-noon Sat. **No credit cards.**
The WAM prides itself on having been the first American museum to purchase work by Claude Monet and Paul Gauguin. It has a good eye for the new and presents small but often rewarding contemporary exhibitions alongside selections from its large permanent collection, which ranges from Egyptian antiquities and Roman mosaics to Impressionist paintings and contemporary art.

The **Isabella Stewart Gardner Museum.**

University collections

Boston College

McMullen Museum of Art

140 Commonwealth Avenue, at College Road, Chestnut Hill (552 8100/www.bc.edu/artmuseum). Chestnut Hill T. **Open** *Sept-May* 11am-4pm Mon-Fri; 11am-6pm Sat, Sun. *June-Aug* 11am-3pm Mon-Fri. **Admission** free.
This is a somewhat conservative but genuinely erudite place. It was the only North American venue, for instance, to show the recently discovered Caravaggio, *The Taking of Christ*, and has recently mounted a significant exhibition of Edvard Munch's paintings and prints.

Brandeis University

Rose Art Museum

415 South Street, Waltham (1-781 736 3434/ www.brandeis.edu/rose). Commuter Rail Brandeis/Roberts Station. **Open** noon-5pm Tue, Wed, Fri-Sun; noon-9pm Thur. **Admission** free.
This facility offers a fine collection of 20th-century art, with a focus on post-WWII American art including work by de Kooning, Johns, Rauschenberg and Warhol, and also has a terrific programme of changing exhibitions. In mid-2001, the Rose was undergoing a major renovation. It is scheduled to reopen in autumn 2001, if work proceeds as planned, in expanded and improved quarters.

Harvard University

Arthur M Sackler Museum

485 Broadway, at Quincy Street, Cambridge (495 9400/www.artmuseums.harvard.edu). Harvard T. **Open** 10am-5pm Mon-Sat; 1-5pm Sun. **Admission** with Fogg Art & Busch-Reisinger Museums $5; $3-$4 concessions; free under-18s. Free to all Wed and 10am-noon Sat. **Credit** AmEx, Disc, MC, V. **Map** p311 B2.
Houses the widest collection of Chinese jades outside China, an unrivalled collection of Korean ceramics, sculptures and paintings, and an outstanding collection of Thai illuminated manuscripts.

Fogg Art Museum & Busch-Reisinger Museum

32 Quincy Street, at Broadway, Cambridge (495 2397/www.artmuseums.harvard.edu). Harvard T. **Open** 10am-5pm Mon-Sat; 1-5pm Sun. **Admission** with Arthur M Sackler Museum $5; $3-$4 concessions; free under-18s. Free to all Wed and 10am-noon Sat. **Credit** AmEx, Disc, MC, V. **Map** p311 B2.
With a permanent collection that ranges from the African to the European baroque, the Fogg regularly hosts important travelling exhibitions. Contiguous to the Fogg is Harvard's Busch-

The Calderwood Courtyard of the **Fogg Art Museum** at Harvard University. *See p115.*

Reisinger Museum, the only museum in the western hemisphere devoted to the art of German-speaking Europe; contains in its permanent collection works by Klee, Kandinsky, Beckmann and Klimt.

Peabody Museum of Archaeology & Ethnology

11 Divinity Avenue, at Kirkland Street, Cambridge (496 1027/www.peabody.harvard.edu). Harvard T. **Open** 9am-5pm daily. **Admission** $6.50; $4-$5 concessions. Free to all 9am-noon Sun and after 3pm Wed (Sept-May only). **Credit** AmEx, MC, V. **Map** p311 C2.

This impressive Harvard museum features fossils and artefacts from as far back as the Paleolithic period, with exhibitions on North American Indians and Central America. Despite its scientific bent, the building retains the Victorian character of early museum exhibits by displaying artefacts with descriptive rather than interpretive label text. Overall, it makes for a unique and enjoyable learning experience.

Sert Gallery

24 Quincy Street, in the Carpenter Center for the Visual Arts, Cambridge (495 9400/ www.artmuseums.harvard.edu). Harvard T. **Open** 10am-5pm Mon-Sat; 1-5pm Sun. **Admission** free. **Map** p311 B3.

Provides exhibition space for modern and contemporary art in a uniquely beautiful site. The Sert has become known as one of the best contemporary art museums in the region, particularly in the area of photography.

MIT

Compton Gallery

77 Massachusetts Avenue, at MIT Campus, Cambridge (253 4444). Kendall/MIT T. **Open** 9am-5pm Mon-Fri. **Admission** free. **Map** p306 D4.

Features rotating shows that draw on MIT's historical collection of art and scientific objects. Note that MIT's campus itself also merits attention: sculpture by Louise Nevelson, Alexander Calder and Henry Moore dot its grounds, and buildings by Eero Saarinen, Alvar Aalto and IM Pei are to be joined by a new Frank Gehry structure.

List Visual Arts Center

20 Ames Street, at Main Street, Cambridge (253 4680). Kendall/MIT T. **Open** noon-6pm Tue-Thur, Sat, Sun; noon-8pm Fri. **Admission** free. **Map** p306 E4.

The List has been a hotbed for challenging contemporary art – often with a strong political thrust – and is currently bursting with curatorial energy in the form of a new director and new curator who are mounting significant exhibitions of contemporary art at MIT.

MIT Museum's Strobe Alley

Fourth floor, Building Four, 77 Massachusetts Avenue, at MIT Campus, Cambridge (253 4629). Kendall/MIT T. **Open** 24 hours daily. **Admission** free. **Map** p306 D4.

This facility presents an indefinite show of the photographs of Harold ('Doc') Edgerton, the pioneer of high-speed photography. (Edgerton was the first to capture on film a bullet in flight and an exploding balloon.) Also on display are the kinetic sculptures of Arthur Ganson – ingenious, frequently hilarious machines that seem to have minds of their own. And since you might expect a little eccentricity from one of the world's finest institutions of scientific research, the museum also features an outstanding collection of holographic art, as well as an exhibition about the, um, exciting evolution of the slide rule.

Art schools

Massachusetts College of Art

Bakalar, Huntington & President's Galleries
621 Huntington Avenue, at Longwood Avenue, Fenway (879 7333/www.massart.edu). Longwood T. **Open** 10am-6pm Mon-Fri; 11am-5pm Sat. **Admission** free. **Map** p306 D7.

The only publicly funded school in the US solely dedicated to the fine and decorative arts. Not only do its galleries showcase artists with international reputations, but its student and faculty shows can offer similar excitement without the name-recognition factor.

School of the Museum of Fine Arts

Grossman Gallery
230 The Fenway, next to the Museum of Fine Arts, Huntington Avenue, Fenway (267 6100). Museum of Fine Arts T. **Open** varies according to exhibition. **Admission** free. **Map** p306 D6.

Across the street from the MFA, also boasts a worthy exhibition programme, showcasing established artists as well as students.

Other museums

Boston Athenaeum

10½ Beacon Street, between Bowdoin & Somerset Streets, Beacon Hill (227 0270). Park Street T. **Open** 8.30am-5.30pm Tue-Fri; 9am-4pm Sat. **Admission** free. **Map** p308 G4.

Founded in the early 19th century as a literary society, the Boston Athenaeum published America's first literary magazine and acquired an extensive library of books and works of art. By the dawn of the 20th century, the Athenaeum had helped establish Boston's Museum of Fine Arts and moved into its current home, a giant five-storey building on Beacon Street. The Athenaeum is closed in 2001 as it undergoes restoration. It should reopen in early 2002.

Boston Public Library

For listings see p79.

This is America's oldest public library. The original structure, an Italian Renaissance-style building designed by Charles McKim, was extended when an annexe designed by Philip Johnson was built in the early 1970s. Along with plenty of books and periodicals, the BPL features several galleries exhibiting everything from rare books and manuscripts to photographs of Boston's changing cityscape. Of more interest, perhaps, are permanent fixtures such as the bronze doors designed by Lincoln Memorial architect Daniel Chester French and several newly restored murals by John Singer Sargent.

Top five Museums

Fogg Art Museum
Excellent permanent exhibitions and intriguing travelling shows. *See p115.*

Isabella Stewart Gardner Museum
An outstanding collection housed in a charming Venetian-style villa. *See p114.*

MIT Museums
Covers everything from high-speed photography to cutting edge contemporary works. *See p116.*

Museum of Fine Arts
The granddaddy of 'em all. *See p114.*

John F Kennedy Library & Museum
Everything there is to know about America's controversial slain president. *See below.*

John F Kennedy Library & Museum

Columbia Point, at Morrissey Boulevard, Dorchester (929 4500/www.jfklibrary.org). JFK/UMass T. **Open** 9am-5pm daily. **Admission** $8; $4-$6 concessions; free under-12s. **Credit** AmEx, Disc, MC, V.

A looming concrete-and-glass monolith designed by IM Pei, the Kennedy Library overlooks the outer harbour from the top of the Columbia Point peninsula. Inside is an extensive display of memorabilia dedicated to the murdered 35th US president. Included in the permanent exhibition is a timeline of the Kennedy family, films of JFK press conferences and the president's desk. Along with JFK memorabilia, the museum also contains books and manuscripts that once belonged to Ernest Hemingway.

The **Arthur M. Sackler Museum** at Harvard.

Sightseeing

Museum of Afro American History

African Meeting House, 8 Smith Court, off 46 Joy Street, Beacon Hill (742 5415/www.afroam museum.org). Charles/MGH or Park Street T. **Open** 10am-4pm Mon-Sat. **Admission** free. **Map** p308 G4.

This museum is essentially two structures of historical significance – the African Meeting House, which once housed the first classroom for black children in Boston and remains the oldest black church in the country; and the Abiel Smith School, which is where the New England Anti-Slavery Society was founded in the 1830s. Though there are exhibitions about African-Americans in New England on display at the African Meeting House, the museum is primarily used as a historic landmark.

Museum of Science & Charles Hayden Planetarium

Science Park, between Storough & Memorial Drives, West End (723 2500/www.mos.org). Science Park T. **Open** 9am-5pm Mon-Thur, Sat, Sun; 9am-9pm Fri. **Admission** $10; $7 concessions; Charles Hayden Planetarium $5.50-$7.50; Mugar Omni Theater $5.50-$7.50. **Credit** AmEx, Disc, MC, V. **Map** p308 F3.

From the Gemini Space Ship capsule (which orbited the Earth more than 200 times in 1965) to the Thomson Theatre of Electricity (which houses a giant Van de Graaf generator), Boston's Museum of Science is committed to providing an interactive and educational experience, making science accessible to the average person through exhibitions that explain all things scientific in straightforward terms, and via hundreds of different hands-on installations. At the Charles Hayden Planetarium, audiences relaxing in ergonomic seats watch the dome-shaped ceiling as the Zeiss Star Projector creates a believable night sky before their eyes.

Museum of Transportation

Larz Anderson Park, 15 Newton Street, Brookline (522 6547/www.mot.org). Cleveland Circle or Reservoir T, then 51 bus. **Open** 10am-5pm Tue-Sun. **Admission** $5; $3 concessions; free under-5s. **No credit cards**.

Located in Brookline's Larz Anderson Park, this museum is at its best in the warmer months, when it hosts weekend get-togethers for classic car buffs and the parking lot fills with rare automobiles. Inside you'll find displays detailing the history of America's favourite form of transport.

USS Constitution Museum

Charlestown Navy Yard (426 1812/ www.ussconstitutionmuseum.org). North Station T. **Open** *Summer* 9am-6pm daily. *Winter* 10am-5pm daily. **Admission** free. **Map** p308 G3.

In 1974 Charlestown Navy Yard was decommis-

Exquisite John Singer Sargent ceiling murals at the **Boston Public Library**. *See p117*

Going public

Public art in Boston falls into two distinct categories: the execrable and the extraordinary. Some of the very best monuments in the city are concentrated on the mall on Commonwealth Avenue and in the Boston Public Garden. Others are scattered around. In the area around the Museum of Fine Arts are several extraordinary outdoor statues (*pictured right*).

Among the best in town is Olin Levi Warner's statue of the abolitionist **William Lloyd Garrison** on Commonwealth Avenue. It captures the spirit of the man who burned a copy of the Declaration of Independence on the State House lawn to protest against slavery and was punished by being dragged by a horse over Boston's cobbled streets until his flesh tore away.

One of the outstanding figures in the Public Garden depicts the writer and minister **Edward Everett Hale**. Bela Lyon Pratt's 1913 statue caused a stir at the time of its erection because Mr Hale is shown with a walking stick and wearing no hat, as if he were strolling in the Garden along with the rest of us.

On the lawn of the State House, overlooking the Public Garden, is one of the city's most poignant statues, Sylvia Shaw Judson's 1959 memorial to the Quaker martyr **Mary Dyer**. Dyer was hanged on nearby Boston Common for challenging Puritan religious laws and her seated figure suggests unimaginable strength.

Directly across the street from Mary Dyer is arguably the most outstanding work of public art in the United States, Augustus Saint-Gaudens' tribute to Civil War **Colonel Robert Gould Shaw** and his infantrymen. Shaw, a white man and abolitionist who came from a wealthy Boston home, is seen leading a regiment of African-American men, all of whom were killed in the assault on Fort Wagner, South Carolina, in July 1863. Although the marching soldiers and the horse-riding Shaw crowd the space they're allotted in the towering bas relief, Saint-Gaudens' memorial renders each man with a haunting peculiarity.

Somewhat off the beaten path (along the Southeast Expressway, which heads out of the city towards Cape Cod), stands Boston's most peculiar and genuinely arresting public monument, a huge gas tank that Corita Kent turned from an urban eyesore into something magnificent when she painted it in 1971. At first glance, the tank appears to have had alternating colours of paint poured over it from the top so that it resembles a crude rainbow. It took people a while to realise that the seemingly randomly dripping blue band actually had the outline of the face of **Ho Chi Minh**, leader of the North Vietnamese forces with whom the US was at war at the time. Despite years of complaints, the piece remains a public pleasure.

Stealing beauty

On 18 March 1990, as all of Boston was blearily wrapping up the city's famed St. Patrick's Day celebrations, two thieves were quietly perpetrating the greatest art theft in the nation's history at the Isabella Stewart Gardner Museum (*see p114*). At 1.24am, two men wearing police uniforms and fake black mustaches strolled into the museum, over-powered the guard and walked out with $300 million worth of art.

While a dollar figure has been applied to the pieces, in reality they were priceless. Stolen was Jan Vermeer's 'The Concert', one of only 35 known works by the great Dutch painter. The thieves also took two Rembrandt paintings (including the only known Rembrandt seascape) and one Rembrandt etching, a Manet painting, and five works on paper by Degas.

More than a decade later, the crime remains unsolved. It is still near the top of the FBI's most-wanted list, but a reward of $5 million has been on offer for 10 years now with no takers.

Because Mrs. Gardner's will doesn't allow anything in the museum to change, the spots where the stolen works once hung remain bare.

sioned by the US Navy and turned into a historic site. One of the Navy Yard's most celebrated guests was the USS *Constitution*, a battleship built in Boston and nicknamed 'Old Ironsides' when it emerged victorious from a battle with the British Navy during the War of 1812. The Navy Yard also houses a museum that features historical exhibitions about shipbuilding. *See p98.*

Outside Boston

Basketball Hall of Fame

1150 West Columbus Avenue, Springfield (1-413 781 6500/www.hoophall.com). **Open** 10am-5pm daily. **Admission** $10; $6 concessions; free under-6s. **No credit cards.**

Springfield doesn't have an NBA team, so this might seem a strange place to put the nation's largest museum devoted to the sport of basketball, but here it is nonetheless. This is the home of the official Basketball Hall of Fame, which is showcased inside a giant three-level facility. The building features a cinema and dozens of displays. Everything from the Harlem Globetrotters to the Houston Rockets is celebrated here. This place is for true fans.

Concord Museum

Cambridge Turnpike, at Lexington Road, Concord (1-978 369 9763/www.concordmuseum.org). **Open** *Apr-Dec* 9am-5pm Mon-Sat; noon-5pm Sun. *Jan-Mar* 11am-4pm Mon-Sat; 1-4pm Sun. **Admission** $7; $3-$6 concessions; $16 family; free under-5s. **Credit** MC, V.

A lantern hung at the Old North Church to warn the local Minutemen of the British Army's approach is on display here, as are furniture and other artefacts documenting life in Concord as far back as the pre-Revolutionary War era.

Kendall Whaling Museum

27 Everett Street, Sharon (1-781 784 5642/ www.kwm.org). **Open** 10am-5pm Tue-Sat; 1-5pm Sun. **Admission** $4; $2.50-$3 concessions; $10 family; free under-6s. **Credit** AmEx, Disc, MC, V.

Heaven knows it's not the most PC of subjects, but whaling is a part of local history and this museum features a number of items relating to the practice of hunting the great mammals of the sea.

Massachusetts Museum of Contemporary Art

87 Marshall Street, North Adams (1-413 664 4481/ www.massmoca.org). **Open** *June-Oct* 10am-6pm daily. *Nov-May* 11am-5pm Mon, Wed-Sun. **Admission** $6; $2-$4 concessions; free under-6s. **Credit** AmEx, MC, V.

Located in downtown North Adams in a vast mill complex, MASS MoCA presents contemporary art in a unique setting. It opened to the public in May 1999 in a sprawling complex of 19th-century factory buildings used to produce electronic components before North Adams fell on hard times in the 1970s. Exhibitions by exciting newcomers like Laylah Ali and contemporary masters such as Joseph Beuys and Mario Merz are theatrically staged in this expansive space.

Norman Rockwell Museum

9 Glendale Road, Stockbridge (1-413 298 4100/ www.nrm.org). **Open** *May-Oct* 10am-5pm daily. *Nov-Apr* 10am-4pm Mon-Fri; 10am-5pm Sat, Sun. **Admission** $10; $7 concessions; free under-18s. **Credit** AmEx, MC, V.

The world's largest collection of Norman Rockwell's paintings is housed here, in a museum dedicated to exploring the life and work of one of America's most beloved illustrators.

Peabody Essex Museum

East India Square, Salem (1-800 745 4054/ www.pem.org). **Open** *Apr-Oct* 10am-5pm Mon-Sat; noon-5pm Sun. *Nov-Mar* 10am-5pm Tue-Sat; noon-5pm Sun. **Admission** $10; $8 concessions; free under-16s outside school hours. **Credit** AmEx, MC, V.

If you're looking for a more scholarly, less Disney-style examination of the Salem Witch Trials than the touristy places, this place is your ticket. Featuring 30 galleries and a research library, the museum contains displays that explore the witch trials along with America's history on land and sea.

Eat, drink, shop

Restaurants & Cafés **122**
Pubs & Bars **156**
Shops & Services **171**

Feature boxes

The best brunch spots 127
The best alfresco 136
Top five top tables 143
Find your java joy 144
Top five cheap eats 147
A truly local coffee shop 151
The best lobster spots 153
It's a short way to Tipperary 158
Don't miss bars 159
Play that funky music 184
Shopping by area 186

Restaurants & Cafés

Just because they call it 'Beantown' doesn't mean you can't have lobster.

Maybe it's because Boston was a little late in getting its culinary act together, and as such the traditions and channels aren't as deeply entrenched. Maybe it's because the spotlight isn't as intense here as it is in some other cities. Most probably though, it's simply the chefs, the sous chefs and the waiting staffs who make it happen. They may work dogs' hours, but peek in any kitchen and you're still more likely to see smiles than frowns. Even as they rake in the awards, they joke. At **Centro**, a three-star Italian restaurant in Central Square, all of the sous chefs have the same style of facial hair (goatees). The kitchen staff at **Hamersley's Bistro**, a wildly acclaimed hotspot in the South End, wear baseball caps and serve sausages during Red Sox season.

Whatever the reason, this much is true: when food is fun, eating is fun. It has been reported that the average Bostonian eats out 2.6 times a week and spends $25 per person per pop. They must be having a good time or they wouldn't keep going back out there.

The main ingredient in Boston's diet is undoubtedly seafood. Fish caught in the morning is on plates by sundown. Some fanatical chefs even have their own boats and commercial fishing licences. At the same time, this being New England, and therefore subject to dramatic changes of season, everyone from highly praised chefs to the gifted burrito spinners at **El Pelon Taqueria** must constantly tweak their menus to reflect what is available. So what ends up on your plate largely depends on what time of the year it is. In the autumn, chefs make use of hard squash, corn, figs, quail and pheasant. In the winter, apples, potatoes and turnips take the spotlight. Spring brings fiddlehead ferns, fava beans and English peas. Summer's the time for heirloom tomatoes, verbena, wild oysters and all kinds of berries and mushrooms.

You can blow a few hundred on a terrific meal in Boston. You can also happily push your belly button far and away from your backbone on ten bucks or less. With that in mind, just remember that the key to eating well in Boston is not simply knowing where to go, but being ready and willing to try something new when you get there. This city refuses to be pigeonholed. There's a little bit of everything here. Enjoy!

Back Bay

American contemporary

Audubon Circle

838 Beacon Street, at Park Drive (421 1910). Kenmore T. **Open** 11.30am-1am Mon-Fri; 5pm-1am Sat, Sun (food served until 11pm daily). **Main courses** $13. **Credit** AmEx, DC, Disc, MC, V. **Map** 306 D5/6.

The only outdoor sign for this sleek, modern bar is a cryptic circle and a dot, and the interior is just as understated. The food is nothing less than a miracle for the price: an excellent pressed turkey and bacon sandwich; white bean paste with fresh grilled bread; a thick pork chop with garlic butter and grits, all for a handful of change. Everything works, and nothing's expensive. The low-profile approach here meant business was slow to build at first, so now everyone packing the bar thinks it's their own little discovery.

Clio

Eliot Hotel, 370 Commonwealth Avenue, at Massachusetts Avenue (536 7200). Hynes/ICA T. **Open** 5.30-10pm Mon-Thur, Sun; 5.30-10.30pm Fri, Sat. **Main courses** $25-$34. **Credit** AmEx, MC, V. **Map** p306 E5.

Chef Ken Oringer's cooking is a nose-thumbing to the profuse and ingredient-intensive cuisine that earned Boston its spot on the gastronomic map. It's also very, very good. His focused flavours and small, sculptural presentations wouldn't be out of place in New York: a dramatically spare plate of foie gras; steak seared with spices and served over a little vegetable ragout; two perfect scallops on pedestals of salt. The dining room is quiet and attracts an older crowd than the trendy Newbury Street spots nearby. For the **Eliot Hotel**, *see p48.*

St Botolph

99 St Botolph, at West Newton Street (266 3030). Prudential T. **Open** 5-10pm Mon-Wed; 5-11pm Thur-Sat; 11am-3pm, 5-11pm Sun. **Main courses** $9-$25. **Credit** AmEx, DC, MC, V. **Map** p306 E6.

Lounge, bar, formal, informal, upmarket dining, comfort food; St Botolph's is all that. Downstairs is the hip bar where you can get a big burger or a nice simple piece of fish. Upstairs is a somewhat more sophisticated restaurant, where you can still get a burger or a nice simple piece of fish. Eat, drink, be merry … it's all so easy here.

Get your Prada on and warm up the mobile phone for **Sonsie**. See p125

Sonsie

327 Newbury Street, between Hereford Street & Massachusetts Avenue (351 2500). Hynes/ICA T. **Open** 7am-1am daily. **Main courses** $13-$27. **Credit** AmEx, DC, MC, V. **Map** p306 E5.

The eminently tasteful Sonsie is possibly the premier hangout spot for the Newbury Street elite and those who want to meet them. The restaurant is crowded elbow-to-elbow with Back Bay's beautiful people. The eclectic menu features Northern Italian pasta dishes and American specialities. The front of the restaurant has tables facing windows, so everybody can keep an eye on who's promenading along chic Newbury. The service here is extraordinary.

Stars

393 Huntington Avenue, at Forsyth Street (536 3232). Northeastern University T. **Open** 7am-10pm Mon-Thur, Sun; 7am-11pm Fri, Sat. **Main courses** $9-$19. **Credit** AmEx, DC, Disc, MC, V. **Map** p306 D6.

Some smart folks out there distilled the best parts of eating at a hip, white tablecloth bistro – complete with giant liquid screen televisions, metallic counters, bamboo placemats and nitrogen-charged cruvinets – and played it to the tune of griddled corned beef hash for breakfast, cheeseburgers for lunch and maple-glazed meatloaf for dinner. Sure, there's a well-selected wine list. And, they've got a spice-rubbed skirt steak on the menu; but it comes with a pile of Tatertots. For dessert – what else? – chocolate chip cookie ice-cream sandwiches with cookie-dough ice-cream and warm fudge.

Vox Populi

755 Boylston Street, between Exeter and Fairfield Streets (424 8300). Copley or Hynes/ICA T. **Open** 11.30am-1am daily. **Main courses** $18-$24. **Credit** AmEx, DC, Disc, MC, V. **Map** p306 E5.

The people have spoken: they want their profiteroles! Or was it the roasted pork loin with calvados apples and Camembert butter? The populist, 'Cicero was here' theme of this restaurant may hold no bearing on, well, anything, but that doesn't mean Vox Pop isn't worth a visit. The atmosphere is sophisticated and lively; the food is a fresh, creative and moderately priced mix – a sort of Paris-meets-Boston. Bonus: giant floor-to-ceiling windows offer excellent people watching, all the more fun since it is located directly across the street from the Boston Duck Tour drop-off spot.

American traditional

Capital Grille

359 Newbury Street, at Hereford Street (262 8900). Hynes/ICA T. **Open** 5-10pm Mon-Wed, Sun; 5-11pm Thur-Sat. **Main courses** $17-$32. **Credit** AmEx, DC, Disc, MC, V. **Map** p306 E5.

There's a carpenter in Vermont who makes a living simply from providing restaurants like this one with their wood panelling. You can imagine the rest: giant Martinis in the bar; porterhouse steaks dry-ageing in a meat locker; a list of major-league and expensive red wines. In classic steakhouse fashion, you order vegetables separately, if at all.

Can't afford a trip to the Himalayas? Head to **Kashmir**. *See p127.*

Flash's

310 Stuart Street, at Columbus Avenue (574 8888). Arlington T. **Open** 11.30am-1am Mon-Wed; 11.30am-2am Thur, Fri; 5pm-2am Sat; 5pm-1am Sun. **Main courses** $8.95-$18.95. **Credit** AmEx, DC, MC, V. **Map** p306 F5.

Simple food; well thought out. That's the idea behind Lynette Mosher's creative, eclectic, but thoroughly neighbourhood-aimed menu at Flash's. She takes wickedly good french fries, for example, and tosses them with garlic confit, lemon and fresh thyme. Everything is made from scratch – not just the house-cured and smoked pork tenderloin, but the ketchups, vinaigrettes and pastas as well. The atmosphere is the height of retro-lounge, complete with cocktail motifs and large communal tables.

Grill 23 & Bar

161 Berkeley Street, at Stuart Street (542 2255). Arlington T. **Open** 5.30-10.30pm Mon-Thur, Sun; 5.30-11pm Fri-Sat. **Main courses** $25-$37. **Credit** AmEx, DC, Disc, MC, V. **Map** p306 F5.

Cigar-chomping fat cat heaven. The steaks here are dry-aged in-house; the wine list is so vast, it's like a coffee table book; the waitstaff could'nt be more attentive if you married them. Very clubby. Very good.

Oak Room

Fairmont-Copley Plaza, 138 St James Avenue, at Dartmouth Street (267 5300). Copley T. **Open** 5.30-10pm Mon-Thur, Sun; 5.30-11pm Fri, Sat. **Main courses** $35-$40. **Credit** AmEx, DC, Disc, MC, V. **Map** p306 F5.

Rich, dark oak, mirrored walls, vaulted ceilings and twin Waterford crystal chandeliers make this joint easily one of Boston's clubbiest. To eat? Thick steaks, chops and fresh Atlantic seafood.

The Palm

200 Dartmouth Street in the Westin Hotel (867 9292). Copley or Back Bay T. **Open** 11.30am-10.30pm Mon-Fri; 5-11pm Sat; 5-9.30pm Sun. **Main courses** $14-$31. **Credit** AmEx, DC, MC, V. **Map** p306 F5.

Okay, it's a haven for Martini-swilling former newscasters. And it's a business traveller's dream. But the Palm also happens to serve some of Boston's most tender, juicy steaks and far and away the city's most exceptional creamed spinach. You'll be cursing us for putting you in such an obvious tourist trap – until you start eating. Then your doubts will melt like so much butter in a mashed potato gratin, and you'll know why all the famous faces caricaturised on the walls are smiling.

Asian

Brown Sugar

129 Jersey Street, at Boylston Street (266 2928). Kenmore T. **Open** 11am-10pm Mon-Thur; 11am-11pm Fri, Sat. **Main courses** $9. **Credit** DC, Disc, MC, V. **Map** p306 D6.

The best Thai food in town is served in this pretty-but-casual room in the quiet West Fens, just across the park from the Museum of Fine Arts. Appetisers are particularly vivid and sharp and the Thai iced coffee and tea are absolutely standard-setting. The small amount of free parking is a real bonus in this small neighbourhood of residents-only spaces.

Kashmir

279 Newbury Street, at Gloucester Street (536 1695). Hynes/ICA T. **Open** 11.30am-11.30pm Mon-Fri; 11.30am-midnight Sat, Sun. **Main courses** $13-$19. **Credit** AmEx, MC, V. **Map** p306 E5.

This below street-level spot is probably the best Indian restaurant in the city – not quantum distances beyond the competition, but still the most handsome with the finest food. Curries are delicate, balanced and energetic; specials such as tandoori rack of lamb are presented with flair.

The best Brunch spots

Judging by the wait at most Boston area restaurants on Saturday and Sunday mornings, it's safe to say that brunch is a ritual for many Bostonians. They do it very well here. So if eggs and champagne are your thing, join the queue.

Claremont Café

Start the day off right and join the eclectic group who turn waiting for a table at this tiny eatery into a stylish pastime. *See p133.*

Johnny D's

While the music gets your toes to tapping, Johnny's varied menu will make everybody very happy. *See p154.*

S&S Deli Restaurant

If you want to do brunch like a local, make a beeline for this place, grab a number from the old lady at the door and commence your wait. *See p153.*

Café Fleuri

When you feel like living it up a little, this place claims the city's most extensive, and expensive, brunch menu. *See p136.*

East Coast Grill

Good seafood and grilled meats to chomp on and the DIY Bloody Mary Bar should bring out the creative bartender in you. *See p149.*

Kebab-n-Kurry

30 Massachusetts Avenue, at Marlborough Street (536 9835). Hynes/ICA T. **Lunch served** noon-3pm daily. **Open** 5-11pm daily. **Main courses** $9.95-$14.95. **Credit** AmEx, DC, MC, V. **Map** p306 E5.

As the name would imply, Kebab-n-Kurry is all about straight-up, no-fuss, tasty Indian food. The garlic nan bread may not be worth writing home about, but it is at least worth ordering another basket. There is a nice sized assortment of special pan-baked Indian breads like nan, roti and poori with which to soak up the subtle curries and to wrap around tandoori-style kebabs. Situated in a sedate basement-level space and frequented largely by brainiacs from MIT, Kebab-n-Kurry is a great place to calm the nerves and listen to a bunch of people discussing things that don't interest you at all.

Pho Pasteur

119 Newbury Street, at Clarendon Street (617 262 8200). Copley T. **Open** 11.30am-10pm daily. **Main courses** $8.50-$12.95. **Credit** AmEx, MC, V. **Map** p306 F5.

Vietnamese food is to Boston what Mexican food is to Los Angeles and curry is to London: the best value in high-flavour ethnic cooking. Duyen Le, with his formula of fresh ingredients, spot-on cooking and low prices, has almost single handedly brought Vietnamese cooking out of Chinatown. The enormous menu includes huge bowls of elegant beef soup (pho), excellent spring rolls and sharp-tasting plates of grilled pork, beef and shrimp.

Shino's Express Sushi

144 Newbury Street, at Dartmouth Street (262 4530). Copley T. **Open** noon-9pm Mon-Sat; 1-9pm Sun. **Lunch specials** $6-$7.50 (12 pieces). **Dinner specials** $15-$25 (18 to 32 pieces). **Map** p306 F5.

Shino's Express Sushi is the equivalent of a sushi diner. The waitresses here snap gum as they take your order. The chefs – visible slicing and dicing from every seat in the restaurant – sport skateboarding T-shirts and can look a bit scruffy at times. The decor is pretty bare, and track lighting bounces off Formica counters. Most important, though, this joint is cheap, quick and always busy – a good thing, as the turnover is key whenever raw fish is involved.

Cafés & coffeehouses

Armani Café

214 Newbury Street, at Exeter Street (437 0909). Copley T. **Open** 11.30am-11.45pm Mon-Thur, Sun; 11.30am-12.45am Fri, Sat. **Main courses** $18-$34. **Credit** AmEx, DC, Disc, MC, V. **Map** p306 E5.

Cell phone central; waiters in black, black, black. Giorgio Armani's restaurant doesn't sell clothes – the boutique is next door – but it does sell attitude by the tableful. It's where to go when you want to feel rich and European and 20 years old, and where the rich and European and 20-year-olds go to feel at home. Excellent people watching. Outdoor seating in warm weather.

Espresso Royale Caffe

44 Gainsborough Street (859 7080). Symphony or Northeastern University T. **Open** 7am-11pm Mon-Fri; 8am-11pm Sat, Sun. **Main courses** $2-$4. **No credit cards. Map** p306 E6.

With Northeastern, the Berklee School of Music, Mass Art, Boston University Theater School, the Museum of Fine Arts and the symphony within a stones throw, Espresso Royale has taken on a role as a 'great place to meet.' Also good for settling down with a friend over checkers, chess or Jenga – all of which the sociable counter help will provide. The sandwiches aren't recommended, but all the liquids – especially the flavour shots – are.

Branch: 286 Newbury Street (859 9515).

Tealuxe

108 Newbury Street (927 0400/1-888 832 5893 www.tealuxe.com). Copley T. **Open** 8am-10pm Mon-Wed, Sun; 8am-11pm Thur-Sat. **Main courses** $5.50-$6.95. **Credit** AmEx, DC, Disc, MC, V. **Map** p306 F5.

'Where there's tea,' said Sir Arthur Pinero, 'there's hope.' Or: 'I got nasty habits,' said Mick Jagger. 'I take tea at three.' And so it is at Tealuxe, where everyone from little old ladies to pierced and painted punks can choose from hundreds of bins full of leafy goodness and share in the pleasures of a nice pot of tea. The Newbury Street location also offers tasty grilled sandwiches and scones.

Branches: Zero Brattle Street, Harvard Square (441 0077); 256 Harvard Street, Brookline (739 4832); 1223 Center Street, Newton (244 3155).

Trident Booksellers and Café

338 Newbury Street, at Hereford Street (267 8688). Hynes/ICA T. **Open** 9am-midnight daily. **Main courses** $2-$4. **Credit** AmEx, DC, Disc, MC, V. **Map** p306 E5.

If you're the type whose idea of a good time is getting a bite to eat, sipping a cup o' joe or a carrot juice with ginger and flipping through a vast selection of magazines, say hello to your new home. The staff here genuinely does not mind you treating the place like a reading library; just try not to break the spines of the magazines.

European

Ambrosia on Huntington

116 Huntington Avenue, at Belvidere Street (247 2400). Prudential T. **Open** 11.30am-2pm, 5-10pm Mon-Thur; 11.30am-2pm, 5.30-11pm Fri; 5-10pm Sun. **Set price dinner** $32. **Credit** Amex, DC, Disc, MC, V. **Map** p306 E6.

Chef Tony Ambrose was one of Boston's original wild-chefs. Impeccably groomed from his work under many of the world's top chefs, Ambrose forged his own style, and has been racking in awards since Ambrosia opened. On the wild side, his provincial French/Asian fusion dishes have been known to resemble anything from the Tower of Pisa to Gustav Klimt's 'The Kiss'. These days, Ambrose's

Tapeo has it all: ambience, tapas and enormous glasses of Spanish wine.

presentation is a bit tamer, but his food still rocks. His signature dish, the Saint Pierre, is a very delicate white fish, steamed in bamboo, served with a yam gallette, stewed leeks and finished with a glaze made from 14 Asian spices.

Brasserie Jo

Colonnade Hotel, 120 Huntington Avenue, at Belvidere Street (425 3240). Prudential T. **Open** 6.30am-2.30pm, 5-11pm Mon-Fri; noon-4pm, 5-11pm Sat; noon-4pm, 5-10pm Sun. **Main courses** $6-$25. **Credit** AmEx, DC, Disc, MC, V. **Map** p306 E6.

The Boston sequel to a successful Chicago restaurant, Brasserie Jo is big, busy and French in a way you don't necessarily expect in an American city: in addition to quirky specialities such as shrimp in a pastry bag, the menu also includes kidney, omelettes and blood sausage. Desserts are to die for. For the **Colonnade Hotel** *see p47.*

Café Louis

234 Berkeley Street, at Newbury Street (266 4680). Arlington T. **Open** 11.30-3pm Mon-Sat; 3-10pm Tue-Sat. **Main courses** $15-$28. **Credit** AmEx, DC, MC, V. **Map** p306 F5.

Gourmet magazine describes Café Louis as 'part boutique canteen, part destination restaurant, part rarefied neighborhood pizzeria'; what it doesn't tell you is that the food in this understated little place will absolutely blow your mind. Its specials are astonishing. It recently offered sweet potato with pumpkin lasagna, in which the noodles were homemade and tossed with black olive rosemary butter, while the pumpkins were grown organically on a small local farm and slow roasted for upwards of 12 hours. Does it make a difference in the end? If you have to ask.

L'Espalier

30 Gloucester Street, at Newbury Street (263 3023). Hynes/ICA T. **Open** 6-10pm Mon-Sat. **Set meals** $65, $82. **Credit** AmEx, DC, Disc, MC, V. **Map** p306 E5.

Chef-owner Frank McClelland serves toweringly exquisite food at equally towering prices in a Back Bay brownstone. Known for its intimacy, hyper-attentive service and an unequalled seven-course set-price meal, L'Espalier is the location of up to three marriage proposals a night (be very careful who you bring with you) and is not quite matched by anything else in the city.

Tapeo

266 Newbury Street, between Gloucester & Fairfield Streets (267 4799). Copley or Hynes/ICA T. **Open** 5.30-10.30pm Mon-Wed, Sun; noon-11pm Thur-Sat. **Main courses** $18-$24; *tapas* $5.40-$7.50. **Credit** AmEx, DC, MC, V. **Map** p306 E5.

Fun, sexy and tasty in a way perhaps only a Spanish restaurant can be; Tapeo is the only place to go for tapas in the Back Bay. Downstairs is a kitschy-fun Spanish sherry bar. Upstairs is a spacious dining-room with witty decor. The menu is consistently excellent, especially if you like garlic. Tapas are as simple as marinated olives and as outré as an $18 plate of baby eels. You don't really need to order entrées, though there's a spectacularly presented baked fish in salt. The list of Spanish wines is extensive and very nicely presented. The place is often crowded, so arrive early or book a table.

Torrefazione Italia Café

85 Newbury Street, at Clarendon Street (424 0951). Copley T. **Open** 7am-9pm Mon-Fri; 8am-9pm Sat; 9am-9pm Sun. **Main courses** $5-$10. **Credit** AmEx, DC, Disc, MC, V. **Map** p306 F5.

Don't hate this place because it's beautiful. In fact, go on and embrace the loveliness that is Torrefazione. All of the plates and glasses are gorgeous Raffaellesco ceramics, and the more sophisticated, well-kempt types that tend to hang out on the 'early' blocks of Newbury populate the joint. Plus, the tea and coffee are fine – when you get what you ordered, that is, which is never a guarantee here.

Latin

Bomboa

35 Stanhope Street, at Clarendon Street (236 6363) Back Bay T. **Open** 5.30pm-1am Tue-Fri; 5.30pm-midnight Sat; 5.30-10pm Sun. **Bar** until 2am Mon-Sat; until midnight Sunday. **Main courses** $17-$21. **Credit** AmEx, MC, V. **Map** p306 F5.

'Bomboa' is a term a construction worker in Brazil might use when a sexy lady passes by; it's an exclamation of love for beauty. Fittingly, few lists of 'What's Hot?' in Boston go by without paying homage to this sexy, swanky French-Brazilian restaurant. In addition to the cast of attractive and well-heeled patrons who hang out at the bar getting lit off caipirinhas and mojitos, Chef E Michael Reidt is getting plenty of attention for his passionate cuisine. Join the queue.

Casa Romero

30 Gloucester Street, at Newbury Street (536 4341). Arlington T. **Open** 5-10pm Mon-Thur, Sun; 5-11pm Fri, Sat. **Main courses** $12.50-$24. **Credit** Disc, MC, V. **Map** p306 E5.

This restaurant is such a hidden jewel that most locals can't even find it. Everyone's heard of it, of course, but its behind-the-beaten-path entrance (located in an alley between Newbury Street and Commonwealth Avenue) helps to keep this upmarket Mexican restaurant obscure enough that you can still get a table without a reservation on most nights. The house specialty, *puerco adobado*, is a cut of pork marinated in oranges and smoked *chipotle* peppers, spicy and sweet at the same time. You can wash down all this fine fare with the brilliant sangria and tasty Margaritas.

El Pelon Taqueria

92 Peterborough Street, at Kilmarnock Street (262 9090). Fenway or Kenmore T. **Open** 11.30am-9.30pm daily. **Main courses** $5.75. **Credit** AmEx, MC, V. **Map** p306 D6.

El Pelon may be small, but this tiny Fenway taqueria packs a punch. Every item on the menu here makes extraordinary use of ordinary ingredients and blows the doors off the bland, gloppy super-chain Mexicana. The salsa here, for example, is good enough to eat with a spoon. The kitchen burns through 12 gallons of the smoky fire-roasted blend every four days, plus tons of vibrant *salsa fresca*. When the cilantro jumps up and dances on your tongue, that's when you know the stuff is fresh.

Seafood

McCormick and Schmick's

Boston Park Plaza Hotel, 34 Columbus Avenue (482 3999). Arlington T. **Open** 11am-2am daily. **Main courses** $10-$40. **Credit** AmEx, Disc, MC, V. **Map** p306 F5.

Inside the miles of clubby dark wood and soft lights of their new restaurant (opened in October 2000), McCormick and Schmick have made a religion of fresh. Offerings here are so fresh that they print two menus each day. Atop each menu is a list of around 40 species of seafood delivered that day, including not only the name of the species, but its origin. Continuing the fresh concept, the restaurant uses no frozen goods or additives; all fruit juices are squeezed fresh for each drink; even the potatoes are mashed with a frequency bordering on fanaticism. Social hour, 4-6pm daily, has a special $1.95 menu.

South End

African

Addis Red Sea

544 Tremont Street, at Clarendon Street (426 8727). Back Bay or Copley T. **Open** 5-10.30pm Mon-Wed; 5-11pm Thur, Fri; noon-11pm Sat; noon-10pm Sun. **Main courses** $8-$13. **Credit** AmEx, DC, MC, V. **Map** p306 F5.

This ten-year-old veteran on Tremont Street may still be Boston's most exotic place to eat. Low wooden stools surround woven-grass tables; food is delivered on wide plates without silverware. *Injera*, the spongy sourdough bread of Ethiopia, serves as both utensil and mild-tasting foil for the spicy chicken, lamb and lentil stews. Don't miss the red pepper cottage cheese as an appetiser, and use the diced tomato salad to cool your palate. A delicious experience.

American contemporary

The Dish

253 Shawmut Avenue, at Milford Street (426 7866/www.southenddish.com). Back Bay T.

Eat with your hands at **Addis Red Sea**. *See p131.*

Open 5-11pm Mon-Thur; 5pm-midnight Fri, Sat; 5-10pm Sun. **Main courses** $11.95-$15.95. **Credit** AmEx, MC, V. **Map** p306 F6.
The epitome of a neighbourhood restaurant. Small, intimate, loud, full of personality and staffed by spunky locals who would just as soon quit as serve a plate that didn't look right. The miscellaneous menu and eclectic handpicked wine list are to match.

Hamersley's Bistro

553 Tremont Street, at Clarendon Street (423 2700). Back Bay or Copley T. **Open** 6-10pm Mon-Fri; 5.30-10.30pm Sat; 5.30-9.30pm Sun. **Main courses** $23-$35. **Credit** AmEx, DC, Disc, MC, V. **Map** p306 F6.
Chef Gordon Hamersley is the most famous alumnus of Todd English's kitchen at Olives (*see p143*). He struck out on his own several years ago and now runs this spacious first-rate 'bistro', with an open kitchen and a largely middle-aged, power-suited clientele. His garlic-roasted chicken is powerfully flavoured and moist throughout; service is informed and not overbearing.

Icarus

3 Appleton Street, at Tremont Street (426 1790). Back Bay T. **Open** 6-9.30pm Mon-Thur; 6-10.30pm Fri; 5.30-10.30pm Sat; 5.30-9.30pm Sun. **Main courses** $24-$32. **Credit** AmEx, DC, Disc, MC, V. **Map** p306 F6.
Long before the South End was overrun by bistros du moment, Icarus had staked out this distinctive, romantic below-street-level spot for Chris Douglass's fancy-but-not-frivolous New American cooking.

On the Park

1 Union Park, at Shawmut Street (426 0862). Copley or Arlington T. **Open** 9am-3pm, 5.30-11pm Sat; 9am-3pm Sun. **Main courses** $15-$24. **Credit** AmEx, MC, V. **Map** p306 F6.
So small, quiet and unassuming is this place that one almost forgets it's there. Reasons to remember include a litany of playfully delicious dishes, a nice-and-tight wine list and an atmosphere so civil and relaxed that you'll forget what day it is. They are best known for their popular weekend brunch, but the dinner hour is also well attended.

Tim's Tavern

329 Columbus Avenue, at Dartmouth Street (437 6898). Back Bay T. **Open** 11am-11pm Mon-Sat. **Main courses** $7-$15. **No credit cards**. **Map** p306 F6.
It's not much to look at from the outside – or from the inside for that matter – but this little joint knows how to make a good old-fashioned American cheeseburger better than just about anyone else in town. In fact, Tom's has been voted best burger by nearly every independent study ever done in Boston.

American traditional

Bob the Chef's Café

604 Columbus Avenue, at Massachusetts Avenue (536 6204). Massachusetts Avenue T. **Open** 11.30am-10pm Tue, Wed; 11.30am-11pm Thur-Sat; 11am-9pm Sun. **Main courses** $9-$14. **Credit** AmEx, DC, MC, V. **Map** p306 E6.
A few years ago, Bob's was a funky caféteria-style soul food restaurant and cult favourite. After a protracted renovation it emerged in almost unrecognisable form, with the sponge-painted walls and four-person tables of a bistro. There are probably better soul food restaurants in the world, but this is the one with the local reputation.

Asian

Jae's Café and Grill

520 Columbus Avenue, at Worcester Street (421 9405). Symphony or Massachusetts Avenue T. **Open** 11.30am-4pm, 5-11pm Mon-Fri; 11.30am-11pm Sat; noon-11pm Sun. **Main courses** $8.25-$16.95. **Credit** AmEx, DC, Disc, MC, V. **Map** p306 E6.
An endlessly popular and consistently delightful sushi/Korean/Thai café. Servers speak of 'Jae's menu' with near-reverence, and it is worshipped by a large cult of well-turned-out Bostonians.

Pho Republique

1415 Washington Street, at West Dedham Street (262 0005). Back Bay T. **Open** 5.30pm-12.30am daily. **Main courses** $14.50-$19. **Credit** AmEx, MC, V. **Map** p306 F5.

Imagine what it would feel like to step into a restaurant off a crowded street in Hanoi and find a modish crowd dining on pho and drinking lemongrass Martinis like tomorrow would never come. That's pretty much the vibe at Pho Republique, plus a DJ in the corner on some nights and random flame jugglers passing through on others. The food here is healthy and hearty; the drinks are inspirational; the decor is as funky as you're going to see in Boston; and there's usually a pretty hip scene happening.

Cafés & coffeehouses

Claremont Café

535 Columbus Avenue, at Massachusetts Avenue (247 9001). Mass Ave T. **Open** 7.30am-3pm Tue-Sat; 9am-3pm Sun; 5.30-10pm Tue-Thur; 5.30-10.30pm Fri, Sat. **Main courses** $14-$24. **Credit** AmEx, MC, V. **Map** p306 E6.

This place has been eclipsed in fame by the slew of high-ambition bistros in the neighbourhood. But this is unfair, as this very consistent restaurant turns out good, sharp-flavoured food – particularly on the appetiser menu – at moderate prices. There's seating outside during warm weather.

Franklin Café

276 Shawmut Avenue, at Hanson Street (350 0010). Back Bay T. **Open** 5.30pm-1.30am Mon-Sat. **Main courses** $12-$16. **Credit** AmEx, DC, MC, V. **Map** p306 F6.

Small, full, warm and constantly abuzz, the Franklin Café's clientele (both gay and straight) and its snappy, updated comfort food give it the feel of the perfect neighbourhood bar in the city's hippest restaurant neighbourhood.

Garden of Eden Café

571 Tremont Street (247 8377). Back Bay T. **Open** 7am-10.30pm Mon-Fri; 7.30am-11pm Sat; 7.30am-10pm Sun. **Main courses** $5-$13. **Credit** AmEx, MC, V. **Map** p306 F6.

It's a greengrocer, cheese shop, patisserie, gourmet shop and deli counter, but first and foremost it is the South End's king café, offering the idle Illy coffees and the hungry a tasty list of cheese and pâté plus a host of daily specials from garlic-pistachio saucisson salad to baked macaroni and cheese.

European

Aquitaine

569 Tremont Street, at Union Park (424 8577). Back Bay or Copley T. **Open** 5.30-10pm Mon-Wed, Sun; 5.30-11pm Thur-Sat. **Main courses** $17-$26. **Credit** AmEx, MC, V. **Map** p306 F5.

The wine racks stretch to the ceiling and the crowd stretches the imagination at this South End hotspot. The food has an undeniably Continental feel, like a good French restaurant in London. A 'tartlet' takes caramelised onions and rich Gruyere and tops them with richer bacon; big ravioli are filled with minced duck and foie gras, bathed in a sauce of Madeira and truffle oil. The wine list is expensive and flashy; the clientele is under 40 and South Endy, which means about as well dressed as Bostonians get.

Talk with your hands at the **Claremont Café**.

Le Gamin

550 Tremont Street, at Dartmouth Street (654 8969). Back Bay T. **Open** 10am-midnight Mon-Fri; 8am-midnight Sat, Sun. **Main courses** $5-$20. **Credit** MC, V. **Map** p306 F6.

The crêpe returns to Boston in a very Parisian little incarnation, a below-street-level café where you can eat a very serviceable meal for $10 a head and not feel as though you're slumming. The elaborate cold salads and drinks are good too.

South End Galleria

480A Columbus Avenue, at West Newton Street (236 5252). Prudential or Massachusetts Avenue T. **Open** 5.30-10pm Mon-Thur, Sun; 5.30-11pm Fri, Sat. **Main courses** $16-$23. **Credit** AmEx, MC, V. **Map** p306 E6.

'The Girls' – as friends and co-owners Rita D'Angelo and Marisa Iocca are known around town – have recently taken control of this place, and the locals are going wild. The setting is intimate; the help enthusiastic and knowledgeable; the espresso Martinis absolutely perfect. Their loving approach to creating a full-blown Italian food experience comes through in every dish.

Truc

560 Tremont Street, at Clarendon Street (338 8070). Back Bay T. **Open** 6-9.30pm Tue-Thur; 6-10.30pm Fri-Sun. **Main courses** $23-$26. **Credit** MC, V. **Map** p306 F6.

A treat for lovers of French food with some money in their pockets. Chef Amanda Lydon, one of *Food & Wine* magazine's top ten chefs of the year for 2000, turns out some very accomplished French classics: cassoulet, trout meuniere, a buttery soft rabbit loin, pork rillettes served with a mustard pot and cornichons. There's a wine list made up almost entirely of French bottles, and the restaurnat's decor is understated (green walls, black and white paintings) but handsome.

Latin

Botucatu Restaurant

57 West Dedham Street, at Tremont Street (247 8394). Back Bay T. **Open** 11.30am-10pm Mon-Thur; 11.30am-11pm Fri, Sat; 3-10pm Sun. **Main courses** $10-$12. **Credit** Disc, MC, V. **Map** p306 F6.

Tell a Brazilian that you're going out for an authentic, no-frills South American/Brazilian supper and he or she will probably ask you, Why? Well, Botucatu is why. The food is cheap and true to its roots: spicy-chicken- and ground-beef-stuffed empanadas, fried tostones with carrot sauce, fresh heart of palm salads, and a Brazilian version of chicken-fried steak called 'bife a Milaneza.' What makes the experience even more special is an 'anything can happen' atmosphere that rarely fails to deliver. People start singing. The waitress dances to a song playing in her head. Free Brazilian beers or snacks are brought to the table for no apparent reason. It's all too wonderful.

Downtown & the Financial District

American contemporary

Radius

8 High Street, at Summer Street (426 1234). South Station T. **Open** 11.30am-2.30pm Mon-Fri; 5.30-10pm Mon-Thur; 5.30-11pm Fri, Sat. **Main courses** $22-$36. **Credit** AmEx, DC, MC, V. **Map** p307 G5.

Chef Michael Schlow and his partner Christopher Meyers presented Radius to Boston just a few years ago. It was regarded as a hotspot even before it opened; it has not disappointed. Gorgeous fashion-bound twenty-somethings out on daddy's credit card are treated with equal care and laugh just as loud as the tuxedoed gentry whom you would be more likely to imagine could afford fare this rich. And it is easy to get carried away among the piles of foie gras and divine plays on regional New England cuisine that Schlow's kitchen offers. If some things are worth hocking your granny's ring for, this may well be one of them.

Silvertone Bar & Grill

69 Bromfield Street, at Downtown Crossing (338 7887). Downtown Crossing T. **Open** 11am-11pm Mon-Fri; 6-11pm Sat. **Main courses** $10. **Credit** AmEx, DC, Disc, MC, V. **Map** p306 G4.

The dining-room side of this funky subterranean place plays host to a hip audience appreciative of the eclectic wine list and the kitchen's finesse with ordinary, everyday dishes such as grilled chicken and macaroni and cheese. Nothing too fancy or out of control here; just consistently tasty – and good-sized – portions of updated comfort foods. The space is dimly lit and tightly packed, but somehow rarely gets stuffy. And the vibe here is that evergreen type of cool that never has to prove itself.

Cafés & coffeehouses

Finale

1 Columbus Avenue, in the Park Square Building (423 3184). Boylston or Arlington T. **Open** 11.30am-3pm, 6-10pm Mon-Fri; 6pm-midnight Thur-Sat; 4-11pm Sun. **Main courses** $5.95-$30. **Credit** AmEx, DC, Disc, MC, V. **Map** p306 F5.

There are those nights when you just can't wait for dessert. Well, Mom's not looking. When Bostonians crave one thing and one thing only – and that one thing is dessert – they head for this sweet tooth temple. This place is a fashionable restaurant entirely dedicated to the art of luscious delight. The reams of velvet and romantically dim lighting set the tone for artfully plated towers of chocolate and ponds of rich sauce. And, as if that weren't enough to get your motor running, Finale also lays claim to a fine selection of dessert wines and cordials by the glass.

European

Café Fleuri & Julien

Le Meridien, 250 Franklin Street, near Post Office Square (451 1900/1-800 543 4300). State/Citizen's Bank T. **Open** *Café Fleuri* 7am-10pm Mon-Fri; 7.30am-10pm Sat, Sun. *Julien* 6-10pm daily. **Main courses** *Café Fleuri* $18-$20. *Julien* $25-35. **Credit** AmEx, DC, Disc, JCB, MC, $TC, V. **Map** p307 G4.

Famous for the most extensive (and expensive) Sunday brunch menu in the city, the first floor Café Fleuri, in the atrium of the Le Meridien hotel, feels not unlike an office building, with white walls, pink marble and a vast paned skylight. The rest of the week, the restaurant's sandwiches and New American entrees offer a slightly less expensive alternative to the hotel's elegant main dining room, Julien – which produces an expensive but noteworthy menu of consistently excellent European dishes and may be the city's grandest restaurant.

Les Zygomates

129 South Street, at Kneeland Street (542 5108). South Station T. **Lunch served** 11.30am-2pm Mon-Fri. **Open** 6-11pm daily. **Main courses** $18-$24. **Credit** AmEx, DC, Disc, MC, V. **Map** p307 G5.

This Francophile bistro, complete with tile floor, zinc bar and rockin' live jazz has two owners: one, a Parisian-trained American cook who turns out straightforward versions of French classics such as rabbit, venison and sweetbread *vol-au-vents*; the other, a European oenophile who keeps the wine list stocked with new names and unusual varietals and hosts weekly wine tastings on Tuesdays. Wine is available by the 'taste' (two ounces) as well as by the glass and bottle, so a good bet is to sit at the bar, order appetisers and taste your way down the list.

Sel De La Terre

255 State Street, at Long Wharf (720 1300). Aquarium T. **Open** 11.30am-2.30pm daily; 5.30-10pm daily. **Main courses** $21. **Credit** AmEx, DC, Disc, MC, V. **Map** p307 H4.

Even among the throngs of tourists that bump into Sel on their way home from the Aquarium, the restaurant shines. This less-expensive sister restaurant to the acclaimed L'Espalier in the Back Bay (*see p129*), this place sets the tone with an accomplished artisan breadbasket and with salads that will make you fall in love with vegetables all over again. Later it kicks into gear with authentic Provençal cuisine described by fans as 'transcendent'. The menu here is structured so that all entrées cost the same.

The best Al fresco

Spanked by inclement weather conditions for two out of the four seasons, locals take every chance they can get to escape outdoors for some fresh air that doesn't create frost on their nose hairs. Eating outdoors, al fresco, en plein air, offers them a chance to proclaim their resilience. 'That's right Mother Nature,' they silently yell. 'You ain't got a thing on us! We eat you for breakfast (lunch, dinner, etc.)!' These are their favourite places to do just that:

Tealuxe

Decompress from the hectic pace of Newbury Street at this sweet little tea shop, where the teas are complicated and the scones are fresh. *See p128.*

The Travis Restaurant

135 Newbury Street, at Dartmouth Street, Back Bay (267 6388). **Open** 7am-4.30pm daily. **No credit cards. Map** p306 E6.

Amid the thick of Newbury Street's salon madness, these may be the best people-watching seats in the city. Don't miss the fantastic fresh-squeezed lime-rickeys.

Maison Robert

Live jazz, a nice wine bar all in an idyllic garden setting among tall buildings. Spend a few dollars and they'll make you feel like you're worth a million. *See p143.*

Bella Luna

There's a pleasantly disorientating aspect to discovering this scruffy little courtyard that makes every meal here an exciting one. *See p147.*

Seafood

Legal Seafoods

26 Park Plaza, at Park Square (426 4444/ www.legalseafoods.com). Boylston or Arlington T. **Open** 11.30am-11pm Mon-Thur; 11.30am-midnight Fri, Sat; 11.30am-10pm Sun. **Main courses** $20-$30. **Credit** AmEx, DC, Disc, MC, V. **Map** p306 F5.

Legal is that rare thing, a tourist magnet that hasn't lost credibility with locals. This huge and thronged restaurant has enjoyed years of success by following one simple rule: start with something fresh out of the ocean and don't screw it up.

Branches: 255 State Street (227 3115); Copley Place (266 7775); Prudential Center, 800 Boylston Street (266 6800).

Ye Olde Union Oyster House

41 Union Street, at Faneuil Hall (227 2750). Gov't Center or Haymarket T. **Open** 11am-9.30pm Mon-Thur, Sun; 11am-10pm Fri, Sat. **Main courses** $17-$33. **Credit** AmEx, DC, Disc, MC, V. **Map** p307 G4.

A recent survey by the *Boston Globe* found this 175-year-old restaurant is where most hotel concierges send tourists for the 'real Boston experience'. While

Boston stalwart **Legal Seafoods**. *See p136.*

it's debatable whether baked scrod is a contemporary experience or not, the semi-circular oyster bar, whitewashed booths and open lobster pond here fit well with the traditional tourist view of the city as an honest slice of living American history.

North End

Cafés & coffeehouses

Café Graffiti

307 Hanover Street, at Commercial Street (367 3016). Haymarket T. **Open** 6am-midnight Mon-Sat; 9am-midnight Sun. **Coffee and pastry** $6. **No credit cards. Map** p306 H3.

Graffiti is seamlessly Italian, from the cigarette smoke haze to the unsurpassed espresso to the loud guys with slicked back black hair and the hots for your girlfriend. Always busy. Always a good place to hang out and get wound up; or listen and learn.

Caffe Vittoria

296 Hanover Street at Prince Street (227 7606). Haymarket T. **Open** 9am-midnight daily. **Main courses** $6. **No credit cards. Map** p306 H3.

Vittoria claims to be the oldest Italian café in the North End, and they've got the 'practice makes perfect' goods to back it up. It's a bit of a tourist trap, but the pastries and desserts are incredible and the cappuccinos are the best and most perfectly proportioned in Boston.

European

Mamma Maria

3 North Square, at North & Prince Streets (523 0077). Haymarket T. **Open** 5-10pm Mon-Thur, Sun; 5-11pm Fri, Sat. **Main courses** $20-$23. **Credit** AmEx, DC, Disc, MC, V. **Map** p307 G3.

Top-notch Italian food is cooked extraordinarily well at this romantic corner restaurant. There are flowerboxes in the windows, candles on the tables and chairs upholstered in rich flowered tapestry.

Monica's

143 Richmond Street, at Hanover Street (227 0311). Haymarket T. **Open** 5.30-10pm Mon-Thur, Sun; 5.30-10.30pm Fri, Sat. **Main courses** $14-$24. **Credit** AmEx, MC, V. **Map** p307 H3.

Inspired by the food and traditions of their Argentinean/Italian family cooking, the Mendoza family has grown their North End empire over the past few years to include three warm and inviting businesses. Monica's Restaurant is the flagship property; their home-made pastas and soups make for comfortable Italian eats without hitting too deep in the wallet. Monica's Salumeria sells imported and domestic food, including freshly prepared selections prepared daily. And Monica's Pizzeria boasts the 'Best Sauce in The North End.' Note the quirky framed etchings and watercolours by Juan and Patrick – the family artists.

Pizzeria Regina

11 Thatcher Street, at North Margin Street (227 0765). Haymarket T. **Open** 11am-11.30pm Mon-Thur; 11am-midnight Fri, Sat; noon-11pm Sun. **No credit cards. Map** p307 G3.

One thing that strikes most visitors to the North End is that there's no pizza. But that's a misconception. There's pizza; it's just hiding. Pizzeria Regina has become a chain; but this is the original. The untameable. This is pizza at its best, and it's even better when it's washed down with a pitcher of either Budweiser or root beer. You'll smell it from around the corner, where the queue begins.

Pomodoro

319 Hanover Street, at Prince Street (367 4348). Haymarket T. **Open** noon-11pm daily. **Main courses** $13-$17. **No credit cards. Map** p306 G/H3.

The smell of sizzling garlic permeates this tiny storefront restaurant, owned by the Italian-food expert Siobhan Carew. The simple, excellent specials and pasta dishes stand out from those found at the run-of-the-mill Italian joints that clutter Hanover Street.

Prezza

24 Fleet Street, at Hanover Street (227 1577). Haymarket T. **Open** 5-10pm Mon-Thur; 5-10.30pm Fri, Sat. **Bar open** from 4.30pm Mon-Sat. **Main courses** $19-$28. **Credit** AmEx, MC, V. **Map** p307 H3.

Here's what's beautiful about this new restaurant: the sexy setting, the hip people who eat there, the bold, earthy food of Abruzzi, and the fact that it's just far enough off of the main drag so waits aren't overly absurd. As for dessert, you'd have to be crazy to go anywhere else.

Sage Restaurant

69 Prince Street, at Salem Street (248 8814). Haymarket T. **Open** 5.30-10.30pm Mon-Sat. **Main courses** $18-$25. **Credit** AmEx, DC, Disc, MC, V. **Map** p307 G/H3.

Chef Tony Susi may not be famous, but he has attracted a well-deserved cult following for the bright, herb-happy Italian food he serves in this tiny (eight-table) North End eatery. Make a reservation and get ready for something special.

Trattoria A Scalinatella

253 Hanover Street, at Richmond Street (742 8240). Haymarket T. **Open** 5-11pm daily. **Main courses** $18-$34. **Credit** AmEx, MC, V. **Map** p307 H3.

Climbing the steps to this North End cult-classic puts you into another world entirely. A world of homemade pastas, nightly meat and fish specials and significant red wine sauces. A world where the chef knits his brow – if he's in a good mood – at requests for salt or extra cheese. Not to mention one of the most exclusive, unique wine lists going. Exactly because of its easy-to-miss location, few tourists would think to try this wonderful place.

If you like 'em cold and slimy, **Ye Olde Union Oyster House** has the best. *See p136.*

Chinatown

Asian

Apollo Grill & Sushi

84 Harrison Avenue, at Kneeland Street (423 3888). Chinatown T. **Open** 11.30am-2.30pm, 5pm-4am Mon-Fri; 11.30am-2.30pm Sat, Sun. **Main courses** $17. **Credit** AmEx, DC, Disc, MC, V. **Map** p307 G5.

A pit in your table is set ablaze and an elegant Asian waitress appears baring platters of meat, lettuce, rice, bean paste and *kim chee*. The rest is up to you. Now this is living. Korean barbecue is to American barbecue what Sumo wrestling is to the World Wrestling Federation. Just as exciting, but drenched in tradition and a hell of lot classier. It's also an extremely tasty repast, and the Apollo's got it nailed. Most fun in groups of three or more.

Banh Mi

696 Washington Street, at Kneeland Street (350 6283). Chinatown T. **Open** 8am-7pm daily. **Sandwiches** $1-$2.50. **No credit cards**. **Map** p307 G5.

This little hole-in-the-wall joint derives its name from the sandwich that makes it worth visiting – a French bread stuffed with shredded carrot, radish, cilantro and spicy fish and chile sauces. The summer rolls, vermicelli and sticky rice in banana leaves are also excellent. The best part is you can eat yourself silly and barely break a ten-dollar bill.

Chau Chow City

83 Essex Street, at Ping On Street (338 8158). Chinatown T. **Open** 8am-3am daily. **Main courses** $8-$15. **Credit** AmEx, DC, Disc, MC, V. **Map** p307 G5.

Dim sum enthusiasts swear by Chau Chow City. If you're in the mood for a real Chinatown experience, you'll check it out too. Carts of luscious *shui-mai*, soups and other tasty nibbles get wheeled around while the ever-maddening crowd eats it up and shouts constantly. Unless you know your dim sum, you won't know what anything is, or what it costs. Luckily, it always ends up being pretty cheap, and what you don't know can't hurt you.

King Fung Garden

74 Kneeland Street, at Harrison Avenue (357 5262). Chinatown T. **Open** 11am-10pm daily. **Main courses** $4.75-$28. **No credit cards**. **Map** p307 G5.

It's a rundown looking shack that's too bright inside, and if you want a beer you'll have to bring your own, but this off-the-beaten-path dive also happens to be the first place where those in-the-know will look for a table. The breathtaking scallion pancakes and dumplings are rumoured to be purchased by far fancier places around town and sold at ten times what King Fung charges. For the ultimate treat, call 24 hours in advance and tell them to get a Peking duck ready – it easily serves four and costs less than a slice of duck breast across the street.

Ocean Wealth Restaurant

8 Tyler Street, at Beach Street (423 1338). Chinatown T. **Open** 11am-4am daily. **Main courses** $6.95-$10. **Credit** AmEx, MC, V. **Map** p307 G5.

Boston's not known as a particularly late-night city, but Chinatown is the exception. When it's 2am, the bars are closed and you're still hungry, you'll be glad you know of a Hong-Kong style restaurant where the fish is so fresh it's still swimming, the 'cold tea' – nudge, nudge, wink, wink – flows, and the vibe only gets more happening as the sun starts getting closer to the horizon.

Suishaya

2 Tyler Street, at Beach Street (423 3889). Chinatown T. **Open** 11.30am-2am Mon-Thur, Sun; 11.30am-3.45am Fri, Sat. **Main courses** $10.95-$27.95. **Credit** AmEx, Disc, MC, V. **Map** p307 G5.

It may not look like much, but the things they serve in this restaurant under the bright yellow awning might scare the pants off of less adventurous eaters. Half Japanese, half fiery Korean, Suishaya is famous for satisfying everything from cravings for all-you-can-eat sushi and *una don* (broiled eel) to an innate desire to conquer wonderfully mysterious bubbling cauldrons of deliciousness.

Beacon Hill

American contemporary

Beacon Hill Bistro

Beacon Hill Hotel, 25 Charles Street, at Chestnut Street (1-888 959 2442/www.beaconhillhotel.com). Charles/MGH or Arlington T. **Open** 7-10am, 11.30am-3pm, 5.30-11pm Mon-Fri; 7.30-10am, 11am-3pm, 5.30-11pm Sat; 7.30-10am, 11am-3pm, 5.30-10pm Sun. **Main courses** $13.50-$18.50. **Credit** AmEx, DC, Disc, MC, V. **Map** p306 F4.

This place is sexy, smart, delicious and you don't have to take out a loan to make it all yours. Owners Peter and Celia Rait have given their restaurant a nimble feel that makes it great for a date or an old friend. Not to mention, if things are going really well, the front desk doubles as the hotel's reservation station, and breakfast is free if you book a room. So what are you waiting for?

The Federalist

XV Beacon, 15 Beacon Street, at Park Street (670 1500/www.xvbeacon.com). Park Street T. **Open** 7-10.30am, 11.30am-2pm, 5.30-10.30pm Mon-Fri; 8am-2pm, 5.30-10.30pm Sat, Sun. **Main courses** $31-$45. **Credit** AmEx, DC, Disc, MC, V. **Map** p307 G4.

Though the press in Boston at times likes to use the Fed as a whipping boy, this restaurant is a genuinely fun yet elegant fine dining experience. Yes, it's expensive. And the room would seem stuffy were it not for the almost palpable spirit of pleasure and celebration that presides. If you can afford to eat here, it goes to reason, you can afford to be happy and enjoy your meal. The food can be extravagant and

sometimes outrageous, but every bite rings true. The service is so good it's almost comical. Just don't try charging the meal to a room you're not really staying in – it may add up to grand larceny.

Asian

Istanbul Café

37 Bowdoin Street, at Beacon Street (227 3434). Gov't Center or Park Street T. **Open** 11am-10pm Mon-Wed; 11am-11pm Thur-Sat; noon-10pm Sun. **Main courses** $12-$18. **Credit** MC, V. **Map** p307 G4.

There realy isn't much Turkish food in Boston, but even without competition this basement café behind the State House still does a decent job with Turkish favourites such as *barek*, *houmous* and a fine kebab plate: shawarma-style meat layered with tomato sauce and yoghurt over toasted cubes of bread. There are Turkish posters adorning the walls; Efes beer comes in bottles.

Lala Rokh

97 Mount Vernon Street, at Charles Street (720 5511). Charles/MGH or Arlington T. **Open** noon-3pm, 5.30-10pm Mon-Fri; 5.30-10pm Sat, Sun. **Main courses** $14-$18. **Credit** AmEx, MC, V. **Map** p306 F4.

A remarkable warren of rooms on a Beacon Hill side-street, this place serves pretty, piquant food from the Persian recipes of the owner's mother, who also mails packets of hard-to-find spices over from the Middle East. Dishes feature unusual ingredients such as pomegranate juice and sturgeon; service is helpful and the experience is one of the most unique and romantic in the city.

European

Maison Robert

Old City Hall, 45 School Street, between Tremont & Washington Streets (227 3370). Gov't Center or State/Citizen's Bank T. **Open** 11.30am-2.30pm, 5.30-10pm Mon-Fri; 5.30-10pm Sat. **Main courses** $18-$24. **Credit** AmEx, DC, MC, V. **Map** p307 G4.

This stalwart of haute-cuisine Boston is now on its second generation of French Robert family. The food recently went through a period of almost-fusion and now seems to have settled back into a more solid, classic style.

No 9 Park

9 Park Street, at Beacon Street (742 9991). Park Street T. **Open** 11.30am-2.30pm Mon-Fri; 5.30-9.30pm, Mon-Sat. **Main courses** $28-$40. **Credit** AmEx, DC, Disc, MC, V. **Map** p307 G4.

This spare and pretty Italian restaurant, chef/owner Barbara Lynch's first solo effort, is the city's most inventive-bistro-of-the-moment; the walls are clean and moss-coloured, but dining plates are crowded with fancy things such as lobster *vol-au-vents* and pheasant served with chanterelle flan. This is an excellent dining spot.

Charlestown

American contemporary

Figs

67 Main Street, at Monument Avenue (242 2229). Community College T. **Open** 5.30-10pm Mon-Thur; 5.30-10.30pm Fri; 5-10.30pm Sat; 5-9.30pm Sun. **Main courses** $11-$19. **Credit** AmEx, DC, MC, V.

After Todd English moved his influential bistro Olives (*see below*) into its current digs in City Square, he promptly opened an upmarket pizzeria in its tiny original space, making the city's connoisseurs of clam-and-oregano pizza very happy indeed. Plus, more recent expansion means he's making them happy in Beacon Hill and Newton too. This place is popular and is nearly always full, so expect to wait for a table.

Branches: 42 Charles Street (742 3447); 1208 Boylston Street, Newton (738 9992).

Olives

10 City Square, at Main Street (242 1999). North Station T. **Open** 5.30-10pm Mon-Thur; 5.30-10.15pm Fri; 5-10.15pm Sat. **Main courses** $19-$30. **Credit** AmEx, DC, MC, V.

Todd English has influenced Boston cooking like nobody since culinary grande dame Julia Child. His totally unrestrained and powerfully flavoured approach to Italian ingredients and sauces, his layers of taste upon taste, create a kind of magic that has kept the house full every night for years while inspiring all kinds of imitators. Although, be warned, no reservations are taken for parties smaller than six; the insider move is to show up the minute the restaurant opens, put your name on the list and find something else to do for a couple of hours. English's 'empire,' as it's called, is big now – a chain of Figs pizzerias; Olives in Aspen, New York and Washington, DC – and his divided attention takes its toll here and there. Still, there's nothing quite like it.

Top five: Top tables

Radius
See p135.

L'Espalier
See p129.

The Federalist
See p141.

No 9 Park
See p143.

Grill 23 & Bar
See p127.

Waterfront

American contemporary

Aura

Seaport Hotel, 1 Seaport Lane (385 4300). South Station T. **Open** 6.30am-2.30pm, 5.30-10.30pm daily. **Main courses** $11-$29. **Credit** AmEx, MC, V. **Map** p307 H5.

It's unusual that a young, talented chef like Ed Doyle should find himself in such an obscure location as this. Maybe Doyle has got the foresight to see beyond the Big Dig that surrounds his restaurant. Certainly he seems to thrive on the resources and built-in audience of a booming hotel backing him. Tasty, playful, strictly pure and seasonally fresh items – and death-defying desserts – make his menu worth the cab fare. If this place were in a trendier location, it would be the talk of the town. As it is, few locals seem to have even heard of it.

Seafood

The Barking Crab

88 Sleeper Street, at Northern Avenue (426 2722). South Station T. **Open** 11.30am-9pm daily. **Main courses** $9-$24. **Credit** AmEx, DC, MC, V. **Map** p308 H5.

Without being outright wacky, the Barking Crab is its own kind of fun. Especially in the summertime, when this is an outdoor lobster tent providing bench seating, beer in plastic cups, lobster in a paper basket and steamer clams in a bucket. In winter, the food moves indoors to a marine-themed room with a fireplace. This is not the city's best or most reliable seafood restaurant, but it remains a perennial favourite with both tourists and a large contingent of locals.

Allston/Brighton

Asian

Rangoli

129 Brighton Avenue, at Harvard Avenue, Allston (562 0200). Harvard Avenue T. **Open** 11.30am-3pm Mon-Fri; 5-10.30pm Mon-Thurs, Sat, Sun; 5-11.30pm Fri. **Main courses** $10-$11. **Credit** AmEx, DC, Disc, MC, V.

While most of Boston's Indian restaurants serve North Indian staples such as chicken tikka masala and tandoori dishes, Rangoli – a pleasant but unassuming storefront on busy Brighton Avenue – was the first to make a speciality of South Indian food. Others have followed, but Rangoli is still a bargain and a treat, with foot-long *dosai* (fried chickpea-flour pancakes) wrapped around potatoes and chicken.

Find your java joy

Even though Boston is well known as a mecca for students and bohemian types, it does seem to lack a particularly strong coffee culture. This is not to say that quality, independent coffeehouses do not exist; they do. You just have to hunt around a bit to find them. Bostonians themselves usually attribute this shortage to the Starbucks siege they've endured for the past few years. There are dozens of the ubiquitous green-and-white shops, with their large, cushy chairs. On Newbury Street alone there are three, all of which serve the usual pastries, bagels and, for the most part, high quality caffeine substances that the chain is famous for. Starbucks obviously fills a need in the coffee community, but in Boston and Cambridge it's not known for being a great place to meet a friend, or to kick back and do some studying. And don't even *think* about lighting a cigarette in one.

For all of those purposes, there are several indie coffee options centrally located in Back Bay. One is the famous **Trident Café** (*see p128*), where you can relax over coffee, tea or a vegetarian meal among an eclectic and literary crowd. Trident offers an impressive selection of hard-to-find art, literary and design magazines, as well as a full-service book store.

The **Other Side Café** (407 Newbury Street, at Massachusetts Avenue; 536 9477), on Newbury across from Tower Records is a popular hangout for artsy and musician types. There are several couches on the first floor, and table service on the ground floor. The OSC is veggie-friendly, and in addition to potent coffee, they offer an impressive selection of smoothies with add-ins like bee pollen and gingko biloba. At night it becomes a bar as well, so you can segue smoothly from coffee or carrot juice to beer, if you so choose.

For a more straight-up coffee experience, try **Torrefazione Italia Coffee** (*see p131*) on lower Newbury. Here you'll find strong Italian coffee and espresso, as well as pastries, sandwiches and an array of sodas. It's also a prime spot to sit solo, read the paper and watch people strut by on Newbury.

If people watching is your main focus, though, head over to **Café Graffiti** (*see p137*)

Eat, Drink, Shop

Latin

Tasca

1216 Commonwealth Avenue, at Washington Street, Brighton (730 8002). Washington Street T. **Open** 5-11pm Mon-Thur; 5pm-midnight Fri, Sat; 4-11pm Sun. **Tapas** $1-$5.95. **Credit** AmEx, Disc, MC, V.

What happens when an Irishman opens a tapas bar? You get a friendly, convivial Spanish-looking restaurant serving a slightly blander version of the salty and piquant tapas available downtown. The dishes are a dollar or two cheaper than other tapas bars, and the free valet parking is a convenience.

Brookline

American traditional

Washington Square Tavern

714 Washington Street, at Beacon Street, Brookline (232 8989). Washington Square T. **Open** 5.30-10pm Mon-Thur, Sun; 5.30-11pm Fri, Sat; 11.30am-2.30pm Sun. **Main courses** $10-$16. **Credit** MC, V.

Twinkling Christmas lights, bookshelves, groovy tunes and an avant-garde menu that fuses new American cuisine with French and Asian influences attract a flood of food adventurers to this hip and sparkling little jewel in the middle of nowhere.

Zaftigs

335 Harvard Street, at Babcock Street, Brookline (975 0075). Coolidge Corner T. **Open** 8am-10pm daily. **Main courses** $9.95-$12.95. **Credit** AmEx, DC, Disc, MC, V.

Maybe the most popular breakfast spot in Brookline, if not the whole Boston area, Zaftigs updates the Jewish deli for a 1990s, slightly more calorie-conscious crowd. There's a huge menu and a 45-minute wait for a table on Saturday or Sunday mornings. Book if you can (in advance at weekends).

Jamaica Plain

American contemporary

Perdix

597 Centre Street, at Pond Street, Jamaica Plain (524 5995). Green Street T. **Open** 5.30-10pm Mon-Thur, Sun; 5.30-10.30pm Fri, Sat. **Main courses** $14-$20. **Credit** AmEx, MC, V.

It's not a bistro, brasserie or a bodega; it's just a cool little place (10 tables) with great food. The lovechild of a local husband and wife team, Perdix is the epitome of a neighbourhood restaurant. The service is personal and comfortable. The wine list – all available by the bottle or the glass – hosts a number of surprises. And the accessible menu ranges on any

in the North End. This is the traditional meeting spot for animated North End natives. The atmosphere here harkens back to an earlier age. It's decorated with mementoes from Italy, and smokers can enjoy a cigarette, a cappuccino and a Italian liquor all at the same time. As a bonus, it's open till 1am.

Over in Cambridge and Somerville, there's less of an urban feel to the coffee shops, but what they lack in flash, they make up for in true coffee clout. The **1369 Coffee House** (*see p153*), is a lovely spot to sit and sip high-grade caffeine while trying home-made pastries, bagels and a small selection of sandwiches. Down the street on Prospect Avenue, **Carberry's Bakery and Coffeehouse** (*see p154*) is a popular meeting spot for Central Square residents. Local writers and students while away the hours gazing out Carberry's floor-to-ceiling windows, or munching on one of its Scandinavian pastries. They also have hearty home-made soups in the wintertime, and they offer gourmet, made-to-order sandwiches year-round.

given night from buttered club steak with potato purée to seared salmon with warm potato salad, slab bacon and chive oil.

European

Bella Luna

405 Centre Street, at Perkins Street, Jamaica Plain (524 6060). Stonybrook T. **Open** 11am-10pm Mon-Wed, Sun; 11am-11pm Thur-Sat. **Main courses** $12-$21. **Credit** AmEx, DC, Disc, MC, V.
Definitely funky. This colourful restaurant is strong in the pizza, pasta, sandwich department, and even stronger in the daily specials. Downstairs from the restaurant is a cool candlepin bowling alley – yes, there is such a thing – called the Milky Way that also serves the full Bella Luna menu and has live bands at night. Karaoke on Tuesday nights.

Latin

El Oriental de Cuba

416 Centre Street, at Paul Gore Street (524 6464). Stonybrook T. **Open** 8am-9pm Mon-Thur, Sun; 8am-10pm Fri, Sat. **Main courses** $7-$8. **Credit** MC, V.
When a restaurant has been in a neighbourhood for many years and there's still a queue out the door, chances are it's a winner. El Oriental de Cuba is just such a champion. For non-Spanish speakers, the spicy sauces and overall Cubano experience can be an adventure, culinary and cultural. For the Hispanic clientele, it's just a well-executed meal. Their Cuban sandwich – a hot pressed roll packed with roast pork, ham, Swiss cheese, lettuce, tomatoes and other condiments – is the real deal.

Cafés & coffeehouses

Coffee Cantata

605 Centre Street, at Pond Street, Jamaica Plain (522 2223). **Open** 7am-10pm Mon-Fri; 8.30am-10pm Sat; 9am-6pm Sun. **Main courses** $3.
No credit cards.
Just to step inside this zero-pretension bistro-and-beans is to be blown away. The aroma of fresh brewing coffee mixed with the rest of this café's tasty offerings is so delicious you'll be ready to eat the air. The reality that follows is pretty good too.

JP Licks

659 Centre Street, at Green Street, Jamaica Plain (524 6740). Heath Street T, then 39 bus.
Open *Oct-Apr* 6am-11pm Mon-Thur, Sun; 6am-midnight Fri, Sat. *May-Sept* 6am-midnight daily.
No credit cards.
This wild, cow-patterned café is far more than a creative frozen yoghurt shop with an 'alternative' bunch of pierced and painted employees. It also serves as a gathering place for the morning bagel-and-coffee club, as well as Jamaica Plain's unofficial town centre. Every season here has its upside: winters, get cosy by the (faux) fire. Summers are pleasant when spent *al fresco,* petting the dogs that aren't allowed inside. Medium ice-cream $4.
Branch: 352 Newbury Street, at Hereford Street (236 1666).

Top five: Cheap eats

El Pelon Taqueria
See p131.

Flash's
See p127.

Rangoli
See p144.

The Galley Diner
See p147.

Common Market
See p153.

South Boston

American traditional

Amrheins

80 West Broadway, at A Street, South Boston (268 6189). Broadway T. **Open** 11am-10pm Mon-Thur; 11am-11pm Fri, Sat; 9am-8pm Sun. **Main courses** $8.95-$16.95. **Credit** AmEx, Disc, MC, V.
Map p308 G6.
You don't stay in business 110 years without doing a few things right. Amrheins, one of Boston's oldest restaurants, happens to do a lot of things right. Amrheins had the first draught beer pump system in Boston. And while folks at some of the new 'organic pubs' in Charlestown are getting their elbows wet on some newfangled bar, Southie's finest can still rest their beers on the oldest hand carved bar in America. Amrheins draws the neighbourhood with waitresses who call everyone 'buddy', and hometown favourites including the enormously popular giant free-form home-made chicken pie and self-proclaimed 'Boston's Best' lobster and scallop pie. Dessert? Boston cream pie or Guinness, naturally.

The Galley Diner

11 P Street, at East First Street, South Boston (464 0141). Broadway T, then 9 or 11 bus. **Open** 5am-8pm daily. **Main courses** $6-$7. **No credit cards.**
'This is not Burger King,' reads the sign on the wall. 'You don't get it your way. You take it my way. Or you don't get the damn thing.' It's no joke either. Exceptional is the order that is delivered as ordered; but that's part of the charm. It's all good here (especially the Southie omelette made with home-made corn beef hash). As for the service with a grin rather than a smile, well, that's just their spe-

Elegance at its best at **Rialto**.

cial way of expressing gratitude for your patronage. When it comes down to it, these folks could hardly be nicer.

Cafés & coffeehouses

Café Arpeggio

398 West Broadway, at F Street (269 8822). Broadway T, then 9 bus. **Open** 6am-10pm Mon-Fri; 7am-10pm Sat, Sun. **Main courses** $3. **No credit cards**.

This nice clean peaceful oasis, pleasantly out of place in its surroundings of pizza joints and pharmacies, provides respite for residents of South Boston looking for a fresh brewed cup of gourmet snicka-doodle, home-baked pastries, home-churned ice-creams and tasty sandwiches. Plenty of light to read by and comfortably upholstered chairs to boot.

Cambridge

American contemporary

Blue Room

1 Kendall Square, between Hampshire Street & Cardinal Madeiros Avenue, Cambridge (494 9034). Kendall/MIT T. **Open** 5.30-10pm Mon-Thur; 5.30-10.30pm Fri, Sat; 11am-2.30pm, 5.30-10pm Sun. **Main courses** $18-$24. **Credit** AmEx, DC, Disc, MC, V.

Kendall Square's purple, green and peach-themed Blue Room brings New American fusion to the grill, pairing seared tuna with tomatillos or enlivening beef skirt with *kim chee*. The seasonal menu, elegant brunch and lively bar keep the clientele faithful. The menu here changes monthly as chefs make use of fresh local produce.

East Coast Grill

1271 Cambridge Street, at Prospect Street, Cambridge (491 6568). Central T. **Open** 5.30-10pm Mon-Thur, Sun; 5.30-10.30pm Fri, Sat. **Main courses** $6.50-$23.50; **Credit** AmEx, Disc, MC, V.

This high-minded grill joint began the gentrification of Inman Square, and its shift towards seafood over recent years promises the colourful, always-packed ECG (and its patrons) a long life. Everything is fresh, well-spiced (although not always hot) and the hungry regularly queue up for more than an hour for grilled oysters and ingenious side dishes, such as the Asian-inspired slaws. Regular 'hotter than hell' nights bring out the macho element, as does the Sunday brunch Bloody Mary bar, with its assortment of peppers and salsas.

Henrietta's Table

Charles Hotel, 1 Bennett Street, Cambridge (661 5005). Harvard T. **Open** 6.30-11am Mon-Fri. Sun; noon-3pm Mon-Fri, Sun; 5.30-10pm Mon-Fri, Sun; 5.30-11pm Sat. **Main courses** $9-$15. **Credit** AmEx, DC, MC, V. **Map** p311 B2.

Set in the Charles Hotel, this upmarket take on a New England farmers' market focuses on fresh and honest fare. That means the chef doesn't buy so-called Frankenfoods, and that every bite offers the entire true flavour of nature. It also makes every meal here a popular one, so make reservations.

Rialto

Charles Hotel, 1 Bennett Street, Cambridge (661 5050/www.rialto-restaurant.com). Harvard T. **pen** 5.30-10pm Mon-Thur, Sun; 5.30-11pm Fri, Sat. **Main courses** $20-$36. **Credit** AmEx, DC, MC, V. **Map** p311 B3.

Relax on one of the overstuffed banquettes and enjoy the latest in chef Jody Adams' offerings: Mediterranean/Italian-influenced combinations of tuna, veal and what have you, meticulously prepared and fancifully presented by waiters who know their stuff cold. Many swear by desserts, such as the stellar hot chocolate cream.

American traditional

B Side Lounge

92 Hampshire Street, at Windsor Street, Cambridge (354 0766/www.bsidelounge.com). Kendall T. **Open** 5.30pm-midnight Mon-Thur, Sun; 5.30pm-1am Fri, Sat. **Main courses** $10-$15. **Credit** AmEx, MC, V. **Map** p306 D3.

It's the hippest, most happening, hardest to find restaurant in Boston – and it's in Cambridge. Though this funky place with great food, rough-sexy waitstaff and killer musical arrangements has gone a little more upscale of late, they still have free hard-boiled eggs at the bar. The menu is whimsical and seasonal, tweaking the familiar where you'd least expect it. Think chicken fried steak sandwich, steamed mussels with lime, ginger and white wine sauce, and divine baked gouda.

Cambridge Common

1667 Massachusetts Avenue, at Sacramento Street, Cambridge (547 1228). Harvard or Porter T. **Open** 11am-1am Sun; 11.30am-1am Mon-Wed; 11.30am-2am Thur-Sat. **Main courses** $5.95-$9.95. **Credit** AmEx, DC, Disc, MC, V. **Map** p311 B1.

Handy for comfort food such as chicken pie and meat loaf, all at family prices. The only frills come in the amount of blue cheese melted on the blue chips or the generous size of the Cosmopolitans, but few complain when they slide into the big wooden booths at this welcoming retreat.

Central Kitchen

567 Massachusetts Avenue, at Salem Street, Cambridge (491 5599). Central T. **Open** 5.30-11pm daily. **Main courses** $14-$22. **Credit** AmEx, MC, V. **Map** p311 C3.

On a good night, this is your all-around all-time great vibrant bistro complete with waiters with good attitudes who love food and wine. And a chef who laughs. And chalkboard specials that are very hard to choose between. On a bad night, it's none of those things, though. There is one dish here, however, that does everything right and will never change, never go away and never fail to please if not redeem: the fabulous Mussels from Brussels. This is a huge bowl of mussels and *frites* drizzled with such a tasty sauce that you'll be slurping up when the food is gone regardless of how crude you look. Oh yeah.

Chez Henri

1 Shepherd Street, at Massachusetts Avenue, Cambridge (354 8980). Harvard or Porter T. **Open** 6-10pm Mon-Thur; 5.30-11pm Fri, Sat; 5.30-9pm, Sun. **Main courses** $18-$29. **Credit** AmEx, DC, MC, V. **Map** p311 B1.

Sometimes the French and Cuban fusion comes together wonderfully, for instance when a moist, tangy duck tamale garnishes a meal-sized warm spinach salad. At other times, this popular little bistro splits its dishes with flair – as in the bouillabaisse with a side dish of *tostones* (fried plantain).

A truly local coffeeshop

Ask any Bostonian how they feel about the coffee and doughnut chain **Dunkin' Donuts**, and chances are the response you get will be anything but lukewarm. Whether they love it or hate it, Boston residents either gleefully or begrudgingly acknowledge that Dunkin' Donuts is a local institution. It certainly feels like there is a distinctively pink and silver D&D branch on every other block. That's, at least in part, because the nationwide branch started just down the road.

The first Dunkin' Donuts opened in 1950 in Quincy, Massachusetts. Its founder, William Rosenberg, opened a coffee shop there called the Open Kettle in 1948. Two years later he renamed it Dunkin' Donuts. The name, by the way, was allegeldy inspired when the actress Mae Murray accidentally dropped a doughnut into her coffee while dining at Lindy's Deli on Broadway in New York.

Some Bostonians love this greasy spoon chain. In fact, they swear by it. Dunkin'

aficionados run the gamut from construction workers to punk rockers, postal workers and seemingly the entire police force in the city of Boston.

In part, this has little to do with the doughnuts. The attraction is the coffee here, which is legendary. A 'regular' coffee comes doused with cream and sugar. Fair warning: it's addictive. And a heck of a lot cheaper than the java served in many of the trendier coffee shops in Boston.

Truly Original
Time Out
LONDON'S
LIVING GUIDE
EVERY WEEK
timeout.com

Quieter in the summer, with tall open windows, and boisterous in the winter, Chez Henri and its adjoining bar qualify as a first-class neighbourhood secret.

House of Blues

96 Winthrop Street, at John F Kennedy Street, Cambridge (491 2583). Harvard T. **Open** 11.30am-11pm daily. Gospel brunch on Sundays, 3 seatings: 10am, noon, 2pm. **Main courses** $7-$18. **Credit** AmEx, DC, Disc, MC, V. **Map** p311 B2.

The food reflects the music on the first floor of this small Harvard Square club, the first of the national chain. That means Southern, with a rich, if somewhat unimpressive tomato-packed, jambalaya, jalapeno-studded cornbread and a respectably dark gumbo. The acts upstairs can be seen and heard via video monitors, so you can linger over your bread pudding. *See also p223.*

S&S Deli Restaurant

1334 Cambridge Street, at Prospect Street, Cambridge (354 0777). Lechmere T, then 69 bus. **Open** 7am-11pm Mon-Wed; 7am-midnight Thur, Fri; 8am-midnight Sat; 8am-10pm Sun. **Main courses** $10. **Credit** AmEx , MC, V.

A great, basic deli where breakfast is served until closing time. Join the queue at this 80-year-old Inman Square institution for bagels and overflowing omelettes on Sunday mornings, or slide into a booth for late-night comfort food and ridiculously rich desserts. Fancier daily specials are sometimes overambitious and seafood is often overcooked, but basics such as onion-packed chopped liver and piled-on pastrami never fail.

Asian

Common Market

1815 Massachusetts Avenue, at Porter Exchange, Cambridge. Porter T. **No credit cards**. **Map** p311 B1.

Actually a conglomerate of six small restaurants, this mini-mall in the Porter Exchange shopping building is the heart of Little Asia for North Cambridge and serves excellent Japanese fare at rock-bottom prices. Sit down at the sushi bar at Kotobukiya (492 4655; open noon-8.30pm Mon-Sat; noon-6.30pm Sun) for fast, fresh nori rolls. Or belly up to big bowls of noodle soups at Tampopo (868 5457; open noon-9pm Mon-Sat, noon-8pm Sun) or a curried cutlet at Café Mami (547 9130; open noon-9pm Mon-Sat, noon-7pm Sun. Main courses $7).

Korea Garden

20 Pearl Street, at Massachusetts Avenue, Cambridge (492 9643). Central T. **Open** noon-10.30pm Mon-Sat. **Main courses** $10. **Credit** Disc, MC, V. **Map** p311 C3.

Tucked in among Central Square's ethnic restaurant enclave, this family-run storefront Korean has been delivering cheap and hearty food to garlic-loving locals for almost two decades. With big bowls of the egg, meat and veggie *bi bim bap* and sweet-hot *bulgogi* barbecue for comfort, as well as the eye-stinging heat of *yuk kai jang* soup, this fine little restaurant sustains the Seoul of the city.

Cafés & coffeehouses

1369 Coffee House

1369 Cambridge Street, at Hampshire Street, Cambridge (576 1369). Lechmere T, then 69 bus. **Open** 7am-11pm Mon-Fri; 8am-11pm Sat; 8am-10pm Sun. **Coffee and pastry** $4. **No credit cards**. **Map** p306 D2.

This is as much a hangout for bicycle couriers on break and Cantabridgian musicians as anything else. The 1369s know how to crank out high-power java. The scene here is always buzzing.

Branch: 757 Massachusetts Avenue at Inman Street, Cambridge (576 4600).

Carberry's Bakery and Coffeehouse

74 Prospect Street, at Massachusetts Avenue, Cambridge (576 3530). Central T. **Open** 6am-8pm daily. **Coffee and pastry** $3. **Credit** AmEx, DC, Disc, MC, V. **Map** p311 C3.

The best Lobster spots

It's really hard to mess up a lobster. It's even harder to make a crustacean stand out in Boston's lobster crowd. Here are five worth breaking out the bib out for:

Legal Seafoods

The sheer volume they crank out guarantees amazing freshness. *See p136.*

Ye Olde Union Oyster House

Watch 'em swim in an open pit before you eat 'em. *See p136.*

Ambrosia on Huntington

Have you ever seen a martini with a giant saki marinated lobster claw reaching out of the glass? It's a beautiful thing. *See p128.*

The Barking Crab

Served New England style with corn and butter, and startlingly cheap. *See p144.*

Amrheins

They've been cooking the little monsters for more than a century. *See p147.*

Eat, Drink, Shop

For an Icelandic bakery set in a former auto supply shop just off Central Square, Carberry's has caught on fast. It could be the outsize fruit-studded scones, the marzipan-rich pastries or simply the huge windows, which make the café tables inside almost as light and airy as those lining the parking lot.

International

Baraka Café

80 Pearl Street, at Williams Street, Cambridge (868 3951). Central T. **Open** 11.30am-3pm Sun-Tue; 5.30-10pm Tue-Sun. **Main courses** $17. **No credit cards**. **Map** p311 C4.

How this amazing, lusty, colourful, exotic Tunisian restaurant remains such a secret to even Central Square locals is as much a mystery to us as how the owner here sometimes manages to cook for and wait on eight tables while simultaneously yapping away into a cordless phone crunched between her head and shoulder. Everything from the fresh mint green tea to the ever-evolving, savoury menu and the astonishing flourless chocolate torte with star anise, black pepper, saffron and ginger is lovingly and perfectly prepared.

Centro

720 Massachusetts Avenue, at Pleasant Street, Cambridge (enter through the Good Life) (868 2405). Central T. **Open** 5.30-10pm Mon-Thur; 5.30-11pm Fri, Sat; 4.30-9pm Sun. **Main courses** $12-$19. **Credit** AmEx, DC, MC, V. **Map** p311 C3.

Meet the little restaurant that could. The triumph and pride of all Central Square, this tiny ten-table Italian restaurant doesn't even have its own door in the winter. It shares a kitchen and a bar with an ever-happening jazzy nightclub. And it rocks so hard that even the most notoriously venomous local restaurant reviewer couldn't help but bestow upon it three stars (out of four). So, what's to love? Everything, really. But especially pork chops that open your eyes; soft polenta that will make you close them and sigh; and service that treats you the same whether you're wearing a slutty she-devil outfit or a tux.

Latin

Forest Café

1682 Massachusetts Avenue, at Sacramento Street, Cambridge (661 7810). Porter T. **Open** 11.30am-2.30pm Mon-Sat; 5-10pm Mon-Thur, Sun; 5-11pm Fri, Sat. **Main courses** $11-$15. **Credit** AmEx, DC, Disc, MC, V. **Map** p311 B1.

The closest many Cantabridgians will come to Mexico's two coastlines is this long, narrow barroom. Here the daily catch comes served with sauces of pumpkin seed and cilantro (coriander) while shrimp soak up garlic and herbs. Non-fish-eaters can enjoy a smoky mole chicken or enchilada, and it all comes at barroom prices.

Midwest Grill

1124 Cambridge Street, at Norfolk Street, Cambridge (354 7536). Lechmere T, then 61 bus. **Open** 11.30am-11.30pm daily. **Main courses** $14.95-$18.95. **Credit** AmEx, DC, Disc, MC, V.

This Brazilian restaurant is a carnivore's dream. In the churrascaria tradition of primal dinner theatre, everything is grilled and the spits taken from table to table, where waiters lop off peppery sausages and crispy chicken parts or carve from melting tenderloins and joints. The accompanying salad bar – with rice, beans and hearts of palm – is the only concession to nutritional balance.

Somerville

American contemporary

Eat

253 Washington Street, at Somerville Avenue, Somerville (776 2889). Central or Harvard T. **Open** 6-10pm Mon-Thur; 6-10.30pm Fri, Sat; 5.30-9.30pm Sun. **Main courses** $14-$19. **Credit** DC, Disc, MC, V.

This cosy eclectic place is so eager to feed that its name insists that you nourish yourself. The menu draws upon various influences, from Cajun-style catfish and jasmine rice to Italian antipasto and pasta. At Eat, nothing is fancy. The theme is one of comfort – the old armchairs make you feel at home.

Gargoyles on the Square

215 Elm Street, at Russell Street, Somerville (776 5300). Davis T. **Open** 5.30-10pm Tue-Thur, Sun; 5.30-10.30pm Fri, Sat. **Main courses** $14-$21. **Credit** AmEx, Disc, MC, V.

Perhaps the snazziest restaurant in Davis Square, Gargoyles has a moderately priced menu of well-presented and excellently prepared American food. The intimate tables make this a good spot for a date. The Martinis can make even a bad date bearable.

American traditional

Johnny D's

17 Holland Street, Somerville (776 2004). Davis T. **Open** 4.30-9.30pm Tue-Sat; 9am-2.30pm Sat, Sun. **Main courses** $9-$15. **Credit** AmEx, Disc, MC, V.

Mostly known for its eclectic live music schedule, Johnny D's also serves up creative Southern fare spiced up with a grab bag of ethnic influences. So, alongside chicken wings and sweet potato fries, there's a daily risotto and aubergine tagine.

Redbones

55 Chester Street, at Elm Street, Somerville(628 2200). Davis T. **Open** 11.30am-10.30pm Mon-Thur, Sun; 11.30am-11.30pm Fri, Sat. **Main courses** $8-$19. **No credit cards.**

Ranked among the best of the Boston area's barbecue spots, this Davis Square favourite is stocked with slow-cooks succulent ribs and brisket in the

At **Dali** the waiters eat and *you* serve *them*. Just kidding. Clearly they serve themselves.

classic Southern style. Flaky fried catfish, spongy cornbread and spicy corn pudding are among the 'lighter' offerings. Huge platters, such as the nearly foot-high pile of ribs and brisket called the 'Barbecue Belt', will put you in a meat coma. As good as Southern cooking gets this far north.

Rosebud Diner

381 Summer Street, at Elm Street, Somerville (666 6015). Davis T. **Open** 8am-11pm Sun-Thur; 8am-midnight Fri, Sat. **Main courses** $5.95-$13.95. **Credit** AmEx, MC, V.

A restored dining car from 1941, Rosebud Diner is a beacon of old-fashioned Americana in the gentrified Davis Square neighborhood. Traditional diner fare (hamburgers, clam chowder, steak tips) is served in an atmosphere of shiny chrome and pink neon that's straight out of *American Graffiti*.

European

Dali

415 Washington Street, at Beacon Street, Somerville (661 3254). Harvard T. **Open** 5.30-11pm daily. **Main courses** $18-$23. **Tapas** $3.50-$25. **Credit** AmEx, DC, MC, V. **Map** p311 C2.

Dali, decidedly one of the best eateries in the Boston area, also features some of the best flamenco-dancing waiters you'll find this side of the Atlantic. The atmosphere is animated, from the chatter at the bar to the lively Spanish music. There's usually a queue (reservations are only accepted for large parties) for those waiting to try the dizzying array of savoury and creative tapas. The sangria's great here, but don't miss the exceptional list of wines and sherries. Ask for one of the booth tables if it's intimacy that you're after.

Evoo

118 Beacon Street, at Washington Street, Somerville (661 3866). Harvard T, then 87 bus. **Open** 6-10pm Mon-Thur; 6-11pm Fri; 5-11pm Sat. **Main courses** $16-$27. **Credit** AmEx, Disc, MC, V. **Map** p311 C2.

An acronym for extra virgin olive oil, Evoo is *the* Mediterranean spot in Somerville, featuring a wild ensemble of tastes in its wide array of dishes. Chef Peter McCarthy cooks up adventurous variations of seafood, quail, soups, beef tenderloin and chicken. All the buzz since its opening, this is perhaps the only Somerville restaurant that can get away with charging South End prices.

Pubs & Bars

Spend all your money on whiskey and gin in the hub of the Irish pub universe.

Drinks for all my friends at the **Bukowski Tavern**. *See p157.*

As Boston's economic boom continues, so too does the proliferation of the Hub's pubs and bars. It can be hard to keep up as the places that are deemed fashionable can change before you've downed your triple-chocolate yoghurt martini with a twist of guava, munched on your asparagus pizza and politely asked the guy next to you to stop blowing smoke in your direction.

A few years ago, Irish pubs were the rage. Then it was brew pubs. Today, discerning bar-hoppers flock to the polished lounge bars that have popped up all over the city. Next week – who knows? They could all be sipping *piva* at Russian-style *kioskis*. Guessing what's next is half the fun. Drinking, of course, is the other half.

ALCOHOL AND THE LAW

The legal drinking age in Boston is 21, but carry photo ID if you look anything under 30.

SAFETY

The MBTA ends the subway service at 12.30am – a good half an hour before most bars' last call. If you miss the T, cabs are plentiful and relatively easy to hail. *See chapter* **Directory** for cab companies.

Back Bay & South End

An Tua Nua

835 Beacon Street, at Milner Street (262 2121). Kenmore T. **Open** 11am-1am Mon-Wed; 11am-2am Thur-Sun. **Credit** AmEx, DC, Disc, MC, V.

Formerly known as RíRá, this Fenway favourite recently rechristened itself An Tua Nua (Gaelic for 'the new beginning'). The name may have changed, but it's still the same hybrid of Irish pub and dance club, meaning that it's a fine place to either stop in for a quiet afternoon pint or shoehorn yourself into a seething mass of sweaty BU co-eds bumping and grinding to the latest dance hits.

Audubon Circle Restaurant Bar

838 Beacon Street, at Park Drive (421 1910). Kenmore T. **Open** 11.30am-1am Mon-Fri; 5pm-1am Sat, Sun. (Food served until 11pm.) **Credit** AmEx, DC, Disc, MC, V.

With its angular slate counters, wooden bar-back and subdued lighting, Audubon is one of the more stylish drinking establishments in Boston. It's a comfortable distance from student-riddled Kenmore Square and has an agreeable laid-backness to it. It does terrific food too. (*See p122*).

Barcode

955 Boylston Street (421 1818). Hynes/ICA T. **Open** 11.30am-2am daily. **Credit** AmEx, DC, Disc, MC, V. **Map** p306 E5.

This swanky bar for people who can't be bothered to verbalise names – the name is technically an unpronounceable symbol – caters to the nouveau riche and international student sets that are currently overrunning the Hub. Technically more of a restaurant than a bar, Barcode is still stocked with all the expensive booze a yuppie could hope for.

Beacon Hill Tavern

228 Cambridge Street, at Charles Street (742 6192). Government Center T. **Open** 11am-2am daily. **Credit** AmEx, DC, MC, V. **Map** p307 G4.

A place where young urban professionals and State House denizens gather to compare power suits, the Tavern is something of an upstart among Boston bars, and, judging by the enormous weekend crowds, a surprisingly popular one.

Bill's Bar

5 Lansdowne Street, at Brookline Avenue (421 9678). Kenmore T. **Open** 9pm-2am Mon, Wed-Fri; 10pm-2am Tue, Sat, Sun. **Credit** AmEx, MC, V. **Map** p306 D5.

Among the hip nightclubs dotting Lansdowne Street, Bill's offers welcome respite from the clang and clatter of their dark and sweaty dance floors. If there's no live music, you can actually hear yourself think in here – not necessarily a good thing for many teen-something clubgoers.

Boston Beer Works

61 Brookline Avenue (536 2337). Kenmore or Fenway T. **Open** 11.30am-1am daily. **Credit** AmEx, MC, V. **Map** p306 D5.

Across the street from Fenway Park, BBW can be overrun with fans from April through September. But it's worth popping in here any time of year, if only for the beer they brew on premises: hearty, dark brews like the Beantown Nut Brown Ale and the Buckeye Oatmeal Stout. At any given time, there are between 12 and 16 of their creations on tap. They're all perfect complements to the menu of above-par burgers and munchables.

Bukowski Tavern

50 Dalton Street, at Boylston Street (437 9999). Hynes/ICA T. **Open** 11.30am-2am daily. **No credit cards. Map** p306 E5.

This tiny bar, wedged between the Mass Pike and the Cheri cinema, used to be a dive called Jack Lynch's Webster Lounge. Refurbished and renamed (after the poet Charles Bukowski, the patron saint of the types who used to frequent Lynch's), the bar caters to a hip, young crowd, plus a smattering of old regulars and the occasional businessman. So large is the bar's beer selection (over one hundred different kinds) the staff have set up a wheel of indecision, which, when spun, will make the choice for you. Though the bar serves wine, there are no spirits. As one employee put it: 'It's all about beer.'

Clery's

113 Dartmouth Street, at Columbus Avenue (262 9874). Back Bay or Copley T. **Open** 11am-2am daily. **Credit** AmEx, DC, Disc, MC, V. **Map** p306 F6.

Large, labyrinthine and lively, Clery's attracts a refreshingly mixed crowd. Business types and the megahip lean over frothing pints and heaped plates of grilled meat. If this place is anything to go by, we can all get along just fine.

Daisy Buchanan's

240A Newbury Street, at Fairfield Street (247 8516). Copley T. **Open** 11.30am-2am daily. **No credit cards. Map** p306 E5.

A favourite haunt of the romantically challenged, Daisy Buchanan's often resembles the set of the television game show *The Dating Game*. Though it can be interesting watching guys with enormous pecs pursue girls with enormous, um, eyelashes, if you are not large of pec or lash, you should probably keep walking. If you do stay, keep an eye peeled for the occasional Red Sox or Celtic star.

Delux Café

100 Chandler Street, at Clarendon Street (338 5258). Back Bay T. **Open** 5pm-1am Mon-Sat. **No credit cards. Map** p306 F5/6.

A shrine to all things kitsch, Delux is a good place if you're in the mood to cosy up with the young and hip. And cosy up is right, too: the place is as small as it is popular, the latter thanks largely to some fine micro-brews and even finer food. The decor in the toilets is worth checking out.

Jillian's

145 Ipswich Street, at Lansdowne Street (437 0300). Kenmore T. **Open** 11am-2am daily. **Credit** AmEx, DC, MC, V. **Map** p306 D5.

A whizz-banging, whirring, ding-donging megaplex, Jillian's is the kind of place where beer is barely necessary for those seeking intoxication. With a full arcade, a mock-casino, pool tables galore, and other assorted amusements, the sensory overload alone at this three-storey fantasy land is hangover-inducing before you've even started drinking.

Lava Bar

575 Commonwealth Avenue, at Kenmore Square (267 7707). Kenmore T. **Open** 10pm-2am Tue, Thur-Sun. **Credit** AmEx, MC, V. **Map** p306 D5.

The top floor of a Howard Johnson's is the last place you would expect to find a trendy dance club. But here, at the top of the Kenmore Square HoJo, is the Lava Bar, with its breathtaking vistas of the city, a close-up view of the famous neon Citgo sign, and nary a business suit in sight. Cover can be steep, but the ride up the elevator is oddly satisfying. And, should you need a short respite from getting down with your bad self, huge comfy couches await you and your Cosmopolitan.

The Oak Room

Fairmont Copley Plaza, 138 St James Avenue, at Dartmouth Street (267 5300 ext 1638). Back Bay or

It's a short way to Tipperary

It should be no surprise to anybody that Boston's streets are lined with Irish pubs. The city is so proud of its Celtic heritage you feel you should be treading on shamrocks and dodging leprechauns as you walk down the street. Admittedly, the Irish thing can get a little cloying – especially considering that Boston is so multi-cultural nowadays – however, when it comes to pubs, the Irish ones are the best in town. From the new swank Irish-lounge hybrids (God help us), to the traditional Guinness-and-Harp versions, it seems there actually is an Irish pub for everyone, just as Bostonians believe, with endless optimism, that there's a little Irish in all of us. It's worth noting that many of Boston's most successful Irish-oriented drinking establishments can be traced back – or, depending on your perspective, blamed on – the **Brendan Behan Pub** in Jamaica Plain. This was sort of the granddaddy of local pubs. Many of the city's best sit-and-drink facilities – including the **Thirsty Scholar Pub** in Somerville (*see p170*) and the **The Field** in Cambridge (*see p167*) – were either founded by the folks who gave us the Behan, or by their family and friends.

Brendan Behan Pub

378 Center Street, at Sherridan Street, Jamaica Plain (522 5386). Stony Brook T. **Open** 11.30am-1am Mon-Sat; 11am-midnight Sun. **No credit cards.**

Whether coming here for a quiet game of afternoon cribbage or for its nightly standing-room-only seisúns, fans of the Behan rank the small Irish bar alongside the polio vaccine in the benefit-to-mankind stakes. Dimly-lit, smoky, often packed to the gills with a young, lively crowd, the success of this pub paved the way for the spate of Irish bars that subsequently engulfed the JP area. The Borstal Boy would be proud.

Copley T. **Open** 4.30pm-1am daily. **Credit** AmEx, Disc, MC, V. **Map** p306 F5.

So this is how the other half live. From the high ceilings and the panelled walls to the plush furniture, the Oak Room (in the Plaza Hotel) simply oozes class. Sink back into an easy chair, light up a cigar (if you are so inclined) and slurp down one of the bar's delicious cognacs out of a magnificent snifter. Then get the hell out of there before you spend your entire holiday allowance. A Martini costs $15, but is served in a miniature pitcher, resting on ice in a gorgeous bowl, with the biggest olives you've ever seen. (*For the* **Fairmont Copley Plaza** *see p48*).

Other Side Cosmic Café

407 Newbury Street, at Massachusetts Avenue (536 9477). Hynes/ICA T. **Open** 10am-midnight Mon-Thur; 10am-1am Fri-Sat; noon-midnight Sun. **No credit cards. Map** p306 E5.

At the tail end of Newbury Street, across Mass Ave from the trendy parts of Back Bay, the Other Side has become a sort of Galapagos Island of Newbury Street bars, attracting a whole different kettle of clientele. Scruffy, bohemian and often goateed, this crowd is equally at home sipping carrot-based cocktails or beer. If you feel that you can't even bear to look at another Martini (and God help you, if that's the case), then this is the place to head for.

Sevens Pub

77 Charles Street, at Mount Vernon Street (523 9074). Charles/MGH T. **Open** 11.30am-1am Mon-Fri; noon-1am Sat, Sun. **No credit cards. Map** p306 F4.

Though often prohibitively crowded, this unpretentious little pub is also a good spot to seek respite from a day of relentless sightseeing. Find a booth in the corner, settle down with a Guinness or a Bass and you may find the Freedom Trail ends right here.

Sonsie

327 Newbury Street, between Hereford Street & Massachusetts Avenue (351 2500). Hynes/ICA T. **Open** 7am-1am daily. **Credit** AmEx, DC, MC, V. **Map** p306 E5.

Known mainly as a restaurant, the tasteful Sonsie is possibly the premier hangout spot for the Newbury Street elite and those who want to meet them. The bar is usually packed to the gills with the chattering classes. The service here is phenomenal. No matter how busy it is, you could hold your breath when you enter and be served before you expire. (*See also p122*).

29 Newbury Street

29 Newbury Street, at Arlington Street (536 0290). Arlington T. **Open** 11.30am-1am daily. **Credit** AmEx, DC, Disc, MC, V. **Map** p306 F5.

Though primarily a restaurant, 29 also has a thriving little bar area where Boston's PR and media power players get together to chug Martinis and call each other darling. With its cast of regulars, the place is almost like a classy, upscale *Cheers*. There's no Norm, though.

Wally's Cafe

427 Massachusetts Avenue (424 1408) Massachusetts Avenue T. **Open** 9am-2am Mon-Sat; noon-2am Sun. **No credit cards. Map** p306 E6.

Around since 1947, this dimly lit little jazz club has hosted some of the giants. And it as as close as you will get in Boston to the classic smoky grottoes of yesteryear. The first saxophone usually starts at 9pm nightly, with special Sunday afternoon sessions from 3.30-7.30pm. The beer is cheap, cover is nonexistent and space is tight. So, what are you waiting for, hep cat?

Whiskey Park

54 Arlington Street, at the Park Plaza Hotel (542 1482). Arlington T. **Open** 4pm-2am daily. **Credit** AmEx, MC, DC, V. **Map** p306 F5.

Founded by Cindy Crawford hubby and baby food heir Randy Gerber, this swank new spot has nothing to do with babies. No, this bar, the Boston branch of a group of sleek drinkeries in New York, LA and Chicago, is very adult. A playground for the rich and sometimes famous, Whiskey Park features plush, overstuffed leather furniture, subdued lighting, and quality, but expensive, drinks.

Downtown & Government Centre

Backstage

245 Quincy Marketplace Building (726 1110). Government Center or Haymarket T. **Open** noon-2am daily. **Credit** AmEx, MC, V. **Map** p307 G4.

In the heart of Quincy Market, Backstage is a sign that trendier days are coming to this stuffy old tourist spot. The bar's cavernous space thrums with dance music, flickers with chaotic lights and heaves with the bodies of the young and supple. The staff spend their spare time practising Tom Cruise-like bottle-flinging moves (one bartender catches them in her cleavage).

Bell in Hand Tavern

45-55 Union Street (227 2098). Government Center or Haymarket T. **Open** 11.30am-2am daily. **Credit** AmEx, MC, V. **Map** p307 G4.

Built in 1795, this is 'the oldest tavern in the US', as a plaque outside attests. Yet there's little 'Ye Olde' nonsense going on here. The clientele is largely young regulars and you'll find them nose to elbow Tuesday through Saturday when the bar has live music. Perhaps they're drawn by the unpretentious decor, which has been described as Woolworthian. Outside the window stands Boston's hauntingly beautiful Holocaust Memorial.

Bishop's Pub

21 Boylston Place, between Charles & Tremont Streets (351 2583). Boylston T. **Open** 5pm-2am Mon-Fri; 7pm-2am Sat. **Credit** AmEx, MC, V. **Map** p306 F5.

In 'the Alley' – an area with lots of clubs – Bishop's is something of a pit-stop for the giggling clouds of hairspray that float from club to club. Things don't really get started in here until after 11pm and then you'll be lucky if you can breathe, let alone move.

The Black Rose

160 State Street, at Commercial Street (742 2286). Gov't Center or State/Citizen's Bank T. **Open** 11.30am-2am Mon-Fri, Sun; 8am-2am Sat. **Credit** AmEx, DC, MC, V. **Map** p307 G4.

There are Irish Republican proclamations adorning the walls. And the faces of Republican patriots gaze down with stern dignity. But don't let that put you off. If you fancy a singsong, this is your place to head. The bar has live Irish music '364 nights a year' (it's closed on Christmas day). From Thursdays to Saturdays the bar opens its upstairs section for music and dancing.

Brew Moon

115 Stuart Street, at Tremont Street (523 6467). Boylston T. **Open** 11.30am-12.30am daily. **Credit** AmEx, MC, V. **Map** p307 G5.

Every brewery-restaurant has to distinguish itself somehow, and Brew Moon was the first to break from the Brit pack and go modern. Its clean steel tanks and inexpensive New American menu have been so successful that the place has cloned itself in Cambridge and even Hawaii. This was the original, and it's still busy. As with most brewpub beer, the

Don't miss Bars

Plough and Stars
A Cambridge classic. Watch UK football on Saturday afternoon as sunlight filters through cigarette smoke and plays on the red walls. *See p169.*

Sunset Grill
Beerward, ho! Decor is minimal, but the selection (450 brands) is immense. *See p165.*

The Black Rose
A tad touristy? Perhaps. But with its flag bedecked rafters and traditional music, it's a Boston Irish legend. *See p159.*

Toad & Lizard Lounge
It may be small, but cram yourself inside for great nightly music. *See p170.*

Lock-Ober
See what Boston was like in 1875 when Brahmins ruled. *See p162.*

Doyle's
A place where cops and politicians go to drink. Boston at its best. *See p166.*

Thirsty Scholar Pub
Catering to some of the best and brightest in Cambridge – and the world. See p170.

product tends towards the bitter; to play it safe try the sampler of five small glasses in a steel rack. **Branch**: 50 Church Street, Cambridge (499 2739).

Bristol Lounge

Four Seasons Hotel, 200 Boylston Street, at Arlington Street (351 2071). Arlington T. **Open** 11am-11pm Mon-Thur; 11am-midnight Fri, Sat; 10am-11pm Sun. **Credit** AmEx, DC, Disc, MC, V. **Map** p306 F5.

A proper-attire-required kind of a place in the swanky Four Seasons Hotel. The bar is full of the sort of antique furniture that low-tier royalty might own. And there's no telling just whom one might see here: George Clooney reclining in one of the bar's plush armchairs, Ted Kennedy sipping a glass of Jameson's, Gwyneth Paltrow enjoying subtle jazz.

Bull and Finch Pub

84 Beacon Street, at Arlington Street (227 9605). Arlington T. **Open** 11am-2am daily. **Credit** AmEx, DC, Disc, MC, V. **Map** p306 F4.

Though this place is credited with providing the inspiration for the ridiculously popular TV sitcom *Cheers*, expect no Sams, Norms or Carlas. They don't know your name here, nor do they really want to. And they're only glad you came if you brought your wallet with you. Line up with the dozens of other tourists waiting for a spot inside to eat expensive hamburgers and drink pricey beer in a place that looks absolutely nothing like the bar in the television show. The only part of this pub that was copied for that show was the stairwell. You'll probably go anyway, but don't say we didn't warn you.

Emily's

48 Winter Street, at Tremont Street (423 3649). Park St T. **Open** 5pm-2am Tue-Thur. 4pm-2am Fri. 9pm-2am Sat. **Credit** AmEx, MC, V. **Map** p307 G4.

When MTV's *Real World* filmed in Boston, Emily's was the place the cast chose to hang. The bar certainly has a Gen-X feel to it, with its faux lounge décor and a DJ playing dance hits at ear-splitting volume. If you haven't a cutie to cuddle up to on one of the bar's dimly lit sofas, you might want to try your hand at playing pool on a table conveniently located on the dance floor. Don't try to get in, however, sporting ripped jeans or athletic wear (and that includes trainers and baseball caps).

The Good Life

28 Kingston Street, at Summer Street (451 2622). Downtown Crossing T. **Open** 11am-2am Mon-Fri; 5pm-2am Sat. **Credit** AmEx, MC, V. **Map** p307 G5.

One of several upmarket bars and restaurants that has helped to drag downtown Boston out of a late-night wasteland. This is one of the most popular – and for good reason. With its orange vinyl walls, wood panelling, Rat Pack soundtrack and *Goodfellas* ambience, the Good Life manages to be a smirky tribute to lounge bars. It's the kind of place where one might feel inadequate for not smoking. This is especially true downstairs, where there's rockabilly on Wednesdays, and live jazz from Thursday to Sunday (no cover) and bohemians and businessmen nurse their drinks while octogenarian drummers beat the hell out of tired-looking drum sets. Yeah. **Branch**: 720 Massachusetts Avenue, Cambridge (868 8800).

The Green Dragon

11 Marshall Street, at Union Street (367 0055). Gov't Center T. **Open** 10am-2am daily. **Credit** AmEx, DC, MC, V. **Map** p307 G4.

A stone's throw from the Bell in Hand (*see p163*), this bar dates back (though not in its present form) to 1773. The spot on which it stands is 'the birthplace of American freedom', a place where the sons of liberty gathered over a few pints to plot the downfall of the British. There's a glass case on the wall containing some of the implements – muskets and so on – used to achieve that end. This is a congenial gaff with live music, attentive staff, carpeted nooks and faded wallpaper. It shows British football, too.

Hennessy's

25 Union Street, at Quincy Market (742-2121). Government Center T. **Open** 11am-2am daily. **Credit** AmEx, DC, MC, V. **Map** p307 G4.

A brightly lit place, warm with peat fires and *seisiún* music, and a welcoming refuge from the bustle of nearby Quincy Market. It has a well-appointed bar offering some pricey top-shelf Scotches and very expensive champagne. The 'pub shop' tucked behind a section of the bar sells Batchelor's baked beans, Lyon's tea and Lucozade. And, should you meet the guy or girl of your dreams on your trip, Hennessy's hosts weddings and receptions.

Hibernia

25 Kingston Street, at Summer Street (292 2333). Downtown Crossing or South Station T. **Open** 11am-2am Mon-Sat. **Credit** AmEx, MC, V. **Map** p307 G5.

Across the road from the Good Life (*see above*) and adjacent to JJ Foley's (*see below*), Hibernia is one of the many Irish bars that have popped up in Boston over the past few years. This one, though, has forgone the ubiquitous Irish seisiún for a dancefloor and DJs spinning the latest house hits. The decor blends ancient Celtic symbols and modern geometric shapes. And though the bartenders can pour a pint of Guinness with the best of them, they also serve a decent Martini.

JJ Foley's

21 Kingston Street, at Summer Street (338 7713). Downtown Crossing T. **Open** 8am-2am Mon-Sat; 10am-2am Sun. **Credit** AmEx, MC, V. **Map** p307 G5.

This low-key Irish bar is an institution in Boston – a hangout for bike messengers, tattooed masses, business suits and borderline bums. Anyone who has lived in Boston for long has met someone at Foley's, or broken up with someone at Foley's, or met and broken up with them at the same time there – or knows someone who has. At night it's packed, smoky and brimming with energy. The historic Freedom Trail may have its merits, but this is the place to see personal history being created.

Hey! You with the guitar! Pass the bar nuts! Join the fray at **JJ Foley's**. *See p161.*

The Kinsale

2 Center Plaza, Government Center (742 5577). Government Center T. **Open** 11am-2am Tue-Sat; 11am-1am Sun. **Credit** AmEx, MC, V. **Map** p307 G4.

Built in Ireland and shipped to the Hub piece by piece, the Kinsale is Irish pub as theme park, but one could do a lot worse. The Guinness is top notch, and the Irish staff are unfailingly pleasant. The Kinsale's central location means it can get crowded fast, especially when there's a game on TV, but great pub grub and occasional live music more than make up for any stepped-on toes or spilled suds.

The Littlest Bar

47 Province Street, at Bromfield Street (523 9667). Downtown Crossing or Park Street T. **Open** 8.30am-1am daily. **No credit cards. Map** p307 G4.

There may be smaller bars than this one (it measures 16ft/5m from end to end), but we don't know of any. Maximum occupancy: 34. And it's not just the bar's size that makes it such an intimate setting. The place draws a crowd of doggedly loyal regulars, some of whom are members of Boston's political and cultural elite (note the 'Seamus Heaney peed here' sign outside the men's room). That said, the patrons seem more than willing to make a place at the bar for newcomers – or they would if they could.

Lock-Ober

3 Winter Place, at Tremont Street (542 1340). Park Street T. **Open** 11am-3pm, 5.30-10pm, Mon-Fri; 5.30-10pm Sat. **Credit** AmEx, DC, Disc, MC, V. **Map** p307 G4.

The smell of cigars permeates this top-drawer Yankee hangout – a sea of leather, white linen and the mythical Boston Brahmin. The smart staff's deference can be unsettling, and, yet, oh so wonderfully enjoyable. Be prepared to shell out.

Mr Dooley's

77 Broad Street, at State Street (338 5656). South Station or Downtown Crossing T. **Open** 11.30am-2am Mon-Fri; 11am-2am Sat, Sun. **Credit** AmEx, DC, Disc, MC, V. Map p307 G5.

Named after the fictional, opinion-rich barkeep of writer FP Dunne's syndicated newspaper columns, this financial district mainstay has bartenders who are no less garrulous or affable than the imaginary version. It has a loyal clientele of journalists and politicians and lives up to its own billing as 'a great place for a pint and a chat'.

Oskars

107 South Street, at Kneeland Street (542 6756). South Station T. **Open** 11.30am-2am Mon-Thur; 5.30pm-1am Fri; 7pm-1am Sat; 10am-1am Sun. **Credit** AmEx, DC, MC, V. **Map** p307 G5.

Though better known as a restaurant than a bar, it's worth having a drink here just to get a whiff of how those with real money drink. The staff are friendly and efficient, and the glasses have an irresistible weight to them. Oskars is a prime spot for beautiful people watching, and a night sipping cocktails in its ruggedly chic environs may have you vowing to contact a plastic surgeon first thing in the morning.

Pravda 116

116 Boylston Street, at Tremont Street (482 7799). Boylston T. **Open** 5pm-2am Mon-Sat. **Credit** AmEx, MC, V. **Map** p307 F5.

As well as being its street number, there are 116 different vodkas on offer here. The bar hosts occasional Russian nights, in which much vodka is swigged, many das are uttered and those funny hats are all the rage. But fear not, brown liquor aficionados, there's beer too. It has a dress code – so save the jeans, boots and flannels you were planning on donning for tomorrow's hangover.

Silvertone

69 Bromfield Street, at Tremont Street (338 7887). Downtown Crossing T. **Open** 11.30am-2am Mon-Fri; 5pm-2am Sat. **Credit** AmEx, Disc, MC, V. **Map** p307 G4.

With its nifty 1940s-ish decor (check the vintage radios and backlit aquatints), pleasing jazz soundtrack (Billie Holiday and Miles on our last visit) and affable bar-staff, Silvertone has attracted a loyal cadre of followers. Tucked away on a gloomy side street near Downtown Crossing, it's not really the kind of place you stumble across. But those who find it come back. It sells reasonably priced wine and excellent food (try the 'dirty' spaghetti).

Les Zygomates

129 South Street, at Kneeland Street (542 5108). South Station T. **Open** 11.30am-1am Mon-Thur; 6pm-1am Fri, Sat. **Credit** AmEx, DC, Disc, MC, V. **Map** p307 G5.

Pronounced Zee-go-maht, this is one of Boston's most elegant wine bars. Some visitors may be intimidated by the upmarket atmosphere and the telephone directory-sized wine list (*see p136*) at Les Zyg's (as nobody ever calls it).

North

Grand Canal

57 Canal Street, at Causeway Street (523 1112). Haymarket or North Station T. **Open** 11am-1.30am daily. **Credit** AmEx, DC, Disc, MC, V. **Map** p307 G3.

The Grand Canal boasts one of the finest façades in the city. There's something very English about the place and it doesn't take too much suspension of disbelief to imagine that you're enjoying a pint in deepest West London. Live music and a cheery pub atmosphere have made this bar enormously popular among young people.

Irish Embassy

234 Friend Street, at Causeway Street (742 6618). North Station T. **Open** 11.30am-1am daily. **Credit** AmEx, DC, MC, V. **Map** p307 G3.

Live British football on Saturdays, artery-choking Irish breakfasts on weekends (mmm, black pudding) and an authentic pub atmosphere draw to the Irish Embassy one of the highest concentrations of British and Irish expats in the city. A good place to hear a colourful range of referee abuse.

Allston

Big City

138 Brighton Avenue, at Harvard Avenue, Allston (782 2020). Harvard T. **Open** 11.30am-1am daily. **Credit** AmEx, DC, Disc, MC, V.

Housed in what used to be a bank, Big City lives up to its name. Urban visual gags abound: a working

Size doesn't matter at **The Littlest Bar**. *See p162.*

Well, they had to have one someplace. Wave your flag at **the Irish Embassy**. *See p163.*

traffic light sits in the corner, parking meters perch on the raised bench tables. Rooms surrounding the bar contain some of the nicest pool tables in town, but this is also a fun place to just sit and have a drink. There are 82 beers on tap and the bar menu consists almost entirely of pizza – including the 'Eye Opener', with bacon, eggs and home fries, and the peanut butter and (we're not kidding) jelly pizza.

Model Café

7 North Beacon Street, at Cambridge Street, Allston (254 9365). Union Square T. **Open** 2.30pm-2am daily. **No credit cards.**

The Model has had an interesting life. It started off as an unpretentious little neighbourhood dive and then one day, through no fault of its own, it was suddenly enormously pretentious, playing host to the cream of the counter-cultural community (who inexplicably started calling it the 'Mow-DELL'). Nowadays, the trendy crowd and the divey neighbourhood crowd share the place, with grandmotherly types serving Bud bottles to the pierced, tattooed masses. It's quite sweet, really. And the jukebox is among the best around.

Sunset Grill

130 Brighton Avenue, at Harvard Avenue, Allston (254 1331). Harvard T. **Open** 11.30am-1am daily. **Credit** AmEx, DC, Disc, MC, V. **Map** p311 A5.

For the no-nonsense ale lover, this may be the only place in town. The beer menu is ridiculous: 450 beers, 112 of them on tap. The decor is nothing spectacular, and unless you have a thing about college students, the clientele won't knock your socks off. But with all that ale inside you, who cares?

The White Horse

116 Brighton Avenue, at Harvard Avenue, Allston (254 6633). Harvard T. **Open** 11.30am-2am Mon-Sat; 10am-2am Sun. **Credit** AmEx, MC, V. **Map** p311 A5.

Though this pub can get rather crammed at weekends, its massive size makes it a perfect place for those times when you need privacy. Sit at the huge bar and look around: that couple over in the corner talking in hushed tones could be breaking up or just getting to know each pther better. The beauty of the White Horse is that you and everyone else are sitting too far away to tell.

Drink a toast to the Borstal Boy at the **Brendan Behan Pub**. See p158.

Wonder Bar

186 Harvard Avenue, at Commonwealth Avenue, Allston (351 2665). Harvard T. **Open** 5pm-2am daily. **Credit** AmEx, Disc, MC, V. **Map** p311 A4.
Though Allston hasn't exactly felt the cleansing fire of progress yet, there are definite signs that the area is picking up. On the premises of what used to be a famously grungy music club, Wonder Bar makes no bones about wanting to move in higher circles. At the door a dress code proclaims, among other things, that 'shirts must be tucked and buttoned'. Inside, the bar's black-and-white tiled floor, slo-mo ceiling fans and jazz trio all attest to the encroachment of Martini sensibilities on a Bud Lite neighbourhood.

Jamaica Plain

Doyle's

3484 Washington Street, at Williams Street, Jamaica Plain (524 2345). Green Street T. **Open** 9am-1am daily. **No credit cards**.
One of the oldest Irish pubs in Boston, Doyle's has been in the business for more than a century and it shows. There is an effortless charm about the place. It doesn't rely on 'DUBLIN 23 MILES' signs to promote its Irishness, but quietly goes about the business of pulling a great pint and serving hearty food at low prices. It's a rambling place, with high ceilings, huge murals and invariably a chatty crowd.

Flann O'Brien's

1619 Tremont Street, at Wigglesworth Street, Jamaica Plain (566 7744). Brigham Circle T. **Open** 11am-1am daily. **No credit cards**.
Though somewhat out of the way in the Brigham Circle area, O'Brien's is worth the trip. Irish immigrants and locals alike have found this an ideal spot in which to let their hair down and have a bit of mad fun. Portraits of Irish literary heroes festoon the walls, often lit up by flickering disco lights. The sounds of laughter and loud music compete for air space. Dancers and drinkers somehow mingle with barely a drop of spillage.

Cambridge

B-Side Lounge

92 Hampshire Street, at Windsor Street, Cambridge (354 0766). Central Square or Kendall Square T. **Open** 5.30pm-1am Mon-Wed, Sun; 5.30pm-2am Thur-Sat. **Credit** AmEx, MC, V.
Formerly the Windsor Tap (a real dive), the B-Side is now a faux dive, replete with red-neon decor and hard-boiled eggs free at the bar. Don't fill up on eggs, though, because the menu is out of this world (lobster mashed-potatoes anyone?). Wash it all back with a bottle of Pabst Blue Ribbon, and you'll feel at home with the trendy Cantabridgians who flock here.

Cambridge Brewing Company

1 Kendall Square, Building 100, at Hampshire Street, Cambridge (494 1994). Kendall/MIT T. **Open** 11.30am-12.30am Mon-Fri; noon-12.30am Sat; 3pm-12.30am Sun. **Credit** AmEx, MC, V.
Located in the industrial-turned-entertainment complex of One Kendall Square (the Kendall Landmark Theater is a stone's throw away, as are a number of very good restaurants), this bar boasts some of the finest home-brew in the region – the Tall Tale Pale Ale is a winner. In the summer you can sit at the tables outside, where trees adorned with twinkling fairy lights create a romantic setting. Or maybe that's just the beer talking.

Cambridge Common

1667 Massachusetts Avenue, at Sacramento Street, Cambridge (547 1228). Harvard or Porter T. **Open** 11.30am-1am Mon-Wed; 11.30am-2am Thur-Sat; 11am-1am Sun. **Credit** AmEx, DC, Disc, MC, V. **Map** p311 B1.

This is a low-key, get-a-couple-down-you kind of place. Off the beaten track (between Harvard and Porter Squares), it attracts mostly regulars, as well as the poets, jazz players and Marlene Dietrich lookalikes who frequent the downstairs club.

Crimson Sports Bar & Grille

59 JFK Street, at Eliot Street, Cambridge (868 5900). Harvard Square T. **Open** noon-1am Mon-Wed, Sun; noon-2am Thur-Sat. **Credit** AmEx, Disc, MC, V. **Map** p311 B2.

This bar has no pretensions to being anything other than a sports bar, which is just fine with the hordes of Harvard and Boston College kids who throng here on weekends (and weeknights – this is a college bar, after all). Nonetheless, you could do worse on a weekend afternoon than to munch appetisers and sip beer while taking in a baseball or (American) football game on one of the bar's innumerable TVs.

The Field

20 Prospect Street, at Massachusetts Avenue, Cambridge (354 7345). Central T. **Open** 11.30am-1am Mon-Sat; 1pm-1am Sun. **No credit cards. Map** p311 C3.

This place manages to give the feel of a real Dublin pub, probably because it doesn't try too hard. Irish and American kids jostle and bob along happily to the music in the front room, or sit in the considerably more sedate back room and have a natter.

Grafton Street

1280 Massachusetts Avenue, between Linden & Plympton Streets, Cambridge (497 0400). Harvard T. **Open** 11am-1am daily. **Credit** AmEx, DC, MC, V. **Map** p311 B2.

This relative newcomer to the Irish pub set overflows in summer, when its big French windows allow interaction with Harvard Square's brilliant parade. Serves decent pub grub.

Grendel's Den

89 Winthrop Street, at JFK Street, Cambridge (491 1160). Harvard Square T. **Open** 11am-1am Mon-Sat; 4pm-1am Sun. **Credit** AmEx, Disc, MC, V. **Map** p311 B2.

Directly across the street from the House of Blues is this unpretentious little basement bar, which recently underwent a major overhaul. From 5-7.30pm, anything on the menu (excluding their famous cheese fondue and certain specials) is $2.50 after the purchase of a $3 beverage. That means succulent mussels and stuffed potato skins for less than the price of a pint. Easy on the wallet, heaven in the gullet and packed with chattering Harvard students.

John Harvard's Brew House

33 Dunster Street, at Massachusetts Avenue, Cambridge (868 3585). Harvard T. **Open** 11.30am-12.30am Mon-Wed; 11.30am-1am Thur; 11.30am-1.30am Fri, Sat; 11.30am-midnight Sun. **Credit** AmEx, DC, MC, V. **Map** p311 B2.

Long a favourite of Harvard's student body, this large underground bar offers some basic American cooking, delicious micro-brewed beer and the opportunity to be surrounded by, erm, the bodies of Harvard's student body.

Hong Kong

1236 Massachusetts Avenue, at Plympton Street, Cambridge (864 5311). Harvard Square T. **Open** 11.30am-2am daily. **Credit** AmEx, DC, Disc, M, V. **Map** p311 B2.

Despite the kitsch 1950s-style sign out front, this Chinese restaurant-cum-bar, a Harvard institution, is lacking in eye-candy decor. The downstairs restaurant is Chinesey enough, but the first-floor bar is a modest affair where darts, Budweiser and wonton soup are not strange bedfellows.

House of Blues

96 Winthrop Street, at JFK Street, Cambridge (491 2583). Harvard Square T. **Open** 11.30am-1am Mon-Wed, Sun; 11.30am-2am Thur-Sat. **Credit** AmEx, Disc, M, V. **Map** p311 B2.

As the proprietors never miss the opportunity to remind us, this is the original House of Blues. You'll recognise it immediately, because a) it is literally a blue house, and b) there is almost always a line of people milling about outside by the gift shop. For those willing to brave the crowds, steamy blues jams, mediocre food and ice-cold beer await within.

Miracle of Science Bar & Grill

321 Massachusetts Avenue, at Putnam Avenue, Cambridge (868 2866). Central T. **Open** 11.30am-1am daily. **Credit** AmEx, DC, Disc, MC, V.

Sister bar to Audubon Circle in Boston (*see p122*), the Miracle of Science has huge windows looking out onto Mass Ave, an ultra-modern design, good beer and a comfortable (though too bright) atmosphere. In honour of the many MIT students who frequent the place, the bar serves drinks in laboratory beakers. It's an MIT thing.

People's Republik

880 Massachusetts Avenue, at Lee Street, Cambridge (492 8632). Central or Harvard T. **Open** noon-1am Mon-Wed, Sun; noon-2am Thur-Sat. **No credit cards. Map** p311 C3.

In the spot that used to house the divey little bar Drumlins, the People's Republik has jazzed things up considerably. With inspirational posters from Russia and Red China on the walls and a giant bomb above the window, the bar plays around with a revolutionary theme, which has led local wags to rename the place 'Kremlin's'.

Phoenix Landing

512 Massachusetts Avenue, at Brookline Street, Cambridge (576 6260). Central T. **Open** 11am-1am daily. **Credit** AmEx, DC, Disc, MC, V.

Invariably packed, loud and steamy, the Phoenix was one of the first Irish pubs in the area to realise the potential of combining a dance club with an Irish pub. It offers live music as well as showcasing some of the area's up-and-coming young DJs. And the bartenders pull a decent pint, too.

Better red than sober at the **People's Republik**. *See p167.*

Plough & Stars

912 Massachusetts Avenue, at Hancock Street, Cambridge (441 3455). Central T. **Open** 11.30am-1am daily. **No credit cards. Map** p311 C3.

The spiritual forefather of Greater Boston's thriving pub business, the Plough has been going for 30 years and many of the regulars who line the bar (and whose ink-on-napkin portraits adorn the walls) have been around since the beginning. In the daytime, the Plough offers the best pub grub in town, contentious games of cribbage and live UK and European football games on the television. At night the tiny bar is transformed into a hotbed of smoke, elbows and live music. Getting to the bathrooms when a band is on can be an interesting challenge, not least because you have to push your way past the bass player to get through the door. *See also p225.*

Rialto

1 Bennett Street, at the Charles Hotel, Cambridge (661 5050). Harvard T. **Open** 5-11pm Mon-Thur, Sun; 5-11.30pm Fri, Sat. **Credit** AmEx, DC, MC, V. **Map** p311 B2.

Not your let's-pop-in-for-a-quickie kind of place, Rialto serves hefty cocktails (not to mention excellent food) and has prices to match. Nestled in the elegant Charles Hotel and a stone's throw from Harvard's John F Kennedy School of Government, it's a place where you're equally likely to find yourself sipping a G&T beside foreign dignitaries, expense account-wielding out-of-towners and well-heeled locals. *See also p149.*

Shay's Lounge

58 John F Kennedy Street, at Mount Auburn Street, Cambridge (864 9161). Harvard T. **Open** 11am-1am Mon-Sat; noon-1am Sun. **Credit** AmEx, DC, MC, V. **Map** p311 B2.

Owned and operated by English expats, Shay's is one of the nicer bars in the area. Sunk a few feet below the sidewalk and with a nifty outdoor patio, the bar itself is rather pokey. It attracts a lively brew of academics, artists and die-hard regulars, and bar-side banter can range from the Middle East peace talks to why the Red Sox suck. Though many quaff from Shay's extensive beer menu, this is primarily a wine bar and there are no spirits.

Temple Bar

1688 Massachusetts Avenue, Cambridge (547 5055). Harvard or Porter T. **Open** 11am-1am daily. **Credit** AmEx, DC, MC, V. **Map** p311 B2.

Emblematic of the current vogue for snappy neo-lounge bars, this place attracts the nouveau-riche, mobile-phone-wielding, Martini-clinking crowd. The atmosphere is serene and classy, with arty light fixtures, a gleaming bar and enormous old European advertising posters. Despite its name, an Irish pub this certainly ain't.

Toad & Lizard Lounge

1667 Massachusetts Avenue, at Porter Square, Cambridge (499 6992). Porter T. **Open** 5pm-1am Mon-Wed, Sun; 5pm-2am Thur-Sat. **No credit cards. Map** p311 B1.

You'd miss Toad if you blinked. But if you want to get intimate with Cambridge residents, this friendly, low-key little bar is the place. Toad defies physical laws by successfully combining live music (every night), enormous popularity and minuscule size.

Somerville

Aquarium

65 Holland Street, at Davis Square, Somerville (623 3200). Davis Square T. **Open** 11am-1am daily. **Credit** AmEx, MC, V.

This trendy restaurant/bar is the latest addition to a rejuvenated Davis Square. The theme, as you might guess, is aquatic – evidenced by the gigantic tanks filled with neon-hued sea creatures behind the bar and at the centre of the room. Then there's the fishbowls-for-two filled with a brightly coloured mystery drink – a perfect way to get tanked.

The Burren

247 Elm Street, at Davis Square, Somerville (776 6896). Davis T. **Open** 10am-1am daily. **Credit** AmEx, MC, V.

Since its opening a few years ago, the Burren has enjoyed enormous success – so much so that it has expanded, opening up a huge back room to accommodate the pub's many devotees. In the daytime, a scattering of people can be found eating beef-and-Guinness stew at the bar's wooden tables. At night the place is packed largely by students from nearby Tufts University, who show up to hear classy Irish musicians jam in the pub's incomparable *seisiúns*.

PJ Ryan's

239 Holland Street, at Teele Square, Somerville (625 8200). Davis T. **Open** 4pm-1am Mon, Tue; 11.30am-1am Wed-Sun. **Credit** AmEx, Disc, DC, MC, V.

A relative newcomer to Somerville, PJ's does the Irish pub thing right. No shamrocks on the wall here, instead, just a couple of Jack Yeats paintings, a perfectly pulled pint and live music (of the troubadour-with-an-acoustic-guitar-covering-Van-Morrison variety) on the weekends are enough to get the mood across. With its intimate size, dark wood panelling and homey feel, it's the perfect place to grab a beer, have a bite and watch the world go by through its large front windows.

Sligo Pub

Elm Street, at Davis Square, Somerville (no phone). Davis T. **Open** 9am-1am daily. **No credit cards.**

Its spruced-up new sign and façade notwithstanding, the Sligo is one of the last bastions of Davis Square's aforementioned blue collar traditions. It's a throwback – from the oldies on the jukebox to the small glass that accompanies your bottle of Miller High Life. And though the number of Buddy-Holly-bespectacled Tufts students has increased here lately, this is still the kind of place where your grandfather drank; serving generous shots of the hard stuff to guys who look like they've been regulars since Eisenhower was president.

Practise your Gaelic at **Tir na Nog**.

Thirsty Scholar Pub

70 Beacon Street, at Washington Street, Somerville (497 2294). Harvard T. **Open** 11am-1am daily. **Credit** AmEx, MC, V. **Map** p311 C2.

With its exposed brick walls, and its little nooks and crannies, the Thirsty Scholar is the perfect place for an intimate drink. Not that you'd particularly want to shut yourself off from this pub's patrons, who rank among the friendliest in the area. And they may just be the most literate pub-goers around as well. Once a month, distinguished local writers have an informal get-together, and, true to its name, the pub plays host to many readings.

Tir na nog

366A Somerville Avenue, at Union Square, Somerville (628 4300). Washington Square T. **Open** 11.30am-1am daily. **Credit** Disc, MC, V.

This is a terrific little pub, with bookcases lining the walls and a marvellous mahogany bar. But it's tiny, and on nights when it hosts live Irish or folk music it can begin to feel like the inside of a bean burrito. And yet you couldn't hope to have the life squeezed out of you by a nicer bunch of people.

Shops & Services

From bland brands to eccentric emporia – where to flash your cash.

Boston is not the kind of city to which people travel for miles in order to shop. Its downtown malls and shopping districts are crowded with the same big chain outposts and designer boutiques you'll find in practically any US city these days. And many downtown shopping streets are dominated by extraordinarily expensive designer shops.

Still, shopping here does offer some rewards. The large student population and influx of tourists helps. You can still find quirky boutiques and sophisticated independent retailers squeezed in between the Gaps and Niketowns. Shopping for vintage and used clothing, musical instruments, pop culture ephemera and antiques can be great, though some of the best hunting grounds are a little far flung. If you persevere, you're likely to find both high fashion and cheap knock-offs; New York chic and New England sturdy.

SALES TAX

There is no sales tax on clothing in Massachusetts (there is a 5% sales tax on other goods), making it a much better place to shop, in terms of price, than many of its surrounding states, most of which have high sales taxes.

SHOPPING AREAS

For an easy one-day trip, stick to the major shopping areas. The **Back Bay** has the highest concentration of shops in Boston, with two large malls and the city's most famous shopping strip, **Newbury Street**, all within easy walking distance. Unfortunately, the prices tend to reflect the area's high rents. Around Massachusetts Avenue, the stores tend to be a little funkier and more affordable – most of the CD stores and non-chain bookstores are clustered in this area. The most upmarket retailers are at the Arlington Street end, including **Louis Boston**, which is the city's answer to Barney's in New York or Harvey Nichols in London.

A short walk from Newbury Street is the **Prudential Center** mall, filled with national chain stores and overpriced mall fixtures. One of the Pru's better features is the glassed-in bridge that connects it to the upmarket **Copley Place** mall, enabling shoppers to cross from one to the other without having to deal with traffic or bad weather. South of Copley is the **South End**, where the shops are tiny, stylish and eclectic, but, unfortunately, not always clustered conveniently together.

The industrial-looking, crowded **Downtown Crossing** is the first stop for many people, most of whom are succumbing to the siren's call of **Filene's Basement**. Washington Street, the main drag in this area, is dominated by chain stores, although busy vending carts and stalls add some character, and a few old bookshops and ancient independent retailers can be found tucked away on the side streets.

Although it's just across Boston Common, **Beacon Hill** feels like the other side of the world from Downtown Crossing. Blessed with antique and gift shops, gourmet grocers and boutiques, prices here tend to be sky-high.

Further downtown, near the waterfront, the **Faneuil Hall/Quincy Market** area is one of the region's most popular shopping attractions. It's often uncomfortably crowded on fine days, but the cobblestoned setting is charming and there are lots of boutiques and stores. From here, you can head north to investigate the romantic, old-world Italian charm of the **North End** nearby.

In **Cambridge**, some of the more interesting shops are located on the walk up Massachusetts Avenue between Central and Harvard Squares, including offbeat record stores and bookshops, ethnic and pop-culture shops, and furniture and homeware stores. Other Cambridge shopping destinations include the **Porter Square** area, where the shops become more interesting as you head north on Massachusetts Avenue but are perhaps a little too spread out for easy, uninterrupted window-shopping.

A short ride on the T will get you to the happening little neighbourhood of Davis Square in **Somerville**, which is virtually chain-store-free and loaded with cool little antique shops. Another decidedly boho shopping experience can be had in **Allston**. Along Harvard Avenue are Vietnamese grocers, cheap furniture outlets, musty antique shops and a host of subculture shopping spots.

Department stores

Filene's

426 Washington Street, at Summer Street, Downtown (357 2100). Downtown Crossing,

Head to **Fanueil Hall** for touristy buys.

Park St or State/Citizen's Bank T. **Open** 9.30am-7.30pm Mon-Sat; 11am-7pm Sun. **Credit** MC, V. **Map** p307 G4.

Perhaps the country's most famous store for bridalwear. Women have been known to have fistfights over some of the dresses here. You should be above all that, however, and just buy one politely. Also sells brand-name clothing, cosmetics, china, crystal furniture, homeware and jewellery.

Lord & Taylor

760 Boylston Street, at Exeter Street, Back Bay (262 6000). Copley T. **Open** 10am-9pm Mon-Fri; 10am-8pm Sat; 11am-7pm Sun. **Credit** AmEx, Disc, MC, V. **Map** p306 E5.

Designer and brand-name men's, women's and children's clothing, shoes, cosmetics, jewellery and accessories. The end-of-season sales offer huge savings (up to 75% off).

Macy's

450 Washington Street, at Summer Street, Downtown (357 3000). Park St or State/ Citizen's Bank T. **Open** 9.30am-7.30pm Mon-Sat; 11am-7pm Sun. **Credit** AmEx, MC, V. **Map** p307 G4.

Some people are addicted to this store. Macy's has got so much of everything that people practically need therapy to quit buying here. Brand-name clothing, cosmetics, housewares, china, crystal, furniture all feature, and there's also a good selection of lingerie. Alterations available.

Neiman Marcus

5 Copley Place, at Boylston, Back Bay (536 3660). Back Bay or Copley T. **Open** 10am-8pm Mon-Sat; noon-6pm Sun. **Credit** AmEx, DC. **Map** p306 F5.

Neiman's doesn't refer to itself as a department store ('high-end speciality store' is preferred) but has several departments nonetheless, including furs, precious jewellery, designer clothing and shoes. The gift shop is referred to as a 'gallery'.

Saks Fifth Avenue

Prudential Plaza, Back Bay (262 8500/ www.saksfifthavenue.com). Copley T. **Open** 10am-8pm Mon-Sat; noon-6pm Sun. **Credit** AmEx, DC, Disc, MC, V. **Map** p306 E5.

Top-quality men's and women's clothing, sportswear, shoes, jewellery, lingerie and cosmetics. Its designer lines include Armani, Donna Karan, Calvin Klein and Michael Kors.

Discount

Filene's Basement

426 Washington Street, at Summer Street, Downtown (542 2011). Downtown Crossing or Park St T. **Open** 9.30am-7.30pm Mon-Fri; 9am-7.30pm Sat; 11am-7pm Sun. **Credit** AmEx, Disc, MC, V. **Map** p307 G4.

The famous automatic markdown store, where shopping can be fierce (shove and be shoved) but fruitful. Filene's sells mid-range to designer label clothing, jewellery, homeware and bridal attire at discounts of up to 70%. The truly spectacular steals are a matter of luck and fortitude, but keep looking. On our last visit we found a $98 Jones New York skirt for $9. Gets the heart pounding, that does.

Marshall's

500 Boylston Street, at Clarendon Street, Back Bay (262 6066). Arlington or Copley T. **Open** 9am-9pm Mon-Sat; 11am-7pm Sun. **Credit** AmEx, Disc, MC, V. **Map** p306 F5.

Stocks an impressive selection of brand-name men's, women's and children's clothing, plus gifts, fine cutlery, shoes and accessories. Reductions range from around 20% to 40%.

Branch: 350 Washington Street, Downtown (338 6205).

TJ Maxx

525 Harvard Avenue, Brookline (232 5420). Coolidge Corner T. **Open** 9.30am-9.30pm Mon-Sat; 11am-6pm Sun. **Credit** AmEx, Disc, MC, V. **Map** p311 A5.

Sells mid-range brand-name and designer clothing (think Liz Claiborne, Polo, Tommy Hilfiger) for men, women and children. It also sells accessories, gifts, homeware and linens, at discounts of 20% to 50%.

Branch: 198 Alewife Brook Parkway, Cambridge (492 8500).

Antiques & collectibles

Antique Revival

1 Harvard Avenue, at Cambridge Street, Allston (787 4040). Harvard Avenue T. **Open** 11am-6pm daily. **Credit** AmEx, MC, V. **Map** p311 A4/5.

One of Allston's most reliable treasure-hunting grounds, selling decently priced antique wooden furniture, lamps and decorative pieces.

Brodney Gallery

145 Newbury Street, at Dartmouth Street, Back Bay (536 0500). Copley T. **Open** *summer* 10am-6pm Mon-Sat; noon-5pm Sun; *winter* 10am-6pm Mon-Sat. **Credit** AmEx, MC, V, DC. **Map** p306 F5.

This elegant, family owned shop stocks 18th- to 20th-century antiques, artwork, fine rugs and jewellery from around the world.

Cambridge Antique Market

201 Monsignor O'Brien Highway, Cambridge (868 9655). Lechmere T. **Open** 11am-6pm Tue-Sun. **Credit** Disc, MC, V.

Antique furniture, homeware, china, toys, clothing and decorative pieces fill the numerous stalls in this dusty, five-level warehouse. The London Café on the fourth floor serves light lunches on weekends.

India Antiques, Art and Music

279 Newbury Street, at Gloucester Street, Back Bay (266 6539/www.indiaantiquesboston.com). Hynes/ICA T. **Open** 11am-6pm daily. **Credit** AmEx, Disc, MC, V. **Map** p306 E5.

A treasure trove of Far Eastern curiosities, including traditional musical instruments, decorative wooden pieces, fabrics and tapestries, plus saris and kurtas. It's also the only place in town where you can get a henna tattoo.

JMW Gallery

144 Lincoln Street, at Beach Street, Downtown (338 9097/www.jmwgallery.com). South Station T. **Open** 11am-6pm Tue-Fri; 11am-5pm Sat. **Credit** Disc, MC, V. **Map** p307 G5.

JMW sells some particularly fine examples of furniture, lighting, artisan pottery, metalwork, textiles and woodblock prints.

Machine Age

354 Congress Street, at A Street, South Boston (482 0048/www.machine-age.com). South Station T. **Open** noon-5pm Tue-Sat. **Credit** AmEx, MC, V. **Map** p307 H5.

A giant showroom with an exceptional selection of classic modern designs – Herman Miller, Charles Eames, George Nelson and the like – and a sprawling miscellany of 20th-century artefacts.

Marcoz Antiques

177 Newbury Street, between Dartmouth & Exeter Streets, Back Bay (262 0780). Copley T. **Open** 10am-6pm Mon-Sat. **Credit** AmEx, Disc, MC, V. **Map** p306 E/F5.

Not cheap, but tasteful, elegant and well worth a look. Its 18th- and 19th-century European furniture and stylish decorative arts are specialities.

NV53

260 Elm Street, Davis Square Plaza, Somerville (776 0848). Davis T. **Open** 11am-6pm Thur-Sun; Tue and Wed by appointment only. **Credit** AmEx, MC, V. **Map** p311 B1.

A real gold-mine for classic 20th-century design. Furniture by top modern designers in addition to Danish pieces are sold for about 30% below LA/NY market prices. It also sells vintage clothing and decorative objects. Cheap parking is available at the rear of the store.

Sadye & Co

182 Massachusetts Avenue, at Albany Street, Cambridge (547 4424). Central or Kendall/MIT T. **Open** 11am-6pm Mon-Sat; noon-5pm Sun. **Credit** AmEx, MC, V. **Map** p306 D4.

An inviting clutter of mostly 20th-century furniture, watches, fountain pens, jewellery, musical instruments, with the occasional, remarkably cheap find. Now into its 67th year, this family-owned business sells sneakers, sweatshirts, work clothes, boots, fatigues, flak jackets, watchcaps, Timberland and Chippewa lines – all at 10% to 20% discount.

Art supplies

The Art Store

401 Park Drive, at Landmark Center, South End (247 3322). Fenway T. **Open** 9am-9pm Mon-Sat; 11am-6pm Sun. **Credit** AmEx, Disc, MC, V. **Map** p311 C5.

OK, so the Art Store might be little on the pricey side but it's well stocked in supplies and accessories in most media.

Johnson Paint and Art Materials

355 Newbury Street, at Massachusetts Avenue, Back Bay (536 4244). Hynes/ICA T. **Open** 7.30am-5.30pm Mon-Fri; 8.30am-1pm Sat. **Credit** AmEx, Disc, MC, V. **Map** p306 E5.
Not the cheapest supplier, but conveniently located in Back Bay and well stocked with the basics and some speciality items.

Pearl Art & Craft Supplies

579 Massachusetts Avenue, between Essex & Pearl Streets, Cambridge (547 6600). Central T. **Open** 9am-7pm Mon-Thur, Sat; 9am-8pm Fri; noon-6pm Sun. **Credit** AmEx, Disc, MC, V. **Map** p311 C3.
The largest art supplier in the Boston area, with the best prices and friendliest staff. Three floors of art and crafts supplies in all media, from children's fingerpaints to professional drafting boards.

Bookshops

Barnes & Noble

395 Washington Street, at Bromfield Street, Downtown (426 5184/www.barnesandnoble.com). Downtown Crossing or Park St T. **Open** 9am-8pm Mon-Sat; 11am-6pm Sun. **Credit** AmEx, DC, Disc, MC, V. **Map** p307 G4.
The largest downtown branch of the biggest bookseller in the USA. Has just about every book you've ever heard of, plus every book you've never heard of.

Border's Books and Music

10-24 School Street, at Washington Street, Beacon Hill (557 7188). Gov't Center, Park St or State T. **Open** 7am-9pm Mon-Sat; 10am-8pm Sun. **Credit** AmEx, Disc, MC, V. **Map** p307 G4.
This large downtown branch of the massive chain store is a cosy place to browse. The relaxed atmosphere is aided by comfy reading areas and a café.

Brookline Booksmith

279 Harvard Avenue, at Coolidge Corner, Brookline (566 6660). Coolidge Corner T. **Open** 8.30am-11pm Mon-Fri; 9am-11pm Sat; 10am-8pm Sun. **Credit** AmEx, MC, V. **Map** p311 A5.
Award-winning independent bookstore with a busy schedule of readings and special events.

Comicazi

380 Highland Avenue, at Cutter, Somerville (666 2664/www.comicazi.com). Davis T. **Open** 11am-9pm Mon-Sat; noon-6pm Sun. **Credit** AmEx, MC, V.
Vintage and modern comics, plus pop, superhero and sci-fi memorabilia fill this shop, just two blocks out of Davis Square.

Grolier Poetry Book Shop

6 Plympton Street, at Massachusetts Avenue, Harvard Square, Cambridge (547 4648). Harvard T. **Open** noon-6.30pm Mon-Sat. **Credit** AmEx, Disc, MC, V. **Map** p311 B3.
A local institution since 1927, the Grolier is dedicated exclusively to poetry. It was once a cliquey hangout that relied on the trust fund of one of the owners' wives for financial support, but by the 1950s the Grolier had become a profit-making operation. Today the business continues to thrive, as does its annual award, the prestigious Grolier Poetry Prize.

Harvard Book Store

1256 Massachusetts Avenue, across from Harvard University, Cambridge (661 1515). Harvard T. **Open** 9am-11pm Mon-Thur; 9am-midnight Fri, Sat; 10am-10pm Sun. **Credit** AmEx, Disc, V, MC. **Map** p311 B2.
Selling new books, publishers' overstock and used paperbacks, this store specialises mainly in academic texts. Good prices, great customer service and an intelligent clientele distinguish this shop.

WordsWorth Books

30 Brattle Street, Harvard Square, Cambridge (354 5201). Harvard T. **Open** 9am-11.15am Mon-Sat; 10am-10am Sun. **Credit** AmEx, Disc, MC, V. **Map** p311 B1/2.
A well-stocked discount bookshop with more than 100,000 titles. Selected titles are discounted by anything from 10% to 40%.

Avenue Victor Hugo Book Shop. *See p175.*

Second-hand & rare books

Avenue Victor Hugo Book Shop

339 Newbury Street, between Hereford Street & Massachusetts Avenue, Back Bay (266 7746). Hynes/ICA T. **Open** 10am-10pm Mon-Sat; noon-10pm Sun. **Credit** MC, V. **Map** p306 E5.

A dusty retreat complete with sleepy and petulant resident cats, the Victor Hugo sells second-hand and new books on all subjects, rare and first editions and magazines dating back to 1850. Fiction, science fiction and history are a speciality.

Brattle Book Shop

9 West Street, at Washington Street, Downtown (542 0210). Downtown Crossing or Park St T. **Open** 9am-5.30pm Mon-Sat. **Credit** AmEx, MC, V. **Map** p307 G5.

Established in 1825, this cosy general bookshop boasts a fine antiquarian selection.

Cameras & videos

Bromfield Camera & Video

10 Bromfield Street, between Washington & Tremont Streets, Downtown (426 5230). Park St T. **Open** 8.30am-6pm Mon-Fri; 9am-5.30pm Sat. **Credit** AmEx, Disc, MC, V. **Map** p307 G4.

Sells and repairs new and second-hand cameras, video and digital equipment, and stocks a decent selection of hard-to-find photographic equipment.

Calumet Photographic

65 Bent Street, at First Street, Cambridge (576 2600). Lechmere T. **Open** 8am-6pm Mon-Fri. **Credit** AmEx, Disc, MC, V. **Map** p306 E/F3.

Considered the best stockist by local pros, Calumet offers professional photographic equipment for sale or rent. Its digital department is impressive.

CDs, tapes & records

Boston Beat

279 Newbury Street, at Gloucester Street, Back Bay (247 2428). Copley T. **Open** 11am-9pm Mon-Thur, Sun; 11am-10pm Fri, Sat. **Credit** AmEx, Disc, MC, V. **Map** p306 E5.

A comprehensive shop that stocks house, techno, ambient and lounge tunes on vinyl and CD. It also sells a range of DJ equipment.

HMV

1 Brattle Square, at Mount Auburn Street, Cambridge (868 9696). Harvard T. **Open** 10am-10pm Mon-Thur; 10am-midnight Fri, Sat; 11am-9pm Sun. **Credit** AmEx, Disc, MC, V. **Map** p311 B2.

A well-stocked store, as you'd expect from this international chain. Features a good classical department.
Branch: 24 Winter Street, Downtown (357 8444).

Newbury Comics

332 Newbury Street, between Hereford Street & Massachusetts Avenue, Back Bay (236 4930). Hynes/ICA T. **Open** 10am-10pm Mon-Sat; 11am-8pm Sun. **Credit** AmEx, Disc, MC, V. **Map** p306 E5.

A hip regional chain that started as a humble comic-book store, but now sells reasonably priced CDs too.

Other Music

90 Winthrop Street, at John F Kennedy Street, Cambridge (491 4419). Harvard T. **Open** 11am-9pm Mon-Sat; 11am-7pm Sun. **Credit** AmEx, MC, V. **Map** p311 B2/3.

The Boston branch of a Manhattan collector's haven specialises in imports and rare underground and experimental music.

Tower Records

360 Newbury Street, at Massachusetts Avenue, Back Bay (247 5900). Hynes/ICA T. **Open** 9am-12.30pm Mon; 9am-midnight Tue-Sun. **Credit** AmEx, Disc, MC, V. **Map** p306 E5.

A multi-level monolith, well stocked in every genre. The cult-conscious book and magazine department attracts a late-night crowd of enthusiasts.

Computer rental

Kinko's

187 Dartmouth Street, between Stuart & St James Streets, Back Bay (262 6188). Back Bay or Copley T. **Open** 24 hours daily. **Credit** AmEx, Disc, MC, V. **Map** p306 F5.

Oh, glorious Kinko's – a saving grace to anyone on the road with reprographic needs. Offers full copy and print services, plus hourly rentals of Internet-ready Mac and IBM computers. Kinko's also does colour laserprints, scanning, transparencies, lamination, binding and mounting. The round-the-clock opening hours can be a life- (or at least a job-) saver.
Branches: 10 Post Office Square, at Milk Street, Downtown (482 4400); 2 Center Plaza, Government Center (973 9000); 1 Mifflin Place, Cambridge (497 0125).

Electronics

Bang & Olufsen

30 Newbury Street, at Arlington Avenue, Back Bay (262 4949). Arlington T. **Open** 10am-6pm Mon-Sat; noon-5pm Sun. **Credit** AmEx, Disc, MC, V, DC. **Map** p306 F5.

High-end, Danish-designed audio, video and telephone equipment and accessories. Looks like art, costs as much.

Tweeter Etc

350 Boylston Street, at Berkeley Street, Back Bay (262 2299/www.tweeter.com). Arlington T. **Open** 10am-7pm Mon-Sat; noon-6pm Sun. **Credit** AmEx, Disc, MC, V. **Map** p306 F5.

As well as its moderate to high-end inventory of audio, video and telephone equipment, Tweeter offers a 30-day price guarantee: if your purchase sells for less elsewhere, it refunds the difference.
Branch: 874 Commonwealth Avenue, Brookline (738 4411).

Fashion

Boutiques

Alan Bilzerian

34 Newbury Street, between Arlington & Berkeley Streets, Back Bay (536 1001). Arlington T. **Open** 10am-6pm Mon-Wed, Fri, Sat; 10am-7pm Thur. **Credit** AmEx, MC, V. **Map** p306 F5.

A posh boutique with men's and women's attire from the world's top designers. It has exclusive Boston selling rights on Yohji Yamamoto, Ann Demeulemeester, John Galliano and Olivier Theyskens, and US rights on Tokyo's Jipi Japa label.

Allston Beat

348 Newbury Street, between Hereford Street & Massachusetts Avenue, Back Bay (421 9555). Hynes/ICA T. **Open** 11am-9pm Mon-Thur; 11am-10pm Fri, Sat. **Credit** AmEx, MC, V. **Map** p306 E5.

This local alternative institution, owned by a Brit, is club clothes central, selling Pimpgear, Doc Martens, Lip Service and other trendy lines in artificial fabrics. Good spot for funky accessories and body jewellery.

Hermès – not for light wallets.

Betsey Johnson

201 Newbury Street, between Exeter & Fairfield Streets, Back Bay (236 7072). Copley T. **Open** 11am-7pm Mon-Sat; noon-6pm Sun. **Credit** AmEx, MC, V. **Map** p306 E5.

Famously funky designer of affordable to top-of-the-range separates, evening wear, shoes, accessories and jewellery. The clothes are known for their body-conscious design and sumptuous colour.

Dorothy's Boutique

190 Massachusetts Avenue, at Huntington Avenue, South End (262 9255). Hynes/ICA or Symphony T. **Open** 9.30am-6.30pm Mon-Sat. **Credit** AmEx, MC, V. **Map** p306 E6.

Whether you're a transvestite street walker or just an average Jane looking to tart up a little, Dorothy's is one-stop shopping. Wigs, 'large shoe sizes', garter belts, accessories, glitter, French maid aprons and more, all at throwaway cheap prices.

Hermès

22 Arlington Street, at Boylston Street, Back Bay (482 8707). Arlington T. **Open** 10am-6pm Mon-Sat. **Credit** AmEx, Disc, MC, V. **Map** 306 F5.

Classic, understated design from the world-famous French fashion house. Men's and women's suits, leather goods and those famous silk scarves.

Intermix

186 Newbury Street, at Berkeley Street, Back Bay (236 5172). Arlington T. **Open** 11am-7pm Mon Sat; noon-6pm Sun. **Credit** AmEx, MC, V. **Map** p306 F5.

The new Boston outpost of the trendy, spendy New York boutique, carrying such high-end *Sex in the City* faves as Jimmy Choo shoes, and hip, non-designer labels at relatively low prices.

Jasmine Boutique and Sola Men

37 Brattle Street, at Church Street, Cambridge (354 6043). Harvard T. **Open** 10am-7pm Mon-Wed; 10am-8pm Thur, Fri; 10am-7pm Sat; noon-7pm Sun. **Credit** AmEx, DC, Disc, MC, V. **Map** p311 B2.

Jasmine, a women's boutique, and its brother store, Sola Men, are among the most popular fashion retailers in town, with lively, youthful collections culled from New York and international clothing labels. They also sell shoes and accessories.

Riccardi

116 Newbury Street, between Clarendon & Dartmouth Streets, Back Bay (266 3158). Copley T. **Open** 11am-7pm Mon-Sat. **Credit** AmEx, MC, V. **Map** p306 F5.

Caters to a Euro-chic clientele, selling men's and women's sportswear, evening wear, coats, shoes and accessories by prominent European and Japanese designers. Its collection includes Boston exclusives on lines by Vivienne Westwood, Thierry Mugler, Comme des Garçons, D&G and Chrome Hearts.

Serenella

134 Newbury Street, between Clarendon & Dartmouth Street, Back Bay (266 5568).

Open 10am-6pm Mon-Sat. **Credit** AmEx, MC, V. **Map** p306 F5.
As well as established European labels (including a Boston exclusive on Narciso Rodriguez), Serenella sells up-and-coming designer lines for women.

Mainstream chains

Banana Republic

Copley Place, Copley Square, Back Bay (424 7817). Back Bay or Copley T. **Open** 10am-8pm Mon-Sat; noon-6pm Sun. **Credit** AmEx, Disc, MC, V. **Map** p306 F5.
This upmarket arm of the Gap empire sells quality casualwear and business attire.
Branches: Faneuil Hall Marketplace, Downtown (439 0016); 28 Newbury Street, Back Bay (267 3933).

Brooks Brothers

46 Newbury Street, at Berkeley Street, Back Bay (267 2600). Arlington T. **Open** 9am-7pm Mon-Fri; 10am-6pm Sat; noon-6pm Sun. **Credit** AmEx, Disc, MC, V. **Map** p306 F5.
The province of preppies for generations, Brooks Brothers remains a bastion of American conservative style, although efforts have been made in recent years to relax the look (to negligible effect).
Branch: 75 State Street, Cambridge (261 9990).

The Gap

200 Newbury Street, at Exeter Street, Back Bay (267 4055). Copley T. **Open** 10am-9pm Mon-Sat; 11am-6pm Sun. **Credit** AmEx, Disc, MC, V. **Map** p306 E5.
The American standard in affordably priced casualwear. For additional branches, check the phone book – they're everywhere.

Lucky Brand

229 Newbury Street, at Fairfield Street, Back Bay (236 0102/www.luckybrandjeans.com). Copley T. **Open** 10am-7pm Mon-Sat; noon-6pm Sun. **Credit** AmEx, Disc, MC, V. **Map** p306 F5.
This California-based jean company specialises in funky, West Coast-style washes and details.

The Original Levi's Store

800 Boylston Street, Prudential Center, Back Bay (375 9010). Copley or Prudential T. **Open** 10am-8pm Mon-Sat; noon-6pm Sun. **Credit** AmEx, Disc, MC, V. **Map** p306 E5/6.
Full range of jeans and casual separates by the San Francisco original. The shop offers a custom-made jeans service, so you can even get your hands on a discontinued line.

Urban Outfitters

11 John F Kennedy Street, at Massachusetts Avenue, Cambridge (864 0070). Harvard T. **Open** 10am-10pm Mon-Thur; 10am-11pm Fri, Sat; noon-8pm Sun. **Credit** AmEx, Disc, MC, V. **Map** p311 B2.
Inexpensive, trendy designs for hip youngsters and young-at-heart hipsters who don't mind a loose thread or two. It also sells funky homeware, gifts and toys. The late-night hours are a bonus.
Branch: 261 Newbury Street, Back Bay (236 0088).

Betsey Johnson's super clobber. *See p177.*

Speciality

Louis Boston

234 Berkeley Street, at Newbury Street, Back Bay (262 6100/www.louisboston.com). Arlington T.
Open 10am-6pm Mon, Tue, Fri, Sat; 10am-8pm Wed, Thur. **Credit** AmEx, MC, V. **Map** p306 F5.
One of the finest clothing shops in the US, Louis has three floors of men's clothes and two of women's. As well as a collection of top designers from around the world, it sells an upmarket house label and employs 'personal consultants' to help customers. Its chi-chi café is frequented by local socialites.

Vintage & second-hand

Bobby from Boston

19 Thayer Street, at Harrison Avenue, South Boston (423 9299). NE Medical Center or Broadway T.
Open noon-6pm Mon-Sat. **No credit cards**. **Map** p307 G6.
The best-kept secret in Boston is well known to Japanese jeans collectors, movie wardrobe professionals and local rockers. Bobby Garnett is Boston's guru of hip vintage men's fashion and collectible Levi's. Here you'll find both $20 501's and $500 'big E' red-tags, vintage American sportswear (those sought-after Champion sweatshirts) and lots of cool men's suits, including English labels from the 1960s.

The Closet

175 Newbury Street, between Dartmouth & Exeter Streets, Back Bay (536 1919). Copley T. **Open** 10am-6pm Mon-Sat; noon-6pm Sun. **Credit** AmEx, MC, V. **Map** p306 E5.
Contemporary designer resale shop for both men and women, selling styles no more than two years old. Though not every day is a great day here, couture comes through regularly enough, at pretty serious discounts.

The Closet Upstairs

223 Newbury Street, between Exeter & Fairfield Streets, Back Bay (267 5757). Copley T. **Open** 11am-6pm Mon-Sat; noon-6pm Sun. **Credit** Disc, MC, V. **Map** p306 E5.
A small upper-floor shop with friendly, knowledgeable staff who will gladly guide you through the crowded racks without attitude or leave you alone to browse in peace. The stock comprises funky vintage clothes from the 1920s to the early 1980s, plus a few Victorian pieces, contemporary Gothic/Renaissance garments and costume accessories – full-scale angel wings of real feathers, anyone?

Garment District and Dollar-a-Pound Plus

200 Broadway, at Davis Street, Cambridge (876 5230). Kendall/MIT T. **Open** *Garment District* 11am-7pm Mon, Tue, Sun; 11am-8pm Wed-Fri; 9am-7pm Sat. *Dollar-a-Pound Plus* 9am-7pm Mon-Fri; 7.45am-7pm Sat, Sun. **Credit** AmEx, Disc, MC, V. **Map** p306 D3.

Get a hip hairdo at **Ecocentrix**. *See p184.*

This second-hand department store is a regular haunt for the city's student and hipster populations. The draw is a huge selection of vintage and designer-restyled gear, along with racks and racks of old blue jeans. It also sells cheap new clothing and accessories. The Dollar-a-Pound adjunct is for those who don't mind stains and missing zippers. Friday is 50-cents-a-pound day.

Great Eastern Trading Co

49 River Street, Central Square, Cambridge (354 5279). Central T. **Open** noon-7pm Mon-Fri; 11am-6pm Sat; 1-5pm Sun. **Credit** AmEx, Disc, MC, V. **Map** p311 C3.
Along with Oona's (*see p180*), this was one of the first vintage stores in the city, and still maintains a high standard of vintage used clothing and accessories, mostly from the 1970s.

Keezer's

140 River Street, between Massachusetts Avenue & Memorial Drive, Cambridge (547 2455). Central T. **Open** 10am-6pm Mon-Sat. **Credit** MC, V. **Map** p311 B/C3/4.
Established way back in 1895, Keezer's is the oldest used-clothing store in the country and a cherished local resource. Max Keezer started the company by going into Harvard dorms in order to buy barely-worn fine clothing from allowance-starved heirs. The shop now sells second-hand and end-of-the-line men's suits (members of the

Eat, Drink, Shop

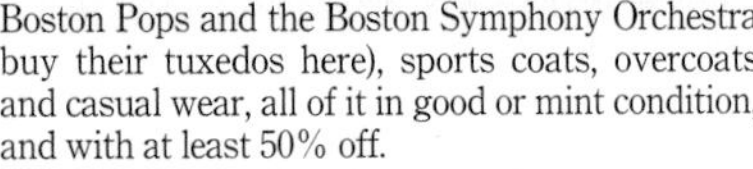

Hubba Hubba – naughty!

Boston Pops and the Boston Symphony Orchestra buy their tuxedos here), sports coats, overcoats and casual wear, all of it in good or mint condition, and with at least 50% off.

Oona's

1210 Massachusetts Avenue, between Quincy & Bow Streets, Cambridge (491 2654). Harvard T. **Open** 11am-7pm Mon-Sat; noon-6pm Sun. **Credit** AmEx, MC, V. **Map** p311 B2/3.

A landmark store selling 'experienced' (translation: used) clothing from the 1920s to the 1970s. Although some of the stock could be considered a little too experienced for its own good, the owner has a keen eye for what's back in style, so it's well worth a look.

Fetish & sex

Eros Boutique

581A Tremont Street, between Dartmouth & Clarendon Streets, South End (425 0345/ www.erosboutique.com). Back Bay T. **Open** 10am-10pm Mon-Sat; noon-8pm Sun. **Credit** AmEx, Disc, MC, V. **Map** p306 F6.

This friendly fetish boutique is possibly the least intimidating place to shop for nipple clamps in the city (the charming and discreet staff will take you behind a curtain to show you how things work, if you're the blushing type). The extensive stock includes rubber and leather clothing, restraints, toys, vibrators and much more.

Grand Opening!

Suite 32, 318 Harvard Street, at Beacon Street, Brookline (731 2626/www.grandopening.com). Coolidge Corner T. **Open** 10am-7pm Mon-Wed; 10am-9pm Thur-Sat; noon-6pm Sun. **Credit** AmEx, Disc, MC, V.

A small 'sexuality' boutique selling sex toys and tools especially, though not exclusively, for women.

Hubba Hubba

534 Massachusetts Avenue, between Brookline & Pearl Streets, Cambridge (492 9082). Central T. **Open** noon-8pm Mon-Sat. **Credit** AmEx, Disc, MC, V. **Map** p311 C3.

A locally renowned sexual fetish store that caters to almost every conceivable kink. Come here for all your leather, latex and PVC needs.

Film processing

Most pharmacy chains offer fast, inexpensive film developing and there's an **Osco** or **CVS** located in just about every part of town (check the phone book for your nearest branch).

Colortek

727 Atlantic Avenue, at Beach Street, Downtown (451 0894). South Station T. **Open** 8.30am-7pm Mon-Fri. **Credit** AmEx, Disc, MC, V. **Map** p307 G5.
A highly regarded professional chain with several conveniently located branches. Services include film and digital processing, E6 slide processing, slide duplication and exhibition-quality copy work. There's also a full mini-lab. Larger branches sell equipment and supplies.
Branches: 636 Beacon Street, Beacon Hill (236 4400); 251 Newbury Street, Back Bay (267 6503); 290 Main Street, Cambridge (868 6606).

Copley Photo

441 Stuart Street, at Dartmouth Street, Back Bay (859 8922). Back Bay or Copley T. **Open** 8am-6pm Mon-Fri; 10am-4pm Sat. **Credit** AmEx; Disc, MC, V. **Map** p306 F5.
Colour or black-and-white film developing, plus printing, passport photos, enlargements and a one-hour photo lab.

Florists

Lotus Designs

547 Columbus Avenue, at Claremont Park, South End (262 7031). Mass Ave T. **Open** 8am-6pm Mon, Tue; 8am-7pm Wed-Sat. **Credit** AmEx, Disc, MC, V. **Map** p306 E/F6.
A South End neighbourhood favourite, this florist sells only top-quality and exotic flowers and can mix an outstanding bouquet in virtually any price range.

Winston Flowers

131 Newbury Street, between Dartmouth & Clarendon Streets, Back Bay (541 1100/ www.winstonflowers.com). Copley T. **Open** 8am-6pm Mon-Sat; 9am-5pm Sun. **Credit** AmEx, Disc, MC, V. **Map** p306 F5.
With five branches in and around Boston, Winston Flowers specialises in contemporary floral design.

Food & drink

Cardullo's

6 Brattle Street, at John F Kennedy Street, Cambridge (491 8888/www.cardullos.com). Harvard T. **Open** 8am-8pm Mon-Fri; 9am-9pm Sat; 11am-7pm Sun. **Credit** AmEx, Disc, MC, V. **Map** p311 B2.
The staff at Cardullo's are so friendly and helpful you won't feel foolish if you don't know your foie gras from your elbow. The shop sells gourmet produce from around the globe.

Cremaldi's

31 Putnam Avenue, between Green & Franklin Streets, Cambridge (354 7969). Harvard T. **Open** 10am-7pm Mon-Sat. **Credit** AmEx, Disc, MC, V. **Map** p311 C3.
An old-fashioned speciality food store selling imported delicacies, desserts, herbs and spices, barrels of pasta, plus fresh meat and fish. The shop also creates and delivers beautiful gift baskets.

DeLuca's Back Bay Market

239 Newbury Street, at Fairfield Street, Back Bay (262 5990). Copley or Hynes/ICA T. **Open** 7am-10pm Mon-Sat; 7am-9pm Sun. **Credit** AmEx, MC, V. **Map** p306 E5.
Established in 1905, Boston's oldest gourmet grocer sells superior quality fruit and veg, meat, fish, caviar, champagne, freshly baked bread and more. Its motto is 'What we don't have, we get'.

Garden of Eden

577 Tremont Street, between Dartmouth Street & Union Park, South End (247 8377). Back Bay or Copley T. **Open** 7am-9pm Mon-Fri; 7am-6pm Sat, Sun. **Credit** AmEx, Disc, MC, V. **Map** p306 F6.
A stylish South End shop boasting a fine selection of imported cheeses and meats. Garden of Eden also stocks French pastry, plus readymade meals, a limited line of gourmet foods, fresh bread, coffee beans and tea.

The Seasonal Table

61 Massachusetts Avenue, at Commonwealth Avenue, Back Bay (236 7979). Hynes/ICA T. **Open** 7am-9pm Mon-Sat; 9am-4pm Sun. **Credit** AmEx, Disc, MC, V. **Map** p306 E5.
The city's newest gourmet speciality store, this remarkable shop promises to make gluttons of us all. It offers all continents and every imaginable flavour on a plate, to go. Artisan cheeses, smoked fish, freshly baked breads and pastries all sit alongside their own extensive prepared food offerings. You can take it all with you or relax in its attractive café. It also sells interesting wine and beer choices and whole-bean coffee. Come on, your guests will never know.

Italian bakeries

Bova's Bakery

134 Salem Street, at Prince Street, North End (523 5601). Haymarket T. **Open** 24 hours daily. **Credit** AmEx, MC, V. **Map** p307 G3.
Owned by the same family for 80 years, this all-night bakery creates classic Italian pastries, freshly made pizza and an extensive deli counter. It's renowned for its fresh bread.

Mike's Pastry

300 Hanover Street, between Prince & Parmenter Streets, North End (742 3050). Haymarket T. **Open** 8am-9pm Mon-Wed; 8am-10pm Thur, Sun; 8am-10.30pm Fri; 8am-11pm Sat. **No credit cards**. **Map** p307 G3/4.
The best known of the North End bakeries, Mike's is a 55-year-old family business selling traditional Italian pastries. It also has a pleasant café.

Modern Pastries

257 Hanover Street, between Cross & Richmond Streets, North End (523 3783). Haymarket T. **Open** 8am-9pm daily. **No credit cards**. **Map** p307 G/H3/4.

The North End old-timers' choice for strictly authentic Italian torrone, cakes and pastries: not too gooey, sweet or Americanised.

Liquor stores

Bauer Wine and Spirits

330 Newbury Street, between Hereford Street & Massachusetts Avenue, Back Bay (262 0363). Hynes/ICA T. **Open** 10am-11pm Mon-Sat. **Credit** AmEx, Disc, MC, V. **Map** p306 E5.

Established in 1960, this is one of Boston's most highly respected vintners. Manager Howie Rubin, a famous local wine connoisseur, selects fine wines from every (important) region in the world, and has a well-stocked liquor department to boot. Domestic and imported beers and cigars are also sold.

Blanchard's

103 Harvard Avenue, at Commonwealth Avenue, Allston (782 9500). Harvard Avenue T. **Open** 9am-11pm Mon-Sat. **Credit** MC, V. **Map** p311 A5.

Blanchard's not only takes pride in its comprehensive wine selection, but also claims to stock the largest selection of beer in the whole of New England. There's a wine-tasting room and wine consultants on the staff. Delivery is available within the Greater Boston area.

Marty's

193 Harvard Avenue, at Commonwealth Avenue, Allston (782 3250). Harvard Avenue T. **Open** 9am-11pm Mon-Sat. **Credit** AmEx, Disc, MC, V. **Map** p311 A5.

A large, comprehensive liquor store with an extensive selection of discounted fine wine, liquor, beer, handrolled cigars and gourmet food. Delivery service to Greater Boston.

Health & beauty

Barbers

Blade

603 Tremont Street, at Dartmouth Street, Back Bay (267 2200). Back Bay T. **Open** 11am-8pm Tue-Fri; 9am-5pm Sat. **Credit** MC, V. **Map** p306 F6.

A stylish shop offering traditional clipper cuts, hot lather shaves and facials, at reasonable prices.

Gregory's Barbershop

745 Boylston Street, between Fairfield & Exeter Streets, Back Bay (236 4885). Copley T. **Open** 9am-8pm Mon-Fri; 9am-6pm Sat; noon-5pm Sun. **Credit** AmEx, Disc, MC, V. **Map** p306 E5.

Gregory's is an excellent choice for luxurious men's grooming, including haircuts, hot lather shaves, facials, manicures, pedicures, foot massages and shoeshines. Every haircut includes a scalp and shoulder massage, and VIP haircuts in private rooms are available – Tom Hanks and Dave Matthews have had their locks lopped and their shoulders seen to here.

Beauty supplies

Colonial Drug

49 Brattle Street, at Church Street, Cambridge (864 2222). Harvard T. **Open** 8am-7pm Mon-Fri; 8am-6pm Sat. **No credit cards. Map** p311 A2.

A unique, family-run business, this apothecary still looks just as it did in the 1950s, but these days it carries more heavenly substances than bromide and hot water bottles. In particular, it specialises in fine imported fragrance and beauty lines. It stocks beauty products by the likes of Beauté Pacifique, Clarins, Decléor, Orlane, Christian Dior and Stendhal; and fragrances by Hermès, Caron, Guerlain and Patou.

Desana

211 Newbury Street, between Exeter & Fairfield Streets, Back Bay (450 9599). Copley T. **Open** 11am-6pm Mon-Thur; 11am-7pm Fri, Sat; noon-6pm Sun. **Credit** AmEx, MC, V. **Map** p306 E5.

The only shop in Boston to offer custom-blended fragrances, Desana stocks over 200 perfume oils from African Gold to Ylang Ylang. It also sells scented beauty products and a selection of decadent accessories for bath and boudoir, including candles, vintage kimonos and antique perfume atomisers.

E6 Apothecary

167 Newbury Street, between Dartmouth & Exeter Streets, Back Bay (236 8138/ www.e6apothecary.com). Copley T. **Open** 10am-7pm Mon-Sat; noon-6pm Sun. **Credit** MC, V. **Map** p306 E5.

A sleek beauty boutique selling hard-to-find skincare products from brands such as Shu Uemura, Philosophy, Tarte, Bliss, Watosa and LeClerc. Friendly, utterly unintimidating staff will help you pick and choose. Ships all over the world.

Fresh

121 Newbury Street, between Clarendon & Dartmouth Streets, Back Bay (421 1212). Copley T. **Open** 10am-7pm Mon-Sat; noon-6pm Sun. **Credit** AmEx, Disc, MC, V. **Map** p306 F5.

With an excellent selection of imported products and fragrances, plus its own range of natural cosmetics, Fresh has carved out a spot as one of Boston's most popular beauty stores. So popular, in fact, that its gorgeous goodies are now sold in two New York branches and at such prestigious cosmetics counters as Barney's New York and Colette in Paris.

Hairdressers

Newbury Street has about 70 hair salons, so if you feel inspired to transform yourself while shopping, snagging a walk-in appointment shouldn't be a problem. Some of Boston's prestigious salons charge through-the-roof prices, but the average price for a cut by skilled stylists is between $40 and $60.

Play that funky music

Smash City Records – vinyl heaven.

The band Kiss may have called Detroit 'rock city', but they were wrong. (About lots of things, actually. Take that stitched-on tongue, for instance. But that's another story.) Boston seems to have 20 rock bands for every square block of space. It's not surprising, then, that music stores, record shops and CD stores jostle for position on its blocks.

This is an outstanding place to shop for used musical instruments, second-hand CDs, vinyl and tapes in every musical genre, most in pristine condition.

Used LPs sell for anything from a few dollars for bargain-bin items to collector's prices for rarities. Cassette tapes are usually dirt-cheap (as they should be). Second-hand CDs, DVDs and videos will usually cost about half their retail prices.

There are more music resellers in the Boston area than there's room to list here, so keep your wits about you. Most are worth ducking into, if only for a quick glance around. The city's music interest is impressively diverse. There's very little you can't find here with a little perseverance. These are a few very worthwhile places to try.

Disc Diggers

401 Highland Avenue, at Grove Street, Somerville (776 7560). Davis T. **Open** 10am-9pm Mon-Sat; noon-7pm Sun. **Credit** Disc, MC, V.

At this Somerville location, Diggers stocks what it claims is New England's largest selection of second-hand and discounted CDs and cassettes. We didn't count, but they looked honest.

Looney Tunes

1106 Boylston Street, at Massachusetts Avenue, Back Bay (247 2238). Hynes/ICA T. **Open** 10am-9pm Mon-Sat; noon-8pm Sun. **Credit** AmEx, Disc, MC, V. **Map** p306 E5.

You'll recognise this place (at least in fair weather) by the bargain-cassette concession on the sidewalk outside and the bored, scruffy rock musician sitting behind it. The aisles between the second-hand CDs and the better-stocked record bins are a bit narrow in here, and working your way around the store in a crowd of two or more can be an exercise in contortionism, but the clientele generally adheres to a polite passing policy. Rare classical and jazz CDs are a strong speciality here, and the rock dance and funk inventories are satisfyingly dense.

Mars Records

299 Newbury Street, between Gloucester & Hereford Streets, Back Bay (266 4270). Hynes/ICA T. **Open** noon-8pm daily. **Credit** AmEx, Disc, MC, V. **Map** p306 E5.

Deuxieme at Safar

235 Newbury Street, at Fairfield Street, Back Bay (247 3933). Copley T. **Open** 9am-5.30pm Mon, Tue, Sat; 9am-7pm Wed-Fri. **Credit** AmEx, MC, V. **Map** p306 E5.

The perfect place to go to fix a botched colour job, but you're going to have to pay. Deuxieme, a luxurious, Philippe Starck-style salon on two floors of the spa-sized Safar salon, specialises in serious colour, charging about $185 to $300 a head. Safar offers facials, manicures, pedicures and waxing.

Ecocentrix

30 Newbury Street, between Arlington & Berkeley Streets, Back Bay (262 2222). Arlington T. **Open** 9am-4pm Mon; 9am-7pm Tue-Fri; 9am-5pm Sat. **Credit** Disc, MC, V. **Map** p306 F5.

Local award-winners with a reputation for hip, style-savvy cuts and colour.

A small, independently owned shop staffed by honest, friendly music fans. The selection of new and used CDs and vinyl here is strongest on reggae, hip hop, lounge, electronica and punk rock, with a smaller inventory of jazz and blues titles.

Mystery Train II

306 Newbury Street, between Gloucester & Hereford Streets, Back Bay (536 0216). Hynes/ICA T. **Open** 10.30am-7.30pm daily. **Credit** AmEx, Disc, MC, V. **Map** p306 E5.

On the same stretch of Newbury as the above two shops, MT offers an impressive inventory of collectibles. The staff can discuss arcane details of rock history – and will, if they're in the mood. Headphone set-ups allow you to check out the records for scratches.

Skippy White's

538 Massachusetts Avenue, between Norfolk & Prospect Streets, Cambridge (491 4455). Central T. **Open** 10am-6pm Mon-Wed, Sat; 10am-9pm Thur, Fri; 11am-5pm Sun. **Credit** MC, V.

This shop in Cambridge's Central Square has been an institution for collectors of R&B, blues, jazz, gospel, soul and oldies since 1961. It's also worth wandering across the street to **Cheapo Records**, which has a huge selection of oldies in every category from African to zydeco.

Smash City Records

304 Newbury Street, between Gloucester and Hereford Streets, Back Bay (536 0216). Hynes/ICA T. **Open** 10.30am-9pm Mon-Thur; 10.30am-10.30pm Fri, Sat. **Credit** AmEx, Disc, MC, V. **Map** p306 E5.

A few doors away from Mars, Smash City offers a seemingly endless collection to choose from. The truly committed record collector can dig through a huge stock of dollar records and a free bin.

James Joseph Salon

168 Newbury Street, between Dartmouth & Exeter Streets, Back Bay (266 7222/ www.jamesjosephsalon.com). Copley T. **Open** 10am-7pm Mon-Fri; 9am-5pm Sat; 10am-6pm Sun. **Credit** MC, V. **Map** p306 E5.

Popular with the international college crowd, this trendy Back Bay salon can accommodate virtually any colour, cut and styling request from punk to conservative. You can get it all here.

Niall Roberts

253 Newbury Street, at Fairfield Street, Back Bay (536 7243). Copley T. **Open** noon-8.15pm Mon; 11am-7.15pm Tue; 10am-7pm Wed; 9.45am-8pm Thur, Fri; 8.45am-5pm Sat; 10am-6.15pm Sun. **Credit** AmEx, Disc, MC, V. **Map** p306 E5.

Reasonable prices, competent cut and colour services and a relaxed vibe are the distinguishing factors of this Newbury Street salon.

Olive's Beauty Salon

565 Columbus Avenue, at Massachusetts Avenue, South End (247 3333/www.olivestextures.com). Mass Ave T. **Open** 9am-6pm Tue, Thur, Fri; 11.30am-7pm Wed; 9am-2pm Sat. **Credit** AmEx, MC, V. **Map** p306 E6.

Specialising in curly hair, Olive's offers hair relaxing, cutting and colour, as well as body massage, manicures and pedicures.

Spas & salons

Candela Laserspa

28 Arlington Street, between Boylston Street & St James Avenue, Back Bay (426 6999/ www.candelaspa.com). Arlington T. **Open** 5.30am-9pm Mon-Fri; 8.30am-6pm Sat, Sun. **Credit** AmEx, MC, V. **Map** p306 F5.

Offers hair and skin services, a laser clinic, manicures and pedicures, plus a whirlpool and lap pool.

Giuliano

338 Newbury Street, between Hereford & Massachusetts Avenue, Back Bay (262 2220). Hynes/ICA T. **Open** 9am-6pm Mon; 8am-8pm Tue-Fri; 8am-5pm Sat; 10am-6pm Sun. **Credit** AmEx, Disc, MC, V. **Map** p306 E5.

Giuliano styles itself as a 'full-service salon and wellness center'. If this description doesn't mean much to you, the best way to get a handle on what looks like advertising gibberish is to pop along for a treatment. No detail is omitted: after your haircut, you can visit a board-certified plastic surgeon or, if you're feeling less adventurous, maybe just a cosmetic dentist.

Le Pli Salon and Day Spa

Charles Hotel, 5 Bennett Street, Cambridge (547 4081). Harvard T. **Open** 9am-5.30pm Mon-Wed; 9am-7.30pm Thur, Fri; 9am-5pm Sat; 10am-5pm Sun. **Credit** AmEx, MC, V. **Map** p311 B2.

Hair and skin treatments in an elegant spa setting in Cambridge.

Saks Fifth Avenue Salon and Spa

Saks Fifth Avenue, Prudential Plaza, Back Bay (262 8500). Copley or Prudential T. **Open** 10am-6pm Mon, Sat;10am-8pm Tue-Fri. **Credit** AmEx, DC, Disc, MC, V. **Map** p306 E5.

Comprehensive spa skin-care services and massage. Half- and full-day packages include 'Essential Elements', which offers an anti-ageing facial, eye-contour treatment, manicure, shampoo and style and make-up refresher, for $140.

Shopping by area

Back Bay

Antiques, art & collectibles

Brodney Gallery *see p173*; **India Antiques, Art and Music** *see p173*; **Johnson Paint and Art Materials** *see p174*; **Marcoz Antiques** *see p173*.

Books, music & more

Avenue Victor Hugo Book Shop *see p175*; **Boston Beat** *see p175*; **Daddy's Junky Music** *see p188*; **International Poster Gallery** *see p188*; **Jack's Drum Shop** *see p188*; **Looney Tunes** *see p184*; **Mars Records** *see p184*; **Mystery Train II** *see p185*; **Newbury Comics** *see p175*; **Smash City Records** *see p185*; **Tower Records** *see p175*.

Fashion

Alan Bilzerian *see p177*; **Aldo** *see p189*; **Allston Beat** *see p177*; **Banana Republic** *see p178*; **Betsey Johnson** *see p177*; **Brooks Brothers** *see p178*; **The Closet** *see p179*; **The Closet Upstairs** *see p179*; **Cuoio** *see p189*; **The Gap** *see p178*; **Hermès** *see p177*; **Intermix** *see p177*; **John Fluevog** *see p189*; **Lord & Taylor** *see p172*; **Louis Boston** *see p179*; **Lucky Brand** *see p178*; **Marshall's** *see p173*; **Neiman Marcus** *see p172*; **The Original Levi's Store** *see p178*; **Riccardi** *see p177*; **Saks Fifth Avenue** *see p172;* **Serenella** *see p177;* **Thom Brown** *see p189*; **Walker's Riding Apparel** *see p190*.

Food & drink

DeLuca's Back Bay Market *see p181*; **The Seasonal Table** *see p181*; **Bauer Wine and Spirits** *see p183*.

Health & beauty

Blade (barber) *see p183*; **Candela Laserspa** (spa) *see p185*; **Desana** (beauty supplies) *see p183*; **Deuxieme at Safar** (hairdresser) *see p184*; **E6 Apothecary** (beauty supplies) *see p183*; **Ecocentrix** (hairdresser) *see p184*; **Fresh** (beauty supplies) *see p183*; **Gregory's Barbershop** (barber) *see p183*; **Giuliano** (spa) *see p185*; **James Joseph Salon** (hairdresser) *see p185*; **Niall Roberts** (hairdresser) *see p185*; **Saks Fifth Avenue Salon and Spa** (spa) *see p185*; **Salon Nordic** (spa) *see p186*.

Jewellery

Cartier *see p186*; **Dorfman Jewelers** *see p186*; **John Lewis** *see p186*; **Shreve, Crump & Lowe** *see p186*; **Tiffany & Co** *see p187*.

Services & necessities

Back Bay Laundry and Dry-cleaning Emporium *see p187*; **Bang & Olufson** *see p175*; **Buried Treasures** *see p189*; **Cigar Masters** *see p190*; **Copley Photo** *see p181*; **Gloucester Street Cigar Company** *see p190*; **Kinko's** *see p175*; **LM Peretti Co, Inc** *see p190*; **Time and Time Again** *see p190*; **Tweeter Etc** *see p175*; **Willowbee & Kent Travel Company** *see p187*; **Winston Flowers** *see p181*.

Salon Nordic

221 Newbury Street, between Exeter & Fairfield Streets, Back Bay (421 9551). Copley T. **Open** 10am-6pm Mon-Fri; 9am-5pm Sat. **Credit** MC, V. **Map** p306 E5.

Facials, massage, eyelash tints and body waxing in a private, quiet salon, by appointment.

Jewellery

Cartier

40 Newbury Street, at Arlington Street, Back Bay (262 3300). Arlington T. **Open** 10am-6pm Mon-Sat. **Credit** AmEx, MC, V, DC. **Map** p306 F5.

This venerable jewellery house has a sleekly redesigned Boston store (the only Cartier store in New England) to go with its youthful new direction.

Dorfman Jewelers

24 Newbury Street, between Arlington & Berkeley Streets, Back Bay (536 2022). Arlington T. **Open** 10am-5.30pm Mon-Sat. **Credit** AmEx, DC, MC, V. **Map** p306 F5.

An elegant boutique selling unique jewellery in contemporary and classic styles.

John Lewis

97 Newbury Street, at Arlington Street, Back Bay (266 6665). Arlington T. **Open** 11am-6pm Tue-Sat. **Credit** MC, V. **Map** p306 F5.

This Boston original has been around for nearly half a century. Natural designs and organic shapes define the John Lewis style.

Shreve, Crump & Lowe

330 Boylston Street, at Arlington Street, Back Bay (267 9100). Arlington T. **Open** 10am-5.30pm Mon-Sat. **Credit** AmEx, MC, V. **Map** p306 F5.

This traditional old jewellery and luxury gift shop is Boston's own purveyor of the Tiffany level of grace and service. Whether you're buying a diamond bracelet or a bottle of fountain-pen ink, your patronage is always welcomed here.

Downtown

Antiques, books & collectibles

Barnes & Noble *see p174*; **Brattle Book Shop** *see p175*; **JMW Gallery** *see p173.*

Fashion

Filene's *see p171*; **Filene's Basement** *see p172*; **Macy's** *see p172.*

Services & necessities

Bromfield Camera & Video *see p175*; **Colortek** *see p181*; **Jack's Joke Shop** *see p187.*

Cambridge & Somerville

Antiques, art & collectibles

Cambridge Antique Market *see p173*; **NV53** *see p173*; **Pearl Art & Craft Supplies** *see p174*; **Sadye & Co** *see p173.*

Books & music

Comicazi *see p174*; **Disc Diggers** *see p184*; **Grolier Poetry Book Shop** *see p174*; **Harvard Book Store** *see p174*; **HMV** *see p175*; **Other Music** *see p175*; **Skippy White's** *see p185*; **WordsWorth Books** *see p174.*

Fashion

Berk's *see p189*; **Garment District and Dollar-a-Pound Plus** *see p179*; **Great Eastern Trading Co** *see p179*; **Jasmine Boutique and Sola Men** *see p177*; **Keezer's** *see p179*; **Oona's** *see p180*; **Urban Outfitters** *see p178.*

Services & necessities

Alpha Omega *see p190*; **Cardullo's** *see p181*; **Calumet Photographic** *see p175*; **Colonial Drug** *see p183*; **Cremaldi's** *see p181*; **Grand Opening** *see p180*; **Hubba Hubba** *see p180*; **Le Pli Salon and Day Spa** *see p185.*

Other neighbourhoods

Antiques, books & music

Antique Revival (Allston) *see p173*; **Border's Books and Music** (Beacon Hill) *see p174*; **Brookline Booksmith** (Brookline) *see p174*; **Machine Age** (South Boston) *see p173*; **Nostalgia Factory** (North End) *see p188.*

Fashion

Bobby from Boston (South Boston) *see p179;* **Dorothy's Boutique** (South End) *see p177;* **TJ Maxx** (Brookline) *see p173.*

Food & drink

Bova's Bakery (North End) *see p181*; **Garden of Eden** (South End) *see p181*; **Mike's Pastry** (North End) *see p181*; **Modern Pastries** (North End) *see p181*; **Blanchard's** (Allston) *see p183*; **Marty's** (Allston) *see p183.*

Services & necessities

The Art Store (South End) *see p173*; **Eros Boutique** (South End) *see p180*; **Lotus Designs** (South End) *see p181*; **Olive's Beauty Salon** (South End) *see p185.*

Tiffany & Co

Copley Place, Back Bay (353 0222). Back Bay or Copley T. **Open** 10am-6pm Mon-Sat; noon-5pm Sun. **Credit** AmEx, Disc, MC, V. **Map** p306 F5.

Its location in the busy and very touristy (albeit swanky) Copley Place mall saps the glamour from the experience of shopping at Tiffany's; but you still get the little blue box.

Jokes

Jack's Joke Shop

38 Boylston Street, between Tremont & Washington Streets, Downtown (426 9640/ www.jacksjokes.com). Boylston or Chinatown T. **Open** 9am-5.30pm Mon-Sat. **Credit** AmEx, MC, V. **Map** p307 G5.

Established in 1922, Jack's is the oldest joke shop in America. The rascally old owner-operators flog their huge supply of jokes, pranks, novelties and magic to a wonderfully diverse clientele.

Laundry & dry-cleaning

Back Bay Laundry and Dry-cleaning Emporium

409A Marlborough Street, at Massachusetts Avenue, Back Bay (236 4552). Hynes/ICA T. **Open** 7.30am-11pm daily. **Credit** MC, V. **Map** p306 E5.

A coin-operated laundry with dry-cleaning and wash-and-fold service. Pick-up and delivery is available in greater Boston.

Luggage

Willowbee & Kent Travel Company

519 Boylston Street, between Berkeley & Clarendon Streets, Back Bay (437 6700/ www.willowbeekent.com). Copley T. **Open** 10am-7pm Mon-Sat; noon-6pm Sun. **Credit** AmEx, Disc, MC, V. **Map** p306 F5.

A one-stop shop for travellers: the Malmberg Travel

The inimitable **Daddy's Junky Music**.

Agency arranges bookings and travel services, while a comprehensive store sells luggage, travel clothing, adventure gear and accessories.

Musical instruments

Daddy's Junky Music

159-165 Massachusetts Avenue, between Boylston Street & Huntington Avenue, Back Bay (247 0909). Hynes/ICA T. **Open** 11am-9pm Mon-Fri; 10am-7pm Sat; noon-6pm Sun. **Credit** AmEx, Disc, MC, V. **Map** p306 E6.

A regional chain that grew from a single music shop in New Hampshire. There's a large selection of new and second-hand gear, with best price guaranteed on keys, drums, guitars, amps, PA systems and more. Also offers rentals and repair.

Branch: 2238 Massachusetts Avenue, Cambridge (497 1556).

Jack's Drum Shop

1096 Boylston Street, at Massachusetts Avenue, Back Bay (266 4617/www.jacksdrumshop.com). Hynes/ICA T. **Open** 11am-7pm Mon-Fri; 10am-6pm Sat; 1-5pm Sun. **Credit** AmEx, Disc, MC, V. **Map** p306 E5.

The nation's oldest drum shop, Jack's has been a busy purveyor of percussion since 1945. The friendly, knowledgeable staff will guide you through the large selection of new and used drums, cymbals, percussion instruments and accessories as well as vintage snares and kits. The shop also offers comprehensive on-site repairs.

Posters

International Poster Gallery

205 Newbury Street, between Exeter & Fairfield Streets, Back Bay (375 0076/ www.internationalposter.com). Copley T. **Open** 10am-6pm Mon Sat; noon-6pm Sun. **Credit** AmEx, MC, V. **Map** p306 E5.

With around 3,000 images in stock, this upmarket gallery offers a huge selection of beautiful retro and contemporary posters, including vintage advertising designs, theatre posters, political propaganda from 1900 to World War II, and a few more modern pieces from the 1960s to the 1980s.

Nostalgia Factory

51 North Margin Street, at Thatcher Street, North End (720 2211). Haymarket T. **Open** 10am-5pm Mon-Sat. **Credit** AmEx, Disc, MC, V. **Map** p307 G3.

A treasure trove of movie memorabilia, including posters, stills, press packs and collectors' cards.

Shoes

See also p177 **Fashion**.

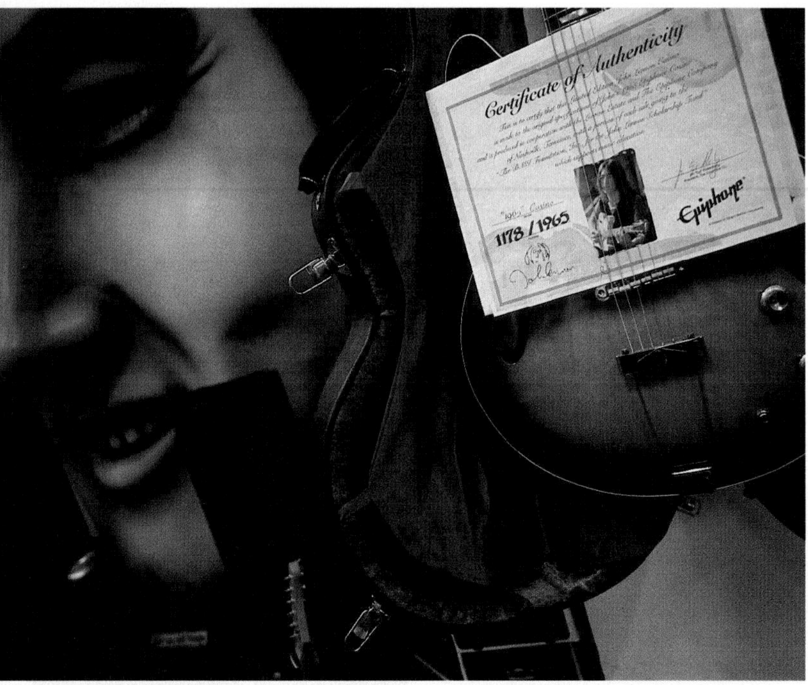

Aldo

180 Newbury Street, at Exeter Street, Back Bay (266 0501). Copley T. **Open** 10am-7pm Mon-Thur; 10am-8pm Fri, Sat; noon-6pm Sun. **Credit** AmEx, Disc, MC, V. **Map** p306 E5.

Clunky, funky fashion shoes for men and women.

Berk's

50 John F Kennedy Street, at Winthrop Street, Cambridge (492 9511/www.berkshoes.com). Harvard T. **Open** 10am-9pm Mon-Sat; 11am-7pm Sun. **Credit** AmEx, DC, Disc, MC, V. **Map** p311 B2/3.

An exceptional, fashion-led range of shoes, boots and sneakers, including Doc Martens, Camper and London Underground.

Cuoio

115 Newbury Street, at Clarendon Street, Back Bay (859 0636). Copley T. **Open** 10am-6pm Mon-Sat; noon-5pm Sun. **Credit** AmEx, Disc, MC, V. **Map** p306 F5.

Stylish European and hard-to-find labels.

Branch: 170 Faneuil Hall Marketplace, Downtown (742 4486).

John Fluevog

302 Newbury Street, between Gloucester & Hereford Streets, Back Bay (266 1079/ www.fluevog.com). Hynes/ICA T. **Open** 11am-7pm Mon-Sat; 1-6pm Sun. **Credit** AmEx, Disc, MC, V. **Map** p306 E5.

The Canadian-based Fluevog line is fun, funky and sometimes downright silly. Most styles are unisex. The shop holds sales in January and July.

Thom Brown

331 & 337 Newbury Street, between Hereford Street & Massachusetts Avenue, Back Bay (266 8722/wwwthombrown.com). Hynes/ICA T. **Open** 10am-7pm Mon-Fri; 10am-8pm Sat; noon-7pm Sun. **Credit** AmEx, Disc, MC, V. **Map** p306 D5.

This popular shop has a trendy selection of good-quality footwear. Frequent sales are a plus.

Smoking

Buried Treasures

28 Haviland Street, between Massachusetts Avenue & Hemenway Street, Back Bay (247 1011). Hynes/ICA T. **Open** 11am-8pm Mon-Sat; noon-6pm Sun. **Credit** AmEx, MC, V. **Map** p306 E5/6.

The tie-dye clothing and reggae posters might give you a clue to the kind of smoking supplies you're going to find here: but be careful what you ask for and remember what prudes New Englanders can be: 'water-filtration devices' are sold by the dozen, but don't ask for a bong or they'll show you the door.

Cigar Masters

176 Newbury Street, between Dartmouth & Exeter Streets, Back Bay (266 4400). Copley T. **Open** 9am-midnight Mon-Sat; noon-11pm Sun. **Credit** AmEx, DC, Disc, MC, V. **Map** p306 E5.

A storefront space that feels like a private club room, Ciger Masters is both a tobacco shop, selling fine cigars, cigarettes and accessories, and a quirky retreat, with a little back bar serving beer, wine and port.

Gloucester Street Cigar Company

34 Gloucester Street, at Newbury Street, Back Bay (424 1000). Copley or Hynes/ICA T. **Open** 10am-8pm Mon-Thur; 10am-10pm Fri, Sat; noon-6pm Sun. **Credit** AmEx, Disc, DC, MC, V. **Map** p306 E5.

European cigarettes, cigars from around the world, pipes, humidors, men's shaving kits, lighters and other macho supplies.

LM Peretti Co, Inc

2½ Park Square, at Charles & Boylston Streets, Back Bay (482 0218). Arlington or Boylston T. **Open** 8.30am-8pm Mon-Fri; 8.30am-7pm Sat. **Credit** AmEx, DC, Disc, MC, V. **Map** p306 F5.

Established in 1870, Peretti's is the oldest family-owned tobacconist in the US. It specialises in handblended tobacco, makes and repairs pipes on the premises and sells an exhaustive selection of imported and domestic cigars and cigarettes.

Watch repair

Alpha Omega

57 John F Kennedy Street, at Winthrop Street, Cambridge (864 1227/www.alphaomegajewelers.com). Harvard T. **Open** 10am-6pm Mon-Fri; 10am-5pm Sat; noon-5pm Sun. **Credit** AmEx, DC, Disc, MC, V. **Map** p311 B2.

Vintage and fine Swiss watches are bought and sold and a large selection of designer jewellery is stocked. On-site repairs are available.

Time and Time Again

172 Newbury Street, between Dartmouth & Exeter Streets, Back Bay (266 6869/www.timepiece.com). Copley T. **Open** 10.30am-6.30pm Mon-Sat. **Credit** AmEx, MC, V. **Map** p306 E5.

An impressive stock of second-hand watches, including the largest selection of used Rolexes in Boston. It also buys and repairs vintage timepieces.

Western

Walker's Riding Apparel

122 Boylston Street, at Tremont Street, Back Bay (423 9050). Boylston T. **Open** 10am-6pm Mon-Sat; 1-5pm Sun. **Credit** AmEx, Disc, MC, V. **Map** p307 G5.

Rockers, country and western dudes and riders of both hogs and horses have been kitting themselves out at Walker's since 1932. The shop specialises in Western wear (fancy fringed shirts aplenty) and all types of leather for motorcycle riders and equestrians (both English and American styles).

Filene's Basement – what fun! *See p172.*

Arts & Entertainment

By Season 192
Children 198
Dance Clubs 203
Film 206
Galleries 210
Gay & Lesbian 214
Music: Rock & Roots 221
Performing Arts 227
Sport & Fitness 234

Feature boxes

Put your back into it! 195
Top five events most outsiders miss 197
Top five kid things 201
The best clubs 205
Location, location, location 209
What a drag 219
Pop go the classics 230
Fenway Park 240
The Curse of the Bambino 242

By Season

Doing it all, from Christmas to tea to witchcraft.

The **John Hancock Tower** overlooks it all.

'I guess God made Boston on a wet Sunday,' Raymond Chandler wrote. While Chandler had a point – leaky clouds and drippy skies certainly aren't unusual in Boston – the city isn't nearly as notorious for rain as, say, Seattle. But rain it does.

Still, whatever the weather when you arrive in New England, there is always plenty going on to keep you occupied. The events and festivals listed below are held annually. Precise dates are difficult to pin down in advance because they're often weather-dependent. The best way to confirm the specifics of an event is by phoning the **City of Boston Special Events Line** (1-800 822 0038).

Winter

Winter, of course, is the bleakest season in New England. If you ever wondered what made the Puritans so grumpy, spend a February here. The days at this time of year are grey and dreary. Temperatures are often below freezing so sleet, snow and ice are seemingly permanent inhabitants in Boston. But there's nothing more serene than the sight of the city blanketed in snow: it looks downright Dickensian. Unfortunately, urban living (read: pollution, cars and road sand) turns two-day-old snow into brown slush, so by the time February plods in, the novelty has worn off and new snow flurries bring shrugs of resignation rather than snowball fights.

Christmas Tree Lighting

Prudential Center (1-800 746 7778/236 2366). Prudential or Hynes/ICA T. **Date** 1st Sat of Dec. **Admission** free. **Map** p306 E5/6.

The Prudential Center has the most magnificent tree in the city, swaddled in colourful lights. The lighting is the semi-official kick-off for the holiday season and there's usually a sing-along.

Boston Common Tree Lighting

Boston Common (635 4505). Park Street T. **Date** 1st weekend in Dec. **Map** p307 G4.

Fifty of the Common's trees are strung with fairy lights. A nativity scene and menorah are usually set up near the Park Street Station. A local dignitary (often the mayor) flicks the switch.

Boston Tea Party Re-enactment

Boston Tea Party Ship and Museum, Congress Street Bridge (338 1773/482 6439/ www.bostonteapartyship.com). **Date** 13 Dec (or the nearest Sun). **Map** p307 H5.

'Patriots' gather for a town meeting at the Old South Meeting House to scream about nasty old King George III. Fife and drum in hand, the excitable group marches to a replica tea ship on the waterfront and does the dirty deed.

First Night

Events at locations throughout the city (542 1399/ www.firstnight.org). **Date** 31 Dec. **Admission** $15.

Boston was the first city in the country to offer this alcohol-free alternative to ringing in the New Year, back in the 1970s. First Night is celebrated citywide with pageants, parades, performances and outdoor art. Main events include the Grand Procession and the Perrier Irrepressible Laser Light Show on Boston Common. It all culminates in a midnight fireworks display on the harbour. Leave the bubbly at home.

Boston Wine Expo

World Trade Center Boston, 164 Northern Avenue, at B Street (1-877 946 3976/ www.wine-expos.com/boston). South Station T. **Date** 2nd weekend in Jan. **Admission** 1-day $70, 2-day $92. **Map** p307 H5.

Spit, but don't swallow at this gigantic boozer. Held at the harbourside World Trade Center, this grape fest features tastings from 400 domestic and international wineries, celebrity chef demonstrations and educational seminars.

No, really, it was a very historic event. The Tea Party is played out each year. *See p192.*

Chinese New Year

Beach and Tyler Streets (536 4100/1-888 733 2678/ www.bostonusa.com). Chinatown T. **Date** late Jan or early Feb, depending on lunar calendar. **Admission** free. **Map** p307 G5.

Three weeks of festivities take place every year in celebration to the first day of the Chinese calendar. The event is filled with colour and interest for those of all nationalities, most are attracted by the dragon dancing and fireworks. The nation's third largest celebration of the Chinese New Year. Most of the action takes place around Beach and Tyler Streets.

Beanpot Hockey Tournament

FleetCenter, Causeway Street (624 1000/ www.fleetcenter.com). North Station T. **Date** 1st & 2nd Mon in Feb. **Admission** $20-$30. **Map** p307 G3.

Sweaty ice skaters from Harvard, Northeastern, Boston University and Boston College go helmet-to-helmet in this annual ice-capade. It's the only sports match in Boston where you'll hear anything chanted other than 'bullshit', as an audience of rival college students assault one another with fusillades of jeers and cheers. The winning team gets a trophy shaped like, um, a beanpot.

New England Boat Show

Bayside Exposition Center, 200 Mount Vernon Street, at Morrissey Boulevard (1-800 225 1577/ 242 6092/www.naexpo.com). JFK/UMASS T. **Date** last week in Feb. **Admission** $8; $3 concessions.

The dinghies come out to play, along with propellers, yachts and salty seafarers at the largest showcase of its kind in the Eastern US. This annual tradeshow focuses on the latest in sailing and motorised craft, though vintage and antique boats also dock here. Grab your fishing hat and float over to the Bayside Exposition Center on Mount Vernon Street.

Boston Massacre Re-enactment

Old State House, State Street, at Washington Street (720 1713/720 3290/www.bostonhistory.org). State T. **Date** 5 Mar. **Admission** free. **Map** p307 G4.

A gathering to watch the 'cowardly' Redcoats take potshots from the balcony of the Old State House at five Patriot heroes below. Costumes, muskets and – hopefully – blanks are supplied courtesy of the Massachusetts Council of Minutemen and Militia.

New England Spring Flower & Garden Show

Bayside Exposition Center, 200 Mount Vernon Street, at Morrissey Boulevard (536 9280/www.masshort.org). JFK/UMASS T. **Date** 2nd week in Mar. **Admission** $7-$20.

Hyping itself as the third largest flower show in the world, this century-old tradition celebrates shrubs, bushes, and blossoms. The Massachusetts Horticultural Society sponsors five acres (two hectares) of landscaped gardens, flower arrangements and horticultural displays at the Bayside Exposition Center on Mount Vernon Street.

St Patrick's Day Parade & Evacuation Day

Dorchester Street and Broadway (536 4100). Broadway T. **Date** 17 Mar. **Admission** free. **Map** p307 H7.

They call Boston the capital of Irish America – as such, every nook and cranny of the Hub wears a shamrock on St Paddy's Day, making Boston both the best and worst place to be on the 17th. A legal holiday for the city, the day begins with the Irish community of South Boston hosting one of the largest St Patrick's Day parades in America, complete with floats, marching bands, war veterans and, of course, waving politicians. Evacuation Day also gets a formal nod when a smaller ceremony commemorates the day the British left town in 1776. But the real festivities begin in the late afternoon, when local pubs froth with green beer, bibulous merry-making and high cover charges. By midnight, the downtown streets are so full of soused pedestrians that the act of hailing a taxi is tantamount to catching a flyball at Fenway.

Spring

For the heat-averse, spring is gentler than summer or winter, but less predictable. The weather is erratic; temperatures can vary wildly from day to day, careening from near freezing to t-shirt weather. Chilly rain is chased by silky warm days. But most would agree those lovely warm days make it all worthwhile. Still, you take your chances in this season.

Lantern Hanging

Salem Street at Hull Street (523 6676/www.oldnorth.com). Haymarket or North Station T. **Date** Sun before 19 Apr. **Admission** free. **Map** p307 G3.

Two lanterns are ceremoniously hung in the steeple of the Old North Church to commemorate sexton Robert Newman's warning that the British troops were headed for Concord 'by land'.

Patriot's Day Re-enactments

Various sites in Concord and Lexington (1-978 459 6150/1-800 443 3332/www.merrimackvalley.org). **Date** 3rd Mon in Apr. **Admission** free.

In Boston, Paul Revere gallops around, yelling about British invasion. In Lexington, on Lexington Green, there's a full-scale re-enactment – complete with uniforms and muskets – of the skirmish that produced the 'shot heard round the world'.

Boston Marathon

Finishes at Copley Square (236 1652/www.bostonmarathon.org). Copley T. **Date** 3rd Mon in Apr. **Admission** free. **Map** p306 F5.

These days, Patriot's Day in Boston has more to do with athleticism – or heavy legs and wheezing breaths – than nationalism. The race begins in Hopkinton (southwest of Boston), wraps around the campus of Boston College and finishes in Copley Square – and at least one running Elvis makes the arduous trek. Thousands of spectators come out to sniff the adrenaline.

James Joyce Ramble

Starts and finishes at Endicott Estate on East Street, Dedham (1-781 329 9744/www.ramble.org). **Date** last Sunday in Apr.

Promoting itself as 'A Convergence of Active Hearts and Minds', this annual 10-kilometre (six-mile) run/walk descends upon Dedham (a south-western suburb of Boston) every spring. While the event is fundamentally a road race, the James Joyce Ramble pays tribute to its namesake by punctuating the contest with an ensemble of Joyce-reading players. Mile one features *Finnegan's Wake*, Mile three *Portrait of the Artist* and Mile six, appropriately, *The Dead*. Past post-race festivities have featured an awards ceremony, a small concert, free food and perhaps, purely in homage to Joyce of course, free beer.

Harvard Square Book Festival

Various locations in Harvard Square (441 2884/1-800 862 5678/www.bookfestival.com). Harvard T. **Date** 2nd week in May. **Admission** free to $85. **Map** p311 B2.

A couple of years ago, even Salman Rushdie showed his threatened and balding head for this scholarly soirée. A major event for literary junkies, and their hangers-on, the Harvard Square Book Festival celebrates all things literary by inviting notable authors for panels, discussions and readings. The week-long series includes authors' luncheons, book signings and children's events. The seminars are often fascinating, even for those with just a passing interest.

Lilac Sunday

Arnold Arboretum, Arborway at Centre Street, Jamaica Plain (524 1717/ www.arboretum.harvard.edu). Forest Hills T. **Date** 2nd Sun in May. **Admission** free.

The name says it all: 400 varieties of fragrant lilacs are in bloom and it's Sunday.

Summer

This is the time of year that the locals love most – students have scattered, the subway is less congested and warm temperatures encourage cool temperament. Although the weather can get uncomfortably warm, many consider it a good time to visit, as the city is somewhat less crowded and the many parks are so inviting.

Lesbian & Gay Pride Festival

Various locations throughout the city (520 3350/ www.bostonpride.org). **Date** 1st week in June.

Beginning with an AIDS awareness walk around the Charles River Basin, the week's festivities include lectures, concerts, readings, performances and parties. It all culminates in a parade through the South End on the Saturday and a carnival on the Sunday.

Central Square World's Fair

Central Square, Cambridge (868 3247). Central T. **Date** 1st weekend in June. **Admission** free. **Map** p311 C3.

Gospel music makes the balloon animals sway, as plates of Indian curry sit comfortably beside houmous. Or uncomfortably. Whatever. It sits there. This day-long street fair in Cambridge's Central Square mingles the neighbourhood's diverse population, rendering it one of the few area events that still summons the community spirit.

Nantucket Film Festival

Various locations in Nantucket (1-508 325 6274/ www.nantucketfilmfestival.org). **Date** 3rd week in June. **Admission** $50 one day, $400 week.

Agents, actors and fans converge on Massachusetts' most exclusive vacation spot, Nantucket Island, for an insider's look at the silver screen. Screenwriting workshops and social events punctuate movie screenings.

Cambridge River Festival

Memorial Drive, between Central and Harvard Squares (349 4380/www.ci.cambridge.ma.us/~CAC). Central or Harvard T. **Date** mid June. **Admission** free. **Map** p311 B3.

An international festival along the Cambridge side of the Charles. There's music and dance, an international bazaar, visual arts and crafts and various children's activities.

Bunker Hill Celebrations

Various locations in Charlestown (242 5669/ www.nps.gov/bost). North Station T. **Date** 3rd weekend in June. **Admission** free.

A re-enactment of the famous battle – complete with military costumes and muskets. The event kicks off with a parade in Charlestown and carries on over at the Charlestown Naval Yard.

Boston Harborfest

Various locations in Boston (227 1528/ www.bostonharborfest.com). **Date** 4th week in June. **Admission** varies.

A maritime festival of fireworks, open-air concerts and (yet more) historical re-enactments, this waterfest plops itself into more than 30 harbourside venues. The Chowdahfest (a celebration of all the many variations of clam chowder) is the best part.

Put your back into it!

Some consider it an annual example of man's desire to conquer water by hanging out in vaguely phallic-looking boats and showing off, but the Head Of The Charles Regatta, held on the Charles River each fall, is actually the world's largest two-day rowing event, attracting skilled rowers from across the globe. Hundreds of thousands of people line the river and watch the boats swish by in what is, on a sunny day, an undeniably gorgeous scene.

Even when there isn't any cheering, rowing is omnipresent along the 60-mile (97-km) Charles. Kayaks, sculls and canoes are a permanent fixture here; they usually belong to college crew teams, with Harvard, Boston University or Boston College being the most prominent. Others on the river are often local prep schools and members of private rowing organisations like **Community Rowing** (455 1992) and **Cambridge's Riverside Boat Club** (492 1869/ www.riversideboatclub.com).

Although rowing has typically been a sport for the privileged – available only to folks with club memberships, cash to burn or old school ties – oar-pushing has become more accessible within the past decade. Inner-city high school girls now partake in crew, thanks to a public programme called G-Row (Girls Row Boston).

Casual athletes rent boats by the hour from **Charles River Canoe and Kayak** (965 5110/ www.ski-paddle.com). So, if you fancy yourself as Steve Redgrave, here's your chance to put your money where your mouth is.

'Old Ironsides', the **USS Constitution**.

Boston Pops Fourth of July Concert

Charles River Esplanade (266 1492/ www.bso.org/pops). Arlington or Copley T. **Date** 4 July. **Admission** free. **Map** p306 F4.

The Boston Pops are an institution here, and this concert is the centre of the universe for fans. Frantically territorial families show up at dawn to claim their grassy patch for the day. Independence Day attracts as many as a million visitors, all of who plant themselves along the banks of the Charles River. Technically, the event is non-alcoholic, but regulars are savvy enough to conceal their drinks in plastic cups. In the early evening – after everyone is tuckered out from a day of guarding blankets (and hiding beer) – the Pops play, their finale always includes the *1812 Overture* and an incredible fireworks display.

Turning of USS Constitution

Viewing along Boston Harbor (426 1812/ www.ussconstitutionmuseum.org). **Date** 4 July. **Admission** free. **Map** p307 G3.

'Old Ironsides', still a commissioned naval vessel, makes her annual sail around Boston Harbor to turn around and re-dock in the opposite direction at the Charlestown Naval Yard – an act undertaken to insure the ship weathers evenly.

Bastille Day

French Library and Cultural Center, 53 Marlborough Street, at Berkeley Street (266 4351/ www.frenchlib.org). Arlington T. **Date** 14 July. **Admission** $20. **Map** p306 F5.

This evening of traditional French food, wine and song on Marlborough Street in Back Bay may be a little on the expensive side, but, like escargots, it's worth trying once.

Edgartown Regatta

Edgartown, Martha's Vineyard (1-508 627 4361). **Date** 2nd weekend in July.

The Edgartown Yacht Club sponsors races for four categories of vessels. Even for those who do not have a boat, it offers an excuse to take the short ferry ride out to the white sand beaches of Martha's Vineyard and wander around the holiday island.

Feast of the Blessed Sacrament

New Bedford (1-508 992 6911/ www.portuguesefeast.com). **Date** last weekend in July. **Admission** free.

The largest Portuguese cultural event in America. The harbour town of New Bedford hosts this city-wide celebration – it features a parade, entertainment and music.

Gloucester Waterfront Festival

Various locations in Gloucester (1-978 283 1601/ www.capeannvacations.com). **Date** mid Aug.

One of the towns that put Boston's fishing industry on the map, Gloucester puts on this annual festival in celebration of the sea, with a Yankee Lobster Bake, whale watching and musical entertainment.

Provincetown Carnival Week

Various locations in Provincetown (1-508 487 2313/ 1-800 637 8696/www.ptown.org). **Date** 3rd week in Aug. **Admission** varies.

This very gay-friendly town celebrates itself each year with a small, Mardi Gras-like event marked by extravagant costumes, wild antics and a parade down Commercial Street. Though the carnival is not strictly gay, expect drag queens and high camp.

King Richard's Faire

Carver (1-508 866 5391/1-952 238 9915/ www.kingrichardsfaire.net). **Date** weekends from Labor Day to third weekend in Oct. **Admission** $20; $10 concessions.

Drink from the chalice of the 16th century with wenches, beggars, jugglers and knights. Packed with period revelry, Carver's re-creation of an English marketplace teems with fire eaters, street brawls, singing executioners and Siberian tigers.

Caribbean Carnival

Franklin Park, Dorchester (524 8383/ www.bostoncarnival.com). Forest Hills T. **Date** Sat before Labor Day. **Admission** free.

Franklin Park hosts a celebration of Caribbean culture, that runs to ethnic foods, arts, crafts and dance. Make the trip to the Dorchester end of Roxbury to hear calypso, soca and steel drum.

Autumn

Weatherwise, most visitors think this is the best time to visit – temperatures are cool but not cold, and skies tend to be clear. Essentially, it's gorgeous. Sadly, what this means is that the city becomes suffocatingly crowded at this time of year. It's like winter on the Riviera here, as thousands of students descend upon the more than 60 colleges in the city at the same time as hundreds of business conventions swing into town. Simultaneously, foliage gazers arrive by the coachload to view the famously beautiful

Top five Events most outsiders miss

Chinese New Year
With dragons and fireworks, not to mention outstanding food, this is First Night with better food and fewer tourists. *See p193.*

Central Square World's Fair
It's either heaven or hell, depending how you feel about a day full of eclectic music and oh-so-hip globalism. The food is outstanding, and the music can be amazing. *See p195.*

James Joyce Ramble
Runners, *Ulysses* and beer, oh my. *See p194.*

Mass Cann's Freedom Rally
Take large group of kids add marijuana and cops – need we say more?*See below.*

Harvard Square Book Festival
Go on. Get in touch with your inner intellectual. *See p194.*

scenery as the leaves turn, and it all makes for miserable overcrowding. Naturally, prices escalate and hotel vacancies are in short supply. But, hey, at least the weather's nice.

Boston Film Festival

Loews Copley Place, 100 Huntington Avenue, at Dartmouth Street (1-781 925 1373/ www.bostonfilmfestival.org). Copley or Back Bay T. **Date** 2nd week in Sept. **Admission** $9 per film. **Map** p306 F5.

An annual festival of lectures, panels and screenings, this two-weekend showcase integrates both feature-length and independent works. There's a strong, local contingent of participants, many from nearby colleges. Past entries include Oscar-winning *American Beauty* and David Guterson's *Snow Falling on Cedars.*

Massachusetts Cannabis Reform's Freedom Rally

Boston Common (1-781 944 2266/ www.masscann.org). Park Street T. **Date** 2nd or 3rd Sat in Sept. **Admission** free. **Map** p307 G4.

Every year, the city of Boston broods over issuing permits to this annual drug fest. Nonetheless, the rally always takes place, and thousands of stoners sneak spliffs onto the Boston Common, a handful of edgy bands play and booths manned by left-leaning activist groups preach to the converted. It goes without saying, but people inevitably end up getting arrested. Bring your lawyer's phone number.

Lowell Celebrates Kerouac! Festival

Various locations in Lowell (1-877 537 6822/ ecommunity.uml.edu/lck/index.htm). **Date** 1st week in Oct. **Admission** varies.

Most famous for *On the Road*, an American travellers' ode to wanderlust, whiskey and boisterous escapades, Jack Kerouac was born and buried in Lowell. While he never claimed to have taken much from Lowell, once a year this industrial township commemorates its sole tie to the Beat Generation with a five-day festival of open mikes, sleek jazz, book signings and poetry readings.

Harvard Square Oktoberfest

Harvard Square (491 3434/ www.harvardsquare.com/events/oktoberfest). Harvard T. **Date** mid Oct. **Admission** free. **Map** p311 B2.

Harvard Square is transformed for a weekend into a Bavarian township, with bands, dancers, ethnic food and, of course, beer gardens. Some 200 regional artisans and merchants display their wares.

Head of the Charles Regatta

Charles River, between the Eliot Bridge and the Boston University Bridge (868 6200/www.hocr.org). Central or Harvard T. **Date** 2nd weekend in Oct. **Admission** free.

This is one of the most spectacular boat races anywhere. The hundreds of thousands of fans lining the bridges and river banks along the Charles are a sight to be seen, as are the thousands of rowers who converge on Cambridge for this world-class regatta. Fans bring blankets and picnic baskets to the banks of the Charles to cheer their favourite teams.

Salem's Haunted Happenings

Locations throughout Salem (1-978 744 0013/ www.salemhauntedhappenings.com). **Date** 2nd half of Oct. **Admission** varies.

A haven for Pagans, Salem does Halloween like no other Massachusetts haunt. A huge costumed parade kicks off two weeks of Jack-o-lantern carving, haunted house tours, candlelight vigils, modern witchcraft ceremonies, magic shows and a psychics' fair. Leave your scepticism at home.

Christmas on Cape Cod

Various locations on Cape Cod (1-888 332 2732 1-508 862 0700/www.capecodchamber.org). **Date** 4th week in Nov. **Admission** free.

Experience an old-fashioned New England Christmas by attending the series of open houses, parades and lighting of the Pilgrim Monument in Provincetown.

► For tourist information offices, public transportation and climate information, *see Chapter* **Directory**.

Children

To-dos for tykes.

Whether it's educational – playing around at the **Museum of Science** – or gastronomical – creating an ice-cream sundae at **JP Licks** – there's plenty to keep the little ones entertained in Boston. In the winter you can join the locals skating on the **Frog Pond** in Boston Common, or pose for photos with the country's largest teddy bear in front of the **FAO Schwarz** toy store. In the summer you can catch a puppet show or a baseball game in the park.

For additional ideas, try the Calendar section in Thursday's edition of the *Boston Globe*, which offers a selection of children's activities for the week. Or check out the *Parents' Paper* (www.BostonParents.com), available at select newsstands and street boxes.

Another good source is the **Greater Boston Convention & Visitors Bureau**'s *Kids Love Boston* publication ($3.25), a font of useful tips (1-888 733 2678/www.bostonusa.com).

At the airport

Kidport

Logan Airport, Terminal C (561 1212). Airport T. **Open** 7am-9pm daily. **Admission** free.

A hands-on interactive waiting area designed by the **Children's Museum** (*see p201*). Features include a climbing structure, a baggage claim slide, a play area, a magnetic poetry wall and a toy shop.

Babysitting

Nanny Poppins

100 Cummings Center, Beverly (978 927 1811). **Open** 8.30am-5pm Mon-Fri. **Rates** $25 call-out fee per day ($50 overnight), then $9-$15 per hour. **Credit** AmEx, Disc, MC, V.

Nanny Poppins must have one of the most stringent screening processes around. All sitters are looked into by a private detective, and state criminal (as well as driving and federal) records are checked. Nannies who speak a range of languages, including sign language, are on the books.

Parents in a Pinch

45 Bartlett Crescent, Brookline (1-800 688 4697/739 5437). Washington Street T. **Open** 8am-5pm Mon-Fri. **Rates** $10 per hour per first child ($1 per hour each extra child, plus up to $15 transportation reimbursement); agency charge $60 per weekday, $40 per evenings and weekends. **Credit** AmEx, MC, V.

This 15-year-old agency can refer up to 150 nannies offering short-term child care.

Eats & treats

These restaurants will entertain kids' taste buds (and, sometimes, their imaginations, too).

Fire & Ice

50 Church Street, Harvard Square, Cambridge (547 9007). Harvard T. **Open** 11.30am-11pm Mon-Thur; 11.30am-midnight Fri, Sat; 1pm-11pm Sun. **Main courses** $7.50-$15.95. **Credit** AmEx, DC, Disc, MC, V. **Map** p311 B2.

Don't let the sleek, trendy interior fool you. Picky children can choose the ingredients themselves and watch the meal cooked right before their eyes. Although it's all-you-can-eat, kids' appetites may not justify the $15.95 fixed dinner cost.

Branch: 205 Berkeley Street, Back Bay (482 3473).

Friendly's

41 Boylston Street, at Chestnut Hill Plaza, Brookline (731 1095). Chestnut Hill T, then 60 bus. **Open** 8am-10pm Mon-Thur, Sun; 8am-11pm Fri, Sat. **Credit** Disc, MC, V.

This ever-popular chain offers a plethora of splits, ice-cream sundaes, shakes and malts.

Full Moon

344 Huron Avenue, at Fresh Pond Parkway, Cambridge (354 6699). Harvard T. **Open** 11.30am-3pm Mon-Sat, 5-9pm Sun-Thur; 5-9.30pm Fri, Sat; 9am-3pm Sun. **Main courses** $8-$16. **Credit** MC, V.

Twice winner of the Parents' Paper Clean Plate Club Award, Full Moon is filled with lots of baskets of educational toys, a chalkboard, doll's houses, etc. While the kids play and munch, you can sample the butternut squash soup washed down with a glass of Chianti. Booking is recommended.

Hard Rock Cafe

131 Clarendon Street, at Stuart Street, Back Bay (353 1400). Back Bay T. **Open** 11am-midnight Mon-Wed, Sun; 11am-1am Thur-Sat. **Main courses** $13. **Credit** AmEx, DC, Disc, MC, V. **Map** p306 F5

Noisy and boisterous – the kids can fuss all they want in one of the most popular burger joints in town and nobody will get angry.

JP Licks

674 Centre Street, at Seaverns Avenue, Jamaica Plain (524 6740). Green Street T. **Open** 6am-11pm Mon-Wed, Sun; 6am-midnight Fri, Sat. **Medium ice-cream** $4. **No credit cards.**

Let the kids scream – about ice-cream. Don't be surprised if your bill's a bit high; it's worth it. *See p147.*

Branches 311A Harvard Street, Brookline (738 8252); 352 Newbury Street (236 1666); 46 Langley Road, Newton Centre (244 0666).

P-p-pick up on the penguins and sharks at the **New England Aquarium**. *See p200.*

Another brick in the wall at the **Children's Museum**. *See p201.*

Marché Movenpick Boston

Prudential Center, 800 Boylston Street, Back Bay (578 9700). Prudential or Hynes/ICA T. **Open** 7.30am-2am daily. **Main courses** $3-$20. **Credit** DC, Disc, MC, V. **Map** p306 E5.
Filled with different food stations, from the Pasta Island to the Seafood Bar and the Grill & Rotisserie.

Rainforest Cafe

75 Middlesex Turnpike, Burlington Mall, Burlington (1-781 272 7555). **Open** 11am-10pm Mon-Thur; 11am-11pm Fri; 10.30am-11pm Sat; 11am-9pm Sun. **Main courses** $10-$20. **Credit** AmEx, DC, Disc, MC, V.
You need a car to get to this place, but the theme, wildlife characters and the thunderstorms every 22 minutes rank big with the little ones.

Entertainment

Amazing animals

As well as the **New England Aquarium** (*see p70*), here are other places to observe some animals outside of your own family.

Franklin Park & Zoo

One Franklin Park Road (541 5466/ www.zoonewengland.com). Forest Hills T, then 16 bus. **Open** *Oct 1-Mar 31* 10am-4pm daily; *Apr 1-Sept 30* 10am-5pm Mon-Fri; 10am-6pm Sat, Sun. **Admission** $7; $4 concessions. **Credit** AmEx, MC, V.
The Tropical Forest, complete with gorillas, pygmy hippos, leopards and tropical birds, is the main draw here. There is also the Kalahari Kingdom's lions, and wallabies and emus on the Outback Trail. And little ones can meet llamas, goats and chickens out in the Contact Corral.

Marino Lookout Farm

89 Pleasant Street, at Route 16, South Natick (1-508 651 1539). **Open** 8am-8pm daily. **Admission** free.
The oldest working farm in the country has horses, ostriches, reindeer and sheep – and fresh produce.

Get on up

John Hancock Observatory

Trinity Place, at St James Street, Back Bay (247 1977). Back Bay or Copley Square T. **Open** *Nov-Apr* 9am-10pm Mon-Sat; 9am-5pm Sun. *May-Oct* 9am-11pm daily. **Admission** $6; $4 concessions. **Map** p306 F5.
Spot landmarks from the 60th floor (740ft/225m) of Boston's tallest building. *See p79.*

Bunker Hill Monument

Monument Square, Charlestown (242 5641). Community College T. **Open** 9am-4.30pm daily. **Admission** free. **Map** p308 G3.
This is the site of the Revolution's first major battle – the 221ft (67m) granite obelisk affords a great view. *See p98.*

Museums

Boston is filled with museums – and there are some wonderful ones for kids. In addition to the ones listed below, the **Museum of Science** (*see p117*) has many memorable options for children while the **Museum of Fine Arts** (*see p114*) hosts a 'Family Place' programme, on weekends from October until June, featuring a variety of entertaining children's activities.

Children's Discovery Museum

177 Main Street, Acton (1-978 264 4200). **Open** *Oct-June* 1-4.30pm Tue, Thur, Fri; 9am-6pm Wed; 9am-4.30pm Sat-Sun. *June-Sept* 9am-4.30pm Tue-Sun. **Admission** $7. **Credit** MC, V.

This Victorian house is filled with exhibits in every nook and cranny. Children can explore the colourful Rainbow room or serve up a meal in 'Bessie's Diner', and go from a safari to outer space to the ocean in a matter of minutes.

Children's Museum

300 Congress Street, at Museum Wharf, Downtown (426 8855/www.bostonkids.org). South Station T. **Open** 10am-5pm Sat-Thur; 10am-9pm Fri. **Admission** $7; $2-$6 concessions; 5-9pm Fri $1 for everyone. **Credit** AmEx, DC, Disc, MC, V. **Map** p307 H5.

Four floors of fun. Kids can shop in the Supermercado, play with bubbles, climb the big maze, board the Minnow and learn about boats, explore doll's houses, an old Japanese home or the costumes in Grandma's 1959 attic. The changing exhibits are always educational, but kids will be having too much fun to notice. There's also a recycle shop selling cheap crafts and a gift shop.

Imagination Works

1282 Worcester Road, Route 9 East, Natick (1-508 647 6212). **Open** 9.30am-5.30pm daily. **Admission** $8 child; $4.50 adult. **Credit** MC, V.

This may be worth the drive, if only because it's a hands-on heaven, featuring eight separate areas for young ones. Activities include computer finger painting and (sort of) real rock climbing.

On the boards

Instead of acting up, let the kids act out – or at least watch others who do – at these theatres which specialise in performances geared towards children of all ages.

Artbarn Community Theatre

Coolidge Corner Theater, 50 Sewall Avenue, at Beacon Street, Brookline (975 0050). Coolidge Corner T. **Show times** and **prices** vary.

A new theatre specialising in providing affordable opportunities for kids to get involved. From toddlers to high schoolers, these diverse young actors work to build confidence and self-esteem.

Boston Children's Theater

647 Boylston Street, at Dartmouth Street, Back Bay (424 6634). Copley T. **Open** 9am-5pm Mon-Fri. Call for performance times. **Tickets** $10-$16. **Credit** MC, V. **Map** p306 F5.

One of the country's oldest theatre organisations, the BCT puts on three main stage shows a year in a number of venues around the city. Productions, by kids for kids, coincide with the school holidays. Acting classes are offered all year. Performances for under-5s in Copley Square on Wednesday nights in the summer.

Puppet Showplace Theatre

32 Station Street, at Washington Street, Brookline (731 6400/www.puppetshowplace.org). Brookline Village T. **Box office open** 10am-4pm daily. Call for show times. **Tickets** $8. **Credit** MC, V.

Some of the most popular fairy tales, from *Cinderella* to *Jack and the Beanstalk*, are shown here, along with more contemporary stories – all performed by the professional puppeteers.

Wheelock Family Theatre

Wheelock College, 180 The Riverway, at Plymouth Street (734 4760/www.wheelock.edu/wft.html). Longwood Avenue T. **Box office open** noon-5.30pm. Call for specific performance dates and times. **Tickets** $10-$15. **Credit** MC, V.

Has been serving up family fare for the past two decades; performances have included an introduction to Shakespeare in a kids' version of *The Tempest*.

Outdoor outings

Blue Hills Reservation

Hillside Street, Milton (698 1802). **Open** dawn-dusk daily. **Admission** free.

Trailside Museum *1904 Canton Avenue, Route 138, Canton.* **Open** 10am-5pm Tue-Sun. **Admission** $3, $1.50 concessions.

Pack some sandwiches and the kids and head for the

Top five

Kid stuff

Boston by Little Feet
Give them a kids-eye view of the city. *See p202.*

Red Sox game
Scream at something besides the kids for a change. *See p234.*

Charles River Canoe & Kayak
If they wear themselves out paddling, they'll fall asleep early. *See p202.*

Children's Museum
They'll never know they're learning. *See p201.*

Blue Hills Reservation
For flowers in the summer and snow in the winter. *See p201.*

Blue Hills, just outside of the city. Summer is perfect for a picnic and some hiking among this woodland reservation, full of wild flowers and wildlife. You may be able to sneak in a round of golf while the kids explore the Trailside Museum. Check out the view from the top of one of the Blue Hills.

Charles River Canoe & Kayak

Soldier's Field Road, Boston side of the Charles River, upstream of Eliot Bridge (462 2513/ www.skipaddle.com). Harvard T, then 86 bus to Smith Playground. **Open** *May-Oct* 10am-sunset Sat, Sun; *June-Aug* 1pm-sunset Fri. **Rentals** $5-$72. **Credit** Disc, MC, V.

Paddle around Boston's waterways. Renting a canoe or kayak is $40 for the day, or $10 an hour. If you're feeling adventurous, try taking one of the day trips with a guide.

Swan Boats

Public Garden, opposite the Ritz-Carlton, 15 Arlington Street at Newbury Street, Back Bay (522 1966/www.swanboats.com). Arlington T. **Open** *15 Apr-20 June* 10am-4pm daily; *21 June-1 Sept* 10am-5pm daily; *1 Sept-17 Sept* noon-4pm Mon-Fri; 10am-4pm Sat, Sun. **Admission** $2; $1 concessions. **No credit cards. Map** p306 F5.

The swan boats, a staple of the Gardens since 1877, often prove irresistible to children. The Lagoon that they navigate isn't very big, but the 15-minute cruise is still an essential Boston tourist experience. Need to cool off? Swing through the Common and let the kids play in the Frog Pond. In winter, five bucks gets a pair of skates and an afternoon of skating fun.

Tours

Boston by Little Feet

Meet at the Samuel Adams statue on Congress Street (367 2345/367 3766/www.bostonbyfoot.com). State House T. **Tours** *May-Oct* 10am Mon, Sat; 2pm Sun. **Tickets** $6. **No credit cards.**

This hour-long tour for kids aged 6-12 is organised by the Boston by Foot tour group. It provides a child's-eye view of sites along the Freedom Trail.

Charles Riverboat Cruises

100 Cambridgeside Place, at Charles Street, Cambridge (621 3001/www.charlesriverboat.com). Lechmere T. **Departs** Cambridgeside Galleria Mall. *Apr-Sept* 6pm Thur-Sat. **Admission** $10; $7 concessions.

An inexpensive way to see the city from the water.

Duck Tours

Prudential Center Court, 800 Boylston Street, at Fairfield Street, Back Bay (723 3825/ www.bostonducktours.com). Hynes/ICA or Prudential T. **Open** *Apr-Nov*, tours depart every half hour 9am-sunset. **Tickets** $22, $12-$19 concessions. **Credit** Disc, MC, V. **Map** p306 E5.

At $22, it's pricey for adults, but the children's price is a better deal. The highlight of this 80-minute trip, for kids, is when the Ducks take a swim. *See p111.*

Make Way For Ducklings Tour

Historic Neighbourhoods Foundation, 99 Bedford Street, at Kingston Street, Downtown (426 1885/www.historic-neighborhoods.org). Downtown Crossing T. **Tours** *Apr-June* 9am, 10am, 11.30am, noon Mon-Fri. **Tickets** $7, $5.75 concessions. **No credit cards. Map** p308 G5.

Trace the route of Jack, Kack, Mack, Nack, Quack, Pack and Mr and Mrs Mallard from Robert McCloskey's celebrated book, *Make Way For Ducklings*. The tour quacks and waddles through Beacon Hill and Boston Common, where you'll have the chance to take pictures with bronze statues of the book's main characters.

New England Ghost Tours

Meet at the Visitor's Centre in the Boston Common, 147 Tremont Street, Back Bay (1-781 235 7149). Park Street T. **Tours** depart at 7.30pm on select evenings, reservations required. **Admission** $12, $9 concessions. **Map** p306 F5.

A 75-minute tour of Boston's haunted hotspots.

Shops

Curious George Goes To WordsWorth

1 John F Kennedy Street, at Harvard Square, Cambridge (498 0062/1-800 899 2202). Harvard T. **Open** 9am-11.15pm Mon-Sat; 10am-10.15pm Sun. **Credit** AmEx, Disc, MC, V. **Map** p311 B2.

Named after the little monkey whose creator, Margret Rey, once frequented the old WordsWorth book store. This colourful bookshop is full of friends such as Madeline, Thomas the Tank Engine and Winnie the Pooh. You'll also find stuffed animals, toys and art.

FAO Schwarz

440 Boylston Street, at Berkeley Street, Back Bay (262 5900). Arlington T. **Open** 10am-7pm Mon-Sat; 11am-6pm Sun. **Credit** AmEx, DC, Disc, MC, V. **Map** p306 F5.

Bring the kids here for a romp through toy heaven – two floors of stuffed animals, gadgets, educational items – and, of course, the latest toys. The giant bronze teddy bear outside (the country's largest) is a favourite backdrop for tourist snaps.

No Kidding

19 Harvard Street, at Boylston Street, Brookline (739 2477). Brookline Village T. **Open** 9.30am-6.30pm Mon-Sat; noon-5.30pm Sun. **Credit** MC, V.

Stocks a selection of imaginative toys and books. The children can amuse themselves with the train set, playhouses and Lego sets that dot the place.

Stella Bella Toys

1360 Cambridge Street, Inman Square, Cambridge (491 6290). Lechmere or Harvard T, then 69 bus. **Open** 9.30am-7pm Mon–Sat; 10am-5pm Sun. **Credit** AmEx, Disc, MC, V.

A quaint store that specialises in a wide array of educational developmental toys. It also offers fun activities such as sing-a-longs and storytellers.

Dance Clubs

Shake your money maker all night long, or at least until 2am when it all closes.

After years of a seemingly schizophrenic format, switching from season to season at the whim of fleeting trends, Boston's dance clubs have settled down to more regular, tried-and-tested schedules. As a general rule of thumb, the Euro clubs play international house, the mainstream clubs play Top 40 and dance house and the cooler joints keep up with what's hot in London and New York. But the scenes can still change from night to night in any club, so if you care to avoid a particular segment of humanity it might be best to call ahead to check the current demographics.

THE CODE

To get into most clubs you must be 21 – or at least aged 19; the law allows entry for 18-year-olds, but the clubs usually like to know that their clientele has finished high school. Dress codes are looser than they used to be, and tend to be enforced at the discretion of the doormen. As a good general rule, avoid caps, sneakers, athletic wear of all kinds – basically, anything that might identify you as an idiot prone to bar fights, racism or sexual harassment.

THE SCENE

There are two main club districts in Boston. Lansdowne Street, a one-block stretch bordering Fenway Park and packed with nightclubs, is the city's main club row, with a neon-lit, carnival-like atmosphere. The street has some great, revamped industrial spaces and hit music programmes, but hordes of college students and suburbanites descend at the weekends, so enter the area with some trepidation on those nights.

Downtown, in the Theatre District near Chinatown, is club headquarters for the jet-setting international crowd, though they also frequent scenes elsewhere in the city. Here you'll normally find a high concentration of seemingly perfect looking people with money to burn. If that's your scene, then it's your place.

Nearby, Boylston Place (known to its fans as 'the Alley') offers a sort of a club mall, with bars, restaurants and clubs lining the street from one end to the other. And, on most weekend nights, drunken twentysomethings wobbling from one club to another.

Join the swirl at **Avalon** on Lansdowne Street. *See p204.*

Aria

246 Tremont Street, at Stuart Street, Back Bay (338 7080/www.ariaboston.com). Boylston T. **Open** 11pm-2am Tue-Sat, Sun. **Admission** varies. **Credit** AmEx, DC, Disc, MC, V. **Map** p306 F5.

Small enough that it's both exclusive and jam-packed, this velvet-upholstered dance club under the Wilbur Theater is popular with Boston's status-obsessed international set. Be gorgeous. Wear Prada.

Atlas Bar & Grill

145 Ipswich Street, at Lansdowne Street, Fenway (437 0300). Kenmore T. **Open** club 10pm-2am Fri, Sat. **Admission** $7. **Credit** AmEx, DC, MC, V. **Map** p306 D/E5.

Located on the first floor of Jillian's, a massive entertainment complex with several floors of pool tables, darts, a video arcade that looks and sounds like Vegas and virtual-reality amusements, Atlas is a modern bar and grill with a deco-influenced, futuristic decor. The dance floor is in a back room, in front of a wall of giant video screen. The music is a mix of Top 40 and dance hits from the 1970s to the present. The atmosphere is casual, in the sense that no one will look at you sideways if you're not in Gucci.

Avalon

15 Lansdowne Street, at Ipswich Street, Fenway (262 2424). Kenmore T. **Open** 10pm-2am Thur-Sun. **Admission** $10-$15. **Credit** AmEx, Disc, MC, V. **Map** p306 D/E5.

With a capacity of 2,000, this is the biggest venue on Lansdowne, so be prepared to boogie en masse. There's a regular schedule of big-name live shows, but they almost always flush out the rockers in time to usher in the disco crowd at 10pm. Friday's well-entrenched Avaland is the biggest dance night in town, with international DJs, regularly scheduled fashion shows and special events, and a racially mixed crowd of gay and straight 19- to 25-year-olds. Saturday is called Downtown, with a mix of city-dwellers and bridge-and-tunnel (read: suburban) types. The Sunday gay night, now in its twenty-first year, is the most interesting dance night here. When it merges with Axis next door, the club becomes a huge complex with three dance floors.

Axis

13 Lansdowne Street, at Ipswich Street, Fenway (262 2437). Kenmore T. **Open** 10pm-2am Mon, Thur-Sat. **Admission** $10. **Credit** AmEx, Disc, MC, V. **Map** p306 E5.

Axis is one of the cooler venues on the street, with a strong tradition in cutting-edge dance trends. Thursday's Chrome programme draws guest DJs from around the world, serious dance fanatics and a mixed urban/college/gay/straight crowd. Friday's Spin Cycle event features house and progressive dance. The Saturday X-Night is a perennial scene, with contemporary dance and industrial beats downstairs and a shifting playlist of trendy genres upstairs. Monday is Static gay night features a mixed dance crowd and local drag performers.

The Big Easy

1 Boylston Place, between Charles & Tremont Streets, Back Bay (351 7000). Boylston T. **Open** 9pm-2am Thur-Sat. **Admission** $5-$8. **Credit** AmEx, MC, V. **Map** p307 F5.

A large, New Orleans-style dance club with DJs and cover bands playing alternative and Top 40 dance, Motown, and old and new R&B and soul. Two lounges upstairs offer nuzzling room and pool.

Chaps

100 Warrenton Street, at Stuart Street, Back Bay (695 9500). Boylston T. **Open** 3pm-2am Mon-Sat; noon-2am Sun. **Admission** $3-$5. **No credit cards. Map** p308 G5.

One of the most famous gay clubs in Boston, Chaps has mellowed from an implicitly exclusive gay men's club to more mixed scene. These days a few straight people frequent the club, especially on Tuesday – an oldies dance night with spins from the 1970s to the early 1980s – and on Thursday, when the hip hop Mocha programme brings in a racially and sexually mixed crowd. On Friday and Saturday DJs spin high-energy dance music. The Sunday Tea Dance (6-10pm), featuring disco classics and modern house spins, is a time-honoured tradition.

The Club at Il Panino

295 Franklin Street, at Broad Street, Downtown (338 1000). Downtown Crossing or State/Citizen's Bank T. **Open** 9pm-2am Fri, Sat; 11pm-2am Sun. **Admission** varies. **No credit cards. Map** p307 H4.

A five-storey club where the international crowd is not averse to ordering a bottle of decent champagne at top prices. On Sunday, there's underground house on the fourth and fifth floors and Latin house on the third floor. On Friday and Saturday, the spins are international – Latin and progressive house music. The crowd is older on Friday and Saturday (about 25 to 55) than on Sunday (21 to 30).

Embassy

36 Lansdowne Street, at Ipswich Street, Fenway (262 2424). Kenmore T. **Open** 10pm-2am Thur-Sat. **Admission** $10-$15. **No credit cards. Map** p306 D5.

Dark and crowded, with reserved tables and a VIP elevator, the Embassy club, located upstairs from

When Avalon gets boring, you can wander next door to **Axis**.

Avalon, is Euro, Euro, Euro and young, young, young. Thursday is Latin lounge night, with free passage to the bigger club below. Friday is Latin and Eurohouse; Saturday is the king of the classic Euro nights. Tip: stop in early and have a few drinks at the Modern Lounge downstairs at Avalon, and ask the bartender for free passes to Embassy.

Hibernia

25 Kingston Street, at Summer Street, Downtown (292 2333). Downtown Crossing T. **Open** 3pm-2am Mon-Sat; noon-2am Sun. **Admission** $5-$10. **Credit** AmEx, DC, MC, V. **Map** p308 G5.

An Irish-owned restaurant and dance club with an international crowd and a sleek, architectural decor, Hibernia is recommended for its lively crowd of South American habitués and down-to-earth Irish staff. On Thursday, it's a funky house/jazz night. Friday is deep house; Saturday techno and trance.

Karma

9 Lansdowne Street, at Ipswich Street, Fenway (421 9595). Kenmore T. **Open** 10pm-2am Thur-Sat. **Admission** $10-$15. **Credit** AmEx, Disc, MC, V. **Map** p306 D5.

This remarkable-looking club, decorated in rich fabrics and carved woodwork, much of it from India and the East, is a weekend dance club with three very distinct musical identities and a generally sophisticated customer base. Thursday's Speed features R&B and classic hip hop; on Friday, it's American Top 40 and classic dance; Saturday is Elements of Life, with a rotating schedule of NY DJs.

Lava Bar

575 Commonwealth Avenue, at Kenmore Square, Fenway (267 7707). Kenmore T. **Open** 10pm-2am Thur-Sun. **Admission** $5-$10. **Credit** AmEx, MC, V. **Map** p306 D5.

The dance club with the best view in Boston, Lava Bar is a hip, dark, comfortable club on the penthouse level of the Kenmore Square Howard Johnson's hotel, with three walls of windows overlooking the Charles River and the Back Bay skyline. The promoter is emphatic about offering a sophisticated, fun, inclusive alternative to the attitude you get at some of the bigger, more corporate nightclubs. The crowd is a little older (as in, over 22), urban and mixed – Euros, yuppie hipsters, mods, gays and straights tend to get along happily here. Sunday's Pandora's Box mod night, featuring obscure and classic garage rock, Brit pop and Motown spins by one of Boston's coolest DJs, is a blast – striped flares and go-go boots are optional.

The best Clubs

To get on top of things

Perched high above the HoJo in Kenmore Square, the **Lava Bar** offers a bird's-eye view of Boston. *See p205.*

To down a Guinness

The Irish ex-pats who run Central Square's **Phoenix Landing** regularly book DJs into their snug, wood-panelled pub. *See p205.*

To hear your fave DJ

The biggest DJs on the planet – Armand Van Helden, Sasha & Digweed and Paul Oakenfold – regularly stop by **Axis** and **Avalon**. *See p204.*

To feel ugly

Boston's international students are a notoriously beautiful and moneyed crew, and they hang at **Aria.** *See p204.*

Man Ray

21 Brookline Street, at Green Street, Cambridge (864 0400). Central T. **Open** 9pm-1am Wed; 9pm-2am Thur, Fri; 10pm-2am Sat. **Admission** $5. **Credit** AmEx, MC, V. **Map** p306 D4.

This underground club has the most interesting queues outside on Wednesday and Friday nights – lots of shrouds, corsets, hip boots and full vinyl ensembles laced up tight. As well as the dedicated Goth/industrial nights, there's a Thursday gay night and a campy disco/new wave night on Saturday, but the Goths and fetishists don't always stick to the schedule. The dress code is strictly enforced, to keep out potential troublemakers and overexcitable voyeurs (there's an in-house whipping post, and a lot of flesh on view). Wear black and only black.

Phoenix Landing

512 Massachusetts Avenue, at Brookline Street, Cambridge (576 6260). Central Square T. **Open** 11am-1am daily. **Admission** free-$5. **Credit** AmEx, DC, Disc, MC, V. **Map** p311 C3.

The dance floor's not huge at this Irish dance pub (yes, we said Irish dance pub), but the DJs are some of the hippest in town, spinning a mix of jazz, funk, techno, drum and bass and reggae. The music is always fresh, and the crowds are friendly. Regulars here are thoroughly mixed in age and background, with a core group of fun-loving Irish and American kids getting to know each other – fast.

Film

Whether you're shooting the film or simply sitting and watching, these days Boston is movie-central.

Over the past couple of years, Boston has suddenly found itself dazzled by the bright lights of Hollywood. Although it has long been known for its art-house theatres and academic film-making, the city has recently become a mainstream filming hotspot, which it doesn't mind at all. Never one to shrink from opportunity, Boston has embraced the film industry wholeheartedly.

LEARN TO FILM

Film programmes at Boston's arts-oriented universities – Emerson College, Boston University and the Mass College of Art – have always been popular, but now post-graduates, adults and even teenagers are attending film classes. Film, it seems is a cottage industry in these parts. The **Boston Film and Video Foundation** (1126 Boylston Street, Suite 201; 536 1540/www.bfvf.org), for example, which has been serving the local film community for 25 years, offers challenging classes to adults and high-school students, taught by professional film-makers. It also rents editing suites, camera equipment and everything else needed to shoot a film. Would-be directors and cinematographers can also take classes at **CityScape** (Film Shack Studio, 227 Roxbury Street, Roxbury; 989 0588). CityScape's laudable mission is to 'engage students in real-world projects with real-world deadlines.'

WHERE TO WATCH

With all the filming taking place in and around Boston, there are a wide variety of screening venues where movie lovers can catch a flick, whether that's a mainstream feature, a local short or a foreign film. The city's arthouses are among the country's best. The oldest of these is the **Coolidge Corner Theater**, a double-screen art deco venue in Brookline. Built originally as a church, the Coolidge was renovated into a movie palace in 1933, and has served as both a film theatre and stage for music performers ever since.

Another Boston film landmark is the **Brattle Theatre** in Cambridge. The oldest of the city's alternative screening theatres, the Brattle features a large single screen and a balcony. Like the Coolidge, it's decidedly no frills, and sightlines can be challenging, but the incredible programming organised by the Beacon Cinema Group make the Brattle a reliable choice.

For newer independent releases, Boston cinephiles usually go to the (relatively) newly built **Kendall Square Cinema** in Cambridge. Also very popular is the **Nickelodeon**, the only theatre in Boston proper showcasing newly released independent feature films.

For the location of the nearest cinema, or for information on films currently showing, check local listings or call the free MovieFone Line at 333 FILM.

Art-house screens

Brattle Theatre

40 Brattle Street, Harvard Square, Cambridge (876 6837/www.beaconcimena.com/brattle). Harvard T.
Tickets $7; $4 concessions. **No credit cards.**
Map p311 B2.

Built in 1890 for theatrical use by the Cambridge Social Union, the Brattle serves only as a movie house now. The Queen Anne-style building with a gambrel roof has seen many famous folks pass through its doors, especially during the 1940s, when it served as a resident theatre company and hosted the likes of TS Eliot, Paul Robeson and, later, Zero Mostel and Jessica Tandy. Moviegoers enjoy second-run independent features, classic foreign film series and classic revivals and restorations.

Coolidge Corner Cinema

290 Harvard Street, at Beacon Street, Brookline (734 2501/www.coolidge.org). Coolidge Corner T.
Tickets $8; $4 concessions. **No credit cards.**

This non-profit theatre might be looking a little shabby – it could use some newer seats with better sightlines – but it still feels like a grand theatre. The Coolidge screens an eclectic mix of foreign films and underground features, and sponsors Video Balagan, a screening series devoted to showing work by local film-makers. Best of all, tickets are cheap and it's easily accessible by public transport.

Harvard Film Archive

Carpenter Center for the Visual Arts, 24 Quincy Street, at Broadway, Cambridge (495 4700/www.harvardfilmarchive.org). Harvard T.
Tickets $7; $5 concessions. **No credit cards.**
Map p311 B2.

The Archive sponsors series by directors like Fassbinder and Truffaut, as well as classic film revivals. Like the Museum of Fine Arts (*see p114*), serious film-watching is encouraged, which means food and drink are forbidden. No giggling, please.

Brattle Theatre – Cambridge's century-old cinematic landmark. *See p206.*

Kendall Square Cinema

1 Kendall Square, at Broadway, Cambridge (Information 621 1202 or 494 9800/Tickets 333 3456/www.landmarktheaters.com). Kendall/MIT T. **Tickets** $8.50; $5.50 concessions. **Credit** AmEx, MC, V. **Map** p306 E4.

This clean, faux-art deco theatre has six screens, coffee and gourmet pastries for sale and a friendly, artsy staff. On weekends and holidays it's best to buy tickets several hours in advance as queues can be long and seating limited.

Loews Nickelodeon Theater

606 Commonwealth Avenue, at Sherborn Street, Fenway (424 1500/www.enjoytheshow.com). Blandford Street T. **Tickets** $8; $5 concessions. **Credit** AmEx, Disc, MC, V. **Map** p306 D5.

In the heart of the Boston University campus, the Nick is home to several scampering rats, and the seats could do with replacing, but it's convenient and has been around for years.

Museum of Fine Arts

465 Huntington Avenue, at Museum Road, Fenway (369 3770/369 3306/www.mfa.org). Museum T. **Tickets** $7. **Credit** AmEx, MC, V. **Map** p306 D6.

The MFA promotes an intellectually stimulating programme. The focus is on local films, foreign films and documentaries. However, what the venue offers in terms of quality film-making, it lacks in terms of a traditional film-watching atmosphere: it's airy, large and comfortable, but drinks and snacks (even popcorn) are not permitted.

Other screens

Loews Theater Cheri

50 Dalton Street, opposite the Sheraton Hotel, Back Bay (536 2870/ www.enjoytheshow.com) Hynes/ICA T. **Tickets** $8; $5 concessions. **Credit** AmEx, MC, V. **Map** p306 E5.

Modern large cinema, well-located in Back Bay, and therefore handy – that's all it's got going for it.

Circle Cinemas

Cleveland Circle, 399 Chestnut Hill, at Beacon Street, Chestnut Hill (566 4040). Cleveland Circle T. **Tickets** $5-$8. **Credit** Disc, MC, V.

Cleveland Circle is at the nexus of the Boston University/Boston College area as well as the classier enclaves of Brookline and Newton. This first-run cinema has the advantage of comfortable high-backed, deep-cushioned tilting chairs.

Copley Place

100 Huntington Avenue, at Dartmouth Street (266 1300). Copley T. **Tickets** $5-$8. **Credit** AmEx, MC, V. **Map** p306 F5.

This honeycomb of tiny auditoriums in the Copley Place shopping mall began as an arthouse complex, but now features big commercial first-runs. The crowds can make it hellish, especially when kids pack the place for animated features, but you can't beat the location.

General Cinema Fenway Theater

Landmark Center, 201 Brookline Avenue, at Beacon Street, Fenway (424 6266/www.generalcinema.com). Fenway T. **Tickets** $9; $6 concessions. **Credit** AmEx, MC, V. **Map** p306 D5.

This venue has all the modern conveniences you could ever want – comfy seats, huge screens and great sight lines. On the down side, the line-up is often a highly disappointing mix of blockbuster hits and cheesy Hollywood dramas.

Loews Cineplex Harvard Square

10 Church Street, at Massachusetts Avenue, Cambridge (864 4580/www.enjoytheshow.com). Harvard T. **Tickets** $8; $5 concessions. **Credit** AmEx, MC, V. **Map** p311 B2.

This four-screener was fashioned out of a former single-screen beauty and has wicker chairs in the first rows of the balcony and a nice repertory programme. The main auditorium has retained its huge screen, though poor conditions for years made it the scourge of first-run fanatics.

Festivals

Though it's still a long way from becoming the home of the next Sundance, Boston does have its share of film festivals. In the autumn, Loews theatres and the *Boston Globe* sponsor the **Boston Film Festival** (for more information visit the website at www.bostonfilmfestival.org or call 266 2533). This two-week event takes place in mid September at the Copley Square Cinema in Boston and the Kendall Square Cinema in Cambridge. It shows a substantial roster of short films, as well as features. There's also the **New England Film Festival**, which offers an extensive programme of independent shorts, features and documentaries. It gives special recognition to film-makers based in New England. Taking place over six days in April, the festival is sponsored by the Boston Film and Video Foundation, and is held at the Coolidge Corner Cinema (for more information visit www.newenglandfilmfestival.com.

The **Nantucket Film Festival**, held every June, is a favourite mid-summer excursion for Boston film lovers. Billed somewhat dramatically as the festival 'Where Screenwriters Inherit the Earth', this five-day event has a strong programme of independent feature films, as well as shorts, documentaries and staged readings of un-produced scripts (for further details call 1-508 325 6274 or try www.nantucketfilmfestival.org).

Film lovers who prefer rare movies will enjoy the **Boston Jewish Film Festival**. Held in November at the Coolidge Corner Cinema and at the Museum of Fine Arts, the JFF screens up to 40 films from 15 different countries, all centred on a Jewish theme (for information call 781 899 3830 or try the website www.bjff.cyways.com).

Location, location, location

Although Boston doesn't have even a fraction of the film and TV studios boasted by its bigger brothers, it is the hot place to shoot right now (or at least to get quaint establishing shots to make it look as if something was filmed here). And for good reason. Hollywood has just discovered that there are plenty of attractions here. Boston is picturesque, with diverse geography that includes an urban warehouse district, a waterfront and university campuses. It's possible to shoot one scene in a tough, urban neighbourhood like East Boston, then drive ten minutes downtown and be on Beacon Hill, where rows of gorgeous brownstones line cobblestone streets.

In large part, it was television producer David E Kelley who spurred the recent Boston craze. He set all three of his popular US programmes – *Ally McBeal* (pictured), *The Practice* and *Boston Public* – in Beantown. While most of the shows are taped elsewhere, the dramatic aerial shots of State Street, the Financial District, Fenway and the Back Bay interspersed in the shows made many in Hollywood give the city a second look. Boston is also the setting of other shows including *Gideon's Crossing* and *Sabrina the Teenage Witch*.

Feature film companies have also jumped on the Boston bandwagon. Several Hollywood features were recently shot in and around the city. MGM's *What's the Worst that Could Happen?*, starring Danny DeVito and Martin Lawrence, was shot in the South End and Back Bay. *Prozac Nation*, featuring Christina Ricci, Anne Heche, Jason Biggs and Jessica Lange, spent several weeks filming in Cambridge and at Wheaton College in Newton, while *Legally Blonde*, with Reese Witherspoon, was shot in Cambridge. Local director Brad Anderson (*Next Stop Wonderland*, *Happy Accidents*) filmed his newest venture, *Session 9*, in and around Boston proper while former film festival sweethearts Khari Streeter and Demane Davis shot their movie *Lift* in Roxbury.

But Boston is more than home to the movies. It's also home to the movie makers. Robert Gardner, Richard Leacock and Frederick Wiseman, three of the underground leaders of *cinéma-vérité*, are natives of Boston, as are documentary film-makers Laurel Chiten (*The Jew in the Lotus*), Jane Gillooly (*Leona's Sister Gerri*), Ross McElwee (*Sherman's March*) and David Sutherland (*The Farmer's Wife*). One of America's most famous documentarians, Erroll Morris (*The Thin Blue Line; Fast, Cheap and Out of Control*), resides in Cambridge.

David Mamet, writer and director of *The Spanish Prisoner*, lives in Newton. He shot his recent hit film, *State and Main,* in Manchester-by-the-Sea. And then there is the Cinderella story – local director Brad Anderson signed a $6 million deal with Miramax after his tiny, Boston-based, independent, romantic comedy *Next Stop Wonderland* did well at the box office and won raves at Sundance.

Galleries

Though it may not boast an art scene the size of London's or New York's, Boston has plenty of interesting spaces, thank you very much.

The city's best-known galleries are on elegant Newbury Street.

The gallery scene in Boston traditionally orbits around upmarket Newbury Street. A burst of new galleries opening off the beaten track is bringing fresh art and attitude into the mix, but Newbury is still the heart of the Boston art scene, and for good reason. It's a charming stretch of blocks running alphabetically from Arlington to Gloucester Streets (and a bit beyond), where swanky shops and chic restaurants exist side by side with a bevy of art galleries, many located in townhouses and converted brownstones. Don't be afraid to take the inevitably slow elevators up past the designer hair salons and boutiques in pursuit of artists of repute (as well as to discover emerging local talent), but do try to avoid the vanity galleries and schlocky paintings of sunset on Cape Cod. Some of the best galleries in town can be found here, but beware: they are mixed in with some of the worst.

While some galleries can be found further afield, the truth is you need only walk a few blocks to be off what's considered the beaten track in Boston, and some new paths are worth beating. Recent developments have seen a concentration of galleries take hold in Boston's South End, as well as a handful of art outposts in Allston and Jamaica Plain. Though these alternative spaces, member-owned galleries and ambitious start-ups can be hit or miss, they keep these developing scenes interesting and constantly changing.

Newbury Street

Barbara Krakow Gallery

10 Newbury Street, at Arlington Street (262 4490/ www.barbarakrakowgallery.com). Arlington T.
Open 10am-5.30pm Tue-Sat. **Admission** free.
Map p306 F5.

This is one of the longest lasting and most prestigious galleries in the city. Krakow's continued enthusiasm for the new – both local and international – along with her good taste in well-established contemporary artists guarantees there's a whole lot worth seeking out here, from Sol LeWitt to Annette Lemieux and Julian Opie.

Chappell Gallery

14 Newbury Street, between Arlington & Berkeley Streets (236 2255/www.chappellgallery.com). Arlington T. **Open** 11am-5.30pm Tue-Sat. **Admission** free. **Map** p306 F5.

Shows the output of Asian, European and American artists working in glass, with pieces that range from the meditative to the playful, from the comfortingly utilitarian to the disturbingly abstract. The commitment to an international roster of artists is a sign of the zeal and knowledge of director Alice Chappell.

Copley Society of Boston

158 Newbury Street, at Dartmouth Street (536 5049). Copley T. **Open** 10.30am-5.30pm Tue-Sat. **Admission** free. **Map** p306 F5.

Don't let the old-fashioned name mislead you – the Copley Society, the country's oldest non-profit art association, focuses on encouraging the talents of new artists as it draws on a pool of more than 700 members for participation in its frequently changing exhibitions. And although exhibitions here can be uneven, this odd double-decker space sometimes yields excellent work, if you enjoy trying to pick out the winners from those who are still getting there.

Gallery NAGA

67 Newbury Street, at Berkeley Street (267 9060/www.gallerynaga.com). Arlington T. **Open** 10am-5.30pm Tue-Sat. **Admission** free. **Map** p306 F5.

Besides its fine line-up of Boston and New England-based contemporary painters, including Ken Beck, George Nick and pioneer holographer Harriet Casdin-Silver, NAGA is best known for presenting the work of furniture makers – exhibiting unusual pieces that, while not always functional, are always a pleasure to look at.

Howard Yezerski Gallery

14 Newbury Street, at Arlington Street (262 0550/www.howardyezerskigallery.com). Arlington T. **Open** 10am-5.30pm Tue-Sat. **Admission** free. **Map** p306 F5.

Howard Yezerski has been a fixture on the Boston art scene for more than 20 years, and his style is distinctive. Here, you might find an entire exhibition given over to monochrome paintings or abstract concoctions of cotton and glass – and whether the work on display is to your liking or not, you can count on a Yezerski show to be intelligent and provocative.

Judy Ann Goldman Fine Art

14 Newbury Street, at Arlington Street (424 8468). Arlington T. **Open** 10.30am-5.30pm Tue-Sat. **Admission** free. **Map** p306 F5.

Director Goldman is an articulate guide to the often-challenging work she shows. This adventurous gallerist has brought avant-garde artists from LA, Japan, Miami and introduced them to the Boston art scene. At the same time, it has made a name for itself introducing young talent that is being grown and nurtured right here in the city.

Mercury Gallery

8 Newbury Street, at Arlington Street (859 0054/ www.mercurygallery.com). Arlington T. **Open** 10am-6pm Mon-Sat. **Admission** free. **Map** p306 F5.

This gallery warrants a visit not only for its art, but also for its singular interior architecture – it was a car dealership in the late 1920s, a fact reflected in the unconventional architectural details of the space. The Mercury specialises in American figurative expressionism and includes works from as far back as the 1930s, but also features artists who are hard at work right now, notably including respected photographer Phillip Jones.

MPG

285 Newbury Street, at Gloucester Street (437 1596). Hynes/ICA T. **Open** 1-5pm Mon, Sun; 10am-5.30pm Tue-Sat. **Admission** free. **Map** p306 E5.

Presents an eclectic mix of contemporary art, with work by talent such as Helen Frankenthaler, Louise Bourgeois and Henry Moore, as well as by emerging Boston artists. The results can be inconsistent, but this comparative newcomer is worth a visit.

Nielsen Gallery

179 Newbury Street, at Exeter Street (266 4835/ www.nielsengallery.com). Copley T. **Open** 10am-5.30pm Tue-Sat. **Admission** free. **Map** p306 E5.

One of the Newbury Street elite, where the odds are good for taking in memorable work. Among the Nielsen's unabashedly painterly painters are the bold Joan Snyder, the bolder Sam Messer and, perhaps the boldest, John Walker – whose collective gusto is balanced by the deceptively quiet Maureen Gallace and the sadly departed Gregory Gillespie.

Pepper Gallery

38 Newbury Street, at Berkeley Street (236 4497/ www.peppergalleryboston.com). Arlington T. **Open** 10am-5.30pm Tue-Sat. **Admission** free. **Map** p306 F5.

Devoted almost entirely to painting, and to representational painting at that, the Pepper gallery slyly interrupts the traditional with the unexpected; accomplished still-life painters coexist with quirky artists (such as the collaborative team of Kahn and Selesnick) in this gallery's stable .

Pucker Gallery

171 Newbury Street, at Dartmouth Street (267 9473/www.puckergallery.com). Copley T. **Open** 10am-5.30pm Mon-Sat; 1-5pm Sun. **Admission** free. **Map** p306 F5.

When director Bernard Pucker gets it right, the results can be breathtaking, as with the mobiles of Mark Davis, the ceramic work of Tatsuzo Shimaoka and the evanescent landscapes of Gunnar Norman. Pucker is also distinct among Newbury Street galleries for showing unschooled and primitive art, in particular Inuit carvings.

The **Howard Yezerski Gallery** is always intelligent and provocative. See p211.

Robert Klein Gallery

38 Newbury Street, at Berkeley Street (267 7997/ www.robertkleingallery.com). Arlington T. **Open** 10am-5.30pm Mon-Fri; 11am-5pm Sat. **Admission** free. **Map** p306 F5.

Devoted exclusively to fine art photography, this gallery deals in established 19th- and 20th-century photographers such as Edward Weston, Charles Sheeler, Sally Mann and William Wegman. Boasting over 3,000 images in its inventory, there are bound to be pleasant surprises here for even the most knowledgeable of collectors.

South End

Berenberg Gallery

4 Clarendon Street, near Tremont Street (536 0800). Back Bay T. **Open** 10am-6pm Tue-Sat. **Admission** free. **Map** p306 F6.

Just across from the Boston Center for the Arts (*see p113*), this recently opened gallery is remarkable in that it focuses on contemporary folk art. In particular, the gallery exhibits the work of self-taught artists. some of whom are elderly or from rural locales, while others have little formal education or are physically or mentally challenged. The result is a moving and unique collection that has become a hit on the Boston art scene. Owner Lori Berenberg energetically searches the country to find unusual art for her gallery, and usually succeeds in locating extraordinary pieces that cannot be found elsewhere in the city. Worth a visit.

Bernard Toale Gallery

450 Harrison Avenue, at Thayer Street (482 2477/ www.bernardtoalegallery.com). NE Medical Center T. **Open** 10.30am-5.30pm Tue-Sat. **Admission** free. **Map** p307 G6.

Bernie Toale's place on the Boston art scene is solid, chiefly because of his unimpeachable taste. There is a great deal to discover below the surface at the South End's anchor gallery. A visit here promises riches, including the seditious eroticism of Debra Bright's oversized colour photos of a plastic horse wearing mascara.

Clifford-Smith Gallery

Third floor, 450 Harrison Avenue, Thayer Street (695 0255/www.cliffordsmithgallery.com). NE Medical Center T. **Open** 11am-5.30pm Wed-Fri. **Admission** free. **Map** p307 G6.

This gallery retains the freshness of a new arrival, although it has been a welcome feature of the South End's art scene for several years now. Rare is the established space – let alone the unestablished – that is as willing to take such informed, exciting risks. From David Kelley's dynamic, dotty abstractions to Joy Episalla's intense, larger-than-life photographs of upholstery, Clifford-Smith offers a unique vision.

Genovese/Sullivan Gallery

47 Thayer Street, at Harrison Avenue (426 9738). NE Medical Center T. **Open** 10.30am-5.30pm Tue-Sat. **Admission** free. **Map** p307 G6.

This merits a visit not only because it is one of the most art-friendly spaces in the city (the rooms are expansive, the ceilings tall), but also because of the curatorial acumen of its owners, David Sullivan and Camellia Genovese. Among the outstanding artists affiliated with the gallery is the sculptor Pat Keck, who creates diabolical works of seeming simplicity and extraordinary complexity, like *Big Head*, which appears to be no more than an inanimate four-foot decapitated wooden head – until you look into one of its eyes, where there's a headless man drumming his fingers while attempting to play solitaire.

Allston

On the outskirts of Cambridge, Allston has become a burgeoning arts community.

Allston Skirt Gallery

129 Braintree Street, 2nd floor, at Harvard Avenue (254 7027/www.allstonskirt.com). Harvard Avenue T. **Open** noon-5pm Wed-Sat; by appointment Mon, Tue, Sun. **Admission** free.

This space can be found down a long hallway on the second floor of a large, industrial-looking building. The focus is on mixing it up – emerging artists with established artists, painting with sculpture, sound art with photography – and on challenging expectations with lively group exhibitions and more tightly focused two-person shows.

Dietrich von Buhler Gallery

16 Ashford Street, near Brighton Avenue (783 2421) Harvard Avenue T. **Open** 2-4pm Sat; by appointment Mon-Fri, Sun. **Admission** free.

In a sprawling Victorian house, this gallery has emerged as a dynamic experimental space in a city with few venues catering to installation art and new media. A painter, performance artist and musician herself, co-owner Cynthia von Buhler brings her multi-media sensibility to this promising new venue.

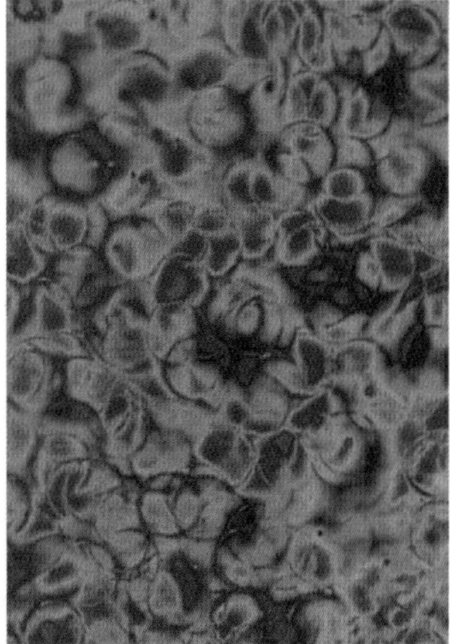

The Clifford-Smith Gallery. See p212.

Elias Fine Art

120 Braintree Street, near Harvard Avenue (783 1888). Harvard Avenue T. **Open** noon-5pm Wed-Sat. **Admission** free.

EFA is in what appears to be a nondescript garage, but looks are deceiving. The gallery shows great contemporary art, from the likes of Christian Boltanski and Sigmar Polke, and talented locals such as Shellburne Thurber and Frank Egloff.

Local Idea Council

107 Brighton Avenue, 2nd floor, at Linden Street (562 0840/www.localideacouncil.org). Harvard Avenue T. **Open** 7-9pm Tue-Thur; by appointment Sat. **Admission** free.

This tiny space has existed as an alternative art venue for more than ten years, quietly and rather subversively presenting unusual projects, and consistently creative works. Some are worthwhile just for their titles, like the recent exhibition called 'Universal Aliens Phenomenological Experiment: One Year Media Blackout by Test Human.'

Jamaica Plain

Another somewhat far-flung neighbourhood, Jamaica Plain features two galleries for which art lovers will travel miles.

The Gallery@Green Street

141 Green Street, at Amory Street (522 0000/ www.jameshull.com). Green Street T. **Open** 6-9pm Tue; noon-9pm Wed, Thur; noon-5pm Fri, Sat. **Admission** free.

In a subway station on the Orange Line, this gallery is non-profit, artist-funded and run with a well-tuned eye for the up and the coming. Green Street often features new media and installation art that other galleries find too artistically experimental or technologically daunting to mess with.

Hamill Gallery of African Art

2164 Washington Street, at Melnea Cass Boulevard, (442 8204). Ruggles T. **Open** noon-6pm Wed-Sat; by appointment Mon, Tue, Sun. **Admission** free.

Although somewhat further afield than the other galleries, it's worth making the trip to see the Hamill. Artist and gallery director Tim Hamill has devoted the last decade to building up a showcase that acts as both gallery and educational centre; collectors come to buy, students come to learn. With textiles that range from the bark cloth of the Mboto pygmy to the exotic, bright cotton weaves of the Asante, with sculpture that ranges from the granary doors of the Dogon to the carved posts of the nomadic Tuareg, Hamill's gallery offers satisfaction with works of such depth that, even if you go nowhere else in town, you still won't feel guilty.

Gay & Lesbian

Being gay in Boston is no big deal, but it can be a lot of fun.

Boston is the kind of place where you can walk downtown in a 'Kiss me, I'm queer' T-shirt and no one will bat an eyelid. Having got past its Puritan origins and its 1960s-style radical politics, the newly prosperous city is characterised by a Yankee version of old-fashioned hedonism. Everyone is too busy looking for a good meal, a shopping bargain and a bit of culture to pay any mind to the sexual proclivities of their neighbours. The gay and lesbian population of Boston is one of the largest in the United States, and one of the most integrated.

The downside of this live-and-let-live philosophy is a sense of aloofness, and Boston is infamous among gay travellers for its 'attitude' problem. In reality, many gay and lesbian residents, most of whom are from somewhere else, adopt a frosty demeanour only because it's the local custom, and, given half a chance, they'll lower their guard.

Boston's queer community often feels transient and youth-oriented, but it's rooted in 400 years of history. The first governor of Massachusetts, John Winthrop, wrote love letters to a man he had left behind in England. Later, at least one lesbian from Boston, Deborah Sampson, fought for Independence alongside the Minutemen. Using the name Robert Shurtleff, Sampson wooed many a maiden, and no one knew she was a woman until she was wounded in battle.

In the 19th century, the 'Athens of America' is said to have been rife with literary men loving men. Much has been read into Herman Melville's dedication of *Moby Dick* to Nathaniel Hawthorne, and Ralph Waldo Emerson's diary chronicles an obsession with a Harvard classmate. Better documented are the so-called 'Boston Marriages' – socially sanctioned relationships between women. Writer Sarah Orne Jewett and poet Amy Lowell, among others, took female partners. By the end of the century, Boston's art scene also included a strong queer presence. Isabella Stewart Gardner, the widow who founded the museum bearing her name (*see p114*), surrounded herself with gay admirers including architect Ralph Adams Cram and the painter John Singer Sargent.

Still, gay culture remained underground until after World War II, when Boston's first gay bars started springing up among the strip joints of Scollay Square (this teeming, saucy neighbourhood is no more; it's now the sterile cementscape of Government Center). In a reference to the sleazy area of New York City, lower Washington Street became known as 'Gay Times Square', while Bay Village – sandwiched between Chinatown and the South End – became a haven for same-sex relationships. Most of these areas were razed in a neo-Puritan attempt at 'urban renewal' back in the 1960s, but by then Boston's gay network was well established.

The gay community took to the streets after the 1969 Stonewall riots in New York kicked off gay emancipation across the country, and organised what became one of the country's first annual Gay Pride parades in 1971. For the first few years, the parade involved only a few

Flying the flag on Chandler Street.

hundred people and had a militant tone. These days, Gay Pride lasts for the entire month of June, and includes art exhibits and Boston Harbour party cruises. Parade attendance regularly tops 100,000, and corporate sponsors vie for space at the post-march fair.

In 1972, Bostonian Elaine Noble became the first openly gay or lesbian person to win a seat in any state legislature. Some 15 years later the first two openly gay members of the US Congress (Gerry Studds and Barney Frank) represented suburban Boston. In 1990, Massachusetts became one of the first states to pass a comprehensive gay rights law. More recently, it has been in the vanguard in developing programmes to protect gay youths from harassment in schools. The gay political lobby is still potent, but it's not often tested by strong opposition. The religious right, which carries great influence in many other states, is virtually non-existent in Boston.

NEIGHBOURHOODS

The South End is no longer, as it once was, a magnet for young men wanting to get their first taste of living in a 'gay ghetto', but even if straight couples seem to be buying more condos here than they once did, the South End has by far the largest concentration of gay-owned businesses in Boston. Most shops are adorned with the rainbow-striped flags that signal that they are gay-owned or gay-friendly. The streets are lined with little shops that mix kitsch with quality in equal measures. Gay men set the tone on Tremont Street. Flirting with a waiter or salesperson of the same sex will not always get you better service, but it's still a no-risk strategy.

Two adjacent neighbourhoods also have a large gay presence. To the north, Bay Village is a tiny enclave of small brick houses; to the west, the Fenway has a notorious cruising area called the Fens.

INFORMATION

There are two weekly newspapers, both free. *Bay Windows* is more the paper of record for the gay community, covering local and national news in a fairly straightforward manner. *In Newsweekly* is a bit saucier, with an emphasis on gay nightlife throughout New England. Both are distributed on Thursdays in bookstores, cafés and gay bars throughout Boston, Cambridge and Somerville.

Bars

For a city of its size, Boston has surprisingly few gay bars. The problem doesn't seem to be homophobia; rather, the city's powerful neighbourhood groups make it difficult to open any establishment that might lead to late-night sidewalk loitering. Many gay Bostonians save their club-hopping for trips to New York, Montreal or Provincetown. One encouraging development in Boston's bar scene is that it's becoming more ethnically diverse. And there's a burgeoning club scene, thanks to a handful of discotheques that have finally done away with their 1970s decor. If you're wearing a pair of jeans and a button-down shirt, you'll fit in almost anywhere.

119 Merrimac

119 Merrimac Street, at Causeway Street, North End (367 0713). North Station T. **Open** 10.30am-2am Mon-Sat; noon-2am Sun. **Admission** free. **No credit cards. Map** p307 G3.

Your basic North End pick-up bar, with a DJ, a few pool tables and minimal lighting. South End boys generally don't include 119 on their circuit, which can be a blessing if you're looking for new faces.

Avalon

For listings see p204.

Sunday at Avalon has been Boston's biggest gay night out for as long as anyone can remember. Recently renovated, the club has a huge dancefloor with platforms for go-go boys. The music is mostly techno and hip hop, but the cover charge also grants entry to Axis next door (*see p204*), which offers alternative music. College kids usually dominate the scene here.

The Eagle

520 Tremont Street, at Berkeley Street, South End (542 4494). Back Bay T. **Open** 3pm-2am Mon-Fri; 1pm-2am Sat; noon-2am Sun. **Admission** free. **No credit cards. Map** p308 F6.

Boston's premier 'last call' destination, the Eagle has a decor befitting a leather-and-Levi's bar, but as the evening wears on, it attracts South End professionals looking for a quick one before heading home. At 2am, some patrons pair up in the nightly 'sidewalk sale' along Tremont Street.

Encore Lounge (at the Tremont Hotel)

275 Tremont Street, at Stuart Street, South End (426 1400). Boylston or NE Medical Center T. **Open** 4pm-2am Mon-Fri, Sun; noon-2am Sat. **Admission** free. **Credit** AmEx, MC, V. **Map** p306 F5.

Not gay as such, but a piano bar in the Theatre District isn't going to be totally hetero, is it?

Fritz (at the Chandler Inn)

26 Chandler Street, at Berkeley Street, South End (482 4428). Back Bay T. **Open** 11am-2am Mon-Sat; noon-2am Sun. **Admission** free. **No credit cards. Map** p308 F5.

A neighbourhood bar that attracts all types, including out-of-towners from the Chandler Inn upstairs. Brunch is served till 3pm at weekends.

Drag yourself to **Jacque's Cabaret** for some sparkling entertainment.

Jacque's Cabaret

79 Broadway, Back Bay (426 8902). Arlington T. **Open** 11am-midnight Mon-Sat; noon-midnight Sun. **Admission** $4-$6. **No credit cards. Map** p308 F5.

The oldest gay bar in town, featuring drag shows every night except Monday. It's hardly glamourous, but the filthy banter and discount-store outfits can add up to an entertaining evening, and once in a while there's a performer who's shockingly good. Lots of straight people show up here at weekends, so be careful who you make a pass at.

Lava Bar (at Howard Johnson's)

575 Commonwealth Avenue, at Kenmore Square, Fenway (267 7707). Kenmore T. **Open** 10pm-2am Tue, Thur-Sun. **No credit cards. Map** p306 D5.

On Saturdays, the crowd is largely lesbian at this upper-floor dance club with a nice view of the city. DJs spin house music with a Latin accent. (Don't be misled by another Ho Jo's a few blocks away, across the street from the hyper-masculine Ramrod bar.)

Luxor

69 Church Street, at Park Plaza, Back Bay (423 6969). Arlington T. **Open** 4pm-1am daily. **Admission** free. **Credit** AmEx, Disc, MC, V. **Map** p308 F5.

Skip the often-deserted 'sports bar' and head to the larger upstairs level. In the back, there's a video bar. While the front area has the feel and look of the waiting room at a brothel.

Machine

Below the Ramrod, 1254 Boylston Street, at Ipswich Street, Back Bay (266 2986). Kenmore T. **Open** noon-2am daily. **Admission** free-$8. **No credit cards. Map** p306 D5/6.

This glitzy, expansive dance club opened a couple of years ago, and its popularity scared a couple of other gay bars into cleaning up their own acts. It features a dancefloor with state-of-the-art lighting, a video lounge and a separate room with pool tables. The cover charge also includes the Ramrod bar upstairs (*see below*), which has an older and sometimes predatory clientele.

Man Ray

For listings see p205.

Sexual identities don't mean much at Man Ray, but the official gay night is 'Campus' Thursday, when collegiate types dance to boypop and house music. 'Liquid' Saturday, which features disco and new wave music, is as popular. Both nights are open to those as young as 19 (instead of the usual 21).

Moonshine (at Club Café)

209 Columbus Avenue, at Berkeley Street, Back Bay (536 0966). Back Bay T. **Open** 8pm-midnight Wed; 9pm-2am Thur-Sat. **Admission** free. **Credit** AmEx, DC, Disc, MC, V. **Map** p308 F5.

A popular video bar in the back of Club Café (*see p218*). Cruising is acceptable but not obligatory. The crowd peaks at about midnight, after which people drift towards dance clubs and bedrooms.

Paradise

180 Massachusetts Avenue, just off MIT campus, Cambridge (494 0700). Central T or 1 bus. **Open** 5pm-1am Mon-Wed, Sun; 5pm-2am Thur-Sat. **Admission** free. **No credit cards. Map** p306 D4.

It's just on the other side of the river from Boston, but Paradise has the feel of the only gay bar in a small town. The crowd is racially mixed and includes all age groups. Upstairs, there are porn videos and often-shirtless bartenders, and go-go dancers circulate among the customers. Discreet fondling is available for a suitable tip. Downstairs, there's a small dance floor.

The Ramrod

1254 Boylston Street, at Ipswich Street, Back Bay (266 2986). Kenmore T. **Open** noon-2am daily. **Admission** free. **No credit cards. Map** p306 D5/6.

This is the headquarters of Boston's leather scene, and such master-and-slave groups as the Leather Knights meet here. At weekends, the back room is restricted to men who are bare-chested or wearing leather gear. Because the Ramrod also serves as a neighbourhood bar for the Fenway, the front area isn't quite so intimidating.

Upstairs (at the Hideaway Pub)

20 Concord Lane, near Fresh Pond Rotary, Cambridge (661 8828). Alewife T. **Open** 11.30am-1am Mon-Wed; 11.30am-2am Thur-Sat; noon-1am Sun. **Admission** free. **No credit cards.**

Thursdays and Sundays feature your basic butch scene with pool tables and darts. You know what you're getting in a comforting sort of way: plenty of loud jukebox music and cheap beer. Tends to be favoured by a more mature clientele.

Bookshops

Calamus Bookstore

92B South Street, at East Street, Downtown (338 1931). South Station T. **Open** 9am-7pm Mon-Sat; noon-6pm Sun. **Map** p307 G5.

A replacement for the recently closed Glad Day Bookshop (a victim of rising rents in the Back Bay), this place is spacious, and has all the books, magazines and videos you'll need, but the out-of-the-way location has kept it from re-creating Glad Day's entertaining and cruisey atmosphere.

New Words: A Women's Bookstore

186 Hampshire Street, Cambridge (876 5310). Central T. **Open** 10am-8pm Mon-Fri; 10am-6pm Sat; noon-6pm Sun. **Credit** AmEx, Disc, MC, V. **Map** p306 D3.

The only queer bookshop in Cambridge, where the emphasis and atmosphere are definitely lesbian. Workers here are friendly, smart and helpful.

We Think the World of You

540 Tremont Street, between Berkeley and Clarendon Streets, Back Bay (574 5000). Back Bay T. **Open** 10am-7pm daily. **Credit** AmEx, DC, Disc, MC, V. **Map** p308 F6.

We Think the World of You. *See p217.*

Queer novels, biographies and magazines, plus CDs, greeting cards and lots of gift items emblazoned with rainbows. A small porn section has recently been added. The staff are friendly and attentive.

Gyms & spas

There are no euphemisms in this category, since the city's only '24-hour gym' (read: bathhouse) was shut down by the city in 2000. The nearest establishments of that type are in Rhode Island. The gyms listed below are only gyms.

Étant

251 Shawmut Avenue, at Milford Street, South End (423 5040). Back Bay T. **Open** 10am-9pm Wed-Fri; 8am-6pm Sat; 11am-5pm Sun. **Rates** massage $65, facial $65; manicure $16. **Credit** AmEx, Disc, MC, V. **Map** p306 G5.

Though Étant bills itself as a 'spa for well-being', it's basically a nice little place where you can book a massage, get a facial or 'align your energy systems' through polarity therapy. The menu also includes acupuncture, hair removal and body wraps. Call ahead to make an appointment.

Metropolitan Health Club

209 Columbus Avenue, at Berkeley Street, Back Bay (536 3006). Back Bay T. **Open** 5.30am-11pm Mon-Fri; 9am-9pm Sat; 10am-9pm Sun. **Rates** day pass $15. **Credit** AmEx, MC, V. **Map** p308 F5.

Where the South End boys with attitude work out. The Metropolitan has the latest weight-training and cardio equipment and a very good aerobics staff. It's best at off-peak hours, if you're the type who just wants to get the workout over with. Otherwise, it's a little like a gay bar with weights.

Mike's Gym II

560 Harrison Avenue, at Waltham Street, South End (338 6210). Back Bay T. **Open** 6am-10pm Mon-Fri; 8am-8pm Sat; 9am-6.30pm Sun. **Rates** day pass $12; week pass $30. **Credit** MC, V. **Map** p306 F6.

Where the serious, big boys go. Good if you like places that are a little more ethnically and racially mixed; bad if you're a clean freak. Mike's has all the equipment you could need (with an emphasis on free weights) and a decent aerobics schedule, but the facilities are a little grubby.

Restaurants & cafés

Any restaurants or cafés in the South End are, by virtue of their location, gay-friendly. Those listed below are popular with queer patrons.

Appetito

1 Appleton Street, at Tremont Street, Back Bay (338 6777). Back Bay T. **Open** 5-10pm Mon-Thur, Sun; 5-11pm Fri, Sat; 11am-2.30pm Sun. **Main courses** $21. **Credit** AmEx, DC, Disc, MC, V. **Map** p308 F5.

Hearty Italian food in a relaxed atmosphere. A favourite for first dates and huge birthday dinners.

Blackstone on the Square

1525 Washington Street, at West Brookline Street, South End (247 4455). 1 or 49 bus. **Open** 11.30am-2.30pm Mon-Fri; 5.30-10pm Mon-Wed, Sat; 5.30-11pm Thur-Sat; 11am-2pm Sun. Bar menu available until midnight. **Main courses** $11-$22. **Credit** AmEx, DC, Disc, MC, V.

This is a textbook example of gay gentrification: a swanky restaurant with a marble-topped bar across the street from a Salvation Army headquarters. The menu emphasises seafood, and the clientele is more identifiable as gay than at similar restaurants on Tremont Street. With church-pew booths and other Gothic touches, Blackstone pays homage to the Cathedral of the Holy Cross, a few blocks away.

Club Café

209 Columbus Avenue, at Berkeley Street, South End (536 0966). Back Bay T. **Open** 12.30-2.30pm Mon-Fri; 5.30-10pm Mon-Wed; 5.30-11pm Thur-Sat; 11am-2.30pm, 5-10pm Sun. **Main courses** $10-$22. **Credit** AmEx, DC, Disc, MC, V. **Map** p308 F5.

The restaurant is almost incidental to the bar, which is the only place in town where gay men and lesbians really mix – or at least occupy adjacent bistro tables. Jazz vocalists add a further touch of class at the weekends. The dining area, with a New American menu, is usually filled with couples. But Sunday brunch feels more like a town meeting with South Enders trading stories about the night before.

Diesel Café

257 Elm Street, at Davis Square, Somerville (629 8717). Davis Square T. **Open** 7am-midnight Mon-Thur; 8am-1am Sat; 8am-midnight Sun. **Coffee & cookie** $3. **No credit cards.**

It's easy to deconstruct the name: there's the coffee-as-fuel metaphor, and there's the winking reference to 'diesel dykes', though the crowd is more diverse and welcoming than that label implies. Stop here for caffeine, sweets and light lunches, or try to claim one of the two pool tables. Somehow the combination of coffee and pool really works here. To blend in with the students, stop by the used bookshop next door and grab a volume or two from the Queer Theory section.

Everyday Café

517 Columbus Avenue, at Greenwich Park, South End (536 2119). Mass Ave T. **Open** 7am-8pm Mon, Wed-Fri; 9am-5pm Sat, Sun. **Main courses** $5. **Credit** MC, V. **Map** p306 E6.

A chatty hangout for the neighbourhood's mixed clientele. In addition to coffee, pastries and sandwiches, you can pick up a few gourmet grocery items and check your email.

Garden of Eden

571 Tremont Street, at Clarendon Street, South End (247 8377). Back Bay T. **Open** 7am-11pm Mon-Fri; 7.30am-11pm Sat; 7.30am-10.30pm Sun. **Main courses** $5.50-$12. **Credit** AmEx, MC, V. **Map** p306 F6.

What a drag

Gay Boston's legendary iciness does thaw in the right settings, and some of the chattiest crowds can be found not in bars but in theatre lobbies. While it was long underwhelming, the city's theatre scene is today steadily improving, thanks to the recently robust economy and the perseverance of several theatre companies. As in New York, gays and lesbians make up a strong part of the theatre scene, both as participants and as audience members. Just about any touring show with gay appeal, from *Rent* to *Dame Edna's Royal Tour*, makes a stop in Boston's Theatre District. The city's only full-time piano bar, the Encore Lounge, is also in this area, though straight patrons tend to dominate the place on the busiest theatre weekends.

Boston's cabaret and 'fringe' theatre scene is even more gay-oriented, and you can find a couple of queer-themed shows just about any time of the year outside of July and August —when the most popular performers work in Provincetown. Both of the city's gay newspapers (*see p215*) devote extensive space to Boston theatre, and they'll tip you off to shows in some of the more offbeat venues. In particular, *Bay Windows* previews and reviews practically everything in town.

With three stages and two more on the way, the **Boston Center for the Arts** (*see p233*) is the unofficial headquarters for the city's version of off-Broadway theatre. It also happens to be the geographical centre of Boston's gay community. The plaza in front of the theatre complex is a popular meeting place at any time of the year. In December, it's ablaze with Christmas lights; in June, the lights turn pink in honour of Gay Pride Month. During popular shows, the BCA lobby can get quite raucous. The friendly kissing and backslapping can make for a stark contrast to the cool atmosphere in many of the city's bars.

Resident companies at the BCA include the **Theatre Offensive** (542 4214/www.thetheateroffensive.org), which focuses exclusively on gay and lesbian playwrights and performers. Its Out on the Edge festival, in September, is a wonderfully mixed bag of performance art, comic monologues and full-blown plays. Holly Hughes, Tim Miller and the British duo Bloolips are among the recent offerings. During the rest of the year, the company spotlights local talent.

Among other BCA regulars, the **SpeakEasy Stage Company** often premieres works from New York with gay themes. **Centastage** (536 5981) promotes the work of local playwrights, and its annual Women on Top festival, in February or March, usually includes a fair dose of lesbian content. The BCA also features, on an erratic basis, late-night performances (in Boston, that actually means 10.30pm) that appeal to South Enders. John Kuntz, an openly gay actor and comedian who might be described as Boston's answer to Lily Tomlin (and also arguably the biggest star in Boston theatre) first gained a following with his one-man shows here.

Gay theatre blossoms throughout the city in June, but the Christmas season also brings alternatives for theatregoers who get enough family values entertainment on television. Recent hits includes the drag burlesque *How Mrs Grinchley Swiped Christmas* and the cabaret show *Holidaze: a Christian, a Jew, and a Ho, Ho, Homo Too!*

Yet another café with excellent views of the foot traffic on Tremont Street. It's got all the essentials for breakfast, plus sandwiches, pastries and fresh fruit. Strangers often find themselves sharing the large wood-block tables and making new friends.

Geoffrey's Café-Bar

578 Tremont Street, between Clarendon and Dartmouth Streets, South End (266 1122). Back Bay T. **Open** 9am-11pm daily. **Main courses** $10.95-$15.95. **Credit** AmEx, DC, MC, V. **Map** p306 F6.
The most outwardly gay of the bazillion eateries along Tremont Street, with a huge rainbow flag over the door. The floor-to-ceiling windows make for good boy-watching, and the (rather cramped) dining area lets you listen in on the latest neighbourhood gossip. The overpriced menu ranges from burgers to pasta to grilled entrées.

Mario's

69 Church Street, at Park Plaza, Back Bay (542 3776). Arlington T. **Open** 5.30-10pm daily. **Main courses** $9-$15. **Credit** AmEx, DC, Disc, MC, V. **Map** p306 G4.
If there really is a gay Mafia, this is its headquarters. The waitstaff is divided between hunky young men and motherly types who call everyone 'hun'. Settle into one of the plush robin's egg blue booths and keep things simple with wine and pasta. For light entertainment, look for the occasional straight couple trying to make sense of it all.

Rave

552 Tremont Street, at Waltham Street, South End (426 0008). Back Bay T. **Open** 8am-11pm Mon-Wed; 8am-midnight Thur-Sat; 9am-11pm Sun. **Main courses** $7-$12. **Credit** AmEx, MC, V. **Map** p306 F6.
This one is tough to miss thanks to its corner location and the garish furniture behind large windows. Find a purple chair and watch the boys go by, but remember that you'll be pretty conspicuous yourself. The menu includes soups, frittatas and desserts. The piped-in music, though rather unpredictable, leans toward disco and divas.

To Go Bakery

314 Shawmut Avenue, at Union Park, South End (482 1015). Back Bay T. **Open** 6.30am-5pm Mon-Fri; 7am-4pm Sat; 7am-3pm Sun. **Average** $5. **No credit cards**. **Map** p306 F6.
Locals swear by the coffee at this tiny corner shop, which also offers tasty scones and elaborate cakes. When the weather is nice, customers linger on the benches outside.

Shops & services

Boomerangs

716 Centre Street, Jamaica Plain (524 5120). Green Street T or 39 bus. **Open** 11am-7pm Mon-Wed; 11am-8pm Thur-Sat; noon-5pm Sun. **Credit** AmEx, Disc, MC, V.
A resale store that is operated by the AIDS Action Committee. It offers one-stop shopping for glamourous drag outfits and disco CDs at bargain prices. Another victim of rising rents, the store recently moved from downtown to a much smaller site in Jamaica Plain.

Liquid Hair Salon

640 Tremont Street, at West Newton Street, South End (425 4848). Back Bay T. **Open** 11am-8pm Tue-Fri; 10am-6pm Sat. **Credit** AmEx, MC, V. **Map** p306 F6.
This salon caters to South End queens who like a little atmosphere and chat but don't want to pay Newbury Street prices.

Marquis Leather

73 Berkeley Street, between Chandler & Lawrence Streets, South End (426 2120). Back Bay T. **Open** 11am-1am daily. **Credit** AmEx, MC, V. **Map** p306 F6.
In addition to renting every video known to male homodom, the Marquis supplies the neighbourhood with magazines, toys, leather accessories and lube.

Mike's Movies

557 Tremont Street, at Clarendon Street, South End (266 9222). Back Bay T. **Open** 10.30am-10pm Mon-Thur; 10am-11pm Fri, Sat; 11.30am-10pm Sun. **Credit** AmEx, Disc, MC, V. **Map** p306 F6.
The entire neighbourhood seems to come here for the latest Hollywood blockbusters. Meanwhile, the gay boys make use of a generous porn section at the back. Mostly rental.

The Movie Place

526 Tremont Street, at Berkeley Street, South End (482 9008). Back Bay T. **Open** 11am-11pm daily. **Credit** for rentals over $20 AmEx, Disc, MC, V. **Map** p306 F6.
More exclusively gay, this is the best place in town for hard-to-find camp, plus what appears to be every episode of *I Love Lucy*. Throw in a visit to the porn section, and there's no limit to what you can put together for an evening in front of the box.

Pet Shop Girls

472 Shawmut Avenue, at West Concord Street, South End (262 7387). Mass Ave T. **Open** 10am-6.30pm Mon-Fri; 9.30am-6pm Sat. **Credit** MC, V. **Map** p306 F6.
Offers grooming services and a menagerie of items for pampering your pet.

Santa Fe Styling Company Hair Salon & Tanning

528 & 546 Tremont Street, at Berkeley Street, South End (338 5095). Back Bay T. **Open** 10am-8pm Tue-Sat. **Credit** AmEx, Disc, MC, V. **Map** p306 F6.
Specialising in buff-boy homocuts. The nice thing about Santa Fe is that everybody's welcome and it doesn't cost an arm and a leg to get a few highlights. Just up the street, its tanning centre has both stand-up booths and beds. Products for sale include creams and colour enhancers plus a skimpy line of men's bathing trunks.

Music: Rock & Roots

Filled with students, artists and money, Boston remains a mecca for musicians. Get in line.

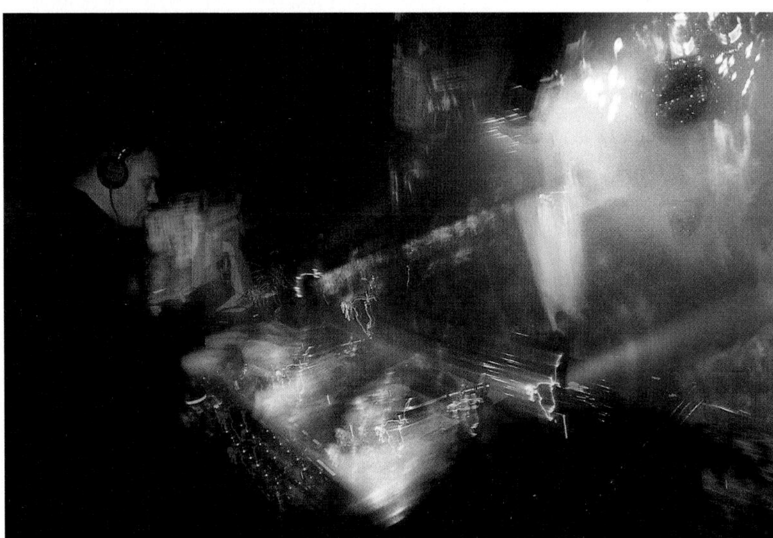

Both bands and DJs rock the house at **Avalon**. *See p222.*

Since the 1960s, Boston has been widely acknowledged as one of the country's most fertile live music environments, and young bands are still moving here from all over the US just to be a part of it. The city's musical pedigree is impressive. The thriving music scene has served as a launch pad for generations of underground legends and a few commercial superstars. Blockbuster 1970s bands Aerosmith, Boston and the Cars all hailed from here, but the city's rock reputation has been secured mainly by less mass-market acts. Boston is, and has been, home to punk and garage-rock royalty. Think that's an oxymoron? Well, consider that Jonathan Richman, the Pixies, Throwing Muses, the Lemonheads and Morphine all come from Boston. If they're not royalty, we don't know who is.

The biggest draw for aspiring rock musicians is the astonishing accessibility of gigs here. Boston's live venues range from arenas, theatres and showcase stages for national and local headlining acts to the humblest of corner bars. The most famous left-of-centre rock club in town is the **Middle East**, in Central Square, with local and national acts seven nights a week on three stages. **Lilli's**, in Somerville, is another premier venue for local and touring bands. It's an enduring tradition in Boston for ambitious young rock promoters to turn dives in crap neighbourhoods into happening club scenes, so don't be afraid of the dumpier addresses.

For a city so far from the south, blues are quite big here. The local bastion of the **House of Blues** chain offers impressive national blues and roots bookings, but, for a truly down-to-earth blues experience check out the scruffy but beloved **Cantab Lounge**.

In general, when it comes to major touring acts, contacting the US ticket leviathan **Ticketmaster** (931 2000) is your best bet. For smaller clubs, deal directly with the venues.

Major venues

Beer and wine are sold at most shows at these big music venues. Cigarette smoking is not permitted anywhere in closed arenas and theatres; open-air venues allow smoking outside the seating areas. As for stronger stuff, proceed with extreme caution, if at all. Security teams tend to be pretty uptight when it comes to illegal substances.

FleetBoston Pavillion

290 Northern Avenue, Fan Pier, South Boston (728 1600). South Station T, then 7 bus. **Open** Box office 10am-5pm Mon-Fri. **Tickets** vary. **Credit** AmEx, DC, Disc, MC, V.

Formerly Harborlights, and since corporatised into name-hell, this is a pleasant, tented venue on the edge of Boston Harbor. The summer schedules tend to be strong on oldies, soul reviews and nostalgia stars – some never to be seen again. Frank Sinatra played here, and the Beach Boys' last Boston show with Carl Wilson was at Harborlights. But there are usually a few contemporary rock shows booked into the season, too (this is where Radiohead stopped on their *OK Computer* tour).

FleetCenter

One FleetCenter, Causeway Street at Friend Street (information 624 1900/tickets 931 2000 www.fleetcenter.com). North Station T. **Open** Box office *Sept-Apr* 11am-7pm daily. *May-Aug* 10am-5pm Mon-Fri. **Tickets** vary. **Credit** AmEx, DC, Disc, MC, V. **Map** p308 G3.

Built next door to the now-demolished Boston Garden – the scene of historic concerts by the Who and the Stones, as well as an Alan Freed package bill that turned into one of the first high-profile rock 'n' roll riots. The new home of the Bruins hockey team and Celtics basketball team leans toward booking mainstream stars such as Tina Turner, Mariah Carey and Ricky Martin, with occasional concessions to rock acts such as AC/DC, Aerosmith and KISS.

Foxboro Stadium

60 Washington Street, Route 1, Foxboro (1-800 543 1776/www.patriots.com/stadium). **Open** Box office *Aug-Dec* 9am-5pm Mon-Sat. **Tickets** vary. **Credit** AmEx, MC, V.

The 50,000-seat home of the New England Patriots football team, suburban Foxboro has also hosted concerts ranging from the Rolling Stones to 'N Sync. A new stadium, with the charming, corporate name **CMGI Field**, is being built next to Foxboro and should open in April 2002.

Orpheum Theater

1 Hamilton Place, at Tremont Street (679 0810/ NEXT Ticketing 423 6398). Park Street T. **Open** Box office 10am-5pm Mon-Sat; NEXT Ticketing 24 hours daily. **Tickets** $20-$50. **Credit** AmEx, MC, V. **Map** p307 G5.

A Boston landmark, built in 1852 as the Boston Music Hall, the 3,000-seat Orpheum was the first home of the Boston Symphony Orchestra; in its early incarnation, the venue's acoustics were said to be the best in the world. Since then, it has been home to everything from movies to boxing matches. These days, it mainly hosts big-name rock and comedy tours.

Somerville Theater

55 Davis Square, Somerville (625 5700/recorded information 625 4988/Ticketmaster 931 2000). Davis T. **Open** Box office 1-9pm daily. **Tickets** $15-$25. **Credit** AmEx, Disc, MC, V.

A converted movie house (though it still serves mainly as a second-run cinema), the Somerville Theater is situated in the middle of the chic Davis Square neighbourhood. It enjoys the patronage of New England's hippie jam-rock underground and is also the gig of choice for top-bill folkies like Arlo Guthrie and Billy Bragg.

Worcester Centrum Center

50 Foster Street, at Worcester Center Boulevard, Worcester (1-508 755 6800). **Open** Box office *summer* 10am-4pm Mon-Fri. *Winter* 9.30am-5.30pm Mon-Sat. **Tickets** vary. **Credit** AmEx, Disc, MC, V.

A slightly less sprawling arena than the FleetCenter – the only regular occupants are the minor-league IceCats hockey team – the Centrum is where you'll see your basic Korn and Limp Bizkit. Although acts who play here often greet their fans with a cheery 'Hello, Boston!' the venue is actually a good hour's drive away, and if you don't plan the route well the directions can be challenging. In other words, allow some time for getting lost.

Music clubs

Abbey Lounge

3 Beacon Street, Somerville (441 9631/ www.schnockered.com). Central T. **Open** *Shows* 9pm-1am Thur-Sat. **Tickets** $3-$7. **No credit cards.**

This is the grungiest of the grungy bars-cum-rock clubs, with a clientele of grizzled neighbourhood regulars on one side of the bar, and a crowd of young rockers in vintage rags on the other, and everyone usually getting along just fine. The drinks are dirt cheap and the live music can be surprisingly strong, with a bent toward garage- and roots-rock.

Avalon

For listings, see p204.

Most nights the massive sound system and slick lighting attract a disco crowd to one of the biggest dance clubs in the city. But its alter-ego as a live music venue is just as strong. From its earliest days as the old Boston Tea Party, this industrial space (with a 2,000 capacity) has hosted almost everybody in the rock pantheon. Contemporary bookings have included Snoop Dogg, Macy Gray, Sonic Youth, PJ Harvey and the Chemical Brothers.

Bill's Bar

For listings, see p157.

A dance club for part of the week, Bill's is the only club left on the Lansdowne strip still to have dedicated live-music nights. It's the live nights that give Bill's its character. 'Monsta' Monday is a long-standing format featuring local and some national hardcore and metal rock.

Cantab Lounge

738 Massachusetts Avenue, at Inman Street, Cambridge (354 2685). Central T. **Open** 8am-1am Mon-Wed; 8am-2am Thur-Sat; noon-1am Sun. **Tickets** $3-$8. **No credit cards.**

The Cantab has been around for at least half a century, virtually without renovation. It looks like a roadhouse, loaded with character – and characters. The star eccentric personality in the joint belongs to Little Joe Cook, a one-time doo-wop chart-topper who's been the resident blues guru here for decades – look for his banana-yellow, souped-up Caddy at the curb. Little Joe Cook plays with his long-time band, the Thrillers, every Thursday, Friday and Saturday night, and he hosts blues jams on Wednesdays and Sundays. Mondays at the Cantab are considerably more restrained, when local folkie Geoff Bartley hosts his open-mike folk and acoustic program. Tuesday is bluegrass night.

Club Passim

47 Palmer Street, at Church Street, Cambridge (492 7679/www.clubpassim.org). Harvard T. **Open** 11am-11pm daily. **Tickets** $5-$20. **Credit** AmEx, Disc, MC, V.

As CBGBs was to New York punk, so Club Passim was to the counter-culture folk scene of the 1960s. This legendary spot was the epicentre of the folk revival even before Joan Baez got her start here (renting the room herself and introducing Bob Dylan between sets). First known as Club 47 and later simply as Passim, it served as an irregularly open but regularly busted jazz joint. Over the past 40 years Passim has been the launching ground for folkies from Baez and Taj Mahal to Suzanne Vega and Shawn Colvin. The vibe is more hippie/vegan than beatnik these days (it's proudly 'alcohol and smoke-free'), but the club still plays host to legions of singer-songwriters in the 1960s tradition.

Emily's

48 Winter Street, at Tremont Street, Downtown (423 3649). Park Street or Downtown Crossing T. **Open** 5pm-2am Mon-Thur; 4pm-2am Fri; 9pm-2am Sat; 10pm-2am Sun. **Tickets** $4-$5. **Credit** AmEx, MC, V. **Map** p308 G4.

Located in second-floor loft space on the end block of Winter Street, Emily's is a relatively obscure but appealing space, decorated to look like somebody's funky apartment. Originally an after-work joint for downtown suits and then a weekend dance club, Emily's has lately begun to book music during the week. Tuesday is an acoustic/folk night; Wednesday it's live local rock.

Harpers Ferry

158 Brighton Avenue, at Harvard Avenue, Brighton (254 9743). Harvard Avenue T. **Open** 1pm-2am daily. **Tickets** $3-$27. **No credit cards.**

Situated right in the middle of student hell, this one-time (and still occasional) biker bar isn't exactly where you'd expect to find Bo Diddley – though it has been known to happen. Other than that, the blues you'll hear is a kind of Chicago-blues-meet-academia mix, mostly played by white guys who make faces when they solo. The sound system is superior, there's plenty of room surrounding the bar and there are pool tables in the room behind the stage. All of which has made Harpers a favourite haunt of local neo-hippie jam bands.

House of Blues

96 Winthrop Street, at John F Kennedy Street, Cambridge (491 2100). Harvard T. **Open** *Shows* 9pm-1am Mon-Wed, Sun; 10pm-2am Thur-Sat. **Tickets** $5 and up. **Credit** AmEx, Disc, MC, V. **Map** p311 B2/3.

A cramped but cosy spot in an alley off Harvard Square, this could be described as the house that blues built. Real-life juke-joint troubadours pass through regularly, and the roster draws better crowds than many rock stars do. The restaurant is downstairs, the ticket counter's in the basement and the blues is in the attic, in a folksy, unpretentious room adorned with folk art commemorating the founders and innovators of the Delta sound.

Jacque's Cabaret

79 Broadway, at Winchester Street (426 8902). Arlington, Boylston or New England Medical Center T. **Open** noon-midnight daily. **Tickets** $4-$6. **No credit cards. Map** p308 F5.

Even though it's just steps away from the Theatre District, Jacque's has remained a well-kept secret and a bastion of surrealism. Local punk and glam acts discovered this seedy transvestite hangout a few years ago and began gigging alongside the drag lip-synch acts. The renovated basement hosts art exhibitions and art-rock bands, ranging from local kids to out-of-town avant-rockers. The mix of patrons has not diluted the place's warped ambience.

Johnny D's Uptown Restaurant & Music Club

17 Holland Street, Davis Square, Somerville (776 2004/www.johnnyds.com). Davis T. **Open** 11.30am-1am Mon-Fri; 9am-1am Sat, Sun. **Tickets** $8-$15. **Credit** AmEx, Disc, MC, V.

The city's best roots music club, family-owned and a favourite hangout for enthusiasts of all stripes. The acts are presented in a lounge/restaurant setting, so get there early and get a table. There's a dancefloor right in front of the stage for spectators, which is also used for the club's Monday salsa dance nights (lessons provided). There's a traditional jazz brunch on Saturday and Sunday, and a Sunday blues jam from 4.30 to 8.30pm.

Kendall Café Alehouse & Grill

233 Cardinal Medeiros Avenue, at Bristol Street, Cambridge (661 0993). Kendall/MIT T. **Open** 5pm-1am Mon-Thur; 11.30am-1am Fri; 3pm-1am Sat, Sun. **Tickets** free-$6. **Credit** AmEx, MC, V.

A compact acoustic room with an insider's taste in singer/songwriters, the Kendall has played host to some pretty big names, from local pop titans such as Letters to Cleo and the Gravel Pit to secret gigs

Arts & Entertainment

Sign of the times: **Bill's Bar**, the only Lansdowne strip club with live music. *See p222.*

by Elvis Costello, Colin Hayes and Bernie Taupin. The club books monthly residences for out-of-town acts, and took an early chance on a then-unknown Alaskan chick named Jewel. Most of the fare here is earnest acoustic folk and low-key electric alt-rock.

Kirkland Café

421-427 Washington Street, at Beacon Street, Somerville (491 9640). Harvard T. **Open** 11am-1am daily. **Tickets** $5-$10. **No credit cards**.

This place is heavy on grunge and plain old rock 'n' roll, with occasional rockabilly and surf nights. Blue collar to the bone, and utterly immune to trends, this is where the local rock dinosaurs go to revisit their musical youth. It has the hootenanny atmosphere that only seems to evolve in places where payday still means something.

Lilli's

608 Somerville Avenue, Somerville (591 1661/ www.lillisclub.com). Porter T. **Open** 8pm-1am daily. **Tickets** vary. **No credit cards.**

Lilli's is named after co-owner Lilli Dennison, a veteran Boston rock booker and manager with a collector's tastes in music and lots of talented friends who show up regularly to lend their cachet to the joint. The atmosphere is lounge/funky, the music bills range from garage rock to electronica, with regular appearances by the likes of Frank Black and the Catholics and the Meat Puppets.

Linwood Grille

81 Kilmarnock Street, at Queensberry Street, Fenway (247 8099). Fenway T. **Open** 6pm-2am daily. **Tickets** $5-$6. **Credit** (bar tabs only) MC, V. **Map** p306 D6.

When Boston's world-famous punk landmark the Rathskellar closed down in 1997, the soundman and a bunch of the regulars moved a few blocks away to this dive/baseball bar, and gradually the Linwood took over the Rat's specialities – the local heavy metal, garage-punk and surf scenes. It has also played host to bands such as Nashville Pussy, Zeke and the Demolition Doll Rods. Recent changes in booking policies have made the bills a crap shoot lately, but considering the average job lifespan of Boston rock bookers, that could change for the better at any moment.

Lizard Lounge

1667 Massachusetts Avenue, at Harvard Street, Cambridge (547 1228). Harvard T. **Open** 9pm-2am daily. **Tickets** $5-$9. **No credit cards**. **Map** p311 B/C2/3.

Situated just below a busy burger-and-brew gaffe, this renovated basement was opened by folks who wanted to emulate the in-the-round set-up of a Nashville club. Decorated to look like a retro-groovy bohemian salon (velvet drapes, gilt mirror frames, red Persian rugs), it's the kind of room where you can choose from several kinds of martinis and catch deft, independent singer-songwriters, as well as out jazz, experimental and rootsy rock acts. The late Mark Sandman of Morphine, one of Boston's most well-respected underground music icons, played here regularly; members of Morphine continue to call this place home.

The Middle East

472 & 480 Massachusetts Avenue, at Brookline Street, Cambridge (492 9181). Central T. **Open** 11am-1am Mon-Wed, Sun; 11am-2am Thur-Sat. **Tickets** $7-$10. **Credit** AmEx, Disc, MC, V. **Map** p311 C3/4.

This is Boston's musical heart. Low-key and friendly, this three-room club is a unique mix of all-around cultural endeavour where you're just as likely to run into the former mayor as, say, former J Geils Band frontman Peter Wolfe. It's a favourite of local heroes and regularly hosts national rock, punk, ska and alternative touring bands. The main live room is frequently the site of shows you won't see anywhere else. The Corner (known locally as the Bakery, for reasons too complicated to explain), has free music seven nights a week (not to mention belly dancing) in a restaurant setting. The upstairs rock room is smaller, and features mostly local rock.

Milky Way Lounge & Lanes

405 Centre Street, Jamaica Plain (524 3740). Stony Brook T. **Open** 6pm-1am daily. **Tickets** $5-$7. **Credit** AmEx, DC, MC, V.

Converted a few years ago from a WWI-era bowling alley – which is still in use – this is a funky, retro-chic bohomian basement club with a clientele of local art-schoolers and off-centre rock types partial to Bettie Paige haircuts and 1970s vintage threads. The live music nights are Thursday and Friday, with alternative and underground rock and funk bands. Saturday is a popular Latin night, and draws a mixed crowd of all ages. Sunday is reggae night.

O'Brien's

3 Harvard Avenue, at Cambridge Street, Allston (782 6245). Harvard Avenue T. **Open** noon-1am daily. **Tickets** $5. **No credit cards**.

The student ghettos of Allston have long harboured a tremendous punk/hardcore/metal scene, and O'Brien's – a pine-panelled relic from decades past – is their neighbourhood stage. Always in danger of being closed down for overcrowding (the capacity is 50), O'Brien's suffers from patchy booking, but you can still find big-draw local bands here.

Paradise Rock Club

967 Commonwealth Avenue, at Babcock Street, Brookline (562 8800/tickets 423 6398). Babcock Street T. **Open** from 7pm Wed-Sat. **Tickets** $8-$20. **Credit** AmEx, MC, V.

If you've just heard their single on the radio, they'll probably play here soon; and if they're playing the FleetCenter, chances are they were here a couple of years ago. U2, Echo and the Bunnymen and Alanis Morissette all played formative gigs here, and the tradition continues. Recent shows have included Nashville Pussy, Cheap Trick and Richard Ashcroft. The upstairs balcony bar is where you'll have the best chance of running into a rock star.

Plough & Stars

912 Massachusetts Avenue, at Hancock Street, Cambridge (441 3455). Central T. **Open** 11.30am-1am daily. **Tickets** free-$3. **No credit cards**. **Map** p311 C3.

The Plough is so cosy it's practically suffocating when the room is full, but local scenesters and Irish regulars don't seem to mind the conditions. There's music here every night, generally of the rootsy, surf-rockabilly variety. The atmosphere here is magical and the staff is lovely, but the squeeze can be too much, especially when you have to shove past the bassist to get to the loo.

Roxy

279 Tremont Street, at Stuart Street, South End (338 7699). Boylston T. **Open** 9pm-2am Thur-Sat. **Admission** $10-$15. **Credit** AmEx, MC, V. **Map** p308 G5.

A 1930s ballroom with dual identities as a concert hall and a dance club, the Roxy's live music events are irregular but often noteworthy, from punk and funk deities such as Joe Strummer and George Clinton to current chart climbers of every genre. A three-sided balcony offers lots of sightlines, but even from the back of the ballroom you can usually get a decent view of the stage.

TT the Bear's

10 Brookline Street, at Massachusetts Avenue, Cambridge (492 2327/tickets 931 2000). Central T. **Open** *Box office* from 6pm daily. *Club* 6pm-1am daily. **Tickets** $4-$8. **Credit** AmEx, MC, V. **Map** p311 C3.

One of Boston's oldest continuous rock venues, TT's has been a regular stop for headliners for more than 25 years. Even today, you simply never know who will turn up to play at this place. Musicians remain as loyal to it as it has been to them. Though the club's been overshadowed by the mighty Middle East next door (*see p224*), it still manages many a booking coup. Despite what are possibly the worst sightlines of almost any major club in the Boston area, TT's stubbornly remains a local favourite.

Western Front

343 Western Avenue, at Putnam Avenue, Cambridge (492 7772). Central T. **Open** 5pm-1am Wed-Sun. **Tickets** $3-$10. **No credit cards**. **Map** p311 C3.

A hotspot for reggae and Caribbean music, with a little avant-jazz thrown in, the Western Front is recommended especially if you like music that feels 'lived in', as oppposed to just stared at. With a couple of bars and comfortable places to hang throughout, and an eclectic, racially mixed crowd of rastas, poets, jazz types and neighbourhood folks, this is an atmospheric, friendly place to be.

Jazz

Hotel lounges

The Regattabar

Charles Hotel, 1 Bennett Street, at Harvard Square, Cambridge (661 5000). Harvard T. **Open** 7pm-1am Tue-Sat. **Tickets** $8-$24. **Credit** AmEx, DC, MC, V. **Map** p311 B2.

This place offers table seating, reasonable covers, a decent light snacks menu and an essential line-up of events. In a typical season, performers include Kenny Barron, Tommy Flanagan, Dave Holland, John Scofield and estimable local artists. Non-jazz fare tends towards blues and Latin music. The 'stage' is in a corner at floor level, under a low ceiling that restricts both sightlines and consistent sound. It's best to book ahead and get a table close to the action if you can.

Groovy, groovy, jazzy, funky – the Charles Hotel's **Regattabar**. *See p225.*

Scullers Jazz Club

Doubletree Guest Suites Hotel, 400 Soldiers Field Road, at River Street (562 4111/783 0090/tickets 931 2000/www.scullersjazz.com). Central T. **Open** for shows only, phone for details. **Tickets** $10-$30. **Map** p311 B4.

High above the Charles River, Scullers has a great view of the water. Unfortunately, its location (at the intersection of two major thoroughfares) cuts it off from public transport and foot traffic. Still, the music can be very impressive, and there are light snacks and cocktail tables to go with the hefty line-up.

Other venues

Bob the Chef's Café

604 Columbus Avenue, at Northampton Street (536 6204/www.bobthechef.com). Massachusetts Avenue T. **Open** 7.30pm-11pm Thur, Sat, Sun. **Tickets** $3-$5. **Credit** AmEx, DC, Disc, MC, V. **Map** p306 E6.

For decades, this South End restaurant has been a favourite late-night stop for authentic soul food. It was expanded and renovated a few years ago and started to introduced jazz nights on the weekends. The combo is worth the trip, although some of the worn-down charm of the old place has been lost.

Good Life

28 Kingston Street, at Summer Street, Downtown (451 2622). Downtown Crossing T. **Open** (for music) 9.30pm-1.30am Tue-Sat. **Tickets** free. **Credit** AmEx, DC, MC, V. **Map** p307 G5.

Opened during the Martini-lounge revival of the 1990s, this place has grown from a self-consciously trendy facsimile of a Rat Pack-era lounge for yuppies to a culturally cross-pollinated favourite, serving up well-priced American comfort food and live jazz in all genres, along with the classic cocktails.

Branch: 720 Massachusetts Avenue, Cambridge (868 8800).

Ryles Jazz Club

212 Hampshire Street, Inman Square, Cambridge (876 9330). Central T. **Open** 7pm-1am Tue, Wed; 7pm-2am Thur-Sat. **Tickets** $6-$12. **Credit** AmEx, Disc, MC, V.

There's jazz in the comfortable downstairs room here, with sandwiches and snacks (as well as a Sunday jazz brunch) and windows looking out onto Inman Square. Jazz trumpeter/promoter Frank Vardaros fills the room with his personal heroes, like Maynard Ferguson and Arturo Sandoval. The action upstairs varies depending on the night – salsa and merengue on Thursday, Brazilian jazz on Friday and Latin dancing on Saturday.

Wally's

427 Massachusetts Avenue, at Columbus Avenue, South End (424 1408). Massachusetts Avenue T. **Open** (for music) 9pm-2am Mon-Sat; 3.30-7.30pm Sun. **Tickets** free. **No credit cards. Map** p306 E6.

This legendary hole-in-the-wall opened in 1947. The sole survivor of the once-thriving jazz and blues district at the edge of Roxbury, Wally's is still owned and operated by the grandsons of original owner James 'Wally' Walcott, and retains its down-to-earth character. Wally's is a haunt for students from Berklee and the New England Conservatory, and when former Berklee-ites like Roy Hargrove or Branford Marsalis drop in, it's easy to see how the club has provided a rite of passage for generations of young players.

Wonder Bar

186 Harvard Avenue, at Commonwealth Avenue, Allston (351 2665). Harvard Avenue T. **Open** 5pm-2am daily. **Credit** AmEx, DC, Disc, MC, V.

The Wonder Bar was renovated recently to cater to the post-grad yuppie crowd that has gentrified the Allston student ghetto. The owner, a saxophonist and fanatical jazz buff, maintains a strong and impressive nightly schedule of intelligent jazz.

Performing Arts

Where to go when you're craving a little culture.

Much like its sports and media worlds, Boston's performing arts scene lives in the shadow of New York. The Beantown theatre scene offers neither the age-old mystique nor the high-tech frills of a night on Broadway. Still, there are plenty of shows in town at any given time of the year, and the NYC gap narrows when it comes to dance and classical music.

Both the **Boston Symphony Orchestra** and, to a lesser extent, the **Boston Ballet**, are leading lights in the international arts community. And the city is full of grassroots performers, including avant-garde DIY theatre troupes and comedians. In addition, in Cambridge, the **American Repertory Theatre** has premiered works by writers such as David Mamet and August Wilson, and the city has spawned more than its fair share of stand-up comics. In terms of sheer variety, Boston's performing arts scene might not stun you with originality, but it has enough to keep you entertained whenever you arrive.

TICKETS

Generally speaking, getting tickets means either travelling to a venue and buying them from the box office, or shelling out some extra dough to buy them over the phone. That probably means dealing with, you guessed it, your old friend **Ticketmaster** (931 2000). Aside from that, tickets for many Theatre District events (plays, musicals and dance performances) are available through an automated service called **TeleCharge** (1-800 447 7400), which is the same kind of corporate behemoth as Ticketmaster, but is at least a slightly smaller maze to crawl through.

When your search for tickets seems impossible but you don't want to seek out touts or scalpers, try **Back Bay Ticket** (40 Dalton Street, at Boylston Street; 536 9666). Sometimes they can make the impossible happen. For last-minute and discounted tickets, the place to go is **BosTix** (723 5181). It has three locations: at Copley Square and Faneuil Hall in Boston, and at 1350 Massachusetts Avenue at Harvard Square in Cambridge. Last-minute tickets go on sale at 11am daily at these booths. Tickets are half price and available only on the day of the performance. You can also buy full-priced tickets for advance shows here, but bear in mind, it's cash only, whatever you're buying.

Theatre

Boston's Theatre District runs south along Tremont Street from the Boylston T stop to the Mass Pike. It's small but vibrant, featuring both travelling shows from New York and works by local groups.

Actors Workshop

40 Boylston Street, between Washington & Tremont Streets, South End (423 7313). Boylston T.
Open box office 9am-7pm Mon-Fri; 10am-7pm Sat. **Tickets** $10-$20. **No credit cards. Map** p308 G5.
Provides a more traditional angle on modern theatre, minus the shocks and surprises that characterise much of the off-off-Broadway fare in Boston.

American Repertory Theatre/ Loeb Drama Center

Harvard University, 64 Brattle Street, at Hilliard Street, Cambridge (547 8300). Harvard T.
Open box office 10am-5pm Mon; 10am-7.30pm Tue-Sun. **Tickets** $23-$55. **Credit** AmEx, MC, V. **Map** p311 B2.
Not at all traditional, this is one of the best theatre companies in the country. Since 1963, the company has consistently broken new theatrical ground, working with the likes of David Mamet and Don DeLillo. Some critics dismiss the ART as too 'out there', but it's hard to argue with the pair of Pulitzer prizes the company earned in 1983 and 1985.

Charles Playhouse

74 Warrenton Street, at Stuart Street, Back Bay (426 6912/www.blueman.com). Boylston or NE Medical Center T. **Open** box office 10am-6pm Mon, Tue; 10am-8pm Wed, Thur; 10am-9pm Fri, Sat; noon-6pm Sun. **Tickets** $39-$49. **Credit** AmEx, MC, V. **Map** p307 G5.
The line-up doesn't change much here, but that does not seem to bother anyone. On one stage you'll find performance artists the Blue Man Group – one of the most popular acts in town. The other stage hosts the semi-improvised comic murder-mystery *Shear Madness*, the longest-running non-musical in the US.

Colonial Theatre

106 Boylston Street, at Tremont Street, Back Bay (426 9366/www.broadwayinboston.com). Boylston T.
Open box office 10am-6pm Mon-Sat; noon-6pm Sun. **Tickets** $25-$75. **Credit** AmEx, MC, V. **Map** p307 G5.
A good place for big musicals, the Colonial was built in 1900 and is the oldest continuously operated theatre in Boston. The fan-shaped auditorium means there's scarcely a bad seat in the house.

The glory of **Symphony Hall**. *See p231.*

Huntington Theatre Company/ Boston University Theater

264 Huntington Avenue, at Massachusetts Avenue, Back Bay (266 0800). Symphony T. **Open** box office 11am-5pm Mon-Fri; noon-4pm Sat, Sun. **Tickets** $10-$54. **Credit** AmEx, Disc, MC, V. **Map** p306 E6.

One of the top companies in town, the Huntington was only founded in 1982, but in that short period it has built a high-profile reputation by balancing a schedule of musicals, new works and theatre classics. The company has premiered countless works over the years, including plays by Tom Stoppard and Willa Cather, and enjoys a reputation as a fairly traditional theatre troupe.

Lyric Stage

YWCA Building, 140 Clarendon Street, at Copley Square, Back Bay (437 7172). Arlington or Back Bay T. **Open** box office 11am-5pm Tue; noon-performance Wed-Sun. **Tickets** $24-$30. **Credit** AmEx, Disc, MC, V. **Map** p307 G5.

One of the city's mid-range theatres. As a response to escalating ticket prices everywhere else in Boston, the Lyric began staging major productions at much cheaper rates.

Peabody House Theater Co-operative

Elizabeth Peabody House, 277 Broadway, at Route 28, Somerville (625 1300). Sullivan Square T. **Open** box office 10am-5pm Mon-Fri. **Tickets** $10-$14. **No credit cards**.

Features small productions by up-and-coming local talent. The shows here are reliably unpredictable. This place has become something of a cult classic. Probably because it's always interesting – expect the unexpected.

Publick Theater

Christian Herter Park, 1175 Soldiers Field Road, Brighton (782 5425). Harvard Square T, then 86 bus. **Open** box office noon-7pm Tue-Sun. **Tickets** $15-$30. **Credit** MC, V.

Pop go the classics

There ought to be a photograph of the Boston Pops in US dictionaries next to the phrase 'national institution'. For decades, their annual patriotic Fourth of July concerts on the Charles River Esplanade have been filmed and broadcast live to the nation, as sort of the US equivalent of the UK Proms.

But not everybody loves the group as much as Middle America does. Most true classical music aficionados find the Pops barely classical at all. This is not news to the Popsters, whose goal is to bring classical music to the masses – to make it approachable to those who might be a bit intimidated by Beethoven. They do this by playing what could be called 'barely classics' – music from films, from Broadway musicals and patriotic tunes with which most US residents are at least vaguely familiar.

It all started in 1885, when – using European garden concerts as his model – BSO founder Henry Lee Higginson programmed a summer season of light classical fare as a way to keep the players in his orchestra employed year-round. Conductor Arthur Fiedler transformed the fledgling group into an institution during his reign (1929-79), initiating the Fourth of July Esplanade concerts and integrating pieces by contemporary American composers into the group's repertoire.

Today, the Pops are more successful than ever before. They sell out nearly every performance, tour the Far East and draw half a million people to the banks of the Charles every year. Whether you love 'em or hate 'em, though, probably will depend on whether or not you're scared of Beethoven.

Has staged both classics and children's theatre since being founded in 1971, and the shows are made more interesting by being performed in the open air in Christian Herter Park. Depending on the season, you'll need a can of bug spray or a warm blanket.

Shubert Theatre

265 Tremont Street, at Stuart Street, Back Bay (482 9393). NE Medical Center T. **Open** box office 10am-6pm Mon-Sat. **Tickets** $15-$60. **Credit** AmEx, MC, V. **Map** p308 G5.

This is the last remnant of a national chain of theatres owned or operated by the theatre-loving Shubert brothers. It hosts its share of musicals and branches out to include performances by the likes of the magic/comedy duo Penn and Teller and pre-Broadway engagements featuring stars like Tom Selleck. Also home to the Boston Lyric Opera.

Wang Center for the Performing Arts

270 Tremont Street, at Stuart Street, Back Bay (box office 482 9393/Boston Ballet 695 6950/ 1-800 447 7400/www.boston.com/wangcenter). NE Medical Center T. **Open** box office 10am-6pm Mon-Sat. **Tickets** $15-$60. **Credit** AmEx, MC, V. **Map** p308 G5.

This is the biggest gun in town when it comes to theatre, and, for that matter, sports. Seating 3,700, the Wang Center has reigned as the regional heavy-hitter since it opened in 1924. Home to the Boston Ballet, large theatre productions, a few mass-appeal concerts and occasional movie screenings, the Wang's calendar runs the gamut of the art world. Performances here range from *Miss Saigon* to Tori Amos. Movies here are shown on the biggest screen in the area – and the choices are always top-notch.

Wilbur Theatre

246 Tremont Street, at Stuart Street, Back Bay (423 4008/www.broadwayinboston.com). Boylston or NE Medical Center T. **Open** box office 10am-6pm Mon-Sat; noon-6pm Sun. **Tickets** vary. **Credit** AmEx, MC, V. **Map** p308 G5.

Like the Colonial, the Wilbur is booked exclusively for travelling Broadway shows. The shows travel through town fairly regularly, so it's very likely there will be something running at any given time year-round. Often the shows that play here are top-quality. Recently it has been the site of pre-Broadway engagements featuring the likes of actors Matthew Broderick and Parker Posey.

Outside Boston

When it comes to theatre, you don't have to stay in Boston to catch an interesting performance. Since 1978, one of the largest theatre companies outside the Boston area has been the respected **Merrimack Repertory Theater** troupe in Lowell, who perform in Liberty Hall at **Lowell Memorial Auditorium** (50 East Merrimack Street; 1-508 484 3926). In Newburyport, there's the **Firehouse Center for the Performing & Visual Arts** (1 Market Square; 1-978 462 7336), which features small-scale, local productions. New Bedford's **Zeiterion Theatre** (684 Purchase Street; 1-508 994 2900) hosts jazz and pop concerts but occasionally stages shows, too. And if you're willing to make the trek all the way to Beverly, the **North Shore Music Theatre** (62 Dunham Road; 1-978 922 8500) puts on large productions.

Dance

Boston Ballet

For listings, see the Wang Center for the Performing Arts, p230.

One of the world's most popular productions of Tchaikovsky's the *Nutcracker* is performed by the Boston Ballet. The company launched its first Sugarplum Fairy in 1963. Today it draws a yearly audience of over 250,000 to see its mostly traditional productions, and particularly its nut cracking.

Dance Complex

536 Massachusetts Avenue, at Brookline Street, Cambridge (547 9363). Central T. **Open** box office 9am-9pm Mon-Fri; 9am-6pm Sat; 9am-5pm Sun. **Tickets** $10-$15. **No credit cards**. **Map** p306 D3.

This community-run group hosts artists-in-residence who teach classes and then perform for the masses. Unconventional, but high-quality.

Dance Umbrella

515 Washington Street, at West Street. Downtown (482 7570). Downtown Crossing T. **Open** box office 9am-5pm Mon-Fri. **Tickets** $28-$65. **Credit** AmEx, MC, V. **Map** p308 G5.

Since 1980, Dance Umbrella has been a forum for contemporary and culturally diverse dance, and has clocked up an impressive number of world premieres. Past performers have ranged from Hip Hop Boston to Sean Curran and Bill T Jones.

Emerson Majestic Theatre

219 Tremont Street, at Boylston Street, Back Bay (box office 824 8000/Ballet Theatre of Boston 262 0961). Boylston T. **Open** box office 9am-6pm Mon-Fri; 10am-2pm Sat. **Tickets** $15-$65. **Credit** AmEx, MC, V. **Map** p308 G5.

This is home to the Ballet Theatre of Boston, founded in 1986 by artistic director Josè Mateo. The troupe has an in-house choreographer who produces original works as well as new interpretations of classics.

Green Street Studios

185 Green Street, at Central Square, Cambridge (864 3191). Central T. **Open** box office 8.30am-6.30pm daily. **Tickets** $10-$15. **No credit cards**. **Map** p311 C3.

Offers small-scale dance performances as well as local theatre.

Impulse Dance Company

179 Massachusetts Avenue, at Boylston Street, Back Bay (536 6989). Hynes/ICA or Massachusetts Avenue T. **Open** box office noon-9pm Mon-Sat. **Tickets** $10-$25. **No credit cards**. **Map** p306 E5.

Hip Hop Over Swan Pond should give you an idea of the kind of genre-bending this company goes in for.

Classical music & opera

Classical music tends towards the highbrow in Boston, where the respected and wealthy **Boston Symphony Orchestra** (BSO) reigns supreme. Opera, meanwhile, has struggled to have its voice heard in recent years. That's about the only thing to complain about in a city bursting with conservatory-trained musicians.

Boston Lyric Opera

(Information 542 6772/bookings 482 9393/1-800 447 7400). **Tickets** $25-$98. **Credit** AmEx, MC, V.

These days, for fully-staged productions, Boston opera-lovers depend on this group, which mounts three performances a year, sometimes drawing brilliant young singers (such as Lorraine Hunt in Handel's *Xerxes* and Dominique Labelle in Verdi's *La Traviata*). The group claims to be the fastest growing opera company in America.

Boston Philharmonic

(Information 496 2222). **Tickets** $12-$60. **Credit** AmEx, MC, V.

The Philharmonic prides itself on its mix of freelance professionals, students and amateurs who play side by side, while Boston audiences value it as an alternative to the BSO. Since its inception in 1978, the orchestra has been lead by conductor Benjamin Zander. His podium style is flamboyant, his interpretations sometimes idiosyncratic (he's gained some notoriety for championing Beethoven's original warp-speed tempo markings). But he's a serious, deeply respected musician and the Philharmonic's performances, especially of Mahler, are highly regarded. It's always worth arriving early to hear Zander's colourful pre-concert lectures.

Boston Pops

(Information 266 1492/bookings 226 1200). **Tickets** $24-$75. **Credit** AmEx, Disc, DC, MC, V.

The Boston Pops are BSO-lite. During the summer season, while the BSO performs out of town at Tanglewood in western Massachusetts (*see p264*), the seats at Symphony Hall are removed and replaced with large circular tables where champagne is served to the accompaniment of pop classics. This is without question middle America's favourite 'classical' music. *See p230.*

Boston Symphony Orchestra & Symphony Hall

301 Massachusetts Avenue, at Huntington Avenue, Back Bay (information 266 1492/bookings 226 1200). Symphony or Hynes/ICA T. **Open** box office 10am-6pm Mon-Sat. **Tickets** $24-$75. **Credit** AmEx, Disc, MC, V. **Map** p306 E6.

The BSO has a long and venerable history, but it really came into its own under the stewardship of Serge Koussevitzky, music director from 1924 to 1949. (Koussevitzsky's most famous personal protégé was the young Leonard Bernstein.) Today, the BSO is one of the nation's premier orchestras. Its performers are top notch (the orchestra's annual trips to Carnegie Hall in New York are invariably sell-outs). The music selection can be conservative, but is still interesting. The 2,600-seat Symphony Hall is an acoustical and architectural marvel.

Emmanuel Music

Emmanuel Church, 15 Newbury Street, Back Bay (536 3356). Arlington T. **Tickets** from $15.50. **Credit** MC, V. **Map** p308 E5.

Craig Smith (best known for his Mozart opera collaborations with stage director Peter Sellars) is a highly regarded Boston conductor. His Emmanuel Music group draws from the cream of Boston's musical crop and delivers compelling concert performances of Mozart's operas, religious choral works on Sunday mornings and an ambitious, multi-season 'Complete Schubert' series.

FleetBoston Celebrity Series

(Information 482 6661). **Tickets** $25-$68. **Credit** AmEx, MC, V.

The Celebrity Series began in 1938 with the likes of Kirsten Flagstad, Marian Anderson, the Ballets Russes de Monte Carlo and Rudolf Serkin. These days the organisation books more than 70 events between October and May each year in venues such as Jordan Hall, Symphony Hall and the Wang Center. Performers include all manner of classical musicians (the St Petersburg Philharmonic, Renée Fleming, Murray Perahia), dancers (Mark Morris, American Ballet Theatre), jazz exponents (Wynton Marsalis, Lincoln Center Jazz Orchestra), and unclassifiables such as the Chieftains or Kodo drummers.

Jordan Hall

290 Huntington Avenue, at Gainsborough Street, Fenway (536 2412). Mass Ave or Symphony T. **Open** box office 10am-6pm Mon-Fri; noon-6pm Sat. **Tickets** free-$100. **Credit** Disc, MC, V. **Map** p306 E6.

It's worth a visit here to catch either a performance in the Celebrity Series or one of the New England Conservatory free faculty/student recitals. The hall's acoustics have traditionally outshone those of Symphony Hall. It was designed and built in 1903 by architect Edmund Wheelwright, and for the past century it has been the premier place to hear vocal and piano recitals as well as chamber music. In 1995, the hall underwent major renovation. Some claim that, despite precautions and acoustical consultation, the hall's perfect balance has been ruined – that brass blares and pianissimo blurs. It's an arguable point, but Jordan is still a jewel of a concert hall.

Early music

Boston Cecelia

1773 Beacon Street, at Dean Road, Brookline (232 4540). Dean Rd T. **Open** box office 9am-5pm Mon-Fri. **Tickets** $11-$54. **Credit** MC, V.

One of the most respected choral groups in town, the group mixes its speciality, Handel, with new work, rarely performed pieces and opera.

Handel and Haydn Society

Horticultural Hall, 300 Massachusetts Avenue, at Huntington Avenue, Back Bay (266 3605). Symphony T. **Open** 10am-6pm Mon-Fri. **Tickets** $20-$60. **Credit** AmEx, Disc, MC, V. **Map** p306 E6.

The name almost says it all. Artistic director Christopher Hogwood leads the Premier Chorus and Period Orchestra of America in H&H as well as a smattering of Bach, Beethoven and others, with annual jazz crossover concerts featuring guests such as Dave Brubeck and the Modern Jazz Quartet.

Isabella Stewart Gardner Museum

For listings, see p114.

Combine a museum visit at this Renaissance palazzo with a concert on Sundays. The series includes new works as well as performances by some of the most respected musicians in Boston and special guest artists such as Musicians from Marlboro and the Chamber Music Society of the Lincoln Center.

Museum of Fine Arts

For listings, see p114.

The MFA's concert series specialises in early music and the baroque, with performances by the resident Museum Trio and recent guest artists such as cellist Pieter Wispelwey, soprano Sharon Baker and the vocal sextet Lionheart.

New music

With the wealth of universities in the Boston area and the number of established composers teaching at them, it follows that all those composers are going to need groups in which to play their music. Here's a sample of just who you should watch out for.

Composer and BU faculty member Theodore Antoniou guides BU's resident contemporary music ensemble **Alea III** (353 3349) through its annual series of engrossing concerts featuring old and new music, while Boulez, Schoenberg and Copland are mixed with estimable Boston composers such as Mario Davidovsky, John Harbison and Scott Wheeler by the **Auros Group for New Music** (323 3430).

Boston Musica Viva (354 6910) director Richard Pittman schedules a balanced mix of 20th-century works, from Prokofiev and Schoenberg to Carter and Harbison, and various world premieres. BMV (founded in 1969) also makes conscious efforts to include world music influences in its programmes.

David Hoose, music director of **Collage New Music** (325 5200), is one of the most respected new music conductors in Boston. In a typical four-concert season series, Collage performs a well-programmed mix of both established composers and world premieres.

A collective of respected local composers and players were behind the founding of the group called **Dinosaur Annex** (482 3852), and they continue to create a stir on the music scene here, presenting an array of thoughtful programmes including works by Babbitt, Davidovsky and artistic director Scott Wheeler.

Schools

Boston University School for the Arts

855 Commonwealth Avenue, near Boston University Bridge (353 3350). BU West T. **Open** box office 9am-5pm Mon-Fri. **Tickets** free-$15. **Credit** AmEx, MC, V. **Map** p306 D7.

Free faculty recitals include performances by early music keyboard specialist Mark Kroll, conductor David Hoose, and resident ensembles such as the Atlantic Brass Quintet, Muir String Quartet and Alea III. Student performances by the Boston University Opera Institute are also highly regarded.

New England Conservatory

290 Huntington Avenue, at St Botolph Street, Fenway (585 1100/newenglandconservatory.edu). Mass Ave T. **Open** box office 9am-5pm Mon-Fri. **Tickets** free-$100. **Credit** Disc, MC, V. **Map** p306 E6.

The big daddy of Boston music schools, founded in 1867, boasts a $33-million endowment and credits itself with supplying 44% of the players of the BSO from its faculty. For the average concert-goer, that means a year-round calendar of excellent (and free) faculty and student recitals, often performed in NEC's lovely Jordan Hall (*see p232*).

Alternative theatre

The **Boston Center for the Arts**' complex in the South End is the hub of fringe theatre in Boston, but small, edgy troupes can be found elsewhere, especially in Cambridge. None is especially prominent, but they all make sure local and otherwise obscure voices are heard.

Boston Center for the Arts

539 Tremont Street, at Clarendon Street (426 5000). Back Bay or Copley T. **Open** 9am-5pm Mon-Fri. **Tickets** $10-$20. **Credit** MC, V. **Map** p306 F6.

Four different companies, each with its own programme and philosophy, are based at the BCA. The SpeakEasy Stage Company and Pilgrim Theater put on small-scale, intimate, contemporary shows, while Theater Offensive centres on gay issues.

Mobius

354 Congress Street, at Dorchester Avenue (542 7416). South Station T. **Open** box office half hour before performance. **Tickets** $4-$12. **No credit cards. Map** p307 H5.

If you really want avant-garde, try Mobius. A combination of art gallery and performance space, Mobius is devoted to the sort of dance, theatre and performance art that isn't ready for primetime and doesn't have much desire to get there. More than 100 local artists perform here each year, and the space is described as 'a laboratory for artists experimenting at the boundaries of their disciplines'.

Tremont Theater

276 Tremont Street, next to the Wang Center (338 4274/www.bostontheatreworks.com). Boylston T. **Open** box office 9am-5pm Mon-Fri. **Tickets** $14-$19. **Credit** AmEx, Disc, MC, V. **Map** p308 G5.

Still small, but on the rise and worth looking out for, are relative newcomers Boston Theatre Works, who perform here. While only now making a name for itself, the group scored a coup in early 2000 by premiering a long-lost Tennessee Williams work.

Comedy

Boston has a well-deserved reputation as a comedy hotspot. Comics the city has spawned range from the high profile (Jay Leno) to the unusual (Steven Wright), the collegiate vitriolic (Denis Leary) to the you'd-know-him-if-you-saw-him (Lenny Clarke). Most earned their stripes at the Ding Ho – a now-defunct Chinese restaurant/comedy club in Cambridge – but the city still supports its share of live venues.

Back Alley Theater

1253 Cambridge Street, at Beacon Street, Cambridge (576 1253). Central T. **Open** from 8pm Fri, Sat; 2pm Sun. **Admission** free-$12. **Credit** MC, V. **Map** p311 C2.

The ever-popular comedy group ImprovBoston always attracts a crowd as they whip up something off-the-cuff here every weekend.

Comedy Connection

Upstairs at Faneuil Hall, at Quincy Market, Downtown (248 9700). Gov't Center T. **Open** 9am-10pm daily. **Admission** $8-$20. **Credit** AmEx, MC, V. **Map** p308 G4.

Deep within the bowels of Faneuil Hall, this is the city's mainstream comedy hotspot. It is also the regular stomping ground for some of the nation's top comics. It's the place to catch the likes of political comedian Jon Stewart, Margaret Cho and established veterans such as Bobcat Goldthwait.

Comedy Studio

Hong Kong Restaurant, 1236 Massachusetts Avenue, at Bow Street, Cambridge (661 6507). Harvard T. **Open** from 8pm Thur-Sun. **Admission** $3-$7. **No credit cards. Map** p311 G3.

This clandestine space picks up where the Ding Ho left off as the city's top haven for alternative comedy. It offers a wide variety of stand-up and sketch routines, and unpredictable humour including the popular 'Thursday Night Fights' series.

Nick's Comedy Stop

100 Warrenton Street, at Stuart Street, Back Bay (482 0930). Boylston T. **Open** 7pm-2am Thur-Sat. **Admission** $10-$14. **Credit** AmEx, MC, V. **Map** p308 G5.

A great place to catch tomorrow's big names. Or tomorrow's bartenders and waiters. Many of the comics here favour raunch for raunch's sake, but sometimes you'll come across a hidden gem.

Sport & Fitness

Whether you play to win, or just like to watch, Boston's got it goin' on.

The Red Sox haven't won a baseball world series since they sold Babe Ruth to the New York Yankees and incurred 'The Curse of the Bambino' in 1919. Larry Bird (now a professional basketball coach) was still playing for the Celtics when that team last won a championship in 1986. The Bruins haven't brought home ice hockey's Stanley Cup since Bobby Orr scored the cup-winning goal for the second time in his career, beating the New York Rangers in 1972. And the New England Patriots have never, ever won a Superbowl. Still, Boston remains undaunted as one of the most sports-crazed cities in America.

Professional sports

Faced with one loss after another, rather than despair, sports fans here maintain a well of inexplicable mad passion and find reason to rejoice beyond the scoreboard. There is no such thing as a casual sports fan in this town. Many have been steeped in sports since birth and are as knowledgeable and argumentative about the fine points of the game as rabbis are about the holy Torah.

In addition to the beleaguered teams already mentioned, Boston also has a professional soccer team, the New England Revolution, but locals have yet to take to the game the rest of the world calls football. College sports too are very popular here, especially Boston College football and basketball, and Boston University hockey. As for gigantic one-time-only sports events, Harvard/Yale football games always draw a crowd, but mostly alumni. The Head of the Charles Regatta (*see p197*) and the Boston Marathon (*see p236*) are both big draws, attracting international crowds by the tens of thousands.

INFORMATION AND TICKETS

For local sporting information, look no further than the two daily newspapers, the *Boston Globe* and the *Boston Herald*. Both have nationally recognised sports sections that report on professional goings-on in great detail. The *Globe* also publishes daily listings of local and national television and radio broadcasts of games and sports talk shows, and it has a free pro sports score information line (265 6600). Sports radio is also popular, particularly WEEI at 850 AM.

The easiest way to get tickets is to phone or visit the box office of the team you want to see. If the game is sold out, many fans purchase tickets (illegally) from touts (scalpers) who sell them at inflated prices in front of the stadiums before the game. Not that we're encouraging illegal activity, but after the game starts these tickets are often sold for much less.

Baseball

The team that the city most longs to see win a championship is the **Boston Red Sox**. If they were to win a World Series the town would be turned upside down. Loyal fans call themselves the 'Red Sox Nation', and despite being disappointed year after year with failed attempts to even achieve a division win, they continue to bow before the 'Green Monster' of historic Fenway Park (*see below*). Once inside the stadium, they'll drink warm, expensive beer and stuff their faces with the park's eponymous tasty tubular treat, the Fenway Frank. *Boston Globe* columnist Dan Shaughnessy penned an excellent history of the team, *The Curse of the Bambino*, which posits that the Sox will never win another title because the team cursed itself by trading Babe Ruth to the New York Yankees (*see p242*). No harm seems to come from just attending a game, however.

The baseball season runs from April to October. Tickets can be purchased by calling the Fenway Park booking line. On game day, tickets can be purchased from touts, but it'll cost you big time for a Red Sox/ Yankees arch-enemies face-off.

Fenway Park

4 Yawkey Way, Fenway (267 9440/bookings line 267 1700/tours May-Sept 236 6666/www.redsox.com). Kenmore T. **Open** box office *Oct-Mar* 9am-5pm Mon-Fri. *Apr-Sept* 9am-5pm daily. **Tickets** $18-$55; tours $3-$5. **Credit** AmEx, Disc, MC, V. **Map** 306 D5/6

Basketball

There was a time in the not-too-distant past when the **Celtics** were gods. Then Larry Bird retired in 1992 and the heavens just seemed to close. A hot young draft pick named Len Bias, Bird's heir apparent, died of a cocaine overdose before he even had a chance to put on a uniform. After that tragedy, a promising all-star named Reggie Lewis died unexpectedly of a heart ailment. Then the beloved Boston Garden, which nurtured 16 championship-winning Celtics teams, was torn down and replaced with the FleetCenter. The FleetCenter is considered sterile, though the seats are more comfortable and you don't have chunks of asbestos falling on your head anymore. Rick Pitino, once a respected coach at the University of Kentucky, was given the keys to the city in the hope that he might be able to turn things around. He didn't. The city grumbled that the Celtics were paying a bunch of faceless scrubs far too much money. So much so that Pitino finally cracked one night after the Celtics were booed by their own fans. 'All the negativity in this town sucks', he said just months before quitting in January 2001.

A different kind of **Patriot**.

FleetCenter

1 Causeway Street, at North Station, North End (624 1000/www.fleetcenter.com). North Station T. **Open** box office 11am-7pm daily. **Tickets** $10-$85. **Credit** AmEx, DC, Disc, MC, V. **Map** p308 G3

Football

The **New England Patriots** seem to be experiencing a stretch of what fans call 'rebuilding years'. This means the team loses more than it wins, but also that fans revel in the good things, and are more forgiving of what they see as growing pains. The games themselves are important, if only because people win or lose small fortunes betting on the outcome. However, the more important, and fun, part of the game is the time-honoured custom of tailgating. Tailgating, which takes place in the parking lot in front of the stadium, involves a great deal of rowdy eating, drinking and, whenever possible, fire. Fans take this ritual extremely seriously. A typical pre-game checklist would include: meat (hot dogs, chicken, steak tips, burgers, sausages), crisps, nips (little plastic bottles of liquor smuggled into the stadium for illegal consumption), condiments, a grill and propane, tickets, two-way radios (if you're really fancy), lots of beer and, of course, a bottle opener. Regardless of weather conditions, this tradition is acted out before – and to a lesser extent, after – every game. If you don't feel like actually going to Foxboro Stadium (located well outside of Boston in the suburbs) for a game, you can also catch the excitement by watching the action from one of Boston's many sports bars (one of the best is Daisy Buchanan's, *see p157*).

Foxboro Stadium

60 Washington Street, Foxboro (931 2222/1-800 543 1776). **Open** box office 9am-5pm Mon-Sat. **Tickets** $31-$75. **Credit** AmEx, MC, V.

Ice hockey

Once known as the 'mighty, big, bad **Bruins**', this team's rough, fearless style of play struck fear in the hearts of all who entered the rink. That was then; this is now. The current stock is considered lacklustre. Coaches seem to get fired every year or two. There aren't even as many fights in the stands as ticket prices have skyrocketed and the drunken yahoos of old can't afford to get in. The latest blow came in 2000 when a key player named Ray Bourke asked to be traded because, he said, he knew he'd never get a championship Stanley Cup ring playing with the B's. According to the team's fans, the blame for all this misfortune rests with an out-of-town owner who is accused of refusing to hire top-notch talent because of a greater interest in profit than wins. Still, win or lose, Bruins games are enjoyable – though the team is bad, the fans are great. Now that fewer people go to the games … shorter beer lines! Phone the FleetCenter for tickets (*see p235*).

Soccer

The **New England Revolution** (www.anyrevolution.com) play in Foxboro Stadium, also home to the New England Patriots, but the team doesn't enjoy anything close to the popularity of the longtime US football team. Interestingly, the Revolution are a very successful team, and, yet you can almost always get a ticket ($10-$25). Phone the stadium for details (*see p235*).

Racing

Car racing

If you like your fun loud and oily, make a visit to one of the many stock car and drag racing speedways located in New England.

New England Dragway

Route 27, Epping, New Hampshire (1-603 679 8001). **Open** *Apr-Oct* 5-9pm Wed, Fri; 9am-5pm Sat, Sun. **Tickets** $10-$25. **No credit cards.**
This track offers motorcycle and auto racing.

Seekonk Speedway

Route 6, Seekonk, Massachusetts (1-508 336 9959/ www.seekonkspeedway.com). **Open** *May-Sept* 6-10.30pm Sat. **Tickets** $12. **Credit** AmEx, Disc, MC, V.
The Seekonk hosts pro-stock, sportsman, street-stock and Formula 4 racing, as well as truck racing.

Stafford Motor Speedway

Route 140, Stafford Springs, Connecticut (1-860 684 2783/www.staffordspeedway.com). **Open** *Apr-Sept* 7-10.30pm Fri. **Tickets** $2-$32.50. **Credit** AmEx, MC, V.
Stafford hosts professional NASCAR racing. It also has motorcycle, monster truck and off-road racing.

Horse racing

Rockingham Park

Rockingham Park Boulevard, Salem, New Hampshire (1-603 898 2311). **Open** *June-Sept* hours vary; simulcast noon-midnight daily. **Admission** $1-$3.50. **No credit cards.**
Rockingham Park offers simulcast horse racing as well as live racing.

Suffolk Downs

111 Waldermar Avenue (the junction of routes 1A & 145), East Boston (567 3900). Suffolk Downs T. **Open** *Sept-June* 12.45-4.40pm Mon, Wed, Sat, Sun; simulcast noon-midnight daily. **Admission** $2-$4. **No credit cards.**
Live racing takes place on a seasonal basis, but the track is open daily for simulcast racing.

Marathon running

The 100-year-old **Boston Marathon** takes place every April on Patriot's Day (a relatively obscure holiday marking Paul Revere's famous ride through the colonies warning that the British were coming). The city more or less shuts down on the day of the race to prepare for

If you're up for a challenge, try running across the city in the famous **Boston Marathon**.

Arts & Entertainment

the arrival of 37,500 runners (a figure that doesn't include the number of unregistered runners who jump into the race) and tens of thousands of spectators. Great views of the runners can be had in the last four miles of the race. It finishes at Copley Square, but the area is always mobbed. If you walk a mile or so from Copley you can cheer in the winners in slightly less crowded conditions (*see p194*).

Participation sports

The best cities to visit for active sports all have one thing in common: locals who get out there and make it look fun. And though you may not guess it by looking at them after work on the T, Boston boasts some of the most dedicated urban athletes in America. Even inclement weather is no obstacle to these rugged New Englanders as they head out running or in-line skating along the Charles River Esplanade, mountain biking in the Fellsway, rowing or sailing on the Charles River, kayaking along the harbour, playing tennis at the public courts along the Charles River or in the Boston Common, or ice skating on the Frog Pond.

In fact, according to research published in *Shape* magazine, Bostonians are more able-bodied and active than most Americans. The obesity rate here is considerably lower than that of most major other US cities; almost half the residents take a walk at least weekly, and 8 per cent run, far more than the average. Hey, when in Rome …

GENERAL INFORMATION

Metro Sports magazine, a free regional publication available in most sports shops, publishes information about outdoor activities. *New England Runner*, available on newsstands for $3.95, is an excellent resource for local road races and multi-sport events. *The Boston Globe* also publishes activities listings on Saturdays, but it's an incomplete directory of weekend events. If you've left some of your sporting equipment or clothing behind, check out Niketown (200 Newbury Street, at Exeter; 267 3400) or City Sports (480 Boylston Street, between Berkeley & Clarendon Streets; 267 3900), a shop with several locations throughout the city and surrounding areas.

Boating & sailing

Boston Harbor Sailing Club

58 Batterymarch Street, at Rowes Wharf, Downtown (720 0049/www.bostonharborsailing.com). Aquarium T. **Open** 9am-5pm daily. **Rates** rental $75-$387 per day. Lessons $425 per week. **Credit** MC, V. **Map** p308 H4.

The BHSC is popular with locals, particularly with college students, as it offers boat rentals and one-on-one lessons for beginners.

Boston Sailing Center

54 Lewis Wharf, at Atlantic Avenue, Downtown (227 4198/www.bostonsailingcenter.com). Aquarium or Haymarket T. **Open** *Apr-Oct* 9am-sunset daily. **Rates** *Skippered charters* $100-$170 per hour. *Lessons* $620-$1,200 per week. **Credit** MC, V. **Map** p308 H3/4.

Offers boat rentals, one-on-one lessons, or charters in which you can lean back and let them do the work.

Community Boating

21 David G Mugar Way, on the banks of the Charles River, between the Hatch Shell & the Longfellow Bridge, West End (523 1038). Charles T. **Open** *Apr-Oct* 1pm-sunset Mon-Fri; 9am-sunset Sat, Sun. **Rates** 2-day pass $50. **Credit** MC, V. **Map** p308 F4

Offers boat rentals, but requires that customers have some level of boating experience.

Bowling

Massachusetts is famous for candlepin bowling, a breed of the game characterised by smaller balls and more pins. It may not sound exciting, but it's always a good time.

Milky Way Lounge & Lanes

403-405 Center Street, Jamaica Plain (524 3740). Stonybrook T or 39 bus. **Open** 6pm-midnight daily. Rates $2.50 per game; shoes $2; after 8pm there may be an additional cover charge. **Credit** AmEx, MC, V.

Where else can you bowl a few strings, eat food that is genuinely good, drink ice-cold beers, listen to bands and meet cool people? Nowhere, that's where. The Milky Way is a true gem.

Sacco's Bowl-Haven

45 Day Street, Somerville (776 0552). Davis T. **Open** 9.30am-midnight Mon-Fri; 10am-midnight Sat; noon-11.30pm Sun. **Rates** $2 per game; shoes $1; pool $7.50 per hour. **No credit cards**.

Sacco's Bowl-Haven attracts a mix of blue-collar types and urban hipsters, especially after 9pm for the black-light extravaganza that has been so creatively dubbed 'Bowling in the Dark'.

Cycling & mountain biking

Just about everywhere on earth, pedestrians and drivers loathe bike messengers and – by default – recreational cyclists, and Boston is no exception to that rule. That said, there are plenty of dedicated trails – on-road and off – that are good for both cyclists and in-line skaters. And you will see them everywhere.

There are plenty of places to rent bikes or blades throughout the Boston area. Some, such as **Back Bay Bikes and Boards**

(336 Newbury Street; 247 2336) do both. For bike rentals in Boston, try **Community Bicycle Supply** in the South End (496 Tremont Street; 542 8623), or stop by the **International Bicycle Center** in Allston (89 Brighton Avenue; 783 5804). Also, in Cambridge and Somerville, there's the **Bicycle Workshop** (259 Massachusetts Avenue, Cambridge; 876 6555) or **WheelWorks** (145 Elm Street, Somerville; 776 2100). The latter also stocks *Ride*, a locally produced 'zine chronicling the New England bike racing scene.

Fitness centres & gyms

There are over 140 fitness centres and gyms in Boston, with a wide array of prices and workout options. Here is a sampling of different types that accept drop-ins like you.

Boston Body

364 Boylston Street, between Arlington and Berkeley Streets, Back Bay (262 3333/www.bostonbody.com). Arlington T. **Open** 6am-9pm Mon-Fri; 8.30am-4pm Sat, Sun. **Rates** membership $56 per month; $12 drop-in fee. **Credit** AmEx, MC, V. **Map** p306 F5.

In addition to standard workouts, Boston Body offers services such as tanning, nutrition counselling, marathon training and pre- and postnatal training. Also check out their group classes like Ashtanga yoga, Butts & Gutts, circuit training, cardio-boxing, Pilates, Power Sculpt and Step & Jab.

Boston Sport Boxing Club

125 Walnut Street, Watertown (972 1711/ www.bostonboxing.com). Bus 70, 70A or 71. **Open** 2-10pm Mon-Thur; 2-9pm Fri; 11am-5pm Sat. **Rates** $10 drop-in fee (call first). **No credit cards**.

Yo, Adrienne! New England's only full-time boxing facility. Hit the heavy bag. Toss the medicine ball – all ten pounds of it. Jump rope. Smack the hand pads. You can't fully appreciate hand-eye coordination until you try to hit a speed bag. Complete the circuit with leg raises, stretching, shadow boxing, stomach crunches, push-ups and the double-end bag that just might hit back. After your circuit training, if you want to hit something besides a bag, you can step in the ring and take on an opponent.

Metropolitan Health Club

209 Columbus Avenue, at Berkeley Street, Back Bay (536 3006). Back Bay T. **Open** 6am-11pm Mon-Fri; 8am-9pm Sat; 9am-9pm Sun. **Rates** membership $55 per month; $12 drop-in fee. **Credit** AmEx, Disc, MC, V. **Map** p306 F5.

For years MHC has been considered a great place for men to meet men and work out. It offers a wide array of workout options to fit the needs of every athlete. Included are aerobics, elliptical trainers, free weights, massage, personal trainers, pro shop, restaurant and juice bar, rowing machines, spinning, stair climbers, stationary bikes, treadmills, weight machines and cross-country machines.

Health Works Fitness Center for Women

441 Stuart Street, at Dartmouth Street, Back Bay (859 7700). Back Bay or Copley T. **Open** 6am-10pm Mon-Fri; 8am-7pm Sat, Sun. **Rates** $12 drop-in fee. **Credit** MC, V. **Map** p306 F5.

If you're the type of lady who'd rather not shake, rattle and roll in the presence of the opposite sex, this gym's the place for you. Aerobics, child care, climbing wall, day spa, elliptical trainers, free weights, massage, personal trainers, pro shop, restaurant and juice bar, spinning, stair climbers, stationary bikes, steam, sauna, treadmills, weight machines, whirlpools and cross-country machine. All for chicks only.

Golf

Looking to swing a few? No problem. The following are public courses.

Fresh Pond Golf Course

691 Huron Avenue, at Fresh Pond Parkway, Cambridge (349 6282). Alewife T. **Open** *Apr-Nov* 5.30am-dusk daily. **Rates** $16-$29. **No credit cards**.

George Wright Golf Course

420 West Street, Hyde Park (361 8313). Bus 50. **Open** 5.30am-9pm daily. **Rates** $12-$27. **Credit** MC, V.

Leo J Martin Memorial Golf Course

190 Park Road, Weston (1-781 894 4903). Riverside T. **Open** *Apr-Nov* dawn-dusk daily. **Rates** $10-$20. **Credit** Disc, MC, V.

Newton Commonwealth Golf Course

212 Kenrick Street, Newton (630 1971). Boston College T. **Open** dawn-dusk daily. **Rates** $10-$30. **Credit** AmEx, MC, V.

Ponkapoag Golf Course

2167 Washington Street, Canton (1-781 828 4242). **Open** *Apr-Nov* 6am-3pm Mon-Fri. **Rates** $17-$20. **Credit** MC, V.

Putterham Meadows Golf Course

1281 West Roxbury Parkway, Brookline (730 2078/2079). Chestnut Hill T. **Open** *Apr-Nov* dawn-dusk daily. **Rates** $25-$35; lessons $35 per half hour. **Credit** AmEx, MC, V.

Will J Devine Gold Club

Franklin Park, 1 Circuit Drive, Dorchester (265 4084). Bus 22. **Open** dawn-dusk daily. **Rates** $11-$25. **Credit** AmEx, Disc, MC, V.

This is the second-oldest public course in America.

In-line skating/rollerblading

If you like to skate, you've come to the right place. Boston and nearby cities offer a plethora of paved trails and roadways for the inveterate eight-wheeler. Both novices and experienced skaters should check out the **Charles River**

Bike Path or the **Minuteman Bike Trail** (*see p292*). If you want to get in a good workout, hit the trail before 10am on sunny weekend mornings, otherwise you'll run into major traffic in the form of all the other runners, walkers, skaters and bikers with the same idea.

If you want to hire or buy blades, try the **Beacon Hill Skate Shop** (135 South Charles Street; 482 7400).

Polo

Those looking for a taste of sporting action combined with high-class tailgating (think champagne and cheese as opposed to beer and crisps), a trip to the perfectly named **Myopia Polo Grounds** in Hamilton, Massachusetts, is a must. Polo matches are held every Sunday at 3pm throughout the summer and tickets cost $5. Phone 1-978 468 7956 for details.

Pool & billiards

It's not uncommon to find a pool table plunked down in the middle (or off to one corner) of a Boston bar. But if you really want to play, check out **Big City** (138 Brighton Avenue; 782 2020), the **Boston Billiard Club** (126 Brookline Avenue; 536 7665), **Sully's Billiards** in Allston (445 Cambridge Street; 254 9851) and **Flattop Johnny's** in Cambridge (1 Kendall Square; 494 9565).

Rowing

Charles River Canoe and Kayak

2401 Commonwealth Avenue, Newton (965 5110). Riverside T. **Open** *Apr-Oct* 10am-sunset Mon-Fri; 9am-sunset Sat, Sun. **Rates** rental $9-$10 per hour. **Credit** Disc, MC, V.

Rent a slim boat and join the hordes out on the river soaking up the sunshine and showing off.

Running

Local runners flock to the **Minuteman Bike Path** and the **Charles River Bike Path** on the weekend for long runs. The Charles River Bike Path provides an 18-mile (29-kilometre) round trip on asphalt, and you can get in a 22-mile (35-kilometre) run if you do the Minuteman trail both ways, starting at Davis Square in Somerville (with the added bonus that the miles are marked on the path). To run off the beaten path, however, check out the trails in the 2,060-acre (834-hectare) **Middlesex Fells Reservation** (off Route 28 in Malden, Medford, Stoneham and Winchester; 1-781-322-2851).

The annual **Boston Marathon** is held in April (*see p194*). Although you must meet a time qualification in a previous race to register officially, the race sees its fair share of illegal entries every year. Unlike, say, the New York Marathon, it's pretty easy to jump into the Boston Marathon.

Skateboarding

Folks who work for the skateboard magazine *Thrasher* love Boston. With its cobblestone streets, cracked sidewalks and numerous handrails, stairs, curb cuts and ledges all concentrated within a small space, Boston is a great place in which to skate. In addition to the parks listed below, the Metropolitan District Commission (MDC) playground in Brighton (between Soldiers Field Road and the Charles River) features rolling concrete banks and other great obstacles. The area in front of the Boston Medical Center (near the intersection of Massachusetts and Harrison Avenues) has enormous curved brick banks that attract skateboarders from all over the city, and the Christian Science complex on Huntington Avenue (*see p83*) is another good spot.

Eight Ball Skate Park

Route 140, Bellingham (1-508 966 3613). **Open** 3-9pm Tue-Fri; 1-8pm Sat, Sun. **Rates** $5-$10. **Credit** MC, V.

Underground Snowboards

860 Commonwealth Avenue, at Boston University, Brookline (232 8680). BU West T. **Open** 10am-9pm Mon-Fri; 9.30am-6pm Sat; noon-5pm Sun. **Credit** AmEx, Disc, MC, V.

Skiing

Aficionados of the sport have been known to make fun of New England skiing, with its rocky trails and slushy snow, but there is some good downhill action to be had in the northern states. In the last decade most New England resorts – including the big ones, **Killington**, **Sunday River** and **Sugarbush** – have brought the art of snow-making to a new level. In other words, as long as the temperature cooperates, there will be snow to ski on, regardless of snowfall. It's possible for road warriors to zip up Route 93 north to **Loon Mountain** on the Kancamagus Highway or to **Cannon Mountain** in the Franconia Notch Parkway, both in nearby New Hampshire, for a daytrip's worth of skiing, but you'll thank yourself if you set aside a weekend for the excursion.

For those who can't afford to leave the city, try the **Blue Hills** (4001 Washington Street, Milton; 1-781 828 7300). It's not the most challenging terrain and snow conditions are entirely dependent on the weather, but it's just a

Fenway Park

Sports paradise or broke-down palace?

'So many places, they're taking landmarks and just tearing them down', laments George Greenidge, a sausage vendor outside of Fenway Park interviewed in a short film called *Fabulous Fenway*. 'What would we be like if they removed the pyramids?'

Greenidge's are not merely the indiscriminate rumblings of a curmudgeonly sausage vendor. They strike at the heart of a debate regarding the future of historic Fenway Park and its famous homer-stealing left-field wall, the Green Monster. Should Fenway, as the Red Sox would have it, be replaced – at a cost of up to $664 million, much of it subsidised with tax dollars – by a shiny new corporate-sponsored park? Or should the greatest ballpark in the world, as those who oppose the plan insist that it is, simply be polished a little and saved? The controversy rages. In the balance? Some would say it's the very soul of baseball.

Everyone with a soapbox to stand on has an opinion on this issue. Ted Williams, the Red Sox legend responsible for many of the memories fans are afraid of losing, isn't shy about expressing his. 'I can't wait to see the new park when it's done', Williams has been quoted as saying. 'I want Boston to have the best. If ever a city needed a new park, it's Boston. I won't shed a tear'.

The arguments for a new park are many. Fenway is the smallest ballpark in the major leagues. It is also one of the oldest; news of the *Titanic* sinking overshadowed news of the first official Red Sox game at Fenway on 20 April 1912. And while historical value can be charming, there's certainly no pride in suffering obstructed-view seats, antiquated loos, seats too narrow for the bulk of today's wide-bottomed adults and dreary food.

Of course, the main interest in building a new stadium is financial. Proponents say that by expanding the size of the stadium, and thus earning more money in ticket sales, the team will be able to hire better players and win more ballgames.

Those opposing the new park say Fenway epitomises all that is good about baseball and Boston. Boston's mayor, Thomas Menino, is one such believer. 'Why do they draw two million people? Why do they get 30,000 people at the end of the season, even when they're not in it? People come to see the ballpark, to see the Green Monster, to be close to the players. Boston must balance development growth with the preservation of what makes our city so liveable – our historic character, scale and charm. We are distinct from other American cities because we view our buildings as resources, not liabilities,' Menino says.

How this saga will end is unclear. In mid 2001, Fenway's fate was still being discussed – the pros and cons were still being weighed, and no decision seemed eminent. These days, even the team's ownership is in limbo, so Fenway Park's future may not be decided for years to come.

Fenway Park

15-minute drive from Boston and you can get in a few runs in an afternoon before heading back to the city's hustle and bustle.

The **Ski Market** (860 Commonwealth Avenue, near Boston University Bridge; 731 6100) not only sells all sorts of ski and snowboard gear, but can be used as a resource for New England skiing and local events. For more on skiing, *see p274*.

Swimming

When it comes right down to it, your best swimming bet may well be your own hotel. However, the Metropolitan District Commission operates all the public pools in the Boston area. These are open daily from late June to early September. Phone 727 1300 to find out the location of your nearest pool.

Tennis

Based primarily on the fact that this is a winter weather state, tennis is not as big a deal as it is in southern US states. In addition, most tennis playing takes place on private courts located at country clubs, all of which require expensive membership. Still, there are a few public tennis courts in Boston, which can be useful to visitors. Most of these are available on a first-come, first-served basis. The City of Boston operates a number of them, as does the Metropolitan District Commission. The most centrally located court is on **Boston Common**, on Beacon Street (phone the Parks Recreation Department on 635 4505 to book it). For complete listings, consult the phone book or contact the MDC (see above **Swimming**).

The Curse of the Bambino

Does **Babe Ruth** (pictured with his family) haunt Fenway to this day?

In truth, nobody in baseball really believes in the Curse of the Bambino – well, not that many people. But it's one hell of a story. When you've got as much history against you as the Red Sox have, every late-season collapse, every play-off series defeat, even every addition to the regular season 'loss' column, potentially adds to the mythology surrounding the most famous jinx in the history of sport.

It all began in 1919, when the owner of the Red Sox, Harry Frazee, got into mild financial trouble after a few of his theatre productions didn't do as well as expected. To ease his bank balance, Frazee sold a player to the hated New York Yankees for $100,000 cash and a loan to pay the mortgage on the team's stadium, Fenway Park. Not much to write home about under normal circumstances. But the player in question was Babe Ruth, and so began the Curse. Ruth went on to lead the Yankees to their first World Series a few years later and became the greatest player the game has ever seen. Since the trade, New York has won the American League 36 times and the World Series on 25 occasions (including in 2000). The Sox have won just four of the former, and none of the latter. They've certainly come close, but therein lies the Curse. For just when it seems as though the Red Sox are going to banish history forever, something fantastic or just downright ludicrous occurs.

Take 1946, when the Sox took a one game lead in the Series after five games had been played. After losing game six, St Louis stole game seven (of a seven-game series) and thus the championship when St Louis outfielder Enos Slaughter incredibly scored the winning run all the way from first base, on a single to centerfield in the bottom of the eighth – a virtually impossible play. Or take 1967, when the Sox again lost in game seven of the Series, again against St Louis. Or 1975, when Joe Morgan blooped a broken-bat single into centre with two outs in the ninth inning of – you guessed it – game seven, giving Cincinatti the World Series.

Most fans believe that it doesn't matter what the team does. The Red Sox could sign every top player in the sport, and it wouldn't make a difference. Because until some sports priest carries out a serious baseball exorcism in Fenway Park, the Curse of the Bambino will prevent the team from ever winning the World Series.

Trips Out of Town

Getting Started 244
Colonial New England 245
Mass Beaches & Ocean 252
Picturesque Western Mass 260
Heading South 265
Heading North 270

Feature boxes

Top five Mass beaches 258
Having a gay old time 259
Skiing in NE: more trad than rad 274

Getting Started

We don't want to change the world, we're just looking for New England.

The writer F Scott Fitzgerald once described in bittersweet fashion what the world must have thought as the settlers stepped for the first time off their ships and into the New England countryside: 'For a transitory enchanted moment man must have held his breath in the presence of this continent, compelled into an aesthetic contemplation he neither understood nor desired, face to face for the last time in history with something commensurate to his capacity for wonder.' While Fitzgerald embraced the entire nation with his words, it was the wilds and wonders of rural New England that he described.

Much of that glory is long gone, of course, and its loss was what Fitzgerald was writing about. But what remains offers hints of what the writer imagined, and what the settlers saw. Exploring it is a way of bringing the past into the present, and of understanding more than New England – it's a way of understanding this entire country.

Virtually in the shadow of Boston lie the battlefields upon which the Revolutionary War was fought. The city is surrounded by rolling hills, rocky shores and gorgeous rural landscapes. The towns nearby are quaint villages with the white colonial churches and picket fences that have provided settings for countless novels and Hollywood films. It would seem the word Americana was invented to describe this area. Whether you go to **Salem**, where Nathaniel Hawthorne sharpened his quill, or to **Walden**, where Henry David Thoreau explored transcendentalism, it's difficult not to be inspired, as they were, by New England.

TRANSPORT

The classic New Englander's unhelpful direction is, 'you can't get there from here'. But never fear. As the oldest continually settled part of the American continent, New England's network of roadways is extensive and well-maintained. Rent a car and you'll find that the terrors of Boston traffic are but a grim memory. Boston has branches of all the major car rental firms, plus a number of smaller, local outfits. The cars at the latter won't look quite as flash but they are sometimes a good deal cheaper. When shopping around, ask if the rates include tax (often quite high) and insurance. It can also be worthwhile to visit a branch of the **AAA** to stock up on maps and get driving advice.

TRAINS

Amtrak (1-800 872 7245) runs between New Haven, Connecticut and Boston, as well as up the Connecticut River Valley and across northern Vermont. The **Massachusetts Bay Transportation Authority (MBTA)** (222 3200) runs regular Commuter Rail train services to most of the destinations within half an hour of Boston.

BUSES

Major companies that run services to greater New England include **Greyhound** (1-800 231 2222/www.greyhound.com), **Bonanza** (1-800 556 3815) and **Peter Pan** (1-800 237 8747).

► For details of Boston's **airport** and **train** and **bus** stations *see p278*. For **AAA** *see p279*. For **car rental** companies *see p280*. The **Trips Out of Town** map is on *p303*.

Colonial New England

Take a short trip to see the place where it all began.

Whether or not history is your thing, it's difficult not to be struck by the import of what happened in this area of New England. There is something intrinsically moving about standing on an old battlefield, knowing that thousands fought and died there. Whether it's on the battlefields of Lexington and Concord, or in the shady streets of Salem where so many were victims of a witch hunt, being here brings you face to face with the past, all while keeping your feet firmly planted in the region's more pleasant present.

Concord & Lexington

American schoolchildren so closely associate the names of these hotbeds of history that they are often surprised to learn later in life that Concord and Lexington are in fact two separate communities. The reason their names roll so easily off the tongue together is that both are synonymous in the national consciousness with the 'shot heard round the world.' The first true battle in the American Revolution started in Lexington and ended in Concord, thus forever combining the two in the minds of many.

It happened this way: in 1774, the Provincial Congress delegated a division of elite militia soldiers known as the Minutemen. They were authorised to form 'for defence only'. But the Minutemen, in anticipation of future battles, had begun stockpiling weapons in the village of Concord. British generals caught word of the arsenal and sent 700 troops marching the 25 miles from Boston to Concord. Alerted by a trio of rebels – including Paul Revere – sent on horseback to warn them, 77 Minutemen met the troops at Lexington Green. When the British soldiers arrived they ordered the Americans to drop their weapons. The colonists refused, and a battle began. In that first struggle, 18 Minutemen were killed or wounded, while not a single British soldier was injured. Emboldened by their victory, the British didn't stop to rest, but marched on to Concord where, unbeknown to them, more militia

The battlefield at Lexington was the site of the 'shot heard round the world'.

were marshalling. As the American troops awaited the Redcoats' arrival outside Concord, they spotted smoke rising from the town. Convinced that the British were burning their homes, they attacked a British patrol sent out to hold the Old North Bridge. It is said that the colonial troops were so enraged that Captain John Parker told the militia, 'Stand your ground. Don't fire unless fired upon, but if they mean to have a war, let it begin here!' And so it did. Two Americans and 11 British soldiers were killed there. After that fight, of course, the gloves were off, and the war began in earnest (*see p6*).

With so much history in this region, you might expect that every house, field and footstep would be marked with narrative placards and memorial statues. And you'd be right. Tourism is very big business here.

All the major sights of **Lexington** are centred around **Lexington Green**, the triangular plot upon which the battle occurred. Today the green is anchored by the **Minuteman Statue** and dotted with other markers and memorials. The statue is of Captain Parker, and his famous quote is engraved under his feet. Turning right as you come out of the green you'll see the **Buckman Tavern**. It was in this tavern that the Minutemen assembled to await the arrival of the British. It is also the site where they later set up their field hospital. The tavern, one of the oldest buildings in the area, was already 85 years old at the time of the Battle of Lexington Green. It is staffed by perky young guides in period costumes who are highly knowledgeable about the history of the area. A bit of trivia: the tavern's exceptionally high bar is said to have been built at this level in order to prevent underage drinking. If a boy's chin wasn't above the bar, he couldn't buy a beer. Another piece of Buckman trivia courtesy of the guides: the tavern keepers tracked the sales of pints and quarts by marking them in chalk on the wall behind the bar. From this practice the expression 'mind your Ps and Qs' is said to have come.

Just behind the tavern is the small but perfectly informed **Lexington Visitors' Centre**, which has a diorama outlining all the particulars of the battle. It also offers tours of the town's historically significant houses.

Just north of the green on Hancock Street you'll find the **Hancock-Clarke House**. On the night of the battle, largely by coincidence, rebels Samuel Adams and John Hancock were spending the night here, as guests of the owner, the Rev. Jonas Clarke. (They were, in fact, relatives. Clarke's wife was Hancock's cousin.) In the end, Revere did awaken them in time, and they were hustled out of town to safety. He did not, however, warn the soldiers at Concord, as he was captured by the British (*see p8*).

About a mile (1.6 kilometres) east of the Green is the **Munroe Tavern**. This establishment gained fame somewhat ignobly, as it was here that the British troops retreating from Concord stopped to rest and care for their injured, and to shoot the bartender, who tried to flee after serving them. George Washington went some way to redeem the bar's reputation by visiting it after the war, and some items related to his stay are kept here today.

About four miles (6.5 kilometres) from Lexington down Route 62 is its historical soulmate, the village of **Concord**. Along with its role in the War of Independence, Concord is further distinguished by its place in American letters: it was the residence of Ralph Waldo Emerson, Henry David Thoreau, Louisa May Alcott and Nathaniel Hawthorne. Within a few short blocks in this town you'll find a group of homes that once contained an unparalleled flowering of American literary genius.

But the first sites most visitors to Concord feel obliged to see are tied in to the country's earliest days. The most significant of these is the **Minuteman National Historical Park**, which marks the spot where the Battle of Concord took place after the British marched on victorious from Lexington. While there is no way to be completely sure where all parts of the battle took place, it has long been believed that it was here that the Minutemen stood watching the smoke rise over the town. The park is vast and is filled with memorabilia and information related to the battle. Once inside the park it's best to start at the **North Bridge Visitors' Centre**, which stands on a hill overlooking the Concord River and the North Bridge. Inside there is a diorama alongside a collection of Revolutionary War memorabilia, including uniforms, weapons and tools from both sides of the battle. The helpful, knowledgeable park rangers working at the centre provide guided tours of the site. From the centre it's just a short walk to the reconstruction of the **North Bridge**. It's worth stopping along the way to listen to recordings that tell the story of the battle and the area. At one end of the bridge stands another Minuteman statue, while a plaque on the far bank remembers the British dead.

If the weather is fine, walk down to the Lexington end of the park, where you'll find the **Battle Road** section. Lined with informational markers, this section stretches out along the first few miles of the British line of retreat to Lexington and Boston. It has an informative visitors' centre of its own, with extensive displays and a multimedia programme that tells the story of the revolution.

Once you've seen the battle site, calmer scenes await throughout Concord for those interested in its literary history. The **Ralph Waldo Emerson House** is the former home of the essayist who was a key figure in the Transcendentalist movement. He lived here from 1835 until his death in 1882. The house still contains its original furnishings and many of the writer's belongings. The steep colonial roof of the **Old Manse** was constructed by Emerson's grandfather, the Rev. William Emerson, in 1770. It is said that he stood in the yard and watched the Battle of Concord. The roof sheltered both Ralph Waldo Emerson and Nathaniel Hawthorne at different times (the former was living here when he wrote 'Nature', the latter lived here with his wife from 1842-1847), and contains many of their belongings. The stories Hawthorne wrote that were inspired by his time in this house brought him his earliest fame.

Not far away is the **Orchard House**, which once was home to the educator Bronson Alcott, another prominent Transcendentalist. However, its best-known resident was his daughter, Louisa May Alcott. Her most famous book, *Little Women*, was both written about and set at the Orchard House. The house, which is filled with the Alcott family's belongings, attracts thousands of (largely female) fans of the book every year. The entrance fee includes a highly informative tour of the building. Louisa May Alcott also lived for a time at The **Wayside**, where Hawthorne later came to spend his final years.

South of town is one of the state's best-known literary and historical sites. On **Walden Pond**, the naturalist and Transcendentalist writer Henry David Thoreau explored his philosophy of returning to a 'civilized' life by, in essence, leaving civilization. He did so off Route 126 in a one-room cabin where he lived for more than a year, from 1846. He wrote the ground-breaking essay 'Walden' about his experience there. The essay didn't make him famous, however. That happened two years later, in 1849, when he wrote the essay, 'Civil Disobedience.' The house in which Thoreau sought his simple life is long since gone – only a pile of stones marks the spot – but the well-preserved **Walden Pond State Reservation** that now encompasses the area still affords the kind of swimming and hiking that the native seer advocated. Two full-size, exactly furnished replicas of the original cabin can be visited: one is near the reservation car park and the other is in town, at the Thoreau Lyceum, which also houses a collection of the naturalist's letters and memorabilia and is situated at the **Concord Museum** (*see p120*).

Buckman Tavern

1 Bedford Street, Lexington (1-781 862 5598). **Open** *Mar-Oct* 10am-4.30pm daily. **Admission** $4; $2 concessions. **No credit cards.**

Hancock-Clarke House

36 Hancock Street, Lexington (1-781 862 1703). **Open** *Mar-Oct* 10am-4.30pm daily. **Admission** $4; $2 concessions. **No credit cards.**

Minuteman National Historical Park

174 Liberty Street, off route 2A, Lexington (1-781 862 7753). **Open** *June-Sept* 9am-5.30pm daily. *Oct-May* 9am-3.30pm daily. **Admission** free.

Munroe Tavern

1332 Massachusetts Avenue, Lexington (1-781 862 2016). **Open** *Mar-Oct* 10am-4.30pm daily. **Admission** $4, $2 concessions. **No credit cards.**

Old Manse

269 Monument Street, Concord (1-978 369 3909). **Open** *Apr-Oct* 10am-5pm daily. **Admission** $6.50; $4.50-$5.50 concessions. **Credit** AmEx, MC, V.

The Orchard House

399 Lexington Road, Concord (1-978 369 4118). **Open** 11am-3pm Mon-Fri; 10am-4.30pm Sat; 9am-4.30pm Sun. **Admission** $7; $6 concessions. **Credit** MC, V.

Ralph Waldo Emerson House

28 Cambridge Turnpike, Concord (1-978 369 2236). **Open** *Apr-Oct* 10am-4.30pm Thur-Sat; 2-4.30pm Sun. **Admission** *tours* $5; $3 concessions. **No credit cards.**

Walden Pond State Reservation

915 Walden Street, Concord (1-978 369 3254/ www.state.ma.us/dem/parks/wldn.htm). **Open** 8am-5pm daily. **Admission** free.

The Wayside

455 Lexington Road, Concord (1-978 369 6975/ www.nps.gov/mima/wayside). **Open** *May-Oct* 10am-4.30pm Mon, Tue, Thur-Sun. **Admission** tours $4; free under-17s. **No credit cards.**

Where to stay

Concord has two interesting inns: the 19th-century **Hawthorne** (462 Lexington Road; 1-978 369 5610; rates $85-$225) and the 18th-century **Colonial Inn** (48 Monument Square; 1-978 369 9200; rates $135-$189).

Getting there

By car

Lexington is 9 miles (14.4km) north-west of Boston on Route 128 (I-95). Concord is 18 miles (29km) north-west of Boston and 6 miles (9.7km) west of Lexington. Take Route 2A from Lexington, or Route 2 from Boston.

By bus and rail

The MBTA Commuter Rail (*see p279*) service covers both towns, Lexington by bus only, Concord by train only. Awkwardly, there is no public transport connection between the two. Both services leave from Boston's North Station.

Tourist information

Lexington Visitors' Centre

Lexington Green, 1875 Massachusetts Avenue, Lexington (1-781 862 1450). **Open** 9am-5pm daily.

Minuteman National Historical Park Visitors' Centre

174 Liberty Street, off route 2A, Lexington (1-781 862 7753). **Open** *June-Sept* 9am-5.30pm daily. *Oct-May* 9am-3.30pm daily.

North Bridge Visitors' Centre

174 Liberty Street, off Monument Street, Concord (1-781 862 7753/www.nps.gov/mima). **Open** *June-Sept* 9am-5.30pm daily. *Oct-May* 9am-3.30pm daily.

Salem

There are few towns in America, few in the world for that matter, with reputations as dark as that of Salem. While there is more to its history than the notorious Salem Witch Trials of 1692, the mass hysteria that consumed the town during seven months of that year still colours its name more than 300 years later. Few US schoolchildren cannot name Tituba, the Haitian maid whose interest in Voodoo was long blamed for turning the interest of a group of repressed young Puritan girls towards magic and mystery. The tragic end of it all, the executions of more than 20 residents – mostly elderly women – means that Salem's name will forever be tied to madness. The current residents, however, have managed to turn a black mark into both a local industry and a curious point of pride (or at least an identity). The city's police cars and its local newspaper sport caricatures of a witch's profile as their logos. In addition, the local high school calls its football team the Witches.

All silliness aside, Salem is a lovely, if vaguely schizophrenic, town. On one side it is darkly colonial, with red brick buildings and ancient cemeteries dating back to its earliest days. On the other side it is a beach town, with ocean breezes wafting over colourful seaside houses that could easily have been picked up in Florida and plunked down here. It's also the site of Nathaniel Hawthorne's childhood home.

Though Salem is small, it is sprawling enough to make walking from one end to another a bit of a hike. That said, it's a fairly easy hike, and walking really is the best way to get around. The colonial section, well away from the sea, makes a good starting point in terms of chronology because you move towards the more modern buildings as you get nearer the water.

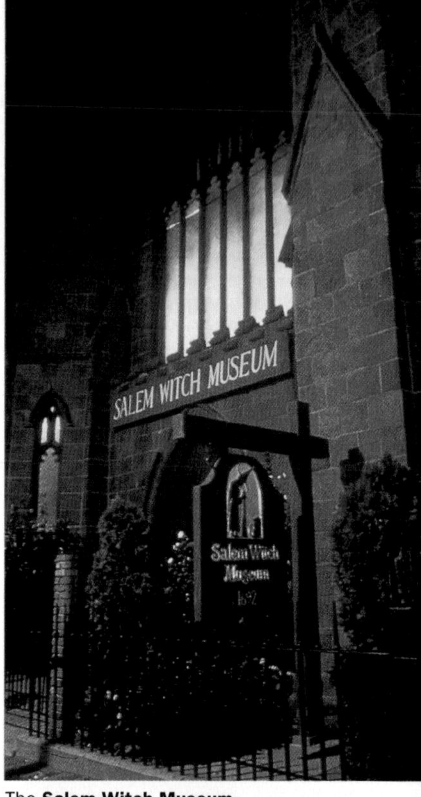

The **Salem Witch Museum.**

Witchcraft-related points of interest are largely scattered around Salem Common, a scenic park in the middle of the oldest section of town. These include the **Witch House**, the site where more than 200 unfortunates suspected of witchcraft during the time of the witch hunts were questioned about their dealings with the devil. The **Salem Wax Museum** is just about what you would expect given the name – wax re-creations of the characters involved in the trials. Nearby, and the best of the lot really, is the **Salem Witch Museum**, which features a very thorough (and scary, if you're under 13) mixed-media re-enactment of the Puritan hysteria.

Old downtown Salem, off the Common, is a National Historic District and boasts a wealth of architecturally interesting streets. In the heart of the area is the **Peabody Essex Museum** (*see p120*), founded by the East India Maritime Company in the late 18th century, when Salem was at the peak of its glory and dominated the shipping trade to China. The Peabody collection documents the history of whaling and merchant shipping, and features a vast collection of exhibits from the sailors' travels; the Essex Institute also serves as the local historical society.

A more fully fleshed-out representation of Salem's sea-going past is found aboard the **Friendship**, a full-scale replica of a three-masted 1797 East India merchant ship. It is docked at the end of Derby Street, amid the nine-acre (3.6-hectare) **Salem Maritime National Historic Site**, which offers tours of reconstructions of wharves, warehouses and stores of the time, as well as the old **Customs House** where Nathaniel Hawthorne worked before he wrote *The Scarlet Letter*.

Salem's most famous native son, Hawthorne took the inspiration for his other great novel from the **House of the Seven Gables**. When you see it, you'll understand why. It's an extraordinary building – large and rather seriously gloomy, with a peaked roof and turrets. Even today it dominates the street. Though it was the home of Hawthorne's cousin rather than the writer himself, it's easy to see how it might have penetrated the thoughts of a scholarly and imaginative boy. Built in 1668, the house is filled with period furniture, much of which is described in the book of the same name. Tours, led, like so many others in town, by guides in period costumes, includes Hawthorne's birthplace, which has since been moved to the grounds, and a detailed description of what it was like to live in the area at that time.

There's more of the same at the **Salem 1630: Pioneer Village**, an interactive museum where the whole Puritan settlement of 1630 has been re-created. Finally, and for sheer entertainment value, don't miss **The Bunghole** (204 Derby Street; 1-978 744 2251), possibly the world's most regrettably named liquor store.

House of the Seven Gables

54 Turner Street, at Derby Street, Salem (1-978 744 0991). **Open** 10am-5pm Mon-Sat; noon-5pm Sun. **Admission** $8; $5 concessions. **Credit** Disc, MC, V.

Salem 1630: Pioneer Village

Forest River Park, at West Avenue (1-978 745 0525). **Open** *June-Sept* 9am-6pm daily. *Oct-May* 9am-5pm daily. **Admission** free.

Salem Maritime National Historic Site

174 Derby Street (1-978 740 1660/ www.nps.gov/sama). **Open** 9am-5pm daily. **Admission** tours $3; $2 concessions. **No credit cards**.

Salem Wax Museum

288 Derby Street (1-978 740 2929/ www.salemwaxmuseum.com). **Open** 11am-4pm Mon-Thur; 10am-5pm Fri, Sat; 10am-4pm Sun. **Credit** Disc, MC, V.

Salem Witch Museum

19 Washington Square, at Route 1A (1-978 744 1692/www.salemwitchmuseum.com). **Open** 10am-5pm daily. **Admission** $6; $4 concessions. **No credit cards**.

Witch House

3102 Essex Street, at North Street (1-508 744 0180). **Open** *Mar-Nov* 10am-4.30pm daily. **Admission** $5; $4, $2 concessions. **Credit** Disc, MC, V.

Where to stay & eat

As it is, in essence, a suburb of Boston, Salem offers fairly extensive dining options. In addition to those listed here, it also is the home of many cheap US chains. The best bet for dining in Salem is **Grape Vine** (26 Congress Street; 1-978 745 9335), a funky, moderately priced 'new American' bistro located right across the street from Pickering Wharf. For a more upscale experience, stop into the building where **Alexander Graham Bell** conducted some of his early telephone experiments, the **Lyceum Bar & Grill** (43 Church Street; 1-978 745 7665), which offers contemporary American cuisine in historical and refined surroundings.

As you might imagine, lodging in Salem features a range of colourful possibilities. Aside from the usual hotel chains and franchises, there are a number of historic choices in this town. One of the best is the **Salem Inn** (7 Summer Street; 1-800 446 2995; rates $119-$270), a complex of two ships' captains' homes both on the National Register of Historic Places. Another option is the **Hawthorne Hotel** (18 Washington Square West; 1-978 744 4080; rates $104-$285), which, while not as old as its name suggests, offers a full hotel service in a grand manner, is close to all the sights, is nicely furnished and reasonably priced. You can save some money a little further off the common at the **Amelia Payson B&B** (16 Winter Street; 1-978 744 8304; rates $75-$130) – an 1845 Greek Revival structure with a piano in the parlour. The **Coach House Inn** (284 Lafayette Street; 1-800 688 8689; rates $80-$130), another 19th-century ships' captain's mansion, is an elegant, alternative choice.

Getting there

By car

Salem is 16 miles (26km) north of Boston. Take Route 193N to Exit 37A (195N) onto Route 128N and follow the signs. The journey takes from 30 minutes to an hour, depending on traffic.

By bus, boat or rail

The journey to Salem by rail takes half an hour by MBTA Commuter Rail (*see p279*) out of North Station. Harbor Express (376 8417) runs a daily ferry service to Salem from Pickering Wharf; the journey takes an hour.

Tourist information

Salem National Visitors' Centre

2 New Liberty Street, Salem (1-978 740 1650). **Open** 9am-5pm daily.

Plymouth

The scenic coast to the south of Boston between Quincy and Plymouth, aka the 'South Shore,' lays claim to a decent chunk of old colonial trails and what has become the hidden, even forgotten, New England. But you'll thank yourself for discovering it.

This part of the coast has been discovered in more dramatic form before, of course. This is the spot where the Pilgrims ultimately landed after their trip from England (in a roundabout kind of way; they stopped at several sites before alighting here). The most famous spot in Plymouth is **Plymouth Rock**, where, according to lore, they first stepped. But they didn't. Historians say that, contrary to what many American schoolchildren were taught, there's no evidence the Pilgrims ever saw the rock, much less stepped on it. Still, the lore exceeds the reality enough that it's worth a look. The actual rock has been moved several times over the years, even broken in two on one such occasion, and it only came to rest at its present location in 1867. The rock itself is rather unimpressive, especially compared to the monstrous, neo-classical monument that both guards and dwarfs it.

A replica of the ship in which the Pilgrims sailed is docked close by. The **Mayflower II** is a full-scale version of the original, with a staff of performers in 17th-century garb who recount the tale of the Pilgrims' struggles. The boat seems tiny, and it's hard to imagine that the initial settlers spent months aboard it, much of that time amid violent storms.

Plymouth itself is a charming town, with narrow streets and 17th- and 18th-century houses, most of which are open to the public, appropriately furnished and staffed by guides in period costume. If, after visiting other colonial towns, you can stomach any more silver-buckled shoes and big, black hats, a visit to **Plimoth Plantation** might be in in order. This in-depth re-creation of the original 1627 settlement includes a village full of actors who speak, work, play, eat and (it would seem) breathe as authentic a re-enactment of 17th-century life as is humanly possible. The site pays painstaking attention to detail, and visitors can watch the 'settlers' stocking firewood, cooking, even shearing sheep. The interactive museum was created by historians and archaeologists, and much of it was based on the writings of the Pilgrim's leader, William Bradford.

Other towns around Plymouth Bay worth visiting are Cohasset, Hull and Hingham. The old Indian trails and coach roads that connect these early coastal towns have a rustic attraction all of their own, and are worth exploring. If your legs are up to it you could consider bringing a bike.

As you're riding around, it's mostly the countryside to be seen here, but there are some quaint sites along the way. For instance, the century-old **Minot's Ledge Lighthouse** in **Cohasset** is a classic piece of New England scenery. Then there's **Hull**, which, like many places in the area, took its name from its English big brother. It was evacuated during the revolution after a military fort was constructed on one of its hills. Thus, today the quaint 18th-century town is perfectly preserved. The fully rigged **Hull Lifesaving Museum** tells the tale of this area's superhuman shipwreck rescues. Nearby, bucolic and peaceful **Hingham** is a good place to kill a few lazy hours. And, once you're there, what the heck, you might as well stop in at **Old Ordinary** (21 Lincoln Street; 1-781 749 0013), a 14-room house museum with period furniture and a taproom, though the name really does say it all. Hingham is also a good place to grab something to eat as it's filled with worthwhile restaurants : **Tosca** (14 North Street; 1-781 740 0080), **Stars On Hingham Harbor** (4 Otis Street; 1-781 749 3200) and **Fireking Baking Co** (19 North Street; 1-781 740 9400) are three of the best.

Hull Lifesaving Museum

1117 Nantasket Avenue, Hull (1-781 925 5433). **Open** *June-Sept* 10am-4pm Tue-Sun. *Oct-May* 10am-4pm Fri-Sun. **Admission** $2; $1.50 concessions. **Credit** MC, V.

Mayflower II

State Pier, Water Street, Plymouth (1-508 746 1622). **Open** *Apr-Nov* 9am-5pm daily. **Admission** $19; $17, $11 concessions. **No credit cards.**

You can travel by land or sea when you're headed Salem's way.

Plimoth Plantation

Warren Avenue, off Route 3A South at Exit 4, outside Plymouth (1-508 746 1622). **Open** *Apr-Nov* 9am-5pm daily. **Admission** $19; $17, $11 concessions. **No credit cards.**

Where to stay & eat

Dining in Plymouth is a briny business. Join the locals for the inexpensive, top-notch fish and shellfish at the **Lobster Hut** (Town Wharf; 1-508 746 2270), a self-service affair with an outstanding view. Stare down your fear of cholesterol and order one of the seafood rolls – fried scallops, clams or prawns in a bun. Or go a bit more upmarket at **Issac's** (114 Water Street; 1-508 830 0001), which offers another great ocean view and more elaborate seafood.

Plymouth has a number of serviceable, if undistinguished, motels within convenient reach of downtown. A more pleasant choice, and one with its own private beach, is the **Pilgrim Sands Motel** (150 Warren Avenue; 1-800 729 72637; rates $60-$130), a few miles out of town. Near the harbour is the **Mabbett House** (7 Cushman Street; 1-800 572 7829; rates $100-$180). Also nearby is **Kimball's-By-The-Sea** (124 Elm Street; 1-781 383 6650; rates $80-$170), a friendly full-service inn with gorgeous views on the harbour's edge.

Getting there

Plymouth is an hour south of Boston by train, or about halfway to Cape Cod by car. As you can imagine, considering the tourist draw of the area, there are numerous organised tours available. Phone the Plymouth Chamber of Commerce (*see below*) for more details.

By car

Plymouth is 40 miles (64km) south-east of Boston on the I-93 (Southeast Expressway) to Route 3. Take Exit 6 (roughly 45 minutes' drive).

By bus or rail

The easiest way to reach Plymouth may well be by public transport. It is an hour by train or bus from Boston. MBTA Commuter Rail (*see p279*) runs daily services from South Station. Buses also leave from South Station (*see p278*)

Tourist information

Plymouth Chamber of Commerce

225 Water Street, Plymouth (1-508 830 1620/ www.plymouthchamber.com). **Open** 9am-5pm daily.

Plymouth Visitors' Centre

130 Water Street, Plymouth (1-508 747 7533/1-800 872 1620). **Open** *Summer* 9am-5pm Mon-Fri, 9am-7pm Sat, Sun. *Winter* 9am-5pm Mon-Sat.

Mass Beaches and Ocean

Hangin' with the Kennedys by the sea, the beautiful sea.

Hit the coast in Massachusetts and you'll see that the communities lining its rocky shoreline are honest towns, many relying still on the Atlantic Ocean in one way or another for their industry and livelihood. Here, you'll find seagulls, sand dunes, salt marshes, lighthouses, clam shacks, fresh air, clear starry nights and seafaring charm. You'll also find drugs, booze, hookers and fisticuffs – if you know where to look. When it comes right down to it, you'll discover the soul of this part of the country. This is what people are talking about when they refer to the 'real' New England.

Cape Ann

There is, it seems, a particular passion – a gruff loveliness, a broken-hearted joy – to Cape Ann. If you really want to know about this peninsula dividing Ipswich and Massachusetts Bays, of course, refer to the work of two former residents: first, Winslow Homer's painting, *Watching the Breakers*, and second, Henry Wadsworth Longfellow's poem, *Wreck of the Hesperus*. This is a beautiful slice of New England that has somehow managed to survive the past couple of centuries with minimal commercial interruption and its pride and soul intact.

The four towns of Cape Ann are Essex, Rockport, Gloucester and Manchester-by-the-Sea. These towns all started off with similar post-Pilgrim seafaring histories – shipbuilding, sailors crossing the Atlantic in dinghies, bravery, terrible wrecks in awful seas and the painters and poets to make it all sound heroic – but have since forged their own reputations.

Gloucester has been getting a lot of attention lately due to the story of the Andrea Gail, a doomed ship caught in a deadly storm in 1991 and documented in Sebastian Junger's best-selling book (then George Clooney's box-office smash movie) *The Perfect Storm*. With its magnificently sheltered harbour, Gloucester has been a centre of the fishing industry since 1623, and some 10,000 Gloucestermen are said to have perished in the big drink over the years. The town's tribute to these men, a bronze statue known as 'The Man at the Wheel', stands guard on the harbour promenade, just off Western Avenue. This sombre history explains why the flood of visitors pinching and poking their way through the 'perfect tour' – The Crow's Nest, Our Lady of the Good Voyage Church – are irritating a few locals, many of whom knew or had relatives lost at sea. Unless you're looking for the perfect sock in the jaw, be sensitive.

For **Essex**, it's all about raking in the clams. The town relies on clamming as one of its principal industries and the sweet, tender Essex clam is almost as famous as a clam can get. There is even a celebration for the bivalve in September at the annual **Essex ClamFest**. In 1914, a clam-digging local named Lawrence 'Chubby' Woodman opened a clam shack called **Woodman's** here. Whether or not Chubby then actually 'invented' the fried clam is not important. What is important is that today, even as fried clams have become the ubiquitous seaside snack and every clam shack along the east coast has its version, the ones at Woodman's are still the best (*see p253*).

Rockport and **Manchester-by-the-Sea** are relatively sleepy, artsy residential towns about eight months of the year. Then summer comes and the population skyrockets. Just sitting on the sandy or rocky beaches and listening to the water lapping at the shore, breathing in the sea air and listening to the locals' accents is entertainment and inspiration enough for many. The town is, in many ways, the quintessential New England beach village. The entrance to Rockport's main harbour is so frequently depicted by artists that it's known locally as 'Motif Number 1'. While in town, stop by the strange edifice of the **Hammond Castle**, the inexplicable full-scale stone replica of a medieval castle.

Among the best beaches on Cape Ann proper are **Wingaersheek Beach**, on the north shore, and **Good Harbour** and **Long Beach**, on the south. South of Gloucester, at **Rafe's Chasm Park**, the granite ledges open to a chasm 200 feet (61 metres) long and 60 feet (18.3 metres) deep, and the tides often produce some striking sights and sounds. East of town,

Pebble Beach offers an unusual shoreline of timeworn stones stretching far to the horizon. **Singing Beach**, some 15 miles (24 kilometres) west of Newburyport, is another local favourite.

For an interesting trip north of Cape Ann take Routes 133 and 1A to **Newburyport**, an old maritime centre that boasts many fine Federal-style mansions. After Newburyport, head over the causeway to **Plum Island**, where a national wildlife refuge includes seven miles (11.3 kilometres) of wide, sandy beach. The dunes and marshes serve as a waystation to tens of thousands of migratory geese and ducks and permanent home to hundreds of other species of flora and fauna.

Hammond Castle

80 Hesperus Avenue, Manchester-by-the-Sea (1-978 283 2080). **Open** *May-Sept* 10am-3pm Sat, Sun. **Admission** $6.50 adults; $4.50 concessions. **No credit cards**.

Where to stay & eat

The most interesting choices in Gloucester include **Rockport's Addison Choate Inn** (49 Broadway; 1-800 245 7543; rates $95-$140), a Greek Revival house from the 1850s, and the **Inn on Cove Hill** (37 Mount Pleasant Street; 1-978 546 2701; rates $71-$101), reputedly built with the proceeds from a discovered cache of pirates' loot. The **Cape Ann Chamber of Commerce**'s hotel booking line (1-800 321 0133) can help with last-minute bookings.

For dining, of course, there's **Woodman's of Essex** (121 Main Street; 1-800 649 1773/ www.woodmans.com). **Evie's Rudder** (73 Rocky Neck Avenue; 1-978 283 7967; closed in winter) in the heart of the Rocky Neck Art Colony, features a moderately priced, eclectic menu, quirky bric-a-brac decor and a festive atmosphere. The **White Rainbow** (65 Main Street; 1-978 281 0017) is a more expensive choice, with nouvelle American dishes served by candlelight.

Getting there

By car

Gloucester is 30 miles (48km) north-east of Boston on Route 1 or I-93; Rockport is 40 miles (64km) from Boston, and 7 miles (11.3km) north of Gloucester on Routes 127 or 127A.

By bus & rail

MBTA Commuter Rail (*see p279*) runs trains to Gloucester from North Station. The bus service on the Cape Ann peninsula is run by the Cape Ann Transportation Authority (CATA; 1-978 283 7916).

Tourist information

Cape Ann Chamber of Commerce

33 Commercial Street, Gloucester (1-978 283 1601/www.cape-ann.com). **Open** 8am-5pm Mon-Fri.

Cape Cod

To Spanky, the bartender at the corner bar, a Cape Codder is a mix of vodka and cranberry juice with a wedge of lime. If Spanky were to add a little Cointreau, the result would be a drink with a far more upmarket name: a Cosmopolitan. That's the Cape right there:

Miles of sand dunes and beaches await on Cape Cod.

sharp, strong, and a mere splash away from being something fancy. And entirely the better for it. Mixologist and writer Denny Lewis once commented: 'The name Cape Codder for the drink of vodka and cranberry juice is born of a sense of pride emanating from the cranberry bogs of south-eastern Massachusetts. You can say "I am from Cape Cod" without danger of sounding arrogant, but try saying, "I am worldly" without someone sneering.' Which is not to hint that Cape Cod is inferior to any of the other capes in New England. Or any less pretty than a postcard.

Early explorers were of dubious creativity, and so it's not surprising they named the area after the mild-flavoured fish found there by English explorer Bartholomew Gosnold. Through its early years, the Cape relied on fishing, whaling, shipping and salt making for economic support. Those industries have long since given way to cranberry growing (the Cape is now the nation's largest producer of the red berries) and to tourism.

Geographically, the 16 towns that make up the Cape are organised into three chunks: Upper (Wareham, Bourne, Sagamore, Sandwich, Falmouth and Mashpee), Mid (Barnstable, Dennis, Yarmouth, Brewster and Harwich) and Lower, or Outer, Cape (Chatham, Orleans, Eastham, Wellfleet, Truro and Provincetown). Within these towns are villages, like Hyannis in Barnstable. Throughout parts of the Cape also runs the **Cape Cod National Seashore**, 43,685 acres (17,686 hectares) of beaches, sand dunes, heathlands, marshes, freshwater ponds and a number of historic sites.

Sandwich was the first established of the Pilgrim's Cape towns. During the 19th century the town became a centre of the American glass-making industry, the local artisans' ovens fuelled by the plentiful surrounding scrub brush. Today its **Glass Museum** contains a wealth of sparkling examples of the work of those craftsmen. At the restored 17th-century **Dexter Grist Mill** at the corner of Main and Water Streets, you can still buy ground corn meal. Not that you would, of course, but you could. Not far away, the **Heritage Plantation** is a hotchpotch of objects ranging from antique cars to Currier & Ives prints and antique firearms. It includes several museums and a Shaker barn built on 76 acres (30.5 hectares) of grounds, and offers children rides on a 19th-century carousel.

Provincetown was the first place where Miles Standish and his *Mayflower* boatload of Pilgrims landed in America on 21 November 1620 (they quickly decided against the site and moved on to Plymouth; *see p250*). Today Provincetown supports a booming tourist trade and a notorious nightlife on three-and-a-half miles of beach. A year-round artist community has sprung up here as well over the years. **The Provincetown Art Association & Museum** has offered exhibitions, lectures and classes since 1914, while **DNA**, a well-respected local gallery, shows daring, recent work. Oh, and, one more thing worth knowing – Provincetown is also one of the gayest places on earth (*see p259* **Having a gay old time**).

Woods Hole, on the Cape's far south-west tip, is one of the world's great centres of maritime research. The **Woods Hole Oceanographic Institute**, which assembled the team that, in 1985, located the remains of the *Titanic*, has a group of exhibitions on the subject of undersea exploration. The more visitor-friendly **Marine Biological Laboratory** offers weekend guided tours and a slide show in summer.

Hyannis, halfway out on the Upper Cape, is the transport hub of the area, with rail and airport services and ferries to both Nantucket and Martha's Vineyard. It came to the forefront of popular awareness as the summer resort home of the Kennedy clan and remains inseparably linked to visions of a suntanned JFK at the helm of a skiff. The family's well-known compound is walled off from view south of town in Hyannisport but there's an extensive photographic display at the **JFK Hyannis Museum**.

Chatham is a chic little town that has been continuously settled since the mid 17th century. In its earliest days, Chatham's perch on the shipping lanes made it a favourite location for 'moon-cussers', bands of pirate wreckers who roamed the beaches with false lights that led boats aground to be pillaged. Chatham's most prominent landmark today is one that guides sailors safely back from the sea, the **Chatham Light** lighthouse. The town still plays host to a substantial population of fishermen and it accommodates the tourist trade in genteel style with an interesting collection of crafts and antiques shops downtown.

For a glimpse of primal New England, head south of town past the Chatham Light onto **Morris Island** and take the ferry to the **Monomoy Island National Wildlife Refuge**. This barrier island, born out of a hurricane some 40 years ago, serves as a stopover point for bird migration in the Atlantic Flyway.

The Atlantic Coast of Cape Cod comprises the aforementioned Cape Cod National Seashore. It is here that you'll find some of Massachusetts' loveliest and liveliest beaches. **Nauset Beach**, at the southern tip outside the town of **East Orleans**, has the best surf and

Sandwich's **Glass Museum.** *See p254.*

draws the youngest, liveliest crowd. This last, narrow stretch of the Cape has escaped most of the horrors of over-commercialisation. **Wellfleet Harbour**, on the bay side, encloses the 1,000-acres (401.5-hectares) that make up the **Wellfleet Bay Wildlife Sanctuary**. Here the Massachusetts Audubon Society sponsors tours and lectures and (for a fee) allows camping. Over the years, both Wellfleet and nearby Truro have developed reputations as artists' and writers' retreats. And deservedly so. Writers have long been attracted by the beauty of the place. Edna Saint Vincent Millay and Edmund Wilson lived in Wellfleet in the 1920s; Edward Hopper liked the bleak light of the high dunes outside Truro. Most recently, Sebastian Junger penned his novel, *The Perfect Storm*, in his Truro vacation house.

DNA

288 Bradford Street, Provincetown (1-508 487 7700). **Open** daily in the summer. **Admission** free.

Glass Museum

129 Main Street, Sandwich (1-508 888 0251). **Open** 9.30am-4.30pm Wed-Sun. **Admission** $3.50. **Credit** Disc, MC, V.

Heritage Plantation

67 Grove Street, Sandwich (1-508 888 3300). **Open** *May-Oct* 10am-5pm daily. **Admission** $9; $8, $4.50 concessions. **Credit** AmEx, Disc, MC, V.

JFK Hyannis Museum

397 Main Street, Hyannis (1-508 790 3077). **Open** *Mar-Sept* 9am-4pm Wed-Sat.

Marine Biological Laboratory

100 Water Street, Woods Hole (508 289 7623). **Open** 8am-5pm Mon-Fri. **Admission** free.

Provincetown Art Association & Museum

460 Commercial Street, Provincetown (1-508 487 1750). **Open** *Summer* 10am-4pm daily. *Winter* noon-4pm Sat, Sun. **Admission** $3; $1 concessions. **Credit** AmEx, Disc, MC, V.

Wellfleet Bay Wildlife Sanctuary

291 State Highway, Route 6A, Wellfleet Harbour (1-508 349 2615). **Open** *May-Oct* 9am-4.30pm daily. *Nov-Apr* 9am-4.30pm Tue-Sun. **Admission** $3; $2 concessions. **Credit** MC, V.

Woods Hole Oceanographic Institute

15 School Street, Woods Hole (1-508 289 2663). **Open** *Apr-Dec* 10am-4pm Fri, Sat; noon-4pm Sun. **Admission** $2 donation requested. **No credit cards**.

Where to stay

Lodging is extremely varied the whole length of Cape Cod. The rule of thumb is that the towns on the Cape Cod Bay side of the peninsula are more interesting and relaxing. Rates tend to drop the further down the Cape you are from Provincetown, though there are bargains there too, if you book well in advance. And of course, off-season rates drop precipitously (and the Cape has a wonderful austerity once the tourists have gone). Far down on the Cape's shoulder, in Sandwich, the **1837 Federal Village Inn** (4 Jarves Street; 1-800 922 9989; rates $75-$105) counts a charming wraparound porch among its amenities. Mid-Cape, in Barnstable, is the **Beechwood** (2839 Route 6A; 1-800 609 6618; rates $90-$170) which nestles among the trees after which it is named and includes a full breakfast in its rate. Chatham's historical district has a number of carefully restored, period-furnished mid 19th-century inns, but they can be expensive in season. Wellfleet is a good place to find inexpensive, if undistinguished, alternatives on the lower Cape. On the other side, the 18th-century **Colonial High Brewster Inn** (964 Satucket Road, Brewster; 1-508 896 3636; rates $90-$210) has beautiful gardens and a rural setting. To be where the action is, head to Provincetown's most luxurious lodging (with prices to match), the **Brass Key** (67 Bradford Street; 1-800 842 9858; rates $100-$325). **The Commons** (386 Commercial Street; 1-508 487 7800) offers slightly lower prices and more history. Out of the centre, the rugged charm of the **White Horse** (500 Commercial Street; 1-508 487 1790; rates $50-$75, studio apartments $90-$125) is a penny-saver's delight.

Where to eat & drink

Dining in Provincetown runs the gamut. Upmarket interpretations of New American cuisine are the order of the day at **Front Street** (230 Commercial Street; 1-508 487 9715); decent contemporary Italian food can be had at reasonable prices at the venerable **Ciro**

and Sal's (4 Kiley Court; 1-508 487 0049); and stylish light fare can be had at **Café Heaven** (199 Commercial Street; 1-508 487 9639). The drive back to Wellfleet is worthwhile for dinner at **Aesop's Tables** (316 Main Street; 1-508 349 6450; closed in the winter), which shows an especially inventive touch with fresh local ingredients. Phone ahead wherever you go, as off-season hours are unpredictable and sometimes non-existent. Provincetown also has a significant Portuguese community, émigrés from the Azores who came to work the fishing boats. Their cuisine is served in interesting surroundings at **The Moors** (5 Bradford Street; 1-508 487 0840), known for its spicy way with swordfish and pork. Or simply grab a loaf of fresh Portuguese sweet bread from the **Provincetown Portuguese Bakery** (299 Commercial Street; 1-508 487 1803) and take a stroll downtown.

Getting there

By car

Cape Cod's gateway, the Sagamore Bridge, is 30 miles (48.3km) south-east of Boston on Route 3, the most direct route.

By bus & rail

The Plymouth and Brockton Bus (1-508 771 6191) operates every hour from Boston's South Station to Hyannis and then on to Provincetown. The Cape Cod Regional Transit Authority (1-800 352 7155) and Bonanza (*see p278*) cover the mid-Cape region by bus. Provincetown runs local shuttle bus services in town during the summer months.

By boat

Bay State Cruises (457 1428) runs a daily ferry service from Boston to Provincetown in the summer months and at weekends in spring and autumn. The journey to Provincetown takes three hours and boats depart from Commonwealth Pier.

Tourist information

Cape Cod Chamber of Commerce

Junction of Routes 6 and 122, Hyannis (1-508 362 3225/www.capecod.com). **Open** 9am-5pm daily.

Martha's Vineyard, Nantucket & New Bedford

Martha's Vineyard, Nantucket and New Bedford were once considered the holy trinity of whaling. It's also worth noting that Martha's Vineyard and Nantucket both sprang from the same glacial activity that created Cape Cod 12,000 years ago. And that the name Nantucket is a Native American word meaning 'faraway island', or 'land far out to sea'. And, heck, you might as well know that in Martha's Vineyard they call tree frogs 'pinkletinks'. But what's really worth knowing is this: if you're visiting Boston in the summer and wondering where all the people are … they're all over here.

The first recreational use of **Martha's Vineyard** was for Methodist camp meetings in the summer of 1835. These days, summer residents include glitterati such as Spike Lee, Walter Cronkite, Carly Simon and former president Bill Clinton. Of the Vineyard's main towns, **Edgartown** is the largest and oldest. A walk along the harbourside, past the stately captains' mansions on Water Street, reveals the prosperity they brought back from the sea. The island's historical society keeps the **Vineyard Historical Museum** replete with scrimshaw, ships' models and other artefacts of local history.

Oak Bluffs has a swell collection of Victorian gingerbread cottages (1 Trinity Park; 1-508 693 7784) and the wonderful **1876 Flying Horses Carousel** (33 Circuit Avenue; 1-508 693 9481), reputedly the country's oldest. A premier example of American folk art, it operates until 10pm for a dollar a ride throughout the summer. Stick to Oak Bluffs for the island's liveliest late-night action, too, chiefly at the **Atlantic Connection** (124 Circuit Avenue; 1-508 693 7129), where celebrity-spotting is part of the fun, and the **Ritz** (1 Circuit Avenue; 1-508 693 9851) for live blues.

Vineyard Haven (also known as Tisbury), on the north coast, was long the island's chief port and is where the old colonial atmosphere is best preserved. And you may have heard of the unparalleled beauty of a town on the western tip of Martha's Vineyard called **Gay Head**. The voters recently legally changed the name of their town to **Aquinnah**, in honour of the area's original Native American population. Aquinnah's public beach, outside town, is famous for dramatic mile-long cliffs of multi-coloured clay and the great views from the trails above them.

Nantucket has a reputation as the Vineyard's prim little sister and it strives to keep it that way. First settled by religious refugees from the Puritan colony, it was the world's foremost whaling port throughout the 18th century. Even in the long period of decline that followed, the picturesque island was a favourite summer retreat for well-to-do holiday-makers. When, after World War II, an explosion of middle-class tourism threatened to change Nantucket's quiet charm, the locals rose up in the cause of historic preservation. These days new construction in most of Nantucket is carefully regulated and must be designed to

Gorgeous vistas are everywhere on Martha's Vineyard.

blend harmoniously with the past. Not surprisingly, the **Nantucket Historical Association** offers a well-organised tour of Nantucket town's historic district. Highlights include the **Jethro Coffin House**, a 17th-century saltbox that is the island's oldest building, the last of the town's 18th-century mills, and the **Old Gaol**, a very civilised one, it is said, from which prisoners were allowed home for the night.

For those who are less turned off by the whole idea than interested in the intricate, exhausting realities and terrors of the whaler's trade, there is the **New Bedford's Whaling Museum** in the heart of the 16 square blocks of the historic waterfront district. The Museum offers a fascinating look into the history of this politically incorrect industry. Interesting note: Herman Melville based his novel *Moby Dick* on the true and tragic tale of the *Essex*, a Nantucket whaling ship rammed by a whale off the coast of South America.

There are also seasonal tours that form at regular intervals across the street from the museum at the old bank building. Volunteer guides offer two dock walks through the real day-to-day labour of fishermen; a historic homes tour; and the **Black Heritage Trail**. The latter includes the blacksmith shop of Lewis Temple, the inventor of a toggle harpoon that revolutionised the whaling industry in the early 1800s. It also includes the home of Sgt. William H Carney, a member of the 54th Massachusetts regiment, on which the film *Glory* was based.

Nantucket Historical Association

15 Broad Street, Nantucket (1-508 228 1894). **Open** *Apr-Sept* 10am-4pm Sat, Sun. **Admission** $12; $8 concessions. **Credit** AmEx, Disc, MC, V.

New Bedford's Whaling Museum

15 Broad Street, Nantucket (1-508 228 1894). **Open** *Apr-Sept* 10am-4pm Sat, Sun. **Admission** $12; $8 concessions. **Credit** AmEx, Disc, MC, V.

Vineyard Historical Museum

59 School Street, Martha's Vineyard (1-508 627 4441). **Open** *Apr-Sept* 10am-5pm Tue-Sat. *Oct-Mar* 10am-5pm Wed-Sat. **Admission** $7; $4 concessions. **Credit** Disc, MC, V.

Where to stay & eat

As a result of the celebrities on Martha's Vineyard, the bluebloods on Nantucket, the tourists and the need to import most produce, good dining on Martha's Vineyard and Nantucket is not cheap. Visitors who wish to take the plunge on Martha's Vineyard go to

Savoir Fare (14 Church Street, Edgartown; 1-508 627 9864; closed in winter), which dishes up New American food that drew Bill Clinton when he was last in the vicinity; **L'Etoile** (27 South Summer Street, Edgartown; 1-508 627 5187) has a renowned contemporary French menu. And, love it or loathe it, the tourist-packed **Black Dog Tavern** (Beach Street Exit, Vineyard Haven; 1-508 693 9223) is a good place to load up on a huge breakfast or to watch the sunset. On Nantucket, the classy village of Siasconset contains **Chanticleer** (9 New Street; 1-508 257 6231), where you'll pay through the nose for great classic French cuisine and an outstanding wine list.

The less finicky budget traveller can find perfectly nice, cheap accommodation throughout the season in hostels on either island. In Nantucket there is the **Star of the Sea Youth Hostel** (31 Western Avenue; 1-800 909 4776, rates $29); while in Martha's Vineyard there is always the **Hostelling International-Martha's Vineyard** (Edgartown, West Tisbury Road, Box 3158; 1-508 693 2665; rates $15-$18). Beyond that, your cost per night is going to be pretty high, if you can even find a room. In the Vineyard, a reasonable blend of comfort and convenience at relatively modest prices can be found in Edgartown at the **Victorian Inn** (24 South Water Street; 1-508 627 4784; rates $105-$325), a former whaling captain's home. Prices run even higher among the swells of Nantucket, but the local landmark, **Jared Coffin House** (29 Broad Street; 1-800 248 2405; rates $65-$210), is not too exorbitant and is packed with history. Nantucket has a wealth of B&Bs listed through services such as **Nantucket Accommodations** (1-508 228 9559).

Get carried away in Provincetown.

Getting there

By boat

The islands of Martha's Vineyard and Nantucket are to the south of Cape Cod. Both are easily reached as they are served by several ferry companies year round. The Massachusetts Steamship Authority (1-508 477 8600) has a year-round service from two Cape Cod locations: the trip from Woods Hole to Martha's Vineyard takes 45 minutes, and the journey from Hyannis to Nantucket takes two hours. There are also several privately run ferries that make the trip from the Cape to the Vineyard in the summer: Island Queen (1-508 548 4800) and Pied Piper (1-508 548 9400) run from Falmouth; Hy-Line (1-508 778 2600) from Hyannis; and the Schamonchi (1-508 997 1688) runs from New Bedford. Hy-Line also has a summer service to Nantucket.

Top five Mass beaches

Plum Island, Newburyport

This island not only has miles of gorgeous sandy beaches, it is also among the premier birding spots in the world. Um, and that's birds as in snowy owl, long-billed dowitcher and brown-headed cowbird. *See p253.*

Aquinnah Beaches, Martha's Vineyard

A short hike up Moshup Trail and you're taking in the surf beneath eminently dramatic mile-long multi-coloured clay cliffs. *See p256.*

Wingaersheek Beach, Cape Ann

Puzzling name, gorgeous beach. One of the best in the Cape. *See p252.*

Long Beach, Cape Ann

The tremendous popularity of this long expanse of beige sand with unusually warm water and calm surf has not yet managed to destroy its beauty. *See p252.*

Nauset Beach, Cape Cod

The heaviest surf and liveliest crowd on the Cape. The strong surf here provides excellent surfing and body-boarding, and its white-sand beckons. *See p254.*

Having a gay old time

There's just something about Provincetown. This town is so laid back it's almost falling down, and that 'anything goes' atmosphere has always had a way of attracting people who like to let their hair down. In the past decade, here on Cape Cod, that has been the gay community.

Everything about P-Town (as aficionados call it) is extreme – even its seasonal shifts are dramatic. In November, P-Town is a sleepy little community; in July, it's the queer version of Disneyland. As straight folks head to Martha's Vineyard, gay people from throughout the country migrate to Provincetown as soon as the days get long.

GETTING THERE

Provincetown is a two-and-a-half hour drive from Boston, usually much longer in weekend traffic. If you don't feel up to the hassle of renting a car, you can fly there (expensive), catch a bus from South Station (cheap), or take the ferry from the waterfront (the most fun). In 2000, the new high-speed ferry service cut the travel time to just under two hours, with a round-trip fare of $40.

You don't really need a car once you're there: the town is tiny, and most people either walk or rent bikes.

RESTAURANTS

For posh meals, check out the **Martin House** (157 Commercial Street; 1-508 487 1327) or **Front Street** (230 Commercial Street; 1-508 487 9715; open summer only). For simpler fare, there's **Fat Jack's** (335 Commercial Street; 1-508 487 4822) or the **Post Office Café** (303 Commercial Street; 1-508 487 3892).

ACCOMMODATION

Though there are any number of queer guesthouses in town, it's always best to book as early as possible for summer stays. A few tried-and-true Victorian B&Bs are **The Sandpiper** (165 Commercial Street; 1-508 487 1928), the **Beaconlite Guest House** (12 Winthrop Street; 1-508 487 9603) and the **Brass Key Guest House** (9 Court Street; 1-508 487 9005).

THE ROUTINE

Whether you're a girl or boy, there seems to be a ritual that everyone follows. First the beach, then the tea dance at the **Boat Slip** (161 Commercial Street; 1-508 487 1669; open summer only). After tea it's the **Pied Piper** – considered by its fans to be America's best lesbian bar (193A Commercial Street; 1-508 487 1527; open summer only) – for a drink and a bit of a jig. Then you're on your own for dinner and a nap before regrouping with friends for drinks at your favourite bar.

At around midnight, just about everybody ends up at the **Atlantic House** (4-6 Masonic Place; 1-508 487 3821) for a final dance. All the bars close at 1am in P-Town, and everyone who hasn't already hooked up strolls over to **Spiritus Pizza** (190 Commercial Street; 1-508 487 2808; open summer only) for a slice and a chat. Nearly half the town's there by the time Spiritus closes at 2 am.

FURTHER INFORMATION

For a free directory of gay- and lesbian-owned hotels, restaurants, bars and services, contact the **Provincetown Business Guild** (115 Bradford Street; 1-508 487 2313/ 1-800 637 8696).

By car, bus & air

Check with the ferry services about transporting cars to the islands, since there are restrictions. Most people find they don't need one, anyway. Both islands have extensive shuttle bus services during most of the year courtesy of the Martha's Vineyard Transit Authority (1-508 627 7448) and the Nantucket Regional Transit Authority (1-508 228 7025). Both islands are suitable for cycling. Besides, all the major car rental firms are found in force if you really need to drive. Better yet, rent a moped at one of the many shops on the islands. They're extremely popular (although, and this is understandable, the locals have mixed feelings about them). Cape Air (1-508 771 6944) has flights from Boston to Hyannis, Provincetown, Martha's Vineyard or Nantucket.

Tourist information

Martha's Vineyard Chamber of Commerce

Vineyard Haven, Martha's Vineyard (1-508 693 0085/www.mvy.com). **Open** 9am-5pm Mon-Fri.

Nantucket Island Chamber of Commerce

48 Main Street, Nantucket (1-508 228 1700/ www.nantucketchamber.org).

New Bedford Area Chamber of Commerce

794 Purchase Street, New Bedford (1-508 999-5231/ www.nbchamber.com).

Picturesque Western Mass

From lesbian villages to art communities, how green is Happy Valley.

After driving through the relatively drab farmland of central Massachusetts, the picturesque villages and leafy countryside of western Mass offer welcome respite. Part of the larger Connecticut River Valley, this area is known as the Pioneer Valley, for it was America's first frontier. Locals often refer to it as Happy Valley, which reveals more about the counter-cultural, neo-hippie vibe of the area than its actual disposition.

Over the centuries, in fact, things have been less than happy here. In the early years, the valley was the site of some of the worst struggles between native tribes and settlers. In the 19th century, entrepreneurs harnessed the river to power the mills of early industry, and factory life still marks the cities of the lower valley. Local manufacturing fell on hard times in the years after World War II and has never fully recovered. Still, the wealth the mills generated in those early years endowed a number of highly regarded colleges that give the area much of its character.

Pioneer Valley

Much of the valley was once the floor of a vast glacial lake that stretched from central Connecticut into Vermont and New Hampshire, and the remains of that sediment-rich floor make the soil exceptionally fertile. That soil drew not only the first European colonists, but the Native Americans who preceded them, which led to a good deal of friction between the two groups. After they had routed the area's native inhabitants, the Puritans cultivated the wild territory into farmland and built what were to become archetypal New England towns, with their village greens, pristine spires and dinky general stores. Meanwhile, a society of independent farmers and artisans blossomed.

The first European settlement was the town of **Deerfield** (just south-west of Greenfield), where the indigenous people's attachment to the land proved very strong. Inter-tribal warfare and waves of epidemic had almost destroyed the Pocumtuck tribe that had occupied the site for several thousand years, and yet they returned to contest the European invasion fiercely. Twice in Deerfield's early years the settlers were overwhelmed in battle and the town was abandoned. The first occasion was during King Philip's War, in the 1670s, after which the land lay vacant for seven years. The second occurred early in the course of the French and Indian wars, when the town was raided and burned to the ground, and the survivors marched off several hundred epic miles into captivity in Quebec.

Tokens of these struggles and other aspects of the period are on display at the village's museum, **Memorial Hall**. The building dates back to 1798, when it first served as part of the elite private school, Deerfield Academy. Much of the rest of the town is of similar age and has been carefully preserved, not as a replica, but as something close to a living shrine to pre-industrial life. The heart of town, known only as 'The Street', is almost entirely made up of houses dating from the 18th and 19th centuries. Most of them are still privately owned, but 14 of them are open to the general public. Tours are conducted by **Historic Deerfield**.

A short drive east of Deerfield on Route 2 is the town of **Shelburne Falls**, where a local group maintains the **Bridge of Flowers**, a 40-foot (12-metre) trolley bridge whose only burden now is flower beds. It's a singularly delightful example of roadside America.

South of Deerfield, **Amherst** alone nurtures three institutions. The most prestigious is **Amherst College** (100 Bolt Wood Avenue; 1-413 542 2000), a small, liberal arts college in the classic mode. It dates from 1821 when it included the lexicographer Noah Webster among its original trustees. More recently, the bard of New England, Robert Frost, was a long-time faculty member. To the north is the immense campus and 25,000-strong student body of 'U-Mass', the **University of Massachusetts** (Massachusetts Avenue; 1-413 545 0306), whose most famous alumnus – the basketball genius Julius Irving (Dr J) – took no doctorate but holds the title just the same. In the hills south of town is **Hampshire College** (Route 116; 1-413 549 4600), which is known for its experimental orientation and counter-culture air. The **National Yiddish Book Center**

(1-800 535 2000), an organisation dedicated to rescuing unwanted and discarded Yiddish books, is located on the grounds of the college. Besides storing over one million volumes in their distinctively designed building – modelled to resemble an 18th-century Eastern European village – the centre features exhibits, concerts and lectures on Yiddish and Jewish culture.

Further south, along Route 116, the town of **South Hadley** consists almost entirely of **Mount Holyoke College** (1-413 538 2000). Founded in 1837, this was the first women's college in the country and is the oldest of the so-called 'Seven Sisters' – the seven elite women's schools that once served as the counterpart of the then all-male Ivy League. The so-called 'Belle of Amherst', Emily Dickinson, was among Mount Holyoke's first graduates, but it was in the town to the north that the poet was born and spent most of her life. **The Dickinson Homestead**, where she spent the final 30 years of her life in seclusion, is now a National Historic Monument.

Another of the Seven Sisters, **Smith College** (1-413 584 2700), is located a little to the north-west, in the city of **Northampton**. The largest women's liberal arts school in the nation, Smith's attractive and expensive red-brick quadrangles cover a good deal of the downtown area. The full pageant of the area's past can be studied in the period homes restored and maintained by **Historic Northampton** (46 Bridge Street; 1-413 584 6011).

Mount Holyoke College.

Northampton is the de facto cultural and shopping centre for the region, with many book stores, boutiques, bars and restaurants scattered throughout the lovely downtown. It also boasts an excellent music scene; local residents include members of the rock bands Sonic Youth and Dinosaur Jr. Partly because of the single-sex Smith College, Northampton is also home to a large lesbian population. Numerous establishments cater to this crowd, making it a tourist destination for the region's gay community. Like a Berkeley of the east, Northampton is a hotbed of progressive politics, alternative lifestyles and neo-hippie musings.

All the local colleges sponsor museums, galleries and individual cultural events that are open to the public, so there's generally something of interest happening every day of the week in the Amherst-Northampton area. Nearby, the countryside is filled with artisans and organic farmers, mostly graduates from local colleges who fell in love with the area called Happy Valley and never left. This academic and artistic population, combined with the significant lesbian community, gives the entire area a left-of-centre feel that is unique to the region.

Further south

The southernmost portion of the Pioneer Valley is less refined and its two chief towns are industrial centres. **Holyoke** is a planned industrial city that was once an important papermaking centre. Though it has fallen on tough times, the glory days are recounted at the exhibition centre at **Heritage State Park**.

Situated further south, **Springfield** has managed much better for itself. It remains the largest city in western Massachusetts and a significant manufacturing centre. The US military bought small arms from here from revolutionary times up until the Vietnam War. This has always been the weaponry capital of the US. In the 1800s, the city was synonymous with its eponymous piece of weaponry, the Springfield Rifle. The **Armory** was closed in 1968 and now houses a museum dedicated to the history of small arms.

Another American mechanical device that has gone out of production and passed into the Valhalla of cult veneration is the Indian Motorcycle. Forget about Harleys; cognoscenti will want to visit the **Indian Motorcycle Museum** (33 Hendee Street; 1-413 737 2624).

But, in the end, Springfield's most successful and enduring (and non-violent) product was a game. It was in Springfield that Dr James Naismith, looking for a form of indoor sport suitable to the long New England winters, suspended two wicker baskets at either end of a gymnasium floor, and invented basketball. The game has come a long way since 1891 and every loving detail and curiosity of its history is explored at the **Basketball Hall of Fame** (*see p120*).

If you want to get the most outrageously large dose of ersatz Americana, make a detour 30 miles (48 kilometres) east of Springfield on I-90 and travel a few miles south on I-84 to **Sturbridge**. Adjoining Sturbridge you'll find **Old Sturbridge Village**, a 200-acre (80-hectare) living museum to which more than 40 19th-century buildings have been moved from all over New England. The structures have been fully restored and populated with costumed interpreters who re-enact the everyday life of rural 1830s New England.

Armory

1 Armory Square, Springfield (1-413 734 8551). **Open** 10am-4.30pm Tue-Sun. **Admission** free.

The Dickinson Homestead

280 Main Street, Amherst (1-413 542 8161). **Open** *Mar-Dec* 10am-4pm daily; tours offered hourly. **Admission** $5; $4, $3 concessions. **No credit cards**.

Historic Deerfield

Hall Tavern, The Street, Deerfield (1-413 774 5581). **Open** 9.30am-4.30pm daily. **Admission** $12; $6 concessions. **Credit** MC, V.

Heritage State Park

221 Appleton Street, Holyoke (1-413 534 1723). **Open** noon-4.30pm Tue-Sun. **Admission** free.

Memorial Hall

8 Memorial Street, Deerfield (1-413 774 3768). **Open** *May-Oct* 9.30am-4.30pm daily. **Admission** $12; $6 concessions. **Credit** MC, V.

Old Sturbridge Village

1 Old Sturbridge Road, Springfield (1-800 733 1830). **Open** 10am-4pm daily. **Admission** $18 adults, $17 seniors, $9 ages 6-15. **Credit** AmEx, Disc, MC, V.

Where to stay & eat

In Deerfield, old-world charm can be found at the **Deerfield Inn** (81 Old Main Street; 1-413 774 5587; rates $148-$254), which dates from 1884. In Northampton, there is the **Hotel Northampton** (36 King Street; 1-413 584 3100; rates $160-$205), and in Amherst the **Lord Jeffrey Inn** (30 Boltwood Avenue; 1-413 253 2576; rates $79-$189).

In Shelburne Falls the **Copper Angel Restaurant** (2 State Street; 1-413 625 2727) features inventive vegetarian dishes. In Amherst, to have a true U-Mass experience, crowd into **Antonio's** (31 North Pleasant Street, Amherst; 1-413 253 0808), a pizza parlour with some of the best slices north of New York. In Northampton there are more options: the **Eastside Grill** (19 Strong Avenue; 1-413 586 3347) specialises in spicy Cajun dishes, while the **Haymarket Cafe** (185 Main Street, 1-413 586 9969) serves eclectic veggie fare.

The nightlife is hottest in Northampton, where **The Iron Horse** (20 Center Street; 1-413 584 0610) is an excellent venue with an eclectic range of live music, and **Pearl Street** (10 Pearl Street; 1-413 584 0610) is a popular dance club.

The rich colours of the Berkshires attract

Getting there

By car

The Pioneer Valley is 90 miles (145km) west of Boston, along the Mass Turnpike (I-90). Route 2 is the most scenic way to explore the Mohawk Trail.

By bus

Greyhound links Boston and Springfield; Peter Pan and Bonanza (*for all, see p278*) both operate between Boston and the major towns of western Massachusetts. The Pioneer Valley Transit Authority (1-413 781 7882) provides local service.

Trips Out of Town

admirers from around the world.

Tourist information

Amherst Area Chamber of Commerce

409 Main Street, Amherst (1-413 253 0700).
Open 8am-4.30pm Mon-Fri.

Greater Northampton Chamber of Commerce

99 Pleasant Street, Northampton (1-413 584 1900).
Open 9am-5pm Mon-Fri.

Greater Springfield Convention & Visitors' Bureau

1441 Main Street, Springfield (1-413 787 1548).
Open 9am-5pm Mon-Fri.

The Berkshires

High and rugged enough to give the land character, low and gentle enough to make it accessible, the Berkshires make westernmost Massachusetts a most inviting retreat. Like the Pioneer Valley, the area has gone through stages of farming settlement and factory growth. It's long been known as the playground of the intellectual elite of both New York and Boston: Hawthorne and Melville picnicked here; Henry James dropped in on Edith Wharton. The Gilded Age's plutocrats built so many of their elaborate 'summer cottages' here that the Berkshires were labelled 'inland Newport'. The residue of all that money and culture is the theatre, dance and music festivals that the region is known for today.

Williamstown, near both the New York and Vermont state lines, is the home of **Williams College** (880 Main Street; 1-413 597 3131). This is another of New England's fine, small, liberal arts schools – the 'little Ivies'. The 200-year-old college has some interesting architecture and a good museum of art, but the town's aesthetic gem is the **Clark Art Institute**, which numbers more than 30 Renoirs in its collection. Then there is the **Williamstown Theater Festival** (1-413 597 3400), a summer-long extravaganza that offers everything from classical drama to contemporary experimentation.

East of Williamstown on Route 2 is the city of **North Adams**, a former industrial centre distinguished by the presence of the impressive **Massachusetts Museum of Contemporary Art** popularly known as Mass MOCA. Opened to great fanfare in 1999, Mass MOCA is a multidisciplinary arts centre built into an impressive 13-acre, 19th-century mill complex. Robert Rauschenberg and Joseph Beuys have exhibited in Mass MOCA's massive galleries, while their performance space has hosted musicians as diverse as Phillip Glass, Merce Cunningham and Los Lobos.

Further south, **Pittsfield** is the region's largest city, and also its geographic and governmental centre. Though not much to look at, the city does hold a few points of interest, and rather a strange brew at that. **Hancock Shaker Village**, 5 miles (8 kilometres) out of town, is a restoration of what was an American Shaker community between 1790 and 1960. Thankfully, the austere life and beautifully spare crafts of the Shakers are exhibited without the otherwise ubiquitous rigmarole of period costume and play acting. Also just outside town is **Arrowhead**, a place for bibliophiles to soak up New England's rich literary tradition. Here, from 1850 to 1863 Herman Melville lived, schmoozed with Nathaniel Hawthorne, peered into the soul of man and the eyes of god, and wrote a book about a whale. The **Berkshire Museum** is right in town, though its sensibility is all over the place: local history, glowing rocks, stuffed birds, Babylonian tablets and live fish.

Lenox, **Lee** and **Stockbridge** cluster above, on and below I-90 respectively. Lenox is gorgeous: a sumptuously tended village of gracious old homes and well-manicured lawns under immense old oaks. Stockbridge is cut from the same silken cloth, trimmed with piping of bohemian funk. Lee is working class: an old paper-making town – and it shows. Each of them is a summer home for one of the muses.

Lenox's star attraction is the famed summer-long series of concerts at **Tanglewood**, a 500-acre (200-hectare) estate south of town. Conductor Seiji Ozawa and the Boston Symphony Orchestra lead the annual charge, with guest reinforcements from everyone who's anyone in classical music. The 5,000-seat 'Shed' hosts performers of the jazz and pop stripe too (1-413 637 5165/www.bso.org).

Long before the music started, Nathaniel Hawthorne stayed here long enough to write his children's classic, *Tanglewood Tales*. Another literary landmark is Edith Wharton's 'cottage', **The Mount**. Here, in the early years of the century, Dame Edith entertained her peers among the ruling class: all the better to dissect them in *The Age of Innocence*.

Lee is the centre of the dance universe for ten weeks every summer, at the **Jacob's Pillow Dance Festival** (1-413 243 0745), 10 miles (16 kilometres) east of town on Route 20. The nation's foremost such event, the 'Pillow' stems jointly from the mama and papa of all modern dance, Martha Graham and Ted Shawn. Besides the usual giants of contemporary dance strutting on the main stage, genre groups take their turn while the fledglings perform for free on the lawns.

For its part, Stockbridge hosts its own **Berkshire Theater Festival** (1-413 298 5576) from late June until late August. The main stage, in a 100-year-old Stanford White 'casino', attracts top-flight thespians in productions of the classics; a newer stage, the Unicorn, shows new and experimental work. And because Norman Rockwell lived for more than 30 years in this town (whose appearance embodies the ideal of his clean-cut vision), Stockbridge contains the mother can of American corn. For better or worse, the **Norman Rockwell Museum** *(see p120*) holds the highest concentration of the artist's work anywhere outside the morgue of the *Saturday Evening Post*. Go and see it, and repent of your cynicism.

Arrowhead

780 Holmes Road, Pittsfield (1-413 442 1793). **Open** 9.30am-5pm daily. **Admission** $5; $1-$4.50 concessions. **Credit** AmEx, MC, V.

The Berkshire Museum

39 South Street, Pittsfield (1-413 443 7171). **Open** 10am-5pm Mon-Sat; noon-5 Sun. **Admission** $6 adults; $4-$6 concessions, free under-3s. **Credit** AmEx, MC, V.

Clark Art Institute

225 South Street, Williamstown (1-413 458 9545). **Open** *July-Aug* 10am-5pm daily. *Sept-Jun* 10am-5pm Tue-Sun. **Admission** $10. **Credit** AmEx, MC, V.

Hancock Shaker Village

Route 20, on corner of Route 41, Pittsfield (1-800 817 1137) **Open** 10am-3pm daily. **Admission** $10 adults, free under-18s. **Credit** AmEx, Disc, MC, V.

Massachusetts Museum of Contemporary Art

87 Marshall Street, North Adams (1-413 664 4481). **Open** 11am-5pm Mon, Wed-Sun. **Admission** $6 adults; $3-$4 concessions. **Credit** AmEx, MC, V.

The Mount

2 Plunkett Street, Lenox (1-413 637 1899). **Open** *May-Oct* 9am-3pm daily. **Admission** $6 adults; $4.50-$5.50 concessions; free under-12s. **Credit** MC, V.

Where to stay & eat

Lodging in the Berkshires is varied. Lenox has a slew of venerable old inns in the centre around Church Street. Stockbridge holds the pre-eminent example of the species, the **Red Lion** (30 Main Street, Stockbridge; 1-413 298 5545; rooms $72-$175). For cheaper rates, phone the **Berkshire Visitors' Bureau** (*see below*) about local motels and B&Bs.

The **Church Street Cafe** (65 Church Street; 1-413 637 2745), in the heart of Lenox, is a local favourite for reasonably priced nouvelle American cooking. For variety, as well as economy, drive the extra few miles to West Stockbridge and the **Truc Orient Express** (3 Harris Street; 1-413 232 4204) and sample the delicate fare of Vietnam.

Getting there

By car

The Berkshires are a good three hours' drive west of Boston on the Mass Pike (I-90) – the distance to Pittsfield is 134 miles (216km). It takes longer on the lesser roads but you get a better sense of the country. If you're continuing on from the Pioneer Valley, consider taking Route 9 from Northampton to Pittsfield, or Route 2 through Shelburne Falls along the Mohawk Trail to Williamstown, both of which are well-maintained roads. Route 7 is the Berkshires' main street, the only highway running the length of the region from north to south.

By bus

As for the Pioneer Valley (*see p262*).

Tourist information

Berkshire Visitors' Bureau

Berkshire Common, West Street, Pittsfield (1-413 443 9186). **Open** 8.30am-5pm Mon-Fri.

Heading South

Into the Mystic.

Going south from Massachusetts you find the land flattening and the greenery changing to a more emerald hue. The towns here are charming; built on rolling green hills and in deep forests. They have names you cannot forget, while they look like some place you should remember. Wandering through this part of the country tends to make part of you wish you'd been born here. It seems it would be nice to have grown up behind those white picket fences. Instead, you learn quickly that you'll never be fully accepted here unless you did grow up in these parts. Don't let it bother you, though, you can still have a lovely time exploring it all before you go back home to the people who really love you.

Harriet Beecher Stowe House. *See p266.*

Connecticut

There are several points of interest clustered around the mouth of the Thames river in Connecticut's south-eastern corner. The first is the hauntingly named town of **Mystic** – an old whaling and shipbuilding centre that has converted 17 acres (6.8 hectares) of its waterfront into the **Mystic Seaport Museum**, a complex of ships, shops, homes and wharves where the life and crafts of 19th-century maritime New England are preserved and re-enacted. More than 400 period crafts are on display, and the repair and restoration of new additions to the collection are part of the show. The town achieved a modicum of fame a decade or so ago, when Julia Roberts made her debut in the independent film *Mystic Pizza,* which was filmed here.

Groton, just a few miles along on I-95, is a one-horse town, that horse being the nuclear submarine. The home of General Electric's Electric Boat division and a major US Navy submarine base, it has been the scene of frequent political demonstrations in the past, but both the protests and their focus have dwindled in the post-Cold War era. The original of these undersea monsters, the USS *Nautilus*, is on display at the **Submarine Force Museum** (Crystal Lake Road; 1-800 343 0079). Nearby, **New London** (further east still and directly on the Thames), is the home of the **US Coast Guard Academy** (15 Mohegan Avenue; 1-860 444 8444), which is open to the public on rare occasions.

North of these coastal towns, on either shore of the Thames, are two anomalous outcroppings of Las Vegas-style recreation. The remnants of two local Native American tribes have opened competing casinos in the towns of **Ledyard** and **Uncasville**. The former is the home of **Foxwoods** (39 Norwich Westerly Road, Ledyard; 1-800 752 9244; open 24-hours daily), run by the Mashantucket Pequot tribe; the latter is home to **Mohegan Sun** (1 Mohegan Sun Boulevard, Uncasville; 1-800 226 7711), run by the, um, last of the Mohegans. The Pequots make a big deal about the money they donate to the preservation of Native American arts and culture, mostly through the nearby **Pequot Museum and Research Center**.

The city of **New Haven**, about an hour's drive to the east, on Long Island Sound, is best known as the home of Ivy League stalwart **Yale University**. Harvard's traditional rival, and something of a conservative counterpoint to the latter's liberalism, Yale has a number of cultural institutions that welcome the public. The **Yale Art Gallery** is strong on French Impressionist and American Abstract Expressionist work; the **Yale Center for British Art** includes fine examples of Hogarth, Constable, Reynolds and Turner; in addition, the **Peabody Museum of Natural History** holds more than nine million specimens from a range of sciences and world cultures. The area around the campus has the eclectic assortment of clubs, bars, restaurants, shops and theatres one would expect, given the fact that college students populate the area.

The overwrought **Mark Twain House.**

The **Nook Farm** neighbourhood, on the east side of town, contains two literary landmarks. Samuel Clemens took the swag he'd earned under a pen name and purchased an immense (and immensely overwrought) Gothic mansion now known as the **Mark Twain House**. This is the home where the writer lived with his family from 1873 to 1897. Nearby at 77 Forest Street, the author of the anti-slavery novel *Uncle Tom's Cabin* lived in what is now called the **Harriet Beecher Stowe House**. Both houses have been restored, and are packed with period artefacts and author memorabilia and have regular guided tours.

In the far north-western corner of Connecticut is an attractive slice of bucolic New England that goes by the name of **Litchfield Hills**. It has a certain cachet as one of the further reaches of settlement for well-to-do New Yorkers who no longer live in New York (meaning that it is filled with New York commuters), but luckily, since the rustic flavour is what drew them here in the first place, they've done a good job of protecting it. So the village greens are undisturbed and the forest lies thick on the land. It's a bit of a drive from Boston – about three hours – but the area has all the charm of the Berkshires with the advantage of even less tourist development.

Harriet Beecher Stowe House

77 Forest Street, Nook Farm (1-860 525 9317). **Open** *June-Sept, Dec* 9.30am-4.30pm Tue-Sat; noon-4.30pm Sun. **Admission** $6.50; $6, $2.75 concessions. **Credit** AmEx, MC, V.

Mark Twain House

351 Farmington Avenue, New Haven (1-860 247 0998). **Open** 9.30am-5pm Mon-Wed, Thur-Sat; noon-5pm Sun. **Admission** $9; $8, $7, $5 concessions. **Credit** MC, V.

Mystic Seaport Museum

75 Greenmanville Avenue, Mystic (1-860 572 0711). **Open** 9am-5pm daily. **Admission** $16; $12 during winter. **Credit** AmEx, Disc, MC, V.

Pequot Museum & Research Center

Route 2, Ledyard (1-860 396 6800). **Open** 10am-6pm Mon, Wed-Sat, Sun. **Admission** $12; $10, $8 concessions, free under-5s. **Credit** AmEx, Disc, MC, V.

The placid beauty of the **Mystic Seaport** is always a draw.

The vivid colours of the **Litchfield Hills**.

Peabody Museum of Natural History

170 Whitney Avenue, New Haven (1-203 432 5050).
Open 10am-5pm Mon-Sat, noon-5pm Sun.
Admission $5; $3 concession. **Credit** MC, V.

Yale Art Gallery

1111 Chapel Street, New Haven (1-203 432 0600).
Open 10am-5pm Tue-Sat; 1pm-6pm Sun.
Admission free.

Yale Center for British Art

1080 Chapel Street, New Haven (1-203 432 2800).
Open 10am-5pm Tue-Sat; noon-5pm Sun.
Admission free.

Where to stay

The Inn at Mystic (Routes 27 and 1; 1-800 237 2415; rates $65-$275) is outside town but a great place to stay for a wonderful ocean view. In New Haven, the **Three Chimneys Inn** (1201 Chapel Street; 1-203 789 1201; all rates $180 plus tax) is a restored Victorian lodging that's moderately expensive but about what you'd expect for an 'old Eli' (read: Yale) traditional lodging. Litchfield, in the hills of the same name, has the **Tollgate Hill** (Route 202 at Tollgate Road; 1-800 445 3903; rates $90-$175), a 250-year-old tavern and stagecoach stop situated on 10 tree-lined acres (4 hectares). **Litchfield Inn** (433 Bantam Road; 1-860 567 4503; rates $105-$200), a colonial-style building ringed by evergreens in winter and extensive flower beds in summer. For B&Bs in the Litchfield Hills, contact the local Travel Council (*see below*).

Getting there

By car

The mouth of the Thames river is about two hours' drive from Boston, west on the Mass Pike (I-90) and south on I-395. New Haven is 142 miles (229km) from Boston: take the Mass Pike and then the I-84 and I-91 at Sturbridge.

By bus or rail

Greyhound and Bonanza (*see p278*) both serve the area by bus; Amtrak (*see p278*) stops at Mystic and New Haven.

Tourist information

Litchfield Hills Travel Council

Telephone enquiries (1-860 567 4506).

Rhode Island

Boston residents looking for a convenient getaway from the city often make the quick drive to Rhode Island, which is less than an hour away. America's smallest state is home to rugged coastline and rolling farmland, and offers a refreshing break from Boston's hustle.

The city of Providence is the capital of Rhode Island and has been a major shipping and manufacturing centre for centuries. The city's College Hill area is home to Ivy Leaguer **Brown University** and the **Rhode Island School of Design (RISD)**. Brown has an innovative course of instruction and a well-known reputation as the hippest of the Ivies; RISD (known locally as 'rizdee') is a hotbed of avant-garde arts training. It is also where David Byrne first assembled the Talking Heads. **RISD's Museum of Art** has a strong collection of Impressionist work. **Benefit Street**, downtown along the river, hosts a concentration of 18th- and 19th-century houses restored and open to the public courtesy of the **Providence Preservation Society** (1-401 831 7440).

About a 30 minute drive to the coast is the city of **Newport**. Well-known as a summer-time party town, Newport was once a thriving commercial port on the level of Boston and New York, but the shipping industry faded here over time. This colonial town is lined with cobblestone streets and buildings dating back to the 17th century. In the early 20th century, Newport was best known for being the summer playground of America's wealthiest industrialists. There is still a touch of that remembered glory today, as the grandchildren of those powerful businessmen drive their Range Rovers down the narrow streets. But it's all a pale imitation of the town's earlier days. At the turn of the century, **Bellevue Avenue** was where the Rockefellers and Vanderbilts built what they modestly called their 'summer cottages'. These massive mansions (the size of English manor homes), are filled with imported Italian marble, miles of gold leaf and so many rooms you wonder how they ever found each other. Some of these monuments to personal wealth are now open to the public. Perhaps the best of them all is the **Breakers**. This 70-room mansion was built in 1895 for Cornelius Vanderbilt and offers a spectacular view of the Atlantic Ocean. Behind the Breakers lies **Cliff Walk**, a path which starts at **Salve Regina College** and passes by the Breakers and several other mansions. The combination of the ocean scenery and all those glorious houses makes a gorgeous view.

Unfortunately, Newport is not all stately homes and history. It's a tourist trap as well. Thus in central Newport on **Thames Street** you'll find block after block of tourist shops, bars and restaurants. If you can make it past all of that, you'll also find the **Museum of Newport History** (Thames Street at the bottom of Washington Square; 1-401 841 8770), which explains, in rather exhaustive detail, the history of the town. This gives you a thorough introduction for your own sightseeing.

Other attractions in Newport include the **International Tennis Hall of Fame**, the world's largest tennis museum, and the **Newport Art Museum**, which offers exhibitions of work by well-known regional artists, both historic and contemporary.

Newport is also the site of one of the world's premier music festivals. The **Newport Jazz Festival** is held each August, as is the **Ben & Jerry's Folk Festival** (1-401 847 3700 for both events). Both attract tens of thousands of music lovers and sun worshippers eager to spend days sitting out in a field listening to top international musical acts.

The Newport area has three beaches to choose from – which are neatly aligned and numerically named as First, Second and Third beaches. Of these, locals tend to think that Second Beach is the nicest. But for true sun worshippers, the best beach experience is a 30 minute drive away in **Little Compton**. The town, which was founded late in the 1600s, refuses to give in to commerce, so what it lacks in strip malls, convenience stores and even hotels, it gains in natural, untainted beauty.

Route 77 is a single lane country road winding along the rugged Atlantic coast. It offers spectacular views of Little Compton's harbour and acres and acres of farmland. It's ideal for bicycling, or for pretending you're in the south of France. Wine lovers can make a pit stop at **Sakonett Vineyards** and get a tour of the winery and a taste of the product. Sakonnet is the oldest and largest vineyard in New England, and is open daily for tours, tastings and wine sales. If you indulge just a bit too much, sober up across the street at the world-famous **Olga's Cup and Saucer**, a charming little café where you can load up on home-made bread, pastries, cookies and pizzas. They've

The **Breakers** – where the other half lived.

also got a pleasant outdoor patio protected by leafy trees for warm days. Patrons at Olga's can lazily sip on their iced coffees while they eye the produce for sale nearby at **Walker's Farm**. Walker's supplies many Boston restaurants with organic produce, and late in summer there are bins packed with ripe tomatoes, corn and blueberries, and every other fruit and vegetable you can imagine, all creating a colourful vista.

Further down Route 77 (also called the Main Road) is **Four Corners**, which consists of precisely that – it is nothing more than an intersection. On one side is an antiques store, on another an art gallery and on the opposite sides are **Grey's Ice Cream** and a gourmet shop called the **Provender**. Grey's offers an eclectic selection of home-made ice-creams and yoghurt, while the Provender sells everything from coffee, cookies, olive oil and pâté to its signature sandwiches on freshly baked bread.

Once you've loaded up, make your way along West Main Road to gorgeous **Goosewing Beach**. Getting to Goosewing is tricky, and it's worthwhile to ask for directions from locals, but it's worth the effort. Goosewing offers five miles of pristine beach surrounded by grassy farmland. It is one of the cleanest beaches in all of New England and is usually free of crowds, even in the heat of summer. Parking costs $5 in spring and $10 during the summer. Grilling food on the beach is permitted, as is surfing and even nudity in some parts. Families would be wise to set their lawn chairs by the rocks near the car park (where there are two public toilets and a food stand). Those looking for more serenity, or even a little romance in the buff, can walk further down the beach and stretch out in one of the alcoves near the high beach grass.

The Breakers

Ochre Point Avenue, Newport (1-401 847 1000). **Open** *Winter* 10am-5pm Sat, Sun. *Summer* 9am-5pm daily. **Admission** $12; $4 concessions. **Credit** AmEx, Disc, MC, V.

International Tennis Hall of Fame

194 Bellevue Avenue, Newport (1-401 849 3990). **Open** 9.30am-5pm daily. **Admission** $8; $6, $4 concessions. **Credit** AmEx, Disc, MC, V.

Newport Art Museum

76 Bellevue Avenue, Newport (1-401 848 8200). **Open** 10am-4pm Mon-Sat; noon-4pm Sun. **Admission** $4; $3, $2 concessions. **Credit** AmEx, Disc, MC, V.

RISD's Museum of Art

224 Benefit Street, Providence (1-401 454 6500). **Open** 10am-5pm Tue-Sun. **Admission** $5; $4, $2, $1 concessions; free under-5s. **Credit** MC, V.

Sakonett Vineyards

162 West Main Road, Little Compton (1-401 635 8486). **Open** 11am-5pm daily. **Admission** free.

Where to eat

Because of its popularity with the higher social circles, the dining and entertainment options here are quite good. The best seafood in town is served by **Scales and Shells** (527 Thames Street; 1-401 846 3474). This casual restaurant tends to be a little noisy but has a good wine list and an extensive menu. If you're looking for a slower pace and a more romantic atmosphere you need only cross the street and hope there's a table available at **Café Zelda** (528 Thames Street; 1-401 849 4002). This candlelit room features cosy tables with dark wood walls, and the food is as good as the lighting. However, it can be just a little expensive. If you're in the mood for quick, cheap American fare, try **Gary's Lunch** (also on Thames Street). Its kitsch vinyl booths are a good place to sit and eavesdrop on the locals over a plate of steaming blueberry pancakes.

The **Newport Jazz Festival**. *See p268.*

Where to stay

There are no hotels or inns in Little Compton, so your best bet is to find lodging in Newport, which is about a 15 minute drive away. Luckily, when you get to Newport you will find there are many modern hotels and quaint, Victorian bed and breakfasts to choose from. One of the more convenient and (relatively) affordable B&Bs is the **Admiral Fitzroy Inn** (398 Thames Street, Newport; 1-800 343 2863 or 1-401 848 8000; rates $85-120 off-season, $165-$215 in summer). It's a charming, European 19th-century building right in the centre of downtown, and it affords a view of the ocean. A good deal can also be found at the **Newport Gateway Motel** (31 West Main Road, Middletown; 1-800 427 9444/ 1-401 847 2735; open Apr-Sept; rates $49-$59 off-peak, $79-109 peak). This two-storey motel is nothing to write home about in terms of its appearance, but it's only a five minute drive to downtown Newport. Those looking for an old-world experience, on the other hand, can alway try the **Hotel Viking** (1 Bellevue Avenue, Newport; 1-401 847 3300/www.hotelviking.com).

Getting there

By car

Providence is 50 miles from Boston on I-95. Newport is about an hour's drive from Boston. Take I-93 south to Route 24, to either Route 114 south, or Route 138 south. To get to Little Compton, look for signs to Tiverton while you are on Route 24. Take Route 77 south toward Tiverton.

By bus or rail

Bonanza (*see p278*) links Boston to Providence by bus; Amtrack (*see p278*) by rail. Buses operating locally are run by the Rhode Island Public Transportation Authority (RIPTA; 1-401 781 9400)

Tourist information

Greater Providence Convention & Visitors' Bureau

1 West Exchange Street, Providence (1-401 274 1636). **Open** 9am-5.30pm daily.

Newport County Convention & Visitors' Bureau

23 America's Cup Avenue, Newport (1-401 466 2982). **Open** *Summer* 10m-5pm Mon-Sat; 10am-3pm Sun. *Winter* 10am-5pm Mon-Sat.

Heading North

Head for the hills.

When you leave Massachusetts you find that the tiny states of New England unfold before you, one after another, like a green and white movie in which frame after frame holds charming colonial churches, craggy coastline, white-capped mountains and stereotypically taciturn locals. This is the area of country that – thanks to history and Hollywood – many non-Americans most closely associate with Americana. It is inhabited by tough fishermen and factory workers, as well as modern business executives and their mobile phones and massive sports utility vehicles. It is the country's past and future combined in an endlessly entertaining, and eminently visitable vista. It is, in other words, well worth the drive.

New Hampshire

New Hampshire has an attractive string of beaches and state parks along its brief stretch of coast, but its most distinctive natural features are inland and high above sea level. The jewel of its coast is the city of Portsmouth, which has a recent veneer of chic and a deep layer of history. First settled in 1623, it was known, enchantingly, as 'Strawberry Banke', for the wild berry that once grew there in abundance. In the old downtown area a museum district of the same name surrounds Market Square, and walking tours of its 18th-century houses are available through the **New Hampshire Chamber of Commerce**. The local citizenry, whose foresight prevented the destruction of the area for 'urban redevelopment' in the 1950s, have transformed Strawberry Banke into a lively shopping district, with a variety of crafts' shops and eating spots.

On the far side of the state and about two hours north-west of Boston on I-93 and I-89 is **Hanover**, New Hampshire's other attractive urban centre. **Dartmouth College** (1-603 646 1110) was founded here in 1769, with a charter from George III 'for the instruction of the youth of Indian tribes', and, while it is mostly a posh, pricey, Ivy League university today, it still provides scholarships for Native Americans. The campus is charming, with rolling green hills and trees. The school's **Hood Museum** and **Hopkins Center for the Arts** sponsor a variety of interesting lectures and events, but the most striking work of art on the campus is in the basement of the **Baker Memorial Library**, where you can see the immense painting *Epic of Western Civilisation*, which the

You can get back to nature in **Bennington**. *See p272.*

Mexican muralist Jose Clemente Orozco painted while teaching here in the 1930s.

The lakes region of central New Hampshire is dominated by the melodically named **Lake Winnipesaukee**, a body of water shaped like some odd experiment in fractal geometry. There's no shortage of stunning views along its 180-mile (290-kilometre) shoreline, but none that will give you a true sense of the lake's size. **Laconia** and the neighbouring lakeside village of **Weirs Beach** (dubbed 'the Coney Island of New Hampshire', for its boardwalk, arcades and rides) are best known to the public for the annual mid-June uproar of Motorcycle Week, in which tens of thousands of two-wheeled 'hog' fanatics from all over the nation pull into town and burn equal amounts of beer and gasoline far into the night. The festivities devolved into a massive street brawl in the summer of 1965, but those days are over. The typical leather boy these days is a stockbroker on a weekend lark – more wannabe than wild one.

There's a more sedate version of American weirdness in **Moultonborough**, on the north side of the lake, where a sinuous, seemingly endless access road leads up through several thousand acres of wooded mountainside to a turn-of-the-century millionaire's folly known as **Castle in the Clouds** (Route 171; 1-800 729 2468; open daily June-October). Tours of this elaborate, stone-walled Xanadu and its grounds are available in season. Those who want to escape urban madness should check into any of the towns a few miles away to the north-west, around **Squam Lake**, the 'golden pond' where Hepburn and Fonda were filmed in the movie of the same name.

The **White Mountains**, spread out over three quarters of a million acres of the state's northern panhandle, are New England's most rugged heights and New Hampshire's pride and defining characteristic. **Conway**, near the Maine state line off Route 16, is the traditional gateway to the area and the terminus of the now-defunct rail service that first opened the mountains to tourism. Nowadays, **Lincoln**, off I-93, is more quickly accessible. Either way, the drive between the two towns along the **Kancamagus Highway** (Route 112) offers countless great views of mountains and waterfalls. Further north on the interstate, outside **Franconia Notch** (they don't have 'passes' or – heaven forbid – 'gaps' here) is the state totem, the **Old Man of the Mountain**. This 40-foot high (12-metre) granite profile, the product of wind and water erosion, was the inspiration for Hawthorne's story *The Great Stone Face*. Though it has come to have sacred status among the citizenry, the famed circus owner PT Barnum once dared offer to buy it.

Dartmouth College. *See p270.*

Obviously, they turned him down. Today it remains untouched, and serves its purpose as the backdrop to a million holiday photos.

North-east of the notch, on Route 3, is the town of **Bretton Woods**, where, in 1944, the powers that were established the Old World Order – the International Monetary Fund and the World Bank. Even mightier forces rage a little further to the east, atop New England's tallest peak, **Mount Washington**, where weather conditions of near Antarctic intensity prevail and winds of more than 200-mile-an-hour (322 kilometre-an-hour) – the world's strongest – are regularly recorded. The peak is accessible by trail, by rail on **Cog Railway** (1-800 922 8825) and roadway, but those 'This Car Climbed Mount Washington' bumper stickers are no idle boast – jalopies and junkers need not apply.

Where to stay

Staying in Portsmouth's historic district is expensive, but lodgings such as **Bow Street Inn** (121 Bow Street; 1-603 431 7760; rates $99-$114) are undistinguished but relatively cheap. Up in the lake country, **Red Hill Inn**

(Route 25B; 1-800 573 3445 or 1-603 279 7001; rates $105-$175), in Center Harbor, is reasonably priced, with a good restaurant. In the White Mountains, **Mount Washington Hotel** (Route 302; 1-800 258 0330; rates $259-$1,259) is decidedly pricey but positively reeks of history, faded glamour and power.

Getting there

By car

The lakes region of New Hampshire is two hours north of Boston (roughly 100 miles/160km); take the Laconia exit off I-93. Conway, in the White Mountains, is about three hours north of Boston (150 miles/240km), off Route 16.

By bus

Concord Trailways (1-603 228 3300) operates services across New Hampshire.

Tourist information

New Hampshire Chamber of Commerce

500 Market Street, Portsmouth (1-603 436 1118). **Open** 10am-6.30pm Mon-Fri.

Vermont

The closest parts of Vermont are a two-hour drive from Boston, and many of the most interesting parts of the state are three hours or more away. It's worth the trek. Visually and culturally, there is no place like it. Enter Vermont from the south and the **Green Mountains** billow up slowly in greeting. It's the perfect, gentle backdrop to the easy pace of the small towns in this part of the country, where the manners of another age linger on. **Brattleboro**, off the I-91, the major settlement closest to Boston, is representative of contemporary Vermont. Its roots are atypical, in that, because of its location on the edge of the Connecticut River, it was an industrial centre in the 19th century. That prosperity faded and left it ripe for a surge of post-1960s gentrification. Consequently, as throughout the state, Brattleboro today vibrates with counter-cultural lifestyles and politics and its old downtown area of winding, riverside streets is a warren of crafts shops and creative cuisine.

Bennington, nestled in a broad bowl in the foothills of the state's south-west corner, is a good introduction to the more classic, mellow Vermont. It was Ethan Allen's mountain redoubt when he first made a name for himself as leader of the resistance to the New York landlords' attempts to stake claims in the Green Mountains. What the Albany sheriffs knew as the 'Bennington Mob' had, within a few years, lead the attack on Fort Ticonderoga as the 'Green Mountain Boys' – it was among the colonists' first key victories. **The Battle Monument** outside town refers to another colonial triumph, however, in which regular forces beat back a British attempt to capture a significant arms store in the area. Another American hero associated with the town is the painter and long-time resident Grandma Moses, 30 of whose primitive landscapes are on display at the **Bennington Museum**. Another of the Seven Sisters, **Bennington College**, is here too; its students (before co-education) were famous for a penchant for black leotards and an artsy cast of mind. With four-year tuition well in excess of $100,000, it is believed to be the single most expensive college in North America.

The drive north from Bennington along Route 7 leads through a good many small, charming Vermont towns – each with its own village green and white-steepled church – and through a broad swath of gorgeous, rolling mountain country. A photographer's delight all year round, it's especially prime when the leaves turn in late September and early October. **Arlington** and **Manchester**, on the southern stretch of the drive, both have charming old inns and some intriguing shops. **Rutland**, about an hour north, is a sad, shabby exception to the state's charm. **Middlebury**, however, half an hour north again, displays all the old virtues and has the added energy of **Middlebury College**, another fine, small liberal arts institution.

Some of Vermont's most recent cultural developments can be appreciated about 20 miles (32 kilometres) over the back roads east of Middlebury, outside the little town of **Hancock**, off Route 100; here the state's longest-running 1960s community survives and thrives. **Quarry Hill** (1-802 767 3902) and its North Hollow Day School have come a long way since the longhairs first huddled in a ramshackle farmhouse, eating brown rice and veg. They're still vegetarian, but the group's primary income these days stems from software development. Visitors are welcome if they call in advance and adhere to the group's dogma and basic rules: 1) Don't hit kids; 2) We can put up with you if you can put up with us; 3) No dishes left in the sink. An understanding of the unity of all living beings is also recommended but not mandatory. And, finally, no drugs allowed.

Another half-hour north on Route 7 from Middlebury is **Burlington**, 'Lake Champlain's Queen City'. This is Vermont's Big Apple, and it's booming. The economy is fuelled by the presence of the University of Vermont, nearby IBM and an assortment of other high-tech outfits. The heart of downtown, **Church Street Marketplace** is a four-block-long pedestrian mall of tasteful shops, several bookstores and varied dining options. The town has a lively bar scene and musical choices ranging from DJ Spooky to Doc Watson and Yo-Yo Ma. The view over **Lake Champlain** at sunset is a dream. Even the crumbling Old North End is on the verge of gentrification. All this and socialism (sort of) too – congressman Bernie Sanders' Progressive Coalition still holds City Hall. What's not to like? (Though old-timers might say, 'I have a feeling we're not in Vermont any more'.)

Bennington Museum

West Main Street, Bennington (1-802 447 1571). **Open** 9am-5pm daily. **Admission** $6; $5 concessions. **Credit** AmEx, Disc, MC, V.

Where to stay

The **Arlington Inn** (Route 7A; 1-800 443 9442; rates $250-$490), just a few miles north of Bennington, is an 1848 Greek Revival mansion in one of the area's loveliest small towns. Just outside Middlebury, the cheaper **Waybury Inn** (Route 124, off Route 7; 1-800 348 1810; $95-$185) has bargain rates. It's so representative of the species that it served as the model for the inn operated by the Bob Newhart character in the TV show of the same name that chronicled the misadventures of an urban refugee in search of country simplicity. South of Burlington, the **Inn at Shelburne Farms** (Harbor Road, Shelburne; 1-802 985 8498; rates $95-$365; open May-October) is an immense Edwardian mansion that dates from 1899 and rests on an estate of almost 1,000 acres (401 hectares). Pricey, but not as much of a splurge as you'd expect.

Getting there

By car

Brattleboro, the settlement closest to Boston, is roughly two hours' drive from the city via the Mass Pike (I-90) and I-91 (116 miles/187km). Bennington is an hour west along Route 9 off the Brattleboro exit off I-91, roughly three hours from Boston.

By bus or rail

Vermont Transit (1-802 254 6066/1-802 864 6811) serves Brattleboro from Boston's South Station twice daily. **Amtrak** (*see p278*) operates services to Burlington (Essex Junction) and Brattleboro.

Tourist information

Bennington Area Chamber of Commerce

Veterans' Memorial Drive, Route 7 (1-802 447 3311). **Open** 9am-5pm Mon-Fri.

Brattleboro Visitors' Information Bureau

Putney Road, Brattleboro (1-802 362 2100). **Open** 9am-5pm Mon-Fri.

Maine

Maine's south coast is a land of old fishing villages and sandy beaches, similar to the Massachusetts shore. The twin towns of

A large collection of Impressionist work is at the **Portland Museum of Art**. *See p276.*

Skiing in NE: more trad than rad

Ok, so it's not Switzerland or even Aspen, Colorado, but skiing in New England has its own cachet nowadays. It's become one of the places where the rich and famous like to swoop. And, what the hell – it's close, there are mountains and it snows here. Why not?

To be fair, skiing is by no means new in these parts. Tourists have been skidding down mountains in New England since the 1930s, when the first rope tow in America was set up on a steep hillside meadow in Woodstock, Vermont. Today, most of the region's leading ski resorts are still located in Vermont, but enthusiasts have good options in New Hampshire and Maine as well. Downhill skiing is the most popular form, but there are plenty of opportunities for cross-country touring as well. **Stratton Mountain**, in Vermont, claims bragging rights as the birthplace of snowboarding, and there is space for boarding at the bigger resorts (Sugarbush's slopes are unrestricted), but, all in all, Yankee skiing is more trad than rad.

Now in its sixtieth year, **Stowe** (1-800 253 4754), on the slopes of Vermont's highest peak, **Mount Mansfield**, is a winter resort complex that has been known for years for its luxurious living and high style. The mountain's Front Four of expert trails are legendary for their challenge, but beginners will find plenty of options there as well. Stowe is also one of Vermont's better locations for cross-country skiing. For après-ski dining, Stowe village is unrivalled in its quality and variety.

Killington (1-800 621 6867), about 60 miles (96 kilometres) south of Stowe, is the largest skiing operation in Vermont and also has a range of difficulty that makes it suitable for all visitors. Without a nearby village to retire to, the nightlife is confined to the mountain's amenities but it's lively enough. The fine dining at nearby **Hemingway's** (Route 4; 1-802 422 3886; four-course set meal $58) has made it the only four-star restaurant in the state.

One of the state's most famous ski resorts, **Sugarbush** (1-800 537 8427), in Vermont's Mad River Valley, provides gorgeous views but, for the most part, gentler skiing. It is also somewhat less lively at night. The towns of the valley have more than their share of scenery and charm, however, and they manage to preserve something closer to the original Vermont ski ambience.

In New Hampshire, the resort of **Wildcat** (1-800 255 6439/1-603 466 3326), situated in the heart of the White Mountain National Forest, has remained particularly unspoilt. Most of the trails are relatively difficult, and the winds coming off Mount Washington can be a real test, but the scenery is lovely and the prices beat those of the larger resorts. New Hampshire also has good cross-country trails at the Black Mountain resort in **Jackson** (1-603 383 4490) and **Mount Washington** (1-800 282 5220/1-603 278 1000).

In Maine, **Sunday River** (1-207 824 3000) is without a lot of flashy amenities, but it's big enough to accommodate visitors in the very height of season and the crews maintain a consistently high quality of surface. More dynamic terrain and a higher degree of challenge are available at **Sugarloaf** (1-800 843 5623), further into the Maine interior.

Other resorts worth investigating include: **Wacheusett Mountain** in Princeton, MA (1-800 754 1234/1-978 464 2300); **Attitash** in Bartlett, NH (1-603 374 2368); **Loon Mountain**, on the Kancamagus Highway, NH (1-603 745 8111); **Mount Sunapee** in Newbury, NH (1-603 763 2356); **Pat's Peak** in Henniker, NH (1-603 428 3245); **Waterville Valley**, NH (1-603 236 8311); **Cannon Mountain** in Franconia Notch Parkway, Franconia, NH (1-603 823 5563); **Mad River Glen** in Waitsfield, VT (1-802 496 3551); **Mount Snow**, VT (1-802 464 3333); **Okemo** in Ludlow, VT (1-802 228 4041); **Pico** in Killington, VT (1-802 422 3333); and **Stratton Ski Resort**, VT (1-802 297 2200).

Kennebunk and **Kennebunkport** are the most famous names in the area, chiefly because of the latter's connection to the 41st president, George Herbert Walker Bush and his 43rd president son, George W. The seaside resort of Kennebunkport evinces a preppy atmosphere that seems appropriate to the former president; while neighbouring Kennebunk has a more proletarian and commercial air. Both towns have their share of history and historic homes. Kennebunkport plays host to the **Seashore Trolley Museum**, where a collection of almost 200 electric streetcars is displayed, vintage and contemporary, from around the world, including an old 'Desire' from New Orleans. The town of **Old Orchard Beach** – half an hour further up the coast – features seven miles (11.3 kilometres) of beach and a touch of honky-

The rocky shores of **Acadia National Park**.

tonk along the pier; its **Palace Playland** amusement park includes a ferris wheel and a working, turn-of-the-century carousel.

Portland is Maine's largest city, though still none too large, with a population of 65,000. It has some outsize culture and cool, partly because of its fine natural setting, bound as it is on three sides by water, and partly because of a strong local historic preservation movement. An added influence is the presence of a sizeable academic community, the 10,000 students of the **University of Southern Maine** and the small but intense **Maine College of Art**.

The city was settled in 1623 but much of it burned to the ground in the Great Fire of 1866. The cobblestoned streets of the **Old Port Exchange**, the city's downtown historic district, are lined with numerous fine examples of the Victorian architecture that rose in the fire's wake. After dark the port lights up in a different kind of blaze, from the heat of young bodies in the thicket of the district's many restaurants, bars and clubs. For more highbrow pursuits, the **Portland Museum of Art** has, in addition to the Payson collection of Impressionist work, a strong selection of paintings by Edward Hopper, Andrew Wyeth and Winslow Homer.

Maine is so big that just to get to the headlands north of **Casco Bay** where the real Maine begins is a three-hour drive from Boston. The satellite roads off Route 1, for hundreds of miles north of here, lead to unspoiled coastal villages of ice-cold waters and granite-bouldered beaches. Those along the **Boothbay Peninsula**, about an hour north of Portland, are the best known, but others (particularly those furthest north) offer the purest examples of old Maine life. Off the coast, in the **Penobscot Bay**, about five hours out of Boston, is the especially virginal and attractive **Deer Isle**, summer home to the highly regarded **Haystack Mountain School of Crafts** (1-207 348 2306). Even further north is **Mount Desert Isle** and its **Acadia National Park** (off Route 3, Bar Harbor; 1-207 288 3338) which is a full day's drive out of Boston, but offers some truly unparalleled coastline – a combination of pounding surf, jagged rock and unbroken pine forest. The isle's chief town, **Bar Harbor**, has a touch of tourist tack these days, but also a hint of its time as an elite resort of the late 19th century.

Seashore Trolley Museum

Log Cabin Road, Kennebunkport (1-207 967 2800).
Open *May-Oct* 10am-5pm daily. **Admission** $7.25; $5.25, $4.75 concessions; free under 5s.
Credit AmEx, Disc, MC, V.

Portland Museum of Art

7 Congress Square, Portland (1-207 775 6148).
Open 10am-5pm Tue, Wed, Sat, Sun; 10am-9pm Thur, Fri. **Admission** $6; $5 concessions; free under-12s. **No credit cards.**

Where to stay & eat

If you're looking for somewhere to stay on the south coast, save yourself a few dollars and forego Kennebunkport for Kennebunk, where the **Kennebunk Inn** (45 Main Street; 1-207 985 3351; rates $65-$155) offers the charm it has accumulated since 1799. In Portland, the **Regency** (20 Milk Street; 1-800 727 3436; rates $119-$219) is right in the historic district (for which you'll pay a premium), while the **Pomegranate Inn** (49 Neal Street; 1-800 356 0408; rates $95-$225), west of the downtown area, is a bit cheaper and delivers a bright mix of 19th-century and contemporary colour.

The outstanding dining choice in Kennebunkport is the **White Barn Inn** (37 Beach Avenue Street; 1-207 967 2321), where inspired interpretations of classic New England dishes are offered in the rustic elegance of a refurbished country barn. Dining in Portland is varied and inventive. In addition to a wealth of ethnic spots, **Street and Co** (33 Wharf Street; 1-207 775 0887) does upmarket contemporary seafood in a converted industrial building, while **Fresh Market** (43 Exchange Street; 1-207 773 7146) offers decent, inexpensive pastas, cafeteria-style.

Getting there

By car

Kennebunk and Kennebunkport are about 90 minutes north of Boston on the I-95 (roughly 80 miles/129km).

By air

Several airlines serve **Portland International Jetport**, including Delta, United Airlines and Continental (*see p278*).

Tourist information

Maine Office of Tourism

Telephone enquiries (1-800 533 9595/ www.visitmaine.com.

Directory

Getting Around 278
Resources A-Z 281
Further Reference 292
Index 294
Advertisers' Index 300

Feature boxes

Winter in Boston: two feet of snow 280
Never say 'pahkin' when you mean parking 282
Colourful forecasting 283
Tourist information 284
Subway ins and outs 287
Useful bus routes 289
Biking & blading in Boston 293

Directory

Getting Around

Arriving

By bus

Most out-of-town services arrive and depart from the **South Station Transportation Center** (700 Atlantic Avenue), which is served by the following bus companies:

Bonanza
720 4110/1-800 556 3815.
For services to Cape Cod.

Greyhound
526 1801/1-800 231 2222.
For national services.

Peter Pan
426 7838/1-800 237 8747.
For the Massachusetts area.

Concord Trailways
426 8080.
For New Hampshire and Maine.

Plymouth & Brockton
773 9401.
For buses to Plymouth and Brockton.

Vermont Transit
1-800 451 3292.
For buses to Vermont.

By train

The national rail service **Amtrak** (1-800 872 7245/ www.amtrak.com) runs from **South Station** and **Back Bay Station** (145 Dartmouth Street, at Stuart Street).

By air

Logan International Airport
(Information 561 1800/ Airport Ground Transportation 1-800 235 6426).
On a spit of reclaimed land to the east of Boston, the airport is just 3 miles (5km) from the downtown area. The airport's five terminals are lettered A to E and connected by a shuttle bus that also runs to Airport T station. By 2003 Logan will be considerably bigger, particularly the international terminal; the work is currently underway.

The airport is served by these major international airlines:

Aer Lingus
1-800 223 6537.

Air Atlantic
1-800 426 7000.

Air France
1-800 237 2747.

Alitalia
1-800 223 5730.

American Airlines
1-800 433 7300.

British Airways
1-800 247 9297.

Business Express/DeltaConnection
1-800 345 3400.

Canadian Airlines
1-800 426 7000.

KLM
1-800 374 7747.

Lufthansa
1-800 645 3880.

Qantas
1-800 227 4500.

Swissair
1-800 221 4750.

United Airlines
1-800 241 6522.

Virgin Atlantic
1-800 862 8621.

To & from the airport

By bus

The **Logan Dart** bus line provides a non-stop transfer between the airport and South Station near downtown Boston. The fare is $5 one way. Buses leave from all five of the airport's terminals every 15 minutes between 6am and 8pm Sunday to Friday.

Departures from South Station are every 15 minutes between 6am and 8pm. They leave the station from Gate 25.

Logan Express (1-800 235 6426) runs a bus service from the airport to Braintree, Framingham and Woburn. One-way fares cost $8.

By taxi

Taxis are directly outside the airport's baggage claim area. The queue can get very long, so prepare to wait. A cab ride to downtown Boston costs $15-$25 (depending largely on traffic), and about $23 to Cambridge, with an extra $1 toll for travelling through the Sumner Tunnel from Logan to Boston.

Station wagons, taxis with disabled access and credit card taxis are all available upon request. For a list of reputable firms *see p279*.

If you want to travel in style, advance booking can be made with **Carey Limousine** (623 8700) and the **Commonwealth Limousine Service** (787 5575).

By boat

Travelling by boat is the most pleasant way of getting to and from the airport and is certainly a good way to say farewell to the city.

The **Logan Water Shuttle** (1-800 235 6426) connects the free terminal shuttle bus with Boston's Rowes Wharf (6am-8pm Mon-Fri, every 15 minutes; 10am-8pm Sat-Sun, every 30 minutes; $10 one way). The journey takes approximately seven minutes.

Harbor Express (1-800 235 6426) runs a similar service between the airport, the southern suburb of Quincy and Long Wharf, in downtown Boston near the Marriott Hotel.

City Water Taxis (422 0392) operates between 1 April and 15 October ($5-$10) and takes passengers from the airport to the World Trade Center, Congress Street (near South Station), Long Wharf (for Government Center and the North End), North Station and Charlestown, among other stops.

By T

The Massachusetts Bay Transport Authority or **MBTA** operates the local subway system known as the 'T'. Access to the Airport station is by the Blue Line, which runs from State/Citizen's Bank or Government Center stations – the journey takes about 15 minutes. Airport shuttle buses numbers 22 and 33 take passengers from the airline terminals to the T station. With the state of traffic in Boston, this is the quickest and cheapest way to access the airport, though it's hard to do with excessive amounts of luggage. Also, it can be incredibly crowded at rush hour, so be prepared.

Photocopied T maps are available from information booths in terminals A, C and E. *See also page 316.*

Disabled transport

Airport Handicap Van
(561 1769) runs a service for the disabled between the airport and various hotels to the Airport T stop. Phone the above number for details. *See also p281*.

Public transport

Public transport in the Boston area is run by the **MBTA** and consists of the T, Commuter Rail and buses.

Visitor's Passports are available for one-day ($6), three-day ($11) or weekly ($22) use, providing unlimited travel on the T and MBTA buses. For those planning longer stays, monthly passes are available for $35. Passes can be bought at the Airport, Gov't Center, Harvard, Alewife and Riverside T stations and North Station, South Station and Back Bay Station, as well as at the Boston Common and Prudential Center tourist information booths (*see p284*).

MBTA

(Information 222 3200/ 1-800 392 6100; pass program 222 5218; complaints 222 5215/ www.mbta.com).

The T

Boston's T was America's first subway, and is efficient, cheap and easy to use. Tokens costs $1 (50¢ for under-12s; 25¢ for senior citizens), though a trip on one of the Green or Red Line surface extensions can cost up to $2.25 (you pay the driver).

Trains run from 5.15am to 12.30am Monday to Saturday and from 6am to 12.30am on Sundays. Free subway maps are available from the larger stations such as Harvard, Gov't Center, North Station, Back Bay, South Station and Park Street.

'Outbound' and 'Inbound' services often have different subway entrances: the direction is in relation to Park Street and Downtown Crossing (*see p287*).

Not many Bostonians (and even fewer visitors) know that each branch colour was chosen to reflect a characteristic of the area that each line covers. The Green Line, for example, was named in honour of the Emerald Necklace, the chain of parks and woods that links Boston and the western suburbs. The Red Line, serving Harvard, pays homage to the Harvard Crimsons, the university's football team colours. The Blue Line is supposed to mirror the colour of the waterfront, and the Orange Line runs along Washington Street, originally known as Orange Street after William of Orange, king of England between 1689 and 1702.

Bus services

The MBTA runs around 150 bus routes in Boston and the suburbs. The flat fare is 75¢ (15¢ for senior citizens), and payment has to be in exact change. Bus transfers good for two hours from time of issue are available for no additional charge.

Buses run from 5.30am to 1am daily. Routes and timetables are available from major T stops or the **MBTA central office** (10 Park Plaza, 120 Boylston Street).

Rail services

Boston has three main train stations: South Station (700 Atlantic Avenue, at Summer Street), Back Bay Station (145 Dartmouth Street, at Stuart Street) and North Station (Causeway Street, at Friend Street). MBTA Commuter Rail runs from North Station and South Station, serving the Greater Boston area and Massachusetts as far away as Providence, Rhode Island.

Taxis & limousines

Taxis can be hailed on the street at any time, providing,of course, that you can find one available. This becomes particularly difficult after 1am, when public transport has closed down for the night. Taxi ranks can be found near major hotels, outside main train stations and in Harvard Square, Cambridge.

Regular meter fares begin at $1.50 for the first quarter of a mile and then 25¢ for each eighth of a mile thereafter. If you have a complaint about a taxi service phone the police department's Hackney Hotline on 536 8294.

The following local taxi companies offer a 24-hour service and most accept major credit cards but it is always best to phone to check first:

All Area Taxi
536 2000.

Bay State Taxi Service
566 5000.

Checker Taxi
536 7000.

Independent Taxi Operators Association
268 1313/426 8700.

Red Cab
734 5000

The **Boston Cab Association** (262 2227/536 5010) also provides limousines (see also *p278*), while **Boston Coach** (387 7676) has vans, coaches, limousines and cars, and if you use **Town Taxi** (536 5000) you might end up being chauffeured by 'Boston's Best Taxi Driver' Bobby Uzdavinis (so voted by readers of *Boston Magazine*).

Lost property

MBTA

The MBTA lost and found department is divided into different sections for each form of transport. If you lose something on a bus, phone 222 5607 (24 hours daily, but you can only pick up valuable items between 9am and 6pm daily). Phone 222 3600 for property lost on Commuter Rail (6.30am to midnight Monday to Saturday; 7.30am to 11.30pm on Sunday).

Each T line has a different number: **Blue Line** (222 5533); **Green Line** (222 5221); **Orange Line** (222 5403); and **Red Line** (222 5317). All are open 24 hours daily.

Taxis

If you lose something in a taxi, phone the police department's **Hackney Hotline** (536 8294). It's open 24 hours daily.

Driving

Until the 'Big Dig' (*see p19*) is completed, driving in Boston is not recommended, but if you must drive, here is some of the information that you may need:

The three main highways that lead into town are the **I-95**, the **I-93** (the Central Artery), which runs all the way to Vermont, and the **I-90** (the Massachusetts Turnpike, or 'Mass Pike'), which is the route taken to and from New York.

The speed limit on most major highways is 55 miles per hour. On sections of the Mass Pike this goes up to 65 miles per hour. Elsewhere in Boston, speed limits range from 20 to 50 miles per hour.

The **American Automobile Association** or AAA (1-800 222 4357) can provide members with maps on request. Some clubs – including the AA and RAC in the UK – have reciprocal arrangements with the AAA, which also entitles you to discounts at certain sights, museums and hotels. The AAA offers a free towing service to members (except on the privately-run Mass Pike, which has its own patrol cars to aid breakdowns).

State law requires the wearing of seat belts. It's also a finable offence to litter: throwing a wrapper out of a car window could cost $1,000 or even your right to drive in the US.

Car rental

If you want to hire a car, check whether an international driver's licence will be required, as some rental companies insist on both a foreign and international licence (available from the AAA, *see p279*).

Many companies also require that a licencee be over 25 years of age, and all insist on payment with a major credit card. Also, the days when you could borrow a parent's or spouse's credit card for this purpose are sadly over. Most companies require the card to be in the driver's name.

Ask about basic US driving rules before heading out. Some rules are different here. If you're driving with children under the age of five they must be in the back seat in an approved child-safety restraint. Car rental rarely includes insurance, so be sure to check exactly what is covered.

Major rental companies include:

Alamo
1-800 327 9633.

Avis
1-800 831 2847.

Budget
1-800 527 0700.

Dollar
1-800 800 4000.

Hertz
1-800 654 3131.

National
1-800 227 7368.

Parking

Parking is difficult, if not all but impossible, in Boston. The number of spaces is trimmed by about five per cent each year, as the city has yet to comply with the Clean Air Act standards. You'll notice right away that, despite the city's ample public transportation, Bostonians still have that American love of cars. Thus, the traffic congestion is dreadful and parking spaces rare. In addition, with extensive parking restrictions, and annual cuts in the number of available spaces, many are available only to locals with special parking decals.

What spaces do exist are metered and only available to non-residents for up to two hours between 8am and 6pm. A fine can cost $20 and retrieving a towed car more than $50. If you do get a ticket, phone the Boston Office of the Parking Clerk (635 4410).

If you must use a car while in Boston, the wisest thing to do with it is leave it in a parking lot and walk. Boston's two main car parks are under Boston Common (on Charles Street, directly opposite the Public Garden; 954 2096) and under the Prudential Center (800 Boylston Street; 267 1002), which offers a discount on parking if you make a purchase at one of the shops in the mall above.

Other garages can be found at: Government Center (50 New Sudbury Street, at Congress Street; 227 0385), the New England Aquarium (70 East India Row, off Atlantic Avenue; 723 1731) and at Zero Post Office Square, Congress Street (423 1430).

Breakdown services

The AAA (1-800 222 4357) offers 24-hour breakdown service (*see p279*). However, in case of a breakdown, your best bet is to contact local police or state highway patrol for help. They will, in turn, contact tow-trucks or local garages to move your car to safety. However, if the vehicle breaks down, it is always a good idea to push it off the road for your safety and for the safety of other drivers.

24-hour petrol stations

Bowdoin Square Exxon

239 Cambridge Street, at Blossom Street (523 3394). **Credit** AmEx, Disc, MC, V. **Map** p306 F4.

Fenway Texaco Service

1241 Boylston Street, at Ipswich Street (247 7905). **Credit** AmEx, Disc, MC, V. **Map** p306 D5/6.

Winter in Boston: two feet of snow

The report on CNN.com on the eve of a snowstorm in the winter of 2001 said it all: 'The Stop and Shop grocery store in Arlington, Massachusetts, was so jammed with people stocking up for the storm that even the store manager was bagging groceries.' This is New England; a place where the uttering of the word 'Nor'easter' (a storm moving down from the north-east) triggers food foraging and the frantic stockpiling of wood. A place where school calendars are padded with snow days, and where Old Man Winter comes on more like an army tank than a thief in the night.

Signs at the edge of the city should read: Welcome to Boston – We get snow here.

The all-time record for snowfall was set during the blizzard of 1978 at 27 inches (69 centimetres). Locals insist that in some places it was deeper. Townies over 30 still talk about that ferocious storm with the braggart nostalgia of a war vet showing off his scars. It attacked in early February, with winds reaching up to 79mph. Electricity was lost state-wide. Traffic halted. Families sledded to the shop for groceries. Unlike most heavy snowstorms that melt within days, that heavy accumulation stuck around for weeks and the temperature hovered below freezing. Life seemed to pause for a month.

Snow isn't usually that imprisoning, but every winter does guarantee at least a few inches of the stuff, plus a series of blustering storms and temperatures that can plummet to -20ºF (-51ºC). It's also a given that, during those times, streets will be barren and you'll think you have the city to yourself. Still, while Bostonians complain endlessly about winter, when it comes right down to it they love it like Sid loved Nancy. It proves how tough they are for living here. And their puritan New England heart thrives on the hardship. If you lack a puritan soul, though, you'd be better off coming in the summer.

Resources A-Z

Business

Convention centres

Bayside Exposition Center
200 Mount Vernon Street, at Morrissey Boulevard (474 6000/ www.baysideexpo.com). JFK/UMass T. **Open** 8.30am-5pm Mon-Fri.

Hynes Convention Center
900 Boylston Street, at Gloucester Street, Back Bay (954 2000/ www.mccahome.com). Hynes/ICA T. **Open** 9am-5pm Mon-Fri. **Map** p306 E5.

World Trade Center
164 Northern Avenue, at Seaport Lane (385 5000/www.wtcb.com). South Station T. **Open** depends on functions. **Map** p307 J5.

Courier services

Local and national messenger services include:

DHL Worldwide Express
1-800 225 5345/www.dhl.com.
Phone for opening hours and pick-up locations.

Federal Express
1-800 463 3339/www.fedex.com.
Phone for opening hours and pick-up locations.

Metro Cab
242 8000.
A taxi company with package delivery 24 hours a day.

Symplex Courier Systems
523 9500.
Provides package delivery service 24 hours a day.

US Postal Service
1-800 222 1811/www.usps.gov.

Office services

Kinkos
10 Post Office Square, at Milk Street (482 4400/www.kinkos.com). Downtown Crossing T.
Open 24 hours daily. **Map** p307 G4.
Services include on-site computer rental, Internet access, typesetting, printing, photocopying, faxing and mailing.
Branches: 2 Center Plaza (973 9000); 1 Mifflin Place, Cambridge (497 0125); 187 Dartmouth Street (262 6188).

Sir Speedy
20 Province Street, at School Street (227 2237/www.sir-speedy.net). State/Citizen's Bank T.
Open 8.30am-5.30pm Mon-Fri. **Map** 307 G4.
Copying, printing, desktop publishing, binding and graphic design services.
Branches: 827 Boylston Street (267 9711); 76 Batterymarch Street (451 6491); 77 North Washington Street (523 7656); 711 Atlantic Avenue (426 3434); 1 Kendall Square, Cambridge (494 0255).

Translation services

Harvard Translations
815 Somerville Avenue, at Porter Square (868 6080). Porter T. **Open** 9am-5.30pm Mon-Fri. **No credit cards. Map** 311 B1.
Offers translation and interpreting services for all major languages.

JKW International
Third floor, 143 Newbury Street, at Dartmouth Street (859 8600). Copley T. **Open** 9am-5pm Mon-Fri. **Credit** AmEx, MC, V. **Map** p306 F5
Offers translation and interpreting services for all major languages. It also provides a multi-lingual secretarial service. Phone for further details.

Consulates

All embassies are located in Washington, DC. Consulate offices based in Boston include the following:

Canada
Suite 400, 3 Copley Place, at Huntingdon Avenue (262 3760). Copley T. **Map** p306 F5.

Republic of Ireland
Third floor, 535 Boylston Street, at Clarendon Street (267 9330). Copley T. **Map** p306 F5.

United Kingdom
25th floor, Federal Reserve Plaza, 600 Atlantic Avenue, opposite South Station (248 9555/www.britain-info.org). South Station T.
Map p307 G5.

Consumer information

Better Business Bureau
(426 9000/ www.bos.bbb.org).
A non-profit public service organisation that is primarily for monitoring businesses for quality. If you are interested in receiving information on a particular company (and know their address) or wish to file a complaint about a US business, you can phone the above number.

Office of Consumer Affairs and Business Regulation
(727 7780).
If you have a complaint to make regarding your consumer rights or a query regarding your responsibilities, OCABR should be able to help. Arbitration services for home improvement and car purchase are provided, as well as basic information on the Boston marketplace. Will make references to mediation or legal services.

Disabled travellers

Boston is generally well equipped for disabled travellers. Hotels must provide accessible rooms, museums and street curbs have ramps for wheelchairs and buses on some routes are wheelchair accessible. However it's always best to phone first to double-check.

Transportation Access Passes (TAP) entitle the disabled passenger to reduced fares on public transport. Passes are available for $3 from the **MBTA Senior and Access Pass Program Office** (Back Bay Station, 145 Dartmouth Street, at Columbus Avenue; 222 5123), and applications must be completed by a licensed health-care professional. The office also supplies a map that shows disabled access points to the T.

For information on access to more than 200 local arts and entertainment facilities contact **Very Special Arts** (Massachusetts China Trade Center, 2 Boylston Street, at Tremont Street; 350 7713/www.vsamass.org).

Access Tours
1-781 322 1610/1-800 557 2047.
This company arranges a number of tours specifically for the disabled. You can either book your travel through them or take part in one of their pre-packaged tours.

Nevah say 'pahkin' when you mean parking

Ever since JFK was president, many Americans have had the false (if quite understandable) misconception that all native Bostonians sound like him. That nasal twang, the lack of Rs, the Ts that sound like Ds – these all made Kennedy's voice distinctive. The Kennedy Boston accent sounds something like: 'Ye-ah, I'm pahkin' the cah ne-ah Hahvid Yahd.' To this day, this is viewed as the quintessential Boston accent. This stereotype has been further perpetuated by the television and film actors who have tried to give their Boston-based characters more authenticity by nailing this accent. This requires them to say things like 'That's wicked pissah!' (translation: really great), that nobody much says anymore.

The sad irony is that the original Irish-American Boston natives who created this accent, some of whom still reside in South Boston and Dorchester, have become a quaint minority in Boston's culturally mixed landscape. In fact, the way natives speak is ever changing, and changing very quickly. Accents in Boston today are based on whatever groups of people are currently migrating to, and forming communities in, the city. Today Boston's population is much more cosmopolitan than it once was. While it is still possible that you might happen upon an authentic-sounding cabby from Southie who spends the entire ride blabbing about 'the Sox', it's likely that your command of Spanish will come in more handy than any guide to traditional local lingo.

However, even though Boston's accent has changed, it is still a city of nicknames, and it can all be a bit confusing, so here is a brief guide to odd pronunciations and quirky names you're likely to hear around town:

Copley Square
Is pronounced 'Cop-ley', not 'Cope-ly'.

Comm Ave
Commonwealth Avenue.

Mass Ave
Massachusetts Avenue.

Dot Ave
Dorchester Avenue.

The Pit
The centre of Harvard Square.

The Pike
The Massachusetts Turnpike.

The Pru
The Prudential Tower.

The Common
Boston Common.

Worcester
Pronounced 'Wooster'.

Gloucester
Pronounced 'Glawster'.

Quincy
Pronounced 'Quinzzie'.

Southie
South Boston.

Rozzie
Roslindale.

Tonic
Old Boston word for soft drink.

Jimmies
Chocolate or multi-coloured sprinkles on top of ice-cream – enormously popular here.

Frappe
A milkshake – pronounced 'frap'.

Spa
Convenience store that serves food.

The T
The local subway – short for the MBTA.

The Sox
Boston's beloved and beleaguered baseball team, the Red Sox. But, then again, you probably knew that by now.

Lift Bus Program

1-800 543 8287.
For queries about bus access.

Massachusetts Office on Disability

727 7440/1-800 322 2020.
This governmental agency is a good source for enquiries into issues like rights enforcement, building access and other information useful for disabled travellers.

Electricity

The United States uses a 110-120V, 60-cycle AC voltage, rather than the 220-240V, 50-cycle AC voltage used in Europe. Laptops and most travel appliances are dual voltage and will work in the US and in Europe, but it is always a good idea to check with the manufacturer before you ever plug them in. Older computers in particular, have been known to blow.

You will also need an adaptor for US sockets; they can be bought at the airport or at pharmacies.

Emergencies

Ambulance, Fire Brigade or Police

For all emergency services in the US, dial 911. The call is toll-free from any payphone. 911 also works from most mobile phones.

Bell Atlantic (telephone) automated hotline
1-800 244 3737.

NStar information hotline
(Gas) 1-800 572 9300; (electric) 1-800 592 2000.

Massachusetts Poison Control Center
1-800 682 9211.

Boston Water and Sewer Commission
330 9400.

Health & medical

Within the United States you will have to pay for any emergency treatment you might need. Welcome to privatised health care. In most cases, emergency rooms will not even see you unless you provide them with a credit card. Be sure to contact the emergency number on your travel insurance before seeking treatment if you can, and you will be directed to a hospital that will deal directly with your own insurance company.

Emergency care

Brigham and Women's Hospital
75 Francis Street, between Huntingdon & Brookline Avenues (732 5500/1-800 294 9999). Brigham Circle T. **Open** 24 hours daily.

Children's Hospital
300 Longwood Avenue, at Brookline Avenue (355 6000/355 6611). Longwood Avenue T. **Open** 24 hours daily.

Franciscan Children's Hospital and Rehabilitation Center
30 Warren Street, at Commonwealth Avenue (254 3800). Warren Street T. **Open** 24 hours daily.

Massachusetts General Hospital
55 Fruit Street, at Cambridge Street (726 2000). Charles/MGH T. **Open** 24 hours daily. **Map** p306 F4.

Mount Auburn Hospital
330 Mount Auburn Street, at Memorial Drive (492 3500). Harvard T. **Open** 24 hours daily. **Map** p311 A2.

New England Medical Center
750 Washington Street, at Kneeland Street (636 5000). NE Medical Center T. **Open** 24 hours daily. **Map** p307 G5.

Dentists

Metropolitan District Dental Society
(1-508 651 3521). **Open** 9am-4pm Mon-Fri.

Tufts Dental School
1 Kneeland Street, at Washington Street (636 6828). NE Medical Center T. **Open** emergency walk-in clinic 9am-10.30pm Mon-Fri. **Map** p307 G5.

Dental Referral Service
(1-800 511 8663). **Open** 8am-8pm Mon-Fri.

Pharmacies (24-hour)

CVS
155-7 Charles Street, at Cambridge Street (523 1028). Charles/MGH T. **Open** pharmacy 7am-midnight daily; store 24 hours daily. **Map** p306 F4.

Check the phone book or phone the number above to find the location of other branches in the Boston area.

Alternative medicine

Langer Chiropractic Group
179 Elm Street, Somerville (625 5350). Porter or Davis T. **Open** by appointment Mon-Thur. **Credit** AmEx, Disc, MC, V.

Dr Langer is a specialist in chiropractic therapy, physiotherapy and massage. In addition, a same-day emergency service is also available.

Market Street Health
214 Market Street, at North Beacon Street, Brighton (787 3511). Cleveland Circle T, then 86 bus. **Open** telephone enquiries 9am-2pm Mon-Fri. **No credit cards.**

Market Street Health has been in practice for 16 years and offers a wide variety of complementary medicine and holistic therapies. Services offered here include acupuncture, colon hydrotherapy, chiropractic therapy, homeopathy, Chinese medicine, flotation, comprehensive massage and yoga.

New England School of Acupuncture
34 Chestnut Street, Watertown (926 4271). Central T, then 70 bus. **Open** 9am-7.30pm Mon-Fri; 9am-3pm Sat. **Credit** varies.

The oldest college of acupuncture and Oriental medicine in the country, this well-known (in the US) school offers a wide array of alternative medicine services including acupuncture, herbal medicine treatments and shiatsu.

Helplines & agencies

AIDS Hotline
(1-800 235 2331). **Open** 9am-7pm Mon-Fri; 10am-2pm Sat.

AIDS Hotline offers telephone advice from counsellors on emotional issues, testing and insurance, as well as referral to support groups for legal assistance, mental health support and financial advice.

Colourful forecasting

The tired cliché, 'If you don't like New England weather, just wait ten minutes', is a cliché for a good reason: Boston's climate is consistently inconsistent.

However, the locals do try to let you know what to expect. In one of the city's most unique architectural elements, the top of the Old John Hancock Tower (the one that looks like the Empire State Building, with a spire on top), changes colour each night based on the weather forecast for the following day.

As the local rhyme goes: solid blue, clear view; flashing blue, clouds are due; solid red, rain ahead; flashing red, snow instead. (Except in summer, when solid red means the Red Sox game has been cancelled.)

Alcohol/drug abuse

Alcoholics Anonymous

(426 9444). **Open** 9am-9pm Mon-Sat; noon-9pm Sun.
Volunteers (recovered alcoholics who have been through the programme) offer counselling and referral to other helplines, detox houses and AA meetings.

Drug & Alcohol Hotlines

(445 1500/1-800 327 5050).
Open 24 hours daily.
This service provides a helpful information and education service on issues including substance abuse, referrals to detoxification centres within Massachusetts and advice on whom to phone for out-of-state information.

Child abuse

Child-at-Risk Hotline

(1-800 792 5200).
Open 24 hours daily.
An emergency service provided by the department of Social Services, this hotline will refer concerned adults or abused children to other agencies for help.

Tourist information

Boston National Historical Park Service

15 State Street, at Congress Street, Downtown (242 5642). State/Citizen's Bank T. **Open** *June-Sept* 9am-6pm daily. *Sept-May* 9am-5pm daily. **Map** p307 G4.
A useful source for information on Boston and New England; there's also a bookshop.

Cambridge Office of Tourism

Office 352, 18 Brattle Street, at Mount Auburn Street, Cambridge (441 2884/1-800 862 5678/www.cambridge-usa.org). Harvard T. **Open** 9am-5pm Mon-Fri. **Map** p311 B2.
For general inquiries on Cambridge. The office also publishes the *Cambridge Visitor Guide*, which has information on local accommodation, sights and attractions as well as maps, a seasonal calendar of events and a walking tour map. The office also runs the Visitor Information Center in Harvard Square, which has a touch-screen service to help you find your way around Cambridge.

Greater Boston Convention & Visitors' Bureau

2 Copley Place, Suite 105, Boston, MA 02116 (536 4100/1-888 733 2678/www.bostonusa.com). **Open** *telephone enquiries* 8.30am-5pm Mon-Fri.
The Greater Boston Convention & Visitors' Bureau (GBCVB) provides information on attractions, restaurants, performing arts and nightlife, shopping and travel services. Its website is also fairly comprehensive. The main office operates as a telephone information service, but the bureau also runs visitor information centres at various locations in the city

Massachusetts Office of Travel & Tourism

(727 3201/recorded information 1-800 447 6277/UK office 020 7978 7429/www.mass-vacation.com). **Open** *Boston office* 8.45am-5pm Mon-Fri. *UK office* 9am-5pm Mon-Fri.
The Office of Travel & Tourism has a telephone information service and also publishes a free magazine called *Getaway Guide*, which includes information about attractions and lodgings, a map and a seasonal calendar of events covering the state of Massachusetts. Also has a useful UK phone number.

Traveler's Aid Society

17 East Street, at Atlantic Avenue, Downtown (542 7286). South Station T. **Open** 8.30am-5pm Mon-Fri. **Map** p307 G5.
A non profit-making social service agency that has been helping travellers since 1920. These days, though, most of the organisation's work is with homeless families. However, volunteers also provide information on Boston and will help out stranded travellers, but only those with serious financial problems.
Branches: Logan Airport, Terminal E (567 5385); Amtrak booth, South Station (737 2880).

Visitor information centres

Boston Common

147 Tremont Street, Back Bay (426 3115/advance information 1-800 888 5515). Park Street T. **Open** 9am-5pm Mon-Fri. **Map** p307 G4.

Prudential Center

Between Boylston Street & Huntington Avenue, Back Bay (advance information 1-800 888 5515). Prudential or Hynes/ICA T. **Open** 9am-5pm daily. **Map** p306 E6.

Cambridge Information Booth

Harvard Square, Cambridge (no phone). Harvard T. **Open** 9am-5pm Mon-Sat. **Map** p311 B2.

Psychiatric emergency services

Massachusetts General Hospital

(726 2994). **Open** 24 hours daily.
Acute psychiatric treatment is offered by the emergency room of Massachusetts General Hospital.

Rape

Rape Crisis

(492 7273). **Open** 24 hours daily.
Rape Crisis is a hotline that takes messages from people who have suffered sexual abuse. A trained counsellor will phone back, usually within five minutes.

Suicide

Samaritans

(247 0220). **Open** 24 hours daily.

Samariteens

(247 8050). **Open** 24 hours daily.
A hotline that offers the same service as the Samaritans, but for teenage callers. Between 2-11pm daily, the line is staffed by teen volunteers.

Immigration & customs

Standard immigration regulations apply to all visitors. During your flight, you will be handed an immigration form and a customs declaration form to be presented when you land at the airport. Fill them in carefully, and ask for another if you make a mistake. Be prepared to queue when you arrive at immigration for anything up to an hour. Expect to explain the nature of your visit (business and/or pleasure). If you don't have a return ticket and are planning a long visit, you will be questioned closely. Usually, you will be granted an entry permit to cover the length of your stay.

US Customs allows visitors to bring in $100 worth of gifts duty free ($400 for returning Americans), 200 cigarettes (one carton) or 50 cigars and one litre of spirits (liquor).

Any amount of currency can be brought into the US, but a form, available from the airport, must be filled in for anything over $10,000. Prescription drugs must be clearly marked (and visitors should be prepared to produce a written prescription upon request).

No meat, meat products, seeds, plants or fruit can be taken through customs. For more detailed information on agricultural produce and customs phone the **US Department of Agriculture** (1-301 734 8295).

UK Customs & Excise allows returning travellers to bring in £145 worth of gifts and goods and an unlimited amount of money, as long as you can prove it's yours.

For further information contact the following agency:

Office of Immigration and Naturalisation

First floor, John F Kennedy Building (565 3879). Gov't Center T. **Open** 7am-3pm Mon-Fri. **Map** p307 G4.

Insurance

It's advisable to take out comprehensive insurance cover before travelling to the United States: it's almost impossible to arrange once you are there. Make sure that you have adequate health cover since medical expenses can be high. *See p283* **Health & Medical** for a list of Boston's hospitals and clinics.

Internet access

Boston is renowned for its IT industry, so getting online is not a problem. The best way to check your email when you're away is to either use one of the public libraries with online facilities or to pay for the use of a computer at a copy/office centre – certain branches of Kinkos, Copy Cop and Gnomon Copy offer high-speed Internet access. The main Boston Public Library at Copley Square offers free 'express' internet access (only 30 minutes at a time for non-members). You need to stop by the computer desk and make a reservation in advance.

For hotels that offer modem or dataport facilities so you can check mail using a laptop (listed under Room Services), *see chapter* **Accommodation**. If you have friends or contacts at any of the area universities, you may be able to gain access to the excellent computer labs on campus. Another good option is to swing by the free Internet terminals in the Prudential Center mall, which are located near the entrance to the Sheraton hotel. Be warned, though: there are no seats, no privacy, and there is often a queue.

The cybercafé trend never really caught on in Boston, and there is only one: **Designs for Living** (52 Queensbury Street, at Jersey Street; Fenway or Kenmore T; 536 6150), in a central location. It has only two terminals for $8 an hour.

Libraries

Boston Public Library

700 Boylston Street, at Copley Square (536 5400). Copley T.
Open *General library & research* 9am-9pm Mon-Thur; 9am-5pm Fri, Sat; 1-5pm Sun; *print department, rare books & manuscripts* 9am-5pm Mon-Fri; *young adults' room* 9am-9pm Mon-Thur; 9am-5pm Fri-Sat.
Map p306 F5.
Branches: North End, 25 Parmenter Street (227 8135); South End, 685 Tremont Street (536 8241); West End, 151 Cambridge Street (523 3957).

Liquor laws

The legal drinking age is 21 and Boston is serious about checking photo identification. Not all forms of out-of-state identification are accepted so it is best to carry your passport with you if you are likely to want a drink or to buy one from a liquor store. Alcohol is sold in liquor stores and a few supermarkets and convenience stores, but it is illegal to purchase alcohol on Sundays unless from a bar or restaurant. The sole exception to this rule is between Thanksgiving and New Year.

Media

Newspapers & magazines

Bay Windows

Weekly newspaper for lesbians and gay men, focusing on Boston news, politics and the arts scene. The cover price is 50 cents, though it's available free from many bars and shops in Back Bay and the South End.

Boston Globe

www.boston.com
The city's oldest and most prominent daily newspaper, the *Boston Globe*'s reputation has fallen since the scandal of 1998, when two prominent columnists (Mike Barnicle and Patricia Smith) were fired for fabricating stories. The *Globe* remains Boston's most popular newspaper and it takes a cautiously liberal line on most subjects, covering local politics quite well, but sometimes lacking on national and international stories.

Boston Herald

www.bostonherald.com
The *Globe*'s main competitor is a raucous and conservative-leaning tabloid in the style of the *New York Post*. It has a strong following among

working-class Bostonians and it has been very successful in unearthing local political scandals. Not surprisingly, the sports coverage is very extensive.

Boston Magazine

www.bostonmagazine.com
A general interest glossy monthly with a mix of lifestyle features, profiles, and occasional strong pieces on city issues; catering mostly to an upmarket audience. The annual 'Best of Boston' issue and the restaurant reviews are highly regarded.

Boston Phoenix

www.bostonphoenix.com
An irreverent free weekly which takes an alternative line on the city's politics and culture. It doesn't cover news exhaustively, preferring longer, strongly worded features on select issues. The arts section is excellent, featuring critical and smart coverage of music, film, theatre, dance and visual art. The entertainment and events listings are the most comprehensive you'll find. Available from sidewalk dispensers, clubs and cafés around the city.

Improper Bostonian

A weekly lifestyle magazine distributed free from sidewalk dispensers on main streets. Newbury Street is the centre of its universe and the desperately enthusiastic and uncritical style and arts features are, well, desperate.

Stuff@Night

A bi-monthly arts and lifestyle magazine published by the owners of the *Boston Phoenix*. The coverage is self-consciously hip, with lots of attention spent on fashion and food. A good place to discover the 'in' bars and nightclubs.

The Tabs

A chain of newspapers that cater towards a particular city or neighbourhood – the Cambridge Tab, the Brookline Tab, etc. Mostly focused on community issues and local arts coverage.

Radio

WERS (88.9 FM)

A very good semi-professional college radio station run by students at Emerson College. Daily slots dedicated to folk, jazz, world music, reggae and hip-hop. Lots of interviews, live performances and local music coverage.

WGBH (89.7 FM)

A public radio station that airs the main NPR (National Public Radio – the US equivalent of the BBC) news shows ('Morning Edition' and 'All Things Considered'), in addition to a mix of classical music, folk, blues and jazz.

WBUR (90.9 FM)

A public radio station dedicated almost completely to news and talk. The very worthwhile nationally syndicated programmes 'Car Talk' and 'The Connection' are just two of the shows that are produced here.

WBOS (92.9 FM)

'Adult Alternative', which means Barenaked Ladies, Sting, Dave Matthews Band and the like.

WJMN (94.5 FM)

Mainstream hiphop and R&B.

WHRB (95.3 FM)

Harvard University's station plays a pleasing combination of classical and jazz during the day, though punk, indie, rock and hiphop take over in the wee hours.

WBCN (104.1 FM)

A long-standing rock station, now focusing on 'alternative' and hard rock, plus a smattering of local music.

WRKO (680 AM)

Talk radio and news programmes.

WEEI (850 AM)

A station for the die-hard Red Sox and Celtics fan. That would be just about everyone in Boston, then.

TV

National networks dominate the airwaves in Boston, however, the local PBS (Public Broadcasting Service, similar to the BBC) station, **WGBH**, is one of the best in the country, producing acclaimed shows such as *Nova* and *Frontline*. Below are the local channels and the national networks with which they are affiliated.

WGBH, Channel 2 and 44, PBS
WBZ, Channel 4, CBS
WCVB, Channel 5, ABC
WHDH, Channel 7, NBC
WFXT, Channel 25, Fox

Money

The US dollar ($) equals 100 cents (¢). Coins range from copper pennies or cents (1¢), to silver nickels (5¢), dimes (10¢) and quarters (25¢). In 2000 the US Mint issued a new 'golden' dollar coin embossed with a portrait of Sacagawea, a Native American woman who acted as a guide to early 19th-century explorers Lewis and Clark. The coin has been so popular with collectors that few have made their way into general circulation. Most vending machines are not set up for them. Very rarely you may also come across the smaller 'Susan B Anthony' one-dollar coin, recognisable by its extra weight and rimmed edges.

Paper money 'bills' come in denominations of $1, $5, $10, $20, $50, and $100, which are confusingly all the same size and colour. To make things worse, the US Treasury has released redesigned bills with larger portraits on them, so you may well end up with bills of the same denomination that look slightly different. Don't worry, everybody's gotten used to them lately, so you won't have trouble spending them.

Since counterfeiting of $50 and $100 bills is a booming business, many small shops will not accept them. If you have to use a $50 or $100 bill, ask first, especially if your payment is only a few dollars. On the whole it is better to restrict your paper money to denominations of $1, $5, $10 and $20.

Banks & bureaux de change

Most banks are open from 9am to 5pm Monday to Friday, and some are open from 9am to noon on Saturday. You will need some kind of photo identification, such as a passport, to transact any business such as cashing travellers' cheques or obtaining cash from a credit card. If you arrive in Boston after 5pm, change money at the airport or, if you have US dollars travellers' cheques, buy something in order to get some change. If you want to cash travellers' cheques at a shop, ask first if a minimum purchase is required. You can obtain cash on a credit card account from certain banks. Check with your credit card company before you leave, and be prepared to pay interest rates that vary daily.

American Express Travel Services

1 State Street, Financial District (723 8400/ www.americanexpress.com). State T. **Open** 8.30am-5.30pm Mon-Fri.

Fleet Bank

100 Federal Street, Downtown (434 5501). South Station or Downtown Crossing T. **Open** 8.30am-5pm Mon-Fri. **Map** p307 G5
Check the phone directory for the location of other branches.

Subway ins and outs

The subway trains travel either 'outbound' or 'inbound', which is determined in relation to the major downtown hubs: Park Street, Downtown Crossing, State/Citizens Bank. Large signs in the stations indicate which tracks are outbound and inbound. If you are unsure whether you need to travel in or out, the direction of each train is also designated by its terminus. For instance, northbound trains on the Red Line will read 'Alewife' (for the last stop on the line in that direction), while southbound trains will read 'Ashmont' or 'Braintree'. Signs on the front and sides of the subway car will list the final destination of the train.

Maps of the entire subway system are posted in numerous locations around each station, plus there are specially designed maps for the inbound and outbound tracks. These maps display only the stops between your current location and the terminus of the line.

Boston Bank of Commerce

133 Federal Street, at Summer Street, Downtown (457 4400). South Station T. **Open** 9am-5pm Mon-Fri. **Map** p307 G5.

Citizens Bank

28 State Street, Congress Street, Downtown (725 5500). Government Center T. **Open** 8.30am-5pm Mon-Fri. **Map** p307 G5.
Check the phone directory for the location of other branches.

Thomas Cook Currency Services

1-800 287 7362.
Phone for exchange rates and the location of the nearest branch.

Travelex

Open 7am-10pm daily.
This bureau de change is located in Terminal C (567 1943) and Terminal E (567 2450) of the airport.

Western Union

1-800 325 6000.
Western Union is still the most reliable way to get money wired from one country to another.

ATMs

Automated Teller Machines (ATMs or cashpoints) are easy to find. Most machines will accept American Express, MasterCard and Visa and selected international debit and cash cards – tap in your usual PIN number. There is a fee, of course – cash on demand has its price. You can get directions to the nearest ATM location by calling Plus System (1-800 843 7587) or Cirrus (1-800 424 7787). If you have forgotten your PIN number or have de-magnetised your card, most banks will dispense cash to card holders. You can also get cash back at supermarkets if you pay with a card bearing the Cirrus or Plus logo (with your usual PIN).

Credit cards

Less disastrous if you're robbed, and accepted almost everywhere, credit (and not debit) cards are required by almost all hotels, car rental agencies and airlines. Your stay will be made much more pleasant if you 'don't leave home with out them'. The major credit cards most often accepted in the US are American Express, Discover, MasterCard and Visa. If you lose your credit card (or your travellers' cheques) call the appropriate number below.

Lost or stolen credit cards

American Express
1-800 221 7282.
Discover
1-800 347 2683.
MasterCard
1-800 307 7309.
Visa
1-800 336 8472.

Lost or stolen travellers' cheques

American Express
1-800 221 7282.
Thomas Cook
1-800 223 7373.
Visa
1-800 227 6811.

Postal services

Post office opening hours in Boston are usually 9am-5pm Monday to Friday, with limited hours on Saturday. Contact the **US Postal Service** (1-800 222 1811/ www.usps.com) for information on your nearest branch and mailing facilities (be ready with a post- or Zipcode). Stamps can be bought at any post office as well as at many hotels, grocery stores and convenience stores. **Western Union** (1-800 325 6000) will take a telegram over the phone and charge it to your phone bill.

Fort Point Station

25 Dorchester Avenue, behind South Station, Downtown (654 5325). South Station T. **Open** 24 hours daily. **Map** p307 G5.
Boston's main post office is open 24 hours daily. If you have no definite address while you are travelling and you're not sure where you will be staying, have it marked General Delivery and posted to Fort Point Station. Proof of identity is needed when picking up mail.

Mailboxes Etc

167 Milk Street, Downtown (734 3744). Government Center T.
Open 8.30am-5.30pm Mon-Fri; 9am-2pm Sat.
This is a very useful national chain offering shipping and packaging services, plus mailbox rentals, office supplies and, oh so many other things that come in handy when you're on the road.

Public toilets/ restrooms

A few public toilets can be found in Boston – in the Cambridge Galleria, Copley Place, Prudential Center and Quincy Marketplace .

Religion

Here are just a few of the many places of in Boston and nearby. Check the Yellow Pages for more.

Baptist

First Baptist Church of Boston

110 Commonwealth Avenue, at Clarendon Street, Back Bay (267 3148). Copley T. **Open** 11am-2pm Mon-Fri. **Service** 11am Sun.
Map p306 F5.

Sacred Heart Church

49 Sixth Street, at Otis Street, Cambridge (547 0399). Harvard T, then 69 bus. **Services** 9am Mon, Wed-Fri; 6.30pm Tue; 7.30am, 9am, 11am Sun. **Map** p306 E3.

Buddhist

Cambridge Zen Center

199 Auburn Street, Cambridge (576 3229). Central T.
Nightly practice at 7pm.

Episcopal

Christian Science Church

215 Massachusetts Avenue, at Huntington Avenue, Back Bay (450 2000). Symphony T. **Services** noon, 7.30pm Wed; 10am, 7pm Sun. **Map** p306 E6.

Church of the Advent

30 Brimmer Street, at Mount Vernon Street, West End (523 2377). Charles/MGH T. **Services** 7.30am Mon-Fri; 9am Sat; 8am, 9am, 11am Sun. **Map** p306 F4.

Old North Church (Christ Church)

193 Salem Street, at Hull Street, North End (523 6676). Haymarket T. **Services** 9am, 11am, 5pm Sun. **Map** p307 G/H3.

Jewish

Jewish Religious Information Services

177 Tremont Street, at Boylston Street, Back Bay (426 2139). Boylston T. **Open** 9am-4pm Mon-Thur. **Map** p306 G5.
The Jewish Religious Information Services is a useful organisation that provides referrals to other groups, organisations, temples and synagogues throughout the area, as well as advice on kosher foods and restaurants.

Temple Israel

Longwood Avenue, at Plymouth Street, Fenway (566 3960). Longwood T. **Services** 5.45pm Fri; 10.30am Sat.

Methodist

Old West Church

131 Cambridge Street, at Staniford Street, Downtown (227 5088). Govt Center T. **Service** 11am Sun. **Map** p307 G4.

Muslim

Islamic Society of Boston

204 Prospect Street, at Massachusetts Avenue, Cambridge (876 3546). Central T. **Services** 6am, 1pm, 2.45pm, 5pm, 7.30pm daily. **Map** p311 C3.
The Islamic Society acts both as a religious organisation and an information service.

Presbyterian

Church of the Covenant

67 Newbury Street, at Berkeley Street, Back Bay (266 7480). Arlington or Copley T. **Services** 10am Sun. **Map** p306 F5.

Quaker

Beacon Hill Friends House

6 Chestnut Street, at Charles Street, Beacon Hill (227 9118). Park St or Charles/MGH T. **Open** office 9am-5pm Mon-Fri; meetings 10.30am Sun. **Map** p306 F4.
The Friends House also has rooms for rent (in the Quaker style) for $50-$75 per night.

Safety

Boston is one of the safest cities in the United States. However, as in any big city, it's wise to be aware of the basic safety precautions. Don't fumble with your map or wallet in public; always plan where you're going and walk with brisk confidence; avoid walking alone at night; avoid parking in questionable areas (if in doubt, use valet parking when you can) and keep your car doors locked when parked and while driving.

Central Boston is generally well lit, but pedestrians should probably avoid Boston Common, the Public Gardens and the walkways along the Charles River after dark. It's also useful to know that the couple of blocks along Washington Street, between Avery and Stuart Streets, are known as the Combat Zone – and that is not a fashion statement.

Smoking

Boston's smoking laws are quite confusing. In 1998, the Boston Public Health Commission implemented a citywide ban on smoking in restaurants that served food and no alcohol. In restaurants that served alcohol, the regulations state, smoking is allowed solely in the bar area, but only if the bar area of the establishment is not more than one-third the total capacity of the restaurant, and only if smokers and non-smokers are separated by a barrier or a buffer zone of at least six feet. Got that? Well, neither did restaurant owners, who tried their best to abide by this confusing law by drawing imaginary lines and mapping out strictly policed smoking areas. Nonetheless, Somerville followed with a similar ruling in 1999 and Cambridge followed suit in 2000. And Brookline boasts the strictest anti-smoking rules in the area – absolutely no smoking in any dining or drinking establishments.

The end result of all this legislation means that smoking is prohibited in coffeeshops and diners; while in restaurants that serve alcohol there may be a smoking section or puffing could only be allowed at the bar; at bars without food, smoking is normally allowed throughout the entire room – except in Brookline. In fact, just forget it. Your best bet is to ask before you light up, or risk being chastised for your perfidy.

Study

As Boston has the world's largest number of colleges and universities per square mile, the choices for study are many. The city is a great place to be a student with loads of youthful activities, and there are a wide variety of courses and summer schools on offer each year. For further details *see chapter* **College Town**.

The following are the most basic address and contact information for some of Boston's largest colleges and universities:

Boston College

40 Commonwealth Avenue, Chestnut Hill, MA 02467 (552 8000).
Founded in 1863, BC is one of the oldest Jesuit universities in the US. Boasting top athletic programmes and high-quality academics, BC hosts more than 13,000 undergrads and graduate students on its 115-acre (46-ha) campus, which is located in the suburbs six miles (9.7km) from downtown Boston.

Boston University

930 Commonwealth Avenue, Boston, MA 02215 (734 0015).
BU is the largest university in Boston and the third largest independent university in the United States. With more than 30,000 students from all 50 US states and 135 other countries, BU offers a range of

Useful bus routes

Though Boston's subway system is efficient for most in-town travel, occasionally it falls short. The distinctive 'X'-shaped design of the T makes travel between certain neighbourhoods (Cambridge and Back Bay, for instance) incredibly time-consuming. This is because it's necessary to transfer at one of the main downtown hubs (Park Street, Downtown Crossing) before heading back outbound.

Certain bus routes can reduce travel time by a great deal. Also, the last bus of the evening generally runs 20 to 30 minutes later than the last subway, which is useful for late-night clubgoers. Bus maps and schedules are available from most major T stops, though the most popular routes (1, 66) run so frequently that a schedule is unnecessary.

1 Mass Ave

This is the most useful route for visitors to the city. Running both directions on Boston's main thoroughfare, Mass Ave, between Harvard Square and Dudley Station, this bus is a quick way to hop back and forth between Cambridge, Back Bay, the Symphony Hall area and the South End. Starting its route right outside the gates to Harvard Yard, it travels south on Mass Ave through Central Square, MIT, Back Bay, the South End, Boston Medical Center and Dudley Station, before turning around to head back north.

47 Central Square – Broadway Station

This route is the quickest way, by far, to jump from Central Square to the Kenmore Square/Fenway area. Beginning at Central Square, the 47 heads immediately across the river to the Fenway T stop, then heads through the Longwood Medical Area, Ruggles T, the Boston Medical Center and Broadway Station, where it turns around.

55 Park Street T, Back Bay, the Fenway

From Park Street T station, this route heads down Tremont Street past the Boylston T stop. Heading through Theatre District on St James Avenue, it passes by the Prudential Center on Huntington Avenue and then crosses over to Boylston Street, continuing out to the Fenway neighborhood. Turning around at Jersey and Queensbury Streets, the route heads back down Boylston Street all the way to Boston Garden, passing by the Hynes/ICA, Boylston Street, and Arlington T stops. It takes a left onto Arlington Street and follows the outer rim of Boston Common past Beacon Hill and the State House before coming back to the Park Street T station.

66 Harvard Square to Dudley Station

Travelling between Harvard Square and Brighton/Allston/Brookline can take over an hour on the subway; the 66 bus reduces this time by half. Beginning in Harvard Square, this route crosses the Charles at the Larz Anderson Bridge, passing through Lower Allston before meeting up with Harvard Avenue. Travelling through the heart of Allston/Brighton on Harvard Ave, the 66 continues through Coolidge Corner, Brookline Village, Brigham Circle, Roxbury Crossing and Dudley Station, where it turns around.

86 Sullivan Square to Cleveland Circle

This is the easiest way to get from central Somerville or Harvard Square to Cleveland Circle or Chestnut Hill. It begins in East Somerville at Sullivan Square and runs through Union Square before stopping in Harvard Square. It then continues across the river through Lower Allston to Brighton Circle and up Chestnut Hill Avenue to Cleveland Circle, where it turns around.

degrees and programmes. It is so large it boasts 52,000 sq ft of bathroom space in its largest residences. It sprawls along Commonwealth Avenue, west of downtown Boston. Famous alumni include Dr Martin Luther King Jr, Geena Davis, Nina Totenberg and *Seinfeld* actor Jason Alexander. Going here isn't cheap, however, annual tuition costs, including fees, room and board, exceed $31,000.

Emerson College

420 Beacon Street, MA 02116 (824 8600).
The nation's only four-year college devoted to the exclusive study of the performing arts and communication, Emerson links education with hands-on experience in studios, editing booths and workshops. It is a fairly small college, with a famously artistic student body. Its radio station, WERS (88.9 FM), consistently earns awards for its programming. Tuition alone costs $17,376 a year here.

Harvard University

Massachusetts Hall, Harvard Yard, off Massachusetts Avenue, Cambridge, MA 02138 (495 1000).
The oldest and most prestigious university in America, enrolling about 6,600 undergrads (in Harvard College) and more than

11,000 graduate students. The Harvard Law, Medical and Business schools are also among the best in the world and the university's massive endowment ($11 billion) and reputation have guaranteed its steady growth and excellence. This is one of the most difficult schools in the world to get into. Undergraduate tuition costs more than $21,000 annually; the total expense per year is more than $33,000.

Massachusetts Institute of Technology

77 Massachusetts Avenue, Cambridge, MA 02139 (253 1000).
MIT is considered one of the top science and technology universities anywhere. More than 4,300 students pay tuition in excess of $33,000 each year to attend. Men at the school bemoan the 61:39 male-female ratio, but there it is anyway. Students are required to take a six-subject core course-load that includes calculus, physics, chemistry and biology; eight terms of humanities; plus laboratory and writing classes. Still, it's primary emphasis is science and technology. Undergrads may also cross-register in courses at Wellesley and Harvard.

Northeastern University

360 Huntingdon Avenue, Boston, MA 02115 (373 2000).
The second-largest school in Boston, enrolling nearly 12,000 undergrads, Northeastern fits neatly into Back Bay between the Museum of Fine Arts and Symphony Hall. Tuition costs $18,000 per year and students are encouraged to participate in 'co-operative education', which combines study with paid, professional employment.

Suffolk University

8 Ashburton Place, Boston, MA 02108 (573 8000).
Located on Beacon Hill, Suffolk sits plum in the heart of Boston. More than 6,000 full- and part-time graduate and undergraduate students are enrolled; Suffolk's Law School is especially renowned.

Tufts University

Bendetson Hall, Medford, MA 02155 (628 5000).
Enrolling more than 8,000 students on three campuses, Tufts is based in Medford, just north-west of Boston proper. Its campus sits on prime real estate, perched on a hill over-looking the city . A private university, it was founded in 1852. Here, too, tuition plus room, board and other costs exceeds $30,000 a year.

University of Massachusetts at Boston

100 Morrissey Boulevard, Dorchester, MA 02125 (287 5000).
Established in 1964, UMass Boston represents one of several branches of the state-wide University of Massachusetts. Everybody, absolutely everybody, calls this system UMass. Situated on the Columbia Point peninsula, UMass is blessed with one of the prettiest campus locations in the city. The university's Boston location enrolls around 12,000 students every year, but it has many more at its other locations throughout the state. More than 37% of the university's students are 30 or older; minority students make up 35% of the population.

Telephones

Dialling & codes

The area code for metropolitan Boston (including Cambridge, Somerville and Brookline) is 617. The first ring of suburbs is in the 781 area code and is considered a local call from metropolitan Boston. The northern suburbs and north coast are served by 978; the western and southern suburbs (including Cape Cod and the islands) are served by 508. These are both long distance calls from metropolitan Boston.

As of April 2001, a new area code 857 (known as an 'overlay' code) is being added to the region. This won't change any of numbers listed in this guide (only new customers will be assigned the 857 code), but it will alter the way that calls are made. All calls made within Eastern Massachusetts (617, 781, 508, 978 and 857) should be dialled using all 10 digits – area code + plus seven-digit phone number. So, when calling from one side of Boston to the other, it is necessary to include 617 before the bulk of the number.

The listings in this guide do not include the 617 area code, so if you're phoning from inside Boston, by mid 2001, you will dial 617, but not a 1 prefix, before the phone number if it is a Boston number. If you are trying to reach a Boston number from elswhere within the US, you will dial 1 + area code 617 before the seven-digit numbers listed. All other area codes are included in the listings, where appropriate.

When calling Boston from abroad, dial the international access code of the country from which you are calling (00 from the UK), followed by the US country code (1), the area code and the number as before. Note that toll-free calls generally start with 1-800 or 1-888, while expensive pay-per-minute calls usually start with 1-900 or 1-976. However, many hotels add a surcharge on all numbers.

Making a call

A local call costs 35¢ and operator, directory and emergency calls are free. Public payphones only accept nickels, dimes and quarters – not ideal for long-distance calls. To make a call from a public phone, pick up the receiver and check for a dial tone before parting with your money; many, many pay phones in the US are broken and battered, and once you put your money in, it's gone. Trying to get the phone company to give you back your change is akin to blues musician Robert Johnson asking for his soul back from the devil. Some phones require you to dial the number first and wait for an operator or recorded message to tell you how much change to deposit. To make a collect (reverse charge) call, dial 0 for the operator followed by the area code and phone number. For help, dial 0 for an operator.

One of the most convenient ways of making a call is to use a phone card. These can be purchased at many retail outlets and range in price from $5 to $50, with a cost as low as 3¢ per minute. Read the card info carefully before buying; some have a 'connection charge'.

European-style prepaid phone cards that you insert directly into public phone booths instead of coins can be used in some special phone booths. Alternatively, you can charge calls to your MasterCard with AT&T (1-800 225 5288) or MCI (1-800 269 2255). Telephone directories are available at most public phones and hotels. If you can't find one, dial directory assistance (555 1212 for local numbers) and ask for the person or location by name.

Useful Numbers

Operator assistance 0.
Emergency (police, ambulance,fire) 911.
Directory assistance 1 + area code + 555 1212.

International calls

To phone abroad from Boston dial 011 followed by the country code, followed by the area code and phone number. Country codes include: UK 44, Australia 61, New Zealand 64. To call other nations, check the White Pages of the telephone book where a full listing of city and country codes is provided.

Mobile phones

Whereas in Europe mobile phones work on the GSM network at either 900 or 1800mHz, the US does not have a standard mobile phone network that covers the whole country. This means that many European handsets will not work, and travellers from Europe may need to rent a handset and service once they arrive. Try **CellularOne** (222 Newbury Street, at Exeter Street; 266 6975), which rents mobile phones on a weekly or monthly basis. US visitors to Boston should check in advance with their service provider as to whether they will be able to use their mobile phone.

Local service providers

Nextel
1-800 639 8359.
AT&T
1-800 462 4463.
Sprint PCS
1-800 480 4727.

Time & date

Massachusetts operates on Eastern Standard Time, which is five hours behind Greenwich Mean Time and one hour ahead of Central Time (from Manitoba to Texas), two hours ahead of Mountain Time (Alberta to Arizona and New Mexico) and three hours ahead of Pacific Time (California).

Daylight Saving Time is observed from the first Sunday in April to the last Sunday in October, when clocks are turned forward one hour.

Also, note that, in the US, dates are written in month, day and year order; so 12/5/99 is 5 December 1999, and not 12 May.

Tipping

Unlike in Europe, tipping is a way of life in the US. The growth of the service industry here is based largely on cheap labour – very cheap in fact. Those in the service industry in the US – particularly waiters and bartenders – often make little more than $2 per hour outside of their tips. In essence, when you're dealing with the service industry – particularly bartenders and waiters – be aware that virtually everything they earn comes in the form of gratuities. Thus, Americans tip much more than do people in other countries. Interestingly, out of this has come the myth that US residents throw their money around trying to impress people by tipping heavily. In reality, they're just aware how much their waiter earns. So, if you want good service and a happy and healthy waitstaff, here are some basic guidelines for tipping in Boston:

Bellhops & baggage handlers
$1-$2 per bag.
Hotel maids
$1 a night.
Hotel concierges
$3-$5.
Bartenders
15% of the bill.
Cabbies, waiting staff, hairdressers & food delivery
15%-20% of the bill.
Valets, counterstaff
$1-$3 depending on the size of the order and any special arrangements
Wait staff
15%-20% if no service is included in the bill.

Visas

Under the Visa Waiver Scheme, citizens of the UK, Japan and all West European countries (except for Portugal, Greece and the Vatican City) do not need a visa for stays in the United States of less than 90 days (business or pleasure) – as long as they have a passport that is valid for the full 90-day period and a return or onward ticket. An open standby ticket is acceptable.

Canadians and Mexicans do not need visas, but they may be asked for proof of their citizenship. All other travellers, including those from Australia and New Zealand, must have a visa. Full information and visa application forms can be obtained from your nearest US embassy or consulate. If you require a visa urgently, apply via the travel agent when you book your ticket.

US Embassy Visa Information Line

Recorded information in the UK 0891 200 290.

When to go

Weatherwise, the best time of year in Boston is the autumn. Temperatures are generally in the low 70s°F and the skies are clear for days. Of course, this also means that the city is packed to bursting-point. Prices soar (even more than usual in this expensive town) and booking a hotel room becomes difficult. It's the time when 60 colleges-worth of students are returning to town, plus their parents; many professional conventions take place at the same time, and fall foliage sightseers are arriving by the busload. In other words, it is, without question, the best of times and the worst of times to find yourself in Boston.

Summer is much quieter, and in general more laid-back. Bostonians are more relaxed and it's a lot easier to get around town. But the downside is that temperatures can soar to the 80s and 90s with almost 100 per cent humidity. In addition, because Boston endures harsh winters for most of the year, many facilities lack any sort of air conditioning. That can make even a moderately warm day seem baking. It can also make sleeping quite difficult. It's worthwhile at this time of year to make sure your hotel has air conditioning.

Spring is also a quieter time of year, when the blossoms appear and the city is quite beautiful. But, the weather can also be very unpredictable at this time of year, and temperatures can range, day-by-day, from the high 40s to the low 70s. It also tends to be a particularly rainy season, so bring the umbrella.

Winter tends to be grey, cold, and dreary, which is why the hotel rates drop. But the city can be downright lovely after a light dusting of snow.

Whichever season you choose to visit Boston, make sure you pack layers of clothing. The old saying 'If you don't like the Boston weather, wait ten minutes' holds true. Hat, mittens, and scarf are essential in winter; and shorts are preferable in the summer. An umbrella or waterproof gear is a good idea for any time of year.

Public Holidays

New Year's Day
1 January.
Martin Luther King Day
Third Monday in January.
Presidents' Day
Third Monday in February.
St Patrick's Day
17 March.
Memorial Day
Last Monday in May.
Independence Day
4 July.
Labor Day
First Monday in September.
Columbus Day
Second Monday in October.
Veterans Day
11 November.
Thanksgiving Day
Last Thursday in November.
Christmas Day
25 December.

Weather forecast

Phone 936 1234 or 637 1212 for free information about the daily temperature. Or check the Massachusetts weather on the web at: www.rainorshine.com.

Further reference

Books

Non-fiction

Jack Beatty: *The Rascal King: The Life and Times of James Michael Curley, 1874-1958*
Thoroughly researched biography of the charismatic Boston mayor and a good reference to big city politics in the US.
Noel Riley Fitch: *Appetite for Life: The Biography of Julia Child*
All about television's America's favourite chef, and a Boston icon.
David Hackett Fischer: *Paul Revere's Ride*
Brilliant account of the legendary ride to Lexington, related as a historical narrative.
Sebastian Junger: *The Perfect Storm*
Gripping tale of a crew of Gloucester fishermen caught up in the 'Hallowe'en Gale' in the North Atlantic in 1991.
Ronald P Formisano: *Boston Against Busing: Race, Class and Ethnicity in the 1960s and 1970s*
The story of the bitter fight over busing that divided the city.
Barney Frank: *Improper Bostonians: Lesbian and Gay History from the Puritans to Playland*
Comprehensive history of homosexuality in Boston.
Doris Kearns Goodwin: *The Fitzgeralds and the Kennedys: An American Saga*
The story behind America's answer to royalty.
Jane Jacobs: *The Death and Life of Great American Cities*
Not exclusively about Boston, but Jacobs cites the North End as a perfect city neighborhood.
Dick Lehr and Gerald O'Neill: *Black Mass*
Story of two former Boston-based FBI agents now facing trial for allegedly befriending Irish Mafia crime boss Whitey Bulger in South Boston.
Walt Kelley: *What They Never Told You About Boston (Or What They Did That Were Lies)*
Local cabbie's humourous collection of facts about the city.
J Anthony Lukas: *Common Ground: A Turbulent Decade in the Lives of Three American Families*
The 1970's busing crisis, through the eyes of an Irish-American, a black and a white middle-class family.
Dan McNichol and Andy Ryan: *The Big Dig*
Tells the story of how the biggest construction job in US history came about, and what it will mean.
Robert S Morse: *25 Mountain Bike Tours in Massachusetts: From the Connecticut River to the Atlantic Coast*
Guidelines and trips for the ambitious recreational biker.
Raymond Mungo: *Total Loss Farm*
Mungo's New England hippie commune drop-out memoir.
Douglass Shand-Tucci: *The Art of Scandal: The Life and Times of Isabella Stewart Gardner*
Biography of Boston's famous patron of the arts and the inspiration behind Isabel Archer in Portrait of a Lady.
Dan Shaughnessy: *The Curse of the Bambino*
Entertaining look at the Red Sox 'curse' by local sports journo.

Fiction

Nathan Aldyne: *Canary; Cobalt; Slate; Vermillion*
Four tongue-in-cheek mystery novels set in the gay communities of Boston and Provincetown circa 1980, featuring bartender and amateur detective Daniel Valentine and his sidekick Clarisse Lovelace.
Nathaniel Hawthorne: *The Scarlet Letter* and *The House of the Seven Gables*
Two American – and New England – classics by the Salem native.
Henry James: *The Bostonians*
The tale of Varena Tarrant, James' Boston feminist.
Henry Wadsworth Longfellow: *The Works of Henry Wadsworth Longfellow*
Includes the famous 'Paul Revere's Ride'.
Robert Lowell: *Life Studies* and *For the Union Dead*
The poet's account of growing up privileged in Boston and hating it.
Daniel Lyons: *Dog Days*
Light-hearted novel about two twenty-something guys living in the North End, prospering off the high-tech industry but despising themselves for it.
Norman Mailer: *Tough Guys Don't Dance*
Boston's ultimate cynic tells another hard-edged tale.
Robert McCloskey: *Make Way for Ducklings*
The classic children's tale about ducks on Boston Common.
Michael Patrick McDonald: *All Souls*
The bittersweet story of a family growing up together in South Boston's Irish ghetto.
Herman Melville: *Moby Dick*
The great American novel. Melville's 19th-century romance with the sea.
Sue Miller: *While I Was Gone*
A haunting novel about a woman living near Boston as her seemingly perfect life begins to crumble.
Henry David Thoreau: *Walden*
The Transcendentalist's most famous work, written while living in isolation in a cabin for two years, two months and two days.
John Updike: *Roger's Version*
The writer's updated version of The Scarlet Letter

Film

Alice's Restaurant (1969)
Woody Guthrie's son Arlo in a hippie pic filmed in the Berkshires, based on Arlo's song of the same name.
Beautiful Girls (1996)
Timothy Hutton and others star in this Mass-based movie about growing older, sort of.
A Civil Action (1998)
John Travolta stars in the real-life table of a town near Boston that was poisoned by a chemical company, sued and lost.
The Crucible (1996)
Wynona Ryder stars in the film version of the Pulitzer Prize winning play about the Salem Witch Trials.
Good Will Hunting (1997)
Academy Award winning film by and about South Boston residents. Filmed on location all over town, particularly in Southie and in Cambridge around MIT.
Next Stop, Wonderland (1998).
Wonderful, low-budget romantic comedy with nods toward Boston's old and new immigrant communities. Filmed all over the city, particularly in Somerville and at the Aquarium, and, of course, Wonderland.
No Cure for Cancer (1994)
Concert film with local comedian Dennis Leary, who both typifies and spoofs Boston's angry young Irish.

TV shows

Ally McBeal
Quirky legal drama, written and directed by the respected writer David E Kelly. Set in, occasionally filmed in Boston.
The Practice
Quirky legal drama, written and directed by the respected writer David E Kelly. Set in, occasionally filmed in Boston. (This is not a mistake. This definition fits both shows perfectly.)
Two Guys and A Girl
Average sit-com. Actually quite dull, really. Doesn't have much going for it but it is set in Boston area.

Biking & blading in Boston

Yeah, we know. Americans and cycling are not supposed to mix. That's the stereotype anyway, and, it's largely true. In many US cities the appearance of a cyclist on the streets would result in their arrest, or at least grave personal harm. Not so in Boston. True, the most significant biking population is the city's many students, but office workers also commute by bike – especially along the 17-mile (27-kilometre) **Paul Dudley White** cycle path, which runs on both sides of the Charles River from near the Science Museum as far as Watertown.

This is one of a number of dedicated cycle routes in the area. From around the Longfellow Bridge on the south side to the Boston University Bridge, it is uninterrupted, high-quality tarmac. On the other side of the river, skaters get extra space on Sundays between April and October, when Memorial Drive is closed to cars from the Eliot Bridge in Cambridge as far as Western Avenue.

Another high-quality route, slightly further out of town, is the ten-mile (16-kilometre) **Minuteman Trail**, which starts near the Alewife T stop and runs out to the historic town of Lexington and on to Bedford. The downside of this route is that at weekends it gets very crowded with cyclists, skaters, skateboarders and pedestrians.

The Southwest Corridor offers an easy four-mile (six-kilometre) ride from the South End around Dartmouth Street into Roxbury, along the **Pierre Lallement Bicycle Path**. Trust Boston to come up with a creative name for a bike path – it's named after the Frenchman who is generally credited with inventing the bicycle. He died broke in Boston in the late 19th century.

If you have a whole day, take a picturesque ride along the old harbour, starting in South Boston at Fort Independence Park and heading for the John F Kennedy Library & Museum. Other biking and skating areas include the **Fresh Pond Reservoir** in Cambridge and Franklin Park, between Dorchester and Roxbury, which has four miles (six kilometres) of paved paths. For off-road trails, you don't have to go too far. In the **Blue Hills State Reservation**, south of Boston, there are miles of mountain bike trails. From downtown, it's about a 40-minute cycle ride to get there. Phone the Metropolitan District Commission (727 5114) for details.

If you buy an MBTA 'Bikes on the T' pass ($5), you can take your bike on Commuter Rail and Orange and Red T services during off-peak hours. Phone the MBTA on 722 5000 for details.

Music

Aerosmith: *Toys in the Attic* (1975)
Essential album by the quintessential '70s rock band before they quit doing drugs.

Alloy Orchestra: *New Music for Silent Films*. (1999)
Popular combo who actually accompany silent films at Boston revival theaters.

The Cars: *Greatest Hits* (1978)
Hugely popular New Wave band from the late 1970s. The US answer to the Buzzcocks.

Dropkick Murphys: *Do or Die* (1998).
Irish-American working class punk anthems to shout along with.

Juliana Hatfield: *Become What You Are* (1993)
Sort of rock, sort of folk from the Boston babe and former leader of Blake's Babies.

Tom Lehrer: *The Remains of Tom Lehrer* (2000)
Box set of snarky satire from Harvard University.

The Lemonheads, *Car, Button, Cloth* (1996)
Funny, sad, wonderful songs by this quirky adorable Boston band.

The Mighty Mighty Bosstones: *More Noise and Other Disturbances* (1992)
The best-known of Boston's many ska bands.

Morphine: *Cure for Pain* (1993)
The quirky Boston rock band with no guitar that was fronted by the late Mark Sandman.

Pixies: *Doolittle* (1989)
Boston's own: on classics like 'Debaser', 'Monkey Gone to Heaven', and 'Here Comes Your Man', these guys (and one girl) had it all – the rock, the quirks and the hooks.

Johnathan Richman and the Modern Lovers: *Modern Lovers* (1988)
Influential band – a Boston-based true musician's band.

Talking Heads, *Fear of Music* (1979)
Formed in nearby Rhode Island, shook the rock world in the 1980s. Too smart for their own good.

Websites

www.bostonphoenix.com
Website of local weekly paper, the *Boston Phoenix*, is a great place to track down what's happening where in the city.

www.justanotherscene.com
Massive site, run entirely by a punk-crazed suburban teenager named Sean Carlson, is ground zero for the local underground rock scene. The place to go for show listings, band sites, and gossip.

www.bostonusa.com
Website of the city's tourism and convention office. Excellent site for all kinds of information about the city.

www.TheInsider.com/boston/
Good site for extensive whats-going-on-in-Boston type information.

www.boston.com/globe/
The website of the *Boston Globe*, the city's daily paper.

www.artsaroundboston.com/
The site to track down information about the city's art scene.

Index

Figures in **bold** indicate sections containing key information. *Italics* indicate photos.

Abiel Smith School 13
accommodation
B&Bs 44, 53, **57**, 59, 259, 264, 267
budget 51-52
gay & lesbian 51, 54-55, 259
guest houses 49-52
out of town *see main page references under specific areas*
renting 20, 38, 57
see also hotels; youth hostels
Acorn Street 72, *72*
Actors Workshop 227
Adams, Samuel 8, 9, 64, 65, 67, 246
Addison Gallery of American Art 113
Afro-American community 12-13, 20, 76, 84, 85, 106
African Meeting House 13, 118
Black Heritage Trail 257
and Civil War 119
galleries & museums 115, 118, 213
and War of Independence 94
see also desegregation; Malcolm X; racism; slavery
AIDS hotline 283
airlines 259, 276, **278**
Airport, Logan 70, 198, **278**
alcohol
helplines 284
laws 19, 101, 156, **285**
liquor stores 19, 183
Alcott, Louisa May 33, 71, 246, 247
Allston 20, 38, 41
art galleries 210, **213**
clubs 225, 226
pubs & bars 163-166
restaurants & cafés 144-145
shopping in 171
Allston Beat 177
Ally McBeal 76, 209, *209*
ambulance 282
American Repertory Theatre 227
Ames-Webster House 26
Amherst 260, 261, 262, 263
antiques 72, 173, 254
Appleton Street 84
aquariums **70**, 97, 136, 170, 199
architecture
17th-century **24**, **30**
18th-century **24-25**
19th-century **25-27**, 79, 80, 84, 87, 256, 276
20th-century **29**, 54, 78, 79, 80, 211
urban renewal 14-15, 29, 65, 76, 214, 270
Arnold Arboretum 29, **88**, 91, 195
Arrowhead 263, 264
art
art deco tour 112
galleries & museums 84, 109, **113-117**, 188, **210-213**, 233
out of town 252, 254, 255, 263, **264**, **269**, 270-271, 272, 276
public 119
schools **117**, 267, 276
supplies 109, **173-174**
theft 120
university collections 104, 265, 267
Arthur M Sackler Museum 115
Asian community *see* Chinatown
Athenaeum 32, 117
autumn 196-197

Babe Ruth 18, 110, 234, 242, *242*
babysitting 198
Back Bay 42, 44, **78-83**, 196, 208, 209
architecture 25-29
Fens 29, **84-85**, 215
history 11-12, 14
hotels 47-52
pubs & bars **156-159**, 215-217, 218, 219
restaurants & cafés 122-131
shopping in 171
ballet 231
banks 286-287
bars *see* pubs & bars
baseball 18, *18*, 76, 167, **234**
see also Fenway Park; Red Sox
basketball **120**, **234-235**, 261-262
Bastille Day 196
Batterymarch 29, 54
Bay Village 214, 215
beaches & coastline **252-259**, 268-269, 270, 273, 276
Beacon Hill 25, 44, **71-73**, 171, 209
history 12, 13, 14-15, 26, 32
hotels 52-53, 58-59
pubs & bars 157
restaurants & cafés 141-143
Beals Street (No. 83) 110
Beanpot Hockey Tournament 193
beauty salons **185-186**
Bell, Alexander Graham 12, 249
Bellow, Saul 36, 38, 41
Bennington 272, 273
Berkeley, The 80
Berklee College of Music 38, **42**, 83
Berkshires, The **263-264**
Beverley Theater 230
'Big Dig' 20-22, *21*, 100
black community *see* Afro-American community
Blackstone Block 69
Blue Hills Reservation **201-202**, 239-240, 293
Blue Laws 18-19
boats & boating **237**
Boat Show 193-194
Boston Duck Tours **111**, 125, **202**
cruises 100, 101, **111-112**, 202
ferries 250, 256, 258, 259
hiring 88, 102, 195, 202, 239
regattas 195, 196, 197, 234
shuttles 278
Swan Boats 64, **202**
water taxis 278
Book Festival **194**, 197
books about Boston 292
bookshops 36, 105, 107, 110, **174-175**
Avenue Victor Hugo Bookshop 81, *174*, 175
children's 202
gay & lesbian 217-218
Old Corner Bookstore 32, 65
Trident Café 81, 128-129, 144
Boston Cecelia 232
Boston Center for the Arts 79, 84, **113-114**, 219, **233**
Boston College **41**, 110, 234, **288**
Museum of Art 115
Boston Common 27, 29, **63-64**, 91, 241
Tree Lighting 192
Boston Duck Tours **111**, 125, **202**
Boston Globe 18, 96, 198, 234, 237, **285**
Boston Harbor 70, 91, 100, 101, 102, 222
hotel 55
Boston Harbor Islands 91, **100-101**
Boston Herald 22, 34, 234, **285**
Bostonian Society museum 25
Boston Massacre 8, 9, 12, 65, 68, 69
Re-enactment 194
Boston Pops 102, **196**, **230**, **231**
Boston Tea Party 9-10, *10*, 65, 67
Re-enactment 192, *193*
Ship & Museum 101, **102**
Boston University 36, 38, **40-41**, 110, 232, 234, **288-289**
theatres 206, **208**, 228
bowling 237
Boylston Street **80-81**
No 500, 29
Brandeis University 42, **115**
Brattleboro 272, 273
Brattle Street 33, 106
Brattle Theatre 105, **206**, *207*
breakdown services 280
Brett, James T 17
Bretton Woods 271
breweries 85-86
brewpubs 159-161
Bridge of Flowers 260
Brighton 38, 41
Publick Theater 229-230
Brookline **109-110**, 118
Coolidge Corner Theater 109, **206**, 208
restaurants & cafés 109, 145
Bryant, William Cullen 34
Buddhism 288
Bulfinch, Charles **25**, 67, 71, 107
Charles Nichols House 73
Faneuil Hall 69
Landmark District 84
St Stephen's Church 93
State House 72, 73
Bull & Finch Pub 62, 72, **75**, **161**
Bunker Hill 10, *11*, 12, 94, **98**
battle re-enactment 98, **195**
Monument 67, 98, **100**, **200**
Pavilion 100
bureaux de change 286-287
Burlington 272-273
Burrage Mansion 26
burying grounds **67**
Copp's Hill Burying Ground 93, 94
Granary Burying Ground 64, **65**, 67

King's Chapel & Burying Ground 64, 65, 67
Mount Auburn Cemetery 107
Old Burying Ground 105, **106**
St Augustine's Chapel 96
Busch-Reisinger Museum 115-116
buses 244, 278, 279, **289**
out of town *see main page references under specific areas*
visitors' passports 279
business services
for conventions 44, 198, **281**, 284
at hotels 47-49, 52-53, 54, 55, 56, 59

c

Cabot, John 7
Cambridge 20, **103-107**, 171, 209
Antique Market 173
Central Square *105*, 106, **107**, 145, 153-154, 195, 197
clubs 105, 223, 224-225, 226
hotels 56-59
Poets **33**
pubs & bars 106, 166-170
restaurants & cafés 106, 145, 149-154
River Festival 195
theatres 105, **206**, *207*, 233
tourist information 284
see also Harvard Square; Harvard University; Kendall Square
camping 100-101
Cannabis Reform's Freedom Rally 197
Cape Ann **252-253**, 258
Cape Cod 7, **253-256**, 258, 259
Christmas on 197
Caribbean Carnival 196
Carmen Park 69
cars & driving *21*, **279-280**
'Big Dig' 20-22, *21*, 100
out of town *see main page references under specific areas*
rental 244, **280**
speedway 236
cashpoints 287
Castle in the Clouds 271
Castle Island 91, **96-97**
Cellucci, Paul 22
cemeteries *see* burying grounds
censorship 34
Chandler, Raymond 192
Chandler Street 84, *214*
Charles (hotel) 56
Henrietta's Table 149
The Regattabar 225, *226*
Rialto (bar) 169
Charlesbank Park 102
Charles Playhouse 227
Charles River *102*, 105
Basin & Esplanade 29, 91, **102**, 230
boat rental 195, **202**, 239
Regatta 195, **197**, 234
Charles River Park (apartments) 14, 29
Charlestown 7, 10, 22, 31, 62, **98**
Navy Yard 98, 118-120, 196
restaurants & cafés 98, 143
USS *Constitution* Museum 98-100, 118-120
Visitor's Center 98
Chatham 254
Cheers 62, 72, 75, 161
chemists 183, 283
Chestnut Hill **110**
Child-at-Risk hotline 284
children's Boston
airport services 198
babysitting services 198
car safety 280
museums 102, 198, **200-201**
outings 200, 201-202
restaurants 198-199
shops 202
theatre 201, 230
tours 202
Chinatown 20, **70**, 141
Chinese New Year **193**, 197
Christian Science Center 29, 83, 87
Christmas 192, 197, 219
Christopher Columbus Park 69, 94
churches **93**, **287-288**
Arlington Street Church 80, 93
Christ Church (Cambridge) 105, **106**
Christ Church (North End) *see* Old North Church *below*
Church of the Immaculate Conception 84
Ebenezer Baptist Church 84
Emmanuel Church 232
First Baptist Church 27, 81, **83**, *83*, 93
First Church of Christ *see* Mother Church *below*
First Church of Roxbury 85
King's Chapel & Burying Ground 64, **65**, 67
Mother Church (Christian Science) 29, 83, *87*, 93
New Old South Church 27
Old North Church 8, 93, **94**, *94*, 120, 194
Park Street Church 64, **65**
Sacred Heart Church **90**
St Augustine's 96
St Leonard's 93
St Stephen's **93**
Trinity Church 27, *28*, 29, **79-80**, *80*, 93
Villa Victoria Church 84
cinemas **206-208**, 222
Citgo sign 110, 157
City Hall Plaza 29, 65-67
Civil War 87, 100, 101
Clinton, Hillary 23, 23, 42
Clock, West Broadway 96
clubs
comedy **233**
dance 110, **203-205**, 262
gay & lesbian 204, 205, **215-216**, 259
music 105, 107, **222-226**
out of town 259, 262
coffeeshops 128, 133, 135, 137, **144-145**, 147, 149, 153-154
Dunkin' Donuts 151
gay & lesbian 219, 220
student 42
colleges 37-39, 42, 117, 260, 270, 272, 288-290
see also Boston College; Emerson College; Massachusetts Institute of Technology
Colonial Theatre 227
Colonnade (hotel) 47
Brasserie Jo 129
Columbus Avenue 84
Combat Zone 70
comedy 233
Commonwealth Avenue 27, 29, **81-83**, 119
Compton Gallery 116
computer rental 175
Concord 8, 10, 34, **245**, **246-248**
Museum **120**, 247
Connecticut **265-267**
Constitution, USS (ship) 94, *99*, *196*
Museum of 98-100, 118-120
Turning of 196
consulates 281
consumer information 281
Convention & Visitors' Bureau 198
Conway 271
Coolidge Corner Theater **206**, 208
Copley Place 171, 187, **208**
Copley Square 26, 29, **79-80**, 201
hotels 48-49
courier services 281
'Cradle of Liberty' *see* Faneuil Hall
crime 23, 78, 96
safety tips 288
cruises 100, 101, **111-112**, 202
Curley, 'Boss' James 13-14, 31, 34
currency 285, **286-287**
customs 285
Customs House 29, 69
cycling 102, **111**, **237-238**, 239, 250, **293**

d

dance
clubs 110, **203-205**, 262
companies/venues 231
FleetBoston Celebrity Series 232
Dawes, William 8, 10, 105
Declaration of Independence 11, 69
DeCordova Museum & Sculpture Park 114, *114*
Deerfield 260, 262
dentists 283
desegregation 15, 95
Dickinson, Emily 33, 65, 261, 262
disabled travellers **281-282**
airport transport 278, 279
Dorchester Heights Monument 96
Downtown **63-70**
clubs 203, 223, 226
hotels 47-52
pubs & bars 159-163
restaurants & cafés 135-137
shopping in **73-75**, 171
drug abuse hotline 284
ducks 64
Dunkin' Donuts **151**
Dyer, Mary 119

Edgartown 196, 256
electricity 282
Eliot, TS 34, 206
Eliot (hotel) 48
Clio restaurant 122
Eliot Square 87
embassies 281
Emerald Necklace 27-29, 84, 88, 112, 279
emergencies 282-283, 285
Emerson, Ralph Waldo 6, 32, 33, 34, 64, 214
House of 246, **247**
and Parker House 54
Emerson College 41, 289
Emerson Majestic Theatre 231
Emmanuel Music 232
English, Todd 98, 110, 143
Essex 252, 253
Evacuation Day *see* 96, **194**

Fairmont Copley Plaza 26, **48**, *49*
The Oak Room 127, 157-158
fall 196-197
Faneuil Hall 9, 25, **67-68**, **69**, 171, 172
Comedy Connection 233
FAO Schwarz 198, **202**
farm (open to visitors) 200
Feast of the Blessed

Sacrament 196
Fens, The 29, **84-85**, 215
Fenway Park 36, 110, 234, **240-241**, 242
tour 112
festivals & events **192-197**
film festivals 114, 195, 197, 208
music 268
theatre 219, 263, 264
see also Pride; Tanglewood
FFBs *see* First Families of Boston
54th Regiment of Massachusetts 13, 257
Filene's 171-172, 172-173
film **206-209**
festivals 114, **195**, **197**, **208**
industry 206
locations 96, **97**, 105, **209**, 252, 265, 271
memorabilia 188
photographic supplies 175, 180-181
movies set in Boston 292
Financial District **70**
hotels 44, **53-54**, 56
fire 24, 29, 30, 89, 276
fire services 282
Boylston Fire Station 80
First Families of Boston 12, 76
First Night 192
Fishing Pier 100, 102
Fitzgerald, F Scott 244
FleetBoston Celebrity Series 232
FleetBoston Pavillion 222
FleetCenter 76, **222**, 235
florists 181
Flour & Grain Exchange Building 27
Flower & Garden Show 194
Fogg Art Museum 113, **115**, *116*
football
American **235**, *235*
soccer 234, **236**
Fort Independence 96-97
Fort Point Channel 101-102
Fort Warren 100
Four Seasons Hotel 47
Bristol Lounge 161
Fourth of July 11
Boston Pops Concert 102, **196**, **230**, **231**
Foxboro Stadium **222**, 235, 236
Franklin, Benjamin 64, 65, 87
Franklin Park & Zoo 29, **88**, 196, **200**
Freedom Trail 62, **68**, 112

g

Gage, Lt Gen Thomas 9
galleries *see under* art
gardens
Frederick Law Olmsted Historic Site 109
Garden Show 194
James P Kelleher Rose Garden 84
see also Public Garden
Gardner, Isabella Stewart 72, 214
Museum 84, **114**, *115*, 120, 232
Garrison, William Lloyd 64, 119
gay & lesbian community **214-220**
accommodation 51, 54-55, 259
café 133
church minister 93
clubs 204, 205, 215-216, 259
festivals 195, 196
in Northampton 261
in the '60s 14
theatre 219, 233
see also Landmark District; Provincetown
ghost tours 202
Gibson House 72, **73**
Gloucester 252, 253
Waterfront Festival 196
Goethe Institute 72
golf courses 238
Government Center 14, 29, 214
hotels 53-54
Green Mountains 272
Groton 265
gyms 238
gay & lesbian 218

h

hairdressers 97, **183-186**
Hale, Edward Everett 119
Hallowe'en (in Salem) 197
Hamilton, Alexander 83
Hammond Castle 252, 253
Hancock, John 8, 10, 11, 64, 71, 246
Hancock (town) 272
Handel and Haydn Society 232
Hanover 270
Hanover Street **90-91**, 139
Harborfest 195
Harborlights *see* FleetBoston Pavillion
Harbor Towers 29
harbour *see* Boston Harbor
Harrison Gray Otis House 25, 73
Harvard, John 7, 39, 103, 104
Harvard Lampoon Castle 104
Harvard Square *103*, **104-106**, 107
Book Festival **194**, 197
cinema 208
House of Blues 153, **167**, 221, **223**
Oktoberfest 197
Harvard University 37, *38*, **39-40**, **103-104**, **289-290**
Cambridge Poets **33**
football 234, 279
Harvard Film Archive 206
Inn at Harvard 59
John Harvard's Brew House 167
museums 38, 104, **115-116**
theatre 227
tour 112
Widener Library 40, 104
Hatch Memorial Shell 102
Hawthorne, Nathaniel 32, 54, 65, 71, 263
birthplace 249
friendship with Melville 33, 214
The Great Stone Face 271
houses of 246, 247, 248
Tanglewood Tales 264
Haymarket 67
health *see* medicine
Heaney, Seamus 36, 39, 162
helplines 283-285
Hemingway, Ernest 34, 117
hiking 101, 110, 247, 271
Hingham 250
history
17th century 6-7
18th century 8-11
19th century 11-13
20th century 13, 14-15
General:
audio-visual accounts 79, 100
Boston's changes of name 7, **22**, 95
Boston's nicknames 6, 12, **22**
design of South Boston 95
gay & lesbian 93, 214-215
industrial 15, 95, 98, 196
key events 16
see also immigration; Independence, American War of; maritime activities
Ho Chi Minh 23, 119
holidays, public 291
Holmes, Oliver Wendell 22, 32, 33-34, 68, 76
grave 67, 107
Holocaust Memorial 69
Holyoke 261, 262
homelessness 20
Hooker, 'Fighting Joe' 71
Hooper-Lee-Nichols House 106
horses
racing 236
riding apparel 190
hospitals **283**, 284
hostels 51, 52, 52
hotels **44-59**
near airport 56
boutique 58-59
chains 55
jazz lounges 161, 225-226
motels 55, 251, 264
out of town *see main page references under specific areas*
seasonal prices 39, 44, 47
top five 48
see also accommodation
Hull 250
Hull Street (No. 44) 94
Huntington Theatre Company 228
Hyannis 254, 255

ice hockey 234, **235-236**
Beanpot Tournament 193
immigration 285
history of 85, 87, 95, 106, 256
and North End 76, 89, 93
Impulse Dance Company 231
Independence, American War of **10-11**, 83, 214, 244, **245-246**, *245*
Significant buildings/places:
Christ Church 106
Faneuil Hall 67-68
Fort Independence 96-97
The Green Dragon 161
the Green Mountains 272
Massachusetts Hall 103
Old State House 69
Powderhouse Park 107
Shirley-Eustis House 87
see also Boston Tea Party; Bunker Hill; Lantern Hanging; Washington, George
Indians *see* Native Americans
industry 15, 95, 98, 196, 254, 272
finance 19
IT 19, 40, 106, 272, 285
see also maritime activities
in-line skating *see* rollerblading
Inman Square 106
Institute of Contemporary Art 80, **114**
insurance 283, **285**
International Place 29
internet 48, 175, **285**, **293**
Irish community 11, 12, 13, 15, 85, 87, 96
clubs 169, 205, 225
pubs *see* Irish *under* pubs & bars
see also St Patrick's Day
Islam 288
islands *see* Boston Harbor Islands
Italian community *see* North End

Jamaica Plain 13, 20, **87-88**, 210
art galleries 210, **213**
pubs & bars 166
restaurants & cafés 145-147
Jamaica Pond 29, 88

James, Henry 34, 263
jazz 14, 39, 184, 185
  cruises 111
  festival 268
  FleetBoston Celebrity Series 232
  Handel and Haydn Society 232
  venues 86, 88, 159, 161, 166, 218, 223, 224, **225-226**, 264
Jewett, Sarah Orne 214
Jewish community 12, 42, 260-261
  film festival 208
  Semitic Museum 104
  synagogues 76, 288
  Zaftigs restaurant 145
JFK Buildings 29
John Hancock Tower *28*, 29, *78*, **79**, *192*
  Observatory 79, **200**
Johnny D's 107, 127, 154, **223**
Johnson, Philip 29, 79, 117
Jordan Hall 232
Jorge Hernandez Cultural Center 84
Joyce, James 194, 197

k

karaoke 147
Kendall Square 106, 166, 206, 208
Kendall Whaling Museum 120
Kenmore Square 36, 44, **110**
Kennebunk 274, 276
Kennebunkport 274, 276
Kennedy, John F 37, 282
  Birthplace 109, **110**
  JFK Buildings 29
  Hyannis Museum 254
  Library & Museum 29, **117**
  Kennedy family 68, 109, 110, 254
Kerouac, Jack 34, 35, 36
  Lowell Kerouac Festival 197
King, Martin Luther, Jr 41
King Richard's Faire 196
King's Chapel & Burying Ground 64, **65**, 67
Krishna Consciousness 81

l

Landmark District **83-84**
language (local dialect) 62, **282**
Lansdowne Street 40
  clubs 203, **204-205**, 222
Lantern Hanging 8, **94**, 120, **194**
laundry 187
Lee 263, 264
Leno, Jay 23
Lenox (hotel) 48
Lenox (town) 32, 34, 263-264
Lexington 8, 10, **245-248**
  Patriot's Day Re-enactments 194
libraries 29, 40, 104, 117, 270
  see also Public Library
Lilac Sunday 195
limousines 278, 279
List Visual Arts Center 116
Litchfield Hills 266, 267
Little Compton 268, 269
Loews Theater 208
Longfellow, Henry Wadsworth 32, 33, 34, 54, 65
  grave 67, 107
  House of 33-34, 106
  Paul Revere's Ride 8, 33
  Wreck of the Hesperus 252
Long Wharf **69-70**, 100
Loring-Greenough House 87
lost property 279
Louis Boston 81, 171, **179**
Lowell, Amy 32, 214
Lowell, James Russell 32, 34
Lowell, Robert 34
luggage
  shops 187-188
Lyric Stage 228-229

Macy's 18, 93, **172**
magazines **286**
  Atlantic Monthly 32, 33-34, 76
  gay & lesbian 215, 217, 218, 219, 285
  North American Review 32, 34
  outlets 104, 175
  sports 18, 237, 238, 239
Maine **273-276**
Malcolm X 31, **86**
Manchester-by-the-Sea 252
Mapparium 83
Marathon (race) **194**, 234, 236-237, 239
  training 238
Mariners' House 90
maritime activities 8, 11, 14, 98, 100
  out of town 249, 250, 252, 253, 254, 256, 265, 267
  research 254, 255
  see also whaling
markets 69, 75, 106, 112, 240
Marlborough Street 83
Martha's Vineyard **256-259**
  Edgartown Regatta 196
Massachusetts Avenue **83**, 171
Massachusetts College of Art 117
Massachusetts Institute of Technology 38, **40**, *41*, 106, **290**
  Media Lab 29
  Miracle of Science Bar 167
  museums & galleries 106, **116-117**
  University Park Hotel 56-59
Massachusetts Museum of Contemporary Art **120**, 263
Massachusetts, University of 260, **290**
Mather, Cotton 14, 32, 64, 94
Mayflower 7, 254
  replica 250
MBTA (transport authority) 278, **279**
McCloskey, Robert 64, 202
McCole, Dan 97
McKim, Charles 26, 79, 117
McMullen Museum of Art 115
medicine 12
  alternative 109, **283**
  chemists 183, 283
  emergencies 282-283, 285
Melville, Hermann 32-33, 214, 257, 263
memorials
  Battle Monument 272
  Bunker Hill 67, 98, **100**, **200**
  Civil War 87
  Dorchester Heights 96
  Franklin, Benjamin 64
  Hale, Edward Everett 119
  Hamilton, Alexander 83
  Harvard, John 104
  Holocaust Memorial 69
  Hooker, 'Fighting Joe' 71
  Minutemen 246
  Revere, Paul 93
  Shaw Memorial 119
  Washington, George 64, 94
Menino, Thomas M 17, 20, 22-23, 240
Méridien, Le (hotel) 53
  Café Fleuri & Julien 136
Middlesex Fells Reservation 239
Milk Bottle (restaurant) 101
Minuteman National Historical Park 246, 248
MIT *see* Massachusetts Institute of Technology
Mobius 233
molasses 8, **13**, 22, 89
motorcycles
  Indian Motorcycle Museum 261
  leather wear 190, 220
  Motorcycle Week 271
  racing 236
motor racing 236
Moultonborough 271
Mount Washington 271, 274
Muddy River 84-85
Museum of Afro-American History 118
Museum of Fine Arts (MFA) 29, 84, 113, *113*, **114**
  concerts 232
  'Family Place' programme 201
  film screenings 208
  School 117
  statues 119, *119*
Museum of the National Center of Afro-American Artists 115
Museum of Science 76, **118**, 201
Museum of Transportation 118
museums 72, 73, 85, **117-120**
  children's 200-201
  Museum Wharf 102
  out of town *see main page references under specific areas*
  top five 117
  university/college 38, 104, 106, **115-117**
  of visual arts **113-117**, 120
music
  Boston Pops 102, 196, 230, 231
  classical 88, 231-233, 264
  on cruises 111, 112
  at DeCordova Museum 114
  gospel 84
  opera 230, 231-233
  orchestras 222, 230, 231, 264
  schools 38, **42**, 83, **233**
  shops 175, 184, 188
  street musicians 104
  see also jazz; rock, blues & folk music
Mystic 265, 266, 267

Nader, Ralph 23
nanny services 198
Nantucket 11, **256-257**
  Film Festival **195**, 208
Native Americans 7, 22, 256, 260, 265, 270
Nautilus, USS (submarine) 265
New Bedford 11, 196, **257-259**
  Zeiterion Theater 230
Newburyport 253, 258
  Firehouse Center 230
Newbury Street 78, **81**, 171, 183
  art galleries 210-212
  coffeehouses 144
  Guest House 49-51, *51*
  pubs & bars 157,158
  restaurants & cafés 125, 128, 129-131, 136
New England Conservatory 38, 42, 232, **233**
New England Telephone Building 70
New Hampshire **270-272**, 274
New Haven 265, 267
Newport 267-268, 26
newsagents 104
newspapers 18, **285-286**
  gay & lesbian 215, 219, 285
  see also newspapers by name
Nichols, Charles (museum) 25, **73**

Nickelodeon 206, **208**
Nook Farm 266
North Adams 263
Northampton 261, 262, 263
Northeastern University 38, **41-42**, 86, **290**
North End 12, 13, 22, 30, 62, 70, 76, **89-94**
  bakeries 181-183
  gay bar 215
  Italian street fair 90
  market tour 112
  restaurants & cafés **137-139**, 145
North Square **90**

O'Brien, Conan 23, 39
observatory 200
O'Connor, Edwin 31, 34
O'Donnell, Rosie 23
office services 281
Oktoberfest 197
Old Corner Bookstore 32, 65
Old Orchard Beach 274-276
Old South Meeting House 9, **65**, *65*, 192
Old State House 9, **25**, 68, **69**, *69*, 194
Old Sturbridge Village 262
Olmsted, Frederick Law 27, 84, 88
  National Historic Site 109
Olmsted Park 29, 84, 85
Omni Parker House (hotel) 23, **54**
Orpheum Theatre 64, **222**
Otis, Harrison Gray 25, 73
Our House 42

Parker House *see* Omni Parker House
parking 280
Park Plaza (hotel) 44, **47**
  Whiskey Park 159
parks 69, **91**, 94, 102, 230, 239, 247
  US Park Service 109, 110, 284
  see also Arnold Arboretum; Boston Common; Boston Harbor Islands; Basin & Esplanade *under* Charles River; Emerald Necklace; Minuteman National Historical Park; Olmsted Park
Patriot's Day **194**, 236
Peabody Essex Museum **120**, 249
Peabody House Theater 229
Peabody Museum of Archaeology & Ethnology 104, **116**
Pei, IM 29
  Christian Science Center 83, *87*
  Compton Gallery 116
  John Hancock Tower 79
  Kennedy Library 117
  MIT buildings 40
  Wiesner Building 106
pharmacies 183, 283
photocopying 175, 281
photography
  exhibitions 212, 213
  good places for 94, 96, 101, 102, 271
  shops 175, 180-181
Pierce/Hichborn House 24-25, 90
Pilgrims *see* Puritans
Pinebank Estate 88
Pinsky, Robert 36, 38
Pioneer Valley **260-263**
Pioneer Village 249
Pittsfield 32, 263
Planetarium 76, **118**
Plath, Sylvia *31*, 34-36
Plimoth Plantation 250, 251
Plough & Stars 36, **225**
Plymouth 7, **250-251**
Poe, Edgar Allan 12, 96, 97
poetry 12, **33-36**, 174
police 23, **282**
polo 239
pool & billiards 110, **239**
population figures (historical) 14
Portland 276
Portsmouth 270, 271
Portuguese community 12, 196, 256
postal services 281, **287**
Post Office Square Park 70
Powderhouse Park 107
Prado, The 93-94
Prescott, Samuel 8, 10
Pride (festival) **195**, 214-215, 219
Prohibition 19
property prices 20
Providence 267
Provincetown 7, 219, 254, **255-256**, **259**
  Carnival Week 196
  Christmas 197
Prudential Center & Tower 14, 29, **80-81**, 171
  Christmas Tree Lighting 192
Public Garden 27, 29, **64**, *82*
  statues 64, 119
  Swan Boats 64, **202**
Publick Theater 229-230
Public Library **26**, *26*, 29, 32, **79**, **117**, *118*, 285
pubs & bars **156-170**
  in Financial District 70
  gay & lesbian 215-217
  historic 13, 96, 98, 159, 161, 246
  Irish 97, **158**, 159, 161, 162, 163, 166, 167, 170
  sports 235
puppet theatre 201
Puritans 7, 12, 22, 103, 248, 256
  arrival of 6, 250, 254
  graves of 106
  the 'Great Elm' 63
  found Harvard 37
Pioneer Valley 260-263
Pioneer Village 249
poets 32

Quakers 288
Quarry Hill 272
Quincy Market 67, **69**, 171
  Backstage 159

racism 6, 13, 15, *15*
radio stations 41, 234, **286**
Rape Crisis 285
Rathskellar 224
raves 20, 107
red light districts 70
Red Sox *17*, 18, 36, 122
  curse 234, **242**
Regal Bostonian (hotel) 44, *45*, **54**
regattas 195, **196**, **197**, 234
restaurants & cafés 69, 84, 86, 90, 97, 98, 101, 102, 106, 109, 110, **122-155**, 226
  cheap 147
  child-friendly 198-200
  gay & lesbian 133, **218-220**
  good for al fresco food 136
  good for brunch 127
  good for lobster 153
  out of town *see main page references under specific areas*
  smoking policy 288
  top five 143
  see also coffeeshops
Revere, Paul **8**, 9, 25, 68, 98
  foundry 85, 93
  grave of 64, 65, 67
  horseback ride 10, 33, 62, 94, 194, 236, 245
  House of **24**, 25, 89, 90
  Paul Revere Mall 93-94
Rhode Island **267-269**
Richardson, Henry Hobson 26-27, 81-83
Ritz-Carlton (hotel) 44, **47**
rock, blues & folk music
  books about 293
  clubs 107, 204, 205, **222-225**
  cruises 111
  festivals 268
  House of Blues 153, **167**, 221, **223**
  Irish 170
  in Northampton 261
  record shops 184, 185
  venues 105, 170, **221-222**, 256, 263, 264
rock climbing 110
Rockport 252, 253
Rockwell, Norman (museum) **120**, 264
rollerblading 105, 237, **238-239**, **293**
Rose Art Museum 115
Roxbury 15, 20, 31, **85-87**, 196, 209
running 105, 237, **239**
  James Joyce Ramble **194**, 197
  Marathon **194**, 234, 236-237, 236, 239
  training 238
Ryder Cup 109-110

Sacco & Vanzetti Case 6, 90-93
Sackler, Arthur M (museum) 115, 117
St Augustine Chapel 96
St Patrick's Day 96, 120, **194**
Saks Fifth Avenue 172, 185
Salem 7, 13, **248-250**
  Haunted Happenings 197
  witch trials 6, 7, **14**, 32, 65, 94, 120, 248
Samaritans 285
Sampson, Deborah 214
Sandwich 254, 255
Sargent, John Singer 26, 79, 114, 117, 118, 214
schools 13, 23, 33, 109, 195, 260
  racial integration 15, 95
Scollay Square 14, 29, 65, 214
Seaport 56, 100
  hotel 56, 144
Sert Gallery 116
Shakers 254, **263**, 264
Shaw, Robert Gould 119
Shawmut 7, 30
shipbuilding 98, 101, 265
  see also Peabody Essex Museum
Shirley-Eustis House 85, **86-87**
shops **171-190**
  opening hours 19
  shopping areas 73-75, 105, 106, 107, 110, **186-187**
  By subject:
  alcohol 19, 183
  antiques 72, **173**
  art/craft supplies 109, **173-174**
  beauty supplies 183-186
  books *see* bookshops
  CDs, tapes & records 107, 175, 184
  children's 69, 198, 202
  clothes 81, **171-173**, **177-180**, 190
  comics 174, 175
  computer services 175
  department stores 18, 26, 93, 110, **171-173**
  electronics 175
  flowers 181
  food & drink 105, **181-183**
  gay & lesbian 220
  houseware 67
  jewellery/watches 81, 109, **186-187**, **190**

joke/novelty 187
musical instruments 188
photography/video 175, 180-181
posters 188
reprographic 175, 181, 281
sex & fetish 70, 83, 106, **180**
shoes 188-189
smoking supplies 105, **189-190**
sports 237
travel supplies 187-188
see also markets
Shubert Theatre 230
skateboarding 239
skiing **239-240**, **274**, 275
slavery 6, 8, 84
abolition movement 13, 33, 64, 119
smoking **288**
hotel policy 44
supplies 105, **189-190**
snowboarding 274
soccer 234, **236**
Somerville 20, **107**
clubs 222, 223, 224
Peabody House Theater 229
pubs & bars 170
restaurants & cafés 145, 154-155
shopping in 171
Theater 222
South Boston 15, 20, 23, **95-102**, 194
as film location 209
restaurants 147-149
South End 20, 29, 44, **78-79**, **83-88**, 195
architecture 25, 78
art galleries 210, **212-213**
clubs 225, 226
gay culture 214-220
hotels 54-55
pubs & bars 156-159
restaurants & cafés 131-135
shopping in 171
South Hadley 261
Southwest Corridor Park 29
spas 97, **185-186**
gay & lesbian 218
sports **234-242**, 286
Boston Garden arena 76, 235
FleetCenter 76, **222**, 235
Foxboro Stadium **222**, 235
see also specific sports
Springfield 261-262, 263
State House 25, 72, **73**
Mary Dyer statue 119
'Sacred Cod' 7-8, 73
statues *see* memorials
Stockbridge 120, 263, 264
Stowe, Harriet Beecher 65, 266
studying 288-290
Strobe Alley 106, **116-117**
students 37-39, 288-290
hangouts 42
see also colleges; universities
subway *see* T (subway)
Suffolk University 290
surfing 254-255, 268
swimming **240**, 247
hotel pools 47
Symphony Hall *228-229*, 231, 232
synagogue 76

T (subway) 156, 278, **279**, **287**
evening service 156
Orange Line 29, 279
visitors' passports 279
Tanglewood (festival) 231, 264
tattooing 19
henna 173
taxation 8-9
taxis 156, 278, **279**
Taylor, Edward 32
telephones 44, **290-291**
television 282, **286**, **292**
locations 62, 75, 76, 161, **209**, 273
tennis 241
Hall of Fame 269
Thanksgiving 7
theatre **227-230**, **233**
Broadway shows 230
in Cambridge 104
children's 201
festivals 219, 263, 264
gay & lesbian **219**, 233
out of town 230
street performers 104
Theatre District **70**, 215, 219, 227
clubs 203
Thoreau, Henry David 31, 33, 34, 244, 246, 247
ticket agencies
music 221
sport 234
theatre 227
Tiffany, Louis Comfort 55, 80, 93, 187
time, local 291
tipping 44, **291**
toilets 287
tourist information 284
out of town *see main page references under specific areas*
tours **111-112**
Boston Duck **111**, 125, **202**
Boston Harbor 70
botanical 107
children's 202
cycling 111
for disabled travellers 281
Emerald Necklace 84, 112
Freedom Trail **68**, 90, 94
ghost 202
JFK Birthplace 110
out of town 251, 257, 260
trains 244, 278, 279
out of town *see main page references under specific areas*
see also T (subway)
Transcendentalism **33**, 244, 247
translation services 281
transport 244, 278
for disabled 278, 279, **281-282**
out of town *see also main page references under specific areas*
public 279
see also buses; trains
travel agency 187-8
Traveler's Aid Society 284
Tremontaine 7, 72
Tremont House (hotel) 54
Tremont Street 215, 218, 220
Tremont Theater 233
triangular trade 8
Triple O's Lounge 96
trolley tours 112
Tufts University 38, 42, 107, **290**
Twain, Mark 266

u

Union Oyster House, Ye Olde 69, **136-137**, *139*, 153
universities **37-42**, 260, 276, 288-290
see also Boston, Brandeis, Harvard, Massachusetts, Northeastern *and* Yale *universities*

Vermont **272-273**, 274
Verrazano, Giovanni 7
Vertigo (bar) 70
visas 291

Walden 244
Walden Pond State Reservation 247
walking 110
James Joyce Ramble **194**, 197
tours 112
see also hiking
Wally's 42, 226
Wang Center 70, **230**, 231
Washington, George 68, 87, 98, 104, 105, 106
at Dorchester Heights 96
memorials 64, 94
Washington Street 214
waterfront **100-102**, 279
hotels 55-56
restaurants 144
see also Seaport
weather 194, 195, 196-197, 283, **291**
winter 192, **280**
websites 293
Webster, Daniel 9, 32, 87
Wellesley College 42
West End 14, 29, **76**
whale-watching 70, 101, 111, 196
whaling 11, 120, 256, 257, 265
Wharton, Edith 34, 263, 264
White Mountains 271, 272, 274
Whittier, John Greenleaf 34
Wiers Beach 271
Wiesel, Eli 36, 38, 41
Wigglesworth, Michael 32
Wilbur Theatre 230
Aria (club) 204
wildlife 101, 253, 254, 255
Williamstown 263
Wilson, Edward O 39
wine
Expo 192
vineyards 268, 269
Winthrop, John 7, 22, 32, 214
Winthrop building 29
witchcraft 6, 7, **14**, 32, 65, 94, 120, 248
museums 248, 249
women
gyms 238
history of 112
lesbianism *see* gay & lesbian community
liberal arts school 261
suffrage 87
YWCA hostel 52
Worcester
Art Museum 115
Centrum Center 222
World's Fair **195**, 197
World Trade Center 192
writers **31-36**, 37, 71, 170, 246, 255
Saturday Club 54
see also writers by name
Wyndham Boston (hotel) 54

XV Beacon (hotel) **58-59**
The Federalist (restaurant) 59, 141-143

Yale University 265
youth hostels 51
YMCA/YWCA 52, 52

zoos 88, 200

Advertisers' Index

Please refer to the relevant sections for addresses/telephone numbers

Blue Man Group **IFC**

In Context

The Museum at the John F Kennedy Library **4**

Accommodation

Boston Park Plaza Hotel **46**
timeoutny.com **50**
Beacon Hill Hotel & Bistro **92**

Sightseeing

Dreams of Freedom Museum **60**
Isabella Stewart Gardner Museum **66**
Old Town Trolley Tours **74**
CityPass **92**
Greater Boston Convention & Visitors' Bureau **92**
SummerStage **108**

Restaurants

House of Blues **124**
The Seasonal Table **126**
The Restaurants at Prudential Center **130**
Saffron **134**
Flemming's **138**
Cafe Ravello/Bella Vista/ Saraceno/Assaggio **140**
Caprice **142**
Zita **146**
57 Restaurant **148**
Tatsukichi & Goemon **148**
Milano's Italian Kitchen **148**
TONY Eating & Drinking Guide **150**
Time Out Magazine **152**

Pubs & Bars

The Bull & Finch Pub **160**
The Somers Pubs **164**
Bull Run Inn **168**

Shops & Services

The Shops at Prudential Center **176**
HMV Record Stores **182**

Maps

TONY Magazine **302**

Time Out City Guides **IBC**

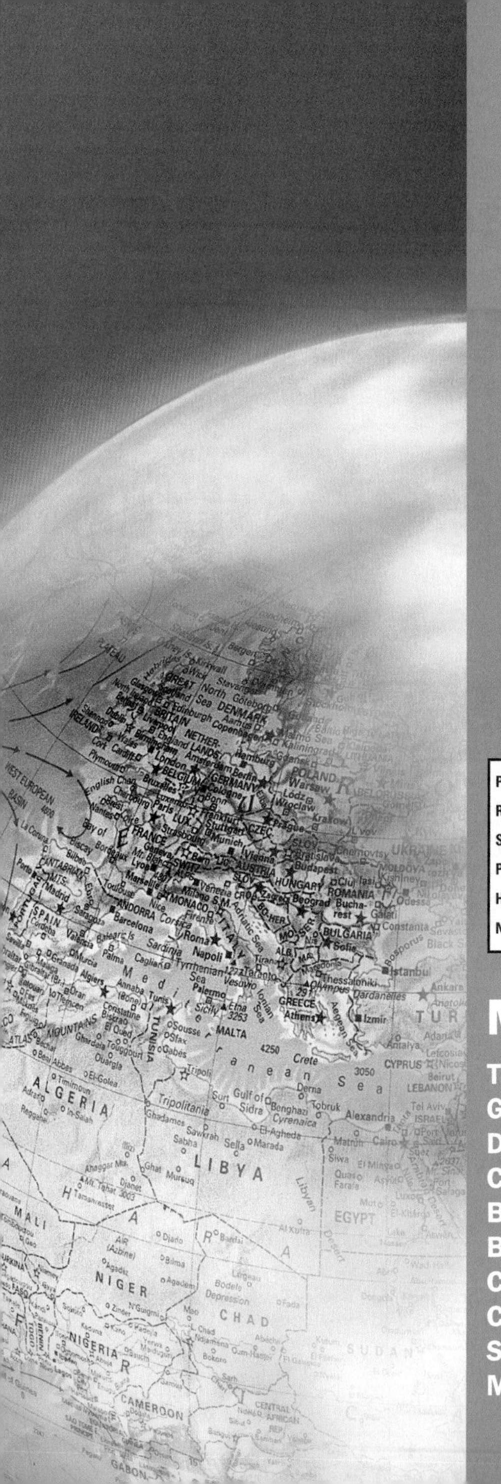

Place of interest and/or entertainment	
Railway stations	
Subway	Ⓣ
Parks	
Hospitals/universities	
Neighbourhood	BACK BAY

Maps

Trips Out of Town 303
Greater Boston 304
Downtown Boston 306
Central Boston 308
Back Bay 309
Beacon Hill 310
Cambridge 311
Coastal Boston 312
Street Index 313
MBTA Subway Map 316

Trips Out of Town

Fresh Pond
Kingley Park
PORTER SQUARE
CONCORD AVE
LOWELL ST
SOMERVILL
HIGHLAND AVE
SOMERVILLE AVE
FRESH POND PKWY
AUBURN ST
BRATTLE ST
Harvard University
HARVARD SQUARE
MT AUBURN
Mt Auburn Cemetery
MEMORIAL DR
KIRKLAND ST
BEACON ST
JFK DR
Charles River
SOLDIERS FIELD RD
CAMBRIDGE
WEBSTER ST
HARVARD ST
Harvard School of Business
WESTERN AVE
CENTRAL SQUARE
ALLSTON
BROADWAY
MASSACHUSETTS AVE
90
CAMBRIDGE ST
MAGAZINE ST
BROOKLINE ST
MAIN ST
BRIGHTON AVE
BRIGHTON
Massachusetts Institute of Technology
VASSAR ST
MEMORIAL DR
HARVARD BRIDGE
See page 311
WINCHESTER ST
HAVARD ST
COOLIDGE CORNER
ST PAUL ST
Boston University
BEACON ST
COMMONWEA
FENWAY
The Fens
BROOKLINE
BROOKLINE AVE
BUCKMINSTER RD
BROOKLINE VILLAGE
HUNTINGTON AVE
BOYLSTON ST
Brookline Reservoir
See pages 306/7
TREMONT ST
MASSACHUSETTS
Leverett Pond
JAMAICAWAY
Olmsted Park
ROXBURY
Jamaica Park
CENTRE ST
Jamaica Pond
POND S
JAMAICA PLAIN
COLUMBUS AVE
0
1 mile
0
1.5 km

Greater Boston

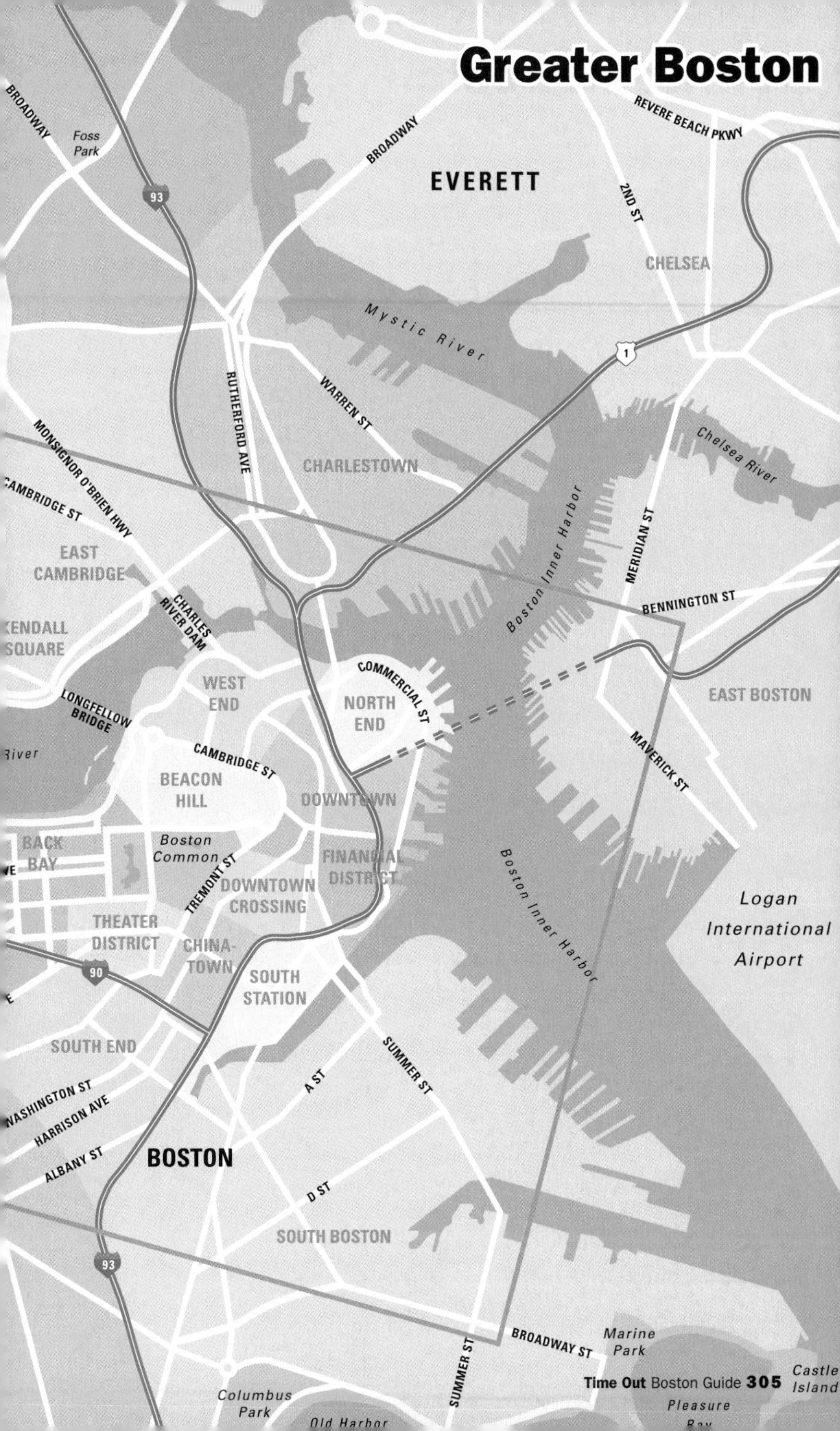

Downtown Boston

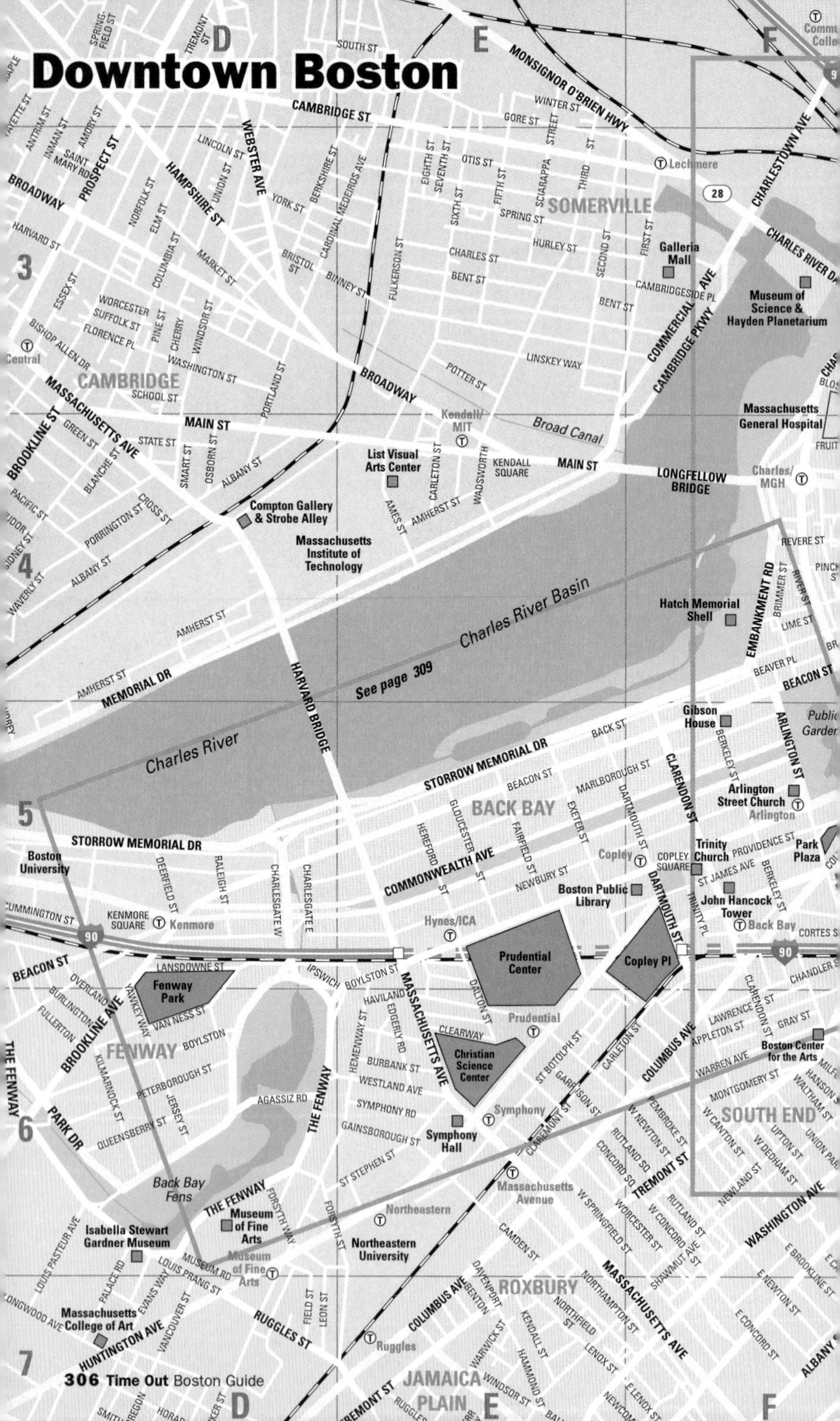

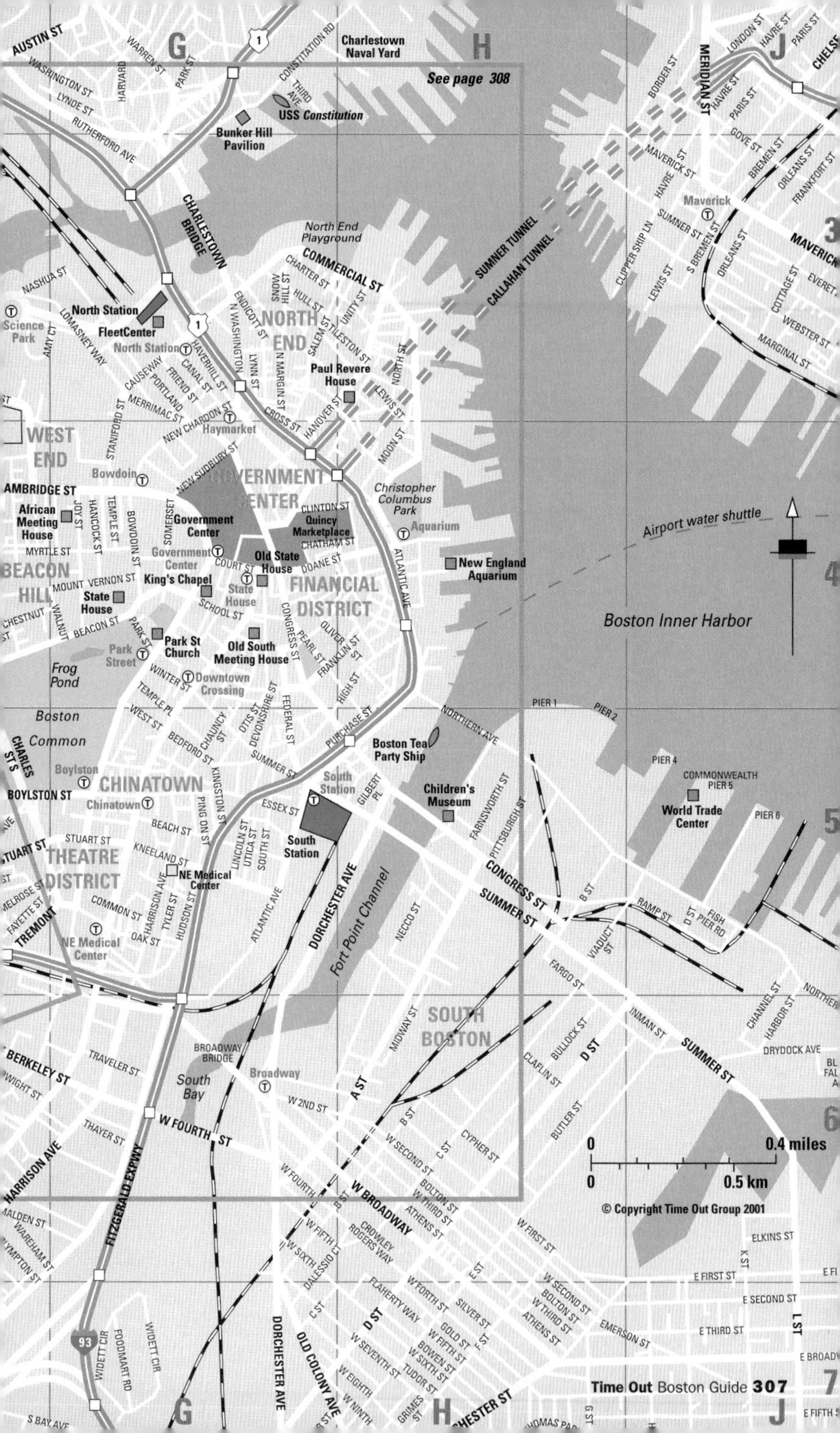

G
H
J
See page 308
Charlestown Naval Yard
USS Constitution
Bunker Hill Pavilion
AUSTIN ST
WARREN ST
WASHINGTON ST
LYNDE ST
HARVARD
PARK ST
RUTHERFORD AVE
CONSTITUTION RD
THIRD AVE
CHARLESTOWN BRIDGE
North End Playground
COMMERCIAL ST
CHARTER ST
HULL ST
UNITY ST
NORTH END
SALEM ST
TILESTON ST
NORTH ST
Paul Revere House
LEWIS ST
HANOVER ST
CROSS ST
MOON ST
N MARGIN ST
LYNN ST
ENDICOTT ST
N WASHINGTON
NASHUA ST
North Station
FleetCenter
North Station
Science Park
AMY CT
LOMASNEY WAY
HAVERHILL ST
CANAL ST
FRIEND ST
CAUSEWAY
PORTLAND
MERRIMAC ST
NEW CHARDON ST
Haymarket
STANIFORD ST
WEST END
Bowdoin
NEW SUDBURY ST
GOVERNMENT CENTER
CLINTON ST
Quincy Marketplace
CHATHAM ST
Government Center
Government Center
Old State House
DOANE ST
COURT ST
State House
King's Chapel
SCHOOL ST
FINANCIAL DISTRICT
CONGRESS ST
PEARL ST
OLIVER ST
FRANKLIN ST
HIGH ST
AMBRIDGE ST
African Meeting House
JOY ST
HANCOCK ST
TEMPLE ST
BOWDOIN ST
SOMERSET
MYRTLE ST
BEACON HILL
MOUNT VERNON ST
State House
CHESTNUT ST
WALNUT
BEACON ST
PARK ST
Park St Church
Old South Meeting House
Park Street
Frog Pond
WINTER ST
Downtown Crossing
TEMPLE PL
WEST ST
BEDFORD ST
CHAUNCY ST
OTIS ST
DEVONSHIRE ST
FEDERAL ST
SUMMER ST
PURCHASE ST
Boston Common
CHARLES ST S
Boylston
BOYLSTON ST
CHINATOWN
Chinatown
KINGSTON ST
PING ON ST
ESSEX ST
BEACH ST
STUART ST
THEATRE DISTRICT
KNEELAND ST
NE Medical Center
LINCOLN ST
UTICA ST
SOUTH ST
South Station
South Station
HARRISON AVE
TYLER ST
HUDSON ST
COMMON ST
OAK ST
MELROSE ST
FAYETTE ST
TREMONT
NE Medical Center
ATLANTIC AVE
DORCHESTER AVE
Fort Point Channel
Christopher Columbus Park
Aquarium
ATLANTIC AVE
New England Aquarium
Airport water shuttle
Boston Inner Harbor
SUMNER TUNNEL
CALLAHAN TUNNEL
Boston Tea Party Ship
NORTHERN AVE
GILBERT PL
Children's Museum
FARNSWORTH ST
PITTSBURGH ST
CONGRESS ST
SUMMER ST
NECCO ST
PIER 1
PIER 2
PIER 4
COMMONWEALTH PIER 5
World Trade Center
PIER 6
B ST
RAMP ST
D ST
FISH PIER RD
VIADUCT ST
FARGO ST
INMAN ST
SUMMER ST
CHANNEL ST
HARBOR ST
NORTHERN
DRYDOCK AVE
SOUTH BOSTON
MIDWAY ST
BULLOCK ST
D ST
CLAFLIN ST
BUTLER ST
CYPHER ST
BROADWAY BRIDGE
South Bay
Broadway
W 2ND ST
A ST
B ST
C ST
W SECOND ST
BOLTON ST
W THIRD ST
ATHENS ST
W FIRST ST
W BROADWAY
W FOURTH ST
W FOURTH
B ST
W FIFTH
W SIXTH
DALESSIO CT
CROWLEY ROGERS WAY
FLAHERTY WAY
W FORTH ST
E ST
SILVER ST
GOLD ST
W FIFTH ST
F ST
BOWEN ST
W SIXTH ST
TUDOR ST
W SEVENTH ST
W EIGHTH
W NINTH
GRIMES ST
D ST
C ST
DORCHESTER AVE
OLD COLONY AVE
DORCHESTER ST
W SECOND ST
BOLTON ST
W THIRD ST
ATHENS ST
EMERSON ST
E FIRST ST
E SECOND ST
E THIRD ST
ELKINS ST
K ST
L ST
E BROADWAY
E FIFTH S
BERKELEY ST
DWIGHT ST
TRAVELER ST
THAYER ST
W FOURTH ST
HARRISON AVE
MALDEN ST
WAREHAM ST
PLYMPTON ST
FITZGERALD EXPWY
93
WIDETT CIR
FOODMART RD
WIDETT CIR
S BAY AVE
MERIDIAN ST
BORDER ST
LONDON ST
HAVRE ST
PARIS ST
CHELSE
HAVRE ST
PARIS ST
GOVE ST
BREMEN ST
ORLEANS ST
FRANKFORT ST
MAVERICK ST
HAVRE ST
Maverick
SUMNER ST
S BREMEN ST
CLIPPER SHIP LN
LEWIS ST
ORLEANS ST
MAVERICK
EVERETT
COTTAGE ST
WEBSTER ST
MARGINAL ST
1
0
0.4 miles
0
0.5 km
3
4
5
6
7

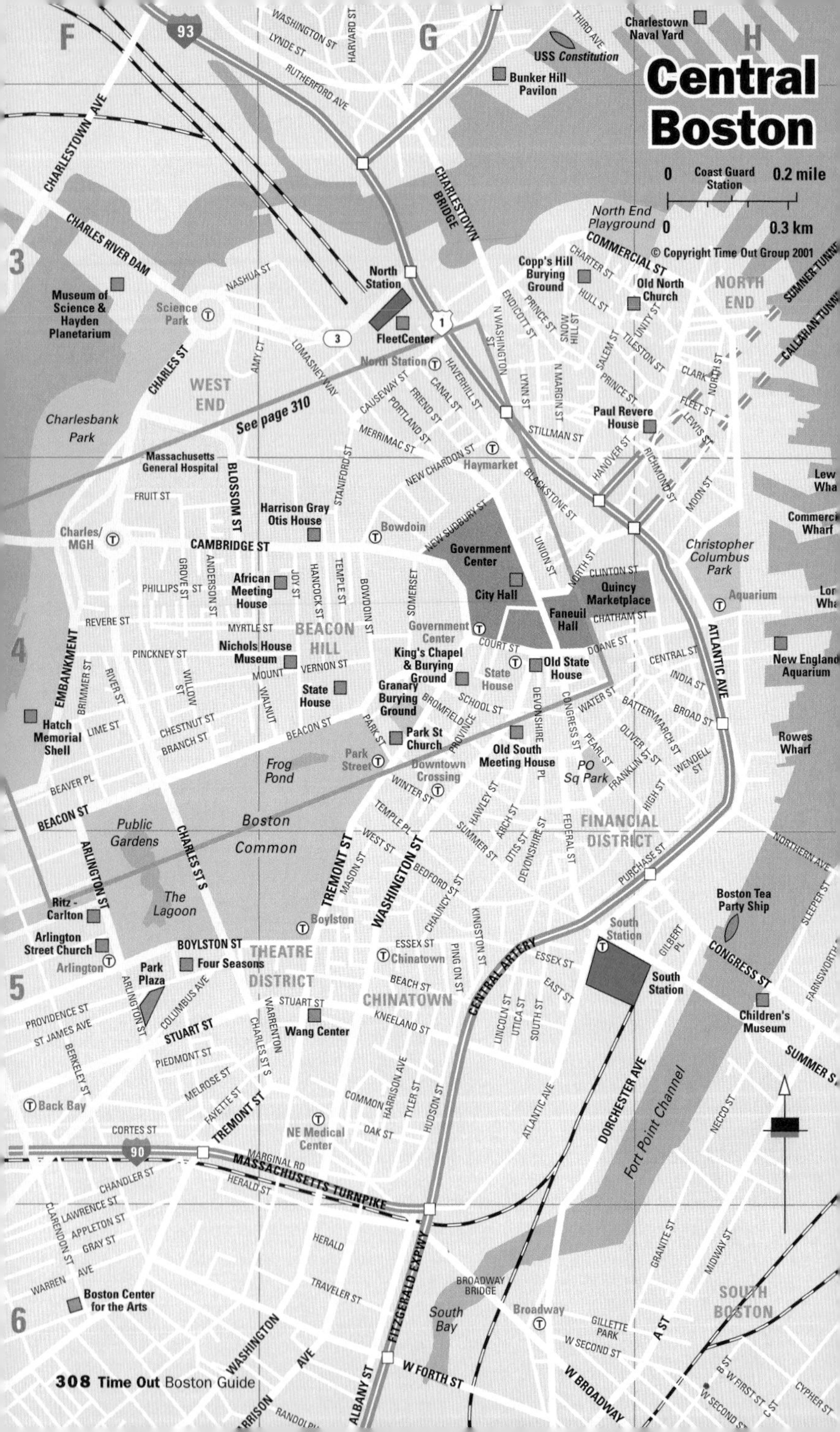
Central Boston
F
G
H
3
4
5
6
0
0.2 mile
0
0.3 km
© Copyright Time Out Group 2001
Charlestown Naval Yard
USS Constitution
Bunker Hill Pavilon
Coast Guard Station
North End Playground
Copp's Hill Burying Ground
Old North Church
NORTH END
Museum of Science & Hayden Planetarium
Science Park
North Station
FleetCenter
WEST END
See page 310
Charlesbank Park
Massachusetts General Hospital
Paul Revere House
Haymarket
Harrison Gray Otis House
Bowdoin
Charles/MGH
Government Center
City Hall
Quincy Marketplace
Faneuil Hall
Christopher Columbus Park
Aquarium
African Meeting House
BEACON HILL
Nichols House Museum
King's Chapel & Burying Ground
State House
Old State House
New England Aquarium
Granary Burying Ground
Park St Church
Old South Meeting House
Hatch Memorial Shell
Frog Pond
Park Street
Downtown Crossing
PO Sq Park
Rowes Wharf
Public Gardens
Boston Common
FINANCIAL DISTRICT
The Lagoon
Ritz - Carlton
Arlington Street Church
Arlington
Boylston
Four Seasons
Park Plaza
THEATRE DISTRICT
Chinatown
CHINATOWN
South Station
Boston Tea Party Ship
Children's Museum
Wang Center
Back Bay
NE Medical Center
Fort Point Channel
Boston Center for the Arts
South Bay
Broadway
BROADWAY BRIDGE
GILLETTE PARK
SOUTH BOSTON
CHARLESTOWN AVE
CHARLES RIVER DAM
CHARLESTOWN BRIDGE
COMMERCIAL ST
CHARLES ST
CAMBRIDGE ST
BLOSSOM ST
ATLANTIC AVE
EMBANKMENT
BEACON ST
ARLINGTON ST
CHARLES ST S
TREMONT ST
WASHINGTON ST
BOYLSTON ST
STUART ST
CENTRAL ARTERY
CONGRESS ST
SUMMER ST
DORCHESTER AVE
MASSACHUSETTS TURNPIKE
FITZGERALD EXPWY
W BROADWAY
W FORTH ST
ALBANY ST
A ST
93
90
1
3

Back Bay

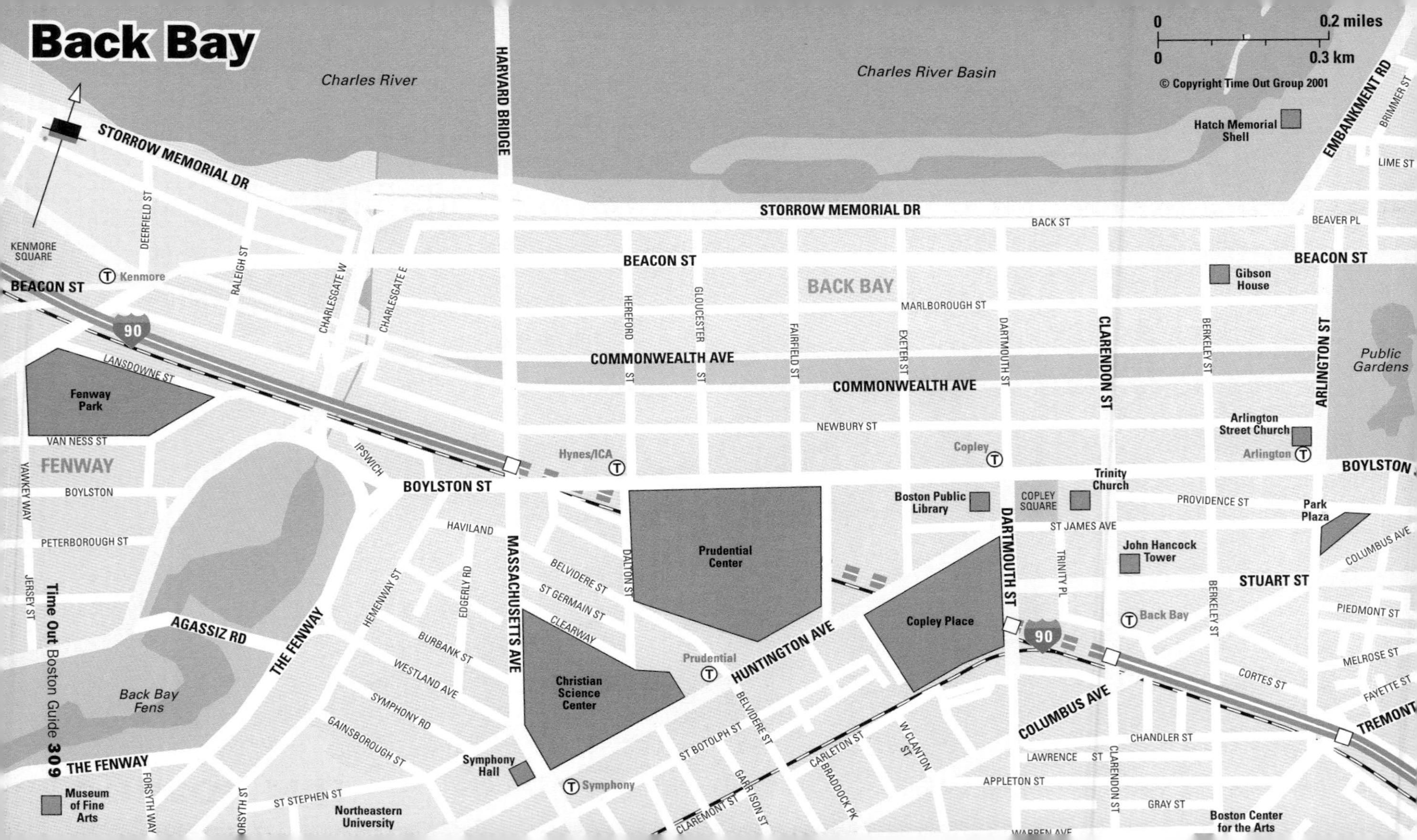

0 0.2 miles
0 0.3 km
© Copyright Time Out Group 2001
Charles River
Charles River Basin
Hatch Memorial Shell
EMBANKMENT RD
BRIMMER ST
LIME ST
STORROW MEMORIAL DR
HARVARD BRIDGE
BEAVER PL
BACK ST
BEACON ST
Gibson House
BACK BAY
MARLBOROUGH ST
COMMONWEALTH AVE
NEWBURY ST
BOYLSTON ST
KENMORE SQUARE
Kenmore
DEERFIELD ST
RALEIGH ST
CHARLESGATE W
CHARLESGATE E
HEREFORD ST
GLOUCESTER ST
FAIRFIELD ST
EXETER ST
DARTMOUTH ST
CLARENDON ST
BERKELEY ST
ARLINGTON ST
Public Gardens
Arlington Street Church
Arlington
Copley
Hynes/ICA
Trinity Church
COPLEY SQUARE
Boston Public Library
PROVIDENCE ST
Park Plaza
ST JAMES AVE
John Hancock Tower
COLUMBUS AVE
STUART ST
TRINITY PL
Back Bay
PIEDMONT ST
MELROSE ST
CORTES ST
FAYETTE ST
TREMONT
Copley Place
Prudential Center
Prudential
DALTON ST
HUNTINGTON AVE
Fenway Park
LANSDOWNE ST
VAN NESS ST
FENWAY
YAWKEY WAY
BOYLSTON
PETERBOROUGH ST
JERSEY ST
IPSWICH
HAVILAND
MASSACHUSETTS AVE
BELVIDERE ST
ST GERMAIN ST
CLEARWAY
EDGERLY RD
HEMENWAY ST
BURBANK ST
WESTLAND AVE
SYMPHONY RD
GAINSBOROUGH ST
AGASSIZ RD
THE FENWAY
Back Bay Fens
Christian Science Center
Symphony Hall
Symphony
ST STEPHEN ST
Northeastern University
FORSYTH WAY
ORSYTH ST
Museum of Fine Arts
ST BOTOLPH ST
GARRISON ST
CLAREMONT ST
CARLETON ST
BRADDOCK PK
W CLANTON ST
CHANDLER ST
LAWRENCE ST
APPLETON ST
GRAY ST
WARREN AVE
Boston Center for the Arts
90

Beacon Hill

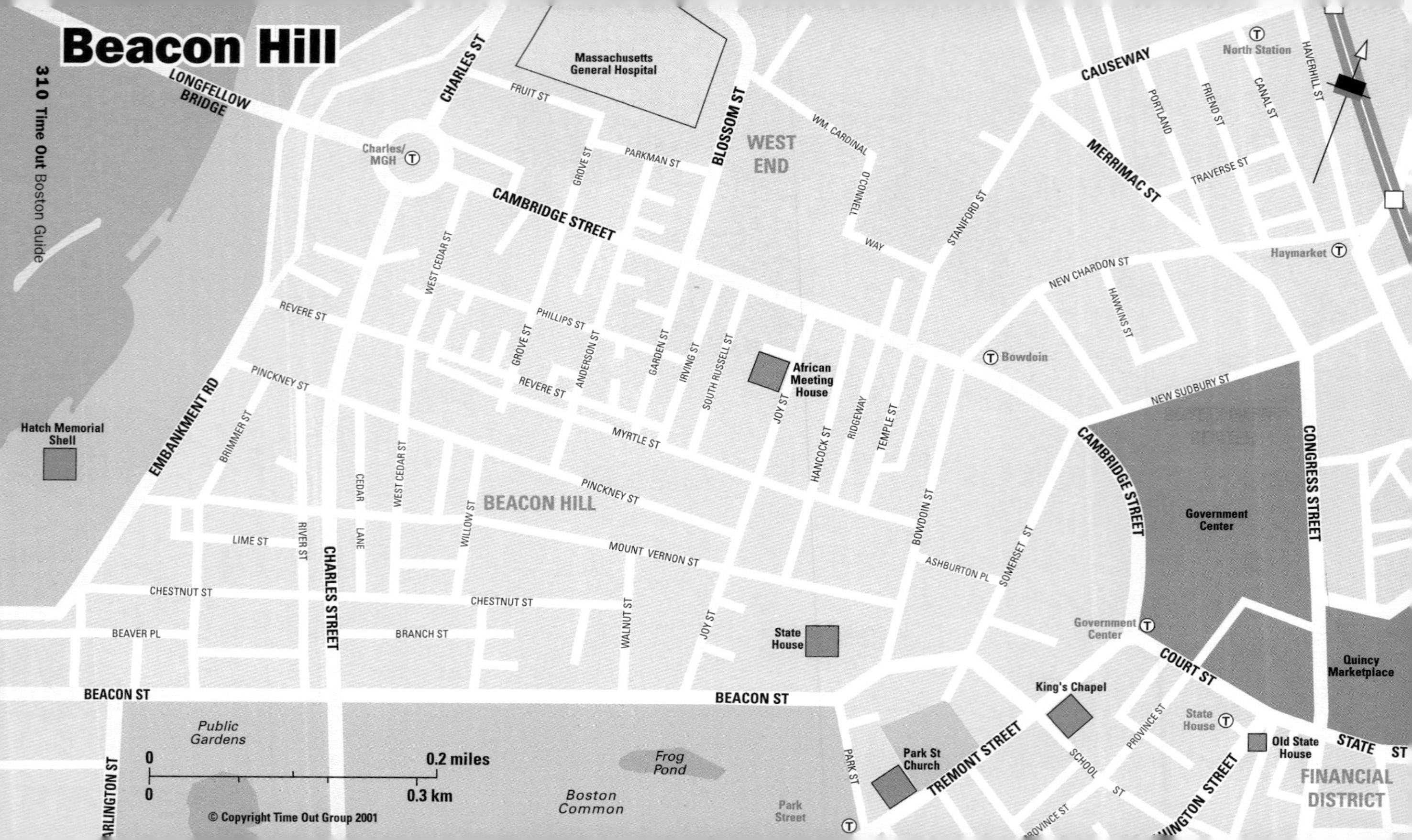

Massachusetts General Hospital
CHARLES ST
LONGFELLOW BRIDGE
FRUIT ST
Charles/ MGH
PARKMAN ST
BLOSSOM ST
WEST END
WM. CARDINAL
O'CONNELL
WAY
CAUSEWAY
North Station
HAVERHILL ST
PORTLAND
FRIEND ST
CANAL ST
MERRIMAC ST
TRAVERSE ST
Haymarket
STANIFORD ST
GROVE ST
CAMBRIDGE STREET
WEST CEDAR ST
NEW CHARDON ST
HAWKINS ST
REVERE ST
PHILLIPS ST
ANDERSON ST
GARDEN ST
IRVING ST
SOUTH RUSSELL ST
African Meeting House
Bowdoin
NEW SUDBURY ST
PINCKNEY ST
JOY ST
RIDGEWAY
TEMPLE ST
HANCOCK ST
MYRTLE ST
EMBANKMENT RD
BRIMMER ST
Hatch Memorial Shell
BEACON HILL
CEDAR
LANE
BOWDOIN ST
CAMBRIDGE STREET
CONGRESS STREET
Government Center
LIME ST
RIVER ST
CHARLES STREET
WILLOW ST
MOUNT VERNON ST
SOMERSET ST
ASHBURTON PL
CHESTNUT ST
BEAVER PL
BRANCH ST
WALNUT ST
State House
COURT ST
Quincy Marketplace
King's Chapel
BEACON ST
Public Gardens
Frog Pond
Boston Common
Park Street
PARK ST
Park St Church
TREMONT STREET
SCHOOL ST
PROVINCE ST
Old State House
STATE ST
FINANCIAL DISTRICT
ARLINGTON ST
0
0.2 miles
0
0.3 km
© Copyright Time Out Group 2001

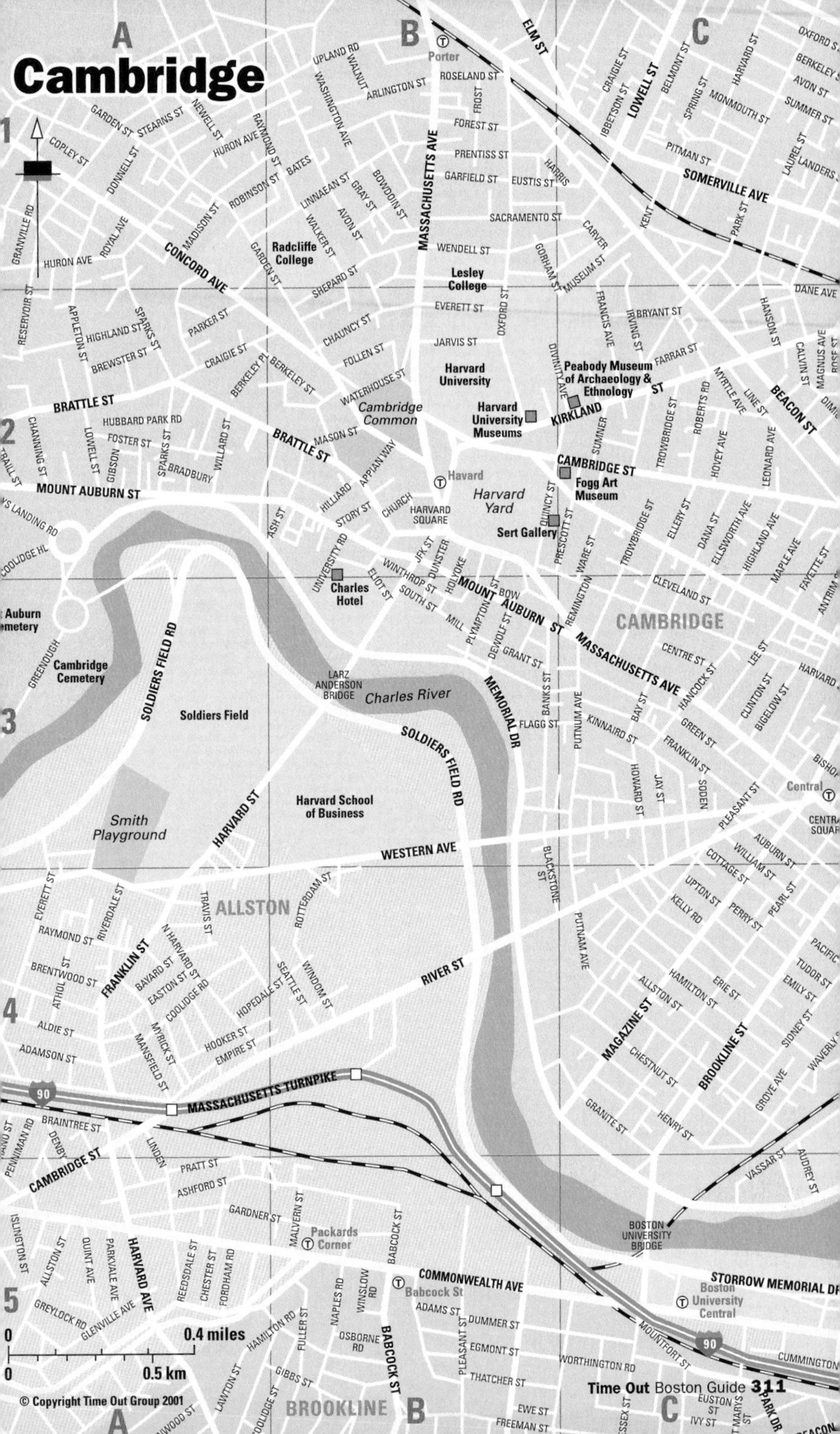

Cambridge
A
B
C
1
2
3
4
5
Porter
Harvard
Central
Packards Corner
Babcock St
Boston University Central
Radcliffe College
Lesley College
Harvard University
Peabody Museum of Archaeology & Ethnology
Harvard University Museums
Cambridge Common
Harvard Yard
Fogg Art Museum
Sert Gallery
Charles Hotel
HARVARD SQUARE
CAMBRIDGE
Auburn
Cemetery
Cambridge Cemetery
Soldiers Field
LARZ ANDERSON BRIDGE
Charles River
Harvard School of Business
Smith Playground
ALLSTON
BOSTON UNIVERSITY BRIDGE
BROOKLINE
CENTRAL SQUARE
MASSACHUSETTS AVE
MASSACHUSETTS TURNPIKE
90
CONCORD AVE
BRATTLE ST
MOUNT AUBURN ST
KIRKLAND ST
CAMBRIDGE ST
SOMERVILLE AVE
BEACON ST
MEMORIAL DR
SOLDIERS FIELD RD
HARVARD ST
WESTERN AVE
RIVER ST
FRANKLIN ST
MAGAZINE ST
BROOKLINE ST
COMMONWEALTH AVE
STORROW MEMORIAL DR
HARVARD AVE
BABCOCK ST
CAMBRIDGE ST
LOWELL ST
ELM ST
PARK DR
UPLAND RD
WALNUT
ARLINGTON ST
ROSELAND ST
WASHINGTON AVE
FROST
FOREST ST
PRENTISS ST
GARFIELD ST
EUSTIS ST
HARRIS
SACRAMENTO ST
CARVER
WENDELL ST
GORHAM ST
MUSEUM ST
EVERETT ST
OXFORD ST
JARVIS ST
DIVINITY AVE
FRANCIS AVE
IRVING ST
BRYANT ST
FARRAR ST
CRAIGIE ST
IBBETSON ST
BELMONT ST
SPRING ST
HARVARD ST
MONMOUTH ST
OXFORD ST
BERKELEY ST
AVON ST
SUMMER ST
LAUREL ST
LANDERS ST
PITMAN ST
KENT
PARK ST
DANE AVE
HANSON ST
CALVIN ST
MAGNUS AVE
ROSE ST
DIMICK
MYRTLE AVE
LINE ST
ROBERTS RD
TROWBRIDGE ST
SUMNER
HOVEY AVE
LEONARD AVE
GARDEN ST
STEARNS ST
NEWELL ST
COPLEY ST
HURON AVE
RAYMOND ST
DONNELL ST
BATES
ROBINSON ST
LINNAEAN ST
GRAY ST
BOWDOIN ST
AVON ST
WALKER ST
MADISON ST
ROYAL AVE
GRANVILLE RD
SHEPARD ST
CHAUNCY ST
FOLLEN ST
WATERHOUSE ST
RESERVOIR ST
APPLETON ST
HIGHLAND ST
SPARKS ST
BREWSTER ST
PARKER ST
CRAIGIE ST
BERKELEY PL
BERKELEY ST
HUBBARD PARK RD
FOSTER ST
CHANNING ST
LOWELL ST
GIBSON
SPARKS ST
WILLARD ST
BRADBURY
MASON ST
APPIAN WAY
TRAILL ST
HILLIARD
STORY ST
CHURCH
ASH ST
UNIVERSITY RD
JFK ST
DUNSTER
HOLYOKE
WINTHROP ST
ELIOT ST
SOUTH ST
MILL
PLYMPTON ST
BOW
DEWOLF ST
GRANT ST
QUINCY ST
PRESCOTT ST
WARE ST
REMINGTON
TROWBRIDGE ST
ELLERY ST
DANA ST
ELLSWORTH AVE
HIGHLAND AVE
MAPLE AVE
FAYETTE ST
CLEVELAND ST
ANTRIM ST
CENTRE ST
LEE ST
HARVARD ST
HANCOCK ST
CLINTON ST
BIGELOW ST
BANKS ST
FLAGG ST
PUTNAM AVE
KINNAIRD ST
BAY ST
GREEN ST
FRANKLIN ST
HOWARD ST
JAY ST
SODEN
BISHOP
PLEASANT ST
AUBURN ST
WILLIAM ST
COTTAGE ST
UPTON ST
KELLY RD
PERRY ST
PEARL ST
PACIFIC
TUDOR ST
EMILY ST
ERIE ST
HAMILTON ST
ALLSTON ST
CHESTNUT ST
SIDNEY ST
WAVERLY
GROVE AVE
GRANITE ST
HENRY ST
VASSAR ST
AUDREY ST
BLACKSTONE ST
PUTNAM AVE
MT AUBURN ST
GREENOUGH
COOLIDGE HL
LANDING RD
EVERETT ST
RAYMOND ST
RIVERDALE ST
TRAVIS ST
ROTTERDAM ST
BRENTWOOD ST
ATHOL ST
BAYARD ST
N HARVARD ST
EASTON ST
COOLIDGE RD
HOPEDALE ST
SEATTLE ST
WINDOM ST
ALDIE ST
ADAMSON ST
MYRICK ST
MANSFIELD ST
HOOKER ST
EMPIRE ST
BRAINTREE ST
PENNIMAN RD
DENBY
LINDEN
PRATT ST
ASHFORD ST
GARDNER ST
MALVERN ST
BABCOCK ST
ISLINGTON ST
ALLSTON ST
QUINT AVE
PARKVALE AVE
REEDSDALE ST
CHESTER ST
FORDHAM RD
NAPLES RD
WINSLOW RD
ADAMS ST
DUMMER ST
EGMONT ST
PLEASANT ST
THATCHER ST
WORTHINGTON RD
MOUNTFORT ST
CUMMINGTON ST
GREYLOCK RD
GLENVILLE AVE
HAMILTON RD
FULLER ST
OSBORNE RD
GIBBS ST
LAWTON ST
COOLIDGE ST
EWE ST
FREEMAN ST
ESSEX ST
EUSTON ST
IVY ST
ST MARYS ST
0
0.4 miles
0
0.5 km

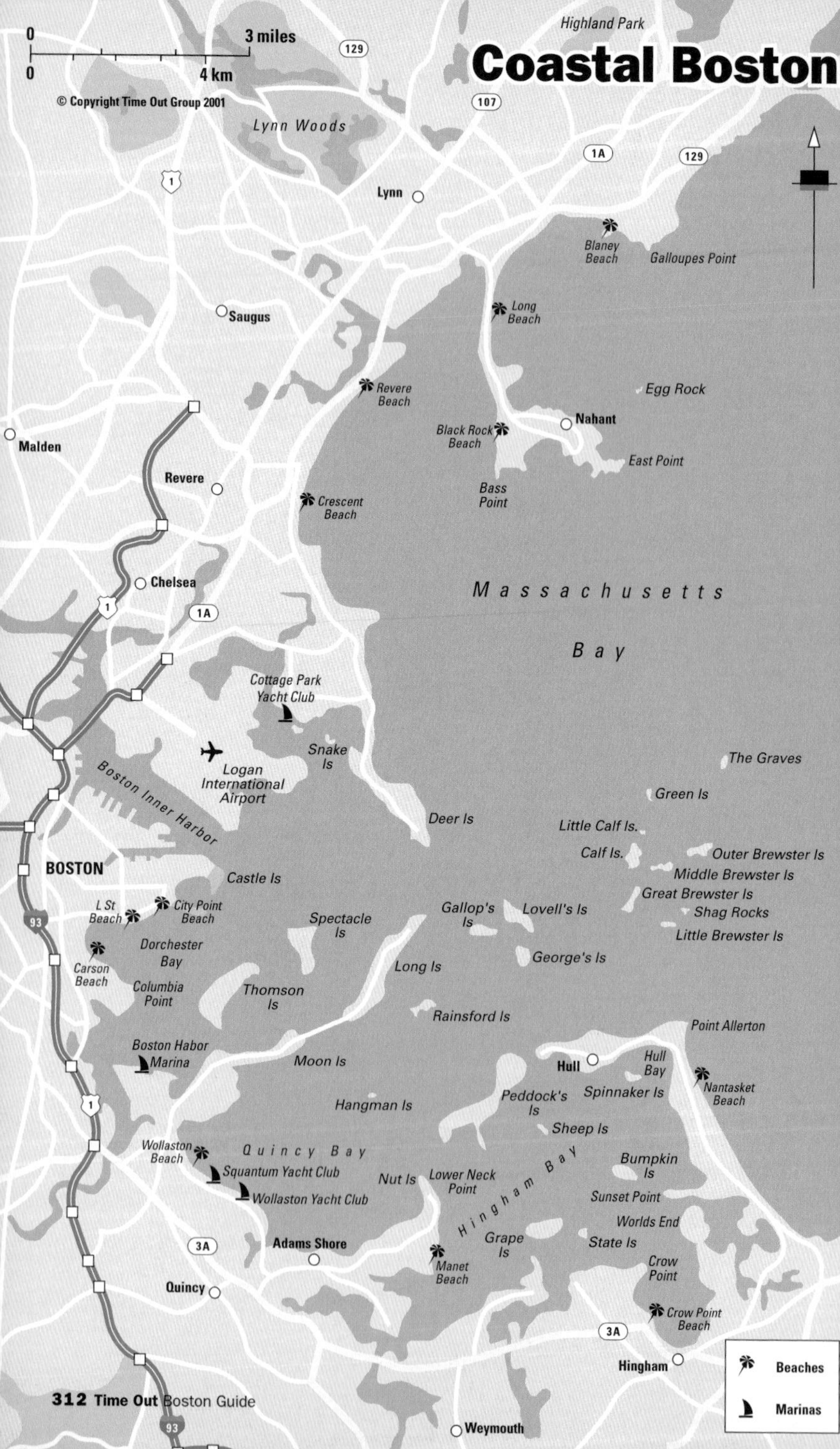
Coastal Boston
0
3 miles
0
4 km
© Copyright Time Out Group 2001
Highland Park
129
107
1A
129
1
Lynn Woods
Lynn
Blaney Beach
Galloupes Point
Saugus
Long Beach
Egg Rock
Revere Beach
Nahant
Malden
Black Rock Beach
East Point
Revere
Bass Point
Crescent Beach
Chelsea
1
1A
Massachusetts
Bay
Cottage Park Yacht Club
Snake Is
Logan International Airport
Boston Inner Harbor
The Graves
Green Is
Deer Is
Little Calf Is.
Calf Is.
Outer Brewster Is
Middle Brewster Is
BOSTON
Castle Is
Great Brewster Is
L St Beach
City Point Beach
Gallop's Is
Lovell's Is
Shag Rocks
Spectacle Is
Little Brewster Is
93
Dorchester Bay
George's Is
Long Is
Carson Beach
Columbia Point
Thomson Is
Rainsford Is
Point Allerton
Boston Habor Marina
Moon Is
Hull
Hull Bay
Nantasket Beach
Peddock's Is
Spinnaker Is
Hangman Is
1
Sheep Is
Wollaston Beach
Quincy Bay
Bumpkin Is
Squantum Yacht Club
Nut Is
Lower Neck Point
Hingham Bay
Wollaston Yacht Club
Sunset Point
Worlds End
3A
Adams Shore
Grape Is
State Is
Crow Point
Manet Beach
Quincy
Crow Point Beach
3A
Hingham
Beaches
Marinas
Weymouth
93

Street Index

A St - P306/7 H6, P308 H6
Adams St - P311 B5
Adamson St - P311 A4
Agassiz Rd - P306/7 D6
Albany St - P306/7 D4, P306/7 F7 P308 G6
Aldie St - P311 A4
Allston St - P311 A5, P311 C4
Ames St - P306/7 E4
Amherst St - P306/7 D4/E4
Amory St - P306/7 D2/3
Amy Ct - P306/7 F3/G3, P308 F3/G3
Anderson St - P308 F4
Antrim St - P306/7 D2/3, P311 C2/3
Appian Way - P311 B2
Appleton St - P306/7 F6, P308 F6 P311 A2
Arch St - P308 G4
Arlington St - P306/7 F5, P308 F5 P311 B1
Ash St - P311 B2
Ashford St - P311 A5
Athens St - P306/7 H6/7
Athol St - P311 A4
Atlantic Ave - P306/7 G5/H4, P308 G5/H4
Auburn St - P311 C3/4
Audrey St - P306/7 D4/5 P311 C5
Austin St - P306/7 F2/G2
Avon St - P311 B1/C1
B St - P306/7 G6/H5/6, P308 H6
Babcock St - P311 B5
Back St - P306/7 E5/F4/5
Ball St - P306/7 E7
Banks St - P311 B3
Bates St - P311 B1
Batterymarch St - P308 H4
Bay St - P311 C3
Bayard St - P311 A4
Beach St - P306/7 G5, P308 G5
Beacon St - P306/7 D5/E5/F4/G4, P308 F4/G4 P311 C2/C5
Beaver Pl - P306/7 F4, P308 F4
Bedford St - P306/7 G5, P308 G5
Belmont St - P311 C1
Bent St - P306/7 E3
Benton St - P306/7 E7
Berkeley Pl - P311 A2
Berkeley St - P306/7 F5, P308 F5 P311 B2 P311 C1
Berkshire St - P306/7 D3
Bigelow St - P311 C3
Binney St - P306/7 D3/E3
Bishop Allen Dr - P306/7 D3 P311 C3
Black Falcon Ave - P306/7 J6
Blackstone St - P306/7 G4, P308 G4 P311 B3/4
Blanche St - P306/7 D4
Blossom St - P306/7 F3, P308 F3/4
Bolton St - P306/7 H6/7
Border St - P306/7 J2
Boston University Bridge - P311 C5
Bow St - P311 B3
Bowdoin St - P306/7 G4, P308 G4 P311 B1
Bowen St - P306/7 H7
Boylston St - P306/7 D6/E5/F5/G5, P308 F5
Bradbury St - P311 A2
Braintree St - P311 A4
Branch St - P306/7 F4, P308 F4
Brattle St - P311 A2/B2
Bremen St - P306/7 J2/3
Brentwood St - P311 A4
Brewster St - P311 A2
Brimmer St - P306/7 F4, P308 F4
Bristol St - P306/7 D3
Broad St - P308 H4, P306/7 H4
Broadway - P306/7 D3/E3
Broadway Bridge - P306/7 G6 P308 G6
Bromfield St - P308 G4
Brookline Ave - P306/7 D5/6
Brookline St - P306/7 D4, P311 C4
Bryant St - P311 C2
Bullock St - P306/7 H6
Burbank St - P306/7 E6
Burlington Ave - P306/7 D6
Butler St - P306/7 H6
C St - P306/7 G7/H6, P308 H6
Callahan Tunnel - P306/7 H3 P308 H3
Calvin St - P311 C2
Cambridge Pkwy - P306/7 F3
Cambridge St - P306/7 D2/E3/F4/G4 P308 F4/G4 P311 A4/5 P311 C2
Cambridgeside Pl - P306/7F 3
Camden St - P306/7 E6/7
Canal St - P306/7 G3, P308 G3
Cardinal Medeiros Ave - P306/7 D3/E3 P311 D3/E3
Carleton St - P306/7 E4, P306/7 E6/F6
Carver St - P311 C1
Causeway St - P306/7 G3, P308 G3
Central Artery - P308 G5
Central Square - P311 C3
Central St - P308 H4
Centre St - P311 C3
Chandler St - P306/7 F5, P308 F5
Channel St - P306/7 J5/6
Channing St - P311 A2
Charles River Dam - P306/7 F3 P308 F3
Charles St - P306/7 E3/F3, P308 F3
Charles St S - P306/7 F5, P308 F5/G5
Charlesgate E - P306/7 D5
Charlesgate W - P306/7 D5
Charlestown Ave - P306/7 F2/3 P308 F2/3
Charlestown Bridge - P306/7 G3 P308 G3
Charter St - P306/7 G3, P308 G3
Chatham St - P306/7 G4/H4 P308 G4/H4
Chauncy St - P306/7 G5, P308 G5 P311 B2
Chelsea St - P306/7 J2
Cherry St - P306/7 D3
Chester St - P311 A5
Chestnut St - P306/7 F4, P308 F4 P311 C4
Church St - P311 B2
Claflin St - P306/7 H6
Claremont St - P306/7 E6
Clarendon St - P306/7 F5/6, P308 F6
Clark - P308 H3
Clearway St - P306/7 E6
Cleveland St - P311 C3
Clinton St - P306/7 G4/H4, P308 G4 P311 C3
Clipper Ship Lane - P306/7 J3
Columbia St - P306/7 D3
Columbus Ave - P306/7 E6/7/F5/6 P308 F5
Commercial Ave - P306/7 F3
Commercial St - P306/7 G3/H3 P308 G3/H3
Common St - P306/7 G5, P308 G5
Commonwealth Ave - P306/7 E5/F5 P311 A5/B5/C5
Concord Ave - P311 A1/2/B2
Concord Sq - P306/7 E6/F6
Congress St - P306/7 G4/H5 P308 G4/5 P308 H5
Coolidge Hl - P311 A2
Coolidge Rd - P311 A4
Coolidge St - P311 A5/B5
Cople Square - P306/7 F5
Copley St - P311 A1
Cornelia Ct - P306/7 D7
Cortes St - P306/7 F5, P308 F5
Cottage St - P306/7 J3 P311 C3/4
Court St - P306/7 G4 P308 G4
Craigie St - P311 A2 P311 C1
Cross St - P306/7 D4 P306/7 G3/4
Crowley Rogers Way - P306/7 H6
Cummington St - P306/7 D5, P311 C5
Cypher St - P306/7 H6, P308 H6
D St - P306/7 H6/7/J5
Dalessio Ct - P306/7 G6
Dalton St - P306/7 E6
Dana St - P311 C2
Dane Ave - P311 C2
Dartmouth St - P306/7 E5/F5
Davenport St - P306/7 E6/7
Deerfield St - P306/7 D5
Denby Rd - P311 A4
Devonshire Pl - P308 G4/5
Devonshire St - P306/7 G4/5 P308 G4/5
Dewolf St - P311 B3
Dimick St- P311 C2
Divinity Ave - P311 B2/C2
Doane St - P306/7 G4/H4, P308 G4/H4
Donnell St - P311 A1
Dorchester Ave - P306/7 G5/7/J5 P308 G5/H5
Dorchester St - P306/7 H7
Drydock Ave - P306/7 J6
Dummer St - P311 B5
Dunster St - P311 B2
Dwight St - P306/7 F6, P308 F6
E 6th St - P306/7 J7
E Berkeley St - P306/7 F6/G6 P308 F6/G6
E Broadway - P306/7 J7
E Brookline St - P306/7 F6/7
E Canton St - P306/7 F6/7
E Concord St - P306/7 F7
E Fifth St - P306/7 J7
E First St - P306/7 J6
E Lenox St - P306/7 F7
E Newton St - P306/7 F6/7
E Second St - P306/7 J7
E St - P306/7 H6/7
E Third St - P306/7 J7
East St - P308 G5
Easton St - P311 A4
Edgerly Rd - P306/7 E6
Egmont St - P311 B5
Eighth St - P306/7 E3

Eliot St - P311 B2/3
Elkins St - P306/7 J6
Ellery St - P311 C2
Ellsworth Ave - P311 C2
Elm St - P306/7 D3,
P311 B1
Embankment Rd - P308 F4,
P306/7 F4
Emerson St - P306/7 H7/J7
Emily St - P311 C4
Empire St - P311 A4
Endicott St - P306/7 G3,
P308 G3
Erie St - P311 C4
Essex St - P306/7 D3,
P306/7 G5
P308 G5
P311 C5
Eustis St - P311 B1
Euston St - P311 C5
Evans Way - P306/7 D7
Everett St - P306/7 J3,
P311 A4
P311 B2
Ewe St - P311 B5
Ewer St - P306/7 G7
Exeter St - P306/7 E5
F St - P306/7 H7
Fairfield St - P306/7 E5
Fargo St - P306/7 H5/6
Farnsworth St - P306/7 H5,
P308 H5
Farrar St - P311 C2
Fayette St - P306/7 D2/3,
P306/7 F5
P308 F5
P311 C2/3
Federal St - P306/7 G4/5,
P308 G4/5
Field St - P306/7 D7
Fifth St - P306/7 E3
First St - P306/7 F3
Fish Pier Rd - P306/7 J5
Fitzgerald Expwy -
P306/7 G6/7
P308 G5/6
Flagg St - P311 B3
Flaherty Way - P306/7 G7
Fleet St - P308 H3
Florence Pl - P306/7 D3
Follen St - P311 B2
Foodmart Rd - P306/7 G7
Fordham Rd - P311 A5
Forest St - P311 B1
Forsyth St - P306/7 D6/E6
Forsyth Way - P306/7 D6
Foster St - P311 A2
Francis Ave - P311 C2
Frankfort St - P306/7 J3
Franklin St - P306/7 G4/H4,
P308 G4/H4
P311 A4
P311 C3
Freeman St - P311 B5
Friend St - P306/7 G3,
P308 G3
Frost St - P311 B1
Fruit St - P306/7 F4,
P308 F4
Fulkerson St - P306/7 E3
Fuller St - P311 B5
Fullerton St- P306/7 D6
G St - P306/7 H7
Gainsborough St - P306/7 E6
Garden St - P311 A1/B2
Gardner St - P311 A5/B5
Garfield St - P311 B1
Garrison St - P306/7 E6
Geneva St - P306/7 J3
Gerrys Landing Rd - P311 A2
Gibbs St - P311 B5
Gibson St - P311 A2
Gilbert Pl - P306/7 H5,
P308 H5
Gillette Park - P308 G6
Glenville Ave - P311 A5
Gloucester St - P306/7 E5
Gold St - P306/7 H7
Gore St - P306/7 E2/3
Gorham St - P311 B1
Gove St - P306/7 J2/3
Granite St - P308 H6,
P311 C4
Grant St - P311 B3
Granville Rd - P311 A1
Gray St - P306/7 F6,
P308 F6
P311 B1
Green St - P306/7 D4,
P311 C3
Greenough St - P311 A3
Greylock Rd - P311 A5
Grimes St - P306/7 H7
Grove Ave - P311 C4
Grove St - P306/7 F4,
P308 F4
H St - P306/7 J7
Hamilton Rd - P311 A5/B5
Hamilton St - P311 C4
Hammond St - P306/7 E7
Hampshire St - P306/7 D2/3
Hancock St - P308 G4,
P311 C3
Hano St - P311 A4/5
Hanover St -
P306/7 G3/4/H3
P308 G3/4/H3
Hanson St - P306/7 F6,
P308 F6
P311 C2
Harbor St - P306/7 J5/6
Harding St - P306/7 D2/E2
Harris St - P311 B1/C1
Harrison Ave -
P306/7 F6/7/G5
P308 F6/G5/6
Harvard Ave - P311 A5
Harvard Bridge -
P306/7 D4/5
Harvard Square - P311 B2
Harvard St - P306/7 D3,
P306/7 G2
P308 G2
P311 A3/B3
P311 C1
P311 C3
Haverhill St - P306/7 G3,
P308 G3
Haviland St - P306/7 E6
Havre St - P306/7 J2/3
Hawley St - P308 G4
Hemenway St - P306/7 E6
Henry St - P311 C4
Herald St - P308 F5/G5/6
Hereford St - P306/7 E5
High St - P306/7 H4,
P308 H4
Highland Ave - P311 C2
Highland St - P311 A2,
P311 B2
Holyoke St - P311 B2/3
Hooker St - P311 A4
Hopedale St - P311 A4
Horadan Way - P306/7 D7
Hovey Ave - P311 C2
Howard St - P311 C3
Hubbard Park Rd - P311 A2
Hudson St - P306/7 G5,
P308 G5
Hull St - P306/7 G3,
P308 G3
Hunting St - P306/7 D2
Huntington Ave -
P306/7 D6/7/E6
Hurley St - P306/7 E3
Huron Ave - P311 A1
Ibbetson St - P311 C1
India St - P308 H4
Inman St - P306/7 D2/3,
P306/7 J6
Ipswich St - P306/7 D5
Irving St - P311 C2
Islington St - P311 A5
Ivy St - P311 C5
Jarvis St - P311 B2
Jay St - P311 C3
Jefferson St - P306/7 E2
Jersey St - P306/7 D6
John F Kennedy St - P311 B2
Joy St - P306/7 G4,
P308 G4
K St - P306/7 J6/7
Kelly Rd - P311 C4
Kendall Sq - P306/7 E4
Kendall St - P306/7 E7
Kenmore Square -
P306/7 D5
Kent St - P311 C1
Kenwood St - P311 A5
Kerr Way - P306/7 E7
Kilmarnock St - P306/7 D6
Kingston St - P306/7 G5,
P308 G5
Kinnaird St - P311 C3
Kirkland St - P311 C2
Kneeland St - P306/7 G5,
P308 G5
L St - P306/7 J6/7
Landers St - P311 C1
Lansdowne St - P306/7 H7
Larz Anderson Bridge -
P311 B3
Laurel St - P311 C1
Lawrence St - P306/7 F6
- P308 F6
Lawton St - P311 A5
Lee St - P311 C3
Lenox St - P306/7 E7
Leon St - P306/7 D7
Leonard Ave - P311 C2
Lewis St - P306/7 H3,
P306/7 J3
P308 H3
Lime St - P306/7 F4,
P308 F4
Lincoln St - P306/7 D3,
P306/7 G5
P308 G5
Linden St - P311 A4/5
Line St - P311 C2
Linnaean St - P311 B1
Linskey Way - P306/7 E3
Lomasney Way - P306/7 G3,
P308 G3
London St - P306/7 J2
Longfellow Bridge -
P306/7 F4
Longwood Ave - P306/7 D7
Louis Pasteur Ave -
P306/7 D6/7
Louis Prang St - P306/7 D7
Lowell St - P311 A2,
P311 C1
Lynde St - P306/7 G2,
P308 G2
Lynn St - P306/7 G3,
P308 G3
M St - P306/7 J7
Madison St - P311 A1
Magazine St - P311 C4
Magnus Ave - P311 C2
Main St - P306/7 D4/E4
Malden St - P306/7 F6
Malvern St - P311 B5
Mansfield St - P311 A4
Maple Ave - P311 C2/3,
P306/7 C2
Marginal Rd - P308 F5/G5
Marginal St - P306/7 J3
Market St - P306/7 D3
Marlborough St -
P306/7 E5/F5
Mason St - P308 G5,
P311 B2
Massachusetts Ave -
P306/7 D3/4/E5/6
P306/7 E6/F7
P311 B1/2
P311 C3
Massachusetts Turnpike -
P308 F5/G5
P311 A4/B4
Maverick St - P306/7 J3
Mcgreevey Way - P306/7 D7
Melrose St - P306/7 F5,
P308 F5
Memorial Dr - P306/7 D4/5,
P311 B3/4/C5
Meridian St - P306/7 J2/3
Merrimac St - P306/7 G3/4,
P308 G3
Midway St - P306/7 H5/6,
P308 H6
Milford St - P306/7 F6,
P308 F6
Mill St - P311 B3
Monmouth St - P311 C1
Monsignor O'Brien Hwy -
P306/7 E2/F3
Montgomery St - P306/7 F6,
P308 F6
Moon St - P306/7 H4,
P308 H4
Mount Auburn St -
P311 A2/B2/3
Mount Vernon St -
P306/7 F4/G4
P308 F4/G4
Mountfort St - P311 C5
Museum Rd - P306/7 D6
Museum St - P311 C1
Myrick St - P311 A4
Myrtle Ave - P311 C2
Myrtle St - P306/7 F4/G4,
P308 F4/G4
N Harvard St - P311 A4
N Margin St - P306/7 G3
N Margin St - P308 G3
N Washington St -
P306/7 G3
P308 G3
Naples Rd - P311 B5
Nashua St - P306/7 F3/G3,
P308 F3/G3

Necco St - P306/7 H5,
P308 H5
New Chardon St -
P306/7 G3/4
P308 G3/4
New Sudbury St - P306/7 G4
P308 G4
Newbury St - P306/7 E5/F5
Newcomb St - P306/7 E7/F7
Newell St - P311 A1
Newland St - P306/7 F6
Norfolk St - P306/7 D3
North St - P306/7 G4,
P306/7 H3
P308 G4
P308 H3
Northampton St -
P306/7 E6/7/F7
Northern Ave -
P306/7 H4/J5/6
P308 H5
Northfield St - P306/7 E7
Oak St - P306/7 G5,
P308 G5
Old Colony Ave -
P306/7 G7/H7
Oliver St - P306/7 G4/H4,
P308 G4/H4
Oregon Ct - P306/7 D7
Orleans St - P306/7 J3
Osborn St - P306/7 D4
Osborne Rd - P311 B5
Otis St - P306/7 E3,
P306/7 G4/5
P308 G4/5
Overland St - P306/7 D5/6
Oxford St - P311 B1/2,
P311 C1
Pacific St - P306/7 D4,
P311 C4
Palace Rd - P306/7 D6/7
Paris St - P306/7 J2
Park Dr - P306/7 D6,
P311 C5
Park St - P306/7 G2,
P306/7 G4
P308 G4
P311 C1
Parker St - P306/7 D7,
P311 A2
Parkvale Ave - P311 A5
Pearl St - P306/7 G4,
P308 G4
P311 C3/4
Pembroke St - P306/7 F6
Penniman Rd - P311 A4/5
Perry St - P311 C4
Peterborough St - P306/7 D6
Phillips St - P308 F4
Piedmont St - P306/7 F5,
P308 F5
Pinckney St - P306/7 F4,
P308 F4/G4
Pine St - P306/7 D3
Ping On St - P306/7 G5,
P308 G5
Pitman St - P311 C1
Pittsburgh St - P306/7 H5
Pleasant St - P311 B5,
P311 C3
Plympton St - P306/7 F6,
P311 B3
Porrington St - P306/7 D4
Porter St - P306/7 J3
Portland St - P306/7 D3,
P306/7 G3
P308 G3
Potter St - P306/7 E3
Pratt St - P311 A5
Prentiss St - P311 B1
Prescott St - P311 C2
Prince St - P308 G3
Prospect St - P306/7 D2/3
Providence St - P306/7 F5,
P308 F5
Province St - P308 G4
Purchase St - P306/7 G5/H5
P308 G5/H5
Putnam Ave - P311 C4
P311 C3
Queensberry St - P306/7 D6
Quincy St - P311 B2
Quint Ave - P311 A5
Raleigh St - P306/7 D5
Ramp St - P306/7 J5
Randolph St - P308 G6
Raymond St - P311 A1
Raymond St - P311 A4
Reedsdale St - P311 A5
Remington St- P311 C3
Reservoir St - P311 A1/2
Revere St - P306/7 F4,
P308 F4
Richmond St - P308 H4
River St - P306/7 F4,
P308 F4
P311 B4
Riverdale St - P311 A4
Roberts Rd - P311 C2
Robinson St - P311 A1
Rose St - P311 C2
Roseland St - P311 B1
Rotterdam St - P311 B4
Royal Ave - P311 A1
Ruggles St - P306/7 D7/E7
Ruth St - P306/7 J3
Rutherford Ave -
P306/7 G2/3
P308 G2/3
Rutland Sq - P306/7 E6/F6
Rutland St - P306/7 F6
S Bay Ave - P306/7 F6/G7
S Bremen St - P306/7 J3
Sacramento St - P311 B1/C1
Saint Mary Rd - P306/7 D3
Salem St - P306/7 G3,
P308 G3
School St - P306/7 D3,
P306/7 G4
P308 G4
Sciarappa St - P306/7 E2/3
Seattle St - P311 B4
Second St - P306/7 E3
Seventh St - P306/7 E3
Shawmut Ave - P306/7 F6/7
Shepard St - P311 B1/2
Sidney St - P306/7 D4,
P311 C4
Silver St - P306/7 H6/7
Sixth St - P306/7 E3
Sleeper St - P308 H5
Smart St - P306/7 D4
Smith St - P306/7 D7
Snowhill St - P306/7 G3,
P308 G3
Soden St - P311 C3
Soldiers Field Rd -
P311 A2/3/B3
Somerset St - P306/7 G4,
P308 G4
Somerville Ave - P311 C1
South St - P306/7 E2.
P306/7 G5
P308 G5
P311 B3
Sparks St - P311 A2
Spring St - P306/7 E3
Spring St - P311 C1
Springfield St - P306/7 D2
St Botolph St - P306/7 E6
St James Ave - P306/7 F5,
P308 F5
St Marys St - P311 C5
St Stephen St - P306/7 E6
Staniford St - P306/7 G3/4,
P308 G3/4
State St - P306/7 D4
Stearns St - P311 A1
Stillman St - P308 G3
Storrow Memorial Dr -
P306/7 D5/E5
P311 C5
Story St - P306/7 H7/J7,
P311 B2
Stuart St - P306/7 F5,
P306/7 G5
P308 F5/G5
Suffolk St - P306/7 D3
Summer St -
P306/7 G4/5/H5/J6
P308 G4/H5
P311 C1
Sumner Rd- P311 C2
Sumner St - P306/7 J3
Sumner Tunnel - P306/7 H3,
P308 H3
Symphony Rd - P306/7 E6
Temple Pl - P306/7 G4,
P308 G4
Temple St - P306/7 G4,
P308 G4
Thatcher St - P311 B5
Thayer St - P306/7 G6
The Fenway - P306/7 D6
Third Ave - P306/7 G2,
P308 G2
Third St - P306/7 E3
Thomas Park - P306/7 H7
Tileston St - P306/7 H3,
P308 G3/H3
Traill St - P311 A2
Traveler St - P306/7 G6,
P308 G6
Travis St - P311 A4
Tremont St - P306/7 D2,
P306/7 E6/7/F5/6
P308 F5
P308 G4/5
Trinity Pl - P306/7 F5
Trowbridge St - P311 C2
Tudor St - P306/7 D4,
P306/7 H7
P311 C4
Tyler St - P306/7 G5,
P308 G5
Union Park - P306/7 F6
Union St - P306/7 D3,
P306/7 G4
P308 G4
Unity St - P306/7 H3
P308 H3
University Rd - P311 B2/3
Upland Rd - P311 B1
Upton St - P306/7 F6,
P311 C4
Utica St - P306/7 G5
P308 G5
Van Ness St - P306/7 D6
Vancouver St - P306/7 D7
Vassar St - P311 C4/5
Viaduct St - P306/7 H5
W 2nd St - P306/7 G6/H6
W Broadway - P306/7 H6/7,
P308 G6
W Canton St - P306/7 F6
W Concord St - P306/7 F6
W Dedham St - P306/7 F6
W Eighth St - P306/7 H7
W Fifth St - P306/7 G6/H7
W First St - P306/7 H6/7,
P308 H6
W Forth St -
P306/7 H6/7/G6
P308 G6
P306/7 G6
W Newton St - P306/7 F6
W Ninth St - P306/7 H7
W Second St - P306/7 H6/7
P308 G6/H6
W Seventh St - P306/7 H7
W Sixth St - P306/7 G6/H7
W Springfield St -
P306/7 E6/F6
W Third St - P306/7 H6/7
Wadsworth St- P306/7 E4
Walker St - P311 B1
Walnut St - P306/7 G4,
P308 G4
P311 B1
Waltham St - P306/7 F6
Ware St - P311 C2
Wareham St - P306/7 F6
Warren Ave - P306/7 F6,
P308 F6
Warren St - P306/7 E2/G2
Warrenton St - P308 G5
Warwick St - P306/7 E7
Washington Ave - P306/7 F6,
P311 B1
Washington St -
P306/7 D3/F2/G2
P308 F6/G4/5/6
P308 G2
Water St - P308 G4
Waterhouse St - P311 B2
Waverly St - P306/7 D4,
P311 C4
Webster Ave - P306/7 D2/3
Webster St - P306/7 J3
Wendell St - P308 H4,
P311 B1
West St - P306/7 G5,
P308 G4/5
Western Ave - P311 B3/C3
Westland Ave - P306/7 E6
Widett Cir - P306/7 G7
Willard St - P311 A2
William St - P311 C3/4
Willow St - P306/7 D2,
P308 F4
Windom St - P311 B4
Windsor St - P306/7 D2/3,
P306/7 E7
Winslow Rd - P311 B5
Winter St - P306/7 E2,
P306/7 G4
P308 G4
Winthrop St - P311 B2/3
Worcester St - P306/7 D3,
P306/7 F6
Worthington Rd - P311 C5
Yawkey Way - P306/7 D6
York St - P306/7 D3

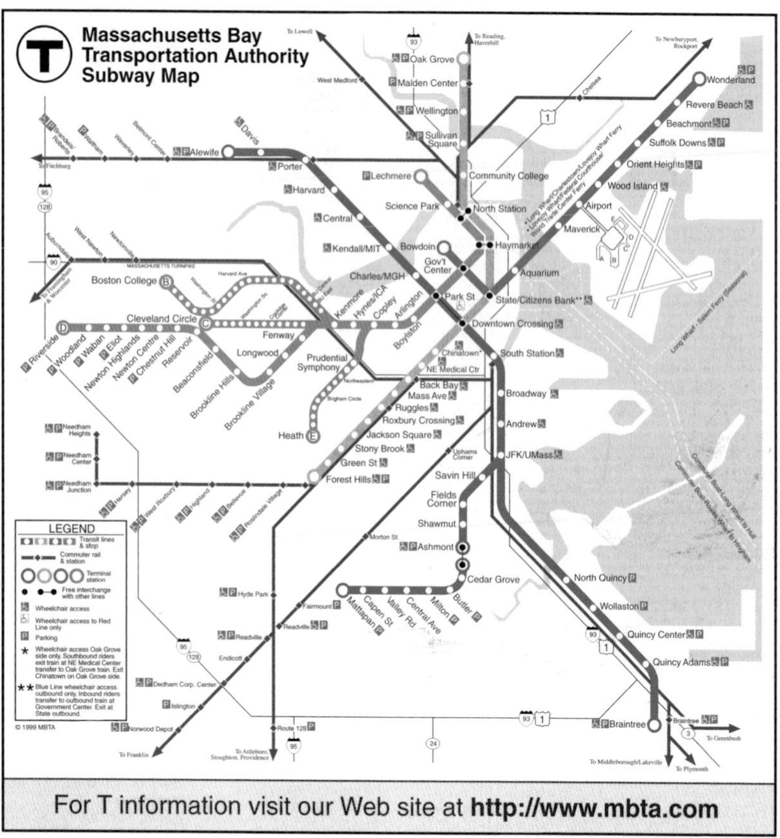

Massachusetts Bay Transportation Authority Subway Map
To Lowell
To Reading, Haverhill
To Newburyport, Rockport
Oak Grove
Malden Center
West Medford
Wellington
Sullivan Square
Chelsea
Wonderland
Revere Beach
Beachmont
Suffolk Downs
Orient Heights
Wood Island
Airport
Maverick
Community College
Lechmere
Science Park
North Station
Haymarket
Bowdoin
Gov't Center
Aquarium
State/Citizens Bank**
Park St
Downtown Crossing
Chinatown*
South Station
NE Medical Ctr
Alewife
Davis
Porter
Harvard
Central
Kendall/MIT
Charles/MGH
Brandeis/Roberts
Waltham
Waverley
Belmont Center
To Fitchburg
Auburndale
West Newton
Newtonville
MASSACHUSETTS TURNPIKE
To Framingham & Worcester
Boston College
Cleveland Circle
Riverside
Woodland
Waban
Eliot
Newton Highlands
Newton Centre
Chestnut Hill
Reservoir
Beaconsfield
Brookline Hills
Brookline Village
Longwood
Fenway
Kenmore
Hynes/ICA
Copley
Arlington
Boylston
Prudential
Symphony
Northeastern
Heath
Back Bay
Mass Ave
Ruggles
Roxbury Crossing
Jackson Square
Stony Brook
Green St
Forest Hills
Broadway
Andrew
JFK/UMass
Uphams Corner
Savin Hill
Fields Corner
Shawmut
Ashmont
Cedar Grove
Butler
Milton
Central Ave
Valley Rd
Capen St
Mattapan
Morton St
North Quincy
Wollaston
Quincy Center
Quincy Adams
Braintree
To Greenbush
To Middleborough/Lakeville
To Plymouth
Needham Heights
Needham Center
Needham Junction
Hersey
West Roxbury
Highland
Bellevue
Roslindale Village
Hyde Park
Fairmount
Readville
Endicott
Dedham Corp. Center
Islington
Norwood Depot
To Franklin
Route 128
To Attleboro, Stoughton, Providence
Long Wharf - Salem Ferry (Seasonal)
Commuter Boat-Long Wharf to Hull
Commuter Boat-Rowes Wharf to Hingham
LEGEND
Transit lines & stop
Commuter rail & station
Terminal station
Free interchange with other lines
Wheelchair access
Wheelchair access to Red Line only
Parking
* Wheelchair access Oak Grove side only. Southbound riders exit train at NE Medical Center transfer to Oak Grove train. Exit Chinatown on Oak Grove side.
** Blue Line wheelchair access outbound only. Inbound riders transfer to outbound train at Government Center. Exit at State outbound.
© 1999 MBTA
For T information visit our Web site at http://www.mbta.com